CONTEMPORARY MUSICIANS

ISSN 1044-2197

CONTEMPORARY MUSICIANS

PROFILES OF THE PEOPLE IN MUSIC

ANGELA M. PILCHAK, Project Editor

VOLUME 47
Includes Cumulative Indexes

GALE®

THOMSON
★
GALE

Detroit • New York • San Diego • San Francisco • Cleveland • New Haven, Conn. • Waterville, Maine • London • Munich

THOMSON

GALE

Contemporary Musicians, Vol. 47

Project Editor
Angela M. Pilchak

Editorial
Noah Schusterbauer, Jennifer York,
Julie E. Bedard

Permissions
William Sampson

Imaging and Multimedia
Dean Dauphinais, Lezlie Light, Mike Logusz

Cover Illustration
John Kleber

Composition and Electronic Prepress
Gary Leach

ISBN 0-7876-6800-1
ISSN 1044-2197

Printed in the United States of America
10 9 8 7 6 5 4 3 2 1

Contents

Introduction ix

Cumulative Subject Index 221

Cumulative Musicians Index 257

Introduction

Fills in the Information Gap on Today's Musicians

Contemporary Musicians profiles the colorful personalities in the music industry who create or influence the music we hear today. Prior to *Contemporary Musicians,* no quality reference series provided comprehensive information on such a wide range of artists despite keen and ongoing public interest. To find biographical and critical coverage, an information seeker had little choice but to wade through the offerings of the popular press, scan television "infotainment" programs, and search for the occasional published biography. *Contemporary Musicians* is designed to serve that information seeker, providing in one ongoing source in-depth coverage of the important names on the modern music scene in a format that is both informative and entertaining. Students, researchers, and casual browsers alike can use *Contemporary Musicians* to meet their needs for personal information about music figures; find a selected discography of a musician's recordings; and uncover an insightful essay offering biographical and critical information.

Provides Broad Coverage

Single-volume biographical sources on musicians are limited in scope, often focusing on a handful of performers from a specific musical genre or era. In contrast, *Contemporary Musicians* offers researchers and music devotees a comprehensive, informative, and entertaining alternative. *Contemporary Musicians* is published six times per year, with each volume providing information on about 70 musical artists and record-industry luminaries from all the genres that form the broad spectrum of contemporary music— pop, rock, jazz, blues, country, New Age, folk, rhythm and blues, Latin, gospel, bluegrass, rap, and reggae, to name a few—as well as selected classical artists who have achieved "crossover" success with the general public. *Contemporary Musicians* will also occasionally include profiles of influential nonperforming members of the music community, including producers, promoters, and record company executives. Additionally, beginning with *Contemporary Musicians 11,* each volume features new profiles of a selection of previous *Contemporary Musicians* listees who remain of interest to today's readers and who have been active enough to require completely revised entries.

Includes Popular Features

In *Contemporary Musicians* you'll find popular features that users value:

- **Easy-to-locate data sections:** Vital personal statistics, chronological career summaries, listings of major awards, and mailing addresses, when available, are prominently displayed in a clearly marked box on the second page of each entry.

- **Biographical/critical essays:** Colorful and informative essays trace each subject's personal and professional life, offer representative examples of critical response to the artist's work, and provide entertaining personal sidelights.

- **Selected discographies:** Each entry provides a comprehensive listing of the artist's major recorded works.

- **Photographs:** Many entries include portraits of the subject profiled.

- **Sources for additional information:** This invaluable feature directs the user to selected books, magazines, newspapers, and online sources where more information can be obtained.

Helpful Indexes Make It Easy to Find the Information You Need

Each volume of *Contemporary Musicians* features a cumulative Musicians Index, listing names of individual performers and musical groups, and a cumulative Subject Index, which provides the user with a breakdown by primary musical instruments played and by musical genre.

Available in Electronic Formats

Licensing. *Contemporary Musicians* is available for licensing. The complete database is provided in a fielded format and is deliverable on such media as disk or CD-ROM. For more information, contact Gale's Business Development Group at (800) 877-GALE, or visit our website at www.gale.com/bizdev.

Online. *Contemporary Musicians* is accessible online as part of the Gale Biographies (GALBIO) database accessible through LexisNexis, P.O. Box 933, Dayton, OH 45401-0933; phone: (937) 865-6800, toll-free: (800) 227-4908.

We Welcome Your Suggestions

The editors welcome your comments and suggestions for enhancing and improving *Contemporary Musicians*. If you would like to suggest subjects for inclusion, please submit these names to the editor. Mail comments or suggestions to:

The Editor
Contemporary Musicians
Gale Group, Inc.
27500 Drake Rd.
Farmington Hills, MI 48331-3535

Or call toll free: (800) 877-GALE

Aaliyah

Singer

In Swahili, the language of East Africa, the name Aaliyah means "highest, most exalted one." Most parents might shy away from burdening their newborn with such a tough name to live up to, but it seems that Michael and Diane Haughton knew from the start that their baby daughter had the makings of a real star. While still a sophomore at Detroit's High School for Fine and Performing Arts, Aaliyah Haughton, known professionally by her first name alone, released her debut album, which created a minor sensation in the recording industry and in time went double-platinum. Her second album quickly went platinum as well, and she later broadened her horizons, adding acting to her resume. Aaliyah's star was burning bright when her life was unexpectedly cut short: Aaliyah and eight others died in a plane crash on August 25, 2001, while returning from a video shoot in the Bahamas.

Born on January 16, 1979, in Brooklyn, New York's Bedford-Stuyvesant neighborhood, Aaliyah Dani Haughton seemed somehow preordained to get into music. She was practically weaned on rhythm and blues and soul, because the Haughton household was almost always filled with music from her mother's extensive collection of recordings. Aaliyah, showing early signs of a talent that would later blossom into a professional career, just couldn't resist singing along to the records of the Isley Brothers, Whitney Houston, and Marvin Gaye.

When Aaliyah was five years old, the Haughton family left Brooklyn behind and moved to a new home in Detroit. It was in the Motor City that Michael and Diane Haughton, impressed by their daughter's raw musical talent, decided to enroll her in vocal classes. When she wasn't learning singing in the classroom, Aaliyah was singing up a storm wherever possible, including school plays and the church choir. Around the age of nine, she began making the rounds, auditioning regularly for television productions and record companies. But the auditions were her idea, she told *Vibe,* not her parents's. "I pushed them. I would talk to my mother every day. After school I'd go to her job and be, like, 'Ma, did anybody call me? Anybody call about signing me?' I was into it." It was at about this time that her mother encouraged her to drop her surname and go with just Aaliyah as her stage name.

An Early Star

While still only nine years old, she appeared on the national television talent show, *Star Search.* Interviewed by *Details* magazine, Aaliyah recalled her TV debut: "It was really, really cute. I sang 'My Funny Valentine,' and I had on a white dress my grandmother made with a little bolero jacket, and special curls in my hair." Unfortunately, Aaliyah didn't win first place, but she gained much-needed experience working in front of a large audience. That experience came in handy a couple of years later when she was signed to perform

For the Record . . .

Born Aaliyah Dani Haughton on January 16, 1979, in Brooklyn, NY; died on August 25, 2001, in the Bahamas; daughter of Michael and Diane (Hankerson) Haughton.

Began actively auditioning as a singer at age nine, appearing on television talent show *Star Search*; shortly thereafter she won her first big professional job, appearing for a week in the Las Vegas show of Gladys Knight; first artist signed by Blackground Enterprises at age 14, 1994; released *Age Ain't Nothing But a Number*, 1994; toured the United States and a number of foreign countries in support of her first album; released *One in a Million*, 1996; performed songs for the soundtracks of several motion pictures, including *Anastasia* and *Dr. Dolittle*, and guested on tracks for albums of fellow performers Nas, Missy "Misdemeanor" Elliott, and Ginuwine; took her first major acting job in film *Romeo Must Die*, 2000; released *Aaliyah*, 2001; posthumous release *I Care 4 U*, 2002.

Awards: MTV Video Music Award, Best Female Video, for "Try Again," 2000; MTV Video Music Award, Best Video from a Film, for "Try Again" from *Romeo Must Die*, 2000; American Music Awards, Favorite Soul/R&B Female Artist, Favorite Soul/R&B Album for *Aaliyah*, 2001, Favorite Soul/R&B Female Artist, 2003; *Source* Award, Female R&B Artist of the Year, 2003.

Addresses: *Office*—Michael and Diane Haughton, Raliah Management, P.O. Box 21847, Detroit, MI 48221.

for a week in Las Vegas with Gladys Knight. Although in the end it was Aaliyah's talent that won her the job with Knight, it didn't hurt that her uncle, Barry Hankerson, who was also her manager at that stage in her career, was Knight's ex-husband. During the week she performed with Knight, Aaliyah sang a solo midway through the show and closed the show in a duet with Knight on "Believe in Yourself."

At the age of 14, Aaliyah signed her first record contract when Hankerson founded his own recording company, Blackground Enterprises. She was the first act to sign with the Blackground label. At about the same time, her uncle introduced Aaliyah to R&B singer/songwriter R. Kelly, who was also managed by Hankerson's Midwest Entertainment Group. Kelly, impressed with Aaliyah's vocal ability, signed on to produce her debut album. Of her first meeting with Kelly, Aaliyah told *Vibe*: "He came to my house, and I sang for him, and from there we went into the studio." Her debut album, entitled *Age Ain't Nothing But a Number*, was released in 1994 and eventually went double platinum. Aaliyah was overjoyed at the success of her first recording venture but less pleased at widespread rumors that she and Kelly were secretly married. She consistently denied that she was married to Kelly, but the rumors persisted. Documents were revealed years later that confirmed the couple married when Aaliyah was 15 and had the marriage annulled shortly thereafter. Not surprisingly, the gossip helped to call attention to Aaliyah's debut recording and in the end gave sales an extra lift. "Back and Forth," the first single released from the album, spent three weeks at number one on the R&B charts, while her second single, "At Your Best (You Are Love)," managed to climb its way to number two.

In support of her first album, Aaliyah spent nearly a year touring in the United States as well as several foreign countries, including Japan, South Africa, and most of Western Europe. In the wake of her debut album's success, she received a number of movie soundtrack and video contracts, including *Low Down Dirty Shame* in 1995 and *All That* and *Sunset Park* in 1996. What was perhaps most amazing was teenaged Aaliyah's ability to juggle her new-found success, concert appearances all over the globe, and interviews while still maintaining a 3.8 grade point average at Detroit's High School for Fine and Performing Arts. Her mother, a school teacher herself, insisted that a tutor accompany Aaliyah whenever she traveled away from Detroit or was otherwise unable to attend school.

One in a Million

Back from nearly a year of touring, Aaliyah began to make plans for her second album. Like a lot of recording artists, she worried that unless she produced a strong follow-up, the public and—even more importantly—movers and shakers in the industry might write her off as nothing but a one-hit wonder. Perhaps still smarting from the media blitz over her relationship with Kelly, Aaliyah decided to work with a team of producers—eight in all—in putting together her second album. She switched distributors, dropping Jive Records to go with Atlantic, a distributor with proven strength in R&B circles. Of the nerve-wracking period leading up to the release of her second album, she later confided in an Atlantic press release: "I was a little anxious. You could even say I was a little afraid. I spoke with my family, and they helped me realize that it wasn't something I should worry about, that I shouldn't overthink the process." In the end, she took her family's advice and followed her instincts, which had proven more than reliable in the past. Although she worked with multiple producers and songwriters in putting together *One in a Million*, her second album, her principal collaborator on the project was Tim "Timbaland" Mosely, one of the hottest producers in hip-hop music.

Any fears that she might be labeled a "one-hit wonder" quickly disappeared after the 1996 release of *One in a Million,* which, like her first album, eventually went double platinum. A number of hip-hop's hottest artists were featured on the album, including Missy "Misdemeanor" Elliott, Slick Rick, and Naughty by Nature's Treach. The first single off the album, "If Your Girl Only Knew," rocketed to number one on the R&B charts. Other successful songs from the album included "Four-Page Letter," a cover of the Marvin Gaye classic "Got to Give It Up," and the title ballad. Her successful collaboration with Timbaland continued in 1997, when the two worked on the track "Are You That Somebody?" for the soundtrack of Eddie Murphy's remake of *Dr. Dolittle.*

Even after the success of her second album and nearly a decade of public appearances, frequently before audiences of thousands, Aaliyah continued to struggle against her basic shyness. So uncomfortable was she around others that she was rarely seen in public without her trademark sunglasses. Even in the recording studio, she felt uneasy being in the spotlight. Talking to an interviewer for *Vibe,* she said, "When I'm in the studio, I have to have the light off—you can't see me 'cause I'm very shy. I don't mind seeing you in the control room, but you can't see me."

In 1997 Aaliyah graduated from Detroit High School for Fine and Performing Arts but postponed plans for college because her career was occupying almost all of her time. For fellow artists Elliott, Ginuwine, and Nas, she contributed tracks on albums they recorded. She continued to work hard on her music but held off on a third album until she found the right combination of elements to make it a sure-fire winner. It was to be a five-year wait until her third album, *Aaliyah,* was released. The album, another collaboration with Timbaland, was scheduled to hit music stores in the summer of 2001.

Impressive Acting Debut

At the end of the 1990s, Aaliyah's career broadened to include acting. She was signed for a starring role in the martial arts thriller *Romeo Must Die,* which was released in the spring of 2000. Costarring with Chinese action film star Jet Li, she made what one film critic termed "a creditable film debut." A single she recorded with producer Timbaland for *Romeo Must Die,* "Try Again," was a smash success, landing Aaliyah her first number one song on the pop charts. Her acting skills obviously made a positive impression on Hollywood's filmmakers, because in short order she was signed to appear in sequels to the wildly popular action film *Matrix* and to play Queen Akasha, "the original vampire," in the film version of Anne Rice's novel *The Queen of the Damned.*

For Aaliyah, her career, particularly the musical side of it, was very much a family affair. Although she was first managed by her uncle, that responsibility was later passed to her parents, who formed Detroit-based Raliah Management for just that purpose. However, Aaliyah still recorded for Blackground Enterprises. Her cousin, Jomo, played the role of executive producer on her second album, while her brother, Rashaad, was her creative consultant.

In an interview with *Billboard* early in 2001, Aaliyah talked a bit about the difficulties of juggling her work in both acting and singing: "I'd literally go from the movie studio to the recording studio. I'm like two different people. Once they say, 'Cut—it's a wrap for the day,' I leave the costumes on the set. I have two different facets to my career. I have to know how to turn it on and off."

With her third album's release, she seemed pleased with the ground she'd covered in just 22 years. She told *Harper's Bazaar* that she is "more controlling now. I have come into my own in the past year, and I really felt it making the new album. I would tell my producers, 'No, no, no. I don't want to do this' or 'Let's take this hook out.' It felt good to be so vocal." She described the third album as "a party album, with a few big, beautiful ballads," and assured the interviewer that her latest effort was definitely not "R&B lite." Timbaland likened their professional relationship to a "musical marriage," saying, "When you feel like someone is part of your family, the work comes naturally."

A Life Cut Short

Aaliyah's promising life came to a halt when she was killed along with seven others on August 25, 2001, when the private plane in which they were traveling crashed after takeoff. She had been shooting a video for the song "Rock the Boat" in the Bahamas and was preparing to return to the United States. The cause of the crash was investigated by Bahamian aviation officials, who later reported that the pilot of the small Cessna plane had traces of cocaine and alcohol in his system at the time of the crash, and that the crash was most likely caused by a pilot error. The plane was also overloaded by at least 700 pounds, most of it sound and video equipment used in the video shoot.

Posthumously, Aaliyah went on to even greater success than she had found in earlier years. In the month following her death, her most recent release, *Aaliyah,* went multiplatinum. Critics unanimously agreed it was her most accomplished work. *All Music Guide* critic Stephen Thomas Erlewine declared, "*Aaliyah* isn't just a statement of maturity and a stunning artistic leap forward, it is one of the strongest urban soul records of its time." Blackground Enterprises released *I Care 4 U* in 2002. The release contained most of Aaliyah's greatest hits as well as six new, previously unreleased tracks, including the poignant first single, "Miss You."

Selected discography

Age Ain't Nothing But a Number, Blackground/Jive, 1994.
(Contributor) *Low Down Dirty Shame* (soundtrack), Hollywood, 1995.
One in a Million, Blackground/Atlantic, 1996.
(Contributor) *Anastasia* (soundtrack), Atlantic, 1997.
(Contributor) *Dr. Dolittle* (soundtrack), Atlantic, 1998.
(Contributor) *Music of the Heart* (soundtrack), Sony/Epic, 1999.
(Contributor) *Next Friday* (soundtrack), Priority, 1999.
(Contributor) *The Nutty Professor II* (soundtrack), Uni/Def Jam, 2000.
(Contributor) *Romeo Must Die* (soundtrack), Blackground/ Virgin, 2000.
Aaliyah, Virgin, 2001.
I Care 4 U, Universal/Blackground, 2002.

Sources

Periodicals

America's Intelligence Wire, November 19, 2003.
Billboard, July 20, 1996, p. 15.
Harper's Bazaar, April 1, 2001, p. 153.
Knight Ridder/Tribune News Service, July 16, 2002.
People, June 23, 1997, p. 130.
Time, April 3, 2000, p. 80

Online

"Aaliyah," *All Music Guide,* http://www.allmusic.com (April 19, 2004).
"Aaliyah Killed in Plane Crash," Eonline, http://www.eonline.com/News/Items/0,1,8731,00.html (August 27, 2001).
"The Rap on R. Kelly," *Chicago Tribune,* http://www.chicago tribune.com (April 14, 2004).

—Don Amerman

Trey Anastasio

Guitarist, composer

AP/Wide World Photos. Reproduced by permission.

Trey Anastasio is a composer and guitarist best known as the co-founder of the unique jam-rock group Phish. He has continued to prolifically compose and expand his musical vocabulary by exploring the limits of improvisation. Apart from his work with Phish, Anastasio has recorded several solo albums and has had success in the trio Oysterhead.

Anastasio was born in Fort Worth, Texas, and grew up in Princeton, New Jersey, where his family moved in 1966. Anastasio's first songwriting was done in collaboration with his mother, who was an editor of *Sesame Street Magazine* and who wrote songs for children's records. His father was an executive for the firm responsible for administering the SAT and other tests.

Anastasio attended Princeton Day School, where he first met Tom Marshall, who would later become his songwriting partner. John Popper of Blues Traveler was another classmate. Anastasio attended Taft High School, and during his high school days he formed the band Space Antelope. Although he played drums as a youth, the guitar became his primary instrument. He continued composing throughout his school years.

While a student at the University of Vermont, he met the musicians who would form Phish: Mike Gordon, Jon Fishman, and Jeff Holdworth. Anastasio co-founded the group in 1983. He transferred to Goddard College, where he studied composition with Ernie Stires, who became an influential mentor for Anastasio throughout his career. The band was signed to Elektra and released its first recording, *Junta,* in 1988. The group's sound is based in rock, but the musicians improvise as jazz musicians might, sometimes placing them in the Grateful Dead-like jam bands category. And like the latter group, Phish has its own devotees who follow them around the country, record and trade their live performances, and memorize minutia about the group and its members.

Since the release of *Rift* in 1993, Phish has released at least one recording a year. The band also undertook a heavy schedule of touring. According to *Rolling Stone,* "Phish remained Anastasio's primary musical outlet for the duration of the '80s and the '90s, as his original work progressed from lengthy prog-influenced compositions, such as 'You Enjoy Myself' of the mid-'80s, to the more focused (though still complex) songs of *Rift.*"

Anastasio formed a free jazz big band in 1996 for his project *Surrender to the Air,* including such musicians as Marshall Allen (Sun Ra), John Medeski (Medeski Martin & Wood), Marc Ribot, and Bob Gulotti. During this period from 1996-98 he moved away from using composition as a basis for creating music, shifting increasingly to improvisation, as illustrated in such Phish recordings as *The Story of the Ghost* and *The Siket Disc.*

The Phish Dry Goods label issued two unusual Anastasio-fronted Phish-related projects that further illustrate his prolific output. *One Man's Trash* consisted of 16 all-Anastasio tracks reportedly "written, produced, recorded and performed by Trey, often in the wee hours at the Fungus Factory or The Barn in Vermont," according to his official website. *Trampled by Lambs and Pecked By the Dove* was essentially a solo album—25 tracks written and recorded by Anastasio with Tom Marshall during a nine-day period in 1997. Of those, ten songs were recorded by Phish on later albums *The Story of the Ghost* and *Farmhouse.*

"Anastasio's ongoing collaboration with Tom Marshall also resulted in new material, far too much for Phish to assimilate into their already gigantic live repertoire," according to *Rolling Stone.* "Though Anastasio brought some of the songs to his newly formed side trio [Oysterhead], he still felt he was holding back." After the release of *Farmhouse* in 2000, the band went on hiatus.

During this break from Phish, Anastasio devoted time to Oysterhead, a trio including Anastasio, Les Claypool (Primus), and Stewart Copeland (ex-The Police), which straddled the jam and prog rock genres. They recorded one album in 2001, *The Grand Pecking Order.* "Over the span of 13 tracks, the trio succeeds admirably at finding the common ground between their seemingly disparate styles. Make no mistake, the characteristic trademarks of each member are still firmly in place," wrote Steve Bekkala in *All Music Guide.* "The musicians seem to be carefully listening and playing off of one another at all times—and enjoying themselves doing so." Anastasio told the Jambands website that there were never concrete plans to continue Oysterhead. "That's the beauty of Oysterhead. … It was the most purely democratic experience musical experience I've ever had by far."

Anastasio's self-titled 2002 solo recording, which included some 30 musicians and vocalists such as Cyro Baptista, Dana Colley (ex-Morphine, Twinemen), and Lisa Fisher (The Rolling Stones), won a Jammy Award for Studio Album of the Year. Anastasio has described his composing process as an organic one. "I do it habitually almost. At times I have a hard time engaging in conversations and whatnot. I'd be much happier locked in the basement with a piano and my guitar," he told the Jambands website. "It makes me feel at peace in a certain way when I try to put notes in their proper place."

Phish announced it was ending its hiatus with a 2002 New Year's Eve show at New York City's Madison Square Garden, and three shows immediately followed at Hampton Coliseum in Hampton, Virginia. Several projects Anastasio participated in during the break were still coming to fruition. While touring in support of *Trey Anastasio,* several of his shows were recorded and culled for the two-disc solo album *Plasma* in 2003, which Elektra called "a series of musical excursions built upon rock-solid and even ferocious grooves." Most notably the album includes a 23-minute version of "Night Speaks to a Woman." In 2004 Anastasio was among the artists announced as backing Dave Matthews's solo project, Dave Matthews & Friends. "I've wanted to play with Trey for a long time," said Matthews in an article originating in the *Boston Globe.*

Selected discography

Solo

Surrender to the Air, Elektra, 1996.
One Man's Trash, Phish Dry Goods, 1998.
Trampled By Lambs and Pecked By the Dove, Phish Dry Goods, 2000.
Trey Anastasio, Elektra, 2002.
Plasma (live), Elektra, 2003.

With Phish

Junta, Elektra, 1988.
A Picture of Nectar, Elektra, 1991.
Lawn Boy, Elektra, 1991.
Rift, Elektra, 1993.
Hoist, Elektra, 1994.
A Live One, Elektra, 1995.

Billy Breathes, Elektra, 1996.
Stash, Elektra, 1996.
Slip, Stitch & Pass (live), Elektra, 1997.
The Story of the Ghost, Elektra, 1998.
Phish, Phish Archives, 1998.
Phish (The White Tape), Phish, 1998.
Hampton Comes Alive, Elektra, 1999.
Farmhouse, Elektra, 2000.
The Siket Disc, Elektra, 2000.
Live Phish, Volumes 01 through 06, Elektra, 2001.
Live Phish, Volumes 07 through 16, Elektra, 2002.
Round Room, Elektra, 2002.
Live Phish, Volumes 17 through 20, Elektra, 2003.
White Tape, Phish Dry Goods, 2003.

With Oysterhead

The Grand Pecking Order, Elektra/Asylum, 2001.

Sources

Books

The Phish Companion: A Guide to the Band and their Music, 2nd edition, Mockingbird Foundation/Backbeat Books, 2000.

Periodicals

Boston Globe, December 16, 2003.
Chicago Daily Herald, May 31, 2002.
Guitar Player, September 1994; May 1996; July 2002.
Los Angeles Times, April 28, 2002.
Relix, April-May 2002; June-July 2002.
Rolling Stone, July 19, 2001.
Washington Post, June 21, 2002.

Online

"Trey Anastasio," *All Music Guide,* http://www.allmusic.com (January 25, 2004).
"Trey Anastasio," *RollingStone.com,* http://www.rollingstone.com/artists/bio.asp?oid=2043760&cf=2043760 (January 25, 2004).
"Trey Anastasio: The Jambands.com Reader Interview," Jambands Online, http://www.jambands.com/Features/content_2002_05_21.10.phtml (January 25, 2004).

—Linda Dailey Paulson

Patti Austin

Singer

RJ Capak/WireImage.com. Reproduced by permission.

A sophisticated vocalist firmly grounded in jazz, Patti Austin enjoyed a period of stardom during the heyday of smooth, expertly produced rhythm-and-blues music in the 1980s. Both before and since this period in the limelight, Austin continued challenging herself, balancing more introspective and/or artistic work with the commercial. Austin has been, in short, a professional's professional.

Austin was born in New York on August 10, 1948, and grew up in show business. Her father was a professional trombone player at the time. The family lived in Bayshore, Long Island. At the tender age of four she made her performing debut, singing a song called "Teach Me Tonight" on the stage of Harlem's famed Apollo Theater during an appearance by vocalist Dinah Washington, who was also Austin's godmother. A child star, she appeared on Sammy Davis, Jr.'s television variety show, worked on stage with such stars as Ray Bolger of *The Wizard of Oz,* and when she was nine she went to Europe with a group led by bandleader Quincy Jones, who would become an immensely influential figure both on Austin's own career and on popular music.

"My friends didn't know I was in show business until I was 16," said Austin. "The rest of the time, I never talked about it, because I wanted people to accept me for me, not based on whether I had a hit record or was highly visible or all that nonsense."

Toured with Harry Belafonte

Austin's first major series of appearances as a mature singer came when she was 16, when she went on tour with pop vocalist Harry Belafonte, then near the peak of his fame. This tour led to a fresh round of television appearances and to a three-year stint as a lounge singer for various international locations of the posh Intercontinental hotel chain. Austin's first recordings were made during this period as well—for Coral Records in 1965. This material was reissued in 1999.

With this wealth of professional experience under her belt before she could even vote, it was not difficult for Austin to decide on a musical career. Recording executives and producers valued the young singer's know-how, and session-work opportunities began to flow her way.

"The first session I did was for James Brown's hit, 'It's a Man's World,' and when I got a nice juicy check from that," Austin recalled in a biographical sketch released by the Concord Jazz label. "I said, 'Hey let me do some more of this stuff.'" Austin became one of pop music's leading session vocalists in the early 1970s, backing both R&B and pop vocalists such as Paul Simon, Roberta Flack, George Benson, and Cat Stevens. With her vocals included on the soundtracks of hundreds of television commercials, Austin became one of America's most heard but least known singers.

For the Record . . .

Born on August 10, 1948, in New York, NY; daughter of Gordon and Edna Austin.

Made debut appearance at age four with vocalist Dinah Washington, her godmother; traveled to Europe with bandleader Quincy Jones, age nine; toured with Harry Belafonte; became leading session and advertising-jingle vocalist, early 1970s; recorded debut LP, *End of a Rainbow*, 1976; recorded four albums for CTI label, late 1970s and early 1980s; signed with Qwest label, 1981; recorded smash *Every Home Should Have One*, which included single "Baby Come to Me," a duet with James Ingram, 1981; released four albums on Qwest, 1980s; signed with GRP label, 1990; signed with Concord Jazz label, 1998; signed with Intersound label, 1999; premiered biographical one-woman show in Sacramento, 2002; released *For Ella*, 2002; nominated for a Grammy, 2003.

Addresses: *Record company*—Playboy Jazz/Concord Records, Inc., 270 North Canon Dr., Ste. 1212, Beverly Hills, CA 90210, website: http://www.concordrecords.com. *Website*—Patti Austin Official Website: http://www.pattiaustin.com.

That began to change when Austin was signed to the jazz-oriented label CTI in 1976, thanks to contacts with industry veteran Creed Taylor and Belafonte's former musical director Bill Eaton. The four albums Austin recorded for CTI helped to raise her profile in the industry and were widely appreciated by the architects of the "Quiet Storm" turn that black popular music took in the early 1980s. One of the albums, *Havana Candy,* was reissued in 1997 and favorably reviewed by *Down Beat*. The magazine pointed to "Austin's appreciation of the jazz legacy as well as her love of various pop styles."

Signed by Quincy Jones

The dawn of the 1980s brought Austin some especially high-profile session assignments: she sang on *Gaucho,* the rock group Steely Dan's complex exploration of the possibilities of soft rock, and, on a lighter note, appeared on the *Blues Brothers* album. She also enjoyed a hit single with "Razzmatazz" on Quincy Jones's Grammy-winning 1980 LP *The Dude,* and in 1981 was signed to Jones's Qwest label. That year, Austin's

Qwest debut album, *Every Home Should Have One,* finally brought her stardom thanks to her chart-topping duet with James Ingram, "Baby Come to Me." The album was produced by Jones and Rod Temperton, the same team that would soon be responsible for Michael Jackson's epochal *Off the Wall* and *Thriller* albums.

"Baby Come to Me" was a perfect showcase for Austin's vocals, which had taken on an exquisite silky quality that blended nicely with the smooth instrumental textures of the period. The song appealed to pop and urban listeners, and was adopted as the theme song of the television soap opera *General Hospital*. Austin and Ingram followed it up in 1983 with another successful duet, "How Do You Keep the Music Playing?"; part of the soundtrack of the film *Best Friends,* the song was nominated for an Oscar, and Austin and Ingram performed it on the Academy Awards television broadcast.

Austin's next Qwest album, *Patti Austin,* was released in 1984, but its assemblage of six separate producers failed to bring together a cohesive whole, and *Rolling Stone* complained that "except on the ballads, Austin's powerful and technically proficient voice lacks distinction." Two more albums for Qwest failed to reach the chart levels of *Every Home Should Have One,* and Austin's career took a dip. She was also shaken by a house fire that destroyed nearly everything she owned and came within seconds of killing her elderly parents.

Strongly Affected by Fire

The accident made Austin reexamine her priorities in life. Recalling her life atop the charts in the early 1980s in an interview with *Essence,* Austin said, "My main concerns were looking good, the parties I would attend and the size of the limousine that would take me to them." Her star-studded circle of associates suddenly seemed less attractive: "Yes, they were the 'happening' people—on the charts and in the news—but they were miserable in their persistent bed-hoppings. They were all doing too many drugs and too much booze. They all had lots of stuff but not much soul or heart." Austin scaled back, built a new home in upstate New York, and reconnected with some of her former jazz associates.

Austin recorded a series of albums for the GRP label in the 1990s. One of them, *Love Is Gonna Getcha,* reunited her with *Havana Candy* producer and keyboardist Dave Grusin, and included the hit "Through the Test of Time." Austin enjoyed a moderate radio presence through the decade, kept up a steady stream of television appearances, and reveled in praise from such luminaries as opera star Kathleen Battle. In 1998 she recorded the *In & Out of Love* album for the Concord Jazz label, and the following year moved to Intersound for *Street of Dreams,* a disc that allowed her to show-case her interpretations of some of her own favorite compositions. Stephen Thomas Erlewine of the *All Music Guide* called the album "a fine latter-day effort from a fine singer."

On the Way to Critical Acclaim

On the Way to Love was released in 2001. "The songs indulge in street argot here and there, but this is an upscale effort for the most part," wrote William Ruhlmann in an *All Music Guide* review. "It's not bad, but Austin can do much better."

In 2002, Sacramento Theatre Company premiered a production with the same title—*On the Way to Love,* a one-person show about Austin, starring Austin. This purportedly "grew out of a meeting with Peggy Shannon, the current artistic director of STC," who had first met Austin a decade prior while working on Shakespeare's Pericles for National Public Radio, according to *Sacramento News & Review.* "My challenge in this show is to tell Patti's stories and dramatize them so that it's not one long monologue with songs—because that's a concert." The production was scheduled to be performed in a couple of regional theatres with the goal being a Broadway run.

Of her 2002 release *For Ella,* a tribute to Ella Fitzgerald recorded in Germany with the WDR Big Band, reviewers were more enthusiastic. "Austin had always had an ear for great material, and she possesses the interpretive tools to makes something special," wrote *Jazziz* reviewer Mark Holston. Austin's previous efforts at recording standards from the jazz canon he says "were compromised by cheesy, popish orchestrations.... There's no scarcity of arresting performances on *For Ella.*"

Ruhlmann said he considers this a sequel to *The Real Me.* "Austin does not, for the most part, attempt to sing in Fitzgerald's style, giving listeners her own interpretations that, in Williams' neo-swing arrangements, nevertheless hark back to the 1950s. ... Austin is better off putting her own stamp on the songs; that she does very well." She was nominated for a Grammy Award for this project and continued to tour in support of it into 2004.

Selected discography

End of a Rainbow, CTI, 1976.
Havana Candy, CTI, 1977; resissued, 1997.
Live at the Bottom Line, Epic, 1979.
Body Language, CTI, 1980.
Every Home Should Have One, Qwest, 1981.
In My Life, CTI, 1983.
Patti Austin, Qwest, 1984.
Gettin' Away with Murder, Qwest, 1985.
The Real Me, Qwest, 1988.
Love Is Gonna Getcha, GRP, 1990.
Carry On, GRP, 1991.
Live, GRP, 1992.
That Secret Place, GRP, 1994.
In and Out of Love, Concord Jazz, 1998.
Street of Dreams, Intersound, 1999.
Best of Patti Austin (Japan), WEA, 1999.
Take Away the Pain Stain—The Coral Recordings, Body & Soul, 1999.
The CTI Collection, Connoisseur, 2000.
On the Way to Love, Warner Bros., 2001.
The Very Best of Patti Austin, Rhino, 2001.
For Ella, Playboy Jazz, 2002.

Sources

Books

Clarke, Donald, editor, *The Penguin Encyclopedia of Popular Music,* Viking, 1989.
Graff, Gary, Josh Freedom du Lac, and Jim McFarlin, *Music-Hound R&B: The Essential Album Guide,* Visible Ink, 1998.
Larkin, Colin, editor, *The Encyclopedia of Popular Music,* Muze UK, 1998.

Periodicals

Asia Africa Intelligence Wire, January 4, 2004.
Billboard, September 26, 1998, p. 25.
Down Beat, December 1997, p. 94.
Essence, March 1993, p. 67.
Jazziz, August 2002.
Knight Ridder/Tribune News Service, March 31, 2003.
People, May 7, 1984, p. 30; May14, 1990, p. 26.
Rolling Stone, March 29, 1984, p. 74.

Online

"Honey for the bees: STC takes a gamble and puts together an original revue, based on the life and times of singer Patti Austin," *Sacramento News & Review,* http://www.news review.com/issues/Sacto/2002-01-17/arts.asp (January 21, 2004).
"Patti Austin," *All Music Guide,* http://www.allmusic.com (January 21, 2004).

—*James M. Manheim and Linda Dailey Paulson*

Les Baxter

Composer

Les Baxter was one of the leading figures in a style of orchestrated music that developed in the 1950s. He is known as the "Godfather of Exotica," a type of lounge music characterized by Latin rhythms and other influences that range from Polynesia to Hawaii to South America. His prolific output of music spanned four decades and included the scores to more than 100 films. The popularity of his music faded for two decades, but by the mid-1990s exotica and other types of lounge music were enjoying a popular revival. Unfortunately, Baxter died before he had a chance to enjoy the full impact of that revival.

Baxter was born on March 14, 1922, in Mexia, Texas. His family soon moved from Texas to Detroit, Michigan. Baxter was considered a child prodigy at the piano, which he learned to play at age five. In addition to piano he also learned to play the clarinet and was a talented singer. He studied at the Detroit Conservatory of Music before leaving the midwest in the 1930s to attend Pepperdine University in Malibu, California, near Los Angeles. While studying composition at Pepperdine, he supplemented his income by playing backup piano and tenor sax in jazz clubs around Los Angeles.

Around 1945, Baxter tired of playing saxophone and joined jazz singer Mel Torme's singing group the Mel-Tones. Baxter performed with the Mel-Tones for a few years and sang on a recording by big band great Artie Shaw. Eventually he left the Mel-Tones and joined NBC Radio. There Baxter performed weekly as a member of a voice quartet that sang Pepsodent commercials for comedian Bob Hope's radio show. Not long afterward,

Baxter began arranging and conducting music for the Bob Hope show as well as for the radio show featuring comedy duo Abbott and Costello. Soon enough he was musical director for those shows and others on NBC Radio.

By the end of the 1940s, Baxter was working for Capitol Records, arranging and conducting for the record company. He worked with many notable performers of the time. Probably his most famous work was on the album that produced Nat "King" Cole's hit "Mona Lisa." In addition to his assigned studio work, Baxter took advantage of the freedom he was given to record whatever he liked in the Capitol recording studios.

Baxter was incredibly curious and adventurous in his compositions and arrangements, experimenting with themes, instruments, and genres. His first release with Capitol was the album *Music Out of the Moon* in 1947. The album was a major style departure from the standard pop album of the time. On it Baxter used a choir, a cello and a French horn, a rhythm section, and one of the first electronic instruments ever invented, the theremin, which used an electromagnetic field over which the instrumentalist moved his hand to create sound. The album sold well enough that Baxter was encouraged to continue recording in a variety of styles.

His next notable work involved compositions and arrangements for noted Peruvian singer Yma Sumac. Sumac had a voice that covered five octaves and Baxter was able to utilize her voice to create the exotic sounds found on her debut album *Voice of the Xtabay.* Almost concurrently Baxter released the album *Ritual of the Savage,* which became the standard on which all future exotica albums were based. Described in the liner notes as a "tone poem of the sound and struggle of the jungle," *Ritual of the Savage* introduced the style and scope of music that would inspire later composers and arrangers such as Martin Denny and Arthur Lyman.

Throughout the 1950s Baxter had chart success with his arrangements of songs like "Because of You," "April in Portugal," and "The Poor People of Paris." In 1955 his "Unchained Melody" was number one on the *Billboard* charts for two weeks. In 1956 "The Poor People of Paris" hit number one for six weeks. His composition "The Quiet Village," which was originally released on *Ritual of the Savage,* was recorded by Martin Denny and became a hit for him in 1959.

In 1953 Baxter scored his first movie, a travelogue called *Tanga Tika.* He was billed as composer for such films as *Untamed Youth* (1957), *Jungle Heat* (1957), and *The Lone Ranger and the Lost City of Gold* (1958). By 1962 Baxter had scored more than 30 films, most of them eventually considered classics of the B-grade movie genre. That year he left Capitol Records and began focusing on movie composing.

For the Record . . .

Born on March 14, 1922, in Mexia, TX; died on January 15, 1996, in Newport Beach, CA. *Education:* Attended Detroit Conservatory of Music, Detroit, MI; attended Pepperdine College, Malibu, CA.

Performed as concert pianist as a teenager; during college played tenor sax and sang; joined the Mel-Tones, 1945; joined NBC radio as a singer for commercials; musical director for Bob Hope and Abbott and Costello radio shows; released first recording, *Music Out of the Moon,* 1947; began composing and arranging film scores, 1953; arranged and conducted recording sessions for Frank Sinatra, Bob Eberle, and Nat King Cole, 1950-60s; left Capitol Records, 1962; composed and arranged for television, mid- to late 1960s.

Most of Baxter's work on film scores during this period was done at American International, the studio run by horror movie director Roger Corman. Baxter scored music for Corman's series of films based on the stories of Edgar Allen Poe, including *The Pit and the Pendulum, Tales of Terror,* and *The Raven.* In the mid-1960s Baxter became the arranger and composer for the series of "Bikini" movies that initially starred teen heart-throbs Annette Funicello and Frankie Avalon. The films from this time period included *Muscle Beach Party, Bikini Beach, Beach Blanket Bingo,* and *How to Stuff a Wild Bikini.*

The 1960s were Baxter's most prolific period. He scored a number of films, and also arranged and composed for television. He is responsible for the well-known whistling theme to the TV show *Lassie.* His other television work included *Music of the Sixties (The Les Baxter Special), Buck Rogers in the 21st Century, The Milton Berle Show,* and *The Gumby Special.*

Baxter's work for films slowed down significantly in the 1970s, and by the 1980s he was keeping himself busy scoring music for theme parks. He also conducted his own works on occasion. One of his last performances was in 1995 at the Century Club in Century City. On January 15, 1996, Baxter died at the age of 73, from a heart attack caused by kidney failure. The music Baxter pioneered had begun making a popular comeback in the 1990s, marked by the 1996 release of Capitol Records' *The Exotic Moods of Les Baxter.* Unfortunately, the artist did not live long enough to enjoy this resurgence of public acclaim for his musical style.

Selected discography

Music Out of the Moon, Capitol, 1947.
Perfume Set to Music, RCA Victor, 1949.
(With Yma Sumac) *Voice of the Xtabay,* Capitol, 1950; reissued, 1956.
Arthur Murray Favorites—Tangos, Capitol, 1951.
Ritual of the Savage, Capitol, 1951.
Thinking of You, Capitol, 1951.
The Passions, Capitol, 1954.
Arthur Murray Favorites—Modern Waltzes, Capitol, 1954.
Kaleidoscope, Capitol, 1955.
Tamboo!, Capitol, 1956.
Caribbean Moonlight, Capitol, 1956.
Skins! Bongo Party with Les Baxter, Capitol, 1957.
'Round the World with Les Baxter, Capitol, 1957.
Midnight on the Cliffs, Capitol, 1957.
Ports of Pleasure, Capitol, 1957.
Space Escapade, Capitol, 1957.
Selections from "South Pacific," Capitol, 1958.
Confetti, Capitol, 1958.
Love is a Fabulous Thing, Capitol, 1958.
African Jazz, Capitol, 1959.
Jungle Jazz, Capitol, 1959.
Wild Guitars, Capitol, 1959.
The Sacred Idol, Capitol, 1960.
Les Baxter's Teen Drums, Capitol, 1960.
Baxter's Best, Capitol, 1960.
Young Pops, Capitol, 1960.
Broadway '61, Capitol, 1961.
Jewels of the Sea, Capitol, 1961.
Wild Hi-Fi Drums, Capitol, 1961.
Sensational, Capitol, 1962.
Original Quiet Village, Capitol, 1963.
The Exotic Moods of Les Baxter, Capitol, 1996.

Sources

Periodicals

Daily Variety, January 19, 1996.

Online

"Les Baxter," Lycos Music, http://www.music.lycos.com/ (January 14, 2004).
"Les Baxter," Space Age Pop, http://www.spaceagepop.com/ baxter.htm (January 14, 2004).

—*Eve M. B. Hermann*

Acker Bilk

Clarinetist, band leader, guitarist

Initially associated with the British traditional or "trad" jazz movement, Acker Bilk rose to prominence in Britain and the United States as the bandleader responsible for the hit instrumental "Stranger on the Shore," which became the theme song of a popular British television series. As a trad jazz musician, Bilk rejected the use of amplified instruments and was also against the use of saxophones—most commonly associated at the time with bop and hard bop jazz—preferring instead the instrumentation most commonly associated with jazz music prior to World War II. As a result, his early recordings featured Bilk on clarinet, with accompaniment on banjo, trumpet, trombone, drums, and piano. As the years progressed, Bilk alienated some of his trad audience by integrating saxophones, string orchestras, and synthesizers into his band lineup. He made up for the loss of his trad followers by recording widely and touring frequently, and by using a humorous form of stage patter between musical numbers.

Born Bernard Stanley Bilk in the Somerset village of Pensford in rural England, Bilk was given the name Acker, Somerset slang for "friend," at an early age. He received piano lessons as a young man, but did not take his musical education seriously. Employed for a period of time at the Willis Tobacco factory, Bilk also engaged in competitive boxing. He began playing the clarinet in 1948 while serving in the Royal Engineers. While stationed in Egypt where he was assigned to guard the Suez Canal, he fell asleep on guard duty. This infraction resulted in imprisonment while awaiting a court martial. He was able to while away his time by practicing on a military clarinet that he was loaned while incarcerated for three months. Due to an early sledding accident, Bilk lacked the finger normally used as a finder on the clarinet, and he developed a unique style as a result. His style was further altered by the lack of two teeth that had been knocked out in a fight. The signature sound he eventually perfected had ample vibrato, and developed a fullness of tone in the clarinet's lower registers.

After returning to England, Bilk moved to Bristol and began performing in various jazz groups. He relocated to London to join a band led by Ken Colyer, but disliked the urban environment and moved back to Bristol, where he formed the Bristol Paramount Jazz Band. He returned to London in 1951 with his band, staying with his wife in a factory attic in Plaistow. His distinctive playing and innate leadership abilities prompted him to drop "Bristol" from the band title and rename it Acker Bilk and the Paramount Jazz Band. The band received its first big break when it was hired to play a six-week gig in Dusseldorf, Germany. This booking gave the group ample time to perfect their timing, musicianship, and repertoire, which consisted of raw blues and ragtime vamps. Returning to England, Bilk outfitted the band in Edwardian England-era attire. Bilk sported a bowler hat and finely trimmed beard that became his signature style on album covers throughout the 1960s.

In 1960 the group enjoyed its first hits with "Creole Jazz" and "Summer Set," an instrumental named humorously after the region where Bilk grew up. The editors of the *Penguin Guide to Jazz on CD* described Bilk as "an impressive middle-register player who seldom uses the coloratura range for spurious effect, preferring to work melodic variations on a given theme. Though he repeats certain formulae, he tends to do so with variations that stop them going stale."

In 1961, Bilk wrote and recorded a song named for his daughter, Jenny. The song languished in obscurity until it was selected as the theme song for a BBC children's program, "Stranger on the Shore." Producer Dennis Preston convinced Bilk to include strings on the recording session, and the Leon Young String Chorale was enlisted to provide the orchestration. The song "Jenny" was re-titled "Stranger on the Shore," and brought Bilk great success on both sides of the Atlantic. He followed up on the success of "Stranger on the Shore" with the theme to the film *A Taste of Honey,* which also registered as a hit. He made numerous television appearances during this period, including a guest appearance on *The Ed Sullivan Show* in 1964, where he was introduced by Sullivan as "the bearded clarinetist, Mr. Acker Bilk."

In an attempt to progress artistically and stave off creative stagnation, Bilk experimented with styles and instruments throughout the remainder of the 1960s. He hired Bruce Turner, a renowned hard bop saxophonist

For the Record . . .

Born Bernard Stanley Bilk on January 28, 1929, in Pensford, England; children: Jenny.

Began playing the clarinet while stationed in Egypt during Suez Crisis, 1948; formed the Paramount Jazz Band, late 1950s; released hit single "Summer Set," 1960; wrote and recorded hit theme song for British television series *Stranger on the Shore*, 1961; recorded theme song for film *A Taste of Honey*, 1963; recorded hit single, "Aria," 1976; named member of the Order of the British Empire, 2001.

Awards: Order of the British Empire, member, 2001; Ivor Novello Award for "Most Performed Work."

Addresses: *Management*—53 Cambridge Mansions, Cambridge Rd., London SW11 4RX, England, phone: 44 (0) 20 7978 5885, fax: 44 (0) 20 7978 5882, e-mail: enquiry@ackermusicagency.co.uk.

who had gained notoriety in the 1950s due to scathingly negative reviews by such trad-friendly critics as Philip Larkin. Turner predictably divided Bilk's audience, but his eventual departure prompted the editors of the *Penguin Guide to Jazz on CD* to write that "Turner's departure was welcomed like the passing of the plague by Bilk's occasionally too vociferous fans, but he added a certain mainstream punch to a band that was in some risk of dead-ending itself."

The Paramount Jazz Band underwent several personnel changes throughout the 1960s. Original trumpet player Colin Smith departed and was replaced by Rod Mason, who in turn was replaced by Mike Cotton. Trombonist John Mortimer was replaced by Campbell Burnap. With this lineup he recorded *Blaze Away*, which included "Aria," his first hit in more than ten years. *Blaze Away* also featured a new recording of "Stranger on the Shore," a composition that Bilk fondly referred to as his pension plan. While "Aria" and "Stranger on the Shore" safely appealed to Bilk's core audience, other compositions, such as "Black and Tan Fantasy," served to appease hardcore jazz aficionados.

In 2001 Bilk was honored by Queen Elizabeth II as a member of the Order of the British Empire, for his musical accomplishments. He continued to record and tour extensively throughout the 1990s and beyond, despite a six-month battle with throat cancer in 1999 and 2000. He has also dedicated much of his time to running a successful music booking and publishing company. He has been a frequent performer at the Edinburgh Festival in Scotland, and has performed in the Giants of Jazz Concerts with Humphrey Lyttelton and George Melly. In 2003 he performed with the reunited Paramount Jazz Band for concerts that also featured the Big Chris Barber Band and Kenny Ball and His Jazzmen. He also guested as a clarinetist on Van Morrison's 2002 *Down the Road* and in a 2003 Blue Note debut *What's Wrong with This Picture?*

Selected discography

Mr. Acker Requests, Nixa, 1958.
Mr. Acker Marches On, Pye, 1958.
Mr. Acker Bilk Sings, Pye, 1959.
Mr. Acker Bilk Requests (Part One), Pye, 1959.
Mr. Acker Bilk Requests (Part Two), Pye, 1959.
The Noble Art of Mr. Acker Bilk, Pye, 1959.
Seven Ages of Acker, Columbia, 1960.
Mr. Acker Bilk's Omnibus, Pye, 1960.
That's My Home, Philips, 1960.
Acker, Columbia, 1960.
A Golden Treasury of Bilk, Columbia, 1961.
Mr. Acker Bilk's Lansdowne Folio, Columbia, 1961.
Stranger on the Shore, Columbia, 1962.
Above the Stars and Other Romantic Fancies, Columbia, 1962.
A Taste of Honey, Columbia, 1963.
Great Themes from Great European Movies, Columbia, 1965.
Acker in Paris, Columbia, 1966.
Blue Acker, Columbia, 1968.
Horn of Plenty, Columbia, 1971.
Acker Bilk and His Paramount Jazz Band, Dixieland, 1971.
Some of My Favorite Things, PRT, 1973.
Love Songs, Bridge, 1973.
That's My Desire, PRT, 1974.
Serenade, PRT, 1975.
The One for Me, PRT, 1976.
Invitation, PRT, 1977.
Meanwhile, PRT, 1977.
Sheer Magic, Warwick, 1977.
Extremely Live in Studio 1, PRT, 1978.
Free, PRT, 1978.
When the Lights Are Low, PRT, 1978.
(With Max Bygraves) *Twogether,* Piccadilly, 1980.
Acker Bilk in Holland, Timeless, 1983.
It Looks Like a Big Time Tonight, Stomp Off, 1985.
Blaze Away, Timeless, 1987.
Acker Bilk Plays Lennon & McCartney, GNP, 1988.
Best of Acker Bilk, GNP, 1989.
Heartbeats, Pickwick, 1992.
Chalumeau—That's My Home, Apricot, 1993.
Love Album, Pickwick, 1993.
Hits Blues & Class, Castle, 1994.
Acker Bilk & Strings, Castle, 1994.
Acker Bilk, Castle, 1994.
Imagine, Castle, 1994.
Some of the Best, Delta, 1996.
More of the Best, Delta, 1996.
The Best of Acker Bilk, Excelsior, 1996.
The Best of Acker Bilk, Prime Cuts, 1997.

The Very Best of Acker Bilk, Taragon, 1998.
Great Moments, Timeless, 1998.
Classic Themes, Crimson, 1998.
Unissued Acker, Harlequin, 1999.
The Frankfurt Concert, Hitchcock, 2000.
Acker, Kenny & Chris, Pulse, 2001.
Sweet Georgia Brown, Trad Line, 2002.
Acker, Lake, 2004.

Sources

Books

Cook, Richard and Brian Morton, *Penguin Guide to Jazz on CD,* 3rd edition, Penguin, 1996.
Larkin, Colin, editor, *Encyclopedia of Popular Music,* 3rd edition, MUZE, 1998.

Online

"Acker Bilk," *All Music Guide,* http://www.allmusic.com (February 9, 2004).

—*Bruce Walker*

Norman Blake

Guitarist

Norman Blake has built his well-deserved reputation as a guitarist extraordinaire over the last 35 years, touring with Joan Baez, recording with Bob Dylan, and participating with the Nitty Gritty Dirt Band's *Will the Circle Be Unbroken* project. Blake has received multiple Grammy nominations over the course of his career. Besides stints with John Hartford and Johnny Cash, Blake has recorded multiple solo and group albums for Rounder and Shanachie Records. "Blake maintains a stolidly original approach to traditional music," wrote Scott Nygaard in *Acoustic Guitar,* "and is well-recognized by the mainstream music world for the integrity of his vision."

Blake was born on March 10, 1938, in Chattanooga, Tennessee, but his family soon moved to Georgia and he grew up in Sulphur Springs and Rising Fawn. Like many rural dwellers, he listened to country radio programs like the *Grand Ole Opry* on WSM out of Nashville, and was influenced by artists like the Monroe Brothers, Roy Acuff, and the Carter Family. At age eleven, Blake started playing the guitar and eventually learned to play the dobro, fiddle, and mandolin, making the young musician a one-man band. At age 16 he dropped out of school and joined the Dixie Drifters. The Dixie Drifters debuted in 1954 on *Tennessee Barn Dance,* a Knoxville radio program, and over the next two years also performed on WDOD radio and WROM-TV in Rome, Georgia. Blake left the group in 1956 and joined the Lonesome Travelers, and in the late 1950s the band recorded two albums with Walter Forbes for Radio Corporation of America (RCA). Although Blake left the band to join Hylo Brown and the Timberliners, he continued to perform with the Lonesome Travelers' banjo player, Bob Johnson, and together, they made several guest appearances on the *Grand Ole Opry.*

Blake was drafted into the United States Army in 1961 as a radio operator and was stationed in the Panama Canal for the next two years. He continued his musical development during this time, forming the Fort Kobbe Mountaineers, a bluegrass band that was voted the Best Instrumental Group of the Caribbean Command. On leave in 1962, Blake recorded *12 Shades of Bluegrass* with the Lonesome Travelers, and in 1963 he returned to civilian life. Blake began giving guitar lessons at a music store in Chattanooga in the mid-1960s, teaching as many as 150 students per week. He also played fiddle at country and western dances several days a week. It was a lucky coincidence that he also learned about a blind guitarist named Doc Watson while working at the store. After listening to Watson's Vanguard albums, he began to develop his flatpicking skills. Blake told Nygaard, "I thought to myself, 'Good Lord, if this is what people like, hell, I could do this. I've been doing this off and on and nobody took it seriously.' So I started taking it more seriously."

In the mid-1960s Blake made a number of excursions to Nashville, recording with the Carter Family and traveling with June Carter's road group. He also befriended country music legend Johnny Cash, and when Blake moved to Nashville in 1969 he became part of the "Man in Black's" band on the summer TV program *The Johnny Cash Show.* Blake became a much-sought-after session player, and performed on Bob Dylan's *Nashville Skyline.* He toured and recorded as part of singer-songwriter Kris Kristofferson's first band—Silver Tongue Devil—and played mandolin on Joan Baez's 1971 hit, "The Night They Drove Old Dixie Down."

Although Blake achieved both respect and fame in Nashville, he grew tired of new country-rock and longed to return to his traditional roots. In 1971 he joined John Hartford's band and contributed to the old-time music classic *Aereo-Plain,* an album that became a touchstone for young players like Sam Bush and John Cowan. The "Aereo-Plain" band soon fell apart, but Blake toured with Hartford for a year and a half and played guitar and dobro on his 1972 album *Morning Bugle.* He then sharpened his bluegrass skills for nine months in Red, White and Blue (grass), and received a gold record for his work on *Will the Circle Be Unbroken* in 1972.

The success of these projects helped Blake launch his solo career the same year with the release of *Back Home in Sulfur Springs* on Rounder Records. "Although he only got better over time," wrote Jim Smith in *All Music Guide,* "this record is among Blake's best."

For the Record . . .

Born on March 10, 1938, in Chattanooga, TN; married Nancy Short.

Joined the Dixie Drifters, 1954, and the Lonesome Travelers, 1956; worked for Hylo Brown and the Timberliners, 1959; hired for *The Johnny Cash Show,* 1969; worked as a session musician on Bob Dylan's *Nashville Skyline,* 1969; joined John Hartford, 1971; initiated solo career, 1972; participated on the Nitty Gritty Dirt Band's *Will the Circle Be Unbroken,* 1972; performed two songs for the soundtrack of the Coen Brothers film, *O Brother, Where Art Thou?,* 2000.

Awards: Grammy Award, Album of the Year for *O Brother, Where Art Thou?* (with others), 2001; Country Music Association Award, Album of the Year for *O Brother, Where Art Thou?* (with others), 2001.

Addresses: *Record company*—Shanachie Records, 37 East Clinton St., Newton, NJ 07860, website: http://www.shanachie.com.

Back Home in Sulfur Springs was listed as one of *Acoustic Guitar* magazine's top ten Bluegrass and Country recordings. He also recorded *Whiskey Before Breakfast* with Charlie Collins in 1976 and *Blake and Rice* with guitarist Tony Rice in 1987.

In 1972 Blake met Nancy Short when her band, Natchez Trace, opened for him at the Exit-In in Nashville. The two married, and in 1974 began a 20-plus-year musical partnership. The Blakes recorded a series of four albums together: *Blind Dog* (1988), *Just Gimme Somethin' I'm Used To* (1992), *While Passing Along This Way* (1994), and *The Hobo's Last Ride* (1996). Each was nominated for a Grammy, along with Blake's solo effort, *Chattanooga Sugar Babe* (1998). In 1998 National Public Radio celebrated Blake's 60th birthday by interviewing the guitarist on *All Things Considered.* Never one to take the familiar path, Blake joined forces with Rich O'Brien for *Be Ready Boys: Appalachia to Abilene* in 1999, and participated on Johnny Cash's *American III: Solitary Man* in 2000.

Blake found himself cast into the spotlight in 2000, when he recorded "You Are My Sunshine" and an instrumental version of "The Man of Constant Sorrow" for the Coen Brothers' film *O Brother, Where Art Thou?* The movie's soundtrack, much like *Will the Circle Be Unbroken* in the early 1970s, found a large audience by returning to country music's roots. "I think people are tired of music that comes out of Nashville," Blake told Seth Rogovoy on the Rogovoy Report website. "They appreciate old-fashioned string music if they have the chance to hear it." Blake also won his first Grammy and a Country Music Association award for *O Brother, Where Art Thou?* Despite multiple awards and a dedicated following, Blake retains a rare modesty concerning his accomplishments. "I never felt like I was technically brilliant," he told Nygaard. "I don't make records with that in mind. I try to make *real* music."

Selected discography

Solo

Back Home in Sulphur Springs, Rounder, 1972.
The Fields of November, Flying Fish, 1974.
Going Places, Flying Fish, 1974.
Live at McCabe's, Takoma, 1976.
Blackberry Blossom, Flying Fish, 1977.
Whiskey Before Breakfast, Rounder, 1976.
Rising Fawn String Ensemble, Rounder, 1979.
Full Moon on the Farm, Rounder, 1981.
Original Underground Music, Rounder, 1982.
Nashville Blues, Rounder, 1984.
Lighthouse on the Shore, Rounder, 1985.
Blake and Rice, Rounder, 1987.
Chattanooga Sugar Babe, Shanachie, 1998.
Far Away, Down on a Georgia Farm, Shanachie, 1999.
Flower From the Fields of Alabama, Shanachie, 2001.

With others

(Contributor) *Will the Circle Be Unbroken,* United Artist, 1972.
(With Nancy Blake) *Blind Dog,* Rounder, 1988.
(With Nancy Blake) *Just Gimme Something I'm Used To,* Shanachie, 1992.
(With Nancy Blake) *While Passing Along This Way,* Shanachie, 1994.
(With Nancy Blake) *The Hobo's Last Ride,* Shanachie, 1996.
(With Rich O'Brien) *Be Ready Boys: Appalachian to Abilene,* Shanachie, 1999.
(Contributor) *O Brother, Where Art Thou?,* Mercury, 2000.
(With Peter Ostroushko) *Meeting on Southern Soil,* Red House, 2002.

Sources

Books

Stambler, Irwin and Grelun Landon, *Encyclopedia of Folk, Country and Western Music,* St. Martin's, 1983.

Periodicals

Acoustic Guitar, October 1999.

Online

"For Norman Blake, Old-Time Music Is Always Just There," Rogovoy Report, http://www.rogovoy.com/ (January 26, 2004).

"Norman Blake," *All Music Guide,* http://www.allmusic.com/ (February 2, 2004).

—*Ronnie D. Lankford, Jr.*

Michelle Branch

Singer, songwriter

A breakout pop star with her platinum debut album *Spirit Room,* Michelle Branch's debut single "Everywhere" hit number 12 on *Billboard*'s Hot 100; the video won MTV's Viewer's Choice Award. She won a Grammy Award in 2003 and saw her second album *Hotel Paper* also go platinum—and all this from a young woman who appears to be breaking the mold of female pop singers. Beth Wood of the Copley News Service wrote, "Hailed by fans and the media as the 'UnBritney,' she was the antidote to sexed-up young girls with slick song-and-dance routines, skimpy costumes and prefab careers."

Branch has struck platinum with an image that borrows more from traditional rock 'n' roll than the smooth choreography of contemporary performers like Britney Spears and Christina Aguilera: She writes most of her own songs, plays the guitar, and is most often seen sporting jeans, a T-shirt, and a pair of tennis shoes. Her lifelong dream to perform has been fulfilled in only a short period of time. She told Jon Bream of the Minneapolis *Star Tribune,* "It's exciting to have this for a job, to play guitar and travel around the world."

Born Michelle Jacquet Branch on July 2, 1983, in Flagstaff, Arizona, her father is a plumber-contractor and her mother is a restaurant manager. She claims that from the age of three she knew she wanted to sing and perform—her first wish was to be on Broadway in musicals like *Cats* or *Oklahoma.* Other influences were found in her parents' record collection, which included bands such as the Beatles and Led Zeppelin and singer-songwriter Joni Mitchell. By the age of eight she was begging her mother to send her to voice lessons.

Branch's family moved to Sedona, Arizona, when she was eleven years old. About that time she started performing at local fairs; she also started writing her own lyrics and recording them, a cappella, on tape. Her focus turned from musical theater to pop when she attended a New Kids on the Block concert and saw the crowd's reaction to the group. After her parents gave her a guitar when she was 14, she told David L. Coddon of the *San Diego Union-Tribune,* "I got a chord book and literally locked myself in my room and kept playing the chords over and over. Two weeks later, I came out … and played a song I'd just written for my parents." Now accompanied by her guitar, Branch continued to record her compositions on tape.

Those tapes would prove instrumental in establishing her career. In 1999 a family friend was showing a condo to a music manager from Los Angeles. The friend called Branch and convinced her to bring the tape over to the condo. Jeff Rabhan was so impressed he helped Branch record her demo album *Broken Bracelet* and booked her on a tour opening for the band Hanson. She soon caught the attention of Maverick Records, the company started by legendary pop star Madonna.

For the Record . . .

Born Michelle Jacquet Branch on July 2, 1983, in Flagstaff, AZ; daughter of a plumber-contractor and a restaurant manager.

Grew up singing at home and at local fairs; taught herself to play guitar, age 14; auditioned for manager Jeff Rabhan and recorded demo album *Broken Bracelet,* 1999; signed with Maverick Records and recorded debut album, *Spirit Room,* 2001; recorded Grammy Award–winning song, "Game of Love" with Santana, toured with Sheryl Crow and Dixie Chicks, and appeared in a cameo role on *American Dreams,* 2002; released second album, *Hotel Paper,* performed in Super Bowl XXXVII pregame concert, and headlined her own world tour, 2003.

Awards: MTV Viewers Choice Award, 2001; Grammy Award, Best Pop Collaboration with Vocals (with Carlos Santana), 2003.

Addresses: *Record company*—Maverick Records, 9348 Civic Center Dr., Beverly Hills, CA 90210, phone: (310) 385-7800, fax: (310) 385-7711. *Home*—Michelle Branch, P.O. Box 20425, Sedona, AZ 86341. *Website*—Michelle Branch Official Website: http://www.michellebranch.net. *E-mail*—michelle@michellebranch.net.

Branch's debut album with Maverick was *Spirit Room,* and it featured songs she'd written before she ever had a record deal. The album's first single, "Everywhere," became a huge hit, landing at number 12 on the *Billboard* Hot 100. The video won an MTV Viewer's Choice Award in 2001. The video for her second single, "All You Wanted," was nominated for Best Female Video and Best Pop Video and became a favorite on MTV's *Total Request Live. Spirit Room* went platinum a year later, and made it as high as number 28 on *Billboard's* charts.

In 2002 Branch's songs were used in the television show *Gilmore Girls* and in the film *American Pie 2.* She toured with female rocker Sheryl Crow and opened for country rock darlings the Dixie Chicks. Her third single from *Spirit Room,* "Goodbye to You," hit the *Billboard* Top 10. She also made a guest appearance on the television show *American Dreams* as 1960s singer Lesley Gore. For the role Branch sported a blonde wig and performed Gore's 1963 hit single "You Don't Own Me."

Branch's sudden rise to fame threw her into the company of some of the music industry's most powerful and popular performers, putting her in awe of her good fortune. As a fan of Crow's, for example, Branch was amazed to find herself in the same building as her idol. She told Alisa Blackwood of the Associated Press, "Little things like that freak me out more than performing because I'm such a fan."

In 2002 Branch was invited to work with guitarist Carlos Santana, who was recording his album *Supernatural.* Her rendition of the song "Game of Love," the result of their collaboration, was an incredible success, reaching number one on the *Billboard* charts and staying there for 13 weeks. Branch and Santana won a Grammy Award in 2002 for Best Pop Collaboration with Vocals.

Branch began 2003 by performing at the Super Bowl XXXVII pregame show. Her second album, *Hotel Paper,* was released in June of that year and promptly hit the charts, eventually reaching number two; the single "Are You Happy Now?" landed in the top ten. The album title reflected Branch's peripatetic life—most of the songs she wrote for the album were composed while on tour the previous year. One track, in fact, was a duet with her former touring partner, Sheryl Crow. That year also saw Branch headline her first tour. Unfortunately, the intense schedule took a toll on her health; toward the end of the year she was forced to cancel several appearances. She recuperated in time to perform at the half-time show of the Major League Soccer Cup championship.

Despite her illness, Branch ended 2003 on a happy note—her second single from *Hotel Paper,* "Breathe," made it into the top ten. *Hotel Paper* went platinum, and her single "Are You Happy Now?" earned her a third Grammy Award nomination for Best Female Rock Vocal Performance.

Branch's career seems to have been blessed. When asked about the ease with which she succeeded, Branch told Blackwood, "It's so funny because it felt so natural and I fell into it so easily. It's one of those things, I felt like I was meant to do this." Though her star rose quickly, she plans to be around for a long time. Speaking of her hopes for the future she told Blackwood, "I really want to establish myself as a writer and have people take me seriously as a writer. ... That's probably the most important thing to me, above singing and guitar playing. ... Maybe in the future I'll even write songs for other people."

Selected discography

Broken Bracelet, Independent, 2000.
Spirit Room, Maverick, 2001.

(With Carlos Santana) *Supernatural,* BMG/Arista, 2002.
Hotel Paper, Maverick, 2003.

Sources

Periodicals

Associated Press, March 10, 2002; July 2, 2002.
Copley News Service, August 4, 2003.
San Diego Union-Tribune, January 23, 2003, p. 2.
Star Tribune (Minneapolis, MN), May 17, 2002, p. 5E.
Times Union (Albany, NY), November 18, 2003, p. F1.

Online

Michelle Branch Official Website, http://www.michellebranch.net (March 3, 2004).
"Michelle Branch: She's 'Everywhere,'" MTV, http://www.mtv.com/bands/b/branch_michelle/news_feature_100601/index.jhtml (February 3, 2004).

—*Eve M. B. Hermann*

Cash Brothers

Country rock duo

Unlike other famous brother duos throughout country and rock music history, Andrew and Peter Cash didn't sing together as a team until they were in their 30s. Instead, both had pursued their own musical paths, one as a punk rocker, the other as a country rocker. When the Cash Brothers finally decided to tie their musical fates together, however, they weren't even sure it would work: what if their voices didn't blend well together? The newly christened duo booked time at a Toronto recording studio to satisfy their curiosity. "I remember going into the control room to hear what it sounded like," Andrew Cash recalled in *All Music Guide.* "We just looked at each other and said: 'Hey, this is going to work.'"

Andrew and Peter Cash were born in Toronto in the early 1960s into a non-musical family. Even as teens, the brothers' paths seldom crossed as they pursued separate interests. Two older brothers influenced their musical development, introducing them to the sounds of Neil Young, the Byrds, and the Flying Burrito Brothers. Besides California country rock, the Cash Brothers listened to British rockers like early Rod Stewart, early Elton John, and the Rolling Stones. Peter Cash eventually started writing, recording, and singing for the Skydiggers, a rootsy alternative country group. Andrew Cash joined L'Estranger with Chuck Angus in 1980, but left the band to pursue a solo career in the mid-1980s. It was only when the two brothers were between projects in 1997 that they decided to record their first track together. "Something about the way we sing together feels really great," Andrew Cash told Elita

Bradley in the *Washington Times,* "even when we're singing out of tune together."

Over the next two years the Cash Brothers built a repertoire of 40 songs, and in 1999 included 11 of those on their first album, *Raceway.* While honing their songwriting skills, the brothers were also careful to build their careers slowly. "We're coming together for the first time," Andrew Cash told Frank Goodman for Pure Music online, "at the point where lots of brothers who worked together aren't speaking to each other anymore.... We've taken it kind of slowly, partially because we've both been in enough bands to know what a grind it can be at some points." Peter Cash concurred. "It helps to have a lot of songs, as far as making the whole ship sail better, or smoother," he told Regis Behe in the Pittsburgh *Tribune Review.* "If something isn't working, we quickly move on, and it's not a bad thing."

The Cash Brothers patience paid off in 2001 when the independent Zoë label gave *Raceway* a facelift, retitling it *How Was Tomorrow?* and making several track changes. With acoustic and jangly electric guitars backing up pristine harmony, the brothers concocted a catchy classic rock sound that harked back to Bruce Springsteen. Indeed, the connections to the "Boss" are made obvious on the cut titled "Nebraska." In the song, the narrator eases his troubled mind after a break-up by driving around town and listening to Springsteen's *Nebraska. How Was Tomorrow?* also generated a strong critical response. Matt Fink in FAME called it "smart, sincere, and extraordinarily consistent," adding that the album "proves that the Cash legacy might be sprouting new branches but from a totally different tree."

How Was Tomorrow?'s well-crafted songs impressed critics. "Night Shift Guru" is a small slice-of-life story about a 7-Eleven clerk killing time by watching himself on the small television screen behind the counter as he munches potato chips. "Guitar Strings and Foolish Things" finds the narrator remembering quiet, elusive moments that occur when he is supposed to be working. Although both brothers compose separately, they attribute each song to the Cash Brothers, partly in realization that composing a song is only half the battle. "Sometimes the writing of the song isn't necessarily the hardest part," Peter told Goodman. "A lot more may be involved to get it arranged and sounding right. Say I write a song, but Andrew spends a lot more time than I did writing it tweaking it in various ways to get it to sound very special on record."

The Cash Brothers also developed a solid reputation for their live shows. Following the release of *How Was Tomorrow?,* they toured the United States, including opening for the Jayhawks in Atlanta. According to Stephen King in the British *Birmingham Post,* "From the moment the pair struck up their chiming guitars and

For the Record . . .

Members include **Andrew Cash** (born in 1962 in Toronto, Ontario, Canada), guitar, vocals; **Peter Cash** (born in Toronto, Ontario, Canada), guitar, vocals.

Formed the Cash Brothers, 1997; recorded *Raceway*, 1999; released *How Was Tomorrow?* on Zoë Records, 2001; recorded *A Brand New Night*, 2003.

Addresses: *Record company*—Zoë Records, One Camp Street, Cambridge, MA 02140, phone: 617-354-4840, website: http://www.rounder.com. *Website*—Cash Brothers Official Website: http://www.cashbrothers.com.

demonstrated their close harmonizing, one knew this was no ordinary outfit."

In 2003 the Cash Brothers released *A Brand New Night*, further enhancing their reputation. "The song writing is the same," Peter Cash told John Hayes in the *Pittsburgh Post-Gazette*, "but the big thing for this record is that we basically [went] a little more electric than the last one. It's to try to give it some variety." *A Brand New Night* also showed the band creating an eclectic repertoire, stretching from mellow ballads like "Fire Dying" and the title track to the funky, brash "Give Me Your Hips." The duo also continued to sharpen its songwriting skills, capturing the small details that make up everyday life. "At their best," wrote Hayes, "Toronto's Cash Brothers' stories are charcoal outlines of vacant emotions, delivered in an acoustic, just-behind-the-beat alt-country whine."

The Cash Brothers' combination of folk, rock, and country harmonies has made the band difficult for crit-ics to categorize. The brother harmony reminds many of older country music, while the combination of acoustic and electric guitar reminds others of folk rock. But Andrew and Peter Cash would rather not be pigeonholed. "There are categories like alt-country or rock or neo-folk, but they don't necessarily apply to what we do," Andrew Cash told Behe. In the end, however, what has mattered is the quality of the Cash Brothers' music itself. Wrote Goodman, "Their classic brothers harmony in both arrangement and execution and their excellent and experienced songwriting are the two factors that shot them to the front of a crowded class."

Selected discography

Raceway, Cash Brothers, 1999; reissued, Universal, 2001.
How Was Tomorrow?, Zoë, 2001.
(Contributor) *Roots Music: An American Journey*, Rounder, 2001.
A Brand New Night, Zoë, 2003.

Sources

Periodicals

Birmingham Post (England), November 29, 2001, p. 15.
Tribune-Review, August 17, 2003.
Washington Times, January 17, 2002, p. 2.

Online

"Cash Brothers," *All Music Guide*, http://www.allmusic.com (February 2, 2004).
"Conversation With the Cash Brothers," Pure Music, http://www.puremusic.com/cash1.html (February 2, 2004).
"*How Was Tomorrow?*," FAME, http://www.acousticmusic.com/fame/p01809.htm (February 2, 2004).
"Music Preview," *Pittsburgh Post-Gazette*, http://post-gazette.com (February 2, 2004).

—*Ronnie D. Lankford, Jr.*

Steven Curtis Chapman

Singer, songwriter

The fast-growing popularity of contemporary Christian music has been greatly helped along by the songs and albums of Steven Curtis Chapman. The winner of four Grammy awards and numerous Gospel Music Association Dove awards, Chapman has gathered a large following of listeners, sometimes attracting more than 360,000 people to a concert. Although he has become a popular singer and performer, his songwriting skills have greatly contributed to his success; he has written most of the songs on his albums. In addition, other well-known Christian and country singers, including Billy Dean, Charlie Daniels, Sandi Patti, and Glen Campbell, have recorded his songs.

A musician from an early age, Chapman began playing the guitar when he was six years old. In his first-grade singing debut, he took the stage with his brother Fred in a school show that featured the boys' versions of Glen Campbell's "Try a Little Kindness" and Mac Davis's "I Believe in Music." The performance established a singing partnership that would last until Fred left for college. Chapman did not concentrate solely on singing, however; he took advantage of being the son of a music store owner by learning to play most of the instruments available to him.

When Chapman graduated from high school he planned on a career in medicine, not because he passionately wanted to be a doctor but because he felt he should pursue something practical. Before embarking on this conventional course, though, he spent the summer performing at the Opryland theater in Nashville, Tennessee. He enjoyed the experience, and during his first semester at Georgetown College in Kentucky, he decided to abandon his premed studies for a musical education. He transferred to Anderson College in Indiana to major in music, tempering the risky move by concentrating on songwriting. Chapman performed each summer at Opryland during his college years, but he continued to feel his best chance at a career in music was as a songwriter. He stuck with that decision after transferring to Belmont College in Nashville.

Gradually, Chapman was persuaded to attempt a performance career. During his college years, several publishing company and record label representatives suggested he could succeed as a recording artist and songwriter. Sparrow Records then confirmed those suggestions by signing the contract that led to Chapman's debut album, *First Hand.* Released in 1987, the LP was the first in a steady string of popular contemporary Christian albums for Chapman. A combination of country, rock, pop, and folk music, *First Hand* contains three songs that made it into the top three of the contemporary Christian music (CCM), or inspirational, charts.

The following year, Sparrow released Chapman's second album, *Real Life Conversations,* which carried the sudden success of the first even further. Several songs

For the Record . . .

Born in Paducah, KY; married; wife's name, Mary Beth; children: Emily, Caleb, Will Franklin, Shaohannah, Stevey Joy. *Education:* Attended Georgetown College, KY, and Anderson College, IN; received bachelor's degree from Belmont College, Nashville, TN.

Signed contract with Sparrow Records, mid-1980s; released debut album, *First Hand,* 1987; released *Real Life Conversations,* 1988; released *More to This Life,* 1989; released *For the Sake of the Call,* 1990; released *The Great Adventure,* 1993; released *Heaven in the Real World,* 1994; released *Music of Christmas,* 1995; released *Signs of Life,* 1996; released *Greatest Hits,* 1997; released *Speechless,* 1999; released *Declaration,* 2001; released *All About Love,* 2002.

Awards: Grammy Awards, Best Pop Gospel Album for *For the Sake of the Call,* 1992, *The Great Adventure,* 1993, *The Live Adventure,* 1994, and *Speechless,* 1999; Dove Awards, Songwriter of the Year, 1989-95 and 1997-98; Contemporary Recorded Song of the Year for "His Eyes," 1989, "Go There with You," 1994, "Heaven in the Real World," 1995, and "Let Us Pray," 1998; Artist of the Year, 1990, 1991, 1993, 1995, 1997, and 2000; Inspirational Recorded Song of the Year for "His Strength Is Perfect," 1990; Southern Gospel Recorded Song of the Year for "I Can See the Hand," 1990; Male Vocalist of the Year, 1990, 1991, 1995, 1997-98, and 2000-01; Contemporary Album of the Year, 1992, 1993, 1995, 1997, 2000, and 2002; Song of the Year for "The Great Adventure," 1993; American Music Award, Favorite Artist in Contemporary Inspirational Music, 2003.

Addresses: *Record company*—Sparrow Records, P.O. Box 5010, Brentwood, TN 37024-5010, website: http://www.sparrowrecords.com. *Management*—Creative Trust, 1910 Acklen Ave., Nashville, TN 37212. *Website*—Steven Curtis Chapman Official Website: http://www.stevencurtischapman.com.

rose to the top five of the CCM charts, with two songs, "His Eyes" and "My Turn Now," reaching number one. "His Eyes" won the Dove Award for Contemporary Recorded Song of the Year. In addition, the album earned him another Dove Award, for Songwriter of the Year, and a Grammy nomination for Best Male Gospel Performance.

From the beginning of his recording career, Chapman has upheld a serious commitment to ministering to people through his music. "Since the fall of certain religious leaders," Chapman commented in *Billboard,* "a lot of people are viewing Christianity with a certain amount of skepticism. How I personally respond to that, how I handle that is important. 'For Who He Really Is' [from the album *Real Life Conversations*] is my heart's cry."

Billboard said of Chapman's 1990 release, *For the Sake of the Call:* "Like previous releases, [it] contains plain-spoken spiritual insights, set to pleasant, hummable AC/pop music. Chapman is an affable and appealing artist, but his lyrics are never lightweight." The musician has explained that his lyrics are developed only after serious research and preparation; for the 1990 album, for example, he acknowledges the influence of Dietrich Bonhoeffer's book *The Cost of Discipleship.*

Although some reviews accused *For the Sake of the Call* of following a Christian-radio formula, listeners made it Chapman's most popular release yet. Five songs rose to number one on the CCM chart, and the LP itself hit the very top of the CCM Top 50 albums chart. The album led once again to his recognition at the Grammys—this time for Best Pop Gospel Album—and at the Dove awards ceremony for songwriter of the year. In addition, *For the Sake of the Call* became Chapman's first LP to win the Dove Award for contemporary album of the year.

The sweep of awards continued for Chapman's next two albums, *The Great Adventure* and *Heaven in the Real World.* Not only did new Grammy awards and Dove awards attest to his popularity, but he received numerous American Songwriter Magazine Awards, CCM Reader Awards, and recognition in the Campus Life Readers' Choice Poll. His Great Adventure tour covered 70 cities, and in some places, he played before crowds of more than 360,000. His mid-1990s Heaven in the Real World tour covered 70 cities in the United States and took him to 30 cities around the world, including ones in South Africa, South America, Europe, and Asia.

The Heaven in the Real World album marked a transition for Chapman into a new level of musical and marketing sophistication. The artist recorded the LP in Los Angeles rather than in Nashville and was joined by veteran studio musicians. Ed Cherney, who has worked with pop stars Bonnie Raitt and Don Was, handled the recording and mixing. With *Heaven in the Real World,* Chapman became one of the first contemporary Christian musicians to benefit from industry-wide SoundScan retail tracking and wider viewing of contemporary Christian videos. Such factors prompted *Billboard*'s Bob Darden to declare that "Chapman is poised to do what [country superstar] Garth Brooks did a few years ago, only in a different genre of music."

Chapman's immense popularity in the contemporary Christian music realm was further cemented in 1995, when he won six Dove awards. The year 1995 also saw the release of Chapman's *Music of Christmas* album. He quickly followed this with *Signs of Life* in 1996. More Dove awards followed, and he landed his fourth Grammy for Best Contemporary Gospel Album in 1999 for *Speechless.* Chapman picked up several more Dove awards for *Speechless,* including the Dove award for Contemporary Album of the Year, Artist of the Year, and Male Vocalist of the Year. His 2001 album, *Declaration,* also won him a Dove award for Contemporary Album of the Year award. In 2003, Chapman took home his first American Music Award, for Favorite Artist in Contemporary Inspirational Music.

Through all of his successes, Chapman has kept sight of his priorities. "My goal isn't just to share what I believe," Chapman proclaimed in a Sparrow Records press biography, "it is to show that belief is important, that it can make a difference, that there can be meaning to all of this we're going through."

Despite the increased sophistication in his production and marketing methods and some speculation over whether he will attempt to "cross over" to the mainstream pop market, Chapman continues to dedicate his musical talent to sharing his religious ideas. In addition to composing and performing music, Chapman has also found time to start a charitable organization with his wife, Mary Beth Chapman. Shaohannah's Hope, named after the couple's adopted daughter, helps orphaned children find homes.

Selected discography

First Hand, Sparrow, 1987.
Real Life Conversations, Sparrow, 1988.
More to This Life, Sparrow, 1989.
For the Sake of the Call, Sparrow, 1990.
The Great Adventure, Sparrow, 1992.
The Live Adventure, Sparrow, 1993.
Heaven in the Real World, Sparrow, 1994.
Music of Christmas, Sparrow, 1995.
Signs of Life, Sparrow, 1996.
Greatest Hits, Sparrow, 1997.
Speechless, Sparrow, 1999.
Declaration, Sparrow, 2001.
All About Love, Sparrow, 2002.

Sources

Periodicals

Billboard, December 10, 1988; December 17, 1988; March 23, 1991; October 31, 1992; April 17, 1993; July 30, 1994; August 6, 1994; February 25, 1995; May 6, 1995.
Cash Box, August 1994.
Detroit Free Press, November 11, 1994.

Online

"Dove Awards History," Dove Awards, http://www.dovea wards.com/history/ (January 21, 2004).
Recording Academy Grammy Awards, http://www.grammy. com/awards/search/index.aspx (January 21, 2004).
Shaohannah's Hope, http://www.shaohannahshope.org (January 21, 2004).
"Steven Curtis Chapman," *All Music Guide,* http://www. allmusic.com (January 21, 2004).
Steven Curtis Chapman Official Website, http://www.steven curtischapman.com (January 21, 2004).

Additional information for this profile was obtained from Sparrow Records publicity materials.

—*Susan Windisch Brown and Michael Belfiore*

Cyrus Chestnut

Pianist, bandleader

© Jack Vartoogian. Reproduced by permission.

Soulful jazz pianist Cyrus Chestnut might just be proof positive of the impact that music has on babies in the womb. Either that, or a life in music was simply in his blood. Chestnut's father, a retired postal employee and the son of a church musician, was the official organist for the local church in Baltimore, Maryland, where Chestnut grew up. Young Cyrus's home was filled with the sounds of the gospel music that his church-going parents played in their home, along with jazz records by artists such as Baby Cortez and Jimmy Smith. Chestnut has said that the roots of his love of music began there, and to this day, Chestnut's ties to the gospel church remain constant. "Growing up, gospel music was what I heard in the house," Chestnut told *Down Beat* magazine.

As a boy Chestnut reached for the piano keys before he could walk, so his father began teaching the earnest five-year-old to play the piano. One of the first songs young Cyrus learned was "Jesus Loves Me." Before long, seven-year-old Cyrus was playing piano in the family church, and by age nine he was promoted to church organist at Mt. Calvary Church in Baltimore, Maryland.

Chestnut, who became known for his improvisational skills and unique jazz-gospel and bop style, has credited his abilities to those formative years when he played at church. And while Chestnut's roots in gospel stemmed from his life at home and in the church, his passion for jazz was born not long thereafter. With his two-dollar allowance, young Chestnut purchased his first album, Thelonious Monk's *Greatest Hits,* simply because he liked the album cover, and thus the young pianist's love of jazz began.

At age nine Chestnut was enrolled in the prep program at the Peabody Institute in Baltimore. He later headed to Berklee College of Music in Boston, where he earned a degree in jazz composition and arranging. Before graduating from Berklee in 1985, Chestnut had received the Eubie Blake fellowship in 1982, the Oscar Peterson scholarship in 1983, and the Quincy Jones scholarship in 1984. In his free time Chestnut studied the history of music and the work of such masters as pianists Bud Powell, Wynton Kelly, and Hank Jones, and the work of gospel artists Clara Ward, Charles Taylor, and Shirley Caesar. In school he studied classical music, writing and performing. A Warner Jazz website article on Chestnut quoted the *New York Times,* which described Chestnut as a "highly intelligent improviser with one of the surest senses of swing in jazz."

After graduating from Berklee, Chestnut went on to work with jazz vocalist Jon Hendricks from 1986-88, and trumpeter Terrence Blanchard and saxophonist Donald Harrison from 1988-90, before joining jazz legend Wynton Marsalis in 1991. But Chestnut really cut his teeth in the business when, one day at Berklee, jazz vocalist Betty Carter arrived to perform. When the

For the Record . . .

Born on January 17, 1963, in Baltimore, MD; son of McDonald (a retired post office employee and church organist) and Flossie (a city social services worker and church choir director) Chestnut; married; wife's name, Ellen; children: Jazzmin Chestnut. *Education:* Attended Peabody Institute, MD; graduated from Berklee College of Music, Boston, MA, 1985.

Toured as pianist for Jon Hendricks, 1986-88; pianist, Terrence Blanchard, 1988-90; pianist, Donald Harrison, 1988-90; bandleader and producer, *There's A Brighter Day Comin'*, 1989; pianist, Wynton Marsalis, 1991; pianist, Betty Carter Trio, 1991-93; recorded *The Nutman Speaks*, 1992, and *The Nutman Speaks Again*, 1993; signed with Atlantic Records, released *Revelation*, 1993; released *Dark Before the Dawn*, 1994; formed Cyrus Chestnut Trio, 1994; toured with opera singer Kathleen Battle, 1995; contributed to soundtrack of Robert Altman film *Kansas City*, 1996; released *Soul Food*, 2001; released *You Are My Sunshine*, 2003.

Awards: Eubie Blake fellowship, 1982; Oscar Peterson scholarship, 1983; Quincy Jones scholarship, 1984.

Addresses: *Booking*—Chriss & Co., 300 Mercer St., Ste. 3J, New York, NY 10003, website: http://www.jchriss.com. *Website*—Cyrus Chestnut Official Website: http://www.cyruschestnut.com.

famous singer found herself without a piano player, the entire auditorium erupted with suggestions for Chestnut to fill in, and he was ushered to the stage. Terrified and nervous, Chestnut took the stage, but when Carter asked him to play *Body and Soul* in the key of G, Chestnut mistakenly played it in C. "I told myself that someday I would make it up to her," Chestnut told *Berklee Today*. After a short stint playing aboard a Caribbean cruise ship in 1985 with a band that included Dizzy Gillespie, Joe Williams, and Tommy Flanagan, Chestnut graduated from Berklee. In 1991 he got his chance to repay Carter when he went on the road for two years as the pianist for the Betty Carter Trio. "She wanted you to create a mode of creating, not re-creating," Chestnut told the *Santa Fe New Mexican*. He

has often said that playing with Carter was a form of graduate school.

For Chestnut, there has always been a deep connection between jazz and God. He believes jazz to be a religious musical genre. "I believe the ability to play music is a gift from God and every time I play, I'm thankful. Every time I sit down to play, for me, is worship and expression," he told *Down Beat* magazine. Fitting this connection, the title of Chestnut's major label debut album was *Revelations,* which he released in 1994 at the age of 30. The album was voted Best Jazz Album by the *Village Voice* and soared on the charts, outselling expectations for piano trio recordings. Prior to that, Chestnut had broken out of his role as an accompanist and band member by forming and leading his own trio. Chestnut's trio recorded two albums on the Japanese label Alfa Jazz, *The Nutman Speaks* and *The Nutman Speaks Again,* in 1992. He also recorded *Nut* in 1992 and *Another Direction* in 1993, both on Evidence.

In 1994 Chestnut released *Dark Before the Dawn* for Atlantic Records. "It's a musical story about me. It's about my life experiences, how I felt at the time, my reactions. Life is not one-sided. A lot of different things happen in life," Chestnut told the *Philadelphia Inquirer*. The album debuted in the sixth spot on the *Billboard Jazz Charts*. The very next year, Chestnut released the critically acclaimed *Earth Stories,* for which he composed nine of the CD's eleven tracks.

Chestnut has earned a reputation for his skillful versatility, his ability for blending sounds and for unabashedly bringing gospel into the club performances he gives. And despite his sense of playful showmanship, he takes jazz very seriously and believes that jazz has great staying power. "Just as Bruce Springsteen has that ability to appeal to a mass audience, I have a vision that jazz can do the same. You can't underestimate the power of this music," Chestnut told the *St. Petersburg Times*.

Throughout his career, Chestnut has worked with an array of artists, including saxophonists James Carter, Donald Harrison and Joe Lovano; trumpeters Roy Hargrove and Freddie Hubbard; jazzman Chick Corea, and opera singer Kathleen Battle, with whom he toured extensively in 1995. More recently Chestnut has collaborated with vocalists Vanessa Williams, Anita Baker, and Brian McKnight. In 2000 he collaborated with Isaac Hayes and the Boys Choir of Harlem on an updated version of Vince Guaraldi's *A Charlie Brown Christmas*. Chestnut also played on bassist Christian McBride's debut album.

Chestnut's 2001 release, *Soul Food,* provided a showcase for his versatility. The album is a blend of jazz, classical, gospel, and R&B. Chestnut was joined on the album by Christian McBride, Lewis Nash, Marcus

Printup, Wycliffe Gordon, Gary Bartz, and James Carter. In 2003 Chestnut released *You Are My Sunshine* on Warner Brothers Records. The album cover featured Chestnut's daughter, Jazzmin, kissing her father on the cheek. Prior to that, Chestnut released a solo piano album, *Blessed Quietness: Collection of Hymns, Spirituals, Carols* in 1996, and followed with *Cyrus Chestnut* in 1998.

The *New York Daily News* once heralded Chestnut as the rightful heir to Bud Powell, Art Tatum and Erroll Garner. In an interview on National Public Radio (NPR) for *All Things Considered,* Chestnut remarked, "If I can send one person home after a performance feeling better than when they arrived, then I've done my job, and I sleep good at night." To this day, Chestnut attends church every Sunday, and whenever he can he plays in the local church in Brooklyn, New York, where he lives with his family. He told *CBS News,* "If I'm not working, you'll find me in somebody's church."

Selected discography

Solo

The Nutman Speaks, Alfa Jazz, 1992.
The Nutman Speaks Again, Alfa Jazz, 1992.
Nut, Evidence, 1992.
Another Direction, Evidence, 1993.
Revelation, Atlantic, 1993.
Dark Before the Dawn, Atlantic, 1994.
Earth Stories, Atlantic, 1995.
Blessed Quietness: Collection of Hymns, Spirituals, Carols, Atlantic, 1996.
Cyrus Chestnut, Atlantic, 1998.
A Charlie Brown Christmas, Atlantic, 2000.
Soul Food, Atlantic, 2001.
You Are My Sunshine, Warner, 2003.

With others

Plays Herbie Hancock, Paddle Wheel, 1987.
(With Michael Carvin) *Between Me and You,* Muse, 1988.
(With Kim Waters) *Sweet and Saxy,* Warlock, 1989.
(With Michael Carvin) *Revelation,* Muse, 1989.
(With Donald Harrison Quintet) *For Art's Sake,* Candid, 1990.
(With Donald Harrison) *Full Circle,* Sweet Basil, 1990.
(With Donald Harrison) *Indian Blues,* Candid, 1991.
(With Jae Sinnett) *Blue Jae,* Valley Vue, 1991.
(With Betty Carter) *It's Not About the Melody,* Verve, 1992.
(With Kim Waters) *Tribute,* Warlock, 1992.
(With Jazz Voice) *Jazz Voice,* Hot Productions, 1992.
(With Ronnie Burrage) *Ronnie Burrage Shuttle,* Sound Hills, 1993.
(With Denise Jannah) *Heart Full of Music,* Timeless, 1993.
(With Freddy Cole) *Circle of Love,* Fantasy, 1993.
(With Roy Hargrove Quintet) *With the Tenors of Our Time,* Polygram, 1993.
(With Joris Teep & the Don Braden Quintet) *Pay as You Earn,* Mons, 1993.

(With Vincent Herring) *Folklore: Live At The Village Vanguard,* Music Master, 1993.
(With Freddy Cole) *Always,* Fantasy, 1994.
(With Jae Sinnett) *House & Sinnett,* Positive, 1994.
(With Christian McBride) *Gettin' to It,* Polygram, 1994.
(With Carl Allen) *Testimonial,* Atlantic, 1994.
(With Gerald Albright) *Giving Myself to You,* Atlantic, 1995.
(With Denise Jannah) *I Was Born in Love with You,* Blue Note, 1995.
(With Kathleen Battle) *So Many Stars,* Sony Classical, 1995.
(With Jeri Brown) *Fresh Start,* Justin Time, 1995.
(With Vincent Herring) *Don't Let It Go,* Music Master, 1995.
(With Dave Young) *Two by Two: The Complete Sessions,* Justin Time, 1995.
(With Tim Warfield Quintet) *Cool Blue,* Criss Cross, 1995.
(With Steve Wilson) *Step Lively,* Criss Cross, 1995.
(With Rodney Whitaker) *Children of the Light,* Koch Jazz, 1996.
(With Tim Warfield) *Whisper in the Midnight,* Criss Cross, 1996.
(With Dave Young) *Side by Side, Vol. 3,* Justin Time, 1996.
(With Dave Young) *Two by Two, Vol. 2,* Justin Time, 1996.
(With Hollywood Bowl Orchestra) *Prelude to a Kiss,* Philips, 1996.
Miles 2 Go, Polygram, 1996.
(With Gary Bartz) *Blues Chronicles: Tales of Life,* Atlantic, 1996.
(With Ge Ann Hampton Callaway) *To Ella with Love,* After 9 Records, 1996.
(With Madeleine Peyroux) *Dreamland,* Atlantic, 1996.
(With Courtney Pine) *Underground,* Verve, 1997.
(With Kansas City Band) *KC After Dark: More Music from Robert Altman's Kansas City,* Polygram, 1997.
(With James Carter) *In Carterian Fashion,* Atlantic, 1998.
(With Freddy Cole) *To the Ends of the Earth,* Fantasy, 1997.
(With Dizzy Gillespie Alumni All Stars) *Dizzy's 80th Birthday Party,* Shanachie, 1997.
(With George Mraz) *Bottom Lines,* Milestone, 1997.
(With Bud Shank) *By Request: Bud Shank Meets the Rhythm Section,* Milestone, 1997.
(With Jae Sinnett) *Listen,* Heart Music, 1997.
(With General Music Project) *General Music Project, Vol. 2,* Evidence, 1998.
(With Bette Midler) *Bathhouse Betty,* Warner Brothers, 1998.
(With Tim Warfield) *Gentle Warrior,* Criss Cross, 1998.
(With Freddy Cole) *Grand Freddy,* Fantasy, 1999.
(With Carla Cook) *It's All About Love,* Max Jazz, 1999.
(With Lincoln Center Jazz Orchestra & Wynton Marsalis) *Live in Swing City: Swingin with the Duke,* Sony, 1999.
(With Sadao Watanabe) *Remembrance,* Verve, 1999.
(With Wynton Marsalis) *Marciac Suite,* Columbia, 1999.
(With Joh Yamada) *Bluestone,* Milestone, 1999.
(With George Mraz) *Duke's Place,* Milestone, 1999.
(With Roy Nathanson) *Fire at Keaton's Bar and Grill,* Six Degrees, 1999.
(With Little Jimmy Scott) *Mood Indigo,* Milestone, 2000.
(With Kevin Mahogany) *Portrait of Kevin Mahogany,* Warner Brothers, 2000.
(With Manhattan Trinity) *Make Me A Memory,* Lightyear, 2000.
(With Dr. John) *Funky New Orleans,* Metro Music, 2000.
(With The Keystone Quartet) *Love Story,* 32 Jazz, 2000.
(With Carla Cook) *Dem Bones,* Max Jazz, 2001.
(With Carla Cook) *Simply Natural,* Maxx Jazz, 2002.
(With Tim Warfield) *Jazz Is,* Criss Cross, 2002.
(With Betty Carter) *Betty Carter's Finest Hour,* Verve, 2003.
(With Little Jimmy Scott) *Moon Glow,* Milestone, 2003.

Sources

Periodicals

Down Beat, March 1997.
New York Daily News, December 1, 1996.
Philadelphia Inquirer, April 19, 1996.
St. Petersburg Times, February 19, 1999.
Santa Fe New Mexican, October 3, 2003.

Online

"Cyrus Chestnut," *All Music Guide,* http://www.allmusic.com (February 5, 2004).
"Cyrus Chestnut," Warner Jazz, http://www.warnerjazz.co.uk/launch.php?page=releasefull.php%Fnid%3D42 (February 5, 2004).
"Piano Stories," Berklee Today, http://www.berklee.edu/bt/123/piano.html (February 5, 2004).

Additional information was obtained from an interview with Cyrus Chestnut on *CBS Sunday Morning* on October 27, 1996, and from an interview on National Public Radio's *All Things Considered* on December 16, 2000.

—*Kerry L. Smith*

Chicks on Speed

The Berlin, Germany-based trio Chicks on Speed emerged on the electroclash scene in the late 1990s. Never claiming grandiose musical ambitions or even an ability to play their instruments, the band started simply as a tongue-in-cheek art-school project, but its multinational trio of women quickly gained a cult following for their remixes and covers, and for the bizarre stage outfits they sewed themselves. The three Chicks, noted *Paper*'s Jennifer Maerz, mix "stark, robotic beats and bubbly, post-disco dance numbers with lyrics about feminist fashion politics and glamour girls alike."

The Chicks coalesced around the Munich Academy of Art scene in the mid-1990s, but their sole German member is Kiki Moorse. Alex Murray-Leslie left Sydney, Australia, to study art in Munich, where she met Melissa Logan, a native of New York. Moorse had a background in fashion magazines, but was part of the art-school scene, and soon the three became friends. The band's origins date to a multimedia art project they conceived for a nonexistent musical group they dubbed "Chicks on Speed," and they first devised the *The Box Set,* which included a tape, a record made from cardboard, a poster, a badge, and a t-shirt. They also delivered a spoof performance in which they pretended to be DJs, but producers in the audience liked it enough to encourage them to make music in earnest.

At the time, the Chicks' energies were spread thin around Munich. They ran an underground bar called "Seppi," and liked to engage in another art project they called the trading post. As Moorse explained to *Week-end Australian* writer Annabel McGilvray, she and the other two women ventured out on to Munich streets with "our personal possessions and swapped them. Things like our passport, some earrings one of us got from a boyfriend. And people really got into it and went home and brought stuff back, and it was real bartering…. Our goal was to communicate with people and prompt people to question the capitalist system a little, and bring it down to a more personal level and see what happens." The group also re-created the stunt for German television cameras.

Not surprisingly, the band's first single released in Germany was titled "I Wanna be a DJ, Baby." It was followed by "Warm Leatherette," a cover of the Grace Jones classic, and a string of other releases whose raw, decidedly un-slick sound caught on in Munich and elsewhere. They also put out some B-52's covers. In 2000, finding Munich too conservative for their tastes, the trio packed up and moved to Germany's capital. "Berlin is really the only place where it is still possible for people to do their own thing, their crazy ideas," Moorse told Maddy Costa of the London *Guardian.* "The city supports the arts a lot…. And there are great audiences here. In Munich, the moment you had a gathering of people, the police would come."

From the start, the Chicks have been candid about their musical abilities, or lack thereof. Never claiming to be actual musicians, they admit to relying heavily on the studio production process to craft the final sound. "We have an idea for a text and a general idea about the music," Moorse told *Time* journalist Benjamin Nugent, "and then the producers finish it." They issued three LPs in 2000, two on their own label: *Chicks on Speed Will Save Us All!, The Re-Releases of the Un-Releases,* and *Monsters Rule This World.* "Steeped in the influence of both avant-garde '70s new-wave bands and slick '90s techno," Nugent wrote, "they have created an irresistible sound, in which synthesizers, samples and drum machines collide with catchy rock hooks and English lyrics that are half sung and half spoken."

An American tour in the spring of 2001 introduced the group to a wider audience, and they also had a hit back home with "Kaltes Klares Wasser," a cover of a song by an early-1980s all-female German punk band called Malaria. The song stayed on the charts for three months. Back in Berlin, they returned to their various art and music projects, including another label and a line of clothing sold on their website. They began to gain a certain amount of art world credibility in Berlin's thriving scene, and even the fashion establishment began to take notice. They worked with designer Jeremy Scott, who designed a stage uniform for them. They liked the new overalls, Murray-Leslie told journalist Vanessa Friedman of the *Financial Times.* "They are much slicker and more perfect than they would have been if we had made them ourselves," she told the paper. "One of the benefits of collaborating with

For the Record . . .

Members include **Melissa Logan** (born c. 1971, in the United States); **Kiki Moorse** (born c. 1968, in Germany); **Alex Murray-Leslie** (born c. 1971, in Australia).

Group formed in Munich, Germany, 1997; released first single, *Euro Trash Girl,* on their own label, Go Records, 1998; released first LP, *Chicks on Speed Will Save Us All!,* on Chicks on Speed Records, 2000; relocated to Berlin, Germany, c. 2000; made first U.S. tour, spring 2001; released *99 Cents,* 2003.

Addresses: *Record company*—Chicks on Speed, Rosenthalerstrasse 3, 10119 Berlin, Germany. *Website*—Chicks on Speed Official Website: http://www. chicksonspeed.com.

someone in a different discipline is they push your creativity in directions you wouldn't normally go. If we had made the overalls they would have looked like Teletubby clothes."

In 2003 the Chicks released their fourth LP, *99 Cents,* which featured a cover of the Tom-Tom Club's "Wordy Rappinghood." The Tom-Tom Club was an early-1980s side project from members of the seminal art-rock band the Talking Heads, and the link was not lost on London *Observer* critic Emma Warren. "The Chicks are direct descendants of Talking Heads' art-rock aesthetic," she noted, "but swap funky bass guitars and outsized suits for purposefully cheap sounding electronic pop, scrawled art, and home-made clothes." Other tracks on *99 Cents* included "We Don't Play Guitars," "Sell-Out," and "Shick Shaving," but Warren declared that its "title track is the kind of liberating electro-pop mayhem that suggests everyone should move to Berlin without delay."

For their 2003 record, the band even shot a video at a prestigious New York City gallery, with Murray-Leslie describing the visual concept to Maerz in *Paper* as "a Chicks on Speed factory sort of thing, with slaves ... It relates to the idea of exploiting people to make luxury goods." Further blurring the line between conceptual art and consumer culture, they put out a book in 2003 titled *It's a Project,* with the help of a respected art publisher, Booth-Clibborn Editions. Known for their frank statements on socio-economic topics, the band members have been scathing in their denunciations of contemporary culture. "We are in a capitalist system and we all know that," Murray-Leslie told Costa. "But we're taking away the greed factor, and creating more competition to companies like Starbucks, which have cannibalised everything.... We're saying to young people that you can do your own record label, do your own gallery, do your own whatever and not rely on the big institutions."

Selected discography

Singles

"Euro Trash Girl," Go, 1998; reissued, K, 2001.
"Mind Your Own Business," Go, 1999.
"Chix 52," Chicks on Speed, 2000.
"Fashion Rules," EFA, 2002.
"We Don't Play Guitars," EMI, 2003.

Albums

Smash Metal (EP), Go, 1998.
Glamour Girl (EP), EFA, 1999.
Chicks on Speed Will Save Us All!, Chicks on Speed, 2000.
The Re-Releases of the Un-Releases, K, 2000.
Monsters Rule This World, Chicks on Speed, 2000.
99 Cents, EFA, 2003.

Sources

Financial Times, January 24, 2004, p. 8.
Guardian (London, England), October 17, 2003, p. 12.
Knight-Ridder/Tribune News Service, October 21, 2002.
Observer (London, England), October 19, 2003, p. 54.
Paper, February 2003.
Time, January 15, 2001, p. 130.
Weekend Australian (Sydney, Australia), January 8, 2000, p. O3.

—Carol Brennan

Edwyn Collins

Singer, songwriter

Scottish singer/songwriter Edwyn Collins began his career as the leader of the Scottish rock band Orange Juice. After the band folded he started a solo career and went on to make international waves with his hit single "A Girl Like You" in 1994. Since then he has settled down to enjoy the more cultish status he had before his signature hit, experimenting with less pop-sounding music that features hard-edged lyrics and his own lush singing voice.

Edwyn Collins was born in Edinburgh, Scotland, on August 23, 1959, and grew up in Glasgow. He was attracted to music at an early age, and as a boy he sold his stamp collection so that he could buy an electric guitar. He began his career in music when he teamed up with four buddies from his school to start a punk band called the Nu-Sonics in 1976. By 1979 they were calling themselves Orange Juice and playing music reminiscent of 1960s independent rock. Collins spoke of the band's new direction to Will Hodgkinson in the Manchester *Guardian,* explaining, "We were smart enough to know that we weren't going to get anywhere as a provincial punk-rock group." Of the origin of the band's new name, Collins wrote in the liner notes of the band's original CD releases, as quoted on his official website, "We thought that the name Orange Juice would annoy people and stand out like the proverbial sore thumb."

Lacking a suitable venue for their recordings, the newly renamed Orange Juice joined with Alan Horne, a well-known Scottish philanthropist, to create their own label, called Postcard Records of Scotland. During its short lifespan, this label produced many popular independent Scottish recording artists, including Aztec Camera and the Go Betweens. The Postcard Records of Scotland recordings were successful enough to prompt the group to move in 1981 to Polydor, a bigger label that could give them broader distribution. The group made four albums with Polydor and produced a thoroughly pop-sounding hit single, "Rip It Up," before disbanding in 1985.

Collins decided to pursue a solo career after the band's breakup, and was signed by the Elevation label in 1986. A pair of singles, "Don't Shilly Shally" and "My Beloved Girl," followed but failed to take off. The label went out of business in 1987, and he was again left without a label. He soon relocated to Germany to record for a small recording studio, and began work on what was to become his first solo album, *Hope and Despair.* The album was released in 1989 on the Demon label, and was well received by fans and critics alike. Buoyed by this success, Collins went to work on *Hellbent on Compromise,* an album that was released in 1990 accompanied by a promotional concert tour.

Hellbent on Compromise failed to fulfill the expectations of Demon's managers, and Collins was subsequently dropped from the label's lineup. On his own

For the Record . . .

Born on August 23, 1959, in Edinburgh, Scotland; married; wife's name Grace; children: William.

Frontman for Scottish rock band Orange Juice, 1976-85; recorded hit single with Orange Juice, "Rip It Up," 1983; started career as a solo artist following the breakup of Orange Juice, 1985; released first solo album, *Hope and Despair,* on the Demon label, 1989; released *Hellbent on Compromise,* 1990; dropped from Demon label, founded own recording studio, 1990; released *Gorgeous George* on the Setanta label, 1994; single from that album, "A Girl Like You," became an international hit, 1994; released *I'm Not Following You,* 1997; co-created and starred in BBC Channel 4 sitcom, *West Heath Yard,* and a feature-length sequel, 1999-2000; released *Dr. Syntax,* 2002.

Addresses: *Record company*—Setanta Records Ltd., 174 Camden Rd., London NW1 9HJ, England, website: http://www.setantarecords.com. *Website*—Edwyn Collins Official Website: http://www.edwyncollins.com.

once again, Collins worked as a producer and arranger during the early 1990s, and started his own recording studio, where he began work on his new album, *Gorgeous George.* The small label Setanta picked up *Gorgeous George* from Collins's homespun label, and it was released in 1994 in the number eight position on the British charts. The album won praise from critics and raves from fans. Especially popular was a single from the album called "A Girl Like You," which quickly became an international hit. The song topped out at the number four position on the British music charts, and played well in France, Germany, Austria, and Australia. It crossed the Atlantic as well, becoming a hit in the United States, reaching the number six position on the *Billboard* Heatseekers chart. It was the first time Collins had had a hit song since Orange Juice's "Rip It Up" topped the charts in 1983. Collins celebrated with a world concert tour.

The international success of *Gorgeous George* gave Collins the breathing room he needed to continue to record his own music exactly the way he wanted to. He relocated and expanded his recording studio, and continued his production work for other recording artists. He released a fourth solo album, *I'm Not Following You,* in 1997. This album, like its predecessor, received raves on both sides of the Atlantic, with Carlo Wolff of the *Boston Globe* calling it a "handsome, versatile album." Many of the album's lyrics were sharply critical of the music industry and the uninspired music that is often its product. But Collins was not above critiquing himself as well. Stephen Dowling of the Wellington, New Zealand, *Sunday Star-Times* quoted his lyrics, "You've got to cow-tow to the corporate cow/To the new superpowers I respectfully bow."

Branching out into television in 1999, Collins co-created a six-episode sitcom on Britain's Channel 4 with his sound engineer, Sebastian Lewsley. Called *West Heath Yard,* the late-night show was named after Collins's recording studio, and depicted Collins and Lewsley dealing with a variety of amusing situations set in a sound studio. The show reportedly had no script, but it was successful enough to spawn a feature-length version, *West Heath House,* which aired in 2000.

Collins released his fifth solo album in the spring of 2002. *Dr. Syntax* took Collins three years to make, along with Lewsley and Paul Cook, the former drummer for the punk band Sex Pistols. The three began work on the album as 1998 drew to a close, and finished it in the winter of 2001. Collins played most of the instruments featured on the album, with Cook contributing his drums to two of the tracks. After its release, the album was praised for its mix of smart lyrics and Collins's able vocals. Barry Didcock in the Glasgow *Sunday Herald* remarked that the album gives "the impression that the world would be a poorer place without [Collins's] vision in it."

Collins lives in West London with his wife, Grace, and their son, William. He has insisted that he will continue to make music that is meaningful to him, without regard to how it will be received by critics or fans. "I don't mind being popular," he told Dowling, "but I don't like populism as a political philosophy, or appealing to the lowest common denominator.... I refuse to try and anticipate the market place."

Selected discography

Solo

Hope and Despair, Demon, 1989.
Hellbent on Compromise, Demon, 1990.
Gorgeous George, Bar/None, 1994.
I'm Not Following You, Epic, 1997.
Dr. Syntax, Setanta, 2002.

With Orange Juice

You Can't Hide Your Love Forever, Polydor, 1982; reissued, 1998.
Rip It Up, Polydor, 1982; reissued, 1998.
The Orange Juice, Polydor, 1984; reissued, 1998.

Sources

Periodicals

Boston Globe, December 18, 1997, p. 26.
Business World (Manila), May 31, 1996, p. 26.
Guardian (Manchester, England), November 8, 2002, p. 26.
Sunday Herald (Glasgow, Scotland), April 28, 2002, p. 6.
Sunday Star-Times (Wellington, New Zealand), October 19, 1997, p. F5.

Online

"Edwyn Collins," *All Music Guide,* http://www.allmusic.com (January 27, 2004).
Edwyn Collins Official Website, http://www.edwyncollins.com (January 27, 2004).

—Michael Belfiore

Marilyn Crispell

Pianist, composer

One of the finest modern jazz pianists, Marilyn Crispell has recorded some of the "most beautiful piano trio records in recent memory," said Adam Shatz in the *New York Times.* Crispell came to prominence as a free jazz player and composer early in the 1980s, and over the next 20 years honed her reputation with the Anthony Braxton Quartet and as a leader of her own ensembles. Influenced strongly by the work of jazz pianist Cecil Taylor, Crispell first charted her own course in jazz piano with her up-tempo, percussive improvisations; in the late 1990s she once again broke new ground with a lyrical, introspective improvisational style.

Crispell took up the piano at the age of seven when she studied at Baltimore's Peabody Institute. After high school she continued her classical piano studies at Boston's New England Conservatory, where she added courses in music composition to the mix. She earned a degree in composition from the New England Conservatory in 1969.

Shortly after graduation, however, Crispell put music aside and focused instead on her marriage and work in the medical field. She took jobs in various hospitals, and even seriously contemplated a career as a physician. This dry spell ended, however, with her divorce in 1974 and a move to Cape Cod. Starting a new life on her own, she took a job in a bookstore, and shortly thereafter met jazz pianist George Kahn, who introduced her to the music of jazz saxophonist John Coltrane, whose 1964 release *A Love Supreme* affected her profoundly. From then on jazz became the all-consuming focus of her life. She found the improvisational nature of jazz the perfect antidote to the regimented, highly rehearsed classical music in which she had been trained.

Recommitted to music—and to jazz in particular—she returned to Boston to study jazz for two more years. In 1979, she moved to Woodstock, New York, where she began teaching at the Creative Music Studios, a collective of free jazz musicians run by pianist and vibraphone player Karl Berger. She never again considered a career in any other field. "I know now," she later told Doug Fischer in the *Ottawa Citizen,* "that music is something I was born to do. I will never not play again."

The Creative Music Studio proved fertile ground for Crispell. It was there that she met reed player and composer Anthony Braxton, leader of the Creative Music Orchestra. Crispell joined the group for a European concert tour and stayed on as a member, contributing to their *Composition 98* album in 1981. She earned a reputation as an innovator in improvisational music, strongly influenced by the work of Coltrane and another of her heroes, Cecil Taylor; her style, however, was entirely her own; Fischer called it excitingly "volcanic."

In the 1980s, Crispell began to come into her own as a soloist, ensemble player, and group leader, both in the studio and in live performances. A member of both the Anthony Braxton Quartet and the Reggie Workman Ensemble for more than ten years, she also played with violinist Billy Bang and drummer John Betsch, bassist Reggie Workman, percussionist Andrew Cyrille, saxophonist Tim Berne, and many others.

Crispell continued to record through the 1990s and into the 2000s, working with fellow Braxton Quartet members Mark Dresser and Gerry Hemingway, as well as drummer Paul Motian, pianist Irène Schweizer, and bassist Gary Peacock, among others. In addition to contributing to the albums of other jazz musicians, Crispell made a number of solo albums, including *Live at Mills College 1995,* and continued to play in jazz and avant-garde music festivals and as a soloist.

During this time Crispell radically changed the direction of her music, adopting a more melodic, and, according to Fischer, more "lyrical [and] meditative" style. *New York Times* jazz critic Adam Shatz likened the change to that of an abstract expressionist painter suddenly deciding to paint like a Dutch master. Crispell herself was content to let her music take its own direction, without much forethought; she was pleased with her new direction, which she has described as her classical training shining through the jazz.

Crispell first displayed her new direction in the studio with her album *Nothing Ever Was, Anyway.* Released in 1997, it was her first effort for the Germany ECM label, and a tribute to composer, poet, and fellow Woodstocker Annie Peacock. The album featured, in addition to Crispell, Gary Peacock (Annie's ex-husband), and Paul Motian. The album was well

Born Marilyn Braune on March 30, 1947, in Philadelphia, PA; divorced. *Education:* Degree in music composition, New England Conservatory of Music, 1969.

Studied classical piano at New England Conservatory of Music, 1960s; became a jazz pianist, late 1970s; joined Creative Music Studios as a teacher, 1979; joined Creative Music Orchestra led by Anthony Braxton; 1979; played on Creative Music Orchestra's *Composition 98,* 1981; played with numerous groups, 1980s through 2000s; worked as a group leader, recorded numerous albums, including *Live at Mills College,* 1990s; signed to ECM label, released *Nothing Ever Was, Anyway,* 1997; released *Amaryllis,* 2001; joined Barry Guy New Orchestra, 2000s.

Awards: New York Foundation for the Arts grant recipient, 1988-89 and 1994-95; composition commission from the Mary Flagler Cary Charitable Trust, 1988-89.

Addresses: *Record company*—Egger Innovations- und Handels-GmbH, Abt. ECM Export, Pasinger Str. 94, Gräfelfing D-82166, Germany, website: http://www. ecmrecords.com. *Website*—Marilyn Crispell Official Website: http://www.marilyncrispell.com.

received, and it led to another Crispell-led release featuring the same musicians in 2001, *Amaryllis.* Named for an African flower that blooms in winter, this continued Crispell's work in her new direction, and showcased a quartet of ballads that were improvised in the studio as the album was recorded.

Crispell finds composing on the spot a liberating experience, and has said that the resulting music has a freer quality than that composed more traditionally. This "spontaneous composing," she told Fischer, has found its way into her live performances as well. She particularly enjoys performing with a musician with whom she has not previously played. Apart from a brief conversation or two beforehand, Crispell and her cohorts do very little planning about what will actually be played in concert. "It's like we're getting on a train that's running, and it takes you where it's going," she explained to Andrew Gilbert in the *San Diego Union-Tribune.*

In the 2000s Crispell became a member of the Barry Guy New Orchestra, and also played frequently with

Guy's London Jazz Composers Orchestra. Crispell's work has also been featured on film; she composed music for *Soul Suitcase,* an independent film directed by Paul DiStefano, and appeared in documentaries about jazz, including *Women in Jazz,* by Gilles Corre. Along with live performances and recordings, Crispell conducts workshops in improvisational music throughout the United States, as well as in Canada, Europe, and New Zealand. She has resolved to do more teaching, telling Fischer in late 2003, "I'm a bit burned out from years of travel." Then 56 years old, she wanted to play fewer road shows and find a semipermanent teaching spot at a college or university.

Selected discography

Spirit Music, Cadence, 1981.
Live in Berlin, Black Saint, 1982.
A Concert in Berlin, FMP, 1983.
Rhythms Hung in Undrawn Sky, Leo, 1983.
And Your Ivory Voice Sings, Leo, 1985.
For Coltrane, Leo, 1987.
Gaia, Leo, 1987.
Labyrinths, Victo, 1987.
Quartet Improvisations, Leo, 1987.
Kitchen Concerts, Leo, 1989.
Live in San Francisco, Music & Arts, 1989.
Live in Zurich, Leo, 1989.
Circles, Victo, 1990.
Overlapping Hands: Eight Segments, FMP, 1990.
Piano Duets, Leo, 1991.
Images, Music & Arts, 1991.
Duo, Knitting, 1992.
Hyperion, Music & Arts, 1992.
Inference, Music & Arts, 1992.
On Tour: Highlights from the Summer of 1992 American Tour, Music & Arts, 1992.
Stellar Pulsations/Three Composers, Leo, 1992.
Cascades, Music & Arts, 1993.
Santuerio, Leo, 1993.
Band on the Wall, Matchless, 1994.
Contrasts: Live at Yoshi's, Music & Arts, 1995.
Live at Mills College 1995, Music & Arts, 1995.
MGM Trio, Ramboy, 1995.
Woodstock Concert, Music & Arts, 1995.
Destiny, Okka Disk, 1996.
Nothing Ever Was, Anyway: The Music of Annette Peacock, ECM, 1997.
Dark Night and Luminous, Musica Secreta, 1998.
Red, Black Saint, 1999.
Amaryllis, ECM, 2001.
Blue, Black Saint, 2001.

Sources

Periodicals

New York Times, September 23, 2001, p. 25, section 2.
Ottawa Citizen, September 23, 2003, p. C8; October 18, 2003, p. K1.
San Diego Union–Tribune, March 14, 2002, p. 10, Entertainment.

Online

"Marilyn Crispell," *All Music Guide,* http://www.allmusic.com (February 3, 2004).
"Marilyn Crispell Biography," Marilyn Crispell Official Website, http://www.marilyncrispell.com (February 3, 2004).

—*Michael Belfiore*

Angèle Dubeau

Violinist

Angèle Dubeau's impressive international career as a classical violinist got off to a flying start when she graduated from the Conservatoire de musique de Montreal. She had studied there with Raymond Dessaintes and had the honor of being named recipient of the First Prize from the school. Previously, she had studied at the esteemed Julliard School of Music in the United States with Dorothy DeLay, but left, in a gutsy and unorthodox career move, to study with Stefan Georghiu in Romania.

Although Dubeau's career took off early, she has avoided the trap of the "young wonder" and remains as popular and acclaimed today as when she emerged on the scene as a "young virtuoso" in the late 1970s. One reason for this may be that Dubeau stood out from the crowd from the very beginning.

"Of all the cliches ground out by performers' agents and concert publicists, surely the most tiresome is 'brilliant young virtuoso,'" Richard Todd wrote in the *Ottawa Citizen* in 1987. "If every artist who bears that label were to send a dollar to the Receiver General, Canada's federal deficit would vanish into the same oblivion that many of these musicians will face before their careers have run their course. Angèle Dubeau need not worry. No one who heard her play Mendelssohn's Violin Concerto in E Minor with the National Arts Centre Orchestra Friday night would slight her with such a description … She is young, a qualified virtuoso, and capable of playing brilliantly, if not flawlessly, but there is much more to her than that."

Dubeau established herself early as the recipient of several prestigious awards, including First Prize at the Canadian Music Competition in 1976, the Montreal Symphony Orchestra Competition that same year, and the Canadian Broadcasting Corporation's Talent Festival in 1979. In addition to her widely recognized talent, Dubeau is known these days for the gloriously rich sound of her exquisite instrument, a Des Rosiers Stradivarius crafted in 1733 and valued more than one million dollars. The instrument was the subject of a legal battle that ended in 1987 when the Quebec Superior Court ruled that the Dubeau family had purchased the violin in good faith and the heirs to the previous owner had taken too long to stake their claim to the instrument, which had been purchased 40 years earlier by shipbuilding magnate Ludger Simard.

Nearly all of Dubeau's extensive catalogue of recordings have been released on the Analekta record label, which was founded by Dubeau's husband, Mario Labbe. The couple met in 1985 at the Festival International de Lanaudiere, an annual event that takes place just outside Dubeau's hometown of St-Norbert, Quebec. Labbe, an agent who had booked the Dave Brubek quartet for the festival, was recruited to give the young violinist a ride back to Montreal. He has been Dubeau's producer since 1988 as well. Dubeau is the successful label's best-selling artist, having garnered the impressive accomplishment of being the first living Canadian soloist to score a gold record for *La Ronde des Berceuses*, a recording of lullabies released in 1994. In addition to the accomplished musicians it supports, the label has received some press attention in recent years for its boycott of the Juno Awards. Labbe claimed Analekta's failure to be nominated even once demonstrates the bias of the Juno selection committee.

Dubeau added a new direction to her career—that of television host—in 1994 when she began anchoring the weekly CBC show *Faites vos gammes* (Do Your Scales). Dubeau approached the CBC with her idea for the show, which features musicians under 21 years of age, while pregnant with her daughter, Marie, who was born in 1990.

"When I was expecting my child, I started to watch television and I saw nothing about classical music," she explained in an interview in the *Globe and Mail*. "So I made a proposal to Radio-Canada, and a few months later I got a call. They said that they liked my idea and wanted me as the hostess." In addition to up-and-coming performers, Dubeau also features celebrities in other fields as musicians on her show. Quebec Liberal MLA John Ciaccia has played a Verdi piano piece and Olympic speed skater Sylvie Daigle performed Chopin on episodes featured in the spring of 1997. Already popular, the show has made Dubeau a household name. "People in the street say, 'Hello, Angèle! and kiss me on the cheek, because they feel they know me," she told the *Globe and Mail*.

Born on March 24, 1962, in St-Norbert, Quebec; daughter of Jules Dubeau and Lucette (Dauphin) Dubeau; married Mario Labbe; children: Marie. *Education:* Graduated from the Conservatoire de musique de Montreal; attended the Juilliard School of Music, 1979-81.

First public performance at the Jeunesses Musicales of Canada contest, 1969; studied with Raymond Dessaints at the Conservatoire de musique de Montreal, 1970s; first public recital, 1977; performed as soloist with Tokyo Philharmonic Orchestra, 1986; recorded albums and toured, 1980s–; created female string orchestra La Pietà, 1997; with La Pietà, released *Let's Dance*, 1999, *Infernal Violins*, 2000, and *Violins du monde*, 2002.

Awards: Canadian Music Competition, First Prize, 1976; Orchestre symphonique de Montreal competition, First Prize, 1976; Radio-Canada National Radio Competition, First Prize, 1979; Canada Art Council's Sylva-Gelber Award, 1982; Tibor Varga International Competition, First Prize, 1983; International Community of French Speaking Radio Awards for Soloist of the Year, 1987; Félix Award, Best Classical Album of the Year, Orchestra and Ensemble category, 1990; Félix Award, Best Classical Album of the Year, Orchestra and Ensemble category, 1993; Félix Award, Best Classical Album of the Year, Soloist and Chamber Music (with Alvaro Pierri), 1993; Félix Award, Best Classical Album of the Year, Soloist and Chamber Music, 1995; Félix Award, Best Classical Album of the Year, 1995; Société Saint-Jean-Baptiste, Prix Calixa-Lavallée, 1996; Félix Award, Best Classical Album of the Year, Soloist and Small Ensemble, 1996; Félix Award, Best Classical Album of the Year, Soloist and Small Ensemble (with La Pietà), 1999; Félix Award, Best Classical Album of the Year, Soloist and Small Ensemble (with La Pietà), 2000.

Addresses: *Management*—Jonathan Wentworth Associates, LTD., 100 Stevens Ave., Ste. 503, Mt. Vernon, NY 10550. *Record company*—Analekta Distributions, Inc., 364, Rue Guy, Bureau G-15, Montreal, Quebec, H3J 1S6. *Website*—Angèle Dubeau Official Website: http://www.angeledubeau.com.

Dubeau launched a second side project in the spring of 1997. She began serving as concertmaster for an all-female chamber orchestra, La Pietà. The group's name comes from the orphanage where Vivaldi conducted an all-female orchestra and wrote much of his work. Despite the wealth of projects she has slated for herself, Dubeau says she is at a time in her life where she can pick and choose offerings, allowing her to spend time with Marie. "I can let my CDs act as calling cards in different countries," she explained in *Maclean's.*

Dubeau and La Pietà won two Félix Awards for Best Classical Album of the Year; one in 1998 for *Berceuses et jeux interdits,* and another in 2000 for *Let's Dance.* Speaking to Helen Butterfly of *Maclean's* soon after the release of *Violins du monde* in 2002, Dubeau shared her feeling on her favorite compositions, many of which were included on *Violins du monde.* The pieces, she said, "express the richness, diversity and beauty of life…. Bach is jazz's neighbor. There shouldn't be any division between styles."

Selected discography

Solo

(Prokofiev, Tchaïkovsky, Kabalevsky) *Violin Concertos,* Analekta, 1989.
(With Les Petits Chanteurs du Mont-Royal) *Adoration: Sacred Music,* Analekta, 1990.
(Schubert) *Three Sonatas for Violin and Piano,* Analekta, 1990.
(Sibelius, Glazounov) *Violin Concertos,* Analekta, 1991.
(de Falla, Paganini, Piazzolla) *Works for Violin and Guitar,* Analekta, 1992.
(Martinú) *Promenades, Five Madrigal Stanzas and other Trio Sonatas,* Analekta, 1993.
(Telemann) *Twelve Fantasies for Violin without Bass,* Analekta, 1993.
La Ronde des Berceuses, Analekta, 1994; released in English as *On Wings of Song,* 1994.
(Telemann) *Sonatas for Two Violins,* Analekta, 1995.
(Mozart) *Opera for Two: Late 18th Century Transcriptions,* Analekta, 1996.
(Mendelssohn) *Violin Concertos,* Analekta, 1997.
(Vivaldi) *Per Archi: Concertos for Strings,* Analekta, 1998.
Opus Québec, Analekta, 1999.
(Fauré, Leclair, Debussy) *French Sonatas for Violin and Piano,* Analekta.
(Brott) *Works by Alexander Brott,* Analekta.

With La Pietà

Berceuses et jeux interdits (Lullabies and Forbidden Games), Analekta, 1998.
Let's Dance, Analekta, 1999.
Infernal Violins, Analekta, 2000; rereleased with bonus DVD, 2003.
Once Upon a Time…, Analekta, 2002.
Violins du monde, Analekta, 2002.

Sources

Periodicals

Globe and Mail, December 7, 1996.
Maclean's, February 10, 1997; January 13, 2003.
Ottawa Citizen, January 24, 1987.

Online

Angèle Dubeau Official Website, http://www.angeledubeau.
  com/ (April 20, 2004).

Eroica Trio

Classical trio

The Eroica Trio comprises cellist Sara Sant'Ambrogio, pianist Erika Nickrenz and violinist Adela Peña. All three are talented and attractive musicians with a natural stage presence. With their combination of looks and talent, they have found it somewhat difficult to be taken seriously in the world of classical music. But after several years of performing together, the trio has been able to develop an excellent reputation as well as an impressive musical repetoire.

The three have played together most of their lives and are so close they call each other sisters. Adela Peña, born in New York City, was a classical music fan from an early age. As she grew up, she shared her parents' love of music and eventually asked to take violin lessons. She was a dedicated student and immediately showed a flair for the material assigned. She studied chamber music at the famed Greenwich House, and then attended Juilliard School of Music, where she won the school's Mendelssohn Violin Competition, giving her the opportunity to represent the United States in an international competition. The result was a solid stint of independent performances in Venezuela.

It was probably inevitable that Erika Nickrenz would love classical music as well. Her father was a respected violist who helped found the Orpheus Trio. Her mother, a busy career concert pianist, also had an ear for music that had brought her three Grammy Awards as a producer. Nickrenz showed such talent early on that she appeared at New York's Town Hall at the age of eleven. She met Peña at the age of nine and Sara Sant'Ambrogio at the age of 12, and the three would not only become friends but would share a similar level of musical talent.

Sara Sant'Ambrogio was set to play classical music from the moment she was born. Sant'Ambrogio is part of a 600-year-old family line that traces its roots to Saint Ambrose, a patron saint of the arts. Her father was a cellist with the esteemed Boston Symphony before he moved on to be principal cellist with the St. Louis Symphony. After studying under her father for years, she won the Bronze Medal at the International Tchaikovsky Cello competition in 1986. The award led to an invitation from world-famous Carnegie Hall to perform at its grand re-opening after extensive repairs and upgrades had kept the famous musical venue closed for years.

With impressive resumes already under their belts, the three attended Juilliard School together, where they decided to start a trio. All were fans of Beethoven's "Eroica," and the idea of three young women being heroic inspired the name. The "a" at the end of the word added a special feminine touch that the women also liked.

With such stellar individual talents and careers, it should not have taken long for the three friends to develop a successful trio. But there were high expectations and prejudice to overcome in order to be taken seriously as an all-female group in a man's world. But with hard work and practice, the Eroica Trio won the esteemed Naumburg Award in 1991. The award allowed them to perform at Lincoln Center to a sold-out audience. The program allowed the trio to perform a variety of musical works, and the final program impressed critics and audience alike. The Eroica Trio had made its first mark in the music world.

The group members were able to depend on each other for the strength and support they needed in order to persevere and succeed. The three artists knew each other well and were able to begin the tough process of working with their individual strengths and weaknesses. They characterize themselves as three very different women with different styles, who come together to make beautiful music. "I wouldn't say competition, but there was certainly a sense of fiercely different approaches to this, and that's kind of what's given us our fire," Peña told *Fanfare*. "We've had our differences, and we've learned to use them to our greatest advantage."

The trio eventually found opportunities to showcase their talents. When EMI signed them on, the three artists decided to develop a five-album strategy that would allow the classical world to get to know them and their array of musical styles and talents. Sant'Ambrogio's love of pop and rock sometimes steered the band toward Mozart, big band music or Piazolla, while Nickrenz's love of the classics led to

For the Record . . .

Members include **Erika Nickrenz** (daughter of Joanna Nickrenz, a concert pianist and record producer, and Scott Nickrenz, a violist; children: Zachary), piano; **Adela Peña** (born in New York, NY), violin; **Sara Sant'Ambrogio** (born in Boston, MA; daughter of John Sant'Ambrogio, a cellist), cello.

Group formed in New York City, c. 1991; released debut album, *Eroica Trio*, 1997; released LP *Dvorak: Trio No. 4; Shostakovich: Trio No. 2, Op. 67*, 1998; released albums *Baroque*, 1999; *Pasión*, 2000; *Brahms: Piano Trios Nos. 1 & 2*, 2002; appeared in documentary *Eroica!* for PBS, 2003; released album, *Beethoven: Triple Concerto, Op. 56; Piano Trio, Op. 11*, on EMI, 2003.

Awards: Naumburg Award, 1991; National Public Radio (NPR), Best Debut Album of the Year for *Eroica Trio*, 1998.

Addresses: *Record company*—EMI, 1290 Avenue of the Americas, New York, NY 10104. *Website*—Eroica Trio Official Website: http://www.eroicatrio.com.

some of the group's more traditional performances. The group also brought Nickrenz's mother on board as producer. Hiring Joanna Nickrenz, one of the premier producers for classical albums, proved to be a successful strategy for the trio.

Their first album, *Eroica Trio,* included works by Benjamin Godard, George Gershwin, Maurice Ravel, and Paul Schoenfield. National Public Radio (NPR) named *Eroica Trio* as its Performance Today Debut Recording of the Year, and the album secured a spot on the *Time Out New York* Top Ten Recordings of 1997. The attractive and talented young women got as much exposure in *New York Magazine* as they did in *Strings.* At first, many in the classical world paid them little mind. But their self-titled debut CD was received so well by the mainstream press that serious classical fans began to take notice.

With the combination of their developing talent, looks, and energy on stage, the trio became a hit with both traditional fans and many new, younger admirers. All three women are committed to education, and in addition to their hectic tour schedule they have given much of their time to traveling to schools in order to perform and answer questions.

Their second album was a slightly more traditional album for the trio, and included pieces by Rachmaninov, Shostakovich, and Dvorák. Positive reviews of the group's second album prompted many in the classical world to take notice. And with all of the attention from the mainstream press, the three have found their way onto television as well as into fashion magazines. However, they have been able to stay focused on their musical careers and on the dynamic they have established as a team.

Their third CD was a Baroque mix, aptly called *Baroque,* and it further enhanced their growing reputation as serious classical musicians. The fourth album, *Pasión,* featured music of Piazzolla, Villa-Lobos, and Turina, all virtuoso pieces in a Latin vein.

Even as the three have expanded their musical focus, they have begun cementing their reputations in the classical world as an active trio in the orchestral performances arena, and have earned a reputation for premiering new and innovative work. At the same time they are becoming known for performing more traditional fare, such as Beethoven Triple Concerto concerts.

In the midst of releasing their fifth album, *Beethoven: Triple Concerto, Op. 56; Piano Trio, Op. 11,* two of the Eroica Trio became mothers. Both women have been able to strike a balance between touring and motherhood and are confident they can continue to stay active in the musical world.

What keeps them going? One favorite moment for the band came after a performance in Japan when a young woman approached them. Peña told *Strings* that she said, "You've really inspired me as a woman, to pursue my own goals with passion and determination." When the band asked the woman what instrument she played she responded, "I'm a graphic artist! But this concert tonight has changed me, it's changed how I think of myself and it's changed the way I intend to approach my career!" Seeing someone so moved by their music has proved to the group that they are making a difference with their music.

Selected discography

Eroica Trio, EMI, 1997.
Dvorák: Trio No. 4; Shostakovich: Trio No. 2, Op. 67, EMI, 1998.
Baroque, EMI, 1999.
Pasión, EMI, 2000.
Brahms: Piano Trios Nos. 1 & 2, EMI, 2002.
Beethoven: Triple Concerto, Op. 56; Piano Trio, Op. 11, EMI, 2003.

Sources

Periodicals

American Music Teacher, February/March 2003.
Fanfare, April 2002.
Strings, January 6, 2004.

Online

"Eroica," Angel Records, http://www.angelrecords.com (February 9, 2004).
"Eroica!," Independent Lens, http://www.pbs.org/independentlens/eroica/ (February 9, 2004).
"Eroica Trio," *All Music Guide,* http://www.allmusic.com/ (February 9, 2004).
"Eroica Trio," Kaos2000 Magazine, http://www.kaos2000.net/interviews/eroicatrio01/ (February 9, 2004).
Eroica Trio Official Website, http://www.eroicatrio.com (February 9, 2004).

—Ben Zackheim

Betty Everett

Singer

"The Shoop Shoop Song (It's in his Kiss)" was first recorded by Betty Everett, and is the song for which she is best known. During the 1960s and 1970s, Everett's powerful voice recorded a string of rhythm and blues hits.

Betty Everett was born on November 23, 1939, in Greenwood, Mississippi, an area known at the time for its local blues scene. She was playing the piano and singing in church by the age of nine, and also sang in gospel choirs. She was in her late teens when she moved to Chicago, Illinois, in 1956, where she turned her attention from gospel music to singing rhythm and blues.

Everett started recording for several small local record labels. In 1957 she recorded "My Life Depends on You" for Cobra. She then signed with C.J., followed by the One-Derful label. While contracted with One-Derful she recorded "I've Got a Claim on You," and "I'll Be There." She had the honor of performing with Magic Sam and the legendary Muddy Waters. She also briefly sang the lead for the all-male group the Daylighters, and together they produced a minor hit, "Why Did You Have To Go?" In 1963 she was signed to Vee-Jay, which at the time also had the American rights for releases by the Beatles. While with Vee-Jay, she had a number of hits, including "You're No Good," which just missed the Top 50 in late 1963. A year later, a Liverpool band called the Swinging Blue Jeans covered it and the song became a smash hit. The song later became a number one hit when Linda Ronstadt recorded it in 1975. Everett also put out an album titled *You're No Good* in 1964. "The Shoop Shoop Song (It's in his Kiss)," written by Rudy Clark and produced by Calvin Carter, made the *Billboard* Top Ten in 1964. At a time of popularity for girl groups, including the Shirelles, the Ronettes, and similar groups who infused gospel and soul into pop, Everett's success placed her firmly within this group of singers.

Duos were very popular at the time, and Everett teamed up with another of Vee-Jay's artists named Jerry Butler, a Mississippi native who had made a name for himself in Chicago, and whose style of rhythm and blues had earned him the nickname "The Iceman." The two covered a romantic, soulful rendition of "Let It Be Me," previously recorded by the Everly Brothers. The Everett/Butler version became a top five hit in 1964. This was followed by another duet, "Smile," also in 1964, which just missed the top 40. They recorded an album together in 1964, entitled *Delicious Together*, which hit the charts at 104.

During the mid-1960s Everett toured England and successfully developed a fan base for her music. In 1965 she recorded on her own, providing the energetic "I Can't Hear You" and "Getting Mighty Crowded." The

Born on November 23, 1939, in Greenwood, MS; died on August 19, 2001, in Beloit, WI.

Moved to Chicago, IL, to pursue singing career, 1956; performed with Magic Sam and Muddy Waters, late 1950s; sang lead for the Daylighters; released single "You're No Good," 1963, and album *You're No Good*, 1964; released "The Shoop Shoop Song (It's in his Kiss)," 1964; released "Let It Be Me" with Jerry Butler, 1964; recorded *Delicious Together* with Jerry Butler, 1964; released "I Can't Hear You" and "Getting Mighty Crowded," 1965; "There'll Come a Time," 1969; *Love Rhymes*, 1974; *Happy Endings,*1975; appeared on PBS special *Doo Wop 51*, 2000.

Awards: BMI Pop Award, "The Shoop Shoop Song (It's in his Kiss)," 1964; BMI R&B Award, 1964; BMI Pop Award, "The Shoop Shoop Song (It's in his Kiss)," 1991; R&B Foundation Pioneer Award, 1995.

latter, a punchy Van McCoy song, was her first chart entry in the United Kingdom at number 29.

During the 1960s Vee-Jay Records struggled with financial difficulties and eventually collapsed in 1967. Everett then signed with ABC-Paramount Records. Her success with ABC was limited, although she produced the single "Love Comes Tumbling Down." She then switched to Uni, where she recorded the album *There'll Come a Time*. The title song reached number two on the rhythm and blues chart in 1969 and hit number 26 on the pop charts. She also recorded "I Can't Say No to You" and "It's Been a Long Time," remaining with Uni until 1970. She then signed with Fantasy Records and recorded "I Got to Tell Somebody." She recorded with Fantasy until 1974.

During the 1970s Everett worked the club circuit in the United States and Europe. She also worked with the prestigious arranger Gene Page and recorded *Love Rhymes* in 1974 and *Happy Endings* in 1975. Her last chart entry was in 1978 with "True Love (You Took My Heart)," which she recorded for United Artists. In the mid-1980s she moved to Beloit, Wisconsin, where she was active in the Fountain of Life and New Covenant churches, as well as with the Rhythm and Blues Foundation. In 1995 she received a Rhythm and Blues Foundation Pioneer Award, and was joined on stage by her former partner Jerry Butler to sing "Let It Be Me."

The *Boston Globe* reported that Everett was nearly in tears onstage as she accepted her award.

Everett's last public appearance was a performance in 2000 on the PBS special *Doo Wop 51*, a program that honored the great a capella groups of the 1950s and 1960s. *The Independent* of London, England, stated, "Partnered by her old friend Jerry Butler, she reportedly brought the house down." Her attorney, Jay B. Ross, accompanied her to the show. "She was nervous because she hadn't performed in quite a while," he stated on the VH1 website. "But once she got into it and saw how much the audience loved her, she just blossomed, and the audience just went nuts."

Throughout her life, Everett continually stated that singing and playing the piano were her two favorite activities. For most of her life she lived very modestly, until she began to gain from her royalties near the end of her life. She won BMI Awards for "Hands Off," "I Need You So," "It's All Right," and "It's in his Kiss."

Everett died on August 19, 2001, at the age of 61. Family members found her at her home at 241 W. Grand Avenue in Beloit, Wisconsin. Her cause of death was not reported to the public.

"The Shoop Shoop Song (It's in his Kiss)" is the song for which she is best remembered, and it was covered by many artists in the decades that followed her original recording. Linda Lewis revived it in 1975 for a top ten hit in the United Kingdom. In 1990, nearly 27 years after Everett first recorded it, Cher recorded her own version of "The Shoop Shoop Song (It's in his Kiss)" for the soundtrack of her hit movie *Mermaids*. Vonda Shepard later covered the song for the Fox television show *Ally McBeal*. Everett will long be recognized as one of the top soul singers of the 1960s and 1970s.

Selected discography

Singles

"My Life Depends on You," Cobra, 1957.
"Ain't Gonna Cry," Cobra, 1958.
"Tell Me Darling," Cobra, 1959.
"I've Got a Claim on You," One-Derful, 1963.
"By My Side," Vee-Jay, 1963.
"Getting Mighty Crowded," Vee-Jay, 1964.
"I'll Be There," One-Derful, 1964.
(With Jerry Butler) "Smile," Vee-Jay, 1964.
(With Jerry Butler) "Let it Be Me," Vee-Jay, 1964.
"You're No Good," Vee-Jay, 1964.
"The Shoop Shoop Song (It's in his Kiss)," Vee-Jay, 1964.
(With Jerry Butler) "Fever," Vee-Jay, 1965.
"Too Hot to Hold," Vee-Jay, 1965.
"The Shoe Won't Fit," Vee-Jay, 1966.
"In Your Arms," ABC, 1967.
"Bye Bye Baby," ABC, 1967.
"Love Comes Tumbling Down," ABC, 1967.
"I Can't Say," ABC, 1967.

"Been a Long Time," Uni, 1969.
"Sugar," Uni, 1969.
"Unlucky Girl," Uni, 1970.
"There'll Come a Time," Uni, 1969.

Albums

You're No Good, Vee-Jay, 1964.
(With Jerry Butler) *Delicious Together,* Vee-Jay, 1964.
The Very Best of Betty Everett, Vee-Jay, 1965.
There'll Come a Time, Uni, 1969.
Black Girl, Fantasy, 1974.
Love Rhymes, Fantasy, 1974.
Happy Endings, Fantasy, 1975.
Getting Mighty Crowded, Charly, 1980.
Too Hot to Hold, Charly, 1982.
The Real Thing, Charly, 1987.
The Fantasy Years, Fantasy, 1995.
The Best of Betty Everett: Let it Be Me, Aim, 1998.

Sources

Books

Clarke, Donald, editor, *Penguin Encyclopedia of Popular Music,* Penguin, 1989.
Gregory, Hugh, *Soul Music A-Z,* Blandford, 1991.
Hardy, Phil and Dave Laing, *Encyclopedia of Rock,* Schirmer, 1988.
Larkin, Colin, editor, *Encyclopedia of Popular Music,* MUZE, 1998.
Nite, Norm N., *Rock On Volume II,* Thomas Y. Crowell, 1978.

Periodicals

Boston Globe, March 2, 1996, p. 27.
Daily Telegraph (London, England), August 23, 2001.
Herald (Glasgow, Scotland), September 8, 2001, p. 14.
Independent (London, England), August 23, 2001.
Times (London, England), September 17, 2001, p. 23.
USA Today, March 4, 1995; February 22, 1996, p. 1.D; August 21, 2001, p. D01.
Wisconsin State Journal, August 22, 2001, p. D1.

Online

"Betty Everett," BMI, http://repertoire.bmi.com (February 4, 2004).
"Betty Everett," The Iceberg, http://www.icebergradio.com/artist.asp?artist=3334 (January 20, 2004).
"Betty Everett," MSN Entertainment, http://www.entertainment.msn.com (January 20, 2004).
"Betty Everett," VH1, http://www.vh1.com/artists/az/everett_betty/artist.jhtml?_requestid=100282 (February 5, 2004).

—Sarah Parkin

Fabolous

Rap musician

Jeffrey Mayer/WireImage.com. Reproduced by permission.

The American Library Association may not approve, but the errant "o" in John Jackson's assumed name ranks among hip-hop's savviest marketing moves. It gives Fabolous an excuse to spell his name in almost every song, and hooks fans, deejays, and journalists into talking about the handsome young rapper from Brooklyn. "Now people get it," Fabolous said of his name in *Jet*. "That's my signature for people to know who I am. I started hearing people's grandmother saying it."

Actually, until 1998 nobody knew who John "Fabolous" Jackson was. A "quiet kid" from Brooklyn's Breevort Houses public housing project, according to his website biography, Jackson wound up performing live on DJ Clue's prominent *Monday Night Mixtape* radio show on New York City's WQHT. The appearance didn't seem significant to him at the time, however. "I thought it was a joke," Fabolous told *Billboard,* several years later. "If I had really believed it, I would have been better prepared. Once I got there, I knew this was my opportunity."

The performance ignited his career, and Clue started featuring Fabolous on his influential mixtape collections. After rapper Lil' Mo heard Fabolous she included him on her "Superwoman, Pt. 2" remix. The resulting MTV video was a smash—Fabolous claimed it transformed him from regular guy to star overnight. He signed with DJ Clue's fledgling Desert Storm record label and spent the summer of 1999 touring with Clue, Jay-Z, Method Man, Redman, and DMX on the Hard Knock Life Tour.

Fabolous's breakthrough came in 2001. After his smash "I Can't Deny It" made him a major hip-hop player during the summer, Elektra signed a productin and distribution deal with Desert Storm and arranged to release his debut album *Ghetto Fabolous.* It jumped quickly to number four on the *Billboard* 200 albums chart. Like Jay-Z, who released his own CD that same day, Fabolous has a knack for spouting coarse language in a nursery-rhyme delivery that's proved popular on pop radio and MTV.

Fabolous, who poses on his album covers in a baseball cap tilted just so, a baseball jersey, and the requisite gold chains and bracelets, knows how to make successful pop music. His style, he told MTV, is "a mixture. It can be street sometimes, but it can be … I don't really want to say commercial, but it can be [a little] commercial. I'm not making it for [the mainstream], but I see the world through both sides. You can't have a street person who don't respect commercial [tastes], and a commercial person who don't respect the street. I'm trying to just bring the two together. Somewhere they can meet and just make some good music."

"You can't make every song a party song," Fabolous continued to *Billboard.* "You may feel like partying all week, but by the end of the week, you're exhausted. So you have to have a little diversity. We have some East Coast joints, West Coast joints like 'Can't Deny It' and some down South joints. We also have two deep songs like 'One Day.' You can't do all of anything—you have to mix it up. That's what makes a good album."

Occasionally Fabolous takes the concept of "street" a little too literally. In early 2003 police arrested him twice in two days—first for allegedly possessing a weapon, the second time for driving without a license. The gun charges were dropped two months later, but Fabolous was arrested a third time in late March when police discovered a loaded nine-millimeter handgun in a car in which he, a bodyguard, and several other people been riding. Fabolous's lawyer denied all the charges and, later in 2003, publicly threatened to sue New York City for $5 million. The suit has yet to be filed.

During that same year Fabolous toured Boys and Girls Clubs around the United States. He also announced that in addition to endorsing products for Nextel, Lipton, Reebok, and EA Sports, he would promote literacy for the American Library Association. Having a spokes-man who fractures the English language for a living, however, seems a bit ironic. "We like anyone who supports kids reading," spokeswoman Laura Clark told the *Houston Chronicle* in 2003. "And maybe the librar-ians get it. Librarians have a sense of irony, too, you know." Fabolous gets it, too, as evidenced in lyrics like these from "Get Smart": "I feel like a genius / Look at it from a playa's position / I got a scholarship, I get smart without payin' tuition / My classes be like two three hours / That's why I'm the smartest young guy since Doogie Howser."

Fabolous released his follow-up album, *Street Dreams*, in March of 2003; it went gold in six weeks and plati-num by early fall. Like all smash hip-hop albums, *Street Dreams* went heavy on celebrity guest appearances. Rappers P. Diddy and Snoop Dogg, respectively, ap-pear on "Trade It All, Pt. 2" and "Up on Things"; R&B singer Ashanti appears on "Into You." During that same year Fabolous was part of the Rock the Mic Tour with headliners 50 Cent and Jay-Z. By early 2004 he was talking about doing movies. "I wanna tackle it all," he told MTV. "I think I can pull off a comedy. I'm really trying to see if I can do a thriller or drama."

Fabolous told MTV he was planning to release his third album in late 2004. "I wanna talk about real situations, real things going on with people's lives, real things going on at a party, real things going on when you're chillin'," he said. "I just wanna be 100 percent real."

Selected discography

Ghetto Fabolous, Desert Storm/Elektra, 2001.
Street Dreams, Desert Storm/Elektra, 2003.

Sources

Periodicals

Billboard, September 8, 2001; September 15, 2001; March 8, 2003.
Chicago Sun-Times, January 18, 2003.
Houston Chronicle, March 24, 2003.
Jet, June 16, 2003.
New York Daily News, March 25, 2003.
Rolling Stone, April 3, 2003.

Online

"Fabolous," *All Music Guide,* http://www.allmusic.com (Feb-ruary 9, 2004).
"Fabolous Completing Third Album, But He Really Wants To Act," MTV, http://www.mtv.com (January 4, 2004).
"Fabolous Dreams Up New Record," *RollingStone.com,* http://www.rollingstone.com (December 10, 2003).
"Fabolous: Ghetto Superstar," MTV.com http://www.mtv.com (September 9, 2003).
Fabolous Official Website, http://www.fabolous.com (Feb-ruary 9, 2004).
"Fabolous Plans To Sue New York For False Arrest," VH1. com, http://www.vh1.com (February 16, 2004).
"Fabolous Strikes Gold," Rap News Direct, http://www. rapnewsdirect.com (April 22, 2004).

—*Steve Knopper*

The
Fat
Boys

Rap group

Early in the not-so-long history of rap music, the Fat Boys made a splash with their self-deprecating humor, large size, and infectious rhythms and rhymes. With a combined weight totaling over 750 pounds, the Fat Boys lumbered onto the rap scene, performing a blend of comedy and music. The trio—Mark "Prince Markie Dee" Morales, Darren "Buff the Human Beat Box" Robinson, and Damon "Kool Rock-Ski" Wimbley—was one of the first rap acts to cross over into mainstream popularity. Although they eventually released one platinum and several gold albums and appeared in films, on television shows, and commercials, their fortunes declined as the 1980s drew to a close, and the trio disbanded in the early 1990s.

Robinson, Morales, and Wimbley grew up on the same block in the New York City borough of Brooklyn, where they began rapping together. As Wimbley later explained to Dennis Hunt in the *Los Angeles Times,* "We used to rap on street corners. We'd practice in basements. ... It was just one of the things we'd like to do together."

Originally known as Disco 3, the Fat Boys first gained national prominence when they won a national talent contest at Radio City Music Hall in 1983. The judges

Paul Natkin/Photo Reserve, Inc. Reproduced by permission.

were especially impressed with Robinson's ability to generate sound effects, producing an astonishing variety, noted Pierre Perrone of the London, England, *Independent,* of "percussive belches, grunts and clicks ... with his mouth."

Their contest win attracted the notice Charlie Stetler, who became the group's manager. In addition to their talents, Stetler was also impressed with his new clients' sheer bulk. Robinson alone tipped the scales at 450 pounds, and the group ran up astonishing restaurant tabs while on the road; one breakfast reportedly cost $350. It was Stetler who suggested that the group change its name to the Fat Boys and use comedy as part of their act.

The Fat Boys also hired Kurtis Blow, an accomplished rap artist in his own right, to produce their first albums. The releases, which blended party tunes and humor set to hip-hop, reggae, and rock music, all played up the Fat Boys' heaviness in their titles. *Fat Boys* debuted in 1984, and went gold. The following year, the group was featured in a hip-hop documentary called *Krush Groove,* which brought them an even wider audience and a three-picture deal with Warner Brothers. The group's sophomore album, *Fat Boys Are Back* was also released in 1985; *Big and Beautiful* followed in 1986.

Meanwhile, rap music itself was becoming increasingly popular, helped by Run-D.M.C.'s 1986 cover of the Aerosmith rock hit "Walk This Way." Sensing an opportunity, the Fat Boys decided to make a splash with their own cover tunes. After moving to the Polydor label,

they released their version of the Surfari's 1963 hit "Wipe Out," backed by the Beach Boys. The song, featured on *Crushin',* the Fat Boys' 1987 platinum album, climbed to number two on the British charts, and hit number 12 in the United States. Following on the success of this effort, the Fat Boys landed starring roles as themselves in the Three Stooges-inspired comedy film *Disorderlies* in the same year. Unfortunately, the film was a critical and box office flop. Writing in the *Houston Chronicle,* film critic Michael Spies called the film "a Three Stooges short pushed to a breaking point that makes the best of Larry, Curly and Moe look extremely tight." Apparently the Fat Boys were not destined to be movie stars.

The Fat Boys' next album, *Coming Back Hard Again,* was similar in style to *Crushin'* and it too featured a hit cover track, called "The Twist (Yo' Twist)." Chubby Checker, who had helped make the original Twist a national craze in 1960, backed the Fat Boys' cover and once again helped propel the song to the top of the charts. Like "Wipe Out," "The Twist (Yo' Twist)" grabbed the number two spot the British charts, and landed in the American top 20. Now bona fide stars, the Fat Boys racked up appearances on TV shows, including *Miami Vice,* and in commercials. They also wrote "Are You Ready for Freddy" for *Nightmare on Elm Street 4: The Dream Master,* and filmed the song's video with Robert Englund.

By the end of the 1980s, however, the Fat Boys' novelty act was losing its edge. They tried unsuccessfully to remake their image in 1989 with a rap opera ("rappera") called *On and On,* after which Morales left the group in 1990 to pursue a solo career. He released his first album in 1992 as Prince Markie Dee and the Soul Convention, scoring a hit single with "Trippin' Out." He also produced and wrote for such high-profile recording artists such as Mary J. Blige, Christopher Williams, and El DeBarge. Robinson and Wimbley fared less well on their own, releasing *Mack Daddy* in 1991 to a lukewarm reception before calling it quits. The pair went on to host MTV's *Yo MTV Rap* and to produce and perform with other rappers. In 1991 Robinson was also tried for sexual abuse of a minor, and his conviction on that charge generated too much negative publicity to overcome. Plans for a Fat Boy reunion album were underway in December of 1995 when Robinson died suddenly at his home in Queens, New York. Only 28 years old, he suffered a fatal heart attack brought on by obesity after a bout of influenza.

Selected discography

Fat Boys, Sutra, 1984.
Fat Boys Are Back, WEA, 1985.
Big and Beautiful, Sutra, 1986.
Crushin', Polygram, 1987.
Best Part of the Fat Boys, Pair, 1987.
Coming Back Hard Again, Mercury, 1988.

Krush on You, Blatant, 1988
On and On, Polygram, 1989.
Mack Daddy, Emperor, 1991
Greatest Hits, Unidisc, 1991.
All Meat No Filler: The Best of the Fat Boys, Rhino, 1997.

Sources

Periodicals

Houston Chronicle, August 17, 1987, p. 1.
Independent (London, England), December 12, 1995, p. 16.
Los Angeles Times, October 2, 1987, p. 10.
Times Union (Albany, NY), December 12, 1995, p. B4 C1.

Online

"The Fat Boys," *All Music Guide,* http://www.allmusic.com (January 27, 2004).
"The Fat Boys," *Rolling Stone,* http://www.rollingstone.com/artists/bio.asp?oid=6399&cf=6399 (January 27, 2004).
"The Fat Boys," VH1, http://www.vh1.com/artists/az/fat_boys/bio.jhtml (January 27, 2004).

—Michael Belfiore

Béla Fleck

Banjoist, composer

Béla Fleck is an acknowledged master of the five-string banjo. An unassuming artist whose virtuoso performances fuse jazz, rock, Irish balladry, and bluegrass, Fleck cannot possibly be confined to a strict genre or even considered "new grass." His is an original style, a hip, urban sound that just happens to come from a uniquely American instrument traditionally stereotyped as being anything but sophisticated. *Time* magazine contributor John Elson called Fleck "the Paganini, or maybe the Jimi Hendrix," of the banjo, noting that the Grammy Award winner has taken "this jangling folk instrument into jazz, classical music, and beyond."

Fleck never touched a banjo until he was fourteen, but by the time he was in his mid-twenties, he was cutting solo albums and picking with the New Grass Revival, a premier bluegrass band. His later work, with Béla Fleck and the Flecktones, is more likely to be heard on jazz radio stations than on country stations. "I wanted to play like pianist Chick Corea," Fleck disclosed in an interview with *Down Beat* magazine. "I could look up and down the banjo neck and everything was there that you needed to play the notes, but no one had come up with the technique to play it. I started working on things most musicians work out on for most instruments, like working on scales, finding a way to play the chords. There was nothing remarkable about the things I did except that they were on the banjo."

Fleck was born and raised in New York City. He and his brother lived with their mother, a public school teacher. "I never met my father," Fleck declared in *Time.* "He taught German for a living but was crazy about classi-cal music. He named me after Béla Bartok, the Hungarian composer. He named my brother Ludwig after Beethoven. It was rough. The torture started in kindergarten."

Fleck was just about ready to start kindergarten when he had his first brush with the banjo. Like many Americans, he initially heard the instrument in the theme music of the 1960s television series *The Beverly Hillbillies.* Fleck recalled in *Time* that he and his brother were watching the show at his grandparents' house. "The theme music started, and I had no idea it was the banjo," he said. "It was Earl Scruggs in his prime. I only remember hearing something beautiful. It called out to me."

Other musical influences intervened, however. Fleck learned to play guitar and was influenced by pop and rock as a youngster. Then, at 14, he saw the film *Deliverance,* with its "Duelling Banjos" bluegrass theme. "The sound of the banjo just killed me," he remembered in *Time.* "It's like hearing mercury."

He got his first banjo at age 15 in 1973. "Some people say banjo is an instrument you either love or hate," said Fleck. "For me I just instantly loved it. I couldn't put it down for days. I didn't want to go to sleep. I got up early to play it. I thought about it in my spare time. On the bus to school I was thinking about it. I was so excited to get home and play it again. I tried to play other instruments, but nothing else ever really caught on, nothing else called out to me that way."

He began to spend up to eight hours a day locked in his room, experimenting with the instrument. He was accepted into Manhattan's High School of Music and Art, but since the banjo was not considered a serious instrument there, he played guitar and studied music theory. He took private banjo lessons with three teachers, Tony Trischka, Erik Darling, and Mark Horowitz. He also learned, as many bluegrass musicians do, from listening to and imitating such bluegrass pioneers as Scruggs and J. D. Crowe. He also was absorbing musical ideas from additional, seemingly disparate, sources such as Yes, Charlie Parker, The Beatles, Joni Mitchell, and Return to Forever.

As soon as he graduated from high school in 1976, Fleck moved to Boston and took a job with the bluegrass band Tasty Licks. In 1979 he moved south to Lexington, Kentucky, to help form the group Spectrum. Fleck confessed to a *Time* correspondent that his first exposure to Southern bluegrass was a "big culture shock." He added: "I was a little cocky, but down South, they didn't think I sounded so great because I lacked tone and I didn't have a great sense of rhythm. They were right." Fleck perfected his technique and cut his first solo album, *Crossing the Tracks,* in 1980.

He joined Sam Bush, John Cowan, and Pat Flynn in the New Grass Revival in 1981. The band, of which he

For the Record . . .

Born c. 1958 in New York, NY; son of a public school teacher.

Played with Boston-based bluegrass band Tasty Licks, 1976-79; member, with Jim Gaudreau and Glenn Lawson, of the group Spectrum, 1979-81; joined New Grass Revival, 1981; group disbanded, 1991; formed group Béla Fleck and the Flecktones, c. 1989 (other members include Howard Levy on keyboards, Victor Wooten on bass guitar, and Future Man (a.k.a. Roy Wooten) on Drumitar). Also cut albums as a solo artist and has done studio work in Nashville with Loretta Lynn, the Statler Brothers, Randy Travis, Sam Bush, and others. Has made television appearances, with the New Grass Revival and the Flecktones, on *Hee Haw, Nashville Now,* and the *Lonesome Pine Specials*; continued exploring limits of the instrument in experimental recordings, including a recording of classic masterworks on banjo and the three-disc *Little Worlds,* released in 2003.

Awards: Named top banjo player in the nation by *Frets* readers' poll more than six times since 1981; Grammy Awards: Best Country Instrumental Performance (with Asleep at the Wheel) for "Hightower," 1995; Best Pop Instrumental Performance (with the Flecktones) for "The Sinister Mister," 1996; Best Instrumental Composition (with the Flecktones) for "Almost 12," 1998; Best Contemporary Jazz Album (with the Flecktones) for *Outbound,* 2000; Best Country Instrumental Performance (with Alison Brown) for "Leaving Cottondale" from *Fair Weather,* 2000; Best Classical Crossover Album for *Perpetual Motion,* 2001; Best Instrumental Arrangement (with Edgar Meyer) for Claude Debussy's "Doctor Gradus Ad Parnassum" from *Perpetual Motion,* 2001.

Addresses: *Record company*—Columbia Records/Sony Music Entertainment Inc., 550 Madison Ave., New York, NY 10022-3211. *Booking*—Joe Brauner, Monterey Peninsula Artists, 509 Hartnell St., Monterey, CA 93940, e-mail: joe@mpanewyork.com. *Management*—David Bendett, David Bendett Artists, Inc., 2431 Briarcrest Rd., Beverly Hills, CA 90210, e-mail: artistsinc@ aol.com. *Website*—Béla Fleck Official Website: http:// www.flecktones.com.

and Flynn were the newest members, were all ready well known for pushing the acceptable musical limits of bluegrass. Throughout the 1980s the New Grass Revival continued to raise the bar and musically experiment. *Stereo Review* correspondent Alanna Nash proclaimed the band "the ultimate progressive supergroup" with "its own unique, indescribable, and innovative blend of jazz, rock, reggae, gospel, rhythm and blues, and whatever else strikes its fancy."

Almost every New Grass Revival album recorded since Fleck's arrival features an instrumental withhim as its principal performer and composer. Among these are the Grammy-nominated "Seven by Seven," "Big Foot," and the popular "Metric Lips."

New Grass Revival disbanded in 1991. Fleck and Bush have played together live and in the studio since on Bush solo releases from 1996's *Glamour & Grits* to Ice Caps: Peaks of Telluride, released in 2000. Bush has reciprocated, appearing as a guest on Fleck's solo and band projects. Perhaps the best example of this synergy is Strength in Numbers, a one-off recording project with Fleck, Bush, Jerry Douglas (dobro), Mark O'Connor (guitar/mandolin), and Edgar Meyer (bass). The group was "sort of the de facto house band" at Telluride for years when they recorded a single album under the moniker. Fleck also performed on various other artists' recordings throughout the decade including Andy Statman, Ginger Baker, Rhonda Vincent, and Dave Matthews Band.

For Fleck, this freedom from the constraints of a band and genre offered him an opportunity to play more jazz-oriented material. As Seth Rogovoy pointed out in a 1996 article, Fleck has taken the banjo, "from its fixed role as a lead instrument in the traditional bluegrass ensemble, restored it to its long-forgotten home in the jazz band, and by recognizing no limitations on its potential, transformed the way it is played and imagined."

He formed Béla Fleck and the Flecktones in 1990 with a pair of brothers, Victor and Roy (a.k.a. Future Man) Wooten, on bass and Drumitar, and added Howard Levy on keyboards and harmonica. Jeff Coffin would join the group well after Levy's 1992 departure. Their music has been embraced enthusiastically by the jam band community. Fleck has recorded with several notable bands in this genre including Phish, Government Mule, and Leftover Salmon and he frequently appears at numerous music festivals, including bluegrass, jazz, jamband, and world music festivals.

After a decade-long relationship with the Warner Bros. label, Fleck signed a five-record deal with Sony's Columbia Records. This package stipulated that he would record two projects for release on Sony Classical, a solo album, and two discs with the Flecktones. The first of these was *Outbound,* released in 2000. William Ruhlmann, writing in an oblique review on *All Music*

Guide, essentially called the project a random mess. "Fleck really offers no defense to the charge of being a musical dilettante, he simply celebrates the surface pleasures of different varieties of music, offering an overlapping series of appetizers," he wrote. "A fan of any particular style is liable to feel that it has been trivialized, but Fleck doesn't mean any harm. His music represents the pursuit of facileness as a musical goal, one that he and his band achieve with alacrity."

Fleck seemed to fare better with the critics with 1995's *Tales from the Acoustic Planet.* This project combined both jazz and bluegrass, featuring guest artists from both worlds: Chick Corea, Branford Marsalis, Douglas, Meyer, and Bush. The credo adopted by Fleck and his mates is virtuosity. If someone can play their chosen instrument expressively, the music being played is incidental. "Béla's bad, man," said Marsalis, who first played on *UFO Tofu* with Fleck, to *Down Beat* in 1997. "Béla just has that thing. When you hear the music, you say, 'Yeah, I'm down,' and that's the true test for me. ... It was one of the original jazz instruments, but it was mostly a strumming, picking instrument. ...Even banjo solos were just like 'chink chinka chink,' which is not what Béla's doing at all. He's playing the goddamn thing."

Perhaps no other album to date has attempted to combine all these influences in one package than 2003's ambitious *Little Worlds.* Guest artists on the three-disc set included Bobby McFerrin, Marsalis, The Chieftains, Douglas, and Bush. Jason MacNeil, music critic for the online publication PopMatters, said it appeared adopted the "everything but the kitchen sink to pad albums and give fans more than they anticipated and, in some cases, even wanted" approach. "Béla Fleck has decided to try the same format." A second single disc was released at the same time. MacNeil called the full project, "Long, average and thoroughly unappealing, unless you are the ultimate Fleck fanatic."

But *Down Beat*'s Jason Koransky observed similarities to Weather Report, the great jazz group of the 1970s and 1980s known for its improvisational prowess. He said the project "stands as a milestone, and ... offers the best song-writing and production of the Flecktones' recording career."

In *The Big Book of Bluegrass,* Fleck discussed his artistic goals and his position in the music business. "I think I just have to follow the path where the music leads me and play as many different kinds of things as I can," he said. "Basically, I try not to take it all too seriously. As Alan Munde once said, 'It's only a banjo.' I mean, how seriously can you take it? It's like being the best kazoo player in the world."

Critics have taken it seriously indeed. Elson concluded that Fleck's work "is pure revelation. ... His technique is always at the service of a sophisticated musical imagi-nation that can make the banjo sound as if it were born to play jazz."

Selected discography

Solo

Crossing the Tracks, Rounder, 1980.
Natural Bridge, Rounder, 1982.
Daybreak, Rounder, 1987.
Places, Rounder, 1988.
Drive, Rounder, 1988.
Tales From the Acoustic Planet, Warner, 1994.
The Bluegrass Sessions: Tales from the from the Acoustic Planet, Vol. 2, Warner, 1999.
Perpetual Motion, Sony, 2001.
Ten From Little Worlds, Columbia, 2003.
Little Worlds (3-CD set), Columbia, 2003.

With the New Grass Revival

Deviation, Rounder, 1985.
On the Boulevard, Sugar Hill, 1985.
New Grass Revival, EMI America, 1986.
Hold to a Dream, Capitol, 1988.
Friday Night in America, Capitol, 1989.
The New Grass Revival Live, Sugar Hill, 1989.
New Grass Anthology, Capitol, 1990.

With Béla Fleck and the Flecktones

Béla Fleck and the Flecktones, Warner Bros., 1990.
Flight of the Cosmic Hippo, Warner Bros., 1991.
UFO Tofu, Warner Bros., 1992.
Three Flew over the Cuckoo's Nest, Warner, 1993.
Left of Cool, Warner, 1998.
Outbound, Columbia, 2000.
Live at the Quick (DVD), Columbia, 2002.

With others

(With Tasty Licks) *Anchored to the Shore,* Rounder, 1979.
(With Spectrum) *Opening Roll,* Rounder, 1980.
(With Spectrum) *Spectrum Live in Japan,* Rounder, 1983.
(With Jerry Douglas, Mark O'Connor, and others) *Inroads,* Rounder, 1987.
(With Strength in Numbers) *The Telluride Sessions,* MCA, 1989.
(With Spectrum) *Too Hot for Words,* Rounder, 1990.
(With Asleep at the Wheel) *The Wheel Keeps on Rollin',* Capitol, 1995.
(With Tasty Licks) *Tasty Licks,* Rounder, 1997.
(With Alison Brown) *Fair Weather,* Compass, 2000.

Sources

Books

Kochman, Marilyn, editor, *The Big Book of Bluegrass,* Morrow, 1984.

Periodicals

Billboard, March 4, 1995; October 10, 1998.

Bluegrass Unlimited, November 1978.

Chicago, December 1986.

Down Beat, July 1986; July 1988; August 1991; March 1997; October 2003.

Guitar Player, February 1989; July 1990.

People, May 25, 1992.

Rolling Stone, July 13, 1989.

Stereo Review, May 1985; January 1988; November 1988; September 1990.

Time, June 11, 1990.

Variety, July 4, 1990.

Online

"Béla Fleck," *All Music Guide,* http://www.allmusic.com (January 26, 2004).

"Béla Fleck and the Flecktones," *All Music Guide,* http://www.allmusic.com (January 24, 2004).

"Béla Fleck & The Flecktones: Little Worlds (Special Edition)," PopMatters, http://www.popmatters.com/music/reviews/f/fleckBéla-littleworlds.shtml (January 25, 2004).

"Béla Fleck: Born To Play Banjo," *The Berkshire (MA) Eagle,* http://www.berkshireweb.com/rogovoy/interviews/fleck.html (January 25, 2004).

—Anne Janette Johnson and Linda Dailey Paulson

Celso Fonseca

Guitarist, producer, composer, singer

Although he's not a household name—even among fans of Brazilian music—Celso Fonseca is nonetheless a direct heir of the bossa nova ("new beat") and MPB (música popular Brasileira) sounds that are synonymous with Brazil. Influenced and inspired by legendary Brazilian composers and instrumentalists Baden Powell (Roberto Baden Powell de Aquino) and Gilberto Gil, singer-songwriter Fonseca is a major force in contemporary Brazilian music. Known for his solo and ensemble work, he has played or recorded with the best musicians in modern MPB—Chico Buarque, Milton Nascimento, Caetano Veloso, Gal Costa, Djavan, Elza Soares, Marisa Monte, João Bosco, Leila Pinheiro, and Jorge Benjor.

Despite his early appreciation for music, Celso José da Fonseca was born into a family with no musical roots an not a single musician in the immediate family tree (other than a grandmother who may or may not have sung in church choir). His father nonetheless instilled in him an interest in classical music. At the age of 10, he found an acoustic guitar at his cousin's house and immediately fell in love with the instrument. "Strangely, it seemed quite familiar to me," he would later recall in his official website biography. "On that day, I decided that it would be my instrument." When Fonseca was 12

Stephane De Sakutin/AFT/Getty Images. Reproduced by permission.

For the Record . . .

Born Celso José da Fonseca on November 15, 1956, in Rio de Janeiro, Brazil; son of a physician.

Guitarist for Brazilian musician Gilberto Gil, 1981; starting producing for musicians such as Gil, Vinícius Cantuária, Virginia Rodrigues, and Daúde, 1986; recorded three albums with Ronaldo Bastos: *Sorte*, 1994, *Paradiso*, 1997, and *Juventude/Slow Motion Bossa Nova*, 2002. Recorded three solo albums: *Minha Cara*, 1986, *O Som Do Sim*, 1993, and *Natural, 2003.*

Awards: Sharp Music Prize, Best Pop/Rock Arranger, 1996.

Addresses: *Record company*—Six Degrees Records, 540 Hampshire St., San Francisco, CA 94110-1417, website: http://www.sixdegreesrecords.com. *Website*—Celso Fonseca Official Website: http://www2.uol.com.br/celsofonseca.

his father gave him a guitar. He began studying the instrument, taking private lessons. His real interest at the time, however, was to learn songs by British rock group the Beatles, and these he ended up teaching himself.

As his musical ability progressed, he became interested in both jazz and electric guitar. He soaked up the vibrant bossa nova that characterized Rio in the early 1960s. "We lived in a beautiful area in the mountains overlooking the city, with a lot of birds, a lot of trees, a lot of sky," he told Britain's *Telegraph* newspaper. "It was a very rich, intense time when people were finding new ways of saying things, not only in music, but in architecture, literature and the visual arts. Jobim and João Gilberto's music was always on the radio—sophisticated music created by the middle class, but you'd hear people everywhere in the streets singing it. I'm still inspired by the atmosphere of that time. I carry it around inside me, and I try to bring it alive in my music."

Although he'd dreamed as a child of becoming a physician like his father, Fonseca briefly attended journalism school. At 19, however, he succumbed to his life-long passion and became a musician. By 1981 he was playing guitar for Gilberto Gil's band and toured with him the following year. "My debut was with him at the Montreaux Festival, in Switzerland," he recalled on his personal website. "At first, I would not go to Europe; I would only play in Brazil. But, after all, I went and that's when my journey with Gil began, which also led me to work with other great artists of the Brazilian music, as a guitar player, producer and arranger." According to his official website biography, he quickly became known as "Gil's guitar player" and was soon touring abroad and playing festivals in the United States, Canada, Japan, and Europe.

In 1986 Fonseca began to work as a producer for artists such as Gil, Vinícius Cantuária, and Virginia Rodrigues. His work on the Daúde's 1996 debut album won the Sharp Music Prize for Best Pop/Rock Arranger. Fonseca also worked on Gil's album *Quanta Live*, which won a Grammy for Best World Music Album in 1998. He also produced Gil's *O Eterno Deus Mu Dança,* Rodrigues's first two solo albums, Gal Costa's *Aquele Frevo Axé,* six tracks on Leo Gandelman's *Brazilian Soul,* and albums by Rosana, Verônica Sabino, Zeca Baleiro, and Adriana Maciel. Fonseca also directed Gil, Veloso, Costa, Buarque, Soares, and Rodrigues in the 1999 show *Since Samba Has Been Samba* at the Royal Albert Hall in London. In 1997 Fonseca and Gil launchd the Geléia Geral record label.

In comparison to his work on others' albums, Fonseca's solo efforts may seem few and far between. He released his first solo album, *Minha Cara* in 1986, and nearly a decade passed before the second, *O Som do Sim,* was launched in 1995 and met with some European success. Fonseca also released a trilogy with Ronaldo Bastos: *Slow Motion Samba, Paradiso,* and *Sorte.* The latter two albums were released simultaneously in Brazil and Japan.

Fonseca always assumed that his comparatively late start as a musician made him unable to compose. "Later, I learned that composing is much more related to hard work than to the wait for that inspiration moment that may happen once in a while, but that is not essential to the composition work," Fonseca said on his website. He wrote his first compositions at age 23, and eventually began to write lyrics to accompany his music, sometimes with the help of his musical partner, Ronaldo Bastos. Other musicians began to take notice, and artists such as Caetano Veloso, Gal Costa, Maria Bethânia, and Milton Nascimento recorded his songs. "Even now I work every day to enhance myself as a composer," he commented.

Fonseca has been credited with modernizing bossa nova, adapting the music of the 1960s for a twenty-first-century audience. "Bossa nova is a way of playing and singing," Fonseca told *Telegraph.* "It's a kind of slowed-down samba, that can be applied to anything. Stevie Wonder songs, Gershwin can all be bossa nova. I've taken the aspects of bossa nova that I love—the spaciousness, the melodic economy—and I've tried to push them towards the future."

In 2003 Fonseca made his international solo debut as a singer-songwriter with *Natural.* "Like the classic recordings of bossa nova, a style in which his music is obviously rooted, [*Natural* is] smooth, smart and casually sensual," said the *Washington Post*. "Backed by a small group, Fonseca's singing rarely needs to rise above the intimate whisper to make its points." Fonseca's acoustic guitar playing, wrote a BBC reviewer, "is understated but sublime throughout and although three tracks with English, rather than Portuguese, lyrics feels a little like one too many, his crooning vocals do suit the material down to the ground in either language." Fonseca's hushed voice and simplicity are reminiscent of the performances of Brazilian icon Caetano Veloso. "Others may go for brass, big bands and backing singers, but Fonseca prefers the minimalist approach," wrote the *Guardian* praising his "mood of gentle, exquisite melancholy."

Selected discography

Minha Cara, WEA, 1986.
O Som Do Sim, Natasha, 1993.
Sorte, Dubas Música, 1994.
Paradiso, Dubas Música, 1997.
Juventude/Slow Motion Bossa Nova, Universal, 2002.
Natural, Ziriguiboom/Crammed/Six Degrees, 2003.

Sources

Periodicals

Guardian, June 18, 2003.
Washington Post, April 20, 2003.

Online

"Celso Fonseca," *All Music Guide,* http://www.allmusic.com (February 4, 2004).
"Celso Fonseca Musica," All Brazilian Music, http://www.cliquemusic.com.br (February 4, 2004).
"Celso Fonseca, Natural," BBCi Music, http://www.bbc.co.uk/music/world/reviews/celsofonseca_natural.shtml (January 17, 2004).
Celso Fonseca Official Website, http://www2.uol.com.br/celsofonseca (February 4, 2004).
"If Niemeyer Made Music, It Would Sound Like This," *Telegraph,* http://health.telegraph.co.uk/arts/main.jhtml?xml=/arts/2003/03/15/bmbrazil15.xml (March 15, 2003).

—*Brett Allan King*

Carl Fontana

Trombonist

Many critics and musicians have called Carl Fontana "the world's greatest trombonist." Bandleaders and fellow trombonists have stated that Fontana "raised the bar and set the standard." Fontana is one of the most well-known and treasured jazz trombonists in music history. When the legendary musician died on October 9, 2003, he left a legacy of musicianship and ingenuity. His life and personality were full of genuine modesty, coupled with a desire to give back by teaching and sharing his gifts with young students and other musicians.

Fontana's biggest contribution to music was perhaps the playing technique he created, known as "doodle tonguing." According to the Monroe, Louisiana, *News-Star,* "It allowed trombonists to play faster and with more precision." Fontana called the technique "a self-defense against saxophone players." This groundbreaking method of playing influenced countless numbers of musicians. According to Jazzmasters, by using this technique Fontana "combine[d] a plump tone with the fast-tonguing of notes that caused a re-thinking of techniques the world over." Fontana was also well known for mixing mainstream jazz with bebop, creating his own signature swing-meets-bop style.

Born on July 18, 1928, in Monroe, Louisiana, Carl Fontana's first trombone was a gift from his father. According to the *News-Star,* Fontana's brother Mickey said Carl "always knew he wanted to be a jazz musician." As a teenager, Fontana played in the local big band that was led by his father, Charles "Collie" Fontana, who also worked as a plumber, saxophonist,

and violinist. While in the band, Fontana worked and played school sports. After graduating from Neville High School, he enrolled at Louisiana State University (LSU). He graduated in 1950 and soon returned to LSU to pursue a master's degree in music. In between his studies, Fontana performed with the Lee Fortier Band. His first big break came when, in 1951, he filled in for Woody Herman's current saxophonist, Urbie Green. Green's wife had gone into labor at the same time the band was due to play New York's Blue Room. After Fontana filled in for him on stage the crowd went wild, and Herman asked him to join the band permanently. After just two years at graduate school, an eager Fontana left his studies to go on tour with Woody Herman's Third Herd Band. Other trombonists in the group included brothers Urbie and Jack Green.

It didn't take long for Fontana's music career to take off. In 1954 he played in a band led by Lionel Hampton, and from 1954-55 he played with Hal McIntyre. In 1955 Stan Kenton hired Fontana. Kenton, who liked to feature Fontana as a soloist, invited Fontana to record with him, and together they recorded eleven albums. Perhaps the best-known track was Fontana's trombone playing on *Fuego Cubano* in 1956. Soon after, Fontana departed for a European tour in Kai Winding's four-trombone band; the tour, which lasted from 1956 to 1957, garnered international attention for Fontana.

In 1957 Fontana re-teamed with Woody Herman for the International State Department Tour. He also performed for many years with Woody Herman, Stan Kenton, and Kai Winding on television shows such as the *Ed Sullivan Show* and the *Tonight Show,* and also performed at Carnegie Hall. Later in 1957, Fontana decided to settle in Las Vegas, where he had been performing with greats such as Lionel Hampton, Duke Ellington, Benny Goodman, and Frank Sinatra. Every year in Las Vegas, Fontana performed in the annual trombone concerts at the University of Las Vegas, as well as at an array of festivals, tours, and all-star jazz parties.

In 1958, Fontana played his most renowned and well-known solo on Woody Herman's song "Intermission Riff." Although the tune contained only three chords, Fontana played it so skillfully that people called his performance a masterpiece. Fontana earned the nickname "Captain Kut-Cha," and he became known as a master of timing.

In the late 1970s Fontana toured Japan with bandleader Georgie Auld, and worked with the group Supersax. The group, which was signed to Blue Note Records, recreated Charlie Parker's solos, and featured Fontana and saxophonists Med Flory and Buddy Clark. He also played with the all-star group the World's Greatest Jazz Band. In 1975 Fontana took center stage again, co-leading a group with Swing drummer Jake Hanna. He made a name for himself in 1985, leading a quintet that included his longtime friend and

Born Charles Fontana on July 18, 1928, in Monroe, LA; died on October 9, 2003, in Las Vegas, NV; son of Charles "Collie" (a plumber, saxophonist, violinist and big band leader) and Mary Fontana; married; children: Felicia, Mark, Scott. *Education:* Graduated from Louisiana State University, 1950.

Trombonist for various bands, including Charles "Collie" Fontana and his big band, 1941-45; Lee Fortier, 1951; Third Herd, 1952-53; Lionel Hampton, 1954; Hal McIntyre, 1954-55; Stan Kenton, 1955-56; Mel Torme, 1956; Kai Winding's four-trombone band, 1956-57; Bill Holman, 1958; toured intermittently as trombonist with Woody Herman band, 1966; trombonist, World's Greatest Jazz Band, 1968; trombonist, Supersax, 1973; trombonist and band leader (with Jake Hanna), 1975; appeared with Dick Gibson's Colorado Jazz Party, 1971; recorded albums with Louis Belson (1984), Al Cohn (1984), vocalist Joni Janak (1993), Arno Marsh (1997), and Jiggs Whigham (1999); released debut album, *The Great Fontana,* Uptown Records, 1985; appeared at Royal Inn Hotel in Phoenix, 1993; soloist on albums featuring Bobby Shew (1995), Andy Martin (1998), Paul McKee (1999), Bill Trujillo (1999), and Bill Watrous (2001).

Awards: International Trombone Association Award, 1998.

Addresses: Record company—Woofy Productions, P.O. Box 272, Phoenix, AZ 85001, website: http://www. woofyproductions.com. *Website*—Carl Fontana Official Website: http://www.jazzmasters.nl/fontana.htm.

fellow musician Al Cohn. By the 1990s, Fontana had regular gigs playing Las Vegas and touring as a soloist.

In 1985 Fontana's first major label release, *The Great Fontana,* featured the artist as quartet leader. Subsequently he released *The Carl Fontana-Arno Marsh Quintet: Live at Capozzoli's* in 1997 and *The Carl Fontana Quartet: Live at Capozzoli's* in 1998. On *Nice and Easy* in 1997, Fontana shared the lead, playing side by side with trombonist Jiggs Whigham. Later he released *First Time Together* in 2002, *Quintet, Vol. 3* in 2002, and *Conte Candoli Quintet (live)* in 2003.

Although he toured extensively, Fontana always maintained close relationships with his family. He married and had three children, who currently reside in Las Vegas. Toward the end of his life, Fontana suffered from Alzheimer's disease. Carl Fontana passed away on October 9, 2003, in Las Vegas. In his later years, Fontana regularly taught clinics and master classes at the University of Nevada and other universities across the United States, including Harvard and Mississippi State College; he was also a featured soloist with the Army Blues Jazz Band. Ken Hanlon, a music professor at the University of Nevada, told the *Los Angeles Times* that Fontana was a phenomenon.

Selected discography

Solo

The Great Fontana, Uptown, 1985.
The Carl Fontana-Arno Marsh Quintet: Live at Capozzoli's, Woofy, 1997.
The Carl Fontana Quartet: Live at Capozzoli's, Woofy, 1998.
Nice 'n' Easy, TNC Jazz, 1999.
First Time Together, Budapest Music, 2002.
Keepin' up With the Boneses, TNC Jazz, 2002.
Quintet, Vol. 3, Woofy, 2002.
Conte Candoli Quintet (live), Woofy, 2003.

With others

(With Stan Kenton) *Retrospective,* Capitol, 1943.
(With Woody Herman) *Early Autumn,* Discovery, 1952.
(With Stan Kenton) *Sketches on Standards,* Capitol, 1953.
(With Stan Kenton) *Cuban Fire!,* Capitol, 1956.
(With Stan Kenton) *Kenton in Hi-Fi,* Capitol, 1956.
(With Bill Perkins) *Bill Perkins Octet on Stage,* Blue Note, 1956.
(With Mel Tormé) *Round Midnight: A Retrospective (1956-1962),* Stash, 1956.
(With Bill Holman) *Big Band in a Jazz Orbit,* Andex, 1958.
(With Bill Holman) *In a Jazz Orbit,* Andex, 1958.
(With Woody Herman) *Concerto for Herd,* Verve, 1967.
(With The Lawson-Haggart Jazz Band, Vol. 1) *World's Greatest Jazz Band, Vol. 1,* Project 3, 1968.
(With Supersax) *Supersax Plays Bird, Vol. 2: Salt Peanuts,* Pausa, 1973.
(With Hanna-Fontana Band) *Live at the Concord,* Concord Jazz, 1975.
(With Jake Hanna) *Live at Concord,* Concord Jazz, 1975.
(With Louis Bellson) *Don't Stop Now!,* Capri, 1984.
(With Paul Cacia) *Alumni Tribute to Stan Kenton,* Happy Hour, 1987.
(With Tommy Vig Orchestra) *Space Race,* Discovery, 1992.
(With Woody Herman) *Scene & Herd in 1952,* Jazz Band, 1995.
(With Bobby Shew) *Heavyweights,* MAMA Foundation, 1995.
(With Don Sickler) *Nightwatch,* Uptown, 1995.
(With Stan Kenton) *Plays Holman Live!,* Artistry, 1996.
(With Bobby Knight/Great American Trombone Co.) *Cream of the Crop,* Jazz Mark, 1996.

(With Stan Kenton) *Jazz Profile,* Blue Note, 1997.

(With Scott Whitfield) *To Be There,* Amosaya, 1997.

(With Woody Herman) *Cool One,* Hindsight, 1998.

(With Louise Baranger) *Trumpeter's Prayer,* Summit, 1998.

(With Stan Kenton) *1950's Birdland Broadcasts,* Jazz Band, 1998.

(With Stan Kenton) *Intermission Riff 1952-1956,* Giants of Jazz, 1999.

(With Paul McKee) *Gallery,* Corridor, 1999.

(With Stan Kenton) *Revelations,* Tantara, 2000.

(With Bill Watrous) *Bill Watrous & Carl Fontana,* Atlas, 2001.

(With Dusko Goykovich) *Belgrade Blues,* Cosmic Sounds, 2001.

(With Woody Herman) *Jazz Swinger/Music for Tired Lovers,* Collectables, 2001.

(With Woody Herman) *Woody Herman's Finest Hour,* Uptown/Universal, 2001.

(With Woody Herman) *Presenting Woody Herman & The Band,* Jazz Band, 2001.

(With Conte Candoli and Carl Fontana) *Complete Phoenix Recordings, Vol. 1,* Woofy, 2002.

(With The Bill Perkins Octet) *Bill Perkins Octet on Stage,* Japanese Import, 2002.

(With Flip Phillips) *Celebrates His 80th Birthday at the March of Jazz 1995,* Arbors, 2003.

(With Woody Herman) *Standard Times—The Third Herd (1951-1952),* Ocium, 2003.

(With Stan Kenton & His Orchestra) *At the Ernst-Merck-Halle, Hamburg,* Sounds of Yesteryear, 2003.

(With Stan Kenton) *Contemporary Concepts,* Capitol Jazz, 2003.

(With Stan Kenton) *Concepts Era Live!,* Artistry, 2003.

Sources

Periodicals

Hollywood Reporter, October 15, 2003.

Las Vegas Review-Journal, October 10, 2003.

Los Angeles Times, June 15, 1992; October 11, 2003.

News-Star (Monroe, LA), January 18, 2003; October 16, 2003.

New York Times, October 15, 2003.

St. Louis Post-Dispatch, May 13, 1999.

Online

"Carl Fontana," *All Music Guide,* http://www.allmusic.com/ (February 18, 2004).

"Carl Fontana Profile," Jazzmasters, http://www.jazzmasters.nl/fontana.htm (October 9, 2003).

"Carl Fontana Profile," Vegas Jazz, http://www.vegasjazz.org/fontanaprofile.html (February 11, 2004).

"Guest Artist—Carl Fontana," Whitworth College, http://www.whitworth.edu/Academic/Department/Music/PerformanceOpportunities/JazzEnsemble/GuestArtists/CarlFontana.htm (February 18, 2004).

—*Kerry L. Smith*

Nelly Furtado

Singer

AP/Wide World Photos. Reproduced by permission.

At the young age of 24, Nelly Furtado was already making waves in the music industry, winning her first Grammy and proudly representing both her Portuguese and Canadian backgrounds. The youngest of three children born to immigrant parents in Victoria, British Columbia, Canada, her father was a landscaper and her mother a chambermaid. As a child, young Nelly was exposed to many different types of music as her mother was also a talented singer and often held choir practices in the family home. Furtado was constantly encouraged to sing and by 12, she had written a few songs of her own. While her mother passed down her singing gifts, Furtado's father and brother also played pivotal roles in her musical development. They both had diverse record collections through which she would often forage. At night, she listened to Billy Joel, Blondie, and the Brazilian star Caetano Veloso.

Furtado's rich ethnic heritage also influenced her musical exploration. "You wouldn't even believe how real the people are on the [Azores]," she told *Entertainment Weekly*'s Neil Drumming. "They're straight-up old world. Going there ever since I was 9 years old really made a mark on me. Just from seeing the old buildings and the wonderful elderly people and their faces and their devotion to religion, or the devotion to keeping their houses looking nice, or their devotion to making the best stew. I have that in me."

In school, she was introduced to hip-hop and R&B. She took to music naturally; it boosted her confidence in a place where she felt she didn't totally fit in. "I'd never see any Portuguese people on TV, and that really struck a major chord with me. And so I was like 'One day I'm gonna be on TV, and Portuguese kids are gonna see me on TV and they're gonna feel proud, they're gonna feel right,'" she told Christopher John Farley in *Time International*.

Furtado had worked hard to develop her singing voice and by the end of high school, she had learned to play the trombone and ukulele as well. She also joined the school's marching band and regularly took part in Victoria's Portuguese cultural festival. When she was just 17, she moved across Canada to Toronto, where she lived with her older sister. With her strong interest in hip-hop, Furtado started the group Nelstar and played local clubs whenever she could. While her live performance skills were sharply honed, she wasn't quite confident enough to record an album, though she did make some quick demos with the production duo Track and Field—Gerald Eaton and Brian West of Canadian indie stalwarts the Philosopher Kings. She soon moved back to the West Coast, however, and enrolled in the creative writing program at Camosun College. She taught herself guitar by listening to her brother's rock albums and she began to write music more proficiently. Back in Toronto, though, her short demo caught the attention of DreamWorks Records.

With an offer to record, Furtado immediately moved back to Toronto to begin work on *Whoa, Nelly!* with Eaton and West.

The result was an amalgam of styles—hip-hop, jazz, reggae, Portuguese *fado* (traditional folk music)—and a pop-chart juggernaut. Among the talents enlisted for the record were guitarist James McCollum, Portuguese *guitarra* player Nuno Cristo, and scratch deejay Jasper "Li'l Jaz" Gahunia who would also perform with Furtado on the subsequent "Burning in the Spotlight" tour.

With a massive promotional push, the 2001 single "I'm Like a Bird" took off on the pop charts, eventually going multiplatinum. The record however, was far more diverse than its first single indicated and Furtado was scared that it gave listeners a shortsighted view of her. "It's always strange when you have this monster single that doesn't sound too much like anything else on your record," she told Drumming. "Because some people may get a different idea of who you are without digging deeper into the record." Not to worry: On top of mountains of fawning press, *Rolling Stone's* James Hunter called *Whoa, Nelly!* "spastic like high-impact hip-hop, melodically durable like big-time pop and soulfully, intelligently, sensuously international."

The following February, Furtado was invited to perform at the Grammy Awards. At the ceremony she received the award for Best Female Vocal Performance for her hit song "I'm Like a Bird." That year she also took home Juno Awards (the Canadian Grammy equivalent) for Best New Solo Artist, Best Single, Best Songwriter, and Best Producer (with Eaton and West). Furtado followed up the record with the aforementioned tour and a few dance-inflected hip-hop collaborations with Missy Elliott, Timbaland, and the Roots.

Her next studio effort, *Folklore* came nearly three years later, and under slightly different circumstances. Her well-oiled production team was still with her but now she was pregnant with Gahunia's child and had admittedly mellowed out a bit. "About a year after my first album came out, I decided I wanted to make a modern folk record," Furtado told Steven Mooallem of *Interview.* "As we started working, I began falling in love with all these stringed instruments—the banjo, the Portuguese ukulele, and the dulcimer, all of which are on this record. And we focused a little more on the songwriting than on frenetically switching the genres five times in one song, the way we did on the last record. There's something so pure about a guitar and a vocalist, or somebody singing in the street, so the idea was to take that essence and make a folk record for 2003 ...."

Unfortunately, *Folklore* wasn't as quickly embraced by the press. "I don't have an 'I'm Like a Bird' on this album, that's for sure," she admitted to Drumming. "DreamWorks would love it if there was a great, bangin' 'Powerless' remix but sometimes it just doesn't make sense. You can't totally reinvent a song," she said of the record's decidedly different tone.

Never terribly fazed by what critics thought of her music, Furtado preferred to let her fans' opinions gauge her popularity. When *Whoa, Nelly!* was released, she had the chance to play in Portugal and, needless to say, was both excited and nervous to perform there. "What are they going to think of me? I'm this kid. I'm Portuguese, but I'm Canadian—and I'm Americanized," Furtado pondered rhetorically to Farley. Starting out with "Onde Estas," a song sung in Portuguese, the crowd erupted in rapturous applause and chanted *Fadista,* meaning *fado* singer. "It was the highest compliment they could have paid me," she said.

Selected discography

Whoa, Nelly!, DreamWorks, 2000.
Folklore, DreamWorks, 2003.

Sources

Periodicals

Entertainment Weekly, November 21, 2003.
Interview, November, 2003.
Rolling Stone, October 12, 2000.
Time International, August 6, 2001.

Online

"Nelly Furtado," *All Music Guide,* http://www.allmusic.com
   (February 4, 2004).
Nelly Furtado Official Website, http://www.nellyfurtado.com
   (March 31, 2004).

—Ken Taylor

Philip Glass

Composer, keyboardist

AP/Wide World Photos. Reproduced by permission.

The American composer Philip Glass continues to have a tremendous impact on contemporary music. His brand of music is often described, much to his chagrin, as minimalism. Glass's music and his approach to creating it are thoroughly modern, even revolutionary, making him one of the most provocative, commercially successful, and controversial composers of his generation. "Glass's music can be found not only at the opera where he reigns supreme as American's most successful living composer, but at the ballet, on television, in symphony halls, films, jazz clubs, and even the occasional sports stadium," wrote William Duckworth in *Talking Music*.

Philip Glass was born on January 31, 1937, in Baltimore, Maryland. His interest in music developed from an early age, thanks to the eclectic tastes of his father who owned a radio repair shop/record store. Glass heard everything from the extremely popular Elvis Presley records to obscure composers such as Foote and Gottschalk. His father typically brought home the 78 RPM records that did not sell. The biggest impressions on Glass during this period were made by Schoenberg, Anton Webern, and Berg.

Glass began playing violin at the age of six, flute by eight. The bright young man advanced quickly as a scholar and musician. "Musicians have something like a calling, a religious calling," he told Duckworth. "It's a vocation. I think it happens before we know it's going to happen. At a certain point you realize that's the only think you can take seriously."

He entered a program for gifted youth at University of Chicago at the age of 15. He quit flute about this same time because he says he knew he could not make a career of it. "Had I not been ambitious, I would not have noticed that it was a limited repertoire. I would have been happy to play the Telemann, Vivaldi, the few Mozart pieces, and the handful of modern works, which of course I tried." In addition to academic subjects, he studied musicology on his own, concentrating on Charles Ives, Webern, and William Schuman. He also began studying piano with Marcus Raskin.

After receiving a bachelor of arts degree in 1956 at the age of 19, he entered the Juilliard School of Music in New York City in 1958 and pursued composition studies with William Bergsma and Vincent Persichetti for five years. (He had mistakenly thought he would be able to study with Schuman, who was the head of the school at the time and did not teach.) He continued to explore Ives's music as well as that of Aaron Copland. Glass also studied with Steve Reich and, later, Darius Milhaud. He served as a composer-in-residence in Philadelphia through a Ford Foundation Grant. During those years alone, he had written 20 pieces and had been the recipient of numerous awards, including a Broadcast Music Industry Award (1960), the Lado Prize (1961), two Benjamin Awards (1961, 1962), and a Young Composers' Award (1964).

Born on January 31, 1937, in Baltimore, MD; married four times; children: three. *Education:* Graduated from the University of Chicago, 1956; graduated from the Juilliard School of Music.

Began playing violin and flute, early childhood; graduated from the University of Chicago, 1956; graduated from Juilliard School of Music in New York City; continued composition studies with Steve Reich, Darius Milhaud, Nadia Boulanger; began creating music for theatre while studying in Paris; worked and studied with Ravi Shankar, 1965-1966; moved back to New York and formed Philip Glass Ensemble, 1967; began prolifically creating pieces including *Music with Changing Parts,* 1971. Other notable pieces include the operas *Einstein on the Beach,* 1976, *Satyagraha,* 1980, *CIVIL warS: a tree is best measured when it is down,* 1984; and film music for *Koyaanisqatsi,* 1982, *Mishima* and *Thin Blue Line*; created symphony based on David Bowie's *Heroes,* 1997. Various other works include the operas *Monsters of Grace,* 1999, and *Galileo Galilei,* 2002; plus scores for the films *The Hours, Naqoyqatsi,* and *The Fog of War,* 2003.

Awards: Broadcast Music Industry Award, 1960; Lado Prize, 1961; Benjamin Award, 1961, 1962; Ford Foundation grant, 1962; Young Composers' Award, 1964; Musican of the Year, *Musical America,* 1985; Golden Globe Award for *The Truman Show,* 1999.

Addresses: *Record companies*—Nonesuch Records, 75 Rockefeller Plaza, 8th Fl., New York, NY 10019, website: http://www.nonesuch.com. Orange Mountain Music, 632 Broadway, Ste. 902, New York, NY 10012, website: http://www.orangemountainmusic.com. *Management*—Dunvagen Music, 632 Broadway, Ste. 902, New York, NY 10012. *Website*—Philip Glass Official Website: http://www.philipglass.com/.

Despite these achievements, Glass increasingly felt that his compositional style, based on 12-tone compositional theory and advanced rhythmic and harmonic forms, was no longer a meaningful. "My twelve-tone period was over by the time I was nineteen, for better or worse," he told Duckworth. To better realize the music he wanted to created, he went Paris in 1964 to study composition with Nadia Boulanger on a Fulbright Fellowship. He was looking to her to provide him with the musical technique he thought he needed. His studies were focused on counterpoint, solfege, and composition analysis. "One standard exercise of Boulanger's was that from any note you had to sing all the inversions of all the cadences in every key," Glass explained to Duckworth. "It takes about ten or twelve minutes to do, and you go through about thirty or forty formulae. So you become a technician in a certain way. Most Americans don't have that."

Reliance on Cyclic Rhythm

Lessons with this famous teacher had less of an impact on Glass than did his exposure to non-Western music. In some respects, Glass notes, it was as if he had discarded everything she taught him. It was while in Paris that he began his long association with Mabou Mines, an experimental theatre company for which he composed music. Outside the theatre, his music was ignored and even reviled. It was this—including physical fights sparked during concerts—that would eventually prompt him to return to the United States.

Glass traveled extensively through India, Tibet, and North Africa, and in 1965 he became a working assistant to the virtuoso sitar player, Ravi Shankar. Through notating his music for Western musicians and studying tabla with the well known Indian percussionist, Allah Rakha, Glass gained an understanding of the modular-form style of Indian music. Shortly thereafter he completely rejected his earlier compositional style and began to rely solely on the Eastern principle of cyclic rhythm to organize his pieces. Harmony and modulation were added later, but these typically consisted only of a few static chords. It was also through watching Shankar, that Glass realized he could indeed make a career as a composer-performer. Before 1966 Glass had composed 80 pieces. Now they all seemed irrelevant. He essentially started anew.

After returning from Europe in 1967 the composer organized the Philip Glass Ensemble, a seven-member group consisting of three electric keyboard players and three wind players with one sound engineer. The ensemble made its debut in New York on April 13, 1968, and embarked on the first of several European tours the following year. Notable works from this period include *Pieces in the Shape of a Square* (1968), *Music in Similar Motion* (1969), *Music for Voices* (1972), *Music in Twelve Parts* (1971-1974), and *Music with Changing Parts* (1971), a double album and the first release by Glass's Chatham Records.

Entered Uncharted Musical Territory

Glass' reputation as a serious composer suffered during this period, in part because he was not an academic composer. Foundations supporting new music compositions snubbed him. Through the early years of the ensemble, Glass worked temporary day jobs—as a crane operator, furniture mover, plumber and taxi driver—to support the group. He wanted to be self-sufficient, independent—"to put myself in a position where I could create what I wanted without having to answer to a council of elders about whether I was a serious composer," he told *Smithsonian*. He would continue to work odd day jobs until 1978 when the combination of a grant and a commission from the Netherlands Opera freed him to fully concentrate on composition.

Glass controlled his music from its creation, including securing the copyright for it, then allowing only the ensemble to play and record it. "I felt that if I had a monopoly on the music, that as the music became known there would be more work for the ensemble," he told Duckworth. "So for the next eleven years, the only people who played my music was the ensemble."

It was this unique approach to the economics of music that also set Glass apart from his peers. "I figured that if I could get the publishing company working, then I wouldn't have to work again. And it turned out to be true. In fact, you can make a living *and* you can do the music that you want; it takes a combination of a lot of different skills. Don't forget I began working in a record store when I was a kid. The first thing I knew about music was that you sold it; in other words, people paid for it."

Slowly, Glass was creating a name for himself. The appearance of the ensemble at the Royal College of Art in London in 1970 drew support for his work. In 1974 the first parts of *Music in Twelve Parts* were released on Virgin Records, a progressive rock label, thereby increasing his exposure to the popular music audience. Glass soon counted such popular performers as David Bowie and Brian Eno among his fans, and his influence could be heard in the rock music of Tangerine Dream and Pink Floyd. His ability to appeal to numerous musical factions caused him to be described as a "crossover" phenomenon. Indeed, according to David Ewen, he is the only composer ever to have received standing ovations at three varied musical venues such as Carnegie Hall, the Metropolitan Opera House, and the Bottom Line, a venerable New York City music club.

Rejected Minimalism as Accurate Description

Although Glass has been inextricably linked with minimalism, he contends critics are choosing one moment in his career that has long since passed. He has said

the most useful description is "chamber music that's amplified."

Minimalism, which was en vogue as a compositional style in the late 1960s, emphasized a simplification of the music rather than complex musical structures such as harmony, melody, modulation, and rhythm. "With minimalism, Philip Glass invented a new kind of music that attracted an enormous group of people who had never listened to classical music before and, in some cases, who still only listen to his form of it," Joseph McLellan, classical music critic emeritus of *The Washington Post* told *Smithsonian* in 2003.

"The difficulty is that the word doesn't describe the music that people are going to hear," Glass told Duckworth in a late 1990s interview. "I don't think 'minimalism' adequately describes it." Even in 2003, Glass was protesting "It's a term invented by journalists. I never liked the word," he told *Smithsonian*, "but I liked the attention! … [T]he term became a kind of shorthand for people who were making music that was a radical return to tonality, harmonic simplicity and steady rhythms."

Glass does indeed utilize repetitive cycles of rhythm, similar to Hindu *ragas,* which change slowly over long periods of time and are said to produce a trance-like state in some listeners. Certainly his work does fuse together the Eastern musical concepts of space, time, and change with Western musical elements such as diatonic harmony.

Einstein on the Beach

Glass's alliance with the visual arts prompted a collaboration with Robert Wilson, the painter, architect, and leader in the world of avant-garde theater. *Einstein on the Beach,* one of Glass's best known works, was enthusiastically received at its premier in Avignon, France, on July 25, 1976 and was a sellout when performed in New York at the Metropolitan Opera. More a series of "events" than an opera, this full-length stage work explores through dance and movement the same concepts of time and change that Glass investigated through music. Several characters appear as Einstein, one playing repetitive motifs on a violin; a chorus intones repetitive series of numbers and clichés; dancers and actors perform repetitive actions such as moving back and forth across the stage in slow motion. *Einstein on the Beach* has less to do with meaning than concept. "Go to *Einstein* and enjoy the sights and sounds," advises Robert Wilson in one interview, "feel the feelings they evoke. Listen to the Pictures."

Glass followed this work with other theater successes. *Satyagraha,* commissioned by the city of Rotterdam in 1980, is the ritual embodiment of pacifist spirituality.

Based on the life of Gandhi, the opera unfolds as a series of tableaux tracing his early life. The libretto is derived solely from the *Bhagavad Gita* and is sung in Sanskrit. It is said to be one of Glass' most lyric works.

Also during this decade, Glass composed *The Photographer,* a chamber opera based on the life of the early 20th-century inventor Eadweard Muybridge (Amsterdam, 1982) and *Akhnaton,* his third opera, produced at the Stuttgart Opera in 1984. In addition, Glass began scoring music for films. Most notable among this early work was *Koyaanisqatsi,* which was successfully received at the New York Film Festival in 1982. It marked the beginning of his collaboration with filmmaker Godfrey Reggio. This was the first in a trilogy of films. The music from this film is an integral part of the ensemble repertoire and continues to frequently be performed by the group live. That same year, he released *Glassworks,* his first and one of the first ever digital recordings. It consisted of short pieces and was mixed specifically to take advantage of a new consumer electronic device called The Walkman. Glass continued composing, including numerous works for Mabou Mines, commissions for opera and art installations, and works for choreographers Lucinda Childs, Alvin Ailey, and Jerome Robbins. Glass also collaborated with Wilson on another opera, *CIVIL warS: a tree is best measured when it is down*, as well as Allen Ginsberg, the beat poet, on *Hydrogen Jukebox.*

Glass continued his collaborative efforts into the 1990s and beyond. He composed three operas based on films by the late Jean Cocteau, French author and movie director. *Orphee,* composed by Glass in 1993, followed the soundtrack of the film closely. In *La Belle et la Bête* (1994), Glass went one step further, stripping the film of its soundtrack and creating a live and carefully synchronized operatic accompaniment that took its place among his finest and most exciting works. In *Les Enfants Terribles* (1996) Glass teamed with choreographer Susan Marshall to tell the story through instrumental music and dance rather than singing.

Since 1983 Glass continued to score for films such as *Mishima* and *Thin Blue Line,* prompting *Billboard* to note that "few classical composers can boast a relationship with film music as innovative and dynamic as that of Philip Glass." He would later add two Academy Award nominations to his long list of accomplishments.

In 1997 Glass composed and recorded a symphony based on the David Bowie album *Heroes.* One reviewer remarked in *New Statesman* that Glass needed to be credited his help in taking a giant hammer to the wall traditionally separating classical and rock music. In the same article Glass commented that, "Just as composers of the past have turned to music of their time to fashion new works, the work of Bowie became an inspiration for symphonies of my own."

Glass released *Aguas de Amazonia* in 1999 that relied heavily on a Brazilian influence, and he also produced his Symphony No. 2 (Nonesuch) which received much critical praise. He continued creating many new works and made a short solo tour of Europe. Also in 1999, Glass created a soundtrack for the film *Dracula,* directed by Bela Lugosi.

Glass continued to find interesting collaborative efforts as the year 2000 approached. He and Wilson worked together again with Kleiser-Walczak Construction Company on a unique digital film-performance project. "Monsters of Grace" combined ancient poetry with modern ideas and technologies.

"Monsters of Grace combines technology, poetry, animation and music into a meditative 3-D opera," explained a contributor to *ComputorEdge* magazine in 1999. "The production, which takes its name from Shakepeare's Hamlet, uses computer animated film rather than live actors, as live musicians perform the score. The production's film is said to rival *Toy Story* or *A Bug's Life* in its digital complexity and is the longest digital film—probably the longest stereoscopic film—to date." It was Glass who "suggested using Coleman Barks translations of the mystic poet Rumi for Monsters of Grace lyrics."

Work Habits Created Prolific Production

Glass works every day. This, he attributes to Boulanger's influence. He typically works from 6 a.m. until noon; afternoons are devoted to working in the studio. He tries to listen to new works one or two times a week, and sets aside one afternoon each week to speak to people. He also uses sampling to help speed the composition process and has said he is limited only by how much music he can write, which seems to still be prolific.

"If we worked bankers' hours we'd get nothing done!" he told Mark Prendergast, writing in *The Ambient Century: From Mahler to Trance—The Evolution of Sound in the Electronic Age*. That pace continued unabated. He was named a featured composer by the Lincoln Center Festival in 2001. That same year he worked on "Shorts"—scoring short films by Reggio, Peter Greenaway and Atom Egoyan—and mounted "White Raven," a five-act opera created with Wilson and originally commissioned in 1998 to celebrate Portuguese explorers such as Vasco da Gama.

Yet Glass continued to explore seemingly cosmic ideas about how history, social consciousness, and music are all interwoven in works such as "Galileo Galilei" (2002), and Symphony No. 5: Requiem, Bardo and Nirmana-kaya, which "encompasses the history of the world in a little more than 90 minutes," according to *The Washington Times.* Some reviewers observed his work has a meditative quality, no doubt linked to his practice of Buddhism.

By 2003, Glass had several more projects on which he was working including his twentieth opera "The Sound of a Voice" with Henry Hwang, and scores for the films including *The Hours,* which earned him a 2003 Academy Award nomination, and *Naqoyqatsi,* the final film in the Reggio trilogy. *American Record Guide,* in a March-April 2003 review said that in this latter soundtrack, that when the music is "yoked with images" the music takes on "a mysterious life." He also contributed the score to *The Fog of War* (2003), a documentary film by Errol Morris about Robert McNamara, former United States Secretary of Defense and was releasing various recordings of his works, including that film's soundtrack, on his Orange Mountain Music label.

Still, there continued to be detractors. Writing in *The New Republic* in 2000, John Rockwell, editor of the Arts and Leisure section of *The New York Times,* took Glass to task for being tired and tedious, writing that his work "has declined in quality, and that decline can be described." Rockwell contends that since about 1984, Glass lost faith or interest in compositional devices such as repetition and periodization, becoming "too restless, too willing to accommodate conventional taste." He added that Glass "now panders nervously to his audience in the fear they may be bored. And his pandering undercuts the radical hypnotic aura of his early music."

"[A]rtists have a way of surprising, and defeating, their critics," continued Rockwell. "At least he is still working. He did not quit while he was ahead, or retire early." There is still no firm opinion as to the legacy Glass will leave. Prendergast observes it is Glass's "contribution to electronic music that is most under-valued. It was Glass who popularized the early Farfisa portable organs and brought the polyphonic synthesizers of the 1970s into concert halls."

David Schiff, writing in *The Atlantic Monthly* in 2001, observed Glass is "probably the only American composer since George Gershwin whose music could work equally well in a cocktail lounge ... or a concert hall. The music world has not yet made up is mind whether this is a good thing."

Selected discography

Music in Similar Music/Music in 5ths, Chatam Square, 1973.
Music in 12 Parts, Virgin, 1975; rereleased, Nonesuch, 1996.
North Star, Virgin, 1977.
Einstein on the Beach, Atlantic, 1979; rereleased, Elektra, 1993.
Glassworks, CBS Masterworks, 1982.
Koyaanisqatsi, Antilles, 1983.

Akhnaten, Columbia, 1984.
Satyagraha, Columbia, 1985.
Mishima, Nonesuch, 1985.
Songs From Liquid Days, Columbia, 1986.
Dancepieces, Columbia, 1987.
Powaqqatsi, Elektra, 1988.
Mad Rush; Metamorphosis; Wichita Sutra Vortex, CBS Masterworks, 1989.
1000 Airplanes on the Roof, Alliance, 1989.
The Thin Blue Line, Elektra, 1989; reissued, Orange Mountain Music, 2003.
Mindwalk, 1990.
Hydrogen Jukebox, Elektra, 1993.
Glassworks, Catalyst, 1993.
Low Symphony, Polygram, 1994.
Music With Changing Parts, Elektra, 1994.
La Belle et la Bête (Beauty and the Beast), Nonesuch, 1995.
Secret Agent, Nonesuch, 1996.
Heroes Symphony, Point, 1997.
Kundun, Elektra, 1997.
Dracula, Elektra, 1999.
CIVIL warS: a tree is best measured when it is down: ACT V; The Rome Section, Nonesuch, 1999.
Piano Music of Philip Glass, Roméo/Qualiton, 2000.
Songs from Liquid Days, Silva Classics, 2000.
Symphony No. 5: Requiem, Bardo, Nirmanakaya, Nonesuch, 2000.
The Music of Candyman, Orange Mountain Music, 2001.
Music in the Shape of a Square, Stradivarius, 2001.
The Hours: Music from the Motion Picture, Nonesuch, 2002.
Naqoyqatsi (soundtrack), Sony Classical/Sony Music Soundtrax, 2002.
Etudes for Piano, Vol. I, No. 1-10, Orange Mountain Music, 2003.
The Fog of War, Orange Mountain Music, 2003.

Sources

Books

Buckley, Jonathan, editor, *Classical Music on CD: The Rough Guide,* Rough Guides, 1995.
Duckworth, William, *Talking Music: Conversations With John Cage, Philip Glass, Laurie Anderson, and Five Generations of American Experimental Composers,* Da Capo, 1999.
Predergast, Mark, *The Ambient Century: From Mahler to Trance—The Evolution of Sound in the Electronic Age,* Bloomsbury, 2000.

Periodicals

American Record Guide, March-April 2003.
The Atlantic Monthly, July-August 2001.
Billboard, July 21, 2001
The Christian Science Monitor, July 20, 2001; June 13, 2003.
ComputorEdge, May 21, 1999.
Daily Variety, January 6, 2003.
High Fidelity/Musical America, April 1979.
The New Republic, April 10, 2000.
New Statesman, February 14, 1997.
People, October 6, 1980.
Smithsonian, November 2003.
Time, June 19, 1978; December 9, 1996.
Washington Times, November 10, 2001.

Online

Orange Mountain Music Website, http://www.orange
mountainmusic.com/ (April 8, 2004).
Philip Glass Official Website, http://www.philipglass.com/
(April 8, 2004).

—*Bar Biszick and Linda Dailey Paulson*

Josh Groban

Singer

In a meteoric rise to success, Josh Groban took the world by storm while he was still a high school student. His strong baritone voice and his unusual mix of pop mixed with opera and romantic classical music has attracted a wide audience and has led music executives to create a whole new way of promoting talent.

Joshua Winslow Groban was born on February 27, 1981, in Los Angeles, California, the oldest of two siblings. His father, Jack, worked as an executive recruiter. His mother, Melinda, was an artist and art teacher. The family enjoyed attending theater productions, but they had no show business connections.

Groban was recognized for his voice as a young boy. As his voice matured and he became a teenager, he was accepted into the Los Angeles County High School for the Arts. He participated in high school plays and had dreams of someday singing or acting on Broadway. When Groban was 17 years old his voice teacher, Seth Riggs, was contacted by multiple Grammy Award-winning producer David Foster, who was looking for someone to sing at charity events. Riggs sent Foster some tapes of some of his students, including one of Groban's voice. "I'm always leery when people send me tapes," Foster was quoted as saying on the ABC News website. "Ninety-nine times out of 100 there's just nothing there.... But [Groban's] tape stuck out like a sore thumb."

Foster booked Groban to fill in for Michael Crawford at the 1999 inauguration of California Governor Gray Davis. A few weeks later, Foster needed someone to fill in for Andrea Bocelli to sing "The Prayer" with Celine Dion at a rehearsal for the 1999 Grammy Awards. Although Bocelli sang at the actual show, Groban was noticed by the host of the Grammys, Rosie O'Donnell, who booked him on her show, calling him "Opera Boy."

Foster continued to book Groban at charity events, and soon David E. Kelley, the creator and executive producer of the television show *Ally McBeal,* noticed the young man. Kelley decided to create a small role for Groban in an episode of the show, and in the 2001 season finale Groban played Malcolm Wyatt, a teenage boy who was suing the girl who backed out of attending the prom with him. "We expanded his part once we realized he could act," said executive producer Bill D'Elia in *Entertainment Weekly.* "I don't think even Josh realized he could act." The Wyatt character ended up singing at his prom and impressing his classmates. Groban also impressed the television audience, and the show received thousands of messages from viewers who wanted to know more about him.

In the meantime, Groban had graduated from high school and was accepted as a student in Carnegie Mellon University's musical theater department. However, he decided to hold off on continuing his formal

Born Joshua Winslow Groban on February 27, 1981, in Los Angeles, CA; son of Jack (an executive recruiter) and Melinda (an artist and art teacher) Groban.

Performed at inauguration of California Governor Gray Davis, 1999; played Malcolm Wyatt on two episodes of the *Ally McBeal* show, 2001; released *Josh Groban*, 2001; performed at Winter Olympics, 2002; released *Josh Groban in Concert*, 2002; released *Closer*, 2003.

Addresses: *Record company*—143 Records, 530 Wilshire Blvd., Ste. 101, Santa Monica, CA 90401. *Agent*—William Morris Agency, 1 William Morris Pl., Beverly Hills, CA 90212. *Website*—Josh Groban Official Website: http://www.joshgroban.com.

education when he was offered a record deal with 143 Records, a joint venture between Foster and Warner Brothers. Executives took some time deciding what to do with him. Some thought he should try to fit in with boy bands such as the Backstreet Boys. Others thought he should sing only in Italian. Finally Groban and Foster came up with a combination of pop, ballads, classical music, and opera, with songs in English, Spanish, and Italian. His first album, titled *Josh Groban,* was released in November of 2001.

Initially, radio stations were unclear on how to handle Groban's hybrid musical style, and it was clear that marketing the new artist would need to take a nontraditional path. "We have to do everything with Josh outside of the traditional channels of how we would market most artists," said Diarmuid Quinn, executive vice president at Warner Brothers Records, in the *Hollywood Reporter.* "There's no MTV, there's no VH1, there's no pop or rock radio. So you're marketing in a different realm."

Groban was asked to return for the holiday episode of *Ally McBeal* in late 2001. He began to appear on talk shows, including *Oprah, Good Morning America,* the *Today Show,* and the *Tonight Show,* and in a major profile on *20/20.* Following the *20/20* profile, his album went from number 108 to number 12 on the *Billboard* 200 chart, and sales figures multiplied by ten. "When Josh goes on television and opens his mouth, there is this magical vulnerable quality about him that drives people nuts," Quinn said in an article in *Billboard.* He also sang at the Nobel Peace Prize Concert in Oslo, Norway, and at a holiday show for the Pope at the Vatican. He was chosen to sing at the closing ceremonies of the 2002 Winter Olympics in Salt Lake City, along with Charlotte Church. At first the two practiced outdoors and at a higher altitude in order to get their voices ready. However, it was finally decided they would lip-synch their performances. "We had about 15 minutes before we went in, and it was the greatest adrenaline rush I've ever had," Groban stated in *Entertainment Weekly.*

Marketers soon found that Groban's records were primarily selling through the Internet, rather than through record stores. An online community calling themselves "Grobanites" developed, boasting a 90,000-fan database. Groban's fan club website, Friends of Josh Groban, offered video footage, music, and advance concert ticket sales for a fee and, in its first three weeks, 7,000 fans signed up. "The music has brought them together and created this community, which has been really cool," Groban stated in *Billboard.* "It's wonderful for me to see the music affect them on such a personal level."

In December of 2002, Groban released *Josh Groban in Concert,* a DVD-CD combo based on a PBS "Great Performances" special. Between this and his debut album, he had become the best-selling new male artist of 2002. Even with all of this success, Groban still longed to sing on Broadway. On September 22, 2003, he got his chance, performing in a one-night-only performance of *Chess* with Lara Fabian and Adam Pascal at the Amsterdam Theater.

Groban worked for seven months on his next album, *Closer,* in which he co-wrote some of the songs and played the piano. "I got back into the studio after two years and just made a list of the things I wanted to explore," Groban said in *Billboard.* "I wanted to step forward in the range of difficulty of the songs. I also had my own point of view and wanted to try and write the kind of songs that I would want to listen to." The new album was released late in 2003, and raced to number four on the *Billboard* 200 chart, with first-week sales of 375,000.

When tickets went on sale for a 2004 tour, they sold out quickly. "We put 40 shows on sale and the seats were filled in less than 30 minutes—every market—which is unbelievable," said Gayle Holcomb, senior vice president for the William Morris Agency, in *Billboard.* He added that "when Ticketmaster went up, people were in a frenzy." Tour stops were scheduled throughout the United States, England, France, Norway, and Sweden. By the time Groban sang at the pre-game show for the 2004 Super Bowl, he no longer had to worry about recognition.

Selected discography

Josh Groban, 143 Records, 2001.
Josh Groban in Concert, 143 Records, 2002.
Closer, 143 Records, 2003.

Sources

Periodicals

Billboard, December 6, 2002, p. 1.
Entertainment Weekly, March 8, 2002, p. 32; December 20, 2002, p. 53.
Hollywood Reporter, November 13, 2003, p. 6.
People, December 1, 2003, p. 46.
Variety, April 28, 2003, p. 4.

Online

"A Star in the Making," ABC News, http://www.abcnews.com (January 12, 2004).
"Josh Groban in Concert," PBS Great Performances, http://www.pbs.org (January 12, 2004).
"Josh Groban tops album chart," CNN, http://www.cnn.com (January 25, 2004).

—Sarah Parkin

Hall
& Oates

Rock duo

Universally hailed as "exponents of blue-eyed soul," Daryl Hall and John Oates began performing as a duo in the late 1960s, but first gained widespread attention with their self-titled 1975 RCA debut album. Many albums and hits followed; but in recent years Hall has been adamant about shedding that moniker, calling it "archaic" and "racist." No matter what label is applied, the rock duo remains the most successful pairing in rock history.

Both halves of the duo loved music from their early years. Hall, born in or near Philadelphia on October 11, 1948, was the son of two classically trained musicians. Though they gave him voice and piano lessons in the hope that he too would follow the classical path, Hall was enchanted by the sounds of rock and roll. By the time Hall was in junior high, he was catching rides to Philadelphia to become involved in the city's vibrant rhythm and blues scene. He hung out on corners with black vocal groups who were impressed enough by his devotion to let him sing with them. Unwilling to disappoint his parents, he continued his classical music education. Hall began to experience success in both genres simultaneously: He would purportedly sing with the Philadelphia Orchestra in the afternoon and at night sing backup for performers like Motown great Smokey Robinson in small city clubs.

John Oates, on the other hand, was born on April 7, 1949, in New York, New York, to parents who liked rock and roll and encouraged his interest in it. His mother even took him to concerts by pioneering rock artists such as Bill Haley and the Comets. Oates started guitar lessons when he was eight years old and eventually perfected a routine in which he imitated Elvis Presley. Like Hall, after Oates's family moved to the Philadelphia area, he often went to the city as a teenager to see soul acts like Sam and Dave or Gary U.S. Bonds. Oates also spent a lot of time dancing at local record hops, in addition to practicing with various bands he formed with his friends. He too eventually became a studio backup singer and musician.

Hall and Oates met in 1967, around the time both attended Temple University. They quickly became friends because of their shared interest in soul and rhythm and blues. Oates also began playing occasional sessions with Hall's rock band, Gulliver. By 1969 they had left Gulliver to perform as a pair. At that time both Hall and Oates were also interested in folk music; their first album on Atlantic, *Whole Oates,* released in 1972, had a predominantly folk sound. Though this effort was generally ignored by critics and fans alike, the two musicians were undaunted. Their next release, *Abandoned Luncheonette,* had more of the "blue-eyed soul" feel that ultimately became their trademark; it fared better, garnering good reviews and scoring a minor hit with "She's Gone."

Ever experimental, Hall & Oates's third release, *War Babies,* which was produced by Todd Rundgren, had a

For the Record . . .

Members include **Daryl Hall** (born on October 11, 1948, in Philadelphia, PA; son of two classical musicians; married Bryna Lublin, divorced), singer, songwriter; **John Oates** (born on April 7, 1949, in New York, NY; married Nancy Hunter, a model; children: one son), singer, songwriter, guitarist. *Education:* Both attended Temple University.

Duo formed c. 1969; released debut album *Whole Oates,* 1972; *Abandoned Luncheonette* released, 1973; chart with single "She's Gone" from that same album, 1973; *War Babies* released, 1974; moved to RCA label for *Daryl Hall and John Oates,* which generated the hit "Sara, Smile," 1975; tour internationally in support of album; *Bigger Than Both of Us* released, 1976; number of poorly received releases issued; *Voices* released, 1980; album spawned hits including "You've Lost That Lovin' Feelin'" and "Kiss on My List"; released *Private Eyes,* 1981; hit singles "Private Eyes" and "I Can't Go For That" made charts, 1981; *H20* released, generated hits "Did It in a Minute," "Maneater," "One on One," and "Family Man," 1982; greatest hits collection, *Rock 'n' Soul Part One* issued, 1983; *Big Bam Boom* released, 1984; album generated hits "Out of Touch" and "Method of Modern Love"; decides to concentrate on solo projects; released *Ooh Yeah!,* 1988; topped the record for number one hits set by the Everly Brothers, late 1980s; *Change of Season* released, 1990; decided to stop touring and returned to work on solo projects, 1991; returned to recording as a duo with *Marigold Sky,* released in 1997; released *VH1 Behind The Music: The Daryl Hall & John Oates Collection,* 2002; released *Do It for Love,* 2003; released "best-of" collection *The Essential Collection,* 2003.

Awards: National Association of Television and Radio Artists, Best Song of the Year for "Sara, Smile"; Best Duo of the Year, c. 1976; NARAS Heroes Award, 2003.

Addresses: *Management*—Robert Norman, CAA, 9830 Wilshire Blvd., Beverly Hills, CA 90212. *Record company*—BMG, 1540 Broadway, New York, NY 10036. *Website*—Hall & Oates Official Website: http://www.hallandoates.com.

harsher, more metallic rock tone, which largely alienated their burgeoning audience. Recalling concert performances of the same period, Hall told Michael Ryan in *People*: "We played a few gigs where people actually threw things at us." The duo returned to a mellow, soul sound for their RCA debut, *Daryl Hall and John Oates.* The album's single, "Sara, Smile," raced up the charts in Europe as well as the United States and Hall & Oates launched a successful world tour. Based on this popularity, interest was generated in their previous efforts, especially *Abandoned Luncheonette.* "She's Gone" belatedly became a much bigger hit. Hall & Oates kept their new found popularity going with the 1976 release of *Bigger Than Both of Us,* scoring another smash with the catchy single, "Rich Girl."

Their next three albums, however, did not fare as well. *Along the Red Ledge* was more rock-oriented than their previous successes, while *X-Static* was influenced by disco. But with the 1980 release of *Voices,* Hall & Oates were back on track and collected a series of platinum albums. *Voices* included a hit remake of the Righteous Brothers's classic "You've Lost That Lovin' Feelin'," along with the chart-climbing "Kiss on My List." The following year *Private Eyes* fared just as well, scoring hits with the upbeat title cut and "I Can't Go For That." Next came *H20,* which featured "Did It in a Minute," "Maneater," the slow ballad "One on One," and "Family Man." Not content when they released the greatest hits collection, *Rock 'n' Soul Part One,* Hall & Oates included new hits on the album as well—"Say It Isn't So," and "Adult Education." In the late 1980s, the duo bested the record for number one hits set by the Everly Brothers, making them the most successful rock duo ever.

Despite their success, after 1984's *Big Bam Boom,* which yielded the hits "Out of Touch" and "Method of Modern Love," and the popular *Live at the Apollo,* the long-time team split to pursue individual projects. Oates helped produce albums for other musical groups, while Hall recorded his second solo effort, *Three Hearts in the Happy Ending Machine.* Hearts, like Hall's previous solo album, *Sacred Songs,* drew respectful remarks from critics, but Hall & Oates fans were disappointed; neither disc sold well.

Nonetheless, as Hall predicted in a 1986 interview with Steve Dougherty in *People,* the duo did re-team to record again and again. In 1988 they released *Ooh Yeah!* on Arista and had the satisfaction of watching two singles, "Everything Your Heart Desires" and "Missed Opportunity," become popular with Top Forty audiences. Not only fans, but critics too welcomed Hall & Oates's reunion effort; Hank Bordowitz in *High Fidelity,* for instance, proclaimed gleefully that *"Ooh Yeah!* attacks the brain and breeds there, causing you to hum incessantly." Hall & Oates's follow-up album, 1990's *Change of Season* also produced a hit with "So Close," co-produced by Jon Bon Jovi and Danny Kortchmar.

By 1991, they decided to stop touring together to focus on solo projects. Hall decamped to England, Oates to Colorado. Hall eventually released *Soul Alone*. But a 1997 interview in *Billboard,* found Hall repeating his predictions from the post *Big Bam Boom* hiatus. The duo did re-team to record again and again. This time, they had "made it an open-ended sort of separation."

Despite the number of times either member has attempted to go it alone, the reception has not been anything approaching that of their combined efforts. As *Billboard*'s Melinda Newman observed in a March 30, 1991 concert review, it is "obvious why the whole is often greater than the sum of its parts. Together, they offer a textbook case of near-perfect pop songwriting and delivery; alone, their weaknesses are glaringly apparent."

In 1997, the duo released *Marigold Sky,* their first album since 1990, to fairly tepid praise. "*Marigold Sky* finds them relaxing into maturity, recording a collection of appealingly smooth, well-crafted soul-pop," stated Stephen Thomas Erlewine, in a review of the album on the *All Music Guide* website. The project generated a single hit, "Promise Ain't Enough," that snuck onto the adult contemporary music charts. Hall said audiences seemed to accept the new material as part of their live performance setlist. *Entertainment Weekly* was not as kind, calling it "over-echoed and old" and "competent, professional dross." Erlewine agreed that there was indeed nothing "unforgettably catchy" on the album, "but it's a well-made album … illustrating that even if Hall & Oates are past their peak, they nevertheless are capable of making engaging music." In a later review of another Hall and Oates release, he said "it wasn't the right album for a comeback."

It would be another six years until their next release. During that period, the pair signed a deal with Columbia Records and began working on a new studio album between touring obligations. They also continued working on solo projects. Oates released his first solo album *Phunk Shui* in 2002. In 2003, he announced he was re-releasing it with three new tracks on his own PS Records label. Critics seemed to regard it as a curiosity more than anything.

Do It for Love was on shelves in February of 2003. Part of the success of this release was attributed to nostalgia, fueled by a Hall & Oates episode of the VH1 program, *Behind the Music*. Erlewine called it "their best album in 20 years," adding that it "hearkens [sic] back to the sensibility of both *Abandoned Luncheonette* and 1975's eponymous debut for RCA. … [N]othing here will erase memories of their biggest hits, yet nearly all of these 14 songs hold their own against many of the album tracks and lesser-known hits from their golden period while also having a unified sense of sound and purpose, adding up to a thoroughly satisfying record, the kind that will please the faithful while winning back those listeners who haven't really listened to the duo since the '80s. A really fine, surprising comeback effort."

With Ruben Blades and Nile Rodgers, Hall & Oates were named recipients of the 2003 NARAS Heroes Awards. The award is given to those deemed "outstanding individuals whose creative talents and accomplishments cross all musical boundaries and who are integral to the vitality of the music community," according to the Associated Press.

Selected discography

Whole Oates, Atlantic, 1972.
Abandoned Luncheonette, Atlantic, 1973.
War Babies, Atlantic, 1974.
Daryl Hall and John Oates, RCA, 1975.
Bigger Than Both of Us, RCA, 1976.
Beauty on a Back Street, RCA, 1977.
Livetime, RCA, 1978.
Along the Red Ledge, RCA, 1978.
X-Static, RCA, 1979; remastered re-release, Buddha, 2001.
Voices, RCA, 1980.
Private Eyes, RCA, 1981.
H2O, RCA, 1982.
Rock 'n' Soul Part One, RCA, 1983.
Big Bam Boom, RCA, 1984.
Live at the Apollo, RCA, 1985.
Ooh Yeah!, Arista, 1988.
Change of Season, Arista, 1990.
Marigold Sky, Push, 1997.
Ecstasy on the Edge, Fruit Tree, 2001.
VH1 Behind The Music: The Daryl Hall & John Oates Collection, BMG Heritage, 2002.
Do It for Love, Image, 2003.
The Essential Collection, BMG (UK), 2003.

Sources

Periodicals

Associated Press, August 22, 2002.
Billboard, March 30, 1991; August 30, 1997; April 4, 1998.
Entertainment Weekly, October 3, 1997.
High Fidelity, July 1988; November 1988.
Mademoiselle, September 1981.
Newsweek, February 20, 1984.
People, May 25, 1981; April 15, 1985; December 15, 1986.
Record (Bergen County, NJ), September 9, 1993.
Rolling Stone, March 22, 1979; January 17, 1985; May 5, 1988.
Stereo Review, April 1978; September 1988.
Times Union (Albany, NY), February 27, 2003.
Virginia Pilot, July 10, 2003.

Online

"Hall & Oates," *All Music Guide,* http://www.allmusic.com (January 23, 2004).

"Hall and Oates Deemed 'Heroes' in Music," *San Jose Mercury News,* http://www.mercurynews.com (January 23, 2004).

—*Elizabeth Wenning and Linda Dailey Paulson*

Jesse Harris

Songwriter, guitarist, singer

AP/Wide World Photos. Reproduced by permission.

Jesse Harris is a musician and songwriter who fronts Jesse Harris and The Ferdinandos, a group with several CDs to its credit. However, he is best known as the Grammy Award-winning songwriter of "Don't Know Why," recorded by Norah Jones in 2002. From this collaboration, Harris achieved recognition within the industry for his songwriting skills and became eagerly sought after for his songwriting talents.

Harris grew up in New York City, where he studied music from an early age. He studied classical piano, but while in his teens he dropped the instrument in favor of the guitar. Some of his earliest musical influences have included Bob Dylan, The Band, Joni Mitchell, and Van Morrison. After graduating from a private high school, Harris attended Cornell University, majoring in English. He counts Walt Whitman, Henry Miller and *The Arabian Nights* among his literary favorites, and critics have noted his literary bent. "I always wanted to be a writer," he said during a National Public Radio (NPR) interview, "but I always loved music.... When I started playing guitar, I was able to bring those two things together, which is a love of writing and a love of music."

Well before he was acknowledged for his talents as a songwriter, he performed with various musical groups, in addition to working day jobs such as typing soap opera scripts and teaching private guitar lessons. His first group was Once Blue, a duo that was signed to EMI, releasing its debut recording in 1995. A follow up project was recorded, but remained unreleased. However, nine of the album's tracks surfaced in 2003 on an EMI/Toshiba rerelease of *Once Blue.*

Harris was playing the East Village club The Living Room one rainy night when a Sony Publishing employee decided to duck into the Lower East Side nightclub, and Harris was subsequently signed to a recording deal. Harris used his advances to make CDs with his next group, The Ferdinandos, with whom he continues to perform and record. The group takes its name from a favorite Italian restaurant. Many of the group's musicians have backgrounds in jazz. "I tend to play with a lot of guys who also play in the downtown instrumental scene," Harris told *Music Connection.* "Kenny Wollesen, outside of my group, doesn't really do other vocal things. He plays with Bill Frisell and Sex Mob; so does Tony Scherr, our guitarist. For lack of a better word, they play with avant garde instrumentalists." Harris and the group recorded original material for their first three releases and stayed with independent companies for distribution. "What records originally were for was for capturing a moment," he told *Paste.* "Now it's about assembling a flawless product—like a soda can or something."

When performing, Harris has tried to create as much space in the room as possible. "I like space, particularly when I'm performing and the audience is talking. If I

For the Record . . .

Born c. 1970 in New York, NY. *Education:* Cornell University, bachelor's degree in English.

Co-founded Once Blue, 1995; debut released, 1995; group dissolved, c. 1997; formed Jesse Harris and the Ferdinandos, c. 2000; contributed songs to Norah Jones's *Come Away With Me,* 2002; won Grammy Award for "Don't Know Why," 2002; released *The Secret Sun,* 2003.

Awards: Grammy Award, Song of The Year for "Don't Know Why," 2002.

Addresses: *Record company*—Verve Music Group, 1755 Broadway, 3rd Fl., New York, NY 10019. *Booking*—Monterey Peninsula Artists, 509 Hartnell St., Monterey, CA 93940. *Management*—Bob Andrews, Undertow Music, 4217 W. Grace St., Chicago, IL 60641. *Website*—Jesse Harris Official Website: http://www.jesseharrismusic.com.

leave a lot of space it makes silence happen and gets their attention," he told *Music Connection.* "It has the power to draw them in." As for his approach to songwriting, Harris explained to *The Philadelphia Inquirer* that he doesn't edit a great deal. "I just write a lot, over and over, until I get to the version that seems to say it best."

Harris became acquainted with Norah Jones in 1998, during a cross-country road trip he was taking with a friend. They stopped in Denton, Texas, to visit friends who were in college there. Harris wound up playing with Jones, who was also a student at the school, in an impromptu jam session. After leaving, he and Jones remained in contact, meeting again when she moved to New York and began performing. Harris contributed several songs to her 2002 debut, *Come Away With Me,* including "Don't Know Why," "Shoot the Moon," "One Flight Down," and "I've Got to See You Again." He also played guitar with her in live performances as well as on the recording.

It was "Don't Know Why" that got the attention from fans and critics, and Harris won a Grammy Award for Song of the Year in 2002. Harris admitted that winning a Grammy against competition from the likes of heavyweights such as Bruce Springsteen was initially daunting. But, as he told Lynn Neary in the NPR interview, he finally figured, "What's one Grammy, more or less, to them?" By mid-2003 the album had sold more than 13 million copies.

The Secret Sun, the Ferdinandos' major label debut, was released in the wake of Harris's Grammy Award win, and the two personalities of Harris and Jones were inextricably entwined in the minds of music critics. Few critics outside of the New York scene were familiar with Harris apart from his work with Jones, but they gave Jesse Harris and The Ferdinandos a fair shake—even if Jones's name appeared in every review. "What do Harris's songs sound like without the sultry voice of Norah Jones? Some would say they sound better," remarked Reid Davis in *Paste.* "While in Jones' hands the songs are sleek, high-priced thoroughbreds, in Harris's hands the songs become favorite old mares—with less pedigree, perhaps, but eminently more approachable."

Critics praised the strength of the songwriting on *The Secret Sun.* "The success of these songs is their universal appeal," wrote Harry Rubenstein in the *Jerusalem Post.* "Most of these carefully constructed ballads would blend into a smoky East Village nightclub, and just as easily into a Nashville dive.… His songs are sketches of life, and paint a cerebral picture of young love, nostalgia and Brooklyn beaches." Other reviewers remarked that although the work is strong, it is clearly the work of an artist with a lot of potential yet to be realized. "Harris stands ready to stake his claim as a singer-songwriter with *The Secret Sun,*" noted a reviewer on the PopMatters Music website. "The attentive listener will be rewarded by the work of a simple storyteller who uses both music and words to create songs that feel like independent film shorts. … The roots-rock flavor of *The Secret Sun* is pleasantly competent and assured, but these songs never blossom beyond coffeehouse sketches of life. There are no memorable melodies or lines and with 12 tracks running at less than 42 minutes, Harris doesn't give himself time to build a good thematic head of steam." The reviewer added that the album is a "work of promise that needs a quicker, stronger follow-up."

Harris's artistry has already earned him some $2.6 million from songwriting and publishing royalties, plus additional earnings from radio airplay on the Jones album. *Philadelphia Daily News* reviewer Jonathan Takiff declared that Harris "could be the next David Gray or John Mayer, both like-minded romantic spirits. But then again, he may be the next Jimmy Webb—revered for his songs though not his performances."

Selected discography

With Once Blue

Once Blue, EMI, 1995; rereleased 2003.

With Jesse Harris and the Ferdinandos

Jesse Harris and the Ferdinandos, Undertow, 1999.
Crooked Lines, 2001.
Jesse's Box, Sony/Columbia, 2002.
Without You, Bean/Undertow, 2002.
The Secret Sun, Blue Thumb, 2003.

Sources

Periodicals

Daily News (New York, NY), June 20, 2003.
Dirty Linen, October-November 2003.
Down Beat, August 2003.
Jerusalem Post, October 21, 2003.
Miami Herald, May 16, 2003.
Music Connection, June 23, 2003.

New York Post, May 27, 2003.
New Yorker, February 3, 2003.
Paste, Autumn 2003.
Philadelphia Daily News, June 23, 2003.
Philadelphia Inquirer, May 18, 2003.
Rolling Stone, March 6, 2003.

Online

"Jesse Harris & The Ferdinandos: *The Secret Sun,*" Pop Matters Music, http://www.popmatters.com/music/reviews/h/harrisjesse-secret.shtml (January 28, 2004).
Jesse Harris Official Website, http://www.jesseharrismusic.com/ (April 14, 2004).

Additional information was taken from a National Public Radio interview on *Morning Edition,* May 12, 2003.

—Linda Dailey Paulson

The Isley Brothers

R&B group

Inducted into the Rock and Roll Hall of Fame in 1992, the Isley Brothers are an enduring rhythm and blues band known to several generations of music fans for a multitude of hits, beginning in the late 1950s. Their biggest single, "It's Your Thing," was released in 1969 and rose to Number Two on *Billboard*'s pop charts. Young audiences in the sixties knew the band for their rollicking "Shout" and "Twist and Shout," the latter of which was later recorded by the Beatles. During the 1970s, the Isley Brothers scored big with their expanded lineup, and in 1990, pop-rocker Rod Stewart revived their 1966 Motown version of "This Old Heart of Mine" in a duet with Ronald Isley to score a top ten pop hit.

When O'Kelly Isley, Sr., first married Sallye Bernice Bell, he announced that he wanted to have four sons who would replace the Mills Brothers, a World War II-era pop group that got their start in Cincinnati, Ohio. The Isley patriarch got his wish when the young Isley Brothers, all born in Cincinnati, began as a trio consisting of brothers O'Kelly, Jr. (known as Kelly), Rudolph, and Ronald. (A fourth brother, Vernon, died tragically in 1954 when he was knocked off his bike while riding to school.) In the early 1950s, the brothers were singing

© Jack Vartoogian. Reproduced by permission.

For the Record . . .

Members include **Ernie Isley** (born c. 1952 in Cincinnati, OH), lead guitar, drums; **Marvin Isley** (born c. 1953 in Cincinnati, OH), bass, percussion; **O'Kelly Isley, Jr.** (born on December 25, 1937, in Cincinnati, OH; died on March 31, 1986), vocals; **Ronald Isley** (born on May 21, 1941, in Cincinnati, OH), vocals; **Rudolph Isley** (born on April 1, 1939, in Cincinnati, OH), vocals; **Chris Jasper**, keyboards.

Brothers Kelly, Rudolph, and Ronald Isley performed gospel music, Cincinnati, OH, early 1950s; established professional singing career, New York City, 1956; recorded first hit, "Shout," RCA Victor, 1959; recorded for various labels including Atlantic, Wand, United Artists, and Tamla; moved to Teaneck, NJ, 1960, and formed own label, T-Neck (distributed by CBS/Epic during most of 1970s and early 1980s); joined by Ernie and Marvin Isley and Chris Jasper for 1969 recording "It's Your Thing"; became sextette with album *3+3*, 1973; Ernie and Marvin Isley and Chris Jasper left group, 1984, to perform separately as Isley/Jasper/Isley; Marvin, Ernie, and Ronald Isley reformed the Isley Brothers as a trio, 1990; recorded album *Tracks of Life,* 1992; signed with DreamWorks Records, 2001; released *Body Kiss,* 2003.

Awards: Grammy Award, Best Rhythm and Blues Vocal by a Duo or Group for "It's Your Thing," 1969; inducted into the Rock and Roll Hall of Fame, 1992; inducted into the Vocal Group Hall of Fame, 2003.

Addresses: *Record company*—DreamWorks, 9268 W. Third St., Beverly Hills, CA 90210, website: http://www.dreamworksrecords.com. *Booking*—Booking Entertainment.Com, 236 West 26th St., Ste. 701, New York, NY 10016, website: http://www.bookingentertainment.com. *Website*—The Isley Brothers Official Website: http://www.theisleybrothers.com.

In 1956 Kelly, Rudolph, and Ronald set out for New York City. When they arrived, they worked odd jobs for fast cash and tried to break into the music business. By the beginning of 1957 they had demonstrated enough talent to land a spot on a bill at the Apollo Theater in Harlem. They made their first record that year, "Angels Cried" on the Teenage label, and toured the East Coast circuit of black theaters from the Howard Theater in Washington, D.C., to the Uptown in Philadelphia.

After making several records in New York for George Goldner, who owned the Mark X, Cindy, and Gone labels, they were searching for their first hit when they found what they were looking for at D.C.'s Howard Theater. Influenced by rhythm and blues pioneer Jackie Wilson's ability to get a crowd going, Ron Isley wrote "Shout," the song that became their first hit when it was recorded by RCA and released in the summer of 1959.

The Isley Brothers developed a reputation for a rousing stage show. One such show was described by singer James Brown in his autobiography: "We saw the Isley Brothers coming from the back of the theater, swinging on ropes, like Tarzan, onto the stage. They hardly had to sing at all. They'd already killed 'em."

After releasing a couple of songs that went nowhere, the Isleys came up with "Twist and Shout" in 1962. It received airplay in England, and the Beatles recorded their version of the song in January of 1963 with John Lennon on lead vocals. The Beatles met the Isley Brothers in person when the Isleys were touring England in 1962, but it wasn't until 1964 that the Beatles' version of the song went to number two on the American charts.

Over the next couple of years the group formed their own label, T-Neck, named after Teaneck, New Jersey, where the family had settled after "Shout" became a hit. In 1964, a young guitarist named Jimmy (later Jimi) Hendrix joined the group for a brief time before skyrocketing to fame on his own. By late 1965 the Isley Brothers had signed with Berry Gordy's Motown Record Corporation. Gordy had high hopes for the band and assigned them right away to his top songwriting-production team of Holland-Dozier-Holland. Their first Motown release—on the Tamla label—was the Holland-Dozier-Holland composition "This Old Heart of Mine (Is Weak For You)." They also released an album featuring ten other Holland-Dozier-Holland songs.

Some of Motown's other acts were reportedly jealous of the treatment given to the Isleys, and they were soon assigned to other producers there. They left the label in 1968 and the next year released their biggest hit, "It's Your Thing," on the T-Neck label. Appearing on the record were the Isleys' younger brothers Ernie and Marvin and brother-in-law Chris Jasper. The success of

gospel music in the churches of southern Ohio and northern Kentucky with their mother accompanying them on piano. Around 1973 they added two younger brothers, Ernie (on guitar and drums) and Marvin (on bass and percussion), and their brother-in-law Chris Jasper (on keyboards) to form the "3+3" lineup.

the song enabled the Isleys to record other groups on their label, and in the summer of 1969 they organized and headlined one of the biggest live performances of their career at New York's Yankee Stadium.

With their new 3+3 lineup, the Isley Brothers opted for a new pop-rock sound. In June of 1971 they covered Stephen Stills's "Love the One You're With," which featured Ernie's acoustic guitar playing. It became a top 20 hit and was included on the album *Givin' It Back,* on which the Isleys chose to record the pop-rock songs of several other artists.

With the younger members of the group studying for their fine arts degrees in music, the group's sound expanded to include a range of musical ideas. According to Marvin, they began to incorporate a jazz idiom based on their studies with jazz pianists Billy Taylor and Ramsey Lewis. The 3+3 lineup became official in 1973 when the group signed with CBS/Epic for distribution of their T-Neck releases and recorded their *3+3* album.

The Isleys were heavily influenced by Stevie Wonder's self-produced 1972 album, *Music of My Mind.* Rather than containing one or two good songs and a lot of filler material, Wonder's was a concept album in which all of the songs were significant. When the Isleys discovered *Music of My Mind* had been recorded in Los Angeles, they decided to go there to record *3+3.* The recording facility was state of the art and allowed them to use a Moog synthesizer and phase shifter, a pedal that Ernie used to alter his guitar sound.

Marvin Isley also noted another influence: "Marvin Gaye and Ronald definitely had influence on each other, because they kind of admired the same people.... When Marvin put that *What's Going On* album out [in] 1971, that became the way of, 'Let's approach our album like these artists are doing now.'"

3+3 was a landmark album for the Isley Brothers, both from a commercial standpoint and from a creative one. The album balanced cover songs of other artists with a selection of original compositions. It made the Isleys one of the first black groups to go platinum, selling over two million units.

The Isley Brothers were one of the top rhythm and blues acts of the 1970s, along with their two main competitors, Earth, Wind, and Fire and the Commodores. Their 1975 hit, "Fight the Power," went to Number Four on the pop charts, and their live performances were held in 20,000-seat arenas such as the Forum in Los Angeles and Madison Square Garden in New York.

In 1984 the six-member 3+3 group split up. Ernie, Chris, and Marvin stayed with CBS to record for them as Isley/Jasper/Isley. Ronald, Rudolph, and Kelly signed with Warner Bros. T-Neck Records closed,

marking the end of an era. In 1986 Kelly died of a heart attack in his sleep in Teaneck, New Jersey.

In addition to the Beatles' version of "Twist and Shout," other songs written by the Isleys became hits for various groups in the 1960s and 1970s. The Outsiders, known mainly for their 1966 hit "Time Won't Let Me," made the Isley Brothers' "Respectable" a top twenty hit later that same year. In addition, the brothers wrote "Work to Do," recorded by the Average White Band, and their earliest hit, "Shout," was revived by Otis Day and the Knights in the film *Animal House.*

The breakup of the six-man lineup was not the end of the Isley Brothers. Aside from Ronald's solo successes, Marvin, Ernie, and Ronald reformed a band in 1990, and by 1992 they released an album titled *Tracks of Life.* "[We] see ourselves as the next generation of Isley Brothers, in touch with the past but looking to the future," Ronald was quoted as saying in a Warner Bros. press release. Part of that future included a 1994 lawsuit against singer Michael Bolton for incorporating elements of their hit "Love is a Wonderful Thing" into his own similarly titled song. In 2000, a Los Angeles federal judge upheld a lower court's $5.4 million dollar ruling against Bolton.

Staying abreast of current trends, the Isley's 1996 album *Mission to Please* was produced by Babyface and R. Kelly. They made a bigger splash signing with DreamWorks in 2001 and releasing the hip-hop oriented *Eternal* and 2003's guest-star laden *Body Kiss,* the latter garnering a Grammy nomination for the group. Collaborations with R. Kelly, Lil' Kim, and Snoop Dogg, among others, raised the group's profile for a whole new generation. Also in 2003, Ronald Isley's collaboration with 1960s pop icon Burt Bacharach *Here I Am: Isley Meets Bacharach* drew critical raves, proving that in one form or another, the Isley's remain a force to be reckoned with.

Selected discography

Singles

"Angels Cried," Teenage, 1957.
"Shout," RCA Victor, 1959.
"Twist and Shout," Wand, 1962.
"This Old Heart of Mine," Tamla, 1966.
"It's Your Thing," T-Neck, 1969.
"Fight the Power," T-Neck, 1975.
"Who Loves You Better," T-Neck, 1976.
"Don't Say Goodnight (It's Time for Love)," T-Neck, 1980.
(Recorded by Rod Stewart and Ronald Isley) "This Old Heart of Mine," Warner, 1990.

Albums

Shout!, RCA Victor, 1959.
Twist and Shout, Wand, 1962.

Twisting and Shouting, United Artists, 1963.
This Old Heart of Mine, Tamla, 1966.
Soul on the Rocks, Tamla, 1967.
It's Our Thing, T-Neck, 1969.
The Brothers Isley, T-Neck, 1969.
Live at Yankee Stadium, T-Neck, 1969.
Get Into Something, T-Neck, 1970.
In the Beginning, T-Neck, 1971.
Givin' It Back, T-Neck, 1971.
Brother, Brother, Brother, T-Neck, 1972.
3+3, T-Neck, 1973; reissued Sony, 2003.
Live It Up, T-Neck, 1974.
The Heat Is On, T-Neck, 1975; reissued, Sony, 2003.
Harvest for the World, T-Neck, 1976; reissued, Sony, 2003.
Go for Your Guns, T-Neck, 1977.
Showdown, T-Neck, 1978.
Timeless, T-Neck, 1978.
Winner Takes All, T-Neck, 1979.
Go All the Way, T-Neck, 1980.
Grand Slam, T-Neck, 1981.
Inside You, T-Neck, 1981.
The Real Deal, T-Neck, 1982.
Between the Sheets, T-Neck, 1983.
Greatest Hits, Volume 1, T-Neck, 1984.
Masterpiece, Warner Bros., 1985.
Smooth Sailin', Warner Bros., 1987.
Spend the Night, Warner Bros., 1989.
Shout!: The Complete Victor Sessions, RCA, 1991; reissued, 1996.
Tracks of Life, Warner Bros., 1992.
Live, Elektra/Asylum, 1993.
Beautiful Ballads, Sony/Legacy, 1994.
For The Love of You, Collectables, 1995.
The Isley Brothers Live, Rhino, 1996.
Mission to Please, Island, 1996.
Shake it Up Baby: Shout, Twist and Shout, Varese Vintage, 2000.
Eternal, DreamWorks, 2000.
Love Songs, Sony, 2001.

20th Century Masters - The Millenium Collection: The Best of the Isley Brothers, Universal, 2001.
Body Kiss, DreamWorks, 2003.
Here I Am: Isley Meets Bacharach, DreamWorks, 2003.
Live It Up, Epic/Legacy, 2004.

Sources

Books

Bianco, David, editor, *Heat Wave: The Motown Fact Book,* Pierian, 1988.
Brown, James, and Bruce Tucker, *James Brown: The Godfather of Soul,* Macmillan, 1986.
Joel Whitburn's Top Pop Singles, 1955-1990, Record Research, 1991.

Periodicals

Goldmine, November 29, 1991.
Jet, May 29, 2000; September 3, 2001; July 14, 2003.
Rolling Stone, August 10, 1978.
Sepia, December 1980.

Online

"Isley Brothers," *All Music Guide,* http://www.allmusic.com (February 20, 2004).
"Isley Brothers," Richard De La Font Agency, Inc., http://www.delafont.com/music_acts/Isley-Brothers.htm (February 1, 2004).
"Isley Brothers," *RollingStone.com,* http://www.rollingstone.com (February 1 2004).
The Isley Brothers Official Website, http://www.theisley brothers.com (February 1, 2004).

—*David Bianco and Ken Burke*

Jay-Z

Rap musician, record company executive

James Devaney/WireImage.com. Reproduced by permission.

Jay-Z is all too familiar with the hard knock life. In his hit single "Hard Knock Life," Jay-Z samples the musical *Annie*'s signature song of the same name. "These kids sing about the hard knock life, things everyone in the ghetto feels coming up," Jay-Z said of the orphans in *Annie* in a *People* feature. "That's the ghetto anthem." The rap star grew up in a single-parent household in the Marcy Projects of Brooklyn, New York. Known for his honesty, Jay-Z has admitted in both his autobiographical lyrics and interviews that he sold drugs as a teenager. For Jay-Z, rap was his way out of the hard knock life. The money that came with a successful rap career would took him out of the Brooklyn projects, and rap music gave him a means to express his feelings about knocks and blows he has taken.

The way, however, was not easy and Jay-Z encountered more hard knocks along the road. When he could not get a record deal, Jay-Z, along with two friends, formed his own record label. He also had run-ins with the law. The timing of Jay-Z's arrest in early December of 1999 for the stabbing of record executive Lance "Un" Rivera at a Times Square nightclub could not have been worse. His much-awaited album, *Volume 3: The Life and Times of S. Carter,* was due to be released right after Christmas and it was uncertain whether the negative publicity from this latest incident would hurt sales. However, for a man who grew up on the mean streets of Brooklyn this was just another one of the hard knocks that has formed his voice in rap.

Jay-Z was born Shawn Carter on December 4, 1970, in Brooklyn, New York, the youngest of four children. He grew up in the well-known Marcy Projects, where the J and Z subway trains run. His mother, Gloria Carter, worked as a clerk in an investment company. Jay-Z's father, Adnis Reeves, left when he was 12. "To me, that was basically the end of our relationship," Jay-Z told *Vibe.* "That was when the hurt and then the healing began for me, from that day right there." Jay-Z's relationship with his father served as fodder for many of his songs, including the *Black Album*'s "Moment of Clarity," in which he forgave Reeves for abandoning his family. Jay-Z reconciled with his father in 2003, six months before his father passed away from a liver ailment.

Founded Roc-A-Fella

When Jay-Z was first starting out in the rap world, he was introduced to Damon "Dame" Dash, who, by the time he was 19, had already gotten record deals for two acts. Dash soon became Jay-Z's manager and Dash's childhood friend, Kareem "Biggs" Burke, was then hired as Jay-Z's road manager. For two years, the three worked unsuccessfully to obtain a record deal. The trio then decided to form their own record company, Roc-A-Fella Records, in which they would all serve as partners. Jay-Z's role was that of marquee artist, Dash ran the company's day-to-day operations,

For the Record . . .

Born Shawn Corey Carter on December 4, 1970, in Brooklyn, NY; son of Gloria Carter and Adnis Reeves.

Released debut album, *Reasonable Doubt,* Roc-A-Fella, 1996; *In My Lifetime, Vol. 1,* Roc-A-Fella, 1997; released *Vol.2: Hard Knock Life,* Roc-A-Fella, 1998; released *Vol. 3: The Life and Times of Shawn Carter,* Roc-A-Fella, 1999; established Rocawear clothing company, 1999; charged with assault, 1999; released *The Dynasty: Roc la Familia,* Roc-A-Fella, 2000; released *The Blueprint,* 2001; released *The Blueprint 2: The Gift & the Curse,* 2002; opened the 40/40 club in New York City, 2003; released *The Blueprint 2.1,* 2003; released *The Black Album,* 2003; retired from rap to focus on business ventures, 2004.

Awards: Grammy Award, Best Rap Album for *Vol. 2: Hard Knock Life,* 1998; MTV Video Music Award, Best Rap Video, for "Can I Get A...," 1999; *Source* Award, Lyricist of the Year, Solo, 1999; *Billboard* Award, Rap Artist of the Year, 1999; *Soul Train* Award, Sammy Davis Jr. Entertainer of the Year, 2001; BET Award, Best Male Hip Hop Artist, 2001; *Source* Award, Best Hip Hop Artist, Solo, 2001; *Soul Train* Award, Album of the Year for *The Blueprint,* 2002; Grammy Award, Best R&B Song (with Beyoncé) for "Crazy in Love," 2003; Grammy Award, Best Rap/Sung Collaboration (with Beyoncé) for "Crazy in Love," 2003; ASCAP Golden Note Award, 2004.

Addresses: *Record company*—Roc-A-Fella Records, 160 Varick St., 12th Fl., New York, NY 10013, phone: (212) 229-5200, fax: (212) 229-5299, website: http://www.rocafella.com.

and Burke, according to *Vibe,* served as "a barometer of the streets." After Roc-A-Fella secured a deal with Priority Records for the distribution of their albums, Jay-Z was ready to release his first record, *Reasonable Doubt.*

Jay-Z rose to fame with his 1996 gold-certified single, "Ain't No N-G-A (Like the One I Got)," a duet with Foxy Brown. The controversy started immediately. The single's title was not the language that even the most daring disc jockeys wanted to play. According to Janine McAdams of *Billboard* in June of 1996, "For now, 'Ain't No N-G-A' has radio production rooms working overtime. None of the stations contacted for this story advocate the use of the n-word over the air, but their solutions are varied: Some edit the word out; others substitute 'brother' or 'player.'" Still, radio stations pointed out that, however reluctant they were to broadcast that and other offensive words, the public knew when it was cut out anyway. In some cases, the change altered the content enough to lose its intended impact and appeal.

Despite the hardcore quality of his first album, as Shawnee Smith of *Billboard,* noted in November of 1999, it was Jay-Z who also began to transform the hip-hop scene from its hardcore "gangsta rap" to something that bears a more refined style—that of "Armani suits, alligator boots, Rolex watches, expensive cars, broads, and Cristel," At the end of 1996, Havelock Nelson reflected on the year in rap for *Billboard.* Jay-Z, Nelson said, "masterfully reinvented himself after receiving battle scars from his previous rhyme life."

Announced His Retirement

In addition to making music, Jay-Z was also interested in the corporate side of the business. Since 1994, Jay-Z had been producing records for other artists as chief of operations for the Roc-A-Fella label. The same handle he had for money in the drug business translated well into the music industry. He talked about his future at that time; "Although my album has already gone gold, it will be my last one. From this point, it's all about the business." Jay-Z did not retire from rap, however. Jay-Z told *Vibe* that he realized his music had a powerful effect on his fans. "There were cats coming up to me like, 'You must have been looking in my window or following my life' ... It was emotional. Like big, rough hoodlum, hardrock, three-time jail bidders with scars and gold teeth just breaking down. It was something to look at, like, I must be going somewhere people been wanting someone to go for a while." So he returned to rap in 1997, with the album *In My Lifetime, Vol. 1.* In 1998 his best-selling *Vol. 2: Hard Knock Life* won him a Grammy Award for Best Rap Album.

In 1999, Jay-Z headlined the Hard Knock Life Tour, which also featured DMX, Beanie Sigel, and others. Jay-Z used his stature as a hit-producing rap star to ensure that the rappers he wanted would be included on the tour. At the outset, there were fears that violence would break out on the tour. The tour concluded without incident, however, and was a resounding success.

A documentary crew joined the tour, filming the rappers as they performed, hung out backstage, and traveled in tour buses. The resulting film, "Backstage," was released in September of 2000. Some reviewers lamented that the documentary did not provide a complete picture of Roc-A-Fella's place in the rap world. Although, Elvis Mitchell of the *Contra Costa Times* noted, hardcore fans are already familiar with the rivalries of the rap business. Mick LaSalle of the *San Francisco Chronicle* said that "The film makes no attempt to guide hip-hop novices. It just tosses the viewer into this musical experience, which will seem vital to some and depressing and repetitious to others."

In 1999, Jay-Z was preparing to release his fourth album. In the December 27, 1999, issue of *USA Today,* Steve Jones wrote that he noticed in a session he sat in on with Jay-Z and rapper Beanie Sigel, that Jay-Z never writes down a lyric. "I don't write songs," Jay-Z explained. "I just sit there and listen to the track, and I come up with the words. It's a gift. A gift from God." In the article Jay-Z also discussed his upcoming album, *Vol. 3: The Life and Times of Shawn Carter.* He talked about how his life had changed in the few short years of his success. "With five million records out there, there are all kinds of things that you have to deal with," he said. "Even though it's just been a year, people think that things change with you and start treating you differently. Street people start thinking that maybe you've gone soft. But I'm the same dude. That's why I did the song, 'Come and Get Me.' I'm still holding firm in my position."

Arrested in Stabbing Incident

In early December of 1999, Jay-Z was charged with first-degree assault and second-degree assault after Untertainment Records executive Lance "Un" Rivera was stabbed once in the stomach and once in the shoulder. According to *Newsweek,* Jay-Z suspected that Rivera had released bootleg copies of his fourth album, an act that would lead to the loss of millions of dollars in rightful profits. When the two came face to face at a record-release party for rapper Q-Tip held in a New York nightclub, eye-witnesses reported that there was an altercation between the two. In the commotion that followed, Rivera was stabbed. At his arraignment in early 2000, Jay-Z pleaded not guilty.

In the weeks between the stabbing incident in New York, and the release of his new album, Jon Caramanica talked about Jay-Z's difficult week in early December of 1999. "After the breakout success of last year's *Vol. 2: Hard Knock Life,* the expectations on Jay-Z were greater than ever," Caramanica wrote. "In fact, it's been speculated that the entire stabbing incident was part of some large marketing conspiracy to guarantee strong buzz and sales. In hip-hop, where crime is often flipped as a marketing tool, having your artist splashed across the cover of the *Daily News* may well work financial wonders, but that option seems absurd for a man in Jay's position. Still, the very existence of such a theory hints at an underlying belief that Jay, of all rappers, is too smart to go out like this.

Business, never personal." Jay-Z commented in *Vibe* in December of 2000 on the fact that, one year after the stabbing incident, a trial date still had not been set. "I feel that if it was any other person," Jay-Z said, "it wouldn't still be dragging on this long." Yet he maintained a positive attitude. He told *Vibe,* "Everything happens for a reason. It's another learning experience for me."

Despite the mixed reviews of *Vol. 3: Life and Times of Shawn Carter* and his legal troubles, Jay-Z was still on top of his game. The album was an instant platinum success, emphasizing that he still had the power to be a number one seller in the genre he helped to define. In 2000, Jay-Z released *Dynasty: Roc la Familia.* He told *Vibe,* "I could make records as long as I have to desire to really dig deep and challenge myself to do it. I can do it for as long as I want." *Dynasty* featured a host of new producers, including Just Blaze and Kanye West, who would go on to produce some of Jay-Z's biggets hits. Jay-Z shared equal mic time with up-and-coming Roc-A-Fella artists on the album, including Memphis Bleek and Beanie Siegel. The album produced a few hits, including the huge success that was "I Just Wanna Love U (Give It To Me)."

Laid *The Blueprint*

Already in the public eye in 2001 with a chart-topping duet with R. Kelly, "Fiesta," Jay-Z dropped what would become an instant classic—*The Blueprint*—on September 18, 2001. Selling nearly a half million albums in less than a week, *The Blueprint* was universally praised by critics and loved by fans. The first track on the album, "Takeover," was a searing attack on New York rapper Nas (Nas would reply with his own track, "Ether," attacking Jay-Z in the following weeks), a five-minute narrative over a blistering, thumping sample of the Doors' "Five to One." But "Takeover," wrote *All Music Guide* critic Jason Birchmeier, was "just one song. There are 12 other songs on *The Blueprint*—and they're all stunning, to the point where the album almost seems flawless." Besides the battle track, the album also showcases Jay-Z's songwriting skills on tracks like "Song Cry" and "Heart of the City." Birchmeier concluded that *The Blueprint* is "a fully realized masterpiece."

In the months that followed, the battle with Nas heated up. In response to "Ether," Jay-Z delivered an exclusive freestyle to a New York radio station, "Super Ugly," that dug deep at Nas. Among concerns that the battle could result in tragedy (as was the case with the Notorious B.I.G. and Tupac Shakur in the 1990s), the battle slowly faded away. "Ultimately, Jay-Z and Nas have too much at stake for foolishness," wrote *Village Voice* contributor Selwyn Hinds, "and together they crafted a piece of hip-hop myth that will live for years to come."

Jay-Z recognized this in an MTV *Unplugged* session. Performing the track "Takeover," he referred to the act of the battle as "the truest essence of hip-hop," but one whose place was solely in recorded material. The MTV session, featuring the Roots as Jay-Z's backing band, was released in late 2001. Jay-Z was the first hip-hop artist to record such an MTV *Unplugged* session, and Jay-Z's material translated to an *Unplugged* session surprisingly well. "Hip-hop with live instrumentation has seldom sounded this good," wrote Hinds in the *Village Voice.*

The Blueprint 2: The Gift & the Curse, a double album with 25 tracks and numerous guest starts including Rakim, Dr. Dre, Lenny Kravitz, and Beyoncé Knowles, followed within a year. The release was generally thought to be unfocused and too long; many reviewers agreed that if Jay-Z had edited the album down to a single disc, it would've been another classic. *All Music Guide* reviewer John Bush observed: "It's clear Jay-Z's in control even here, and though his raps can't compete with the concentrated burst on *The Blueprint,* there's at least as many great tracks on tap, if only listeners have enough time to find them." A few months later, Jay-Z released *The Blueprint 2.1,* featuring the best tracks from *The Blueprint 2* on a single CD.

From Marcy to Madison Square

Jay-Z began talking about retiring from the stage even before releasing *The Blueprint 2.* He told reporters that his next album, the follow-up to *The Blueprint 2,* would be his final official release. The original concept for the release was to make a prequel to *Reasonable Doubt,* with no guest stars and a different producer for each track. What resulted was *The Black Album.* Though somewhat removed from the original concept, Jay-Z often and rightfully referred to the release as his most introspective album. From the track "December 4th" (Jay-Z's birthday), featuring spoken word interludes from his mother, to the bittersweet closing track "My First Song," Jay-Z used his final turn in the studio to make an album that was at times hilarious and heartbreaking, and above all, honest. As he put it himself, "There's never been a n***a this good for this long, this hood or this pop, this hot for this long." If *The Black Album* is indeed Jay-Z's final release, he couldn't have gone out on a better note.

The Black Album was accompanied by an autobiography, *The Black Book*; a line of sneakers for Reebok, the S. Carter Collection; and a final sold-out show at New York's Madison Square Garden. Speaking to MTV's Sway, Jay-Z tried to explain why he planned to retire while still enormously popular. "I'm in the comfort zone as far as making music," he said. "I'm a young guy, and I still have to challenge myself in life. I have to step outside my comfort zone. That's just part of being alive."

Selected discography

Reasonable Doubt, Roc-A-Fella, 1996.
In My Lifetime Vol. 1, Roc-A-Fella, 1997.
Vol. 2: Hard Knock Life, Roc-A-Fella, 1998
Vol. 3: The Life and Times of Shawn Carter, Roc-A-Fella, 1999.
Dynasty: Roc la Familia, Roc-A-Fella, 2000.
The Blueprint, Roc-A-Fella, 2001.
Unplugged (live), Roc-A-Fella, 2001.
The Blueprint 2: The Gift & the Curse, Roc-A-Fella, 2002.
(With R. Kelly) *The Best of Both Worlds,* Universal, 2002.
The Blueprint 2.1, Roc-A-Fella, 2003.
The Black Album, Roc-A-Fella, 2003.

Sources

Periodicals

Billboard, June 29, 1996; November 23, 1996; December 28, 1996.
Contra Costa Times (Walnut Creek, CA), September 7, 2000.
Globe & Mail (Toronto, Canada), December 4, 2003.
Jet, September 27, 1999.
Los Angeles Times, December 27, 1999; December 31, 1999.
Newsweek, December 13, 1999.
New York Times, December 26, 1999; December 30, 1999; January 1, 2000.
People Weekly, April 5, 1999.
Rolling Stone, October 14, 1999.
San Francisco Chronicle, September 6, 2000.
Teen People, June 16, 2002.
USA Today, December 27, 1999; January 3, 2000.
Vibe, December 2000.
Village Voice, December 14, 1999; January 22, 2002; January 1, 2003.
Washington Post, December 14, 1999; January 2, 2000.

Online

"From A- to A," Slate Magazine, http://slate.msn.com/id/2091248 (April 4, 2004).
"Jay-Z," *All Music Guide,* http://www.allmusic.com (April 4, 2004).
"Jay-Z: What More Can I Say?," MTV.com, http://www.mtv.com/bands/j/jay_z/news_feature_112103 (April 5, 2004).

—Laura Hightower and Jennifer M. York

Judas Priest

Heavy metal group

With a dozen albums and nearly three decades of live performance behind them, Judas Priest has proven to be one of heavy metal's most enduring and imitated bands. Their head-banging beat and frenzied guitar harmonies are a concert mainstay and their wardrobe of studded leather and chains has become the fashion uniform of metal heads the world over.

Guitarist K. K. Downing and bassist Ian Hill formed Judas Priest in Birmingham, England, in 1969. Hill recruited vocalist Rob Halford in 1971, eventually marrying Halford's sister. The band performed locally for several years, eventually adding guitarist Glenn Tipton and drummer Alan Moore, and in 1974 Judas Priest signed with Gull Records and released their first album, *Rocka Rolla.* Though sales were low for both it and the group's next album, *Sad Wings of Destiny,* the band had amassed a loyal following.

In 1977 they signed with Columbia and released *Sin After Sin.* The album, produced by ex-Deep Purple bassist Roger Glover, featured dual lead guitar riffs and differed from most heavy metal music of the time by being shorter, with more discernable melodies. Drummer Simon Phillips replaced Moore for *Sin After Sin,* but only remained with the band for that one album.

© David Atlas. Reproduced by permission.

Members include **Les Binks** (group member, 1978-79), drums; **K. K. Downing**, guitar; **Rob Halford** (group member, 1971-92, rejoined group, 2003), vocals; **Ian Hill**, bass; **Dave Holland** (group member, 1979-1989), drums; **Alan Moore** (group member, 1974-77), drums; **Tim Owens** (group member, 1996-2002), vocals; **Simon Phillips** (group member, 1977-78), drums; **Glenn Tipton** (joined group, 1974), guitar; **Scott Travis** (joined group, 1989), drums.

Group formed in Birmingham, England, 1969; signed first recording contract and released debut album *Rocka Rolla,* 1974; signed by Columbia Records, 1977; released Columbia debut *Sin After Sin,* 1977; released first gold album in the United States, *Screaming for Vengeance,* 1982; released *Defenders of the Faith,* 1984; frontman Rob Halford left group, 1992; new vocalist Tim Owens officially joined group, 1996; released *Jugulator,* 1997; Halford returned, 2003; released box set *Metalogy,* 2004.

Addresses: *Record company*—Chipster Public Relations, Chipster Entertainment Inc., 1976 E. High St., Ste. 203, Pottstown, PA 19464. *Website*—Judas Priest Official Website: http://www.judaspriest.com.

Drummer Les Binks joined the band in 1978, but, like Phillips, remained for only one year. His replacement, Dave Holland, proved to be a longer-lasting addition to the band; he joined Judas Priest in 1979 and continued to play with the band for over a decade before Scott Travis took over.

Though album sales gradually increased, Judas Priest's music remained more popular in England than in the United States. Not until the group's seventh album, *British Steel,* did they make it to the top 40 in the United States. *Screaming for Vengeance,* in 1982, became the group's first gold album in the United States.

As their music received more American airplay, the band's live performances were becoming legendary among concertgoers. Roaring on stage astride a Harley Davidson, clad in studded leather and brandishing whips and chains, Halford was a commanding presence, strutting and screaming his way through songs that played off the band's thunderous wall of sound. *Creem*'s Toby Goldstein described the group as "a rampaging quintet of metal marauders."

By the mid-1980s Judas Priest had achieved respectability among critics and peers and many of the new metal bands cited the group as one of their early influences. The members of Judas Priest were duly flattered but made it clear they had no intention of stepping aside to make room for newer blood. With the release of *Defenders of the Faith* in 1984 the band embarked on a gruelling promotional tour. Goldstein described the new album: "Crammed with enough fire and fury to satisfy even the most crazed metal head, the album typifies Judas Priest's concern with crisp, distinctive leads, thundering rhythms and even—never woulda thunk it—melody lines."

The band's success in heavy metal never tempted them to cross over to more mainstream rock in search of a top ten hit. Glenn Tipton told *Creem* that "You have to believe in what you're doing. If you stray from it for one second, it's a sign that you're not genuine. And we are genuine. We believe in heavy metal, we've played it for ten years, we've never strayed from it."

Lyrically, Judas Priest's music had long been a subject of controversy, with many objecting to the graphic violence and fascist overtones. Ironically, it was the music's *undertones* that sparked a series of bizarre accusations by religious groups and concerned parents. A Christian organization leveled a charge of Satan worship against the band, claiming that when Judas Priest records were played in reverse, menacing subliminal messages could be heard. As further evidence they cited the cover of the *Defenders of the Faith* album, which depicted a horned animal. Judas Priest denied all allegations.

Other groups, such as the Parents' Music Resource Center (PMRC), found enough to criticize without resorting to accusations of subliminal messages. Jennifer Norwood, the PMRC executive director, told *Rolling Stone,* "There is no scientific proof that you pick up the lyrics that way." However, the PMRC was vocal in its criticism of Judas Priest's violent and sexually explicit lyrics, particularly those in the song "Eat Me Alive." Halford defended the oft-quoted line from that song, "I'm gonna force you to eat me at gunpoint," by claiming that it was meant to be tongue in cheek. Noting that they had censored the "really obscene" lyrics themselves, Halford told *Creem,* "You should've seen the original lyrics!"

While controversy continued to follow the group, heavy metal in general and Judas Priest in particular enjoyed a surge in popularity during the 1980s, with heavy metal making up a substantial portion of MTV's rotation and metal songs rising into the Top 40 charts. The resurgence of heavy metal was largely a reaction to punk rock. J. D. Considine described the differences between the two genres in *Rolling Stone:* "Punk's world view lunged towards a gleeful nihilism of boredom and no future, but metal somehow clung to its underdog optimism. Sure, life sucked, the music seemed to say, but that's not the whole story. Above all, metal reminded its listeners that, good times or bad, the bands and the fans were all in it together." According to Halford, people found they preferred the metal world view: "Suddenly, everybody looked at this music and said: 'Yeah, this is exactly what I want. It talks about what I want out of life.'"

Judas Priest changed their image somewhat for their 1986 world tour. Gone were the studs and chains and S & M gear. Halford told Sylvie Simmons of *Creem,* "What we've done is take the strong parts of our image—the leather and the tough, aggressive look—and we've tried to make it a bit more stylish, if that's the right word." The band made the change in part because of all the heavy metal bands that had imitated Judas Priest's look. The group also toned down their music for the 1986 release of *Turbo,* which featured some actual singing. Halford told *Creem,* "It's been my first real opportunity, given our type of songs, to sound a little bit less hysterical. Not just yelling at the top of my voice."

The conflict that had been simmering over Judas Priest's music came to a boil in 1986 when two Nevada families brought suit against CBS Records and Judas Priest, claiming that the lyrics on the band's 1978 *Stained Class* album had driven their sons to attempt suicide. On December 23, 1985, 18-year-old Ray Belknap and 20-year-old Jay Vance had been drinking and listening to Judas Priest albums when, reportedly, according to Vance, "all of a sudden we got a suicide message, and we got tired of life." The two went to a nearby park, and each shot himself in the head with a sawed-off shotgun. Belknap died instantly, but Vance, sustaining catastrophic injuries, survived until 1988.

When the families' lawyers learned that similar suits had been dismissed on constitutional grounds, they filed a new complaint, in 1988, claiming that engineers had found subliminal messages urging listeners to "do it." The suit averred that such a message was dangerous to unstable individuals like Vance and Belknap, both abused children and high-school dropouts with police records for various offenses. When the product-liability case came to trial in 1990, the charges against Judas Priest were dismissed. The decision was upheld by the Nevada Supreme Court on May 31, 1993.

Painkiller, Judas Priest's first album after the trial, did not back away from the band's usual frenzied style or violent lyrics. For example, "Hell Patrol" contains the following lines: "Gonna go for your throat as you choke/ Then they'll vaporapeize you.... Gonna cut to the bone as you groan/And they'll paratamize you." Although not all reviewers were so harsh, *Rolling Stone* said of

Painkiller, "Played forward or backward, this is hardly an album that will make you kill yourself; it will merely drive you to distraction."

In 1992, after 20 years as frontman for the band, Halford announced—via a letter to the band's lawyer—that he and drummer Travis were leaving to form Fight, a heavier, more thrash-oriented band. The remaining members of Judas Priest continued without them. "We're musicians," Downing told *Guitar School* magazine, "it's in our blood to play music. I won't give up just because we may have lost a lead singer."

In early 1993 Judas Priest completed work on a compilation of 31 songs—selections from all 12 of their albums. The collection, titled *Metalworks '73-'93,* was presented as a two-CD set, commemorating the group's 20-year anniversary. "This compilation," Tipton told *Guitar School,* "will not only sum up Judas Priest's true capabilities, it will also recall some pretty magical memories for the die-hard fans."

From 1992-1996, while Judas Priest as a band remained mostly dormant on the live and recording front, former vocalist Halford continued to work on solo endeavors. Over the year immediately following his departure through 2003, Halford put out several releases with a variety of newly formed outfits; Fight, Two, and a self-titled group, Halford, to nominal success. In 1996 however the remaining members of Judas Priest finally found a new singer with then unknown Ohio-based vocalist Tim Owens.

Owens was the frontman for a local Judas Priest cover band called British Steel when drummer Scott Travis was passed a tape through a mutual friend. Completely amazed at what they heard, the group flew Owens over to England to audition. After running through a few songs, the band was taken aback by the singer's considerable vocal abilities and Owens was immediately asked to join the group. In 1996, Owens (dubbed "Ripper" after his shining talents on the Priest track of the same name) was officially announced as the new singer of Judas Priest. The band proceeded to release *Jugulator* in 1997 and in 1998 embarked on their first world tour in nearly seven years.

In an odd turn of events, on the evening of the new line-up's sold-out performance at New York's Roseland Ballroom, former vocalist Halford publicly announced for first time that that he was gay. Although initially shocking to many who thought of Priest as ultra-masculine rock provocateurs especially considering their lyrical content and heavy-image, very few dismissed Halford's importance in the metal arena.

In 1998, Judas Priest released an audio momento of their first tour in many years with new vocalist Owens, titled *'98 Live Meltdown.* Two years later, the band released their second effort with Owens, *Demolition* on

Atlantic Records. Unfortunately, despite some European success, *Demolition* didn't do very well in the states. The band proceeded to tour on and off throughout 2002, releasing the live CD and DVD *Live in London* in 2003.

In July of that year much to the delight of the group's long-standing fans it was announced that Rob Halford would finally reunite with Judas Priest. At the same time Owens amicably left the group. In 2004, the band released the high profile box-set *Metalogy,* and embarked on a much anticipated world tour with singer Halford.

Selected discography

Rocka Rolla, Gull, 1974.
Sad Wings of Destiny, Repertoire, 1976.
Sin After Sin, Columbia, 1977.
Killing Machine, Columbia, 1978.
Stained Class, Columbia, 1978.
Best of Judas Priest, RCA, 1978.
Hell Bent for Leather, Columbia, 1979.
Unleashed in the East, Columbia, 1979, reissued, 1985.
British Steel, Columbia, 1980.
Point of Entry, Columbia, 1981.
Screaming for Vengeance, Columbia, 1982.
Defenders of the Faith, Columbia, 1984.
Hero, Hero, RCA, 1985.
Turbo, Columbia, 1986.
Priest … Live, Columbia, 1987.
Ram It Down, Columbia, 1988.
Painkiller, Columbia, 1990.
Rocka Rolla and Other Hits, RCA, 1990.
Metalworks '73-'93, Columbia, 1993.
Jugulator, CMC International, 1997.
'98 Live Meltdown, CMC International, 1998 .
Live in London, SPV, 2003.
Living After Midnight, Columbia, 2003.
Metalogy, Columbia, 2004.

Sources

Books

Rees, Dafydd, and Luke Crampton, *Rock Movers & Shakers,* ABC/CLIO, 1991.
The Rolling Stone Encyclopedia of Rock & Roll, edited by Jon Pareles and Patricia Romanowski, Rolling Stone Press/ Summit, 1983.

Periodicals

Billboard, September 8, 1990; May 23, 1992; June 12, 1993.
Creem, July 1984; September 1986.
Guitar School, May 1993.
Musician, November 1990.
Rolling Stone, July 12, 1990; November 15, 1990; December 13, 1990; October 29, 1992.
Stereo Review, July 1986.
Wilson Library Bulletin, December 1990.

Online

Judas Priest Offical Website, http://www.judaspriest.com (February 6, 2004).

Additional information was obtained from press materials provided by Chipster Entertainment, 2004.

—*Susan Windisch Brown and Nicole Elyse*

Ini Kamoze

Reggae musician, singer, songwriter

Jamaican-born reggae singer Ini Kamoze first gained international prominence in 1983 with his self-titled debut album, released on the Island label. He is best known, however, as the originator of the international smash hit "Here Comes the Hotstepper," which topped the *Billboard* pop charts in 1994, was featured on the soundtrack of a major Hollywood film, and landed on the top five charts in Britain. Although he later changed his appearance and experimented with different musical sounds, including the synthesized beats of dancehall-reggae and hip-hop, Kamoze remained committed to his early reggae roots and to a philosophy that included spreading a message of peace and love through music.

Ini Kamoze was born Cecil Campbell on October 9, 1957, in Port Maria, St. Mary, Jamaica. He made his first recordings in the early 1980s, cutting his first single, "World Affairs," in 1981. He gained a following in his native country, earning the nickname of "Voice of Jamaica." He was picked up by Sly And Robbie, a musical duo who led the Taxi label. With Sly And Robbie as producers, Kamoze released a 12-inch single called "Trouble You Trouble Me," on their label, and the cut was warmly received by fans. Although Kamoze was described at the time as six feet tall and

Born Cecil Campbell on October 9, 1957, in Port Maria, St. Mary, Jamaica.

Recorded first singles, early 1980s; released first album, *Ini Kamoze,* 1984; played in numerous reggae festivals internationally, 1980s; released *Statement,* 1984; released *Pirate,* 1984; made British stage debut at the Reggae Sunsplash festival, 1985; released *Shocking Out,* 1988; released *16 Vibes of Ini Kamoze,* 1992; released international hit single, "The Hotstepper," 1994; released *Here Comes the Hotstepper,* 1995; released *Lyrical Gangsta,* 1995.

Addresses: *Record company*—Elektra Records, 75 Rockefeller Plaza, 17th Fl., New York, NY 10019, website: http://www.elektra.com.

willowy, with untangled hair, and very frail in appearance, he nevertheless burned up the stage with a ferocious stage presence, wowing fans and critics alike during his live performances.

After recording several singles and playing extensively in live shows in Jamaica, Kamoze cut his first full-length album. *Ini Kamoze* was produced by Sly And Robbie and released through Island Records. The album was well received internationally, but Kamoze began to lose cachet among his local fans, who were increasingly turning to the popular, feel-good, DJ-driven dancehall licks instead of the more traditional, message-heavy music favored by Kamoze.

Kamoze made a splash at the 1984 Jamaican Sunsplash festival, however, when he gave the DJs a run for their money with his stage presence. That year also saw the release of Kamoze's next album, *Statement,* which included "Call the Police," a track that was used in the soundtrack for the film *Good To Go.*

As a performer in the lineup of the 1985 Reggae Sunsplash, Kamoze made his British stage debut as part of an event produced by Sly And Robbie. There he shared the stage with such Jamaican dancehall luminaries as Gregory Isaacs and Sugar Minott. The British fans loved Kamoze's style, and when the tour moved on to the Continent, reggae fans in other parts of Europe responded equally well.

Pirate, which included tracks like "Betty Brown's Mother" and an anti-gun song titled "Gunshot," was Kamoze's next recorded effort. This album was not as

well received as his earlier work, but Kamoze remained a strong presence on the international concert circuit. Taxi took him on the road on the Taxi Connection International Tour, putting him on stage alongside fellow reggae artists Yellowman, Half Pint, and the Taxi Gang. A highlight of the tour was a concert at London's Town & Country Club. The concert was taped, and subsequently formed the basis of the album *The Taxi Connection Live in London.* The tour itself was featured on a United Kingdom music show called *The Tube.*

Back home, Kamoze cut loose from the Taxi Gang in 1987 and began to work with the One Two Crew. This proved a fruitful collaboration, resulting in Kamoze's next album, *Shocking Out.* Kamoze also toured with the One Two Crew, who backed him up at such events as the Reggae Fall Fest, which played in the United States, and in solo concerts in New York and other cities. Music critic Jon Pareles, reviewing a Kamoze concert in 1988 in the *New York Times,* called Kamoze a standout reggae performer who "sings in a satin-smooth tenor that's unconcerned with gravity." *Washington Post* critic Ilona Wartofsky praised Kamoze's "irresistible" music after hearing a concert in the Washington D.C. area.

Kamoze then founded his own label, putting out a compilation album called *Selekta Showcase,* which featured a popular Kamoze single titled "Stress." Four years later he released his next album, *16 Vibes of Ini Kamoze,* which sold well and helped Kamoze remain popular with reggae fans, who especially liked the hit single "Another Sound."

In 1994 Kamoze, then 37 years old, found himself with an international hit on his hands. "Here Comes the Hotstepper" was to become the singer's biggest hit single. This "infectious pop-dance hit," according to Tony Moton in the *Omaha World Herald,* was recorded with Philip "Fatis" Burrell, and was featured initially on a compilation of reggae music called *Stir It Up,* produced on the Epic label. It was not an entirely new composition, having its roots in the song "Land of 1000 Dances," which was first recorded by Chris Kenner in 1961 and reprised in 1963 by Fats Domino.

The song won widespread acclaim for Kamoze, especially after it was chosen by major Hollywood director Robert Altman for the soundtrack of *Pret-A-Porter* ("Ready to Wear"), Altman's film about the fashion industry. The soundtrack also featured the work of rock stars such as the Rolling Stones, pop star Janet Jackson, and many other well-known artists. "Here Comes the Hotstepper" rose to the top of the British charts in January of 1995, and earned Kamoze a nomination for the International Reggae Music Awards, held that year in New Orleans.

"Here Comes the Hotstepper" next showed up on record store shelves in 1995 on an album of the same name, featuring the production work of Salaam Remi. The album featured previously released work by Kamoze, along with his hit single. The song leapt to the top of the *Billboard* Hot Singles Chart, where it remained for two weeks. It remained on numerous other charts for close to four months. Kamoze parlayed the song into a music video, displaying a solid, well-muscled physique and long dreadlocks that looked quite different from the anemic appearance often commented on by critics during the 1980s.

The success of "Here Comes the Hotstepper" brought Kamoze a contract with Elektra Records. In keeping with his new image, Kamoze began to move away from his traditional Jamaican sound to embrace a more modern, hip-hop style. He showcased this new sound in concert tours in the Los Angeles area, and also in a new album, *Lyrical Gangsta,* released on Elektra's Asylum label in 1995.

Selected discography

Ini Kamoze, Island, 1984.
Pirate, Mango, 1984.
Statement, Mango, 1984.
Shocking Out, Ras, 1988.
(With others) *Selekta Showcase,* Selekta, 1989.
16 Vibes of Ini Kamoze, Sonic Sounds, 1992.
Here Comes the Hotstepper, Columbia, 1995.
Lyrical Gangsta, Elektra/Asylum, 1995.

Sources

Periodicals

Denver Post, January 9, 1995, p. E8.
New York Times, August 7, 1988, p. 52.
Omaha World Herald, April 30, 1995, p. 12, Entertainment.
Rocky Mountain News (Denver, CO), December 9, 1994, p. 20D.
St. Louis Post-Dispatch, September 24, 1988, p. 5D.
Times-Picayune (New Orleans, LA), March 10, 1995, p. L7.
Washington Post, November 24, 1987, p. D7.

Online

"Ini Kamoze," *All Music Guide,* http://www.allmusic.com (January 28, 2004).
"Ini Kamoze," The Iceberg, http://www.theiceberg.com/artist/3811/ini_kamoze.html (January 28, 2004).

—*Michael Belfiore*

Nigel
Kennedy

Violinist

When he sets foot onstage, Nigel Kennedy raises eyebrows. In his oversized shoes and "punk" attire, Kennedy looks more the waif than the classical violin virtuoso. But when he lifts his bow, it is Kennedy's technical finesse that leaves audiences stunned, dispelling any suspicion that he is anything but a musician of the highest caliber.

Kennedy's unconventional approach to music-making is more than superficial. One of a new breed of classical musician, he has developed a highly individualized style that draws on an eclectic musical background. Inspired by jazz and rock, Kennedy's classical technique is spontaneous and enhanced by his mastery of improvisation.

Born in Brighton, England, Nigel represents a third generation of Kennedys to pursue a career in classical music. Both his grandfather and father were professional cellists—his grandfather a well-respected chamber musician, his father a member of the Royal Philharmonic. Nigel began his musical training at the age of seven when Yehudi Menuhin awarded him a scholarship to attend his highly regarded school in Surrey. It was there that Kennedy turned to the violin

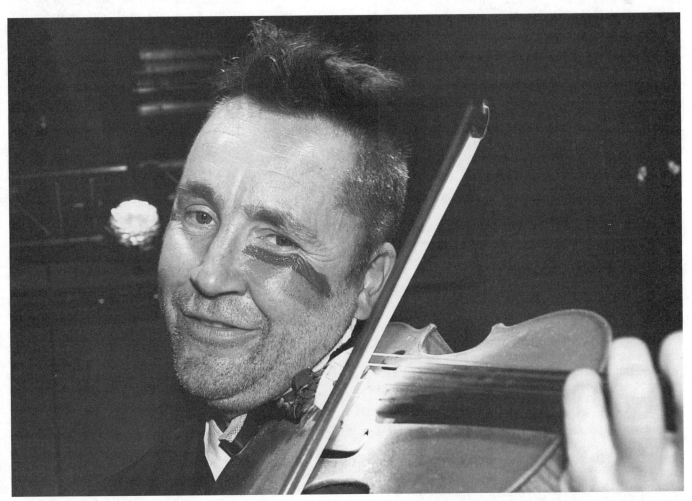

AP/Wide World Photos. Reproduced by permission.

For the Record . . .

Born in 1957 in Brighton, England; son of John (principal cellist for the Royal Philharmonic) and Scylla (a piano teacher) Kennedy; married; wife's name Agnieska; children: Sark (son). *Education:* Attended Yehudi Menuhin School, beginning in 1964, and the Juilliard School, beginning c. 1972.

Classical, jazz, and rock violinist. Made London debut with Philharmonia Orchestra, 1977; launched recording career with *Elgar Violin Concerto,* 1984; conductor of the St. Paul Chamber Orchestra; appeared with major symphony orchestras in North America, Europe, Australia, New Zealand, and the Far East, 1980s-2000s; released best-selling classical album of all time, Vivaldi's *The Four Seasons,* 1989; published *Always Playing* (autobiography), St. Martin's Press, 1992; released numerous albums through the 1990s and 2000s; won recognition for Outstanding Contribution to British Music at the BRIT Awards, 2000, and as Male Artist of the Year at the BRIT Awards, 2001; released *Kennedy Plays Bach,* 2001; released rerecording of *The Four Seasons,* 2004.

Awards: British Record Industry Awards, Best Classical recording and Record of the Year, 1985; British Phonographic Industry BRIT Awards for Outstanding Contribution to British Music, 2000, and Male Artist of the Year, 2001.

Addresses: Record company—EMI Records London, 20 Manchester Square, London W1, England.

---

and developed a preference for the informal performance style that has become his trademark.

Kennedy, as quoted in the *Detroit News,* elaborated on this development: "I had this really rigorous teacher who used to hang out backstage to make sure my tie was on straight and that I was wearing the right jacket. Well, I had a lot of trouble wearing a jacket and tie when I performed. So I would wait until she had closed the door behind me when I walked onstage. And then, in front of the audience, I'd take the jacket off, put it on the floor, loosen my tie, play the gig, get back into the jacket and go back offstage before she could find out. That worked out fine until she noticed that the applause went on a bit too long before I played, because a lot of

the audience identified with what I was doing. The whole thing was a lesson to me in two ways: first, that I could get away with it, and second, that if you showed who you were, the audience was more likely to identify with you, which is what you want anyway."

It was also at the Menuhin School that Kennedy discovered jazz. Yehudi Menuhin encouraged his interest by introducing him to the renowned jazz violinist Stephane Grappelli, with whom he would later make his Carnegie Hall debut at the age of 17. "Nigel didn't really get into the classical stride until after he had liberated himself in the improvised jazz world," Menuhin noted in the *New York Times.* Together, Menuhin and Grappelli had great influence on the development of Kennedy's musical style. From Menuhin he gained technical assurance, and from Grappelli, a fondness for spontaneity and a sly sense of play. "Menuhin had the right spiritual approach, yoga before breakfast and all that," Kennedy contended in *Harper's Bazaar,* adding that "Steph likes to have a whiskey before going onstage, and then enjoy every second of playing. He had a great attitude."

After completing his studies at the Menuhin School, Kennedy became a student of Dorothy DeLay at the prestigious Juilliard School. While at Juilliard he continued to perform as a jazz musician, appearing at Greenwich Village nightclubs with such jazz greats as Stan Getz and Helen Humes.

In 1977 Kennedy made his London debut at the Royal Festival Hall, where he appeared with the Philharmonia Orchestra, conducted by Riccardo Muti. After that, his performance schedule grew to include 120 concerts worldwide each year. He appeared with major symphony orchestras in North America, Great Britain, Europe, Australia, New Zealand, and the Far East, and performed regularly with the National Symphony and St. Paul Chamber Orchestra, which he also conducted. Kennedy has collaborated with such renowned conductors as Vladimir Ashkenazy, Neville Marriner, Antal Dorati, and Andre Previn.

Wherever he performs, Kennedy's technical virtuosity and "everyman" style rarely fail to delight audiences and critics alike. Fans are charmed by his habit of "chatting up" the audience between pieces, addressing its members fondly as "monster," "animal," and "mate." Critics are awed by his sheer artistry. A reporter for the *Detroit News* deemed him "easily the most refreshing, disarming, personal, intuitive, [impetuous] and unorthodox fiddler currently before the public." A *Boston Globe* reviewer described his playing as "technically assured, extremely musical, dashing, elegant, and sweet-toned," while a *Washington Post* critic assessed Kennedy as "gifted not only with an incredible pair of hands but also with a superb set of musical instincts. He is able to play not only with incredible speed, power, and accuracy ... but also with a heart-on-sleeve romanticism when the music requires it."

In addition to maintaining a rigorous performing schedule, Kennedy has recorded extensively. He has an exclusive and unprecedented contract with EMI Records that includes a rock, classical, and jazz repertoire.

Kennedy's rock recordings include collaborations with Paul McCartney, Talk Talk, and Kate Bush, on her album *The Sensual World* and on her single "Experiment IV" from the album *The Whole Story.* He also composed his own progressive rock album *Let Loose* with keyboardist Dave Heath. "Writing rock music really helps me," Kennedy maintained in *Vogue.* "Being involved in compositional techniques yourself makes you appreciate the techniques of the classical composers."

Judging from the critical acclaim his classical recordings have received, Kennedy does indeed appreciate those techniques. His rendition of the Elgar Violin Concerto, recorded with the London Philharmonic, was named best classical recording at the British Record Industry Awards ceremony and was honored as record of the year by *Gramophone* in 1985.

Kennedy then recorded Bartok's Sonata for Solo Violin along with "Mainly Black"—an interpretation of Duke Ellington's orchestral suite "Black, Brown and Beige"—two pieces that were also included on his *Strad Jazz* album. The inspired pairing of these two 1940s classics was hailed by critics for its innovation.

A high point of Kennedy's career came with his recording of Vivaldi's *Four Seasons,* released by EMI 1989. It became the most popular classical album of all time, selling more than two million copies. After he appeared at a recital dressed like a rock star, complete with white face paint and fake blood dribbling out of his mouth, some critics said that the success had gone to his head. And, in 1992, in true rock star form, he trashed a luxury hotel suite where he was staying in Berlin, causing thousands of dollars of damage by smashing champagne bottles against the walls and destroying furniture.

By mid-1992 Kennedy had decided to form his own string quartet and concentrate chiefly on music in the rock and jazz arenas rather than classical. "Others might see it as a giant leap, but I don't," he explained in *Entertainment Weekly.* "If the true test of classical music is being remembered, [rock artists Jimi] Hendrix and Led Zeppelin are the classical artists of their age." In 1996, he released *Kafka,* which includes his own compositions. He followed this in 1999 with *The Kennedy Experience,* a tribute to Jimi Hendrix's band, the Jimi Hendrix Experience.

Kennedy stayed out of the classical arena for five years, finally making a much heralded comeback at London's Royal Festival Hall in April 1997. Particularly in his native Britain, Kennedy was greeted with ovations from audiences and critics alike; the British newspapers gave him front-page coverage, on an equal footing with news of the run-up to the British General Election.

Soon Kennedy was back on the international classical music circuit. He also returned to the studio to record classical music, including EMI's *Classic Kennedy,* in 1999. This album proved that Kennedy was as popular as ever, landing at the top of the UK classical music charts. In 2000, Kennedy won an award for Outstanding Contribution to British Music at the BRIT Awards, and the following year, he won a BRIT Award for Male Artist of the Year. The year 2001 also saw the release of *Kennedy Plays Bach.* He continued to record classical albums into the 2000s, including a much-anticipated new recording of Vivaldi's *Four Seasons,* with the Berlin Philharmonic.

Kennedy has said that simply to play music for an appreciative audience is his greatest wish for his continuing career. He told a correspondent for the *Baltimore Evening Sun,* as reprinted in the *Oakland Press,* "I'm pleased to have a career now because it means I can buy a violin and live in a place with more than one room. But you can't take the music for granted.... The best audience I played for was in a pub in Dublin, elbow to elbow with people and mugs of Guinness. I was playing with a local violinist and the audience was so quiet that you really could've heard a pin drop. That's what I'm after. As long as I get that, the career doesn't matter."

Selected discography

Classical releases

(Elgar, Sir Edward William) *Violin Concerto in B minor, Op. 61,* Angel/EMI, 1984.

(Mendelssohn, Felix and Max Bruch) *Violin Concerto in E minor, Op. 64* (Mendelssohn); *Violin Concerto in G minor, Op. 26* (Bruch), Angel/EMI, 1986.

(Bartok, Bela and Duke Ellington) *Sonata for Solo Violin* (Bartok); *Mainly Black* (Ellington), Angel/EMI, 1986.

(Sibelius, Jean) *Violin Concerto, Symphony No. 5,* Angel/EMI, 1986.

(Walton, Sir William Turner) *Violin Concerto, Viola Concerto,* Angel/EMI, 1987.

(Vivaldi, Antonio) *The Four Seasons,* Angel/EMI, 1989.

Just Listen, EMI, 1992.

Classic Kennedy, EMI, 1999.

(Bach, Johann Sebastian) *Kennedy Plays Bach,* EMI Classics, 2001.

(Vivaldi, Antonio) *Four Seasons,* EMI Classics, 2004.

Non-classical releases

Nigel Kennedy: Let Loose, EMI.

Nigel Kennedy Plays Jazz, Chandos, 1990.

Once Upon a Long Ago, EMI.
Strad Jazz, Chandos.
Kafka, Angel, 1996.
The Kennedy Experience, Sony, 1999.
Plays Jazz, Chandos, 2000.
Nigel Kennedy's Greatest Hits, EMI, 2002.
East Meets East, EMI, 2003.

Sources

Books

Kennedy, Nigel, *Always Playing* (autobiography), St. Martin's, 1992.

Periodicals

Boston Globe, August 6, 1985.
Detroit News, April 11, 1991; April 19, 1991.
Entertainment Weekly, June 26, 1992.
Harper's Bazaar, February 1990.
Guardian, December 23, 1992; April 11, 1997, p. 2
New York Times, April 12, 1992.
Oakland Press (Pontiac, MI), April 19, 1991.
People, March 9, 1992.
Stereo Review, October 1985; January 1986.
Times (London), October 15, 1992.
Vogue, November 1987.
Washington Post, March 2, 1988.
Washington Times, March 3, 1988.

Online

"Kennedy," EMI Classics, http://www.emiclassics.com/artists/biogs/kennb.html (January 22, 2004).
"Nigel Kennedy," *All Music Guide,* http://www.allmusic.com (January 22, 2004).

—Nina Goldstein and Michael Belfiore

Barney Kessel

Guitarist

Barney Kessel was a guitar innovator who came to prominence during the 1940s with the rise of be-bop jazz. Like many players of his time, his primary influence was a young African-American guitarist named Charlie Christian who had joined Benny Goodman in 1939. Unlike most guitarists of the time, Christian relied on electric guitar, making its acoustic counterpoint seem passé to many young players. Christian, however, died of tuberculosis in 1942, and it would be left to electric guitarists like Kessel to explore the progressive chord patterns and emphatic pacing of be-bop jazz.

Kessel was born on October 17, 1923, in Muskogee, Oklahoma, and bought his first guitar at age 12. Two years later he joined a local band, and even though Muskogee was a small town, he found other musicians to jam with, after hours. "Barney absorbed the pulsating beat of jazz," wrote Nat Hentoff in the liner notes to *The Poll Winners,* "the way most of us absorbed the multiplication tables." An opportunity to play with idol Charlie Christian was a life-changing experience for Kessel, inspiring the young protégée to move to Los Angeles a year later. There he found work as a dishwasher while he searched for gigs. Soon Kessel landed a job with the Chico Marx Band, and over the

Born on October 17, 1923, in Muskogee, OK.

next few years he played with Artie Shaw, Charlie Barnet, and Hal McIntyre. He also appeared in *Jammin' the Blues,* an Oscar-nominated movie short.

Kessel's big break came in 1947 when he recorded with one of the innovators of be-bop, saxophonist Charlie Parker. The young guitarist's single note style, like that of Christian's, fit in well with the new musical sound, and Parker allowed him ample room to solo. This provided a launching pad that eventually landed Kessel a steady job with the Oscar Peterson Trio in 1952. Pianist Peterson was a leading light in early 1950s' jazz, and following the induction of its newest member, the trio departed on a 14-country tour with Jazz at the Philharmonic. Kessel also recorded with singer Julie London in 1955, including a celebrated rendition of "Cry Me a River" that became a popular standard.

Kessel recorded *Easy Like* for Contemporary Records in 1953, his first album as a leader. Over the next few years he recorded *Kessel Plays Standards* (1955), *To Swing Or Not to Swing* (1955), and *Let's Cook* (1957) for the label. "Guitarist Barney Kessel's string of recordings for Contemporary in the 1950s," wrote Yanow, "included some of the finest work of his career." In addition to these fine achievements, Kessel recorded a series of albums with bassist Ray Brown and drummer Shelly Manne, including *The Poll Winners* (1957), *The*

Poll Winners Ride Again (1958), and *The Poll Winners Three!* (1959). The albums were initiated when each of the players won *Metronome, Downbeat,* and *Playboy* polls in 1956. Stan Britt noted in the book *Masters of Jazz Guitar* that these albums did an excellent job of "showcasing the guitar trio format and demonstrating how well the guitar could substitute for piano in a jazz setting." Kessel also continued to win *Downbeat*'s Guitarist of the Year until the rise of Wes Montgomery in the 1960s.

Kessel recorded less frequently throughout most of the 1960s, but returned to a higher profile in 1968 to take his place on a European tour as a member of the Guitar Workshop (with George Benson, Larry Coryell, Jim Hall, and Elmer Snowden). In 1969 he moved to London, but returned to the United States in 1970 and busied himself with session work, including completing a soundtrack for an Elvis Presley movie. Kessel soon tired of studio work, however, and happily joined guitarists Herb Ellis and Charlie Byrd for a tour of Australia in 1974. The trio became known as the Great Guitars, and would tour and record together for nearly 20 years. "Great Guitars' portentous name carries enormous expectations," wrote Yanow. "But with world-class talent like these three … the music is usually worthy of the billing, genially swinging and harmonically erudite."

Kessel recorded a series of solo albums for Concord Records in the 1970s, including *Barney Plays Kessel* (1975) and *Soaring* (1976). One of his strongest efforts for the label was a reunion with the Poll Winners, 15 years after the trio's last recordings. Writing about *The Poll Winners Straight Ahead,* Yanow declared, "Overall this is the best all-around recording by the Poll Winners and is easily recommended to bop fans." Kessel also teamed up with guitarist Herb Ellis, a former member of the Oscar Peterson Trio, for *Poor Butterfly* in 1976, and recorded an unaccompanied album, *Solo,* in 1981. Later in the 1980s he released two more albums on Contemporary, *Spontaneous Combustion* (1987) and *Red Hot and Blues* (1988). In 1992, however, while on an Australian tour with the Great Guitars, Kessel suffered a major stroke that left him unable to perform.

On June 25, 1997, a tribute was held in honor of Kessel at the Danny and Sylvia Kaye Playhouse in New York City. "It just might have been the most important night ever in jazz guitar history," remarked Cindy Benedetto in *Jazz Guitar.* Thirty guitar players were in attendance, including newcomers like Howard Alden and Jimmy Bruno, who had developed within the bop tradition. The Great Guitars also made an appearance, with Kessel's spot being filled by the great Tal Farlow. The highlight of the evening came when Kessel himself walked unassisted to the microphone and thanked his friends for the warm tribute. "The tribute was a very moving experience and I don't think anyone there that night will ever forget it," wrote Benedetto. "It's not likely that that many great guitarists will ever be reunited again in one night."

Selected discography

Solo

Easy Like, Contemporary, 1953.
Kessel Plays Standards, Contemporary, 1955.
To Swing Or Not to Swing, Contemporary, 1955.
Music to Listen to Barney Kessel By, Contemporary, 1956.
Let's Cook, Contemporary, 1957.
Barney Kessel Plays "Carmen," Contemporary, 1958.
Some Like It Hot, Contemporary, 1959.
Barney Kessel's Swingin' Party at Contemporary, Contemporary, 1960.
Workin' Out, Contemporary, 1961.
Autumn Leaves, Black Lion, 1968.
Feeling Free, Contemporary, 1969.
Limehouse Blues, Black Lion, 1969.
Yesterday, Black Lion, 1973.
Just Friends, Sonet, 1973.
Barney Plays Kessel, Concord, 1975.
Soaring, Concord, 1976.
Poor Butterfly, Concord, 1976.
Live at Sometime, Storyville, 1977.
Jellybeans, Concord, 1981.
Solo, Concord, 1981.
Spontaneous Combustion, Contemporary, 1987.
Red Hot and Blues, Contemporary, 1988.

With others

(With Ray Brown and Shelly Manne) *The Poll Winners,* Contemporary, 1957.

(With Ray Brown and Shelly Manne) *The Poll Winners Ride Again,* Contemporary, 1958.
(With Ray Brown and Shelly Manne) *Poll Winners Three!,* Contemporary, 1959.
(With Ray Brown and Shelly Manne) *Exploring the Scene,* Contemporary, 1960.
(With Ray Brown and Shelly Manne) *The Poll Winners Straight Ahead,* Contemporary, 1975.
(With Herb Ellis and Charlie Byrd) *Great Guitars,* Concord, 1976.
(With Herb Ellis and Charlie Byrd) *Great Guitars at Charlie's Georgetown,* Concord, 1982.

Sources

Books

Erlewine, Michael, editor, *All Music Guide to Jazz,* Miller Freeman, 1998.
Osborne, Charles, editor, *Masters of Jazz Guitar,* Balafon, 1999.

Online

"Kudos to Kessel," *Jazz Guitar,* http://www.jazzguitar.com/ (January 26, 2004).

Additional information was obtained from the liner notes of *The Poll Winners,* Nat Hentoff, 1957.

—*Ronnie D. Lankford, Jr.*

Kula Shaker

Rock group

Kula Shaker was a rock group whose short, though notable career had a significant influence on the British music scene during the mid-to-late-1990s. Putting a modern edge on a sound that melded Indian folk music, sitars, and spirituality with 1960s psychedelic pop, the group managed to sound like no one else—and everyone else, simultaneously. Like Oasis, Kula Shaker was a promising standout among a crowded field of British exports with worldwide aspirations. For a time, they were poised to become next big thing on either side of the Atlantic. Unfortunately, the group was never able to fulfill its enormous potential.

Crispian Mills, Kula Shaker's flamboyant vocalist, was born on January 18, 1973, into a famous acting family. His mother is actress Hayley Mills, star of such Disney films as *Pollyanna* and *The Parent Trap,* and his grandfather is the veteran British cinema star Sir John Mills. Despite the theatrical culture in which he grew up, Mills started playing guitar in his early teens and decided to make his career in music. His mother's reaction was, not surprisingly, positive. As Mills explained to *The Gate,* "(Haley was) actually, a very supportive mother because she encouraged me as opposed to saying 'Oh, guitar's all right, but get a proper job.' But we were

AP/Wide World Photos. Reproduced by permission.

For the Record . . .

Members include **Alonza Bevan** (born on October 24, 1970, in West London, England), bass; **Jay Darlington** (born on May 3, 1968, in Sidcup, Kent, England), keyboards; **Crispian Mills** (born on January 18, 1973, in Hammersmith, West London, England; son of actress Hayley Mills), lead vocals, guitar; **Paul Winterhart** (born on September 19, 1971, in London, England), drums.

Group formed in England, 1995; signed to Columbia Records, 1995; released debut *K,* 1996; *Peasants, Pigs and Astronauts,* 1999; disbanded after vocalist Crispian Mills left the group, 1999; released *Kollection: The Best of Kula Shaker,* 2003.

Awards: BRIT Award, Best Newcomer, 1997.

Addresses: *Management*—Cowboy Music, c/o 6 Lansdowne Mews, London W11 3BH, England.

never like that, because half the family doesn't have proper jobs—they have circus jobs. So she couldn't say 'Get a proper job,' since it's the family business, getting out and jumping through the hoop."

When he was just 15, Mills joined the psychedelic band the Objects of Desire. That same year he met bassist Alonza Bevan when both were students at Richmond College. Bevan was soon a member of the band and in 1991, future Kula drummer Paul Winterhart joined the Objects lineup as well. By 1993 the band has disbanded, and Mills went to India for several months, a decision that greatly influenced Kula Shaker's future.

Returning to England in June of that year, Mills regrouped with Bevan, Winterhart, and new vocalist Saul Dismont to form the Kays. Eventually, Dismont soon left, and Mills took over vocals and played guitar. After adding keyboardist Jay Darlington the Kays performed for about two years without much fanfare. They even turned down a development deal with independent label Gut Records. One day, however, they had a fateful encounter with, as Mills described it for the NY Rock website "this real wild guy who just came back from India. He was a bit under the influence of ahhh, things, substances, and he told us about this Kula Shaker guy and that since he changed his name to Kula Shaker, he had all the luck in the world. It didn't seem like a bad idea. We had nothing to lose and decided to give it a try and hey, it looks like it really did

work. We read up a bit and this guy Kula Shaker was cool. He was an Indian king from the 9th century. A great poet and a holy man."

Oddly, the band's decision to change their name led to an almost immediate change in their fortune. After playing several notable shows and participating in the British Music Conference In the City, the group found themselves pursued by several major record labels. In September of 1995 they signed with Columbia.

Shortly afterward Kula Shaker released their singles "Tattva" ("truth" in Sanskrit) and "Hey Dude" in Britain. They were enormously successful and propelled the group's 1996 album *K* to number one when it debuted. The band's odd blend of psychedelic melodies, sitar, and Sanskrit chanting (all done by a bunch of guys from England!) made them extremely popular. On the other side of the Atlantic, however, "Tattva" enjoyed only limited success among the American indie crowd, and reception for *K* was equally lukewarm, although it did climb into the *Billboard* Top 200 albums chart. In 1997, however, Kula Shaker won a Brit award (the British equivalent of a Grammy) for Best Newcomer.

Kula Shaker might have risen to great heights had they not made a nearly fatal mistake. The group was known for its eccentric mysticism, spirituality, and superstitions, which seemed harmless, if somewhat affected. As critic Nicole Pensiero summed it up in Philadelphia's *City Paper,* "They're the Brit-pop equivalent of Austin Powers: stuck in Swingin' London, circa 1967. On one level, Kula Shaker's psychedelic, cosmically aware music is a guilty pleasure; on another, it's terribly pretentious. C'mon—singing in Sanskrit?"

Unfortunately, Mills's off-handed remarks to British music news giant *NME*—that he wanted to have "great big burning swastikas onstage" and that "Hitler knew a lot more than he made out. You can see why Hitler got support. It was probably the uniforms that swung it"— were reported by the BBC. The band was brutally attacked in the press for apparently supporting Nazism, losing many fans as a result.

Even though Mills defended his remarks and explained that he was referring to the swastika's original use as an Indian spiritual symbol, the press was unrelenting. As he elaborated to NY Rock, "The ancient Indian swastika symbol is a very positive symbol. That was what I was talking about. It's pro peace, love, and equality beliefs. They failed to mention that I didn't talk about the Nazi symbol at all, but you know how the press is. They decided to make a big deal out of it. I was simply young and too innocent. I really wasn't talking about the Nazi sign. I was so caught up in the Indian mythology, that I didn't even think about how the Nazis perverted that sign."

Despite his protestations the incident continued to overshadow the group's music. In 1998, however, they came back with "Sound of Drums," which became a British top-five single, and a performance at the famous Glastonbury festival that June. Their 1999 follow-up *Peasants, Pigs and Astronauts* took them to Los Angeles to work with rock guru Rick Rubin and onto a barge off the River Thames to record with legendary Pink Floyd and Alice Cooper producer Bob Ezrin. Despite the group's hard work and high-profile help, the record was not nearly as successful as its predecessor.

In September of 1999 Mills decided, without animosity towards his bandmates, that he wanted to leave Kula Shaker to start his own group. As he explained to the BBC News: "I have loved my time with Kula Shaker and have experienced more than I could ever have imagined. The time is now right for me to move on and try new experiences, new musical ideas. I will always consider them to be friends and much, much more."

Selected discography

K, Columbia, 1996.
Peasants, Pigs and Astronauts, Columbia, 1999.
Kollection: The Best of Kula Shaker, Sony, 2003.

Sources

Periodicals

Drop-D Magazine, June 7, 1997.
NME, February 10, 1998; January 5, 1999; March 6, 1999.
Philadelphia City Paper, July 8-15, 1999.
Rolling Stone, November 12, 1996.
Smash Hits, November 20-December 3, 1996.
USA Today, November 26, 1996.

Online

"Interview with Crispian Mills of Kula Shaker," NY Rock, http://www.nyrock.com/interviews/kula_int.htm (February 19, 2004).
"Kula Shaker," *All Music Guide,* http://www.allmusicguide.com (February 2, 2004).
"Kula Shaker," Hip Online, http://www.hiponline.com/artist/music/k/kula_shaker/ (February 4, 2004).
"Kula Shaker," Iceberg Radio, http://www.icebergradio.com/artist/8386/kula_shaker.html (February 4, 2004)
"Kula Shaker," VH1, http://www.vh1.com/artists/az/kula_shaker/bio.jhtml (February 3, 2004).
"Kula Shaker Hushed," BBC News Online, http://news.bbc.co.uk/1/hi/entertainment/452327.stm (February 20, 2004).
"Kula Shaker: Just Where Are They Going?" San Francisco Gate, http://www.sfgate.com/ea/rock/lanham/lanham1028.html (February 22, 2004).
"Kula Shaker [sic]: Still Waiting for Tomorrow," *Circle Magazine,* http://www.circlemagazine.com (March 18, 2004).

—*Nicole Elyse*

Laika

Ambient rock group

While it's hard to pin down Laika's music to one specific genre, their nebulous style is undoubtedly one that has influenced numerous bands and will continue to do so. Incorporating jazz, blues, ambient, trip-hop, and psychedelia, multi-instrumentalist Margaret Fiedler and celebrated producer-programmer Guy Fixsen craft songs in a class of their own. "There isn't a genre for us," Fiedler told *Billboard*'s Jonathan Cohen. "If we were as big as Björk, people would just say, 'Oh, it's another Laika record.'"

In her childhood, Fiedler, the band's vocalist, attended grade school with fellow rocker Liz Phair in Winnetka, Illinois. Fiedler developed a taste for music early, and took up the cello at a young age. During high school, her family moved to Connecticut, and it was there that she befriended a young Richard Melville Hall—later known as Moby. Together they formed the band Child's Play, a post-punk-styled group that had a fondness for the Smiths and Joy Division.

After tiring of the East Coast music and the predominance of pre-riot grrrl punk, Fiedler went to London in 1989, where she quickly immersed herself in the indie rock community. She joined Moonshake in the early 1990s and, through the band's studio, met Fixsen, an established producer-engineer who had worked with shoegaze artists like Chapterhouse and My Bloody Valentine.

When Fiedler was dumped from Moonshake in 1993 she took bassist John Frenett with her. They teamed up with Fixsen and drummer Lou Ciccotelli for Laika's first release, 1995's *Silver Apples of the Moon,* a direct homage to the epic Morton Subotnick album of the same name. Around the same time, Fiedler and Fixsen became romantically involved.

Fielder found the name Laika (Russian for "barker") in an encyclopedia of historical events, where she learned that in the late 1950s Russia sent a dog named Laika into outer space. Fiedler, an animal rights supporter, told Cross Radio, "That image of this little dog was so hopeful but at the same time tragic because they [knew] how to put her up but not to get her back and she died, and it just sort of touched on a lot of things we felt and still feel strong about."

Laika's sound reflected its members' sonic influences: swirly guitars and heavy ambient textures, but reveled in its newfound taste for groovier flavors. "When we started out," Fixsen explained to Mike Wolf of *Time Out New York,* "there were plenty of bands, like My Bloody Valentine and Sonic Youth, pushing the guitar into new areas. We felt we had to find something with more potential, which meant getting into samplers and non-rock music. With a sampler, if you can conceive of a sound, you can make it."

Coming at a time when London's Britpop scene had nearly reached its peak and just about any band from the city was put on a pedestal, *Silver Apples of the Moon* garnered a nice share of critical praise. *Mojo* magazine, quoted on the BBC 1 website, called the album "the missing link between the avant funk of Can and the ambient jungle heard on London's pirate [radio stations]." It also made *Spin* magazine's "10 Best Albums You Didn't Hear" list in 1995.

After a successful support slot on Tricky's North American tour, Laika found themselves in New York City recording their follow-up, 1997's *Sounds of the Satellites,* further embracing their fixation with spacey subjects. Jason Ankeny in *All Music Guide* called *Satellites* "a simultaneous expansion of the band's sonic palette and a brilliant refinement of their past innovations." Josh Klein of *Salon* praised the album as "another subtle masterpiece that smoothly refines the chaotic blast of creativity that formed Laika's first album." The album earned Laika some new high-profile fans, Radiohead, who asked Laika to tour with them as well. It was a mutually satisfying venture, and Radiohead's Thom Yorke later admitted to cribbing some of their style from Laika's hushed electro-tinged soundscapes.

Good-Looking Blues, the band's third major studio effort, was released in 2000, also to much acclaim. Explaining the record's genesis, Fixsen told *Billboard*'s Jonathan Cohen, "At first, we made the album in a similar electronic form [as *Sounds*], although it was more programmed. At that point, we felt it wasn't enough of a move forward. So we decided to make it more 'live.'"

For the Record . . .

Members include **Lou Diccotelli**, percussion; **Louise Elliott**, saxophone, flute; **Margaret Fiedler**, vocals, programming; **Guy Fixsen**, producer; **John Frenett**, bass.

Fiedler and Fixsen formed Laika in London, 1993; signed to Too Pure record label; released *Silver Apples of the Moon,* 1995; *Sounds of the Satellites,* 1997; *Good-Looking Blues,* 2000; *Wherever I Am, I Am What is Missing,* 2003.

Addresses: *Record company*—Too Pure, 3A Highbury Crescent, London N5 1RN, England, website: http://www.toopure.com. *Website*—Laika Official Website: http://www.laika.org. *E-mail*—laika@compuserve.com.

Fiedler had her take on the record as well, as she told the *Onion*: "...for a band that incorporates more electronic stuff, it tends to be that you make a very electronic album and then figure out how to do it live. ...We've never done that.... So this album was a very roundabout record in that we made it at home, a little bit more programmed, but then we went out, played it live, and sort of re-recorded everything more like the way we do it live."

The record also featured the talents of PJ Harvey drummer Rob Ellis and Spleen's Matt Barge, who came along on the supporting tour—a second with Radiohead. *Good-Looking Blues* was a breakthrough recording for Laika, earning them more press and attention than any of their previous albums. Lydia Vanderloo, writing in *CMJ New Music Monthly,* dubbed the record a collection of "Grimm's fairytales for the Palm Pilot generation." That year also saw Fiedler branch out musically as she took a short hiatus from Laika and went on the road to play guitar with PJ Harvey for her *Stories from the City, Stories from the Sea* tour.

In 2003 Laika released their fourth LP, *Wherever I Am, I Am What is Missing*. While forgoing any obvious celestial motifs, the band retained their signature lunar-obsessed sonic sensibility. However, the album was not the full-on collaborative effort that past records had been, perhaps because the relationship that Fiedler and Fixsen once nurtured had gone its course.

"There were two bursts of activity and a lot of empty spaces in between actually," Fixsen said in the band's press materials on the Too Pure website. "A lot of the music was recorded at my place while Margaret was off galavanting [sic] around the world with PJ Harvey and getting drunk, going around Australia and America and hanging around with Bono and s**t, while I was stuck in my little room ... I sort of set myself a task to stop myself from going mad in my little room: 'Today I'm going to write a song from beginning to end and then I'm just going to forget about it,' whereas in the past I would've worked on it over a period of weeks. There is a lot of spontaneity for a record that took three and a half years to make." Despite Fiedler and Fixsen's breakup, the *Toronto Star*'s Ben Rayner praised the album as "Laika making some of the finest music no one ever seems to hear."

Selected discography

Silver Apples of the Moon, Too Pure, 1995.
Sounds of the Satellites, Too Pure, 1997.
Good-Looking Blues, Too Pure, 2000.
Lost in Space, Vol. 1 (1992–2002), Too Pure, 2003.
Wherever I Am, I Am What is Missing, Too Pure, 2003.

Sources

Periodicals

Billboard, August 5, 2000.
CMJ New Music Monthly, September 2000.
Time Out New York, August 24–31, 2000.
Toronto Star, December 18, 2003.

Online

"Focus: Laika," a.v. club, *Onion,* http://www.theavclub.com/avclub3701/bonusfeature1_3701.html (February 18, 2004).
"Interview: Margaret Fiedler—Laika, Cross Radio, http://www.crossradio.org/web/12_03/laika_e.htm (December 19, 2003.)
"Sounds of the Satellites" *All Music Guide,* http://www.allmusic.com (February 18, 2004).
"Sounds of the Satellites: Laika—Too Pure," Sharps and Flats, *Salon,* http://archive.salon.com/may97/sharps/sharps970523.html (February 18, 2004).

—Ken Taylor

Mutt Lange

Producer, songwriter

Despite his attempts to remain modestly out of the public eye, Robert "Mutt" Lange will always be recognized as one of the world's most renowned record producers. His career spans decades and genres, and he holds the distinct honor of working on seven of the hundred top-selling albums of all time.

Lange was the second of three boys born to his parents in Mufilira, Rhodesia (now Zimbabwe). His father was a mining engineer and his mother a cultured woman from a well-to-do German family. Lange's friends called him John—his middle name—but his parents, fond of nicknames, called him "Mutt," a tag that would stick for years to come. From a young age he took an interest in country music, although Africa's mining towns weren't particularly tuned in to American culture. One artist that did, however, transcend the cross-Atlantic boundary was singer Slim Whitman—a favorite of the young Mutt.

Lange first began playing guitar in a band when his parents sent him to boarding school in Belfast, South Africa. After high school, he took a job producing commercials at a recording studio in that country, and he formed the bands Sound Reason and Hocus with some friends near Johannesburg. Hocus was comprised of Lange on bass, vocalist-pianist Stevie Van Kerken (whom Lange soon married), guitarist Steve Mac-Namara, keyboardist Allan Goldswain, and drummer Geoff Williams. During the band's less-than-illustrious career, they released only a handful of singles. When Hocus broke up, Lange decided to concentrate on his production work, scoring a few hits for other artists in South Africa. Within a couple of years, however, he and his new wife moved to London, England.

London in the early 1970s was rife with musical talent and Lange flourished in the city's cultural environment. He immediately found himself with a number of production jobs, his first successes being Graham Parker's *Heat Treatment* and City Boy's self-titled 1976 debut. Lange went on to produce City Boy's next three albums, earning a solid reputation for his work ethic and the incredibly full sound he achieved. Soon Bob Geldof and his band, the Boomtown Rats, enlisted his services for their first record in 1977.

By 1978, Lange's influence was felt all over London. His next work was for the avant-garde pop group XTC and their *White Music* LP. In an interview with an XTC fan site, the band's guitarist-vocalist Andy Partridge commented that on Lange's production of "This is Pop," "Mutt focused in on every sound, every curl, and cooked the groove out of us. We must have played this song well over fifty times, over and over and over. Until the cursing under our breath became louder than our guitars and drums. But he boiled a great take out of us. A zen process, when we stopped thinking about it, out it came, the perfect version."

Around this time AC/DC, who had already built a notable following with their first three albums, were searching for a producer to take their sound to another level. With Lange they produced *Highway to Hell,* their first huge success. After singer Bon Scott died, Lange helped the band find their replacement, Brian Johnson, and produced *Back in Black,* which eventually sold over 19 million copies and dominated radio charts worldwide. Greg Prato of *All Music Guide* commented that "Musically, the band hadn't changed much, although producer 'Mutt' Lange helped the group focus their high voltage rock." With Lange at the helm, AC/DC followed up with the less-successful *For Those About to Rock (We Salute You).*

In 1981 Lange began to branch out, exploring the softer side of rock with Foreigner's album *4.* Throughout the recording sessions, he and guitarist Mick Jones butted heads constantly. But when the record—which included hits "Waiting for a Girl Like You," "Urgent," and "Juke Box Hero"—turned out to be the band's greatest success, the feuds were soon forgotten.

Around this same time, Lange was introduced to the up-and-coming British band Def Leppard through their (and AC/DC's) manager, Peter Mansch. The band was so enamored of Lange's previous work that they postponed recording their second album to allow Mutt to finish the Foreigner record before starting theirs. The band felt that their debut had been rushed and they needed Lange's expertise to achieve the success they desired.

Lange gave his signature treatment to the raw-sounding Def Leppard, and the result was the radio-

Born Robert John Lange on November 15, 1948, in Mufilira, Rhodesia; married Stevie Van Kerken, early 1970s (divorced); married Shania Twain, 1993; children: Eja D'Angelo.

Moved from Africa to London after the breakup of his band Hocus, 1970s; produced hit records for AC/DC, Foreigner, Def Leppard, the Cars, Michael Bolton, Bryan Adams, Celine Dion, Shania Twain, and the Backstreet Boys; Grammy Award for cowriting Bryan Adams's "(Everything I Do) I Do It For You," 1991; Grammy for producing Shania Twain's *The Woman in Me*, 1995; Grammy for cowriting Twain's "You're Still the One," 1998; Grammy for cowriting Twain's "Come on Over," 1999.

Awards: Grammy Awards, Best Song Written Specifically for a Motion Picture or for Television for "(Everything I Do) I Do It For You," 1991; Best Country Album for *Woman in Me*, 1995; Best Country Song for "You're Still the One," 1998; Best Country Song for "Come on Over," 1999.

Addresses: *Record company*—Mercury Nashville, 60 Music Sq. E., Nashville, TN 37203, phone: (615) 524-7500, website: http://www.mercurynashville.com.

friendly *High 'N' Dry*. While the bright and full sound was a bit of a coup for metal purists, the record garnered heaps of praise and yielded a number of charting singles including "Let it Go" and "Bringin' on the Heartache." Lange's collaboration with the band on their third release, *Pyromania,* was much more involved: the album credits list him as a cowriter—sometimes principal writer—on all tracks. The album was constructed with a song-by-song building process that took months in the studio. When it was completed, however, it turned out to be a landmark release for both the band and its producer. They even joked that Mutt had become their de facto sixth member.

Despite the attention he gave to the bands with which he collaborated, Lange shunned the industry's glitz and glamour, opting for an almost reclusive existence. When Def Leppard toured to support *Pyromania,* Lange turned his attention instead to other projects—like new wave popsters the Cars. He left his indelible style on their largely successful *Heartbeat City,* a record that included the hits "Drive," "You Might Think," and "Magic."

Although Lange once again cowrote all the songs on Def Leppard's *Hysteria,* he turned down their request to produce the record, since his intense schedule was both mentally and physically exhausting—at the time, he was also producing AC/DC's *Who Made Who.* When Def Leppard struggled unsuccessfully to find a replacment, Lange took the reins again more than a year later, producing the album that many consider their finest work and one of the best-selling hard rock albums of all time, despite its three years in limbo. Single after single emerged from this record, topping playlists with "Love Bites," "Armageddon It," and one of the 1980s radio's biggest hits, "Pour Some Sugar on Me."

While Lange's success with Def Leppard was definitely his most notable career highlight in the 1980s, he also produced one-off hit makers for Billy Ocean and Huey Lewis and the News. The early 1990s were a period of revitalization for Lange as he produced Michael Bolton's *One Thing* and Bryan Adams's *Waking up the Neighbours.* In 1993, however, Lange's career took its biggest step ever when the then-divorced producer met Canadian country singer Shania Twain. After hearing Twain's debut album, Lange contacted her through Mercury Records; they began a phone relationship, playing and singing songs to one another.

"My manager told me this guy in England had seen my video and was interested in me. I guessed he was a songwriter and so eventually I took a call from him. I didn't know who Mutt Lange was," Twain told American Music Channel. Twain and Lange finally met in person that June and by December they were married.

They immediately set to work on their first collaboration, Twain's 1995 chart-topping *Woman in Me,* writing and producing each track. Among the songs were "Whose Bed Have Your Boots Been Under?" and "Any Man of Mine"—Twain's first number one hit. While the album broke the record for the most weeks spent in the country charts' number-one spot, it paled in comparison to the success of Twain's next record, 1997's *Come on Over.* By the end of 1999 it had sold 36 million copies worldwide and cemented Twain's place in country music history.

The late 1990s found Lange focusing not only on his wife's mounting success but also on his own label, Zomba Records, which launched the careers of both Britney Spears and the Backstreet Boys. He produced the Corrs' *In Blue* was one of the producers of Celine Dion's *All the Way: A Decade of Song.* In August of 2001, Twain and Lange's first child, a son named Eja D'Angelo, was born. The couple had to balance parenthood with the songwriting and production of Twain's *Up!*—another pop-chart smash released the following year.

While Twain still took part in much of the record's promotion, Lange managed to maintain his private lifestyle, staying at their palatial estates in Switzerland and Florida and acquiring the rights to nearly every photo of himself, including those with Twain. It became increasingly common for fans and paparazzi to see Twain alone in public, as she fulfilled her record label's promotion demands. Rumors circulated that the couple were headed towards divorce but Twain assuaged the public's suspicions, explaining her husband's choice to remain out the public eye. She told *People*, "He doesn't want to be a celebrity; he just wants to be a producer."

Selected discography

As producer

(City Boy) *City Boy,* Mercury, 1976.
(Graham Parker and the Rumour) *Heat Treatment,* Polygram, 1976.
(City Boy) *Young Men Gone West,* Mercury, 1977.
(City Boy) *Book Early,* Mercury, 1978.
(Boomtown Rats) *Boomtown Rats,* Mercury, 1977.
(Graham Parker and the Rumour) *Parkerilla,* Malibu, 1978.
(Boomtown Rats) *Tonic for the Troops,* Mercury, 1978.
(XTC) *White Music,* Virgin, 1978.
(Foreigner) *4,* Atlantic, 1981.
(AC/DC) *For Those About to Rock (We Salute You),* Sony, 1981.
(Def Leppard) *High 'N' Dry,* Mercury, 1981.
(Def Leppard) *Pyromania,* Mobile, 1983.
(The Cars) *Heartbeat City,* Elektra, 1984.
(AC/DC) *Who Made Who,* Sony, 1986.
(Def Leppard) *Hysteria,* Mobile, 1987.
(Billy Ocean) *Tear Down These Walls,* Jive, 1988.
(Bryan Adams) *Waking Up the Neighbours,* A&M, 1991.
(Michael Bolton) *One Thing,* Columbia, 1993.
(Shania Twain) *Woman in Me,* Mercury, 1995.
(Bryan Adams) *18 'til I Die,* A&M, 1996.
(Backstreet Boys) *Backstreet Boys,* Jive, 1996.
(Backstreet Boys) *Backstreet's Back,* Jive, 1997.
(Shania Twain) *Come on Over,* Mercury, 1997.
(Celine Dion) *All the Way: A Decade of Song,* Sony, 1999.
(Backstreet Boys) *Millennium,* Jive, 1999.
(The Corrs) *In Blue,* Atlantic, 2000.
(Shania Twain) *Up!,* Mercury, 2002.

Sources

Periodicals

Daily News (Los Angeles, CA), June 5, 1999.
People, June 14, 1999.

Online

"*Back in Black,*" All Music Guide, http://www.allmusic.com (February 4, 2004).
"The Other Half," American Music Channel, http://www.americanmusicchannel.com/interviews/shania.cfm (February 4, 2004).

—Ken Taylor

Loretta Lynn

Singer, songwriter

AP/Wide World Photos. Reproduced by permission.

With 26 number-one songs to her credit and a career that has spanned more than four decades, singer-songwriter Loretta Lynn has become known as the Queen of Country. Many of the feisty performer's works appeal to a female fan base because of their gritty but often upbeat tales of betrayal, hard times, raising kids, and other real-life topics. With a hard-scrabble upbringing, a devoted yet troubled marriage, chronic illness and exhaustion due to her hectic pace, and several tragedies through the years, Lynn's own life often provided the grist for her popular tunes. Her best-selling 1976 autobiography, *Coal Miner's Daughter,* was made into a hit Oscar-winning film starring Sissy Spacek and Tommy Lee Jones. Though she was out of the loop for a few years while taking care of her husband, who died in 1996, Lynn returned to touring in 1998. In 2000 she released her first album since 1988 to contain original solo material.

Born Loretta Webb in Butcher Hollow, Kentucky, Lynn's birthday is April 14, but she is secretive about the year. Most sources put it at 1934, while others have said 1932, 1936, or 1938. She grew up during the Depression. Her father, Melvin, whom everyone knew as Ted, worked on road construction for the Works Progress Administration during the Depression, but when the economy improved, he found a job in the coal mines. Her mother, Clara (Butcher) Webb, was Irish and Cherokee and raised eight children. Lynn was the second child; the youngest, Brenda, changed her name to Crystal Gayle and went on to a successful singing career of her own.

Lynn grew up in a rustic home in the mountains with no electricity or water. Later, after getting a job in the mines, her father was able to buy a four-room home in a big clearing down in the hollow, or "holler," as she calls it. Each week, the family listened to the Grand Ole Opry on a battery-powered radio. "I can't say that I had big dreams of being a star at the Opry," Lynn wrote in *Coal Miner's Daughter.* "It was another world to me. All I knew was Butcher Holler—didn't have no dreams that I knew about." She was 12 before she rode in a car.

While growing up, Lynn helped her mother take care of her siblings, and that is how she began singing. "I'd sit on the porch swing and rock them babies and sing at the top of my voice," she recalled in her autobiography. She got an education in a one-room schoolhouse, and met her husband there at a pie social one night when she was 13. He had already served in World War II, and was dressed in his uniform. He bid a whopping $5 for her pie, which she baked with salt instead of sugar by accident. Despite the mix-up, he walked her home and asked for a kiss, and she fell in love immediately.

Oliver Vanetta Lynn was nicknamed "Mooney" because he once ran moonshine, but Lynn called him "Doo" because of his other nickname, "Doolittle," which he had since age two. "Nobody knows why—maybe

For the Record . . .

Born Loretta Webb on April 14, c. 1934, in Butcher Hollow, KY; daughter of Melvin "Ted" (a coal miner) and Carla (Butcher) Webb; married Oliver Vanetta Lynn (a business manager), 1948; children: Betty Sue, Jack Benny (deceased), Carla, Ernest Ray, Peggy, and Patsy.

Organized her own ensemble, Blue Kentuckians; founder and secretary-treasurer of Loretta Lynn Enterprises, and Loretta Lynn Championship Rodeo; founder and vice-president of United Talent Inc.; founder and honorary board chairman of Loretta Lynn Western Stores; founder of Loretta Lynn Dude Ranch and Loretta Lynn Museum; co-author, with George Vecsey, of best-selling autobiography *Coal Miner's Daughter*, 1976; co-author, with Patsy Bale Cox of a second autobiography *Still Woman Enough: A Memoir*, 2000; released *Van Lear Rose*, 2004.

Awards: *Billboard* Outstanding Achievement Award, 1965; Cashbox Most Programmed Female Artist Award, 1965; Country Music Association Award, Female Vocalist of the Year, 1967, 1972, 1973, Entertainer of the Year, 1972, Vocal Duo of the Year (with Twitty), 1972-75; TNN/*Music City News* Country Awards, Best Female Vocalist, 1967-78, 1980, Best Vocal Duo (with Twitty), 1971-78, 1980-81, Best Album, 1976, Living Legend Award, 1986; Academy of Country Music, Top Female Vocalist, 1971, 1973-75, Best Vocal Group and/or Duet (with Conway Twitty), 1971, 1974-76, Entertainer of the Year, 1975, Pioneer Award, 1995; Grammy Award, Best Country Vocal Performance by a Duo (with Twitty), 1971, Best Children's Recording (with others), 1981; American Music Award, Country Favorite Duo or Group (with Twitty) 1975, 1977, 1978, Country Favorite Female Vocalist, 1977, 1978, Special Award of Merit, 1985; named to Country Music Association Hall of Fame, 1988; Christian Country Music Association Living Legend Award, 1996; Lynn's composition "Coal Miner's Daughter" inducted into the Grammy Song Hall of Fame, 1998; inducted into the Country Gospel Hall of Fame, 1999; inducted into the Kentucky Music Hall of Fame, 2002.

Addresses: *Record company*—MCA Nashville, 60 Music Square E., Nashville, TN 37203, website: http://www.mcanashville.com. *Booking*—Creative Artist Agency, 3310 West End Ave., Ste. 500, Nashville, TN 37206, phone: (615) 383-8787. *Office*—Loretta Lynn Enterprises, Inc., P.O. Box 120369, Nashville, TN 37212-0369.

because he was always a little feller," she noted in *Coal Miner's Daughter*. She pointed out that it was not because he was a layabout; she wrote that he worked hard running their ranch and managing her career and touring schedule.

The pair married on January 10, 1948, a few weeks before Lynn turned 14. She noted in *Newsweek,* "I told Momma, 'I'm getting married so I won't have to rock all them babies.' Momma cried all night. Then bang, bang, bang, bang, I had four children in four years—before I was 18." After having Betty Sue, Jack Benny, Carla, and Ernest Ray, Lynn later gave birth to twins Peggy and Patsy. By age 30, she became a grandmother when her eldest daughter married and had a child.

Soon after they married, Lynn and her husband moved to Washington state, where he had lived when he was young. The coal industry was declining and he found a better job in the timber industry. She helped support the family by picking strawberries with migrant workers and doing laundry. Thanks to the farming family they worked and lived with, she learned how to cook. He later worked as an auto mechanic.

When their oldest daughter was ten, Lynn's husband bought her a guitar. Her brother and two of her sisters were already performing in clubs in Indiana, where the family had moved after her father was laid off from the mines. Doo Lynn had heard his wife singing along with the radio and thought she was talented. "I was proud to be noticed, to tell you the truth, so I went right to work on it," she commented in her autobiography.

Encouraged by Her Husband

At first, Lynn sang Kitty Wells tunes, but soon started writing her own material. After a couple months, her husband suggested she could earn some money by playing for patrons at the local bars. Though she was extremely bashful, she went along with it. "He said I could do it, and he said he'd set me up at some club," Lynn wrote in *Coal Miner's Daughter*. "So I did it—because he said I could. He made all the decisions in those days." She added, "Now that's what I mean when I say my husband is responsible for my career. It wasn't my idea: he told me I could do it. I'd still be a housewife today if he didn't bring that guitar home and then encourage me to be a singer."

Lynn's career began at Delta Grange Hall, where she first appeared at a party with the governor of Washington in attendance. She then started appearing with the Penn Brothers. Soon, with help from her husband, she formed her own group, Loretta's Trail Blazers. Before long, she was playing six nights a week at a tavern and on Sundays would perform at Air Force bases and mental hospitals. After winning first prize at the Northwest Washington District Fair, she and her husband decided to try to make it in Nashville.

A lucky break came after Lynn won an amateur contest on Buck Owens's television show when he was just starting out himself. A Vancouver businessman saw the show and offered to put up the money to cut a record. She went to Los Angeles and managed to get into a studio, where they recorded "Honky Tonk Girl," for the small Zero Records label. Doo Lynn took a picture of his wife and mailed 3,500 copies of the single and Lynn's photo to radio stations around the country. The song made it to number 14 on *Billboard*'s country charts on July 25, 1960. She soon took off on a cross-country promotional tour to talk herself up at radio stations.

First Gold Record

By October of 1960, Lynn was performing with the Grand Ole Opry. She signed a contract with Decca Records and moved to Nashville in 1961. She became good friends with Patsy Cline, one of the reigning country stars of the time, and the two shared secrets and went shopping together. Cline died in 1963 in a plane crash, the year that Lynn's first album, *Loretta Lynn Sings,* went to number one and became the first album by a female country artist to be certified gold. It featured the hit single, "Don't Come Home a Drinkin' (with Lovin' on Your Mind)."

This song was indeed a tribute to Lynn's husband, whom she admits had problems with alcohol. "I think one of the reasons he drinks is he's lonesome when I'm away so much," she told Phyllis Battelle in *Ladies Home Journal*. He even showed up drunk at the premiere of *Coal Miner's Daughter,* and Lynn has hinted that he was not always faithful. But not all of her songs are directly about her life. She admitted that the tune "Fist City," about a woman who plans to fight to keep her man from another woman's attentions, was autobiographical, but said that another, "You Ain't Woman Enough (To Take My Man)" was actually about a distraught fan she met one night backstage.

Indeed, Lynn recounts many tender stories about her husband in *Coal Miner's Daughter*. Just after signing with Decca, Lynn and her husband bought a sprawling 1,450-acre ranch about 65 miles outside Nashville. It was actually an old mill town called Hurricane Mills, and the house on the property reminded Lynn of the house "Tara" in *Gone with the Wind*. Her husband discovered it was structurally unsound, but he worked diligently to get it back into shape because he knew how much she wanted it. But there were other problems, too. "Right after we moved in [in April 1967], I found out the place was haunted," Lynn told Battelle in *Ladies Home Journal*. She refused to be alone in the home after seeing spirits. In 1975, they opened a dude ranch on the property.

Meanwhile, by the mid-1960s, Lynn had racked up several number-one hits and best-selling albums. From the late 1960s to the late 1970s she amassed numerous country awards, including many for duets with Conway Twitty. Rumors abounded that Lynn was responsible for breaking up Twitty's marriage, but in her autobiography she steadfastly denied ever having an affair.

In 1972, Lynn was honored as Entertainer of the Year by the Country Music Association. Before the televised ceremonies, some warned that if she won, she should not to touch presenter, Charley Pride, in order to maintain her "image in rural white America," as George Vecsey wrote in the *New York Times*. She disregarded the advice and embraced him. In 1973, Lynn became the first country artist to appear on the cover of *Newsweek*.

By the late 1970s, spending 10 months a year of the road appeared to be catching up with Lynn. She suffered from exhaustion, illness, high blood pressure, ulcers, and chronic migraines, and began to pass out on stage. Rumors flew that she was drinking heavily or addicted to pills. In her book, she has insisted her troubles were due to an allergy to aspirin, but Dalma Heyn reported in *McCall's* that she was addicted to Valium. Lynn denied this to Bob Allen in *Country Music,* telling him that she did, however, take Librium for nerves. She also has had trouble with unexplained seizures but has said doctors ruled out epilepsy. Also, in 1972 doctors found tumors in her breast and she was in the hospital a total of nine times for that.

As her career was building, Lynn's husband took care of the children for the most part. They had babysitters, too, because he was often on the road with her. She wrote in her book, "If I could start over again, I would still go into show business. But if I could change just one thing, I would be with my children more."

A Year of Tragedy

Lynn was devastated in 1984 when her son Jack drowned in an accident on her family ranch. He went out horseback riding, and the police later found the horse standing beneath a river bluff with Jack's body nearby. She was in intensive care at the time after having one of her seizures on tour. This followed on the heels of plenty of other bad news for the family. The same year, Lynn's other son had a kidney removed, and the previous year, his wife gave birth to stillborn twins. In addition, two of her daughters, including one who married at 15, got divorced.

After the death of her son, Lynn did not record anything for two years and she cut back on her touring. The album *Just a Woman,* which was recorded before the accident, came out in 1985, but then she went back to the studio and released *Who Was That Stranger* in 1988. That same year, she was inducted into the

Country Music Hall of Fame as the most-awarded female in country music history. Subsequently, though, Lynn dropped out of circulation for a few years to take care of Doo Lynn, who had heart surgery in the early 1990s.

Lynn returned to the public eye in 1993 with the trio album *Honky Tonk Angels,* recorded with Dolly Parton and Tammy Wynette, and the following year released a three-CD boxed set chronicling her career. Also, in 1995 she taped a seven-week series on the Nashville Network (TNN) titled *Loretta Lynn & Friends,* and performed about 50 dates that year as well. Doo Lynn died in August of 1996, after suffering from heart disease and diabetes. He had both legs amputated by the time he died.

Lynn went back on the road in 1998 and with Patsy Bale Cox co-wrote another memoir, *Still Woman Enough,* which picks up where *Coal Miner's Daughter* left off. In 2000, she released her first collection of solo original songs in twelve years, *Still Country.* The release features her trademark twang and homespun lyrics. Though some felt her rootsy music was out of place in the new, glitzier Nashville atmosphere, she told Miriam Longino in the *Atlanta Journal and Constitution,* "I never left country music; everybody else did. It's made me a good livin'. Why should I go in another direction?"

Selected discography

Loretta Lynn Sings, Decca, 1963.
Before I'm Over You, Decca, 1964.
Songs from My Heart, Decca, 1965.
Ernest Tubb & Loretta Lynn, Decca, 1965.
Hymns, MCA, 1965.
I Like 'Em Country, Decca, 1966.
A Country Christmas, MCA, 1966.
You Ain't Woman Enough, MCA, 1966.
Singin' with Feelin', Decca, 1967.
Ernest Tubb & Loretta Lynn Singin' Again, Decca, 1967.
Don't Come Home a Drinkin', MCA, 1967.
Fist City, Decca, 1968.
Here's Loretta Lynn, Columbia, 1968.
Who Says God Is Dead!, MCA, 1968.
Your Squaw Is on the Warpath, Decca, 1969.
A Woman of the World, Decca, 1969.
If We Put Our Heads Together, Decca, 1969.
Loretta Lynn Writes 'Em and Sings 'Em, Decca, 1970.
Wings Upon Your Horns, Decca, 1970.
I Wanna Be Free, Decca, 1971.
One's on the Way, Decca, 1971.
You're Lookin' at Country, Decca, 1971.
Coal Miner's Daughter, MCA, 1971.
We Only Make Believe, MCA, 1971.
Lead Me On, MCA, 1971.
God Bless America Again, Decca, 1972.
Here I Am Again, Decca, 1972.
Alone with You, MCA, 1972.
Louisiana Woman/Mississippi Man, MCA, 1973.
Country Partners, MCA, 1974.

Back to the Country, MCA, 1975.
Blue-Eyed Kentucky Girl, Decca, 1976.
I Remember Patsy, MCA, 1977.
Lookin' Good, MCA, 1980.
Two's a Party, MCA, 1981.
Making Love from Memory, MCA Special, 1982.
Lyin' Cheatin' Woman Chasin' Honky Tonkin', MCA, 1983.
Loretta Lynn, MCA, 1984.
Just a Woman, MCA, 1985.
Making Believe, MCA, 1988.
Who Was That Stranger, MCA, 1989.
I'll Just Call You Darlin', MCA, 1989.
Peace in the Valley, MCA, 1990.
The Old Rugged Cross, MCA, 1992.
Sings Patsy Cline's Favorites, MCA Special, 1992.
Hey Good Lookin, MCA Special, 1993.
Honky Tonk Girl: The Loretta Lynn Collection, MCA, 1994.
An Evening with Loretta Lynn, Musketeer, 1995.
Loretta Lynn & Patsy Cline On Tour, Vol. 1 (live album), MCA Special, 1996.
Loretta Lynn & Patsy Cline On Tour, Vol. 2 (live album), MCA Special, 1996.
Honky Tonk Girl, MCA Home Video, 1996.
Still Country, Audium, 2000.
Legends of Country—Loretta Lynn and Patsy Cline, MPI Home Video, 2001.
Coal Miner's Daughter: In Concert, Empire Music Group, 2002.
All Time Greatest Hits, MCA, 2002.
Van Lear Rose, Interscope, 2004.

Sources

Books

Lynn, Loretta, with George Vecsey, *Coal Miner's Daughter,* Regnery, 1976; reissued, Da Capo, 1996.

Periodicals

Atlanta Journal and Constitution, September 10, 2000, p. L1.
Country Music, November-December 1985, p. 40; September-October 1988, p. 30.
Dallas Morning News, June 9, 1997, p. 21A.
Knight-Ridder/Tribune News Service, January 24, 1995.
Ladies Home Journal, June 1984, p. 36.
McCall's, March 1985, p. 88; June 1988, p. 86.
Ms., May 1980, p. 37.
Newsweek, December 4, 1972, p. 67; March 17, 1975, p. 90.
New York Times, October 25, 1972, p. 36.
People, August 13, 1984, p. 38.
Publishers Weekly, December 13, 1999, p. 16.
Reader's Digest, January 1977, p. 83.
Star Tribune (Minneapolis, MN), August 24, 1996.
USA Today, July 21, 1997, p. 5D.

Online

"Loretta Lynn," Internet Movie Database, http://www.imdb.com (January 31, 2004).
Loretta Lynn Official Website, http://www.lorettalynn.com (January 31, 2004).

—Geri Koeppel and Ken Burke

Ziggy Marley

Reggae musician, singer, songwriter

© Jack Vartoogian. Reproduced by permission.

Ziggy Marley is well-known as the son of reggae legend Bob Marley. However, Marley has spent more than 20 years in the music business carving out a name for himself on his own terms. While willing to accept his role as heir to his father's throne as king of reggae, Marley has built on his father's music and life to create a broad eclectic spectrum of reggae sounds that bring in influences from roots rock to hip-hop. Between 1985 and 2000 he released ten albums with three of his siblings, known as the Melody Makers. In 2003, after a decade of falling sales and declining public interest in his music, Marley released his first solo album, *Dragonfly,* which sparked renewed critical attention and praise, with particular notice given to his hit single, "True to Myself."

David Marley was born on October 17, 1968, in Trenchtown, a poor section of Kingston, Jamaica, the oldest son of reggae legend Bob Marley and Rita (Anderson) Marley. Despite his humble beginnings, Marley's life was soon transformed by his father's growing fame. The senior Marley soon moved his family away from the tough Trenchtown streets, but could not entirely shield them from the violence that permeated all of Jamaica during the 1960s and 1970s. Popular around the world, in Jamaica Bob Marley's status neared mystical proportions. He was revered as a poet and a prophet, which was cause for concern among the island's radical political factions. On December 3, 1976, both Bob and Rita Marley were seriously wounded in an assassination attempt.

Banned by his parents from the recording studio during his youngest years, Marley, who was given the nickname Ziggy by his father, grew up playing soccer and fishing in Jamaica. When his father's music business brought the family to the United States, Marley spent several years living and going to elementary school in Wilmington, Delaware. His father taught him to play drums and guitar, and at the age of ten, back in Jamaica, Marley began sitting in on sessions with the Wailers, his father's background group, which included his mother Rita, also an accomplished singer.

Recorded With His Father

When Marley was 11 years old, his father was diagnosed with untreatable cancer. After spending time in the United States attempting to fight the disease, the senior Marley eventually returned to Jamaica to live out his final days. He died in 1981 at the age of 36; Ziggy was 12 years old. In 1979, knowing his death was imminent, Bob called Ziggy into the studio to record a children's song he had written in 1975. "Children Playing in the Streets" was a protest song that dealt with the terrible conditions of poverty under which most of Jamaica's children were raised. Ziggy took lead vocals on the track, with background vocals provided by his older half-sister Sharon (Rita's oldest daughter, adopted by Bob), his younger brother Stephen, and his older sister

For the Record . . .

Born David Marley on October 17, 1968, in Kingston, Jamaica; son of Robert Nesta (Bob) and Alpharita Constantia (Anderson) Marley

Recorded first song with father Bob Marley, "Children Playing in the Streets," 1979; founded the Melody Makers with his siblings, c. 1979; with the Melody Makers, released *Play the Game Right,* 1985; released albums with the Melody Makers, 1980-90s; released solo debut, *Dragonfly,* 2003; voice actor, *Shark Tale,* 2004.

Awards: Grammy Award, Best Reggae Recording for *Conscious Party* (with the Melody Makers), 1988; Grammy Award, Best Reggae Recording for *One Bright Day* (with the Melody Makers), 1989; Grammy Award, Best Reggae Album for *Fallen is Babylon* (with the Melody Makers), 1997.

Addresses: *Management*—Bob Marley Music Inc., 632 Broadway, Ste. 901, New York, NY 10010. *Website*—Ziggy Marley Official Website: http://www.ziggymarley.com.

Cedella. The proceeds from the single were donated to the United Nations Children's Fund. Later Marley recalled the studio session in an interview on the *Relix* website: "I remember it was like a free-for-all. We were just like children expressing. We weren't singing in key. We just sung. We were free and whatever notes came out it was okay. It wasn't even like a big deal. We just went there to sing and we just sing."

Formed The Melody Makers

The four Marley children, who became known as the Melody Makers, began performing at special functions, including their father's state funeral in 1981. Marley began to write songs for the Melody Makers, and in 1985 the group released their first album, *Play the Game Right.* The album was formed around the reggae sound of their father and included the single "Children Playing in the Streets." Along with the title track, other cuts included "Reggae is Now," "What a Plot," and "Naah Leggo." Although the album received mostly positive reviews and attention, album sales were not impressive. Just 17 years old at the time of the album's release, Marley was still finding his place in the music world, dealing with both the privileges and problems of being heir apparent to the vacated throne of the king of reggae. Marley's strikingly similar physical appearance

to his father fueled comparisons and heightened expectations.

Although Marley's lyrics were socially conscious, and many of his songs were written in the political protest vein of his father's music, the Melody Makers were marketed as another teenage kiddie band. Following up their debut album with the release of *Hey World!* in 1986 under the EMI America label, the group once again experienced the disappointment of poor marketing by the record label. Although the album once again earned positive reviews, sales lagged. When EMI pressured Marley to abandon his siblings for a solo career, Marley passionately defended the cohesiveness of the Melody Makers and his complete commitment to performing with his family. Rita, who served as her children's manager, abandoned EMI to sign a deal with the Virgin label, which promised to keep the Melody Makers intact.

The Melody Makers' third album was produced by husband-and-wife team Chris Frantz and Tina Weymouth of the group Talking Heads. *Conscious Party,* released in 1989, became the Melody Makers' breakthrough album, winning a Grammy Award for Best Reggae Recording. The album featured an eclectic mixture of reggae, roots rock, and pop that combined seemingly opposite influences within single tracks. For example, the cut "New Love" melds a dance beat with both a ballad setting and rootsy undertones. Other tracks included the upbeat "Have You Ever Been to Hell," and "Lee and Molly," a roots rock tune about love gone terribly wrong. The album included contributions from some of Jamaica's best-known reggae artists, along with appearances by Keith Richards of the Rolling Stones, Jerry Harrison of the Talking Heads, the Ethiopian band Dalbol, and the cast of the Broadway musical *Sarafina!* For Marley, *Conscious Party* became the proving ground for his own talent and charisma. Previously listened to primarily as Bob Marley's son, *Conscious Party* gave Ziggy a voice all his own.

Matured as Songwriter

The Melody Makers released three more albums on the Virgin label: *One Bright Day, Jahmekya,* and *Joy and Blue. One Bright Day* followed closely on the heels of *Conscious Party* in 1989. As with most of the Melody Makers' albums, Marley was the featured songwriter. He continued to mature as a songwriter, and *One Bright Day* features songs that are uplifting and optimistic without edging over into the preachy and pretentious. According to Jose F. Promis, who reviewed the album for *All Music Guide,* "There is not a single dud on this thoroughly engaging set, which helped cement Ziggy Marley and the Melody Makers as first-rate artists in their own right." *Conscious Party* and *One Bright Day* popularized Marley and the Melody Makers' reggae tunes among the urban crowds in both New York and California.

In the decade that followed Bob Marley's death, Jamaican music turned from reggae to dancehall music, which became very popular among younger Jamaicans. Released in 1991, *Jahmekya* ventured in new directions that reached out to the new hip-hop element with its digitized beats, while continuing to incorporate meaningful lyrics. Stephen, the youngest member of the Melody Makers, took a stronger lead on *Jahmekya,* authoring or co-authoring a number of the tracks. Although Marley himself was beginning to lean toward the more mature sounds of the urban rock scene in the United States, he fully supported the new directions explored by the group on *Jahmekya*. According to *Billboard,* Marley said, "I wanted to change everything with this album. I just wanted it to be different. When we were recording, I would say, 'That sounds too much like me, let's try something new.' I wanted to … stir it up." The album was subsequently nominated for a Grammy Award.

Joy and Blue, released in 1993 when Marley was 25 years old, once again took the group in new directions, dominated by more soulful and personal lyrics. The Melody Makers stepped away from the influence of the Jamaican dancehalls and softened their approach to their roots rock past, bringing to life some of their best lyrics to date. "Mama" is a tribute to Rita Marley, who continued to serve as her children's manager and occasional background vocalist, and the group's soulful cover of "There She Goes" honors their legendary father. Despite slower sales than previous releases, *Joy and Blue* once again proved the eclectic appeal of the Melody Makers and their ability to alter their music as they matured.

Returned to Roots

Disturbed by the slow sales of their previous two albums and unhappy with the publicity efforts of Virgin, in 1995 the Melody Makers switched to the Elektra label to release their seventh album. *Free Like We Want 2 B* looked back to the reggae-dominated beats of *Conscious Party* and *One Bright Day*. The title track "Free Like We Want 2 B" is something of a rebellious song, at least indirectly aimed at shrugging off years of being compared to their father. When asked by the *Michigan Chronicle* yet one more time about living in his father's shadow, Marley responded: "The thing is that it is not my intention to come out of any shadow. My intention is only to make music.… I don't know what they [the public] expect of me. A lot of people expect not what they are getting. The song 'Free Like We Want 2 B' is about becoming a slave to no one."

The album, which introduced small changes in the way of style, provided some sharper-edged political songs, more in line with the protest songs of their father. "Hand to Mouth" addressed the exploitation of the Jamaican worker and the existence of many hungry children in Jamaica. "G7," another politically loaded song, focuses on the exploitation by the seven major world powers who play god and king to the rest of the world.

Marley and the Melody Makers released three more albums under the Elektra label: *Fallen is Babylon, The Spirit of Music,* and *Ziggy Marley and the Melody Makers Live, Vol. 1*. Experiencing declining popularity during the 1990s after peaking in the late 1980s, the Melody Makers were rewarded in 1997 with a Grammy Award for *Fallen is Babylon*. Once again incorporating elements of roots rock, reggae, hip-hop, blues, and even rap, the Melody Makers offered something for everyone on *Fallen is Babylon*. The most popular single to be pulled from the album was the reggae version of Curtis Mayfield's "People Get Ready."

In 1999 Marley, now 31 years old, produced his tenth album, *The Spirit of Music*. Picking up where *Fallen is Babylon* left off, Marley and his siblings fully returned to their father's reggae roots. Covering two of their father's songs, "All Day All Night" and "High Tide or Low Tide," the group filled out the album with pure reggae-driven songs that emphasized faith, love, and harmony. Tracks include "Keep My Faith," "We are One," "Beautiful Day," "Won't Let You Down," and "Jah Will Be Done." However, despite putting out an album referred to by Rosalind Cummings-Yeates in *All Music Guide* as a "must-have for even casual reggae fans," *The Spirit of Music* did not fare well in stores.

Released Solo Album

Despite having left Virgin Records for Elektra in hopes of boosting sales, Marley and the Melody Makers continued to experience declining popularity throughout the 1990s. By 2000 Marley was showing signs of frustration with the music world and was looking for new venues for his creative energies. "The music is there, the message is there," he told the *Los Angeles Sentinel*. "My father say it, me say it; how much more can I say?" Although Elektra released *Ziggy Marley and the Melody Makers Live, Vol. 1,* a compilation of the group's greatest hits, Marley was clearly unhappy with the support he was receiving from the record company. He publicly blamed the record business for pushing flash-in-the-pan artists who had instant fan appeal but no substance to their work, while abandoning artists and groups such as himself and the Melody Makers.

In 2003 Marley released his first single album, *Dragonfly*. This album shelved traditional reggae to depend much more heavily on rock and world-music themes. Although the songs were written in Jamaica, Marley recorded the album in California and Florida, with guest appearances by Flea and John Frusciante from the Red Hot Chili Peppers and Chris Kilmore and Michael Einziger from Incubus. After 18 years with the Melody Makers, Marley's crossover to become a solo artist garnered widespread media attention; however, the 34-year-old Marley has insisted that the Melody

Makers are not defunct, but rather on a break while each member pursues individual interests and projects. No timetable has been set for the group's return to the studio.

With the cut "True to Myself" receiving significant radio air play, Marley took advantage of his increasing exposure in order to step out in new directions. He served as narrator for the film *Life and Debt,* a documentary that examines the social and economic problems of Jamaica, in which he argues that the country's excessive debt load dims any hope for significant recovery. Marley has also worked with the family's Jamaican record label, Ghetto Youths United, producing many of the studio's artists. In 2003 he became involved with DreamWork's animated feature *Shark Tale,* due in theaters in 2004. In this underwater mob film, starring the voices of Robert DeNiro, Angelina Jolie, Will Smith, and Renée Zellweger, Marley lends his thick Jamaican accent to the character of "Ernie," alongside cohort Doug E. Doug as "Bernie." Marley has also confirmed rumors that in the future he may star in a stage production about his father's life.

Selected discography

With the Melody Makers

Play the Game Right, Capitol, 1985.
Hey World!, EMI, 1986.
Conscious Party, Virgin, 1989.
One Bright Day, Virgin, 1989.
Jahmekya, Virgin, 1991.
Joy and Blues, Virgin, 1993.
Free Like We Want 2 Be, Elektra, 1995.
Fallen Is Babylon, Elektra, 1997.
The Spirit of Music, Elektra/Asylum, 1999.
Ziggy Marley & the Melody Makers Live, Vol. 1, Elektra, 2000.

Solo

Dragonfly, Private Music, 2003.

Sources

Periodicals

Billboard, June 1, 1991, p. 32; June 3, 1995, p. 9; May 10, 2003, p. 41.
Caribbean Today, May 31, 2003, p. 16.
Entertainment Weekly, July 21, 1995, p. 65.
Essence, May 2003, p. 128.
Guitar Player, January 2000, p. 25.
Institutional Investor, May 2002, p. 8.
Interview, January 1995, p. 88.
Los Angeles Sentinel, July 19, 2000, p. B6.
Michigan Chronicle, March 12, 1996, p. 1-D.
People Weekly, August 23, 1999, p. 45; May 5, 2003, p. 43.
Sacramento Observer, June 30, 1993, p. E9.
Time, July 19, 1999, p. 81.
Washington Post, June 6, 2003, p. WE08.

Online

"Son of a Bob," *Pulse Weekly,* http://www.pulseweekly.com (August 4, 2003).
"Ziggy Marley," *All Music Guide,* http://www.allmusic.com (August 4, 2003).
"Ziggy Marley," *Relix,* http://www.relix.com/marley (August 4, 2003).
"Ziggy Marley," *RollingStone.com,* http://www.rollingstone.com (August 4, 2003).
"Ziggy Marley: He Talks to Trees," VH1, http://www.vh1.com (May 29, 2003).
Ziggy Marley Official Website, http://www.ziggymarley.com (August 4, 2003).

—Kari Bethel

Mediaeval Baebes

Vocal group

Mediaeval Baebes is an all-female ensemble from the United Kingdom, known in the international media as much for how they dress as for their music. The group originated on a lark and grew quickly, as friends invited friends to sing with the ensemble. Soon after recording a demo, Mediaeval Baebes was signed to the Virgin label, where the group became the fastest-selling act on the label, second only to the Spice Girls. Their vocal musical style, steeped in ancient traditions, has topped the charts.

The group was originally founded by Katharine Blake and Dorothy Carter in 1996 as an a cappella vocal group. Blake, a British classically trained musician who has worked with Michael Nyman and Nick Cave among others, said she founded the Mediaeval Baebes "just for fun." Her idea was to gather women friends to sing a few medieval songs at informal gatherings. While traveling in Germany she met Carter, who played hurdy-gurdy and dulcimer, and who eventually composed music for the group.

Carter's talent for playing hurdy-gurdy, zither, and dulcimer inspired Blake to begin exploring ancient music, and she recruited other friends to join in the project. "Twelve was as many people as you could fit into Katharine's sitting-room," group member Ruth Galloway told the *Independent* in a 1998 interview. When the group was formed in 1996, there were 12 members plus Carter. In addition to Blake and Carter, there were Teresa Casella, who was in the band Miranda Sex Garden with Blake; Audrey Evans; comic writer Marie Findley; Nichole Frobusch; and Ruth Galloway. Other members included Karen Lupton; Claire Ravel; Australian native Cylindra Sapphire; Carmen Schneider; Nichole Sleet; and New Zealander Rachel Van Asch. Members held various day jobs, from actor to computer programmer to clothing and jewelry designer.

Of the group, few had had formal music training, although four of the members were able to read music. Blake, who had attended Purcell School of Music, began serving as the group's musical director. Her selections typically included both religious and secular music. She also composed music for the group based on medieval texts and poems. "The approach is very spirited, as opposed to the emphasis being on perfection," said Blake in *Interview.* "We sound like real people because we are." Costumes and theatrical fantasy also became a part of the Baebes persona. Blake told John Nelson in a National Public Radio (NPR) interview, that "a medieval babe is someone that dresses up in very silly costumes with lots of silly headdresses and sings in about eight or nine different medieval languages. ... We're very clever."

The band was signed by Virgin Records a few weeks after recording its first demo. Within months of its 1997 release in the United Kingdom, *Salva Nos* had sold more than 60,000 copies and stayed at the second position on the charts for months. In a February 1998 feature, *U.S. News & World Report* called the group "the latest—and most brazen—effort to give classical music a hipper image and a wider audience. ... But *Salva Nos* could become the first classical hit to rely mainly on inspired amateurism and pop marketing." Indeed, much of the press compared the group to the manufactured girl pop of The Spice Girls. Blake told *Interview,* "We're signed to the same record label and we're sexy ladies who sing. But that's where the similarities end. We're into fantasy, not getting our faces on crisps packets." Group member Van Asch told *Billboard* that such comparisons were "a horrible piece of sexist nonsense."

The group's music continued to be popular, particularly in the United Kingdom. Van Asch told *Billboard* that she attributes this to jaded ears. "My analogy is that listening to the music is like reading a fairy story. ...Your mind gets taken to a special otherworldly place—a strange place of serenity, magic, and beauty. Certainly in England people are jaded with the same kind of regurgitated Britpop fusion spewing out over the years. But this music is very uplifting and serene and tranquil." *Worldes Blysse,* released in 1998, sold more than 250,000 copies worldwide. It went immediately to top the classical music charts in the United Kingdom, debuting at number one. The success prompted invitations for the group to perform at the 1998 Glastonbury Festival and on the 1999 Lilith Fair tour.

Stephen Pedersen wrote in the *Halifax Herald,* "In spite of the drooling-at-the-mouth publicity, the Baebes are no mediaeval Spice Girls. They sing beautifully, with fresh, sweet voices, performing with elegance and an air of girlish innocence, a mostly 14th-century repertoire of church motets. These are augmented by original settings of middle English poetry from the time of Chaucer, composed by leader Katherine Blake. … Her melodies are haunting, eerily true to the 14th-century style, as are her arrangements in which simple vocal lines are harmonized in fourths, fifths, thirds and sixths, all simple intervals that lend themselves to purity of intonation and tone."

The Baebes began to note that they had a wide base of fans—from pop music aficionados to lovers of goth-rock, and even the club crowd. Several unofficial re-mixes of Baebes songs were reportedly being played in United Kingdom dance clubs in the late 1990s. The next Mediaeval Baebes project, *Undrentide,* was produced in 2000 by John Cale, best known as a member of Velvet Underground. Three members left the group that year—Frobusch, Lupton, and Sleet—and Schneider left in 2002, along with Galloway, who exited with the understanding she might make occasional appearances with the group. Trevor Sharpe, a more recent group member, also left that year. The group released *The Rose* in 2002.

By 2002 the group was singing in a wider variety of rustic dialects, including Mediaeval Welsh and Russian. Their approach had evolved into "taking what we want from the past and making it new," according to Blake in the NPR interview. Mediaeval Baebes was now an eight-vocalist group. During this period they also added percussionist Vince Johnson and Stephen Yates, a classical guitarist who was widely recognized for his work by such publications as *Guitarist Magazine.*

The group mourned the death of Dorothy Carter in 2003. "Dorothy was unique, truly and utterly unique," wrote Findley in a tribute on the group's website. "I was always so impressed that she could do things I suspected I would grow too sensible to do. She was growing old disgracefully and I was proud of her. … She had modesty so deeply ingrained that she hated to take the praise she so rightly deserved." In the fall of 2003, Mediaeval Baebes released *Mistletoe and Wine.* It was their first holiday-themed project, the second produced by Cale, their fifth for Nettwerk America. Among the traditional songs covered by the group were "Greensleeves," "Carol of the Bells," and "Scarborough Fair." They also added a new Baebe, Melanie "Maple Bee" Garside, in December of 2003.

Selected discography

Salva Nos, Virgin, 1998; Nettwerk, 1998.
Worldes Blysse, Virgin, 1998; Nettwerk, 1999.
Undrentide, BMG Classics, 2000; Nettwerk, 2000.
The Rose, Nettwerk, 2002.
Mistletoe and Wine: A Seasonal Collection, Nettwerk, 2003.

Sources

Periodicals

Billboard, August 8, 1998.
Birmingham Post (England), April 18, 2001.
Daily Telegraph, November 20, 1997.
Entertainment Weekly, September 18, 1998.
Halifax Herald (Nova Scotia), December 3, 1998.
Independent, April 18, 1998; October 17, 1998.
Interview, January 1998.
New Statesman, May 20, 2002.
Time International, January 26, 1998.
U.S. News & World Report, February 9, 1998.

Online

"Mediaeval Baebes," *All Music Guide,* http://www.allmusic. com/ (January 17, 2004).
"Mediaeval Baebes," Nettwerk Records, http://www.nett werklabel.com/bio.jsp?artist_id=645 (January 17, 2004).
Mediaeval Babes Official Website, http://www.mediaeval baebes.com (January 17, 2004).

Additional information was obtained from a National Public Radio interview, "Katharine Blake and Rachel Van Asch discuss their musical group Mediaeval Baebes and medieval music," *Weekend Edition,* May 19, 2002.

—*Linda Dailey Paulson*

Molotov

Heavy metal group

The Mexican rap-metal quartet Molotov, like the bomb of the same name, burst onto the Spanish-language rock scene in the mid-1990s with an explosive mix of hard-driving rock, rapid-fire rap, funk, and traditional Mexican influences, combined with controversial, politicized Spanish, English, and "Spanglish" lyrics that targeted corruption and social injustice. Embraced by young Mexicans at a time of political upheaval, the Mexican establishment denounced their music in *Business Week,* as "harmful and offensive trash." The band was also maligned by detractors abroad—Spanish gay groups accused the band of homophobia, and the government of El Salvador barred Molotov's entry into the country on the pretext, quoted by the EFE News Service, that its presence could prove *"inadecuado 'para la salud mental' de los salvadoreños"* (harmful to the mental health of the Salvadoran population).

The band's rise to commercial fame was explosive, moving from the Mexico City underground to a recording contract little more than a year after its inception in September of 1995. Molotov started as a short-lived quartet: Micky "Huidos" Huidobro, Tito Fuentes, Iván Jared (aka La Quesadillera, who left the group on October 10, 1995), and Javier de la Cueva (who left on February 16, 1995). By February of 1996, when the band started playing Mexico City dives, Molotov had established its current lineup: Huidobro, Fuentes, Paco Ayala, Randy "el gringo loco" Ebright, an American immigrant and son of a DEA agent who'd moved to Mexico as a teenager.

The band quickly developed a core audience on the Mexico City underground club circuit, and were soon invited to open for bigger-name groups like the Spanish rock band Heroes del Silencio and Mexican acts like La Lupita and La Cuca. Their big break, however, came at a concert opening for the Argentine pop group Illya Kuryaki and the Valderramas, where representatives from Universal Music Latino saw them and offered them a contract. The group began recording in February of 1997.

Molotov's debut album, *¿Donde Jugarán las Niñas?* (Where will the girls play?) that same year brought instant controversy. Sexually uninhibited and politically scathing, the album was banned by Mexican radio stations and record stores. The band sold its records on the streets, eventually catching the attention of both the public and critics. The band's politicized lyrics found a sympathetic reception at a politically charged time in Mexican history; the southern state of Chiapas had seen the recent uprising of the Zapatista National Liberation Army (EZLN) and millions were captivated by its charismatic spokesman, Subcomandante Marcos. Antipathy toward the Institutional Revolutionary Party (PRI), which had ruled Mexico for more than 70 years, was growing. "Corruption is a fact of life, and so is disillusionment," stated *Business Week* in an article about the band and its political significance. With songs like "Gimme tha Power" and "Voto Latino" (Latin vote) Molotov went for the jugular and attacked the government directly. Despite attempts to silence them, Molotov sold more than 400,000 albums in Mexico and quickly moved into the mainstream.

In 1998 the album earned a Grammy nomination for Best Latin Rock-Alternative Performance, fitting nicely in a new American niche for Spanish-language rock groups, rock en español. New York radio personality Howard Stern began using Molotov's music on his program, and American teens shouted Spanish expletives along with the band at Molotov concerts. By the end of 1998, the album had sold more than 800,000 units worldwide, going platinum in Chile and the United States, and double platinum in Spain. Molotov's Spanish concerts were picketed by gay groups protesting one of the songs on the album, *Puto* which they claimed was homophobic (a charge the band denied). That same year, the band released a remix collection called *Molomix,* which it promoted in the United States.

In 1999 the group released an album of entirely new material. *Apocalyps**t,* produced by Mario Caldato, Jr., who'd also worked with the Beastie Boys. Despite such high-profile help, the album failed to resonate with fans and enjoyed only moderate success. The Molotovs toured the United States as part of the Vans Warped Tour in 1999 and the Watcha Tour, which featured Latin American alternative rock bands, in 2001. The group kept a low profile during the next couple of years, but did collaborate on projects such as a Spanish-language tribute to Queen, an homage to the Mexican

For the Record . . .

Members include **Paco Ayala**, bass, vocals; **Javier de la Cueva** (left group, 1995); **Randy Ebright**, drums, vocals; **Tito Fuentes**, guitar, vocals; **Micky Huidobro**, bass, vocals; **Iván Fuentes** (left group, 1995).

Group formed in Mexico City, Mexico, 1995; released debut album *¿Donde Jugarán las Niñas?*, 1997; released *Molomix*, 1998; released *Apocalyps**t*, 1999; released *Dance and Dense Denso*, 2003.

Awards: MTV Latin Awards, Video of the Year, Best Group or Duo, Alternative Artist, and Best Mexican Artist, 2003; Latin Grammy Award, Best Video, 2003.

Addresses: *Record company*—Universal Music Latino, 1425 Collins Ave., Miami Beach, FL 33139, phone: (305) 604-1300. *Website*—Molotov Official Website: http://www.proteuserp.com/molotov.

band Los Tigres del Norte, and the soundtrack for the Mexican film *Y tu mamá también.*

In 2003 Molotov once again grabbed attention on both sides of the border with the album *Dance & Dense Denso* which, in Spanish can roughly translate to "dance and hit yourselves good." According to the *Houston Chronicle,* "the mosh pit reference is appropriate because the group's searing guitar riffs, pounding drums and loud vocals are as aggressive as ever. But with highhat beats and electric-piano touches, Molotov can instigate hip-shaking as well as head-banging."

The controversial song "Frijolero" ("beaner," a derogatory term for Mexicans) unleashed a cross-border volley of racial epithets at both Mexicans and gringos. The *Village Voice* called the track "a languid, Old West–inspired polka-cumbia" that featured Ayala rapping in Spanish with an affected American accent and Ebright according to the *Houston Chronicle,* "[drawling] his rhymes like a rapping Harry Connick Jr." Interestingly, the video that ran on MTV en Español censored the Spanish-language expletives, but let those in English stand. The video, which also attacked American foreign policy, portrayed falling bombs and Presidents George W. Bush and Vicente Fox dancing with the devil, but the attack wasn't personal, Ayala insisted to *El Universal.* "No somos anti yankis, somos anti ideología del presidente George W. Bush. La gente en-

tendió bien allí el tema del 'Frijolero.'" (We're not anti-Yankee, we're just against the ideology of President George W. Bush. The people up there knew what 'Frijolero' was all about.) [Translation by the author.]

Their songs have a lighter side, too, Huidobro told *La Prensa San Diego.* "We don't want to write solely about social issues or only about politics, because we'd then become bored with ourselves. We also like to drink, we like girls, so we also write songs about those topics." The song "Changuich a la chichona," for example, compares snack foods and female anatomy.

In 2003, after touring Europe and the United States, the band won four MTV Latin Awards: Video of the Year, Best Group or Duo, Alternative Artist, and Best Mexican Artist, and a Latin Grammy Best Video award for "Frijolero."

Selected discography

¿Donde Jugarán las Niñas?, Universal/Surco, 1997.
Molomix, Universal Music Latino, 1998.
Apocalyps**t, Universal Music Latino, 1999.
Dance and Dense Denso, Surco/Universal Music Latino, 2003.

Sources

Periodicals

Business Week, June 26, 2000.
EFE News Services, October 7, 2003.
El Nuevo Herald, September 25, 2003.
La Prensa San Diego, March 28, 2003.
Village Voice, April 23–29, 2003.

Online

"Molotov," *All Music Guide,* http://www.allmusic.com (February 4, 2004).
"Molotov Explode at MTV Latin Music Awards," MTV, http://www.mtv.com/news/articles/1479931/10242003/molotov.jhtml?headlines=true (February 5, 2004).
Molotov Official Website, http://www.proteuserp.com/molotov/ (February 4, 2004).
"Molotov's 'Dance' Incendiary, with No Apologies," *Houston Chronicle,* http://www.chron.com/cs/CDA/story.hts/features/burr/ (February 17, 2004).
"Rechaza Molotov ser 'antiyanki,'" El Universal, http://www.eluniversal.com.mx/pls/impreso/noticia.html?id_nota=146497&tabla=notas (February 7, 2004).
Terra Watcha Tour, http://www.terra.com/especiales/watchatour/molotov/biografia.htm (February 7, 2004).

Additional information was provided by Universal Mexico, January 28, 2004.

—Brett Allen King

Momus

Singer, songwriter

Though not widely known in the pop world, Momus is one of underground music's most controversial and influential provocateurs. From his early days with the Happy Family in the 1980s through his digital troubadour incarnations of the 2000s, Nicholas Currie has lent his style to Pulp, Beck, the Divine Comedy, and others while remaining fiercely political and uncompromising in his artistic vision.

Currie was born on February 11, 1960, in Paisley, Scotland, one of three children born to scholarly parents. His father was an academic that constantly moved the family around the world and by the time Nicholas was 13, he had already lived in Scotland, Greece, and Canada. From a young age, Currie was exposed to music, often in an experimental capacity. For his father's doctoral studies on how children acquire language, the young Nicholas was recorded improvising songs, stories, and other bits of linguistic performance. Though he probably thought little of it at the time, Currie later considered these his first recordings and included fragments of them on in his contentious 1998 LP *Little Red Songbook.*

His intentional (and official) first recordings came during his college years, with the Edinburgh post-punk outfit the Happy Family. Currie temporarily dropped his studies at the University of Aberdeen to form the band with former members of Josef K. Together they recorded the *Puritans* EP and 1982's *Man on Your Street* for London's then-fledgling 4AD label. When the Happy Family parted company later that year, Currie returned to the university to complete his masters degree in English literature—an indication of the direction his music would take.

The Birth of Momus

After graduating, Currie moved to London and reinvented himself as Momus, taking his moniker from the Greek god of blame, ridicule, and criticism. He expanded the political edge he'd honed with the Happy Family and began to delve into more controversial subjects. Despite the praise it earned, his first solo release for él Records, 1986's *Circus Maximus,* wasn't a financial success. It did, however, give Currie a sense of direction, and his critics a taste of the often misogynistic and sexually perverse subject matter he'd tackle in years to come.

In 1987 Momus switched labels, signing with Alan McGee's budding Creation Records—later to be the label of choice for British pop—and released *Poison Boyfriend.* The record dealt with themes that would recur in Momus' works: teen angst, bemusement, and sexual transgression. Currie got his first taste of the rock 'n' roll lifestyle when he toured the album through Germany with Primal Scream, but after encountering typical on-the-road hijinks he realized that he wasn't much of a party animal. The following year he went on the road with Felt and McGee's band, Biff Band Pow, through other parts of Europe.

Upon his return he recorded the Serge Gainsbourg and Jacques Brel–influenced *Tender Pervert,* an homage to sexual perversity intended to defend the rights of the oft-maligned gay community and to destigmatize people afflicted by AIDS. *Tender Pervert* was, according to an audio interview with Currie, "My statement, my ultimate album in the sense of laying out the Momus master plan." Reviewing the album in the *New Musical Express* (*NME*), Len Brown called Momus "[o]ne of the most provocative, intelligent songwriters around; someone who'll tackle sexuality, (im)morality, and the sins of the world with almost embarrassing sincerity."

A voracious consumer of music and art, Currie was interested in all sorts of electronic sounds, specifically acid house and Detroit techno. These were quite evident on his next record, 1989's *Don't Stop the Night,* a biting critique of the upper classes' penchant for power abuse, as well as other topics that most pop artists wouldn't touch, let alone frame in synthy dance music. On this album Momus really began to have fun criticizing popular music, even while wholly embracing it. His ironic "Hairstyle of the Devil" ended up in the number-two spot of the indie charts.

Momus released his first compilation, *Monsters of Love: Singles 1985–90,* a compilation of his early EP songs and a few tracks from *Poison Boyfriend* in 1990. The following year he produced *Hippopotamomus—*

the first of his major controversies. On the album, which was an homage to the notorious French singer-composer Serge Gainsbourg, Momus stretched the envelope even further, as *All Music Guide* noted, billing it as "a record about sex for children." The album tracks reflect Momus' usual scathing wit: "Michelin Man," for example, made a loose comparison between Michelin Tires' mascot and a blow-up doll, which provoked a lawsuit from the company. Settling out of court, Momus was forced to destroy all unsold copies of the album. Later releases appeared with an altered cover graphic and had the offending track deleted. Others found *Hippopotamomus* hard to swallow as well. "Momus is a bit like a mussel: it tastes good when swallowed whole, but examine it too closely and it looks as disgusting as a shriveled, unidentifiable piece of sexual organ. Spit it out immediately," commented Betty Page in *New Musical Express,* assigning the record a zero-out-of-ten review.

Currie followed *Hippopotamomus* with a tour of Japan, where he had a growing fan base, and a pair of albums. To satisfy contractual obligations with Creation, he released *Voyager,* an acid house–inflected clubby affair. To Richmond Records, though, he gave some less dance-oriented cabaret songs, masked as unreleased tracks from a live session recorded in 1910. Those

songs culminated in *Ultraconformist: Live Whilst out of Fashion,* a spellbinding, Kurt Weill–inspired portrait of London's seedy underbelly.

In 1993 Currie returned to Japan for a concert series and to produce an album for the artist nOrikO, who had adopted her stage name the Poison Girlfriend as a tribute to Momus. His shows, promoted with the help of Keigo Oyamada (a.k.a. Cornelius), were sell-out successes. Back in London, though, Currie had begun a relationship with 16-year-old Shazna Nessa, the daughter of a Bangladesh-born businessman. When her father found out about them he sent Nessa off to Bangladesh for an arranged marriage. After much heartache and the *Timelord* record—a message to Nessa like David Bowie's *The Man Who Fell to Earth*—Currie helped her escape back to Britain. There he and Nessa were married, but they soon moved to Paris to keep out of the public eye. As usual, the British press had a fun time with Currie, though this time it had little to do with his music.

American Exposure

Currie's three-year stay in Paris yielded a few hits with Japanese singer Kahimi Karie, and three new albums—*I Am a Kitten: Kahimi Karie Sings Momus in Paris, Philosophy of Momus,* and *Slender Sherbet.* These brought Currie to the attention of Matthew Jacobson, an American who brought Currie overseas to play the United States for the first time to a sold-out crowd in New York City.

Momus signed with Jacobson's young Le Grand Magistery label and released the *20 Vodka Jellies* collection as a primer for potential American fans. Ian Fortman, reviewing the record in the *New Musical Express,* said, "Homoeroticism, inflatable dolls, strychnine and unrequited love are all dealt with, in supremely literate style, so slip into your silk smoking jacket and enter the magnificent Momus mindscape of highballs, harems, and hookahs."

By 1997 Currie had moved back to London to begin working on new projects, among them cowriting and producing records for Jacques and Laila France. He had broken up with Nessa, but the two remained close friends. That same year he released *Ping Pong,* a return to form for the shape-shifting and persona-jumping artist. Peter Robinson of *Time Out* commented, "[H]e writes a scorching tune ... Momus himself may never achieve the success of his impersonators. How depressing."

The following year, Momus toured the States twice with Kahimi Karie. During this time an eye infection caused by a dirty contact lens led to blindness in one eye. (A corneal transplant a year later restored some sight.) The cover of his 1998 album *Little Red Songbook,* and others that followed, showed Momus wearing an eye patch. Recorded in his "analog baroque" style on his new sublabel of the same name, *Little Red Songbook* was a brilliant reinterpretation of classical songwriting twisted through a retro-futuristic lens. Mixing harpsichords, analog synthesizers, and a fondness for powdered wigs, the album became Currie's most controversial record to date.

This time the tempest centered around the track "Walter Carlos," an homage to the pioneering electronic composer who had a sex change operation after the releasing his monumental *Switched-on Bach* album. While Currie intended the song to be a humorous look at what might have happened had Carlos met himself as a woman in a time-travel experiment, Carlos didn't find it amusing. The now-female Wendy Carlos met Momus at one of his New York shows and presented him with a 50-page court document outlining the details of her $22 million defamation suit against him and Le Grand Magistery.

Stars Forever

With legal fees mounting, Currie and Jacobson put their heads together and came up with *Stars Forever,* an album for which Momus created song portraits for 30 patrons willing to donate $1,000 to help the label's cause. Because of its strange genesis and its lyrical brilliance, *Stars Forever* drew plenty of attention in the press and (after an out-of-court settlement with Carlos), saved the label from bankruptcy. Wendy Mitchell of Salon wrote: "Lesser artists might have taken a more literal approach to portraiture, spewing facts in rhyming couplets. But Momus' subversive streak creates songs that people would never have written about themselves.... The fans didn't get exact representations of themselves. They got something better—a chance to become part of Momus' twisted world."

With the lawsuit behind him, Currie moved to New York's grass roots arts and indie music scene. There he recorded *Folktronic,* another electronic collage of Appalachian folk music and Macintosh-inspired digitalia. He extended the record into a month-long residency at Chelsea's LFL Gallery—a one-man performance/installation called "Folktronia."

After touring stints with Stereo Total and Kreidler and the odd academic speaking engagement, Currie started a new label, American Patchwork, through the Darla distribution company. He also recorded *Travels with a Donkey* with his ex-wife Nessa. He spent the following year in Tokyo indulging his interests in kabuki and other Japanese art forms. After touring the United States with American Patchwork artists Phiiliip, Rroland, the Gongs, and Super Madrigal Brothers, Currie returned to Japan and recorded 2003's *Oskar Tennis Champion,* his answer to microsonic glitchy techno, typically delivered via laptop computers.

Currie then moved to Berlin to begin working on his next collaboration with electronic musician Anne Laplantine. Eschewing irony and critical wit, *Summerisle,* released on American Patchwork in 2004, was a sincere examination of Japanese and Scottish folk music, filtered through Currie's voice and Laplantine's computer.

Selected discography

With the Happy Family

Man on Your Street, 4AD, 1982.
Puritans, 4AD, 1982.

As Momus

Circus Maximus, Acme/él Records, 1986.
Poison Boyfriend, Creation, 1987.
Tender Pervert, Creation, 1988.
Don't Stop the Night, Creation, 1989.
Monsters of Love, Singles 1985–90, Creation, 1990.
Hippopotamomus, Creation, 1991.
Ultraconformist, Richmond, 1992.
Voyager, Creation, 1992.
Timelord, Creation, 1993.
Philosophy of Momus, Cherry Red, 1995.
Slender Sherbet, Cherry Red, 1995.
20 Vodka Jellies, Cherry Red/Le Grand Magistery, 1996.
Ping Pong, Cherry Red/Le Grand Magistery, 1997.
Little Red Songbook (original version), Le Grand Magistery, 1998.
Little Red Songbook (post-lawsuit version), Le Grand Magistery, 1999.
Stars Forever, Le Grand Magistery, 1999.
Folktronic, Analog Baroque, 2001.
Forbidden Software Timemachine: Best of the Creation Years,1987–1993, American Patchwork, 2003.
Oskar Tennis Champion, American Patchwork, 2003.
Summerisle, American Patchwork, 2004.

Sources

Periodicals

New Musical Express, July 16, 1988; July 6, 1991; October 12, 1996.

Online

"Momus," *All Music Guide,* http://www.allmusic.com (February 2, 2004).
Momus Official Website, http://www.imomus.com (February 2, 2004).
"Momus: *Stars Forever,*" Salon, http://www.salon.com (February 4, 2004).

Additional information was obtained from an interview conducted with the artist on January 20, 2004.

—Ken Taylor

Nico

Singer, songwriter

One of pop music's most enigmatic and unclassifiable artists, Nico was almost as famous for her associations as she was for her recordings. She remains best known for her brief tenure as a singer with the Velvet Underground and her appearance in Andy Warhol's films and stage productions during the 1960s. As a young woman, her statuesque beauty and aloof demeanor attracted the interest of fashion designers and film directors. By the last decade of her life, however, she had become a cult figure as notorious for her self-destructive habits as her music. Gifted with an unnervingly deep contralto voice, Nico developed into a singer/songwriter of disturbing power, fashioning a unique, austere gothic sound.

A degree of mystery surrounds Nico's early years, because she went to much effort to conceal her age and origins. According to most sources, she was born Christa Päffgen on October 16, 1938, in Cologne, Germany. (Some sources give 1943 or 1944 as the year of her birth; a number give Budapest, Hungary, as her birthplace.) Her father served in the Nazi armed forces and died during World War II, possibly in a concentration camp. After her father's death, Nico and her mother suffered through the Allied bombing campaign in Cologne, sometimes hiding in the bathtub. Towards the end of the war, they moved to Berlin, where at age 15 Nico began to work as a professional model. Moving to Paris soon after, she became a protégé of fashion designer Coco Chanel. Her elegant, sculpted features and ash-blond hair led to assignments as a cover model for *Vogue* and other magazines. Working extensively across Europe, she took the name Nico in the late 1950s.

In the early 1960s Nico landed a small role in Federico Fellini's film *La Dolce Vita.* Hoping to find further work as an actress, she went to New York, where she studied at Lee Strasberg's Actors' Studio. She also became involved in the world of pop music, pursuing romantic relationships with Rolling Stones guitarist Brian Jones and Bob Dylan. In 1965 she moved to London to launch her career as a singer. Later that year, she released her debut single "I'm Not Saying" (written by Gordon Lightfoot) on the Immediate label. Unfortunately, this midtempo folk-rock tune—featuring future Led Zeppelin leader Jimmy Page on guitar— failed to chart in Britain or anywhere else.

From Cabaret Singer to Velvet Chanteuse

While in England, Nico met Pop Art mastermind Andy Warhol, who encouraged her to return to New York and become part of his "Superstar" circle. By late 1965, she was singing at Manhattan's Blue Angel Lounge. On stage and off, her otherworldly beauty and elusive persona fascinated and baffled admirers. "Nico's eyes seem to guard a great mystery which, hidden in aloofness, they do not want anyone to know exists," wrote Gerald Malanga for the arts publication *Status &*

Diplomat in early 1967. "Whether or not a mystery is there, the eyes with the enigma of their absence from what surrounds them eclipse the perfection of features and form to add great magnetism. It is this magnetism, cool and inviolable, which enhances Nico's identification with the Garbo-Dietrich tradition, which elevates her above the genre of uniform Nordic beauties to the elite of an unapproachable mystique."

In early 1966 Warhol added Nico to the Velvet Underground, an avant-garde rock quartet he managed. Known for their decadent songs and abrasive, feedback-laden sound, the New York-based group took her with some reluctance. "We had been through so many changes as a band, we were just settling down and suddenly Andy throws us this red herring," bassist John Cale recalled to writer David Fricke in the liner notes to the 1995 Velvet Underground CD boxed set *Peel Slowly and See.* "But it worked. Sometimes she would love to be on stage in her white outfit, banging away on a tambourine … But part of her modus operandi was being misunderstood, having this very naïve, beatific view of the universe on one hand, and being very tough and dominant on the other."

In 1966, after touring with the multimedia extravaganza dubbed the Exploding Plastic Inevitable, the band recorded its debut album, *The Velvet Underground & Nico,* which featured three tracks written for Nico by Lou Reed, the group's chief songwriter. Her renditions of "I'll Be Your Mirror" and "Femme Fatale" had a wistful delicacy, while her performance of the harder-edged "All Tomorrow's Parties" projected a Teutonic menace. The album, released in 1967, sold relatively few copies at the time of it's release, but went on to become one of the most influential records in rock music history. A few critics at the time took note, including Richard Goldstein, quoted in the *Chicago Sun-Times,* who said "[Nico] sings 'in perfect mellow ovals, like a cello getting up in the morning.'"

Ultimately, Nico and her Velvet bandmates proved an unstable combination. In early 1967 they parted company and Nico began singing at the Dom, a New York night club. Billed as "the Moon Goddess," she was accompanied by a rotating cast of guitarists, including Reed, Cale, and 17-year-old singer/songwriter Jackson Browne, with whom she had an affair. These performances set the stage for her first solo album, *Chelsea Girl,* released in 1967 by Verve Records. Dressed up in baroque string arrangements, *Chelsea Girl* only hints at the musical path she would follow later. The album's songs were written by Browne ("These Days"), Bob Dylan ("I'll Keep It with Mine"), and Tim Hardin ("Eulogy To Lenny Bruce"), among others. Reed cowrote the title track, which doubled as the theme song for a Warhol film of the same name that chronicled the adventures of Nico and others at New York's infamous Chelsea Hotel. The closing track, "It Was a Pleasure Then," cowritten by Nico, Reed, and Cale, was a bleak poetic narrative with screeching guitar accompaniment.

By the end of the 1960s Nico was in Los Angeles. There she embarked on a torrid but short-lived affair with the Doors' Jim Morrison, who she claimed encouraged her to develop her songwriting skills. In typically unconventional fashion, she began to write and compose on the harmonium (a small pump organ), which added to the eeriness of her vague and ominous lyrics. The songs became *Marble Index,* which Nico recorded with Cale and producer Frazier Mohawk (best known for his work with Buffalo Springfield). The album, released by Elektra in 1969, was called "one of the scariest records ever made" by *The Trouser Press Record Guide.* Drawing upon classical and European folk traditions, Nico's spare, two-chord harmonium melodies are given further atmospheric shadings by Cale's dissonant guitar and viola touches. "Lawns Of Dawn" and "Frozen Warnings" come across as gloomy operatic arias, intoned with a chilly seriousness. Darkly fascinating, *Marble Index* invites comparison with the works of Philip Glass, Steve Reich, and similar minimalist composers in its broodingly repetitive soundscapes.

In 1970 Nico continued her recording partnership with Cale with the release of *Desertshore,* and album similar to *Marble Index* in its obsessively dark mood, but one that also included some new sonic touches, such as the Middle Eastern motifs on the title track. One song, "Le Petit Chevalier," featured Nico's young son Ari on vocals. (Fathered by French actor Alain Delon, he was born in 1963.) Two years later, Nico starred in the underground French film *La Cicatrice Intéreiure,* directed by Philippe Garrel. Her next effort, *June 1, 1974,* a concert with Cale, Roxy Music keyboardist Brian Eno, and singer/songwriter Kevin Ayers was recorded live at London's Rainbow Theater. Her rendition of the Doors song "The End" led to a full-fledged solo album on the Island label, with an expanded studio version of "The End" as its title track. Produced once again by Cale, *The End* leans more towards rock than Nico's previous albums, thanks in part to Eno and Roxy Music guitarist Phil Manzanera. Besides the title song, the album included such disquieting originals as "Secret Side" and "Innocent and Vain." Nico closed the album with "Das Lied der Deutschen" (better known as "Deutschland über alles"), invoking memories of her frightening childhood in Nazi Germany.

Decadence and Decline

During the mid-1970s, Nico became addicted to heroin, sending her into a downward spiral. She resurfaced in 1981 with *Drama of Exile,* an indifferent set of songs and performances. To earn money, she played small clubs in Europe and the States during the early and mid-1980s. Among her backup musicians was keyboardist James Young, who described his experiences in his 1992 memoir *Nico: The End,* a harrowing portrait: "Her features, riven by years of narcotic abuse, bore little trace of the 'icy Germanic beauty' that has been chronicled so meticulously [by Andy Warhol] … The 'dark Teutonic soul' that had once added such a puzzling bitterness to the sickly sweet froth of pop seemed to have become an absurd caricature of nihilism, a genuine emptiness."

Despite (or perhaps because of) her air of aimless decay, Nico became an inspiration to the emerging goth-rock subculture. Punk bands like Siouxsie and the Banshees modeled themselves after her morbid mystique, but Nico benefited little from this interest, scraping by on low-budget tours and albums. Several live albums—including 1983's *Live in Denmark*—documented her ragged shows during this period. She reunited with Cale for a final time on the 1985 Beggars Banquet album *Camera Obscura,* cocredited to the Faction (James Young and percussionist Graham Dids). Its tracks matched Nico's vocals to clattering rhythms and dabs of keyboards to mostly successful effect. Standouts included the stark, yearning "Konig" and a somber reading of the Rogers and Hart standard "My Funny Valentine."

In June of 1988 Nico gave her last performance at the Berlin Planetarium. The following month, she fell from a bicycle while visiting the Spanish island of Ibiza and suffered a fatal cerebral hemorrhage. According to Young, she had been free of heroin addiction for some time, though years of abuse had left weakened her health. She was buried in Berlin on August 16, 1988.

Scattered Nico recordings continued to appear after her death, beginning with *Hanging Gardens,* a mixture of live and studio material, in 1990. A comprehensive survey of her recording career, *Classic Years,* and the critically praised 1995 documentary *Nico Icon* also brought her posthumous attention. Insured lasting fame for her involvement with the Velvet Underground, Nico has also maintained a cult following for her solo recordings. In summing up her bizarre and ultimately tragic life, Richie Unterberger praised Nico in the *All Music Guide* for "pursuing a distinctly individualistic and uncompromising musical career that was uncommercial, but wholly admirable and influential."

Selected discography

(With The Velvet Underground) *The Velvet Underground & Nico,* Polygram, 1967.
Chelsea Girl, Verve, 1967.
Marble Index, Elektra, 1969.
Desertshore, Reprise, 1971.
(with Kevin Ayers, John Cale and Brian Eno) *June 1, 1974,* Island, 1974.
The End, Island, 1974.
Drama Of Exile, Aura, 1981.
Live In Denmark, VU, 1983.
Camera Obscura, Beggars Banquet–PVC, 1985.
Behind the Iron Curtain, Dojo, 1986.
Hanging Gardens, Restless, 1990.
Classic Years, Polygram, 1998.

Sources

Books

Bockris, Victor, and Gerald Malanga, *Up-Tight: The Velvet Underground Story,* Omnibus, 1983.
Erlewine, Michael, Vladimir Bogdanov, Chris Woodstra, and Stephen Thomas Erlewine, editors, *All Music Guide,* Miller Freeman, 1997.
Robbins, Ira A., editor, *The Trouser Press Record Guide,* Collier, 1991.
Young, James, *Nico: The End,* Overlook, 1991.

Periodicals

Los Angeles Times, July 23, 1988, p. 26.
New York Times, January 3, 1996, p. B1.

Online

"Nico," *RollingStone.com,* http://www.rollingstone.com (February 12, 2004).
"The Velvet Underground," *Chicago Sun-Times,* http://www.suntimes.com (February 4, 2004).

—*Barry Alfonso*

Nino Tempo & April Stevens

Pop duo

It is difficult to definitively categorize the music of the brother-sister act of Nino Tempo & April Stevens. Today, their sound might best be described as easy listening, but at the height of their popularity their music was placed in the rock 'n' roll category by the Grammy committee in 1963. The duo achieved popularity on the eve of the so-called British Invasion, which would forever change the soundscape and market for American popular music. It disrupted Tempo and Stevens's careers as well, but they continued, undeterred, to record both as a duo and as solo artists.

Antonio "Nino" and Carol LoTempio were both born in Niagara Falls, New York, to Sam and Anna LoTempio. Their father was a grocer. The siblings were a year apart in age. They had separate entertainment careers in their teens: Tempo as an actor; Stevens as a vocalist. According to *MusicHound Lounge: The Essential Album Guide to Martini Music and Easy Listening,* both careers may have been born from their mother's own inability to have a show business career, thanks to the insistence of her traditional Italian husband. According to the book, Tempo began his career as a child vocalist and actor when his mother "put seven-year-old Nino up to fibbing to Benny Goodman [during an appearance in Buffalo, NY] that he had made a $5 bet that he could sing with the band. Goodman bought it, and Nino brought the house down. Goodman had him come back to do the same bit six more nights." Tempo would later portray a character based on the legendary Goodman, in the classic film *The Glenn Miller Story.* After meeting Goodman, Tempo became interested in playing clarinet. He later switched to tenor saxophone, and also learned to play guitar.

During the 1940s the family moved to California, where Tempo began working in films. He made an uncredited film appearance in *The Story of G.I. Joe* in 1945. His first film credit was for an appearance in *The Red Pony* in 1949. During this time he frequently played in high school dance bands, and then embarked on a career as a session musician, while continuing his acting career.

Stevens began a singing career in her teens, after being discovered while shopping in a record store. The single she was asked to record was just suggestive enough to be refused radio airplay, so young Carol decided to adopt a pseudonym. LoTempio, having already proven too difficult for people to pronounce, had been jettisoned by the family in favor of the snappier "Tempo." She chose her stage name by combining her birth month with a name that she thought sounded sufficiently American: April Stevens.

She recorded several singles for Laurel Records and then Society Records. She made her mark with "I'm in Love Again," which she recorded as the featured vocalist with Henri Rene & His Orchestra in 1951. The record made the top ten charts, as did "Gimme a Little Kiss, Will Ya Huh?," and "And So to Sleep Again." Stevens charted again with "Teach Me Tiger," written by Tempo, late in the decade.

Tempo was busy working as an actor and session musician during this period, most notably for Steve Lawrence and Rosemary Clooney, for whom he also served as a composer and arranger. Tempo also worked with noted producer Phil Spector on many of his hits, as part of the session band that would become known as "The Wrecking Crew." It was during a session he was playing for Bobby Darin in 1963 that Tempo was introduced to Ahmet Ertegun, the co-founder and head of Atlantic Records. During this encounter Tempo mentioned he was considering forming a duo with his sister. Ertegun, a fan of Stevens's "Teach Me Tiger," was intrigued and signed the two artists.

In the early 1960s the siblings were signed to the Atco label. The duo's first three singles were not successful, and Tempo begged Ertegun to release "Deep Purple." Ertegun fought against it because he "considered so bad it was embarrassing," according to William Ruhlmann, writing in *All Music Guide.* "Record buyers disagreed. Issued in the summer of 1963 with the billing switched to Nino Tempo & April Stevens, 'Deep Purple' hit number one in November. It also won the 1963 Grammy Award for Best Rock & Roll Recording." This single would become their biggest hit. It was reportedly recorded in about 15 minutes at the end of a session. That it won a Grammy award for best rock recording of the year "says a lot more about the record was released by the independent pop label White Whale, which has since been associated with Los Angeles bubblegum pop music. The duo continued to record in the 1970s for A&M Records, but with chart success limited primarily to the easy listening charts.

Tempo continued to be busy as a session musician, playing saxophone on recordings by artists including Frank Sinatra and Cher. He also worked with Maynard Ferguson as a member of his band. He had a single solo hit called "Hooked on Young Stuff" in 1979 and also contributed to the soundtrack for *The Idolmaker*, which appeared on charts in December of 1980. Stevens retired in 1979. The pair did record the occasional demo work and Stevens recorded vocals on some of Tempo's solo recordings. He took a decade off from recording until Stevens got him back to work with her own *Carousel Dreams*.

Tempo recorded several solo jazz albums in the 1990s. Tempo's revitalized solo career followed his participation in a memorial service for Nesuhi Ertegun, Atlantic Records' co-founder. He was signed to Atlantic and released *Tenor Saxophone, Nino,* and *Live at Cicada*. For *Sweet and Lovely: The Best of Nino Tempo & April Stevens,* a 1996 Varese Sarabande compilation, the siblings reunited to record a new track. They selected "Why Don't You Do Right?," which had been popularized by Benny Goodman and Peggy Lee. As of 2004, both were reportedly living in Arizona in "semi-retirement," occasionally playing reunion shows.

Grammys' questionable grasp of rock than the single, which was at least as much adult pop as rock," according to Richie Unterberger writing in the *All Music Guide*.

"Most of the duo's early and mid-1960s hits were updates of popular standards like 'Deep Purple,' 'Whispering,' 'Stardust,' and 'Tea for Two,'" wrote Unterberger. "They weren't quite in the easy-listening mainstream, though, due to the pop/rock feel of most of their arrangements, and Stevens's breathy, sensual style. ... As pop performers with a bent for Tin Pin Alley material ... [they were] kind of stuck between generations, especially two months after their number one hit 'Deep Purple,' when the Beatles made the top of the hit parade." Their next release was "Whispering." Thanks to the British Invasion, the song didn't crack the top ten pop charts, although at the height of its popularity it reached number eleven.

"All Strung Out" followed in 1966. For this recording, the duo tried to change its musical course to a more mainstream sound. The recording ranked only in the Top 40 in 1966 but, because of its kinship with Spector, it "rates as one of the greatest Phil Spector-inspired productions of all time," according to Unterberger. The

Selected discography

Deep Purple, Atco, 1963.
Nino & April Sing the Great Songs, Atlantic, 1964.
A Nino Tempo/April Stevens Program, Camden, 1964.
Hey Baby, Atco, 1966.
Sweet and Lovely: The Best of Nino Tempo & April Stevens, Varese Sarabande, 1996.
"All Strung Out," White Whale, 1967; reissued, Varese, 1968; reissued, Rev-Ola, 2003.
Deep Purple/Sing the Great Songs, Collectables, 2001.

Sources

Books

Bubblegum Music is the Naked Truth, Feral House, 2001.
Encyclopedia of Popular Music, 3rd edition, Macmillan, 1998.
Guinness Encyclopedia of Popular Music, Vol. 3, Guinness Publishing, 1998.
MusicHound Lounge: The Essential Album Guide to Martini Music and Easy Listening, Visible Ink Press, 1998.

Periodicals

Billboard, January 17, 1998.

Online

"Nino Tempo & April Stevens," *All Music Guide,* http://www. allmusic.com (January 13, 2004).

—*Linda Dailey Paulson*

NOJO

Jazz group

Despite its size, the 16-member Toronto based Neufeld-Occhipinti Jazz Orchestra, or NOJO, is not a typical big band by any stretch of the imagination. Likened more to avant-garde and free jazz artists like Henry Threadgill, Charles Mingus, and Thelonious Monk than to late jazz greats like Count Basie, Woody Herman, or Duke Ellington, the band is known for pushing the musical envelope with its visionary approach to sound and structure.

"Theirs is the most venturesome jazz orchestra in the city, if only for the example they take from writers such as Henry Threadgill and Kenny Wheeler and the influence they have found in the music of various African cultures," wrote jazz critic Mark Miller in the *Globe and Mail.* "It's tough, provocative jazz."

Formed in 1994 by York University classmates Paul Neufeld, a pianist, and Michael Occhipinti, a guitarist—both earned Bachelor of Fine Arts degrees from the university in 1992—the pair was seeking a suitable venue to showcase their extraordinary skills as composers, honed in a jazz composition/arranging class with David Mott. Both played with smaller ensembles on their own—Occhipinti under his own name, and Neufeld with the Rhythm and Truth Brass Band, among others. To their surprise they found that a big band environment, although typically associated with old-style, swing jazz, was the perfect forum in which to combine their multi-layered compositions, which incorporate elements of world-beat, country, blues and experimental music in addition to jazz. "This band started as a workshop for our own material, and it continues to be the place where we teach ourselves and each other about writing music," Neufeld explained in *Words & Music.*

And that music, as some jazz musicians might say, is way out. "Neufeld and Occhipinti obviously enjoy being fractious and unpredictable, filling their compositions with lurching figures, curious turns and sudden developments that have the effect of keeping the musicians perpetually off-balance," Miller wrote in a 1997 review of one of the band's live performances.

While more established musicians were invited to give the group a try when Neufeld and Occhipinti began their venture, the pair ended up going with lesser-known artists to achieve their desired sound. "I think what works to our advantage is that there's a real youth factor to NOJO," Neufeld said. "There's an energy that comes from younger musicians and an open-mindedness that might not exist if we had some mainstream players."

That youth factor has created a sound which has garnered accolades practically from day one. NOJO's first album, which is self-titled, earned the 1995 Contemporary Jazz Album of the Year at the Juno Awards. The band's second release, *FireWater,* was nominated for a 1996 Juno in the same category. In addition, renowned American jazz clarinetist Don Byron sat in with the group for a set of gigs at Top O' The Senator in Toronto in June of 1997. Neufeld and Occhipinti composed some tunes especially for Byron, and also rewrote some older NOJO pieces to feature the clarinetist more prominently. Playing with Byron was a high honor for NOJO. "For us, it's like going three on three with Michael Jordan or playing shinny with Gretzky," Occhipinti told Geoff Chapman in the *Toronto Star.* "With Don's talent we feel we've stumbled onto something really different."

Clarinetist Don Byron became a regular fixture on NOJO recordings, appearing as a guest soloist on their next two releases, *You Are Here* and *Highwire.* Other featured soloists include violinist Hugh Marsh, trombonist Ray Anderson, tenor saxophonists Sam Rivers and Joe Lovano, and trumpeter Kenny Wheeler.

"A lot of time has passed since the mainstream of jazz tradition was established," Neufeld said. "We both have strong feelings about jazz as a living tradition that's got to be relevant to what's happening now. We're not just looking to 1950s' Miles Davis as an inspiration—there are a lot of things that happened in the 1960s and 1970s that changed the way we look at music. It's important to take those things into account so the music's not a museum piece or treated like classical music."

"I love playing standards and I'm glad there are people who do it, but I'm also glad there are people doing newer things," Occhipinti added. "There are other jazz voices that need to be heard, and I think we're one of them."

NOJO signed to True North Records, a label not known for releasing jazz albums, for their third and fourth releases, *You Are Here* and *Highwire.* Speaking in the *Globe and Mail,* Occhipinti was pleased to be associated with the label. "We like the fact that they're not a jazz label. Their idea is, 'We like this record and we don't necessarily listen to a lot of jazz, so other people who don't necessarily listen to a lot of jazz might like it too.'" With the release of *You Are Here,* NOJO reached out to listeners beyond the Canadian border by arranging to release the album in the United States and going

on tour both in the United States and overseas to promote the release. "I enjoy doing this a great deal," Neufeld stated. "So how can I do more of it? There's no way we're going to do this as much as I'd like if we keep being a local band."

After nearly a decade with NOJO, Neufeld spoke to Mark Miller of the *Globe and Mail* about the band's growth. "The modus operandi is still the same. We're trying to have a vehicle to do as freely as possible whatever comes to mind, with no other aesthetic concerns beyond that." Then he added, "The band is much less flappable that it once was. We can throw stuff at the musicians and they get it right away."

Selected discography

NOJO, Auracle, 1995.
FireWater, Auracle, 1996.
You Are Here, True North, 1998.
Highwire, True North, 2002.

Sources

Periodicals

Globe and Mail, February 6, 1995; June 7, 1997; May 25, 1998; November 19, 1998; May 1, 2002.
Performing Arts, Summer 1997.
Toronto Star, February 20, 1995.
Words & Music, May 1997.
York University Alumni Magazine, February 1996.

Online

"NOJO: Artist Homepage," True North Records, http://www.truenorthrecords.com/mainartist.php?artist_id=79 (April 20, 2004).

Nichole Nordeman

Singer, songwriter

It's a rare occasion when someone actually starts their career by winning a contest—but Nichole Nordeman managed to do it. Nordeman, a Christian singer and songwriter, began her career after winning a songwriting competition in Los Angeles. The competition jumpstarted her burgeoning career, and Nordeman has been a staple on the Christian music scene ever since.

Nordeman played piano from a young age in her hometown of Colorado Springs. Her talent was considerable and she often played for family and friends in the local church, where her flair for performing brought her many compliments. But she never really enjoyed being in front of an audience. Putting herself out there for people to judge was difficult for the shy girl. When asked by Mark Fisher in *1340 Mag* about her youth, she responded on her official website, "I think ... that songwriters are by nature introverted. I wasn't the kid who was tap dancing at age 6 or the one that was born with a microphone in my hand. I was always just kind of to myself." Still, she continued to perform for friends and family throughout her teenage years, and has often remarked that the welcoming atmosphere in the church was what gave her the confidence to perform in front of an audience.

By the time she was a sophomore in college, Nordeman knew that she wanted a musical career. She showed a knack for writing songs, which complemented her singing talents. She would lock herself into the school's music room with a piano and pound out tunes, using the personal time to hone her songwriting skills. Deciding that music was the best way for her to communicate with the world around her, she did what many young musicians might do—she went to Los Angeles.

Nordeman, an impressionable teen with a strong Christian upbringing, struggled in the cut-throat, competitive atmosphere of Los Angeles. Like many young hopefuls, she took job as a waitress in order to pay the bills. At night she got out her pencil and paper and wrote songs. Since she could not afford a piano of her own, she sometimes played at a friend's house. Her world was further changed when her parents divorced, but the event prompted Nordeman to evaluate and strengthen her religious faith.

Nordeman's strong love of poetry was evident in her early compositions, as was her newfound commitment to her faith. Many of the lyrics spoke of feeling lost and trying to remember who you are in the midst of a world that doesn't seem to care. Nordeman was able to use her talent to stay in touch with who she was, as she struggled to succeed in her new life. She managed to muster up the $200 entry fee for a contest held by the Gospel Music Association's Academy of Gospel Music Arts. She entered the songwriting contest with a song called "Why," the tale of a girl who watches the crucifixion of Jesus. She ended up playing her own composition, and the combination of the song's intensity and her honest performance won the award.

In a typical fashion she humbly accepted the award, but not without making it clear that she wanted to be a songwriter, not a performer. However, John Mays, a senior vice president of A&R at Starsong Records, felt that she was uniquely qualified to perform her own compositions and convey their spirit, and he urged her to consider the dual role of singer/songwriter. She soon accepted a record contract from Starsong. She had a lot of songs already written, and Mays felt that her strong voice and talent for finding the right words would go over well in the religious community.

Mays assigned Nordeman to Mark Hammond, an experienced producer who had a reputation for helping new artists find their voice. The result of their first collaboration was 1998's *Wide Eyed,* a debut album whose title summed up Nordeman's quick emergence onto the music scene. Many of the tracks showed a deep faith and an even deeper innocence and curiosity. Nordeman's thoughtful lyrics in "To Know You" described her faith as a backbone to be depended upon, but the song also explored moments of doubt and pain. *Wide Eyed* produced many hits, including "Who You Are," "To Know You," "I Wish the Same," and "Wide Eyed." The album sold 130,000 copies and garnered two Dove Award nominations.

The success of Nordeman's first album astounded her. Now she had a chance to make music for a living. She packed her bags and moved from Los Angeles to

For the Record . . .

Born in Colorado Springs, CO; married; husband's name, Errol; children: one.

Signed with Starsong, 1998; released debut album *Wide Eyed*, 1998; released album *This Mystery*, 2000; released *Woven and Spun*, 2002; released *Live at the Door*, 2003; released DVD-single *Legacy*, 2003.

Awards: Dove Awards, Female Vocalist of the Year, 2001; Songwriter of the Year, Pop Song of the Year, Female Vocalist of the Year, and Song of the Year for "Holy," 2003.

Addresses: *Record company*—Sparrow Label Group, P.O. Box 5010, Brentwood, TN 37024-5010. *Booking*—The Breen Agency, 110 30th Ave. N., Ste. 3, Nashville, TN 37203, phone: (615) 777-2227, fax: (615) 321-4656, website: http://www.thebreenagency. com. *Website*—Nichole Nordeman Official Website: http://www.nicholenordeman.com.

Nashville, where the songwriting continued to come to her quite easily. Her second album, *This Mystery,* was produced by Hammond, joined by Charlie Peacock. Reviews in the Christian press were glowing and, supported by a ruthless tour schedule, the album hit the top of the Christian charts.

As she enjoyed the benefits of her hard work, she moved to Dallas, where she got married. But touring, the bane of so many musicians' love lives, presented a challenge to the newlyweds. Nordeman was frequently forced to choose between being home and spending time on the road. The transition was a tough one that appeared to adversely affect the songwriting process. Nordeman's second album had been a smashing success, but her third work hit some serious turbulence. *Woven and Spun* was harder to create. "I wouldn't even call it 'writer's block,' it was like 'God-block,'" she told CMCentral. "I knew I just had to take that time and soak up the silence, instead of resenting it. I had to listen and wait." Her newly discovered attention to words and the focus on her faith made her take a look at who she was. "I just assumed that because what I really wanted to write about was God's goodness and how that goodness is woven into the everyday moments, that the writing would be easy. Instead, I would just sit and stare at the keys for months at a time."

But the struggle to put an album together finally paid off, with the help of a strong production team. *Woven and Spun* became a best-seller on the Christian music charts. Her first single, "Holy," shot to number one, and won the Song of the Year prize at the Dove Awards in 2003. The album garnered three more Dove Awards—including Female Vocalist of the Year, Pop Song of the Year, and Songwriter of the Year. The album also marked her emergence in the mainstream press. Michael Paoletta of *Billboard* wrote of her third album, "[The song] 'Healed' showcases the beautiful poetry that infuses Nordeman's literate, pensive songwriting. 'Legacy' speaks of making a lasting mark beyond what the world sees as success. She has an especially expressive voice that serves her well on these beautiful tunes."

After her son was born she made it clear to her fans that she was going to take it easy for awhile. "I've spent the last five years either in the studio making a record, or on the road touring that record," she wrote on her website. "It has been a very fulfilling experience to get to use music as a vehicle to build the kingdom of God. … a calling that continues to excite me. But ultimately, I had to acknowledge that the desire of my heart was to do a little kingdom building under my own roof this year."

Selected discography

Wide Eyed, Starsong, 1998.
This Mystery, Starsong, 2000.
Woven and Spun, Sparrow, 2002.
Legacy, Sparrow, 2003.
Live at the Door, Sparrow, 2003.

Sources

Periodicals

Billboard, May 6, 2000; November 2, 2002; April 19, 2003; June 14, 2003.

Online

"Nichole Nordeman," *All Music Guide,* http://www.allmusic. com (February 6, 2004).
"Nichole Nordeman," CMCentral, http://www.cmcentral.com/ artists/111.html (February 6, 2004).
Nichole Nordeman Official Website, http://www.nicholenorde man.com (February 6, 2004).
"Shelter Me … But Not Too Much," *Christianity Today,* http:// www.christianitytoday.com (February 6, 2004).
"The Stress of Success," *Christianity Today,* http://www. christianitytoday.com/music/interviews/2003/ nicholenordeman (February 6, 2004).

—Ben Zackheim

Gary Numan

Singer, songwriter, keyboardist

Gary Numan was a pioneer of electropop. His smash single "Cars" spent weeks on the charts in 1980 and paved the way for an entirely new genre of "alternative" music. Spurning the rawness of punk for a slicker, catchier, production-heavy sound, Numan, wrote *Guardian* writer Dom Phillips, "was Britain's first ever synthesizer star, staring coldly at the camera, covered in white make-up, singing in his nasal monotone about isolation, aliens and robots."

Numan was born Gary Anthony James Webb on March 8, 1958 (some sources say 1959), in London, England. He grew up near Heathrow Airport, where his father worked as a baggage handler. Although he claimed to have little serious interest in music until his late teens, he was admittedly fascinated by technology and harbored an early ambition to fly planes. "I taught myself to play guitar," he told Lisa Verrico in a 2001 interview with *Scotland on Sunday,* "but I was always more interested in noise than actual songs." For a time, he wavered between music and flying, but he soon realized, he admitted, that "the academic qualifications to be a pilot became more and more daunting. One I had to be brainy for, the other just lucky."

Numan's academic career was further hampered by his expulsion from two schools for disruptive behavior. He wound up working in an air-conditioner factory for a time, then drove a forklift in a warehouse. Still interested in music, he answered a 1976 ad in a music trade paper for a guitarist, and won the job in a group called the Lasers. "There were three in the band and only one of them liked me, but I not only got in, I took the band over from day one," he told Verrico. With Paul Gardiner, the Lasers' bass player, and his uncle, drummer Jess Lidyard, Numan formed Tubeway Army, a synthesizer-heavy act inspired by the sounds of experimental German rockers Kraftwerk. Still, he was not entirely enthused about the electronic music being made then. He told *Guardian* journalist Will Hodgkinson, "I always associated it with men wearing capes standing on ice rinks, so I wasn't into it at all. But I ended up in a studio and there was a Mini Moog left behind. It had been left on this heavy bass programme, so when I pressed the keyboard this huge sound came out of it, and so it was pure chance that changed everything."

Sudden Pop Stardom

Tubeway Army recorded some singles for the Beggars Banquet label that were not released until some years later as *Plan.* Their eponymous first LP, a Numan-authored mix of punk and glam-rock on which he sang and played both guitar and keyboards, appeared in late 1978. By this time he had changed his name to the more futuristic-sounding "Gary Numan" and fronted their stage shows as a chilly, alien-esque persona. Rechristened "Gary Numan and Tubeway Army" for *Replicas,* their second release in 1979, their single "Are

For the Record . . .

Born Gary Anthony James Webb on March 8, 1958, in London, England; son of a baggage handler and a telemarketer; married; wife's name, Gemma.

Joined the Lasers as guitarist, 1976; formed Tubeway Army, 1977; released singles under the names Valerium, Scarlett, and Rael; changed stage name to Gary Numan, c. 1978; signed to Beggars Banquet label, 1978; released *Tubeway Army,* 1978; "Are 'Friends' Electric" single from *Replicas* reached number one on British charts, 1979; "Cars," from *Pleasure Principle,* also reached number one in Britain and broke the top ten on the American charts, 1980; released three more LPs on Beggars Banquet, early 1980s; formed Numa record label and released *Fury,* 1985; continued to release LPs on Numa and various other labels; subject of tribute album, *Random, Volume 1: A Gary Numan Tribute,* 1997.

Addresses: *Record company*—Beggars Banquet, 625 Broadway, 12th Fl., New York, NY 10012. *Website*— Gary Numan Official Website: http://www.numan.co.uk

'Friends' Electric?," with its compelling hook and buzzy production sound, rocketed to the top of the British charts, where it remained at number one for four weeks. "Even today, its electronic drone sounds powerful," wrote Phillips in the *Guardian.* "In 1979 it landed like a bomb in the dour, post-punk musical landscape." *Replicas* was quickly followed by *Pleasure Principle,* and its massive hit with its single, "Cars" helped launch Numan and the band in North America as well. The track became one of 1980's surprise hits and one of the first "alternative" numbers to break the top ten.

Numan's odd, robotic stage presence only added to his allure as a "replicant," a sci-fi synonym for "android." Actually, Numan told *Scotland on Sunday,* he had terrific stage fright and was simply too frightened to do anything but stare blankly. "I am quite detached by nature," he explained to Verrico. "There's a recognised medical syndrome which is basically an inability to interact with other people. I have a mild form of that. I find it hard to have conversations that aren't about anything in particular." He elaborated further in a 2003 interview with London's *Independent* newspaper, telling journalist Fiona Sturges that he suffered from Asperger's syndrome. "It means I don't say things in the way that other people would," he told the paper. "I

might say things in an abrupt way and therefore seem cold and uncaring. This interview is fine, because our relationship is clearly defined and I know exactly what's expected of me. But if you met me at a party, I probably wouldn't know what to say and you'd think 'what a miserable sod.'"

Derided in the Press

In Britain, Numan was a bona fide pop star, but critical assessments, from a generation of music writers who were ardent rock and punk fans, were often scathing. They mocked his odd persona and massive following, including the fans that copied Numan's hairstyle and clothing. Accused of ripping off David Bowie's arty stage concepts, he was once asked to leave the building when he stayed after a recording session to watch Bowie work. Both he and his family were the target of death threats; his father discovered a gasoline bomb beneath his car, and authorities deemed a kidnap threat to his mother credible enough to place her under police protection for a time. Numan said that his fame became a terrible burden. "People used to walk down the street and shout 'wanker!' at me," he told Sturges in the *Independent.* "I'd think, 'How can you say that? You've never even met me.'"

Telekon was Numan's third LP to reach number one on the British charts, but in 1981 he announced he would end his live performances. He had trained as a pilot by then—an accomplishment that the British music press also mocked as pretentious—and embarked on a round-the-world jaunt. The plane ran into mechanical trouble in India, and Numan and his pilot were forced to make an emergency landing. Because both wore two watches and had cameras with them, authorities arrested them on charges of smuggling and spying, and detained them for four days until the British Foreign Office became involved. Numan began to experience bad luck with his music career as well. His records lost sales to a raft of post-punk, new-wave, New Romantic acts emerging in England at the time such as Echo and the Bunnymen and The Cure. The song "Warriors," from the 1983 release of the same name, was the last of Numan's new releases to make it into the top ten.

Spent Decade in Obscurity

Leaving Beggars Banquet, Numan founded his own label, but ran into severe financial difficulties when its releases failed to sell. A promising deal with IRS Records turned contentious and furthered hampered his career. By the early 1990s he owed $1 million and was nearly forced to declare bankruptcy. This launched a period of intense introspection for him, and when he began to write songs again, "I abandoned all ideas of chart success," he told *Remix*'s Ken Micallef. "That is when this huge weight lifted. My music became much heavier and darker." The result was *Sacrifice* in 1994, which brought out a more industrial side of Numan's songwriting, and surprised the few critics who reviewed it.

The true rebirth of Numan's career began in the years just after *Sacrifice*. He had stopped reading the music press years before, telling Verrico, "I couldn't cope with being slagged off any more. It was too depressing." He was surprised, however, to hear from others that some well-known musicians were mentioning his work and even covering some of his early classics. Nine Inch Nails's Trent Reznor admitted to listening to *Telekon* every day while recording his seminal 1989 debut, *Pretty Hate Machine*; shock-rocker Marilyn Manson covered "Down in the Park," a proto-goth tune from *Replicas* for the B-side of his 1995 single "Lunchbox." In 1997 musicians—including Damon Albarn of Blur—put together *Random, Volume 1: A Gary Numan Tribute*, which featured three versions of "Are 'Friends' Electric?"

Numan still pilots his own plane, which he keeps near his home in Essex, England. He wed one of his long-time fans, Gemma, in the late 1990s, and wrote a 1997 autobiography, *Praying to the Aliens*. Despite swearing off live performances, he still tours occasionally to support studio efforts like *Pure,* a 2000 release that earned enthusiastic critical accolades. In his *Remix* interview he contended that pursuing his own musical direction had probably saved his career, in the end—even if it nearly brought him to financial ruin. "I picked up a lot of respect for not doing the nostalgia thing," he told Micallef. "I did something I was told was suicide, and I was much better off than when I was on a major label and failing. I figured I was finished anyway, so I had nothing to lose."

Selected discography

Tubeway Army, Beggars Banquet, 1978.
Replicas, Beggars Banquet, 1979.
Pleasure Principle, Beggars Banquet, 1979.
Telekon, Beggars Banquet, 1980.
Dance, Beggars Banquet, 1981.
I, Assassin, Beggars Banquet, 1982.

Warriors, Arista, 1983.
Berserker, Cleopatra, 1984.
Fury, Numa, 1985.
White Noise (live), Cleopatra, 1985.
Strange Charm, Big Eye, 1986.
Metal Rhythm, Illegal, 1988.
Automatic, Polydor, 1989.
Skin Mechanic: Live, Illegal, 1989.
Outland, Capitol, 1991.
Machine + Soul, Numa, 1992.
Radial Pair, Salvation, 1994.
Sacrifice, Big Eye, 1994.
Human, Numa, 1995.
Black Heart, Culture Press, 1998.
Exile, Cleopatra, 1998.
Pure, Edel Germany, 2000.
Disconnection, Sanctuary, 2002.
Exposure: The Best of Gary Numan 1977–2002, Universal, 2002.
Hybrid, Artful, 2003.
Numan Factor, Direct Source, 2003.

Selected writings

(With Steve Malins) *Praying to the Aliens,* Carlton, 1998.

Sources

Periodicals

Guardian (London, England), June 13, 1997, p. 14; April 30, 2002, p. 10; December 20, 2002, p. 18.
Independent (London, England), May 19, 2002, p. 8; January 27, 2003, p. 4.
Remix, August 1, 2003.
Scotland on Sunday, February 18, 2001, p. S9.
Times (London, England), July 4, 2003, p. 6.

Online

"Gary Numan," *All Music Guide,* http://www.allmusic.com (February 4, 2004).
Gary Numan Official Website, http://www.numan.co.uk (February 6, 2004).

—Carol Brennan

Mary Margaret O'Hara

Singer, songwriter

Mary Margaret O'Hara may be remembered as a comet who crossed Canada's musical horizon, glowed brightly for a short time, then passed on into oblivion, never to return. She only recorded one album, a four-song EP, and an extremely limited-edition film soundtrack, but they were original enough to send music writers scrambling to their thesauri to find the words to describe her unique voice and style. "O'Hara's voice weds the lilting twang of Patsy Cline to a near-operatic range," music critic Johnny Ray Huston wrote in the *San Francisco Bay Guardian.* "Her original, scat(tered) style doesn't just turn words into objects, it turns them into the possessions of an obsessive: neurotically she picks them up, rubs them, rips them, tosses them away, then picks them up again and tries to piece them back together … Her voice … is riddled with unpredictable stutters and hiccups, it struggles through fractured sentences and sentiments."

Upon its release in Canada and England in 1988, O'Hara's first (and only true) album *Miss America* received rave reviews from both countries in the music press. Britain's *Melody Maker* called her a genius, while *New Musical Express* compared her debut to Patti Smith's *Horses* and Van Morrison's *Astral Weeks.* Chris Dafoe of the *Globe and Mail* wrote, "What emerges after a few listens is an eccentric but engaging record full of strange quirks and out-of-kilter song structures."

Lending credence to O'Hara's ability to deliver a powerful, if somewhat unusual, musical experience, R.E. M.'s Michael Stipe has been quoted as calling her "one of the most powerful singers I've ever heard … a performer of astonishing force." She also numbers among her fans alternative rock star Morrissey, who said she "absolutely, totally stands alone." Tanya Donnelly of alternative pop/rock group Belly put *Miss America* on her list of favorite albums for *Spin*'s Alternative Record Guide.

Artistic Tendencies

O'Hara has been a part of the Queen Street club scene in Toronto since the 1970s. In the early 1970s she studied painting, sculpture, and graphic design at the Ontario College of Art and since then her work has been shown at various galleries in Toronto. A talented graphic artist, she has designed logos for clubs on Queen Street and has seen her artwork appear in publications such as *Rolling Stone* and the *Globe and Mail.* Her playful drawings and calligraphy illustrate the CD booklet of *Miss America.* For much of the 1990s she taught art classes for children in northern Manitoba.

Since she's the sister of well-known comedian and actress Catherine O'Hara (*Home Alone, Best in Show, A Mighty Wind*), it's not surprising that O'Hara has considerable theater experience, as well. She also had a supporting role in photographer Robert Frank's feature film, *Candy Mountain.*

Cult Following on Toronto Club Scene

In 1977 Mary Margaret O'Hara followed her sister Catherine's suggestion and auditioned for a band called Songship at The Jarvis House in Toronto. Catherine was then working with Second City at The Old Firehall Theatre. O'Hara passed the audition and met guitarist Rusty McCarthy, who would work with her for the next decade or more and appear on *Miss America.* Songship broke up and became the Go Deo Chorus ("Go Deo" means "eternal" in Gaelic), keeping most of the same personnel. According to David MacFarlane of *Toronto Magazine,* "The two bands had a fervent cult following in downtown Toronto bars and clubs."

Go Deo Chorus broke up in 1983, and the next year O'Hara signed a contract with Virgin Records of England on the strength of some tapes a friend had sent to the label. Virgin signed her to a seven-record contract, but they would all be at the label's option. That is, Virgin wasn't obligated to release her material if they didn't like it for one reason or another. In fact, artistic differences between Virgin and its newly signed artist delayed the release of O'Hara's debut album for some four years.

O'Hara explained to *Canadian Composer* that Virgin told her she could "do anything [she] want[ed]" as far as changing the music that was on the demo tapes. She

Born Mary Margaret O'Hara in Toronto, Ontario, Canada. *Education:* Studied painting, sculpture and graphic design at the Ontario College of Art, Toronto.

Signed solo recording contract with Virgin Records, 1984; released debut album, *Miss America,* 1988; teacher of art classes for children, northern Manitoba, 1990s; released *Apartment Life,* a film soundtrack and her first studio album in more than a decade, 2003.

Addresses: *Record company*—Maplemusic Records, 30 St. Clair West, Unit 103, Toronto, Ontario M4V 3A1, Canada, phone: (416) 961-4332, fax: (416) 343-9986, website: http://www.maplemusicrecordings.com.

also told the label she wanted to be her own producer, or at least co-produce the first album, but Virgin insisted she work with an established producer. When she finally agreed to a producer, they went to Wales to record. According to *Canadian Composer,* "It was very quickly clear to her and her musicians that the collaboration would be difficult." The producer was soon dismissed, and O'Hara and her band recorded 14 cuts in Wales by Christmas 1984.

O'Hara and her band, which included guitarist Rusty McCarthy, violinist and keyboardist Hugh Marsh, bassist David Piltch, and drummer Michael Sloski, returned to Toronto for overdubbing and remixing. As O'Hara explained in *Canadian Composer,* Virgin became indecisive about going ahead with the album. "They listened to it and thought it was strange, but then they said 'Go ahead.' That happened twice. They didn't want the album, but they didn't drop the album, so we spent years just talking."

The stalemate was broken in the summer of 1988 with the help of musician Michael Brook. After he saw O'Hara perform at Toronto's Music Gallery, he contacted Virgin about helping her finish the album. With Brook's assistance, O'Hara and her band re-recorded four songs in the summer of 1988 and remixed seven of the original cuts from Wales to finish the album.

Music critics in Canada and England praised O'Hara and *Miss America* upon its release in 1988. Perhaps more revealing are the comments of the musicians who worked with her on the album. Piltch told *Canadian Composer,* "The way she thinks of her ideas is not standard, so the musicians have to interpret her ideas

...You can have a very simple song, but her approach is not that simple and her ideas require quite a bit of time to figure out." Marsh, who played violin and keyboards on *Miss America* and was a member of Go Deo, said, "When I work with Mary, the main thing I listen to is her voice, it can go anywhere, it's a real angel's voice—really fascinating. It's as if I'm fencing with her, playing with or against her."

Favorable Critical Reaction

The favorable critical reaction to *Miss America* moved Virgin to commission a video for the album's first (and only) single, "Body in Trouble," which was released in February of 1989. The only recorded follow-up for more than a decade to *Miss America* was the four-song *Christmas* EP, released on Virgin in 1991. On it O'Hara sings one original composition, "Christmas Evermore," and three standards: "Silent Night," "Blue Christmas," and "What Are You Doing New Year's Eve?"

Although no further recordings were issued until well into the next decade, a 1995 poll for the British magazine *Mojo* included *Miss America* among the "Best 100 Albums of All Time," and the March of 1996 issue of Canada's *Chart* magazine ranked *Miss America* #25 in its list of the "Top 50 Canadian Albums of All Time." In July of 1996, Koch Records reissued *Miss America,* then reissued the *Christmas* EP in October of that year.

In a brief return to the recording studio, O'Hara recorded a track for the benefit album *Sweet Relief 2: The Songs of Vic Chestnutt* (Columbia) in 1996. In addition, her vocals were featured on the mostly instrumental album *Puerto Angel* (Bar None) by The Henrys. For the rest of the decade, O'Hara stayed under the radar, working as an art teacher, playing one-off gigs, and, by her own account, recording "zillions" of songs, as she revealed to *Globe and Mail* writer Robert Everett-Green in 2002. Still, a follow-up to *Miss America* did not appear.

And then, with no promotion or support, an album appeared. Titled *Apartment Hunting,* the 14-track album is a soundtrack to a small Canadian film by director Bill Robertson. It was praised by those lucky enough to hear it—the album had no organized distribution, available only over the internet and in a few select Toronto record stores. Her unique, powerful voice hadn't weakened over the past 14 years. Everett-Green of the *Globe and Mail* remarked: "She's a musician of profound contrasts, which begin in the sound of her voice. It's intimate and sweet, with the kind of fast cooing vibrato you might hear on an old 78. But it's also cool and instrumental, and liable at any moment to shuck off the words like satin pumps and dance barefoot into states of artful delirium."

Selected discography

Miss America, Virgin, 1988; reissued, Koch, 1996.
Christmas (EP), Virgin, 1991; reissued, Koch, 1996.
Apartment Hunting, Maplemusic, 2003.

Sources

Canadian Composer, February 1989.
Globe and Mail (Toronto, Canada), November 17, 1988; February 21, 2002; May 25, 2002.
Maclean's, April 22, 2002.
San Francisco Bay Guardian, October 30, 1996.
Toronto Magazine, April 28, 1989.

Pauline Oliveros

Accordion player, composer

© Jack Vartoogian. Reproduced by permission.

Pauline Oliveros is one of the foremost composers of the 20th (and 21st) centuries as well as a pioneer, alongside forerunners like Morton Subotnick, Terry Riley, and Ramon Sender, of electronic music. In addition to performing, teaching, and composing, she has promoted her concept of Deep Listening, a means of becoming attuned to the multitude of sounds in the environment and connecting those sounds to the body.

Oliveros was raised in a musical family; both her mother and grandmother taught piano and she regularly attended concerts by the Houston Symphony. In addition to the classical music she heard at the symphony and on weekly radio broadcasts from the Metropolitan Opera, the New York Philharmonic, and the NBC Orchestra, she was exposed to country and western, Cajun, and swing music.

When Oliveros was a young girl, her mother brought home an accordion intended for her brother. Oliveros became enamored of the instrument, however, and her mother allowed her to keep it. Unable to play accordion in the school band, though she picked up the tuba and the French horn instead. Her first love remained the accordion, though, and she often transcribed her horn pieces to play them on it. By age 16, she knew she wanted to be a composer. After graduating from high school she went to the University of Houston, which offered an accordion major. Seeking greater independence and immersion in a vibrant arts scene, Oliveros left the University of Houston after three years and moved to San Francisco, where she supported herself by teaching private French horn and accordion lessons and working as a file clerk. Eventually, she enrolled in San Francisco State College, completing her composition degree in 1957.

While at San Francisco State, where she studied with Robert Erickson, Oliveros began experimental improvisations with collaborators like Terry Riley, Stuart Dempster, and Loren Rush. In 1958 Oliveros had a creative epiphany when she placed a tape-recording microphone on a window ledge while listening intently to the sounds around her. Upon replaying the tape, she realized she had been unaware of a number of ambient sounds. Her lifelong interest in Deep Listening and recorded sound were born at this moment.

In 1959 Oliveros, Sender, and Subotnick set up a studio at the San Francisco Conservatory with Erickson's help. There they began using tape recorders to augment their improvisations, presenting the results in a 1960 concert called Sonics featuring Riley and Phil Windsor along with Oliveros and Sender. Oliveros's first tape piece, "Time Perspectives," grew out of these experiments.

In *Talking Music,* Oliveros described the potential she saw in the tape studio. "I fell in love with it," she said. "I

Born on May 30, 1932, in Houston, TX. *Education:* Attended University of Houston (1949–52); graduated from San Francisco State College, 1957.

Cofounded San Francisco Tape Music Center with Morton Subotnick and Ramon Sender, 1961; director, San Francisco Tape Music Center, 1966-67; professor, University of California, San Diego, 1967-1981, director, Pauline Oliveros Foundation, 1985–; professor, Mills College, 1996–.

Awards: Gaudeamus Foundation Contemporary Music Center Interpreters Competition Prize for "Sound Systems," 1962; Guggenheim Fellowship, 1973; Dance Theater Workshop Bessie Award for "Contenders," 1991; Society for Electro-Acoustic Music in the United States (SEAMUS) Lifetime Achievement Award, 1999.

Addresses: *Office*—Pauline Oliveros Foundation, Inc., P.O. Box 1956, 73–75 Broadway, Kingston, NY 12402, phone: (845) 338-5984, fax: (845) 338-5986, e-mail: pof@deeplistening.org, website: http://www.pofinc.org.

was very, very happy with what I could do with tape. I had a Silvertone tape recorder from Sears Roebuck which I had to hand wind, so I had manual variable speed. I had fun imagining how things would sound if I dropped them an octave or if I speeded them up. . . . So I used all sorts of acoustic phenomena and milked it in various ways. I worked with that tape recorder in an improvisatory way."

The musicians left the conservatory in 1961 to form the San Francisoco Tape Music Center, where they continued their explorations in electronic improvisation. Oliveros began writing a nonelectronic piece, "Sound Systems," which won the Gaudeamus Foundation Contemporary Music Center Interpreters Competition that same year.

From 1961 to 1966, the Tape Music Center became an integral part of the San Francisco music scene, with a growing subscription audience for its monthly concerts and favorable reviews in the *San Francisco Chronicle.* In 1966 the center moved to Mills College in nearby Oakland, California, with Oliveros as its first director. The following year she accepted a teaching position at University of California, San Diego (UCSD).

While at UCSD, Oliveros began to develop her *Sonic Meditations,* an unconventional composition that issued written directives to musicians instead of using standard notation. The first meditation, "Teach Yourself to Fly," for instance, instructs the musician: "Gradually allow your breathing to become audible. Then gradually introduce your voice. Allow your vocal cords to vibrate in any mode which occurs naturally. Allow the intensity of the vibrations to increase very slowly. Continue as long as possible, naturally, and until all others are quiet, always observing your own breath cycle. Variation: translate voice to an instrument." A later meditation instructs simply, "Listen to a sound until you no longer recognize it." The meditations were greatly influenced by Oliveros's study of t'ai chi, a meditative Chinese martial art that she began to practice in 1969.

In 1971, noting a growing conservatism among her students, Oliveros left UCSD and moved to New York City and from there to upstate New York, where in 1985 she founded the Pauline Oliveros Foundation, an incubator for new and innovative musical works. She also continued to perfect her Expanded Instrument System (EIS), a complex electronic processing system that allows musicians to imbue their instruments with a variety of time- and sound-related effects. The recordings *Crone Music* (1989) and *Roots of the Movement* (1990) both rely heavily on EIS.

In 1988, along with trombonist Dempster and singer Panaiotis, Oliveros performed in the "cistern chapel" near Seattle. A buried, two-million-gallon water tank, the chapel was a unique sound environment for the trombone, didgeridoo, accordion, conch shells, and metal scraps that the musicians played. The performance launched an ongoing exploration of alternative sound environments for the group, which eventually became the Deep Listening Band. Additional performance sites have included a ceramic silo, a power plant cooling tower and Tarpaper Cave in Rosendale, New York, where *Troglodyte's Delight* was recorded. The group returned to the cistern chapel in 1990 to record the *Ready Made Boomerang.*

Oliveros has continued to perfect and promote her Deep Listening concept through annual retreats in New Mexico and classes at Mills College (where she returned to teaching in 1996, often via video relay from New York), and at Rensselaer Polytechnic Institute in Troy, New York, as well. On her Deep Listening website, Oliveros describes the concept: "Listening is noticing and directing attention and interpreting what is heard. Deep Listening is exploring the relationship among any and all sounds. Hearing is passive. We can hear without listening. This is the state of being tuned out—unaware of our acoustic ecology—unaware that the fluttering of a butterfly's wings has profound effect near and in the far reaches of the universe. We can hear sounds inwardly from memory or imagination or outwardly from nature, or from civilization. Listening is actively directing one's attention to what is heard, noticing and directing the interaction and relationships of sounds and modes of attention.... Babies are the best deep listeners."

Oliveros has enjoyed even greater recognition for her contributions to contemporary music in the new millennium. Two of her important but previously unavailable early works, *Electronics I–IV* and *Alien Bog and Beautiful Soop* were released by the Pogus label in 1997. In addition, a variety of younger musicians are recognizing their indebtedness to her works. Sonic Youth commissioned Oliveros to write "Six in New Time (for Sonic Youth)," which appears on their 1999 album *Goodbye 20th Century.* Oliveros has also performed with DJ Spooky.

She continues to utilize new technologies as well, often performing collaborative concerts using simulcasting and other linking devices with musicians in disparate locations. Yet Oliveros remains known for music that comes not from machines, but from the body. As Marc Weidenbaum noted in the *Music Now* newsletter, quoted on the Disquiet Ambient/Electronica website, "Pauline Oliveros has done more to humanize technology than virtually any other living musician in the classical tradition." In 1999 Oliveros was honored with a lifetime achievement award for her work from the Society for Electro-Acoustic Music in the United States (SEAMUS).

Selected discography

Accordion and Voice, Lovely Music, 1982.
Wanderer, Lovely Musc, 1984.
Well and the Gentle, hatArt, 1985.
Roots of the Movement, hatArt, 1988.
Crone Music, Lovely Music, 1989.
Deep Listening, New Albion, 1989.
Ready Made Boomerang, New Albion, 1989.
Troglodyte's Delight, What Next?, 1990.
Pauline Oliveros and American Voices, Mode, 1994.
Sanctuary, Mode, 1995.
(With Deep Listening Band) *Tosca Salad,* self-released, 1995.
Non Stop Flight, self-released, 1996.
Alien Bog and Beautiful Soop, Pogus, 1997.
Electronic Works I-IV, Pogus, 1997.
Suspended Music, Periplum, 1997.
Between/Waves, Sparkling Beatnik, 1998.

Carrier, Deep Listening, 1998.
Live at the Meridian, Sparkling Beatnik, 1999.
Timeless Pulse, Deep Listening, 2002.

Selected writings

Sonic Meditations (score), Smith Publications, 1974.
To Valerie Solanas and Marilyn Monroe in Recognition of their Desperation, for any group or groups of instrumentalists (6 to large orchestra), September 28, 1970, Holland, Michigan, Smith Publications, 1977.
Lullaby for Daisy Pauline: A meditation for Daisy Pauline Oliveros, Smith Publications, 1984.
Software for people: collected writings, 1963–80, Smith Publications, 1984.
Deep Listening Pieces, Deep Listening Publications, 1990.
The Roots of the Movement (book and CD), Drogue Press, 1998.

Sources

Books

Duckworth, William, *Talking Music: Conversations with John Cage, Philip Glass, Laurie Anderson, and Five Generations of American Experimental Composers,* Da Capo, 1999.

Periodicals

San Francisco Chronicle, December 12, 2001.

Online

"Creating, Performing and Listening," New Music Box, http://www.newmusicbox.org/first-person/dec00/2.html (February 8, 2004).
"Deep Listening," Disquiet Ambient/Electronica, http://www.disquiet.com/oliveros.html (April 1, 2004).
"Pauline Oliveros," *All Music Guide,* http://www.allmusic.com (February 1, 2004).
"Pauline Oliveros," ESTweb Index, http://media.hyperreal.org/zines/est/intervs/oliveros.html (February 8, 2004).
"Pauline Oliveros," *Grove Dictionary of Music,* http://www.grovemusic.com (February 1, 2004).
Pauline Oliveros Foundation Website, http://www.deeplistening.org/pauline (January 28, 2004).

—Kristin Palm

Yoko Ono

Singer, composer

AP/Wide World Photos. Reproduced by permission.

Yoko Ono has been sending shock waves through the worlds of art and music since the early 1960s. Although many think she never would have recorded a note if not for her association with John Lennon, Ono had been a musical performer for 11 years before marrying the late Beatle. By the mid-1990s, many critics had reevaluated her musical history, deeming her songs ahead of their time and influential to such cutting-edge musical entities as Public Enemy, Sonic Youth, and the B-52's. In fact, *Onobox,* a 1992 retrospective of Ono's solo work, received widespread critical acclaim. "That she [Ono] made music of marginal worth is repudiated once and for all by this lavish, illuminating six-CD overview of her remarkable pop life," attested David Fricke in *Rolling Stone.*

Born into a prominent Tokyo banking family in 1933, Yoko Ono—"Ocean Child" in Japanese—was burdened with the high musical expectations of a father who had wanted to be a concert pianist. Inevitably, his plans to create a musical prodigy backfired, leading Ono to dislike "accepted" music. After her family moved to the United States in 1951, Ono became fascinated with twelve-tone composers such as Alban Berg while attending Sarah Lawrence College. Her own compositions at school were judged too radical by her music teacher.

In 1957 Ono married composer Toshi Ichiyanagi and moved to a loft in New York City's Greenwich Village. Embracing the avant garde, she began displaying her conceptual art and staging "events" organized by eccentric composer La Monte Young. Young was part of a movement known as Fluxus that attempted to break free from conventional standards of art and music. Ono's creative output was greatly influenced by John Cage, a iconoclastic composer whose work incorporated disorder and randomness. Her first musical performance, in 1961 at the Village Gate in New York, featured mumbled words, laughter, atonal music, and an actor speaking in monotone. Perhaps not surprisingly, Ono's early work was largely ignored, and critics referred to it as little more than screaming or moaning.

After divorcing Ichiyanagi, Ono married avant-garde artist Tony Cox in 1964. The couple made a series of bizarre films in London, including 1967's *Bottoms,* which consisted solely of close-ups of 365 bare backsides. In Paris she met jazz saxophonist Ornette Coleman, who further stimulated her interest in vocal experimentation. Her songs tapped an eclectic blend of inspirations, including Berg's operettas, the Japanese Kabuki singing called *hetai,* Indian and Tibetan vocal techniques, and free jazz. Referring to these antecedents, Kristine McKenna wrote in the *Los Angeles Times,* "Ono synthesized those elements into sound collages that had no precedent and haven't been matched yet in sheer adventurousness."

Ono met John Lennon in 1968 at a London gallery exhibition of her concept pieces. Eight years Lennon's senior, Ono claimed in a *Rolling Stone* interview that she had never even listened to the Beatles' music before meeting the songwriting legend. The outcry against the ensuing liaison was vicious. Although the strains of fame and a desire for individual expression—not to mention growing antipathy among band members—-were already threatening to split up the Fab Four, Ono was blamed for hastening the group's breakup. As quoted in *The Guests Go in to Supper,* Ono recalled, "Our partnership was still great, but mainly our energies were used in fighting the world from splitting us up." Ono and Lennon began collabo-

rating on songs, but the public would not accept her as a legitimate contributor.

Ono signed with Apple Records and continued recording her vocal experimentations. Her 1970 *Plastic Ono Band* set—a sister album to Lennon's identically titled offering of that year—featured the contributions of Lennon, Eric Clapton, Klaus Voorman, and Andy White but was called trash by most critics and reviled by the public. Her follow-up album, *Fly,* demonstrated the influences of her and Lennon's involvement in primal scream therapy. Indeed, Ono persisted in reshuffling the musical deck, integrating everyday sounds into musical patterns and news events into her lyrics. Many of her songs had a strident feminist outlook.

Reunited after a much publicized split in 1974, during which Lennon went on a drunken binge in Los Angeles, the couple had a son, Sean, who was born in 1975 on his father's birthday. Lennon took over child-rearing responsibilities while Ono managed the family's extensive financial empire. Five years later, the couple went back into the studio and created the widely praised *Double Fantasy* album. Soon after the album's release, in 1980, Lennon was gunned down by a psychotic fan outside the couple's apartment building in New York City. Ono—and the world—was devastated.

Ono remained active in various musical, film, and artistic pursuits after Lennon's death. A highlight was "Walking on Thin Ice," a 1981 single that earned her a Grammy nomination. In 1984 Ono released the album *Milk and Honey,* which showcased original material as well as previously unreleased offerings by Lennon. She produced a movie (and soundtrack) entitled *Imagine* in 1988, which incorporated outtakes from other film projects, videos, home movies, and new songs.

A six-CD retrospective of Ono's music, called *Onobox,* was released by Rykodisc in 1992. Ono followed this in 1995 with an album of new work by Ono and her son Sean, called *Rising.* Also that year, Ono's musical play *New York Rock* was produced Off Broadway in New York City. It was accompanied by an original cast recording of the show's music. Two years later, Ono released for the first time an album that she had recorded in 1974 called *A Story.* Still going strong in the 2000s, she released an album of new work, *Blueprint for a Sunrise,* in 2001.

The impact of Lennon and his top-flight musical associates on Ono's career will always be debated. Jerry Hopkins's unauthorized biography, *Yoko Ono,* painted a picture of Ono as an evil, manipulating dictator who used Lennon to fuel her own rise to fame. But others view the much-vilified Ono as a victim whose own artistic development suffered because she was trapped in Lennon's shadow. She has transcended her scapegoating to forge her own musical path, refusing to be deterred by a lack of acceptance by critics or the public. As Fricke said of Ono in *Rolling Stone,* "Her husband may have punched her ticket into the mainstream, but Mrs. Lennon was nobody's rock & roll fool."

Selected discography

Solo

Plastic Ono Band, Apple, 1970.
Fly, Apple, 1971.
Approximately Infinite Universe, Apple, 1973.
Feeling the Space, Apple, 1973.
Season of Glass, Geffen, 1981.
Starpeace, Polygram, 1985.
Onobox, Rykodisc, 1992.
New York Rock (original cast recording), Capitol, 1995.
Rising, Capitol, 1995.
A Story, Rykodisc, 1997.
Blueprint for a Sunrise, Capitol, 2001.

With John Lennon

Unfinished Music No. 1: Two Virgins, Apple, 1968.
Wedding Album, Apple, 1969.
Live Peace in Toronto, Apple, 1969.
Some Time in New York City, Apple, 1972.
Double Fantasy, Geffen, 1980.

Sources

Books

Brown, Peter, and Steven Gaines, *The Love You Make: An Insider's Story of the Beatles,* McGraw-Hill, 1983.

Golson, Barry G., editor, *The Playboy Interviews With John Lennon and Yoko Ono,* conducted by David Scheff, Playboy Press, 1980.
Hopkins, Jerry, *Yoko Ono,* Macmillan, 1986.
Hounsome, Terry, *New Rock Record,* Facts on File, 1983.
Rees, Dafydd, and Luke Crampton, *Rock Movers & Shakers,* ABC/CLIO, 1991.
Seaman, Frederic, *The Last Days of John Lennon: A Personal Memoir,* Birch Lane, 1991.
Sumner, Melody, Kathleen Burch, and Michael Sumner, editors, *The Guests Go in to Supper,* Burning Books, 1986.

Periodicals

Creem, May 1992.
Entertainment Weekly, March 6, 1992.
Interview, February 1989.
Los Angeles Times, April 11, 1993.
Metro Times (Detroit, MI), September 29, 1993.
Musician, April 1992.
New York Times, March 13, 1994.
Oakland Press (Oakland County, MI), September 25, 1993.
People, July 23, 1992.
Publishers Weekly, December 19, 1986.
Rolling Stone, March 19, 1992; February 18, 1993.
Spin, September 1992.

Online

"Yoko Ono," *All Music Guide,* http://www.allmusic.com (January 23, 2004).

Additional information for this profile was obtained from liner notes to *Onobox,* Rykodisc, 1992.

—Ed Decker and Michael Belfiore

Stacie Orrico

Singer, songwriter

Teen singer/songwriter Stacie Orrico has been hailed as one of contemporary Christian music's new breed of crossover stars. Working in the catchy dance-pop segment of the market, Orrico had garnered a steady following by the time her self-titled 2003 release appeared with Virgin Music's marketing muscle behind it. The album was nominated for a 2004 Grammy in the Best Pop/Contemporary Gospel Album category.

Born on March 3, 1986, in Seattle, Washington, Orrico was the third of five children born to missionary parents. After traveling to such remote locales as Ukraine they settled in Colorado, where Orrico became a fan of such mainstream pop divas as Whitney Houston, Mariah Carey, and Celine Dion. At the age of 12 she entered a singing competition at a Christian music seminar in Estes Park, Colorado, and was stunned when she won first place. She was quickly signed to a development deal with ForeFront Records of Franklin, Tennessee, one of the biggest labels in the contemporary Christian entertainment business.

Orrico's parents supported her music career, which she viewed as her ministry, and moved to Nashville, Tennessee, to further it. Her first album, *Genuine,* appeared in 2000 on the Chordant label. It rose to number one on the *Billboard* new artists Heatseekers chart and its single, "Don't Look at Me," topped the Christian charts later that year. Another album track, "Dear Friend," came from her experience with an anorectic friend. In an interview with *Campus Life* writer Mark Moring, Orrico called the experience "devastating to me. We were so close, and then all of a sudden we couldn't talk the way we used to." By writing a supportive song, Orrico felt she could reach out to her friend and others in a way that reflected her religious faith. "I can relate to teens because I am one," she told Moring. "I'm dealing with the same things they're dealing with ... My heart is all about ministering to teens."

In 2001 Orrico toured as an opening act for Destiny's Child and also released a holiday EP, *Christmas Wish.* She had nearly completed her second album when the multimedia entertainment powerhouse Virgin Music signed her to a deal. They added some new tracks and teamed her with experienced producers who had worked with Pink and Matchbox 20. Signing with a mainstream label, however, was a difficult decision, Orrico said, for it made some in the Christian-contemporary scene wonder if she'd compromised her faith for commercial success.

Stacie Orrico and its single, "Stuck," were released by Virgin in 2003. It made top 40 radio play during its first week, and the video featuring Orrico in parody skits from popular teen movies became a favorite on MTV's *Total Request Live.* Orrico had cowritten that particular track as a message to young women in bad relationships, she told MTV's Corey Moss, after her songwriting partner Kevin Kadish asked her what she thought was her peer group's biggest challenge was. "I just said teenage girls end up in these relationships where they're not treated very well and they end up on this emotional roller coaster.... They are stuck." Moss, who called the track "a relationship song," noted that "it also has the young-woman empowerment message common in Christina Aguilera and Britney Spears tunes."

"Stuck" struck a chord with Orrico's target audience, and reached number ten on mainstream top 40 charts. The LP's second single, "(There's Gotta Be) More to Life," was released in the last weeks of 2003 and again proved a surprise crossover hit, hitting the top five. Orrico, who helped write several other tracks, told Moss that she was committed to improving her songwriting abilities, commenting, "I want to reach people my age, and the best way to do it is not to have a 40-year-old man write it."

Some fans worried that Orrico's new *TRL* persona had betrayed the Christian-music ideal, she admitted in an interview with *Denver Post* writer G. Brown. "On the Christian side and on the mainstream side, people are watching very closely for you to make a mistake that they can rally around. I'm not perfect, but I am being put in a situation where I'm a role model. If I'm expected to start dressing in a way I'm not comfortable with and singing songs I'm not comfortable with, that's not worth it for me. I'd rather quit all the music stuff and go back to school than compromise the things I believe in."

Despite such concerns, the success of Orrico's record was part of the phenomenon that prompted *Billboard*

writer Deborah Evans Price to declare 2003 the year of the crossover for Christian contemporary music. Orrico considered it a new era as well, theorizing that both the 2003 war in Iraq and the September 11, 2001, attacks on New York City and Washington, D.C. had opened the door for once-pigeonholed Christian artists like herself. "The events of the last couple of years have made people more open to spiritual things and trying to find answers," she told Price. Furthermore, Christian pop was no longer ostracized by mainstream labels like Virgin—home to Moby and the White Stripes, among other top acts. "I don't think there's [sic] been any stations that decided not to play my music because of my background," she reflected. "If anything, I think they see it as maybe a good thing."

Orrico's major-label promotion helped land her a spot on *American Dreams,* a network series based on the long-running television music showcase, *American Bandstand,* in which she played the lead singer for a 1960s-era girl group, the Angels. She admitted to *Houston Chronicle* writer Nekesa Mumbi Moody that not all marketing ideas were equally wholesome: "My faith … is the foundation for what I do and the decisions that I make as far as what I want to sing about and what I will or won't do or will or won't wear. I don't want to do stuff for men's magazines; I don't really think that's my audience who I'm trying to reach … There are things that I don't want to be a part of." She planned to concentrate on her ministry-through-music for the time being, she told MTV, though she did admit to harboring a fantasy of bringing her message to a wider audience. "I would love to have a talk show or do something like that," she confessed to Moss, "but I've watched so many singers who try to act but have no acting ability whatsoever. I don't think I have any ability."

Selected discography

Genuine, Chordant, 2000.
Christmas Wish (EP), ForeFront, 2001.
Stacie Orrico, Virgin, 2003.
Stuck (EP), Virgin, 2003.

Sources

Periodicals

Atlanta Journal–Constitution, May 18, 2001, p. E1.
Billboard, September 2, 2000, p. 1; November 2, 2002, p. 15; October 25, 2003, p. 3; December 27, 2003, p. 22.
Buffalo News, December 17, 2003, p. N6
Campus Life, November 2000, p. 28; November-December 2001, p. 22.
Christian Reader, November-December 2003, p. 66.
Houston Chronicle, June 12, 2003, p. 1.
Denver Post, March 25, 2003, p. F3.

Online

"Stacie Orrico Goes Looking for More In All the Wrong Places," MTV, http://www.mtv.com/news/articles/1473256/06242003/orrico_stacie.jhtml (February 2, 2004).

"Stacie Orrico Won't Be 'Stuck' with Christian Tag," MTV, http://www.mtv.com/news/articles/1471487/04232003/orrico_stacie.jhtml (February 2, 2004).

—*Carol Brennan*

The Paladins

Rockabilly group

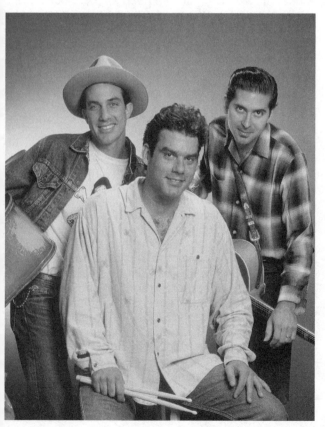

Paul Natkin/Photo Reserve, Inc. Reproduced by permission.

Whether yelping greasy rockabilly, wailing West Coast R&B, crooning Bakersfield-influenced country, or dabbling in small combo swing, the Paladins have kept their roots-music faith alive the hardest way possible—on the road. Despite changing line-ups, record deals gone sour, shifting trends, and heart-wrenching personal problems, the trio continues to earn a solid living as a top attraction in clubs. In the process, this venerable group has become nearly as important to the rockabilly faithful as some of the genre's pioneers.

Group leader Dave Gonzalez's initial influences came from his mother, who listened to such early rock 'n' roll icons as Carl Perkins, Elvis Presley, Roy Orbison, and the Rolling Stones. On the flip side, his father's love of country singers Buck Owens and Merle Haggard also made a strong impression on him. Gonzalez's interest in music turned serious when his cousin Greg Leach gave him his first electric guitar in 1974, along with a Freddie King album. Jamming with older musicians also helped him develop a keen taste for blues as set down by B.B. King, Muddy Waters, and Johnny Winter.

Formed Quartet

Thomas Yearsley was also a guitar player, but switched over to the upright bass so he could play in his high school jazz band at approximately the same time he began playing music with Gonzalez. Eventually, rockabilly buff Whit Broadly befriended the two, and after Gonzalez showed him some chords, he joined the as yet unnamed trio as a guitarist. Getting a drummer for their odd mix of blues, country, and early rock 'n' roll proved somewhat difficult at first, but once Gus Griffin joined, they had a full-fledged quartet ready to take on gigs.

In a Rockabilly Hall of Fame (RHOF) interview, Gonzalez noted that Broadly named the group after an old TV series. "That's exactly where we got it, *Paladin—Have Gun Will Travel.* We were really into rockabilly but we weren't into dressing like modern country and western stars. ...We wanted to look like a cross between Richard Boone and early Elvis."

At the time, neither the band's music nor its sartorial flair were popular with their fellow students. "When we first started out, we all really felt like outcasts, man," Gonzalez laughingly told the ROHF. "We got called all kinds of names and people tried to pick fights with us because we had leather jackets on and greasy hair. People would call us 'Sha-Na-Na' [the kitschy 1950s tribute group] and they didn't know what we were."

Influenced by the Blasters

If the Stray Cats' brief explosion onto the pop charts in 1982 opened some doors for the Paladins, another

For the Record . . .

Members include **Whit Broadly** (group member, c. 1978-83), guitar; **Scott Campbell** (group member, c. 1983-90), drums; **Brian Fahey** (group member, c. 1990-96, 1999), drums; **Gus Griffin** (group member, c. 1978-83), drums; **Dave Gonzalez**, vocals, lead guitar; **Joey Jazdzewski** (group member, c. 1997-2000), upright bass; **Thomas Yearsley** (group member, c. 1978-97, 2001), vocals, upright bass.

Formed as high school quartet in San Diego, CA, 1978; first recording, a cover of "Lonesome Train" by Johnny Burnette & the Rock 'n' Roll Trio, appeared on the *Who's Listening* compilation for Government Records, 1982; their own song "Double Datin'" included on the Rhino compilation *Best of L.A. Rockabilly,* 1983; released single "Slippin' In" b/w "Honky Tonk All Night" on producer Mark Neil's Swingin' label, 1985; released debut album, *The Paladins,* on Wrestler, 1987; recorded for the Chicago-based blues label Alligator, 1988-90; signed with Sector 2 records, 1994; recorded for the punk-gothic label 4AD, 1996; recorded for German-based Ruf Records, 1999-2001; released "El Matador" on Lux Records, 2003.

Addresses: *Record companies*—Alligator Records, P.O. Box 60234, Chicago, IL 60660, website: http://www.alligator.com. Ruf Records America, 162 N. 8th St., Kenilworth, NJ 07033, phone: (908) 653-9700, fax: (908) 653-9702, e-mail: intuneoffice@aol.com. *Website*—The Paladins Official Website: http://www.thepaladins.net. *E-mail*—thepaladins@hotmail.com.

California band, The Blasters, paved the way for their eclectic mix. "They were the ones we really identified with," Gonzalez told the RHOF. "They were kind of rockabilly but they were also R&B, blues, country, and folk all at the same time. To me those guys were the greatest, they smoked everybody." Although they drew from the same inspirational wellspring, the Paladins were generally overshadowed by the Blasters and other up-and-comers such as the Kingbees, Los Lobos, the Fabulous Thunderbirds and Stevie Ray Vaughan, whom they deeply admired. Later they would do two tours with Vaughan, but in the beginning they were still struggling with personnel problems.

Drummer Griffin departed in late 1983, followed by Broadly, who was tired of the poor money and hectic scrambling on the road. With the addition of ex-Red Devil drummer Scott Campbell, the Paladins officially became a trio and started making some inroads in Southwestern clubs while struggling to get a record deal. Mark Neill, whose own eclectic band The Unknowns also had a strong cult following, produced the Paladins' first recordings, and taught them the value of amplifiers, speakers, and recording with vintage equipment. "We still use all old equipment and really try hard to present our whole sound as authentically as we can and make it really sound like how it used to be when the original cats were playing," Gonzalez told the RHOF.

Neill, along with Fabulous Thunderbird leader Kim Wilson, Los Lobos saxophonist Steve Berlin, and engineer Mark Linett shared producing chores for the band's self-titled debut on the Wrestler label. Boasting guest contributions from blues pianist Katie Webster and Anson Funderburgh, the LP created the mold for most of the Paladins' albums to follow. Inspired remakes of obscure old tunes such as "Slow Down," "Daddy Yar," and "Make It," were combined with authentic-sounding Gonzalez-penned originals. Released in 1986, the set was well-loved by the band's fans, when they could find it. Today, Gonzalez wishes he had listened to a friend's warning. "Keith Ferguson from the Tailgaters called one night and said, 'Don't do it. The guy's jive, he won't pay you, he'll rip you off. He owes us a bunch of money.' I said, 'Oh man, we need a record out so bad. We're out here on the road with our little single, we're starving to death and we need to make an album." Their haste resulted in an album, but the band has never been able to collect royalties, even though the album has been kept in constant release.

Hit Early Peak at Alligator

The band did not remain with Wrestler for long. Impressed by their live show, the Chicago-based blues label Alligator Records bought out the remainder of their contract and added the group to their impressive roster. The band would still play rockabilly and bits of country at their live shows, but the accent on their Alligator recordings was blues and R&B. Produced by Berlin and Linett, the Paladins' two discs for Alligator allowed them to survive the demise of rockabilly as a hot underground trend, and helped establish their identities for club owners. Many songs from that era, i.e., the stomping blues of "Let's Buzz," the swinging remake of Brook Benton's "Kiddio," and the grinding R&B of "Goin' Down to Big Mary's," remain often-requested staples of the band's live shows. Equally important in a financial sense, the band attracted a tour sponsor, The Miller Brewing Company.

Let's Buzz! featured legendary saxman Lee Allen, who played on sessions for rock 'n' roll pioneers Fats

Domino, Little Richard, and Lloyd Price. Gonzalez has admitted that the recording remains a high point for the band. However, the young trio—now featuring Brian Fahey on drums—began to resent their label's perceived interference. "I liked working with them a lot, at first," Gonzalez told the RHOF. "I think the first record *Years Since Yesterday* has a good sound—we had control over our production at that time. But then, on *Let's Buzz!,* they started trying to control our sound and productions, so we left." As events turned out, leaving Alligator nearly destroyed their careers as a recording act.

Smaller Labels Stalled Career

The band saw two deals—one with Geffen, the other with Interscope—go down the tubes before they latched on to the relatively small art label Sector 2 in 1994. Produced by Los Lobos guitarist Cesar Rosas, *Ticket Home* reveled in the deftly accented Swing-revival beats of jazz drummer Jeff Donovan. Although it also contained one of the band's best rockers, "Fifteen Days Under the Hood," the poorly distributed disc was mainly available at Paladins' shows. When Sector 2 went belly up, the band added four tracks and leased it to various small companies with the title *Rejivenated.*

Gonzalez refers to 1996's *Million Mile Club* as "my guitar album." Boasting hot renditions of their Alligator recordings, plus two stunning, jazzy instrumentals, it showed the group off at their sweaty in-concert best. However, 4AD, the label that released the album, was primarily known as a punk and gothic label and had no clear idea on how to market the album. Record chains were confused about where to stock the disc and even their most loyal fans had trouble finding it. To compound the problem, group co-founder Yearsley left the band to aid in the fledgling recording career of his wife, the blues-belting ex-stripper Candye Kane. Donovan also departed shortly after. Although they were constantly booked in clubs and at festivals worldwide, it seemed that the Paladins' days as a viable recording act were over.

Revived at Ruf

Undeterred, however, the grouped returned to their musical roots, along with producer Mark Neill. Neill, who had never completely endorsed the band's switch to the blues, accentuated their rockabilly and country leanings, and sharpened their songs' hooks. The result was 1999's *Slippin' In,* a high water mark in their career. Named after the first 45 rpm single they did with Neill—an old Eddie Bond rocker—the disc blended dazzling remakes of Wynn Stewart's "Rain Rain," Gram Parsons' "Strong Boy," and Johnny Bond's "Five Minute Love Affair," with a masterful surf instrumental, and their best-ever original song, "The Hard Way."

Released on the German-based blues label Ruf Records to great acclaim, the album completely restored the group's reputation with the rockabilly faithful, making them a hot act once again. In *Blue Suede News* Gonzalez described the creative process Neill inspired: "When Mark hears a song a lightbulb goes on and he takes over on it. I come in and say, 'Hey, I wrote this kind of country song—or a Sun Records kind of thing.' And he'll say, 'Yeah, it's kind of that, but listen to these records and tell me what you think.'… I write 'em but Mark produces and arranges the whole thing. The guys always jump in there and add their things to it too." Further, the Paladins' leader explained, "Mark's the one playing those [Nashville] baritone-guitar solos, though I have to twist his arm to do it."

Although similar to the first album in style and content, the band's 2001 Ruf album *Palvoline No. 7* displays more gut level emotion. Both Gonzalez and Yearsley had gone through divorces and the impact was felt in their work. The big beat numbers such as Wynn Stewart's "She Tears Me Up," the surf-drenched instrumental "Powershake," and their own "How Long You Gonna Tease Me," were still in evidence. But they infused rocking rants like Jerry Reed's "You Make It They Take It" with palpable anger, and Brook Benton's "Just A Matter of Time" with shades of country heartache. They had become accomplished recording artists at last.

Still Growing Artistically

The combination of Ruf Records and Mark Neill seemed to be a good fit for the Paladins, but Gonzalez complained that his label didn't promote *Palvoline No. 7* with any gusto. The whole record industry was suffering great financial reversals, and Ruf was no exception. Characteristically, the group departed for what they hoped were greener pastures, only to see their 2003 album *El Matador,* a collection of raw, stripped-down performances, released on Yearsley's own Lux Records label.

If the Paladins are discouraged, they don't show it. Still booked for close to 200 dates a year, they continue to draw a unique audience of college kids, rockabilly and blues afficionados, and fellow guitarists seeking to pick up licks by watching Gonzalez work his on-stage magic. Of the group, it is Gonzalez who seemingly never tires. When not touring with the Paladins, he plays jazz with a San Diego ensemble known as the Joint Chiefs, and lays down pure country music with Chris Gaffney, Hank Gallup, and Jimmy Lloyd, who call themselves the Hacienda Brothers. After all the ups and downs, what keeps him going? "The passion that I have for the sounds of old records," he explained in a phone interview. "I keep aspiring to make sounds that match up with all those great old records playing in my head."

Selected discography

Who's Listening, Government, 1982.
Best of L.A. Rockabilly, Rhino, 1983.
The Paladins, Wrestler, 1986.
Years Since Yesterday, Alligator, 1988.
Let's Buzz, Alligator, 1990.
Ticket Home, Sector 2, 1994; reissued as *Rejuvenated,* Hootenany, 2004.
Million Mile Club, 4AD, 1996.
Slippin' In, Ruf, 1999.
Palvoline No. 7, Ruf, 2001.
El Matador, Lux, 2003.

Sources

Periodicals

Blue Suede News #56, Spring 2001.
Country Standard Time, March 2001.

Online

"The Paladins," Rockabilly Hall of Fame, http://www.rockabillyhall.com (February 1, 2004).
The Paladins Official Website, http://www.thepaladins.net (February 1, 2004).

Additional information was obtained from various interviews with Paladins' leader Dave Gonzalez during 2000-01, and in a phone interview conducted on February 5, 2004, from which all quotations were taken.

—*Ken Burke*

The Persuasions

A cappella group

The Persuasions are perhaps the best known and longest-lived a cappella group in the history of pop. The group has been together since 1961, when they first sang on New York City street corners. Their unique sound encompasses all styles, including pop, gospel, doo-wop, and classical. They have been featured in a PBS documentary directed by Spike Lee, performed backing vocals for such musical icons as Paul Simon, Stevie Wonder, and Bette Midler, and have played several world tours. Although the group has yet to score a hit record, as lead singer Jerry Lawson pointed out to Larry Katz in the *Boston Herald,* "we're still out there, still working." No small achievement in the turbulent world of popular music.

The Persuasions started in New York City in the early 1960s, when Jerry Lawson met Jimmy Hayes at the department store where they both worked. They began to sing together at the store, in elevators—every chance they got. The duo soon met Joe Russell, who was so inspired by Lawson and Hayes that he left another singing group to join them. The lineup was completed after they recruited Herbert "Toubo" Rhoad and Jayotis Washington, a partnership that would last until Rhoad's death in 1988.

For the Record . . .

Members include **Jimmy Hayes**, bass; **Jerry Lawson**, lead; **Herbert "Toubo" Rhoad** (died on December 7, 1988, in Davis, CA), baritone; **Joe Russell**, tenor; **Jayotis Washington**, tenor.

Group formed in New York, NY, 1961; played on street corners, in parks, and small clubs, 1960s; signed with Rhino Records, 1968; released first album, *Acappella,* 1970; released numerous albums throughout the 1970s; went on hiatus, 1980s; made a comeback, late 1980s; member Herbert "Toubo" Rhoad died while group was on tour, 1988; released numerous albums through the 1990s and 2000s.

Addresses: *Contact*—Jerry Lawson, P.O. Box 1921, Scottsdale, AZ 85252. *Website*—Jerry Lawson Official Website: http://www.jerrylawson.biz.

The group's chemistry was apparent to everyone who heard their first impromptu concerts. They met in parks, on street corners, and on basketball courts after working their day jobs, and performed for all who would listen. As their audiences grew, so did their ambitions. To achieve wider success, they decided to recruit a guitarist. But as lead singer Jerry Lawson later told Richard Duckett in the Worcester, Massachusetts, *Telegram & Gazette,* "Every time we got a little gig somewhere, the guitarist would get drunk and wouldn't show up." And, he told Hugh Hart in the *Chicago Tribune,* "It got to the point where it was like the Lord telling us, 'Just leave the guitar alone.'"

After they decided to remain a purely vocal group, the question of what to call themselves was settled. If they were to succeed as an a cappella pop group, they would have to "persuade" listeners to overcome their prejudices about what pop music should be.

As predicted, the group had a tough time persuading record executives to back a band an instrumentless band. In the interim, they played gigs in small clubs after working their day jobs. Their following continued to grow, and, finally, their break came in 1968. They were singing in a record store when the man who would become their manager, David Dashev, happened to walk by. As Lawson later explained to Larry Katz in the *Boston Herald,* "He made a phone call, put the phone in the middle of us and told us to start singing. It was Frank Zappa on the other end. A couple of weeks later we had a recording contract and five tickets to LA."

After their 1970 debut, *Acappella,* the Persuasions recorded new albums steadily through the decade, one of the most popular of which was the 1972 release *Street Corner Symphony.* Each song was arranged using a method the group developed as a method of working together. The first step was to have Hayes lay down a bass line. Next, Russell and Washington stepped in to layer on their parts. Finally Lawson's lead vocals were added, with the others supporting him much as an orchestra does a soloist.

The group's output slowed in the 1980s, years during which Jerry Lawson pursued other interests. After a hiatus of about six years, the band reunited again in the late 1980s, playing dates on the East Coast before heading west for a tour in 1988. Still fighting radio and recording formulas that worked against a cappella groups, the Persuasions nevertheless stuck with their winning style.

Tragedy struck during the West Coast tour. Rhoad died of a brain hemorrhage before a concert in Davis, California, in December of 1988. He was 44 years old, and like the others, had been with the group for 26 years. "He was one of the finest baritone singers and one of the finest gentlemen in the whole world," Joe Russell told Rip Rense in the *Los Angeles Times.* Rhoad was survived by a wife and two daughters.

Their number reduced to four, the Persuasions soldiered on. They played the rest of the tour's concert dates, but they left an empty microphone on the stage in Rhoad's place. They believed that was what Rhoad would have wanted them to do—go on singing, no matter what. But a lot of the heart had gone out of their music; they needed to grieve. After completing the tour, five long years passed before they released their next album.

The Persuasions came back from Rhoad's death with the 1993 tribute *Toubo's Song.* Back on their feet, they followed up with a new album, *Right around the Corner,* just a year later. Subsequent releases followed at a steady pace, and the latter half of the 1990s saw a rise in their popularity, culminating in the release of *On the Good Ship Lollipop,* an album of children's music, in 1999.

In 2000 the group had one of its most prolific years ever. The began by recording another tribute album, this time to the man who had given them their first recording contract—*Frankly a Cappella: The Persuasions Sing Zappa.* The group then covered Grateful Dead songs in another release that same year: *Might as Well ... The Persuasions Sing the Grateful Dead.* Following the success of this work, Rounder Records put out a previously unreleased recording of the Persuasion's gospel music called *Sunday Morning Soul* that had been languishing on the studio's shelves. In 2002 came a Beatle tribute, *The Persuasions Sing the Beatles.*

In the new millennium the group expanded their audience to include children, traveling to schools to teach children to sing a cappella. Still going strong in the twenty-first century, Lawson insists that the Persuasions, far from fading, are just hitting their stride. "We're picking up more and more fans every day," he told Duckett. More than that, though, Lawson attributed the group's staying power to their love of what they do. "I wake up every morning, man, and just thank God so much for what he gave us and for what we do, which is to go around the world and make people happy."

Selected discography

Acappella, Rhino, 1970.
We Came to Play, Collectables, 1971.
Street Corner Symphony, Collectables, 1972.
Spread the Word, Collectables, 1972.
We Still Ain't Got No Band, MCA, 1973.
More Than Before, A&M, 1974.
I Just Want to Sing with My Friends, A&M, 1974.
Live in the Whispering Gallery, Hammer N' Nails, 1976.
Chirpin', Elektra, 1977.
Comin' at Ya, Flying Fish, 1979.
No Frills, Rounder, 1984.
Good News, Rounder, 1988.
Toubo's Song, Hammer N' Nails, 1993.
Right around the Corner, Bullseye/Topic, 1994
Stardust, Relic, 1994.

Sincerely, Bullseye Blues, 1996.
You're All I Want for Christmas, Bullseye Blues, 1997.
Man, Oh Man: The Power of the Persuasions, Capitol, 1997.
On the Good Ship Lollipop, Rhino, 1999.
Sunday Morning Soul, Rounder, 2000.
Frankly a Cappella: The Persuasions Sing Zappa, Rhino, 2000.
Might as Well … The Persuasions Sing The Grateful Dead, Arista, 2000.
The Persuasions Sing the Beatles, Chesky, 2002.
A Cappella Dreams, Chesky, 2003.

Sources

Periodicals

Boston Herald, February 2, 2001, p. S21.
Chicago Tribune, April 30, 1992, p. 9.
Los Angeles Times, December 15, 1998, p. 5.
Telegram & Gazette (Worcester, MA), September 19, 2002, p. C1.

Online

"The Persuasions," *All Music Guide,* http://www.allmusic.com (January 26, 2004).

—Michael Belfiore

Suzi Quatro

Singer, songwriter, bassist

American-born singer, songwriter, and bassist Suzi Quatro was one of the first female musicians to front her own band. Diminutive and blond, she sang and played a bass guitar nearly as tall as she was. "I was the first rock 'n' roll successful female who led a band of men and seriously played an instrument," she told Jennifer Selway in a 2002 interview for London's *Express.* "It hasn't been done since either." During the 1970s she was a massive success in Britain and Europe, enjoying a string of glam-rock hits that sold 45 million copies in all; three decades later she still had a cult following. Quatro, asserted Jane Hall of the Newcastle, England, *Journal,* "forged the standard to which all electric guitar-wielding females aspire to [sic] today."

Quatro was born Susan Kay Quatro on June 3, 1950, in Detroit, Michigan, and grew up in Grosse Pointe, a posh suburban lakefront community. Her father, Art, a jazz musician who led his own trio, gave Quatro her stage debut at the age of eight as a conga player with his act. She soon took up the piano, and by age 14 was part of the all-female band the Pleasure Seekers with her sisters Arlene and Patti. The group played at a Detroit-area teen club called the Hideout (which also gave fellow Detroiter Bob Seger his start), and recorded a 1966 single, "Never Thought You'd Leave Me" b/w "What a Way to Die," for a label launched by the club's owner. The single did well and attracted major-label interest. Signed to Mercury, Quatro and her sisters recorded "Light of Love," toured the United States, and even played for American troops in Vietnam. When Arlene dropped out of the band after having a baby,

she was replaced by another Quatro sister, Nancy, and the band continued under the name Cradle.

The fifth Quatro sibling, Michael, became Cradle's manager, and he convinced legendary British music producer Mickie Most to see one of their shows. Most, in Detroit to work with the Jeff Beck Group at the legendary Motown Studios, had discovered the Animals and had produced hits for Donovan, Lulu, and Herman's Hermits (which included Rod Stewart at the time). He liked Quatro's energy and offered her a contract with his own recently launched label, RAK. Elektra Records was also interested at that point, but for Quatro the choice was clear. She told Hall, "According to the Elektra president, I could become the new Janis Joplin. Mickie Most offered to take me to England and make me the first Suzi Quatro—I didn't want to be the new anybody."

Quatro left Detroit and moved to England in late 1971. Her career took off slowly, and in her interview with Hall she described the first few years as "probably the hardest time of my life. I came over with one of my sisters but, after she went home, I felt very, very alone. I had no money … and I was writing at the studio every day. I came home every night and cried myself to sleep because I was so lonely." Her first single, "Rolling Stone" tanked everywhere but in Portugal, where it rose to number one in 1972. Then Most teamed her with songwriting duo Nicky Chinn and Mike Chapman, who would go on to craft a number of bubblegum glam-rock classics of the era, including Sweet's "Ballroom Blitz." They wrote Quatro's first number-one British hit, "Can the Can," which also topped the charts in Europe, Japan, and Australia. It was included on her 1973 debut *Suzi Quatro,* along with her second hit, "48 Crash."

Chinn and Chapman wrote nearly all of Quatro's hit songs of that era, including her signature tune, "Devil Gate Drive," from 1974's *Quatro.* She recorded "The Wild One," and other classic Quatro gems for the LPs *Your Mama Won't Like Me* and *Aggro Phobia.* Her next effort, 1978's *If You Knew Suzi,* showed a more mature, soft-rock sound, and also yielded one of her few American chart successes, a country-tinged duet with singer Chris Norman called "Stumblin' In."

Quatro's American profile was boosted immensely, however, when she did a stint on *Happy Days,* one of the era's top-rated sitcoms. On the popular show, set in the 1950s, she played "Leather Tuscadero," a tough-talking, leather-catsuit-wearing character who proved so successful that ABC offered her a series of her own. She declined the offer. By then married to Len Tuckey, a guitarist in her band, Quatro instead settled into a sixteenth-century manor house in Essex, England. Their daughter was born in 1982, followed by a son two years later. She continued to record and tour, and appeared in two British television series. In 1986 she starred in the London stage revival of *Annie Get Your*

Born Susan Kay Quatro on June 3, 1950, in Detroit, MI; married Len Tuckey (a musician), 1978 (divorced, 1992); married Rainer Haas (a concert promoter), c. 1993; children: two.

Began playing at age 14 with her sisters in a Detroit-area band called the Pleasure Seekers, c. 1964; released the single "Never Thought You'd Leave Me" b/w "What a Way to Die," 1966; signed to EMI; reformed band as Cradle, 1969; signed with British music producer Mickie Most's RAK label and recorded a string of U.K. hits, including "Can the Can" and "Devil Gate Drive"; had top-five U.S. hit in 1979 with "Stumblin' In"; appeared on the ABC sitcom, *Happy Days*, 1977–79; made London stage debut as the lead in *Annie Get Your Gun*, 1986.

Addresses: *Office*—British Broadcasting Corporation, Radio 2, Broadcasting House, London W1A 1AA, England. *Website*—Suzi Quatro Official Website: http://www.suziquatro.com.

Gun. Although her marriage to Tuckey ended in the early 1990s, a few years later she married Rainer Haas, a German concert promoter. In 2000 she became the host of a weekly radio show, *Rockin' with Suzi Q* on Britain's BBC Radio 2.

Quatro still tours occasionally, and compilations of her past hits, including the 2003 EMI release, *What Goes Around,* attest to her enduring appeal. In her later years Quatro claimed to have mellowed considerably from her tough rock-chick-persona days. "Sure, I've wrecked the odd hotel room and I can tell you I made a bloody good job of it," she confessed to Selway in the *Express,* "but that was years ago when I was under a lot of pressure."

Selected discography

Suzi Quatro, Beat Goes On, 1973.
Quatro, Bell, 1974.
Your Mama Won't Like Me, Beat Goes On, 1975.
Aggro Phobia, RAK, 1977.
If You Knew Suzi, RSO, 1978.
Suzi and Other Four-Letter Words, RAK, 1979.
Rock Hard, Dreamland, 1980.
Main Attraction, Polydor, 1983.
Live & Kickin', Alex, 1991.
What Goes Around (compilation) EMI, 2003.

Sources

Periodicals

Daily Mail (London, England), March 2, 1996, p. 46.
Express (London, England), November 21, 2002, p. 28.
Herald Sun (Melbourne, Australia), April 22, 2000, p. 110.
Journal (Newcastle, England) December 31, 2003, p. 34.
Sunday Herald Sun (Melbourne, Australia), January 5, 2003, p. 71.
Times (London, England), September 11, 1999, p. 16.

Online

"Suzi Quatro," *All Music Guide,* http://www.allmusic.com (February 5, 2004).
Suzi Quatro Official Website, http://www.suziquatro.com (February 2, 2004).

—Carol Brennan

Redbone

Rock group

Taking its name from a Cajun epithet for "half-breed," Redbone boasted members of such Native American tribes as Cherokee, Yaqui, Apache, and Shoshone. Remembered primarily as the first commercially successful American Indian rock group, the band attained brief success in the early 1970s for two bona fide pop singles, "Witch Queen of New Orleans" and "Come and Get Your Love." The band's albums, however, were more complex affairs, mingling topical issues—including the Wounded Knee massacre of Sioux Indians by the Seventh Cavalry in 1890 and the Native American protests on Alcatraz Island in 1969—with Native American chants and long, improvisational jams. Following the success of "Come and Get Your Love," which became a huge dance hit, the band increasingly tilted toward dance- and disco-flavored music before disbanding in the late 1970s.

Brothers Pat and Lolly Vasquez were born in Fresno, California. Boasting Yaqui, Shoshone, and Mexican blood, the duo reputedly worked in cotton fields and apricot orchards in the migrant camps surrounding Fresno. Developing as musicians at an early age, the brothers played with Canadian jazz pianist Oscar Peterson at the Monterey Jazz and Pop Festival before relocating to Los Angeles in 1963. Calling themselves the Avantis, the brothers attempted to cash in on the surf craze popularized by Jan and Dean and the Beach Boys, with such songs as "Gypsy Surfer" and "Wax 'em Down" on the Chancellor label, and "The Phantom Surfer" on the Regency label. The Avantis featured future Beach Boy drummer Mike Kowalski, and their recordings earned them an opening slot on a Beach

Boys' tour. The Vasquez brothers also recorded the singles "Let's Go" as the Routers, "Surf Stomp" and "Batman" as the Mar-kets, and "Hotrodders' Choice," "Dawn Patrol," "Double A Fueller," and "Satan's Chariot" as the Deuce Coupes. The 1963 Deuce Coupes' sessions featured impressive session help from Glen Campbell, David Gates, and Leon Russell.

In 1964 the Vasquez brothers recorded as the Sharks, releasing the singles "Big Surf" and "Robot Walk." By the time they had made a musical appearance in the film "It's a Bikini World" in 1965, they had changed their last name to Vegas. They also became members of the Shindigs, the house band on the hit television program *Shindig,* where they performed weekly with band members Leon Russell and Delaney Bramlett. During this period they also performed session work with pop duo Sonny and Cher, and provided instrumental support to Elvis Presley on the soundtrack to the film *Kissin' Cousins.* The brothers also managed a residency at the Los Angeles venue Haunted House, which prompted the release of their first full-length album, *Pat and Lolly Vegas at the Haunted House,* produced by Leon Russell and Snuff Garrett. They became sought-after session musicians and song writers following their studio work on Dobie Gray's hit single "In Crowd" and the 1967 P.J. Proby single "Nicky Hoeky," which was also recorded by Bobbie Gentry and Duane Eddy.

While fulfilling a residency at a Los Angeles nightclub named Gazzarri's, the Vegas brothers met guitarist Tony Bellamy. A Yaqui Indian who had performed with Dobie Gray, and a member of Peter and the Wolves (a San Francisco band that evolved into the psychedelic band Moby Grape), Bellamy had grown up in a family of dancers and musicians. He had learned to play flamenco guitar as part of his musical education as well, and he was recruited by the Vegas brothers to accompany them on session work with Odetta, John Lee Hooker, and the Everly Brothers. According to Pat, it was Jimi Hendrix who talked the musicians into forming an all-Native American rock group. Vegas told *Record Collector* writer Jeremy Isaac, "Hendrix was a friend of ours.... and he was half Indian. Once he knew that we were Indian too he used to come and hang with us because of that. Jimi made me aware of my roots: He'd say 'Native American is beautiful, man, be proud of that.'"

The Vegas brothers and Bellamy rented a house and rehearsed for a year before attempting to land a recording contract. During this period the trio produced and performed on the Jim Ford album *Harlan County,* which featured the Lolly Vegas composition "Working My Way to L.A." While the group was perfecting their sound, they came close to hiring drummer Wayne Bibbey. Bobby Womack, however, suggested that the group hire Pete "Last Walking Bear" DePoe, a Cheyenne drummer from Neah Bay Reservation, Washington. "Bobby said, 'I'll give you my drummer and you give me yours,'" Pat Vegas told Isaac. The

Members include **Aloisio Aguiar** (joined group, 1977), keyboards, drums; **Anthony "Tony" Bellamy** (left group, 1977), guitar; **Peter DePoe** (also known as Last Walking Bear; left group, 1972), drums; **Arturo Perez** (left group, 1973), drums; **Butch Rillera** (group member, 1973-77), drums; **Lolly Vegas** (born Vasquez), guitar, vocals; **Pat Vegas** (born Vasquez), bass guitar.

Brothers Lolly and Pat Vegas formed surf band The Avantis, 1963; brothers recorded as the Deuce Coupes for Del-Fi Records, 1963; brothers performed in film *It's a Bikini World,* 1965; worked with Leon Russell and Delaney Bramlett as house band for the Shindigs on ABC-TV series *Shindig,* 1964-66; released album produced by Leon Russell and Snuff Garrett, *Pat and Lolly at the Haunted House,* 1966; duo wrote "Nicky Hoeky," which became hit for P.J. Proby, 1967; Vegas brothers met guitarist Tony Bellamy, collaborated on Jim Ford album *Harlan County,* 1968; trio hired drummer Pete DePoe and signed band Redbone to Epic Records, 1969; released debut and second album, *Redbone* and *Potlatch,* 1970; released third album, *Message from a Drum,* featuring hit single "Witch Queen of New Orleans," 1972; Arturo Perez replaced drummer DePoe, 1972; Butch Rillera replaced Perez, 1973; released *Wovoka,* featuring single "Come and Get Your Love," 1973; released final studio album for CBS/Epic, *Beaded Drums through Turquoise Eyes,* 1974; released RCA debut, *Cycles,* 1977; group appeared as presenters at Native American Music Awards, 1998.

band adopted the name Redbone from the Cajun epithet Rehbon, which is a derogatory name for half-breed. The group signed to Epic Records in 1969, and released their debut album, *Redbone,* in 1970. A double album, it featured the group's reworking of "Nicky Hoeky," as well as the Cajun-influenced "Danse Calinda" and "Crazy Cajun Cakewalk Band." The album also featured such extended jams as "Jambone," "Suite Mode," and "Things Go Better." The follow-up album, *Potlatch,* featured the song "Alcatraz," which dealt with the 1969 occupation of Alcatraz Island by Native Americans, and a moderately successful single, "Maggie."

In 1971 the band's third album, *Message from a Drum,* hit pay dirt for Redbone. The album featured the Cajun-swamp rocker "Witch Queen of New Orleans," which bore a lyrical and musical resemblance to the swamp-rock songs of Creedence Clearwater Revival. While the song was a success in the United States, it was a monster hit in the United Kingdom, propelling the band to tour as an opening act for such groups as Traffic, Alice Cooper, and the Faces. The death of DePoe's father prompted the drummer to quit the band. "He couldn't stay with us because his family was dependent on him," Pat told Isaac. DePoe was replaced by Arturo Perez on the 1972 album *Already Here.* Perez departed shortly thereafter, however, and was replaced on the 1974 release *Wovoka* by Butch Rillera. *Wovoka* contained the band's most successful single, "Come and Get Your Love," which featured a popping disco bass beat and Leslie-amplifed guitars supporting the husky call-and-response vocals of Pat and Lolly Vegas.

The group was never able to repeat the single's success, however, despite several attempts on subsequent studio releases, including *Beaded Dreams through Turquoise Eyes* and the 1977 album *Cycles.* The latter album marked the recent departures of Bellamy and Rillera, the addition of keyboardist and percussionist Aloisio Aguiar, and the band's new label, RCA. *Cycles* failed to generate much interest, however, and the group disintegrated. A live concert recording in 1977 was eventually released in 1994 as *Redbone: Live.*

The Vegas brothers continued to work as a duo and as solo acts throughout the 1980s. They also did voiceover work for documentaries on Native American history. The brothers attempted to reform the band's original lineup in the early 1990s, but their plans were waylaid by Lolly's illness from a stroke and DePoe's reluctance to tour. Drummer Rillera became unable to perform due to an aneurysm. Despite these setbacks, Bellamy and Pat Vegas continued to work the Native American casino circuit with a group of supporting musicians. In 1998 members of the group appeared as special guest presenters at the Native American Music Awards.

Selected discography

Redbone, Epic, 1970.
Potlatch, Epic, 1970.
Message from a Drum, Epic, 1972.
Already Here, Epic, 1972.
Wovoka, Epic, 1974.
Beaded Drums through Turquoise Eyes, Epic, 1974.
Come and Get Your Redbone, Epic, 1975.
Cycles, RCA, 1978.
Redbone: Live, Avenue/Rhino, 1994.
Golden Classics, Collectables, 1996.
The Essential Redbone, Epic/Legacy, 2003.

Sources

Books

The Billboard Illustrated Encyclopedia of Rock, Billboard
    Books, 1998.
Larkin, Colin, editor, *The Encyclopedia of Popular Music,* 3rd
    edition, MUZE, 1998.

Periodicals

Circus, April 1974.

Additional information was obtained from the liner notes to
The Essential Redbone, Sony Legacy, 2003, and from
Record Collector magazine.

—Bruce Walker

Marie Samuelsson

Composer

At first glance, the Swedish composer Marie Samuelsson might appear hopelessly eccentric and atypical. She has found inspiration in howling wolves; her topics encompass theoretical physics and Magica de Spell (the flamboyant witch from the world of Donald Duck and Uncle Scrooge); her background includes dance, improvisation, multimedia exploration, and rock 'n' roll. Yet Samuelsson is a poet and visionary, a composer whose spellbinding music redefines the experience of listening to music. Indeed, critics have described her work as powerful, irresistible, mysteriously physical, profound, spiritual, suggestive, and richly descriptive. But Samuelsson's powerfully individual and meticulously sculpted works set her apart from most contemporary composers: not only are they accessible and appealing, but they engage the listener in an inner dialogue in such a way that the memory of a Samuelsson composition remains in the listener's consciousness as a secret garden, a magical place to visit and revisit.

With her extraordinary mastery of acoustic and electronic techniques, Samuelsson effortlessly, it seems, translates her deep creative impulse into finely wrought sonic masterpieces, in which irresistible labyrinths lead the listener to unexpected dimensions of moods, inner landscapes, illuminating visions, and profound insights. Exemplifying her brilliant exploration of inner worlds is I Am—Are You?, a piece for French horn, voice, and tape based on a haunting text by the poet Magnus William-Olson. In this piece the words and music effectively become one, as the listener, slowly descending into the mysteriously infinite world of the psyche, first discerns a dialogue of two souls painfully asserting their individuality, only to enter an enigmatic zone where the idea of personal separateness assumes a spectral aura.

Unlike many composers who reach artistic clarity only after many struggles, Samuelsson, it seems, asserted her personality as a composer early in her career. Thus Signal, a work for saxophone quartet and electronics composed during her student days, brought instant international fame. Indeed, the manic, nervous, obsessive energy of this brief composition easily seduces the listener into searching, through obsessive listening, for the elemental source of this explosion of genius. However, what ultimately captivates the listener is not the sonic surface, despite its remarkable charm and fluency, but the composer's inimitable spirit. Regardless of style, structure, instrumentation, mood, and color, any work by Samuelsson provides a glimpse of this extraordinary artist's rich inner world.

As remote as the sonic trajectories may seem, the listener, even when the music seems to be moving in strange directions, always feels the composer's reassuring presence. Often astounding, enigmatic, unsettling, and even overwhelming, Samuelsson's world is reassuringly human: her astonishing originality is strangely familiar. While classical music has often been defined in terms of dichotomies between the intellect and a resistant physical element, Samuelsson prefers an approach based on the idea that human beings exist in a unified world where spiritual and material energies do not oppose each other. Neither cerebral nor physical, her music reflects profound creative impulses that transcend intellectual categories.

With her natural openness to movement, poetry, and the spoken word, Samuelsson redefines music, abandoning the classical idea that music, unlike language, refers only to itself. Indeed, the differences between music and poetry are undeniable, but in a work such as That Night, for example, a choral composition inspired by William-Olson's poetry, the very idea of clear meaning becomes irrelevant, as Samuelsson's music explores the mysterious ambivalence of presence and absence, prompting the listener to confront the paradoxes of life at an experiential level, without resorting to preconceptions and ideas.

Released in 2003, Samuelsson's album Air Drum received immense critical and popular acclaim. The title piece is, in fact, Air Drum III, for orchestra—and three large metal drums that Samuelsson found at a ventilation company. At first glance they threaten to overpower the orchestra, as eerie reverberations quickly invade the composition's sonic space. However, it quickly becomes apparent that Samuelsson had something else in mind. The elemental force in this piece is air, which reduces the drums to simple instruments. Interestingly, she named the work Air Shaft, perhaps wishing to expand the image of a column of air. Although not quite accurate, the English translation has been accepted, apparently even by the composer herself. Works included in *Air Drum* have been performed in Sweden and abroad, and they represent the full range of Samuelsson's genius

Selected compositions

Andra platser (Other places), for alto voice, cello, and percussion, 1989.
Katt: Nio liv (Cat: Nine lives), for woodwind quintet, 1989.
Från Indien till Mars (From India to Mars), dance music for string quartet with guitar improvisation, 1990–91.
Den natten (That night), for choir, 1991.

Signal, for saxophone quartet, 1991.
Ahead, for orchestra, 1992.
La luna, for cello and tape, 1993.
Lufttruma I (Air shaft I), for alto saxophone, piano, and percussion, 1993.
Troll, for orchestra, 1993.
Krom (Chrome), for brass quintet, 1994.
Lufttruma II (Air shaft II), for flute, clarinet, percussion, harp, and double bass, 1994.
Magica de Hex (Magica de Spell), for orchestra, 1994.
Pingvinkvartett (Penguin quartet), for flute, violin, cello, and piano, 1996.
I vargens öga (In the eye of the wolf), for solo saxophone and tape, 1997.
Rotationer (Rotations), for string orchestra, 1997 (revised, 2003).
Lufttruma III (Air shaft III), for orchestra, 1999.
Flow, for chamber orchestra, 2000.
It Takes Two, for two violins, 2000.
I Am—Are You?, for French horn and tape, 2001.
Ö (Island), for solo violin.

Selected discography

(Rydberg, Enström, Samuelsson, Parmerud, Lindwall, and Feiler) *Links* (includes *Signal*), Caprice, 1997.
Air Drum, Suecia, 2003.

Sources

Books

Sadie, Stanley, editor, *New Grove Dictionary of Music and Musicians,* Macmillan, 2001.

Periodicals

Gramophone, February 2004.

Online

"Marie Samuelsson," Music Web, http://www.musicweb.uk.net/classrev/2003/Nov03/Samuelsson.htm (March 29, 2004).
Marie Samuelsson Official Website, http://members.chello.se/marie.samuelsson (March 29, 2004).

—Zoran Minderovic

Ann Savoy

Singer, guitarist, producer

Jim Spellman/WireImage.com. Reproduced by permission.

OffBeat magazine has described Ann Savoy as "Cajun Music's Cultural Ambassador," and she has done much to live up to that title, compiling what many consider to be a definitive reference book on Cajun music, playing Cajun music in the major Hollywood film *Divine Secrets of the Ya-Ya Sisterhood,* and producing a Grammy-nominated recording of Cajun music played and sung by well-known pop stars like Linda Ronstadt and John Fogerty. All of this is in addition to Savoy's extensive recording and live performance career as a Cajun music guitarist and singer with several different bands, including the Savoy-Doucet Band, the Magnolia Sisters, and the Savoy Family Band.

Ann Savoy (pronounced "Sah-vwah") was born Ann Allen on January 20, 1952, in St. Louis, Missouri, and she grew up in Richmond, Virginia, far from the Cajun culture that was to become her passion. She learned to speak French at the age of 13, when she and her family went to live for a year in the French-speaking Swiss Alps, and began playing the guitar at age 12. She majored in French in college, spending her junior year in Paris. Along the way, she developed a strong interest in photography—another calling that would later help her in her career as a Cajun music historian.

Although speaking French and playing music were two of her loves, Savoy didn't discover the joys of playing Cajun music until she met her future husband, Marc Savoy, at Washington, D.C.'s National Folk Festival in 1975. Marc Savoy was an accordion maker and player, and came from deep Cajun roots. He later taught Savoy the rudiments of Cajun guitar and singing, and she fell in love with the man and the music as well. Leslie Berman in *Sing Out! The Folk Song Magazine* reported that Marc's first words to Savoy—in Cajun French—were, "You're so pretty like a little speckled turkey egg." And Savoy recalled to Dan Willging in *OffBeat,* "I fell in love with him instantly." Ann and Marc Savoy were married in 1976, and have been performing together ever since. Together with fiddler Michael Doucet they formed the Savoy-Doucet Band, touring the United States and recording many acclaimed albums, including *Two-Step d'Amédé, Home Music with Spirits,* and *Live! At the Dance,* all on the Arhoolie label.

Cajun music is a folk music form developed by descendants of French-speaking colonists in the bayous of Louisiana. The lively dance music features the accordion, fiddle, guitar, and lyrics in Cajun French as mainstays. It has remained popular in rural Louisiana and is played increasingly in dancehalls throughout the United States and in Europe. Interested not only in playing Cajun music, but in its history as well, Savoy wrote a book titled *Cajun Music: A Reflection of a People.* To complete the book, she conducted interviews with many of Cajun music's brightest stars. In addition to information obtained from interviews, the book features music and lyrics for Cajun songs, in both French and English, including phonetic pronunciations for English speakers, many historical photographs, and

Born Ann Allen on January 20, 1952, in St. Louis, MO; married Marc Savoy (a Cajun accordion player and maker), 1976; children: Joel (a fiddle player and sound engineer), Sarah (a singer), Wilson (a singer and keyboardist). *Education:* Graduated from Mary Baldwin College, bachelor's degree in French.

Formed Savoy-Doucet Band with husband, Marc Savoy, and fiddler Michael Doucent, 1976; toured United States with the Savoy-Doucet Band and cut several albums, including *Two-Step d'Amédé, Home Music with Spirits,* and *Live! At the Dance,* all on the Arhoolie label, 1970s-2000s; author of *Cajun Music: A Reflection of a People,* 1985; formed band the Magnolia Sisters with several other female Cajun musicians, 1990s; released several albums with the Magnolia Sisters, 1990s-2000s; actor and music contributor in Columbia Pictures film *Divine Secrets of the Ya-Ya Sisterhood,* 2002; produced Grammy-nominated *Evangeline Made: A Tribute to Cajun Music,* 2002; released *The Best of the Savoy-Doucet Band,* 2002; formed Savoy Family Band with husband and children, released *The Savoy Family Band,* 2003.

Awards: *OffBeat* magazine, Best Cajun Album of 2000 for *Sam's Big Rooster,* 2001; Best Cajun Album of 2002 for *Evangeline Made: A Tribute to Cajun Music,* 2003.

Addresses: Record company—Arhoolie Productions, Inc., 10341 San Pablo Ave., El Cerrito, CA 94530, website: http://www.arhoolie.com. *Agent*—The Rosebud Agency, P.O. Box 170429, San Francisco, CA 94117.

articles about Cajun music styles and instruments. The book was published in 1985 by Bluebird Press, and has remained a definitive source for learning about Cajun music.

In addition to playing with the Savoy-Doucet Band, Savoy has performed and recorded with the Magnolia Sisters, an all-female Cajun band. In addition to Savoy, the group features Jane Udrine, Tina Pilione, Lisa Trahan Reed, and Christine Balfa. The group's 2000 release, *Chers Amis,* was produced by Savoy.

In 2000 the Savoy-Doucent Band released *Sam's Big Rooster,* which featured both traditional and original songs. Besides the band's usual lineup, the album included Savoy and Marc's son Joel on fiddle. Joel Savoy also engineered the album. *Sam's Big Rooster* was well received by fans of Cajun music and critics alike, and was given *OffBeat* magazine's award for Best Cajun Album of 2000.

In 2002 Savoy made a brief appearance alongside her son Joel as a musician in the major Hollywood film *Divine Secrets of the Ya-Ya Sisterhood,* which starred Sandra Bullock and Ashley Judd. Savoy's music was also featured on the film's soundtrack. Continuing her work in the field of Cajun music scholarship, Savoy contributed a chapter to the book *American Roots Music.* Published in 2001, the book served as the companion volume to a series on the subject that was broadcast on the PBS network. Savoy appeared in the series, and was active in the show's production. She also contributed Cajun music-related photographs— some of which she had taken herself.

Documenting Cajun music through photographs had by this time become something of a passion for Savoy, and she had scoured the Louisiana countryside to find old photos, many of which were featured in the PBS series. She then made copies before they could be lost or destroyed. Speaking of the need to preserve the photos she collected, she explained to Willging that "some of the houses burned down with all the pictures in them shortly thereafter or the people died and their photo collections disappeared." Savoy's photo collection is now recognized as a valuable resource by other scholars of Cajun music and history.

Savoy served as producer for *Evangeline Made: A Tribute to Cajun Music,* an album released by Vanguard Records in 2002. The album featured well-known singers such as Linda Ronstadt and John Fogerty performing Cajun music. At first intimidated by producing an album full of guest artists who did not know Cajun French, Savoy initially refused the project, but finally reconsidered, and plunged into the project with the same passion that has marked all of her efforts. The result was a resounding success, and the album received a Grammy Award nomination for Best Traditional Folk Album. The year 2002 also saw the release of *The Best of the Savoy-Doucet Cajun Band,* which included tracks covering the history of the band going back to 1981.

In 2003 Savoy and her family marked a new direction in their musical careers by releasing an album as the Savoy Family Band. The self-titled debut featured performances by Savoy, Marc, and Joel, and children Sarah and Wilson as well. In addition to new studio tracks, the album featured live performances of several songs, including "Sam's Big Rooster."

Savoy has continued to play music and record with her various bands, and especially with her own family in the Savoy Family Band. Besides playing in concerts throughout North America and Europe, the family plays together at home and at semi-public, once-a-week jam sessions at Marc's music shop, the Savoy Music Center.

Selected discography

With the Savoy Family Band

The Savoy Family Band Cajun Album, Arhoolie, 2003.

With the Savoy-Doucet Band

Home Music, Arhoolie, 1983.
With Spirits, Arhoolie, 1987.
Two-Step d'Amede, Arhoolie, 1989.
Live! At the Dance, Arhoolie, 1994.
Sam's Big Rooster, Arhoolie, 2000.
The Best of the Savoy-Doucet Band, Arhoolie, 2002.

With the Magnolia Sisters

Prends Courage, Arhoolie, 1995.
Chers Amis, Rounder, 2000.

As producer

Evangeline Made: A Tribute to Cajun Music, Vanguard, 2002.

Selected writings

American Roots Music (contributor), Abrams, 2001.
Cajun Music: A Reflection of a People, Bluebird, 1985.

Sources

Periodicals

Advocate (Baton Rouge, LA), March 29, 2002, p. 8.
OffBeat: New Orleans' and Louisiana's Music Magazine, April 2002.
Sing Out! The Folk Song Magazine, Fall 2003.

Online

"Ann Savoy," *All Music Guide,* http://www.allmusic.com (January 29, 2004).
"Contemporary Louisiana Cajon, Creole and Zydeco Musicians: Marc and Ann Savoy," Louisiana State University at Eunice, http://www.lsue.edu/acadgate/music/savoy.htm (January 29, 2004).
"Savoy, Marc and Ann Allen," *Encyclopedia of Cajun Culture,* http://www.cajunculture.com/People/savoymarc.htm (January 29, 2004).

—Michael Belfiore

Giacinto Scelsi

Composer

A biographer's nightmare, Giacinto Scelsi was a mysterious, reclusive, and elusive Italian aristocrat whose music has been described as otherwordly, miraculous, visionary, and life-altering. Refusing the title of "composer," Scelsi regarded himself as a medium through which music, originating in celestial spheres, appeared in the physical realm. Deeply spiritual, Scelsi immersed himself in the great traditions of Eastern and Western wisdom, always seeking a deeper understanding of the universe. He was not, however, a mystic who composed in order to convey certain insights to a wider audience; for him, writing music *was* a mystical act.

As a rule, even esoteric composers express their ideas through more or less traditional musical idioms. Despite his efforts to probe the mysteries of existence, the Russian composer Aleksandr Scriabin, for example, remained within the confines of Western tonality, even as he anticipated atonal music, which relinquished defined keys and the idea of a tonal center—a point of reference that the listener, regardless of his theoretical views about music, still instinctively craves. Rejecting the modern and avant garde quest for new musical forms and languages as superficial, Scelsi decided that, to access the cosmic source of all music, the composer must transcend all musical traditions and concentrate on the primal experience of sound.

The Search for the Hidden Dimension

According to Scelsi, sound—a form of cosmic energy—is a three-dimensional spherical phenomenon. While two dimensions, duration and quality (e.g. timbre) are easily perceived, the third dimension remains hidden within the sphere. What enabled Scelsi to discover this inner dimension were fine, barely perceptible microtonal pitch fluctuations that revealed entire worlds behind the illusion of a monolithic tone. Scelsi noted the profound artistic importance of overtone series, which the German scientist Heinrich Helmholtz analyzed in his writings about acoustics.

As Roger Scruton explained, musical pitch depends on the frequency of the vibration that creates it. Helmholtz observed, however, that when an object vibrates, it sets up subsidiary vibrations that are natural number multiples of the root frequency: 2, 3, 4, 5, 6, etc. The overtone series extends, theoretically, into infinity, suggesting the astonishing idea that every tone is infinte and inexhaustible. Scelsi's intuition that particular acoustical properties of tones opened new creative horizons inspired a group of younger artists, known as known as composers of "spectral music," who used computer technology to further explore the nature of tones. However, musicologists do not define Scelsi's music as spectral, since he eschewed any particular approach, preferring, instead, to experience tones as audible manifestation of a mysterious universe.

Count of Ayala Valva

The last Count of Ayala Valva, Scelsi was born in a castle in 1905 in southern Italy. He discovered the piano at the age of three. As an aristocrat, Scelsi was spared the trials of public education, studying music and the humanities with the best teachers in Italy. In addition, his talent, intelligence, disarming eccentricity, and social status enabled him to move freely among Italy's artistic and intellectual elite. After studying music in Rome, he went to Vienna in the 1930s, to study with Walter Klein, who introduced him to 12-tone music. Also known as serial music, this is a compositional technique invented by Arnold Schoenberg that derived a composition's entire melodic and harmonic structure from a predetermined pattern using all 12 tones of the chromatic scale.

Moving from one European capital from another, Scelsi encountered artists and writers, developed important friendships (particularly with the painter/poet, Henri Michaux and artist Salvador Dali), composed music, and keenly followed the trajectories of surrealism and other artistic movements. Fascinated by oriental mysticism, he also traveled in India and Tibet, returning to Lausanne, Switzerland, in the late 1930s, where he took refuge during World War II. After the war, Scelsi's wife, Dorothy, an English aristocrat related to the royal family, left him; Scelsi never heard from her again. He fell into a state of profound, debilitating despair, which, according to many stories, Swiss doctors were incapable of alleviating. Apparently, Scelsi cured himself by sitting at the piano for hours and playing one note in myriad ways.

Born Giacinto Maria Scelsi on January 8, 1905, in La Spezia, Italy; died on August 9, 1988, in Rome, Italy; married; wife's name, Dorothy.

Discovered the piano at age three; moved to Vienna, 1930s; composed *La nascita del Verbo,* 1948; composed *Quattro pezzi su una nota sole,* 1959; composed String Quartet No. 4, widely considered his greatest work, 1963; continued composing until the late 1970s.

A work symbolizing Scelsi's triumph over despair was *La nascita del Verbo* (The birth of the Word) for choir and orchestra, composed in the late 1940s. Performed in Paris in 1950, this composition established Scelsi as an original force in European music.

Settling in Rome in the early 1950s, Scelsi translated his meditations on the nature of tones into a series of extraordinary compositions, exemplified by *Four Pieces Each on a Single Note* for chamber orchestra. During the 1960s Scelsi continued to explore the resources of various musical instruments and experimented with the expressive potential of the human voice. While all his works represent important facets of his genius, the greatest achievement, according to critics, was his astonishing String Quartet No. 4, in which subtle tonal variations, combined with the mysterious power of small intervals, take the listener into unexpected dimensions of reality.

Blindness, Silence, and Aftermath

In the early 1970s, Scelsi became blind: the man who did not like to be seen (no one was allowed to photograph him) could not see any more. Later in the decade, he stopped composing. After his castle was destroyed in a 1980 earthquake, Scelsi spent his final years in Rome leading a reclusive life. He died in 1988.

After his death, younger composers began seriously studying his music, looking for ideas and insights. Performers, who particularly appreciated his efforts to enlarge the sonic range of traditional instruments, worked assiduously to bring the master's music to wider audiences. In curious twist, however, after Scelsi's death his close collaborator Vieri Tosatti made the outlandish claim that he was the real composer of Scelsi's music. While no one denies Tosatti's role as a scribe, experts have rejected his "revelation." It was Scelsi, and no one else, who composed, often sitting at the piano in a profound meditative trance, music that, to many listeners, evokes worlds beyond the imagination. Scelsi's music, wrote Arved Ashby in *American Record Guide,* "is indescribable: microtonal, arrhytmic, elemental, mysterious, slow-moving, not of our world. Nongrammatical. Visceral. A closed book. It follows no system and defined no audience."

Selected compositions

String Quartet No. 1, 1944.
La nascita del Verbo, cantata for chorus and orchestra, 1948.
Suite No. 8: "Bot-Ba"—Evocation of Tibet with Its Monasteries of High Mountains Summits, Tibetan Rituals, Prayers, and Dances, for piano, 1952
Quattro Illustrazioni: Four Illustrations on the Metamorphoses of Vishnu, for piano, 1953.
Suite No. 9: "Ttai"—A Succession of Episodes Which Express Time, or More Precisely, Time in Motion and Man as Symbolized by Cathedrals or Monasteries, with the Sound of the Sacred Om, for piano, 1953.
Suite No. 10: "Ka"—The Word "Ka" Has Many Meanings, but the Principle One Is "Essence," for piano, 1954.
Action Music, for piano, 1955.
String Trio, 1958.
I presagi (Forebodings), for ten instruments, brass, and percussion, 1958.
Quattro pezzi su una nota sole (Four Pieces Each on a Single Note), for chamber orchestra, 1959.
Hurqualia: A Different Realm, for orchestra with amplified instruments, 1960.
String Quartet No. 2, 1961.
Aion: Four Episodes in One Day of Brahma, for orchestra, 1961.
String Quartet No. 3, 1963.
String Quartet No. 4, 1963.
Duo for violin and cello, 1965.
Anahit (Lyrical poem on the name of Venus), for violin and 18 instruments, 1965.
Uaxuctum: The Legend of the Maya City which Destroyed Itself for Religious Reasons, for vocal soloists, ondes Martenot, chorus, and orchestra, 1966.
Natura renovatur, for strings, 1967.
Konx-Om-Pax: Three Aspects of Sounds—As the First Motion of the Immovable, as Creative Force, as the Syllable "Om," for chorus and orchestra, 1969.
Three Latin Prayers, for voice, 1970.
In nomine lucis, for electric organ, 1974.
Aitsi, for electronically prepared piano, 1974; arranged as String Quartet No. 5, 1985.
Pfhat: A Flash … and the Sky Opened, for choir and orchestra, 1974.

Selected discography

The Complete Works for Clarinet, Cpo, 1997.
Chamber Works for Flute and Piano, Cpo, 1998.
Complete Works for Flute and Clarinet, Col Legno, 2000.
Yamaon, Anahit, I Presagi, Kairos, 2000.

Natura renovatur, Elohim, Kairos, 2001.
Orchestral Works, Mode, 2001.
Piano Works, Mode, 2001.
Streichquartett Nr. 4 (String Quartet No. 4), Kairos, 2001.
Music for High Winds, Mode, 2002.
Action Music, Kairos, 2003.
Quatro Illustrazioni, Col Legno, 2003.

Sources

Books

Kemal, Salim, and Ivan Gaskell, editors, *The Languages of Art History,* Cambridge University Press, 1991.

Read, Gardner, *20th-Century Microtonal Notation,* Greenwood, 1990.
Sadie, Stanley, editor, *Grove Dictionary of Music and Musicians,* Macmillan, 2002.
Scruton, Roger, *Aesthetics of Music,* Oxford University Press, 1999.
Whitall, Arnold, *Musical Composition in the Twentieth Century,* Oxford University Press, 1999.

Periodicals

American Record Guide, January–February, 1998; September 2000; September 2001; January–February 2004.
Village Voice, February 25, 1997.

—*Zoran Minderovic*

Márta Sebestyén

Singer

Márta Sebestyén, one of Hungary's most celebrated music stars, gained a wider international audience when two of her songs were used on the soundtrack to *The English Patient,* the 1996 Academy Award-winning film. Sebestyén has been a performer with Muzsikás, Hungary's best-known folk music ensemble, since the early 1980s. She considers herself "a translator," she told Tim Lloyd, a writer for the *Advertiser* of Adelaide, Australia, "Because people who have never heard folk music in the city at the end of the 20th century need a translator. We are so used to video clips and so on that sometimes we no longer understand the power of the pure voice and pure harmony."

Sebestyén grew up in a small town near Hungary's border with Austria. After a thwarted anti-Communist uprising in 1956, her central European homeland became a frontier of the Iron Curtain, the divide that separated Soviet-controlled Communist Eastern Europe from the rest of the continent. Folk music, like religion, was scoffed at by Communist authorities as a relic of the past and a potentially dangerous expression of nationalist sentiment. However, Sebestyén's mother was an ethnomusicologist who had studied with Zoltán Kodály, the renowned folk music scholar, at the Budapest Academy. "My mother was listening to this music

For the Record . . .

Born in Hungary; daughter of a music teacher; once married. *Education:* Studied at the Budapest Academy, early 1970s.

Vocalist with the Sebö and Halmos group after 1975; also worked with Vujicsics, a folk ensemble, beginning in the 1970s; joined Muzsikás, 1980; toured Europe with Muzsikás during much of 1980s; recorded first solo record, *Apocrypha,* for Hannibal, 1992; two songs by Sebestyén, "Szerelem Szerelem" and "Teremtés," appeared on the soundtrack of the film *The English Patient,* 1996.

Awards: Winner of Hungary's Franz Liszt Prize.

Addresses: *Record company*—Rykodisc USA, Shetland Park, 27 Congress St., Salem, MA 01970, e-mail: info@ rykodisc.com, website: http://www.rykodisc.com.

before I was born," Sebestyén recalled in an interview with the *International Herald Tribune*'s Mike Zwerin. "I was quite literally born into it. It is in the family. But at the same time I have a brother and a sister and they have absolutely no interest in it. I was always mad about folk music."

The fact that much Hungarian folk music survived two world wars, the dissolution of the Austro-Hungarian Empire, and the imposition of state-sponsored socialism has been due in no small part to Kodály and to Béla Bartók, the famous twentieth-century composer. Kodály and Bartók had spent years traveling through rural, Hungarian-settled Transylvania in the early years of the century, taking extensive notes and transcribing the songs. Bartók later invoked many of these melodies in his own modernist works. Sebestyén discovered an example of their efforts when she won an award in a singing contest and was given a recording of old folk songs. "It was a big discovery for me at the age of 12 when I got an album from the archive of original field recordings," she told *Denver Post* writer Jeff Bradley. "I said, 'Oh God, the same song can be done many different ways depending on which region it comes from.' I think that was the moment I decided I wanted to follow this path."

Sebestyén began learning the different vocal techniques and traditional dances of Hungarian folk music, and won a singing contest when she was in high school. She went on to study at the Budapest Academy, where she became involved in a student move-

ment called *tanchaz,* or dance-house. As she explained to London *Times* journalist Nigel Williamson, "It was a folk music revival, young people doing the old folk dances, not in that costumed, choreographed way the regime liked, but with freedom. The authorities couldn't control it, so they decided it was dangerous." By 1975 she was singing with a group formed by Ferenc Sebö and Béla Halmos, two renowned musicians, and she sometimes worked with Vujicsics, another traditional ensemble. She joined the much-heralded Muzsikás ("the village musicians") in 1980. The group, formed by university students in the early 1970s out of the same protest spirit and ethnic pride that fueled the *tanchaz* movement, was immensely popular in Hungary, and with Sebestyén at the forefront, the group began to gain fame outside the country as well.

Muzsikás performed traditional Hungarian folk tunes using such instruments as the bagpipe, zither, violin, and dulcimer. She sang on the group's self-titled 1987 release on Hannibal Records, their first to reach a Western audience, and then went on to record several more for the label, as well as for Hungaroton, the official Hungarian record label. By this time, Hungary had tentatively begun experimenting with some free-market economic reforms, and began to enjoy a reputation as one of the more liberal outposts of the Communist bloc. In the same spirit, Hungaroton began to grant their roster of performers a bit more artistic control over their music. Sebestyén also became involved in a groundbreaking rock opera project, symbolic of this new era, based on the life of Hungary's eleventh-century king, Stephen I.

Sebestyén's first internationally released solo work was *Apocrypha,* issued on the Hannibal label in 1992. It was a "best of" compilation from her previous recordings, culling favorites from her repertoire of Hungarian, Slovak, Bulgarian, and Romanian songs. She won wider fame when director Anthony Minghella approached her personally to ask permission to use her song "Szerelem Szerelem" for his next movie project, a film adaptation of the Michael Ondaatje novel *The English Patient.* The story is set during World War II at a military hospital in the English countryside, where a badly burned Hungarian count, played by Ralph Fiennes, recounts his adventurous past to a war nurse. In one flashback scene, he attempts to seduce Kristin Scott Thomas's character, and plays the haunting Hungarian melody "Szerelem Szerelem," sung by Sebestyén, on an old Victrola. As the singer explained to Williamson, she had made her first recording of "Szerelem Szerelem" while undergoing a marital split in mid-1980s. "I thought it miraculous that Anthony recognised my sorrow and pain through a recording," she reflected.

The English Patient won nine Academy Awards in 1997, including that of Best Picture, and Sebestyén's record label capitalized on the success of the film by issuing *The Best of Márta Sebestyén: The Voice of "The English Patient."* The album featured her solo work as well as songs recorded with Muzsikás and Vujicsics. She also worked with Peter Gabriel, and one of her songs was sampled by the French ambient-techno group Deep Forest for their 1995 release *Boheme.* Despite the wider recognition, Sebestyén told the *International Herald Tribune* that she has tried to steer clear of the commercial side of the music business. "Ordinary people who listen to music on the radio all day long do not know that it is all a lie," she told Zwerin. "It is all noise, the noise of money. I pity people who have grown up never having heard honest music."

For her next solo effort for Hannibal, Sebestyén teamed with acclaimed musician and producer Nikola Parov to create *Kismet.* The 1996 record drew upon the folk traditions of several cultures, and Sebestyén delivered a Hindi lullaby and a Celtic ballad, among other tracks. She worked again with Vujicsics, which specializes in folk tunes found in the southern part of Hungary and in Serbia and Croatia, and appeared on their 2000 release *Southern Slav Folk Music* for Hungaroton. She has remained active in Muzsikás as well, and frequently travels with its members to the remoter regions of Transylvania to expand their repertoire. "We find the best music at weddings," she told *New York Times* writer Johanna Keller, "where the tradition is that the musicians aren't allowed to sleep or stop playing for several days."

Selected discography

(With Muzsikás) *Muzsikás,* Hannibal, 1987.
(With Muzsikás) *The Prisoner's Song,* Hannibal, 1988.
(With Vujicsics) *Vujicsics,* Hannibal, 1988.
Apocrypha, Hannibal, 1992.
(With Muzsikás) *Maramaros: The Lost Jewish Music of Transylvania,* Hannibal, 1993.
(With Muzsikás) *Ketto: Hungarian Folk Music,* Munich, 1995.
Kismet, Hannibal, 1996.
The Best of Márta Sebestyén: The Voice of "The English Patient," Hannibal, 1997.
(As Muzsikás and Márta Sebestyén) *Morning Star,* Hannibal, 1997.
(With Muzsikás) *The Bartók Album,* Hannibal, 1999.
(With Vujicsics) *Southern Slav Folk Music,* Hungaroton, 2000.
Dudoltam, Hungaroton, 2000.
(As Muzsikás and Márta Sebestyén) *Osz Az Ido,* Fono, 2003.
Live at Liszt Academy, Fono, 2004.

Sources

Periodicals

Advertiser (Adelaide, Australia), January 28, 1999, p. 40.
Boston Herald, October 16, 1997, p. 40; September 29, 1999, p. 47.
Denver Post, October 6, 1997, p. F8.
Independent (London, England), May 1, 1997, p. 19.
International Herald Tribune, April 24, 1999.
Nation, April 16, 1990, p. 539.
New York Times, March 30, 2003, p. 34.
Times (London, England), April 25, 1997, p. 36.
Whole Earth Review, Summer 1992, p. 128.

Online

"Marta Sebestyen," The Iceberg, http://www.theiceberg.com/artist/25441/marta_sebestyen.html (February 2, 2004).

—*Carol Brennan*

Russell Simmons

Record company executive, producer

The explosive entry of rap music onto the national music scene in the late 1980s was greatly due to the efforts and vision of rap producer and artist manager Russell Simmons. As co-owner and founder of the rap label Def Jam Records and as head of Rush Artist Management, Simmons, according to Nelson George in *Essence,* took "rap music, an often misunderstood expression of inner-city youth, and established it as one of the most influential forms of Black music." Dubbed by the media as the "impresario" and "mogul" of rap, Simmons began his career as a fledgling promoter of a new breed of street music, and worked his way up to the helm of a multimillion-dollar entertainment company—complete with its own film and television division, as well as several clothing and accessory lines.

Simmons grew up in a middle-class neighborhood in the New York City borough of Queens. As a youth he became involved with a street gang. In the mid-1970s Simmons enrolled at the Harlem branch of City College of New York, where he studied sociology. It was during this time that he became aware of rap music. He saw rappers as they converged in parks and on street corners, taking turns performing rap songs for gathering crowds. These crowds, as Maura Sheehy noted in *Manhattan, Inc.,* found "their power in dancing and dressing styles of the moment; in mimicking the swaggering, tougher-than-leather attitude; and by worshiping their street 'poets.'"

Simmons saw in rap enthusiasts a vast audience that the recording industry had not yet tapped. He thereafter left college and began tirelessly promoting local rap artists, producing recordings on shoestring budgets and organizing "rap nights" at dance clubs in Queens and Harlem. In 1984 he teamed with another aspiring rap producer, Rick Rubin, to form Def Jam Records. The company produced music by new rap groups including Simmons's brother, Joseph's group, rap pioneers Run-D.M.C. CBS Records agreed to distribute Def Jam's records and within three years, Def Jam staples such as the Beastie Boys' *Licensed to Ill,* LL Cool J's *Bigger and Deffer,* and Run-D.M.C.'s *Raising Hell* dominated the black music charts.

Simmons has been described as the "Berry Gordy of his time," comparing him to the man who brought the crossover black Motown sound to pop America in the 1960s. Yet Simmons took a fundamentally different approach. According to Sheehy in *Manhattan, Inc.,* "Like Gordy, Simmons is building a large, diverse organization into a black entertainment company, only Simmons's motivating impulse is to make his characters as 'black' as possible." Simmons was insistent on presenting rap images that are true to the tough urban streets from which rap arose. As a result, his groups donned such recognizable street garb as black leather clothes, high-top sneakers, hats, and gold chains. "In black America, your neighbor is much more likely to be

For the Record . . .

Born on October 4, c. 1957; raised in Hollis, Queens, NY; son of Daniel Simmons (a public school attendance supervisor); married Kimora Lee, 1998; children: Ming Lee, Aoki Lee. *Education:* Attended the City College of New York.

Co-founder and owner of Def Jam Records and Rush Productions, 1985–; owner of Rush Artist Management; founded Rush Communications, 1990; launched Phat Fashions, 1992; started producing *Def Comedy Jam* for HBO, 1991; founded Rush Philanthropic Arts Foundation, 1995; founded Def Pictures with producer Stan Lathan, 1995; director of music videos; published autobiography, *Life and Def: Sex, Drugs, Money and God,* Crown, 2001; organized Hip-Hop Summit Action Network, 2002; launched *Russell Simmons' Def Poetry Jam* on HBO and on Broadway, 2002.

Awards: Peabody Award for *Russell Simmons' Def Poetry Jam,* 2002; Tony Award, Best Theatrical Event for *Russell Simmons' Def Poetry Jam,* 2003.

Addresses: *Record company*—Island Def Jam, Worldwide Plaza, 825 8th Ave., New York, NY 10019. *Publicist*—Rubenstein Communications, Inc., 1345 Avenue of the Americas, New York, NY 10105.

someone like LL Cool J or Oran 'Juice' Jones than Bill Cosby," Simmons explained in the *New York Times.* "...A lot of the black stars being developed by record companies have images that are so untouchable that kids just don't relate to them. Our acts are people with strong, colorful images that urban kids already know, because they live next door to them."

As the manager for all Def Jam acts Simmons has made the authenticity of Def Jam artists a top priority. "Our artists are people you can relate to," he told *Interview.* "Michael Jackson is great for what he is—but you don't know anybody like that. The closest Run-D.M.C. comes to a costume is a black leather outfit.... It's important to look like your audience. If it's real, don't change it."

Some critics found the image of rappers disturbing. "It is the look of many rap artists—hard, belligerent, unassimilated, one they share with their core audience— that puts many folks on edge," noted George. While some objected to Public Enemy's logo of a black teen in the scope of a police gun, Simmons explained to George that the logo was representative of how many black teenagers feel—like "targets that are looked down upon." Simmons added, "Rush Management identifies with them [black teenagers]. That's why we don't have one group that doesn't look like its audience."

The lyrics and antics of some male rap artists have also infuriated women's groups, who found misogynistic messages in many songs and stage acts. Also, public officials have occasionally brought charges of lewdness against some rappers in concert. Despite the controversial nature of many rap lyrics, Simmons refused to censor the content of his rap groups' songs. He told George, "rap is an expression of the attitudes of the performers and their audience."

When critics charged that rap artists were not positive role models for many black youths, Simmons countered these attacks, explaining that many of their listeners are growing up in the same environments the artists spoke about. "If you take a look at the pop cultural landscape or the black political landscape now, there aren't a lot of heroes," he told the *New York Times.* "If you're a 15-year-old black male in high school and look around, you wonder what you can do with your life. (Rappers) opened up a whole new avenue of ambition. You can grow up to be like (them). It's possible."

With the success of his record label and ever-extending reach into the youth and urban culture markets, in 1990 Simmons launched Rush Communications with the intention of putting his wide range of business ventures under one umbrella. In 1991, he produced the Def Comedy series for HBO, which for seven years introduced a mainstream audience to such 'Def' comics as Martin Lawrence and Jamie Fox. In 1992 he created his own very successful men's clothing line, Phat Farm, which later expanded to include a women's line (known as Baby Phat), a children's line, sneakers, and accessories.

Despite his great success in translating urban culture to the masses, Simmons has remained committed to contributing, both socially and economically, to the community in which he was raised. In 1995, Simmons and his brothers, Daniel and Joseph, founded The Rush Philanthropic Arts Foundation, a non profit geared at helping inner city youth. The Foundation funds several initiatives, most notable of which is Rush Arts, a program designed to expose inner city children to the fine and performing arts.

In 1996 Simmons launched *One World* magazine which he later transformed into a syndicated television series, *Oneworld's Music Beat with Russell Simmons* in 1998. The magazine-style program served as a showcase and information bed for hip-hop culture as a whole. "Black culture is universal," he told *Billboard*. "This show won't be targeted just to blacks. I want this show to be inclusive; it will be for everyone who embraces young black culture." With these new endeavors, Simmons brought hip-hop culture to a wider audience. The same year Simmons wed Kimora Lee, longtime girlfriend and host of *Oneworld's Music Beat*. The couple went on to have two daughters, Ming Lee and Aoki Lee.

In 2000 Universal Music Group purchased Simmons's share of Def Jam. He continued to work at Def Jam (now called Island Def Jam), but in a different capacity. Simmons continued to act as a voice of the community. In June of 2001 he organized the historic Hip-Hop Summit. The summit attracted various controversial political and religious leaders including Maxine Waters and Minister Louis Farrakhan. It also flashed major star power with high profile appearances by Sean "Puffy" Combs, Jay-Z, and Mariah Carey. Those in attendance discussed such issues as conflict resolution for artists and greater efforts at accountability for hip-hop's social, political, and economic impact.

Following the Summit, Simmons founded the Hip-Hop Summit Action Network (HSAN). The aim of the HSAN is to take the relevance and impact of hip-hop and use it as a catalyst for education reform and other societal concerns affecting high-risk youth. Over the following years, Simmons remained committed to HSAN, working with New York politicians in an attempt to reform the controversial Rockafeller drug laws, raising money for the state's education budget, and instilling in young people the need to exercise their right to vote.

Russell Simmons' Def Poetry Jam followed in the footsteps of Simmon's former comedy show on the HBO cable network, this time giving a forum to a lauded collective of slam-style poets. The show was granted a prestigious Peabody award in 2002. In November of the same year *Def Poetry Jam* opened on Broadway to critical acclaim, eventually winning a Tony Award for Best Theatrical Special Event.

In 2004 Simmons continued to stretch his unique ability to deliver hip-hop culture, causes, and business ventures to a mass audience, most notably by taking the Hip-Hop Summit on the road to cities around the United States, including Detroit, Philadelphia, and New Orleans, reaching a much larger audience than he was able to in New York. As he explained to *Billboard* magazine, "Hip-hop represents the greatest union of young people with the most diversity—all races and religions—that people have felt in America."

Selected discography

As producer

(Run-D.M.C.) *Run-D.M.C.,* Profile, 1984.
(Run-D.M.C.) *King of Rock,* Profile, 1985.
(Run-D.M.C.) *Raising Hell,* Profile, 1986.
(LL Cool J) *Bigger and Deffer,* Def Jam, 1987.
(Run-D.M.C.) *Tougher than Leather,* Profile, 1988.
(Alyson Williams) *Raw,* Def Jam, 1989.
(Slick Rick) *The Rulers Back,* Def Jam, 1991.
(Boss) *Born Gangstaz,* Def Jam, 1992.
(Afrika Bambaataa) *Presents Eastside,* Obsessive, 2003.

Sources

Books

George, Nelson, *The Death of Rhythm and Blues,* Pantheon, 1988.

Periodicals

Billboard, November 4, 1995; January 31, 1998; August 19, 2000; June 17, 2000; June 16, 2001; February 10, 2001.
Brandweek, May 8, 2000.
Business Week, October 27, 2003.
Daily News Record, June 5, 2000.
Electronic Media, November 20, 2000.
Ebony, January 2001.
Essence, March 1988.
Fast Company, November 2003.
Hollywood Reporter, August 17, 1999.
Interview, September 1987.
Jet, May 28, 1990.
Manhattan, Inc., February 1990.
Newsweek, July 28, 2003
New York Times, August 1987; February 20, 1991.
People, July 5, 1999, pp. 25.

—*Michael E. Mueller and Nicole Elyse*

Tomasz Stańko

Trumpeter, band leader, composer

Tomasz Stańko is Poland's greatest jazz trumpeter, band leader, and composer, whose pioneering work in free jazz shows both European and American influences. The *Times* of London writer Alyn Shipton called him "Europe's most consistently inventive jazz trumpeter."

Tomasz Stańko was born on July 11, 1942, in Rzeszów, Poland. His father, a violinist as well as a lawyer, introduced him to music at an early age with lessons in classical violin and piano. Stańko found his true calling when he began to study the trumpet in 1959 at a Kraków music school. Jazz was new to Poland at the time; Poland's communist government had even outlawed the form until shortly before Stańko began to play. "Jazz," he explained to George Varga in the *San Diego Union–Tribune,* "was outlawed because it was synonymous with the Western and American style of life." Even after playing jazz became legal, it still retained a subversive aura, although an attractive one, because, as Stańko has explained, it represented freedom for both listeners and performers.

Jazz recordings were hard to come by in Poland when Stańko was discovering the form, so his first exposure to jazz was the music he heard on American radio

Born on July 11, 1942, in Rzeszów, Poland. *Education:* Attended music school in Kraków, Poland.

Formed Jazz Darings jazz group, won Polish Jazz Musician of the Year Award, 1962; joined group led by well-known jazz musician and film composer Krzysztof Komeda, 1963; worked with numerous other jazz groups through the 1960s; played with Globe Unity Orchestra throughout Europe, 1960s; formed own quintet, 1968; released *Music for K,* 1970; recorded with numerous other groups, 1970s; formed own quartet, 1974; joined Tomasz Stańko–Adam Makowicz Unit, 1975; began career as soloist, 1978; released *Music from Taj Mahal and Karla Caves,* 1980; appeared on the albums of numerous other artists through the 1980s; formed Freelectronic, 1985; played with Freelectronic at Camden Jazz Festival, 1985; featured on live album made at Montreux Jazz Festival, 1987; played with Cecil Taylor–led European Orchestra, late 1980s; played with numerous other groups, 1990s; founded two new groups, late 1990s; signed with ECM Records, 1990s; released *Leosia,* 1996; *Litania,* 1997; *From Green Hill,* 2000; *Soul of Things,* 2002; awarded European Jazz Prize, 2002; launched first tour of the United States, 2002.

Awards: Polish Jazz Musician of the Year, 1962; European Jazz Prize, 2002.

Addresses: *Record company*—Egger Innovations- und Handels-GmbH, Abt. ECM Export, Pasinger Str. 94, Gräfelfing D-82166, Germany, website: http://www.ecmrecords.com.

broadcasts. He later cited the American jazz musician Chet Baker as his earliest influence, followed closely by Miles Davis. In 1962, when he was 21, Stańko helped form a group called Jazz Darings with Adam Makowicz. At first the band played hard bop, but when Makowicz left and Janusz Manuak replaced him, the group turned to free jazz—an unstructured style pioneered in part by American musician Ornette Coleman. The Jazz Darings became one of the first European free jazz groups and established Stańko as a pioneer in his own right. Stańko won the Polish Jazz Musician of the Year Award in this same year.

From 1963 through 1967 Stańko worked in a group with Krzysztof Komeda, Poland's most famous film composer and jazz musician (known for scoring many of the films of Roman Polanski, including *Rosemary's Baby*). In later years Stańko would call Komeda his mentor and one of his greatest influences, as he told Rob Adams in the Glasgow *Herald,* "I took so much from him, his lyricism, his simplicity—he showed me how to play the music's essentials." Komeda's group made waves with its daring free jazz experiments, and became known to American musicians as well. Komeda emigrated to the United States and planned to bring Stańko over to join him after he got established, but he died in 1969 (some sources say 1968) following injuries sustained in a car accident. Instead of following his mentor to the United States, therefore, Stańko stayed in Europe, where he helped perpetuate Komeda's music in both live performances and his own recordings.

During the 1960s Stańko also worked with Andrzej Trazaskowski (from 1965 to 1969), and with the Alex von Schlippenbach-led Globe Unity Orchestra, which played in Europe's best-known jazz clubs. In 1968, Stańko formed and led a quintet that played in jazz festivals throughout Europe and was acclaimed for its *Music for K,* a tribute to Komeda. During this time, Stańko also recorded with the Studio Jazzowe Polskiego Radia orchestra, with the Don Cherry Eternal Rhythm Orchestra, and in a group led by Michal Urbaniak.

After his quintet disbanded in 1973 Stańko formed a quartet the following year. He also played and recorded with other groups, including ensembles led by Edward Vesala. Stańko teamed up with his old colleague Makowicz in 1974, when they both played in Urbaniak's group. In 1975, they formed the Tomasz Stańko-Adam Makowicz Unit, a group that also included Tomasz Szukalski and Czeslaw Bartkowski. The group toured Germany and cut two albums in the mid-1970s.

In 1978 the quartet disbanded, and Stańko began his career as a soloist, at first playing live concerts, and then recording. In 1980 he made a solo recording in India, at the Taj Mahal, and at the Karla Caves temple. He continued to play in other bands through the 1980s, including in a group led by Edward Vesala called Heavy Life, and in the Sławomir Kulpowicz-led In/formation. In 1981, Stańko teamed with influential American bassist Gary Peacock to cut an album. He appeared on numerous other recordings in the early 1980s, including a 1983 release as a member of the Edward Vesala Trio, and as a guest soloist with the NDR big band in 1984. In addition to playing with these groups, Stańko also performed in a trio consisting of himself, Jack De-Johnette, and Rufus Reid in 1983, and cut an album with the Cecil Taylor-led Orchestra of Two Continents in 1984.

In the early to mid-1980s, Stańko played with an ensemble that also featured Sławomir Kulpowicz. In

1985, Stańko formed Freelectronic, a group that played at the Camden Jazz Festival in 1985, and in 1987 was featured on a live album made at the Montreux Jazz Festival. As the 1980s drew to a close, Stańko again teamed with the pioneering pianist Cecil Taylor to play with the European Orchestra.

The 1990s saw Stańko still going strong, playing with numerous groups, cutting an album in 1991 with a group consisting of himself, reed player Vlatko Kucan, double-bass player Jay Oliver, and American expatriate drummer Billy Elgart. In 1991, 1994, and 1995, Stańko recorded several albums with Nicolas Simion. In 1993 he formed two more quartets, and as the 1990s drew to a close, founded two other groups, one of which specialized in the music of his old collaborator Krzysztof Komeda.

During the 1990s Stańko also signed with the German ECM record label and continued to record solo albums, including *Litania,* a Komeda tribute album. Released in 1997, it included work composed by Komeda for various film projects that had never been recorded as standalone musical compositions. In 2000 ECM released Stańko's *From the Green Hill* in the United States, a work composed by Stańko but heavily influenced by Komeda. *Soul of Things,* released in 2002, was a suite of untitled improvisations

In 2002, at the age of 60, Stańko was awarded the first European Jazz Prize. In the same year the Tomasz Stańko Quartet took its first concert tour of the United States. Starting at a small jazz venue in Philadelphia, Stańko looked forward to introducing American audiences to his work. As he told Tim Blangger in the *Morning Call,* "I am so excited … [t]he United States is the source of this music and the audiences are also the best, very educated." In addition to his extensive work as a performer on stage and in the studio, Stańko has followed in the footsteps of his mentor, Komeda, in composing musical scores for both films and theater productions.

Selected discography

As unaccompanied soloist

Music from Taj Mahal and Karla Caves, Leo, 1980.

As leader

Music for K, Muza, 1970.
Purple Sun, Calig, 1973.
Balladyna, ECM, 1975.
Almost Green, Leo, 1978.
Witkacy-Peyotl, Poljazz, 1984.
Bluish, Power Bros., 1991.
Caoma, Konnex, 1991.
Bosonossa and Other Ballads, Gowi, 1993.
Matka Joanna, ECM, 1994.
Leosia, ECM, 1996.
Litania, ECM, 1997.
From the Green Hill, ECM, 1998.
Soul of Things, ECM, 2002.

Sources

Periodicals

Guardian (Manchester, England), October 17, 1997, p. T18.
Herald (Glasgow, Scotland), July 1, 1999, p. 14.
Morning Call (Allentown, PA), October 26, 2002, p. A53.
San Diego Union-Tribune, November 6, 2002, p. F10.
Times (London), November 25, 2002, p. 17.
Washington Post, November 1, 2002, p. T6.

Online

"Stańko, Tomasz," *Grove Dictionary of Music,* http://www. grovemusic.com (January 29, 2004).
"Tomasz Stanko," *All Music Guide,* http://www.allmusic.com (January 29, 2004).
"Tomasz Stanko Biography," *Polish Jazz Network,* http://www.stanko.polishjazz.com/ (January 29, 2004).

—*Michael Belfiore*

Frank "Andy" Starr

Singer, songwriter, singer

Johnny Cash and Frank "Andy" Starr died on the same day. They never met, but had a few things in common. Both were from the state of Arkansas, made music that reflected the visceral impact of blues and early rock 'n' roll, recovered from lives of excess to become somewhat spiritual men, and both released new albums shortly before their respective deaths. However, Starr was never really able to find his way out of the wilderness of obscurity, although the rockabilly sides he cut in the mid-to-late 1950s still delight archivists with their shuddering, greasy vitality.

Born Franklin Delano Gulledge on October 21, 1932, in Combs, Arkansas, and the youngest of eight children, Starr was raised in abject poverty. In an interview for *Original Cool* he remembered, "My father, bless his heart, he was a rounder—a roustabout. He was hardly ever home; he always went off to Kansas, Missouri, and different places working in the mines and oil fields. He'd come home just long enough to get my mother pregnant again then he was gone again. My father, he drank a lot, and he liked to gamble. I guess that's why he never had any money."

Music Provided Diversion

"If I had not of had an old-fashioned Southern Christian mother to get us all through, I wouldn't even be alive today," he said in the *Original Cool* interview. "She had to raise and garden without hardly anything to farm with. I have nothing but good to say about mother, she was the one thing that held the family together. We had

no money. Once in a blue moon, somebody'd get a hold of a dollar or two, buy a sack of flour, sack of meal, bucket of lard or something like that. It was always a survival game. If it wasn't for rabbits, squirrels, opossums, and raccoons, we'd have never made it."

Starr's brother Bob Gulledge confided that music provided a needed distraction from their sometimes dire circumstances. "For as long as I can remember, our family was a musical one. Mother played an old pump organ, Dad was an accomplished fiddle player, and all the children played an instrument, fiddle, guitars and banjo. I was 7 years old and Frank was 5 when Dad showed us the chords C, D and G on the guitar, and from then on we were hooked. Frank and I sang constantly, and were ever learning new songs, many from listening to the *Grand Ole Opry* on the battery radio." Inspired by such performers as the Skillet Lickers and the Fruit Jar Drinkers, the Gulledge family musicians played raw hillbilly music at local house parties and barn dances.

Serving three years in the Army during the Korean conflict, Starr was a sharpshooter on the front lines who rose to the rank of sergeant. Later he would claim to be the first Korean War veteran to be diagnosed with Post Traumatic Stress Disorder. Although he seemed initially unaffected, the problem would come back to severely haunt him in later life.

An Arkansas Plowboy

After his discharge from the armed services, Starr wanted to make a life in music with his brothers Bob and Chuck. "In 1953, Frank was living with Chuck in Los Angeles, so I joined them there," recalled Bob Gulledge. "We went to one club and asked for an audition, and the manager agreed to let us sing a couple of songs during the current band's intermission. We got a standing ovation, and when the night was over, the manager fired the band he had, and hired us." Billed as the Arkansas Plowboys, the brothers played at several California nightspots including The Chit Chat, Vaughan's Alibi, and George's Round Up.

Although work was steady, the band would not stay together very long. "Sibling rivalry began to surface and Frank demanded to be the front man," explained Gulledge. "He soon quit the band and formed another band, still playing in the area. Chuck and I continued for awhile, but it was never the same, so I packed up and took my family to Idaho. I formed a band in Wallace, Idaho, and was playing at Brownie's Corner. A few weeks later Frank showed up and wanted to play with me. At this time, he played lead for the songs he sung, and I played lead for the ones I sung."

The reunion wouldn't last long, because Starr just couldn't settle down. "Frank soon got restless and feeling the urge to get back into music," recalled

Born Franklin Delano Gulledge on October 21, 1932, in Combs, AK; died on September 9, 2003, in Fayetteville, AK; son of Grover Cleveland (a railroad worker, oil field laborer, miner, and logger) and Tennie (Faubus) Gulledge; married and divorced at least three times; children include: Linda and Teena Gulledge, Jonas Starr.

Played the guitar by age five; joined Army, served in Korea, 1950-53; formed the Arkansas Plowboys with brothers Bob and Chuck, 1953; hosted daily radio show on KDSX in Denison, Texas, 1955; recorded for Joe Leonard's Lin label as Frank Starr and the Rockaway Boys, 1955; as Starr, hosted his own radio program on KWAL in Wallace, ID, 1956; Starr's recordings leased to MGM, who renamed him "Andy Starr," 1956-57; Starr's recordings leased to Kapp and Holiday Inn labels, 1957-62; last single leased to Lin records, 1963; played in California as Frankie Starr and The Blue Notes, 1956-69; returned to radio station KWAL, c. late 1960s; recorded independent releases as Frank Starr, 1972-93; Bear Family released the definitive collection of his early Lin, MGM, and Kapp material as *Dig Them Squeaky Shoes,* 1996; contributed recordings to independent label projects by Bobby Wayne and Don Weise, 1998; recorded for Wild Oats label in Nashville, 2002; full-length posthumous release issued by Wild Oats, 2004.

Awards: Inducted into the Rockabilly Hall of Fame, 2000.

Addresses: *Record companies*—Spitfire Records, 2436 N. Astor, Spokane, WA 99207. Wildfire Records, 2012 West Montgomery, Spokane, WA 99205. Wild Oats Records, P.O. Box 210982, Nashville, TN 37221, website: http://www.wildoatsrecords.com.

Gulledge. "He headed to L.A., and later on to Idaho again." By this time he was beginning to sing a new kind of music—rockabilly.

MGM's Answer to Elvis Presley

"I had a fella go with me who played rhythm guitar. We just took off playing in joints at night and driving through the day," Starr explained to *Original Cool.* "I was just looking for a break; trying to make some records, find a recording contract. I got off in Denison, Texas, and got a job playing on the radio [KDSX]—no money in it, but it was a chance to be heard. So, I cranked up my own little radio show with just me, my guitar, and my buddy. The station manager liked me well enough and he called me in his office and said, 'Frank, I'm going to send you over to Gainesville, Texas, to see Joe Leonard. I believe on my recommendation, you can make records with him.' That's what happened. Joe Leonard had a small label he was trying to make something out of and he signed me to a recording contract. I made my first recordings for him."

Leonard, a canny packager and promoter, dubbed his new artist Frank Starr, and put his debut single, "Dig Them Squeaky Shoes," on his new Lin label. Knowing that his new singer-songwriter was fueled by the same type of talent that drove Elvis Presley, Leonard began shopping Starr to other labels, resulting in another name change. Explained Starr, "When they put me on MGM Records, I got a letter from a lawyer in New York City saying, 'Your new name is now Andy Starr.' That wasn't my idea, I never did like the name Andy Starr, but it's legendary stuff, part of my life."

Billed as Andy Starr and backed by the Texas-based band The Strikes, the singer fashioned some of the best records of the original rockabilly era for MGM: "Rockin' Rollin' Stone," "She's A Goin' Jessie," "Round and Round," and "Give Me a Woman." The latter proved especially popular in Pasadena, California, where a disc jockey reportedly crowed, "You've heard of Elvis the Pelvis, well this is Andy the Dandy."

Despite some hot tunes, a major label, and crowd-inciting appearances on the *Ozark Jubilee* and the *Big D Jamboree,* Starr never scored with anything remotely close to a national hit record. As a result, he spent most of the 1950s working at KWAL radio in Idaho, and grinding away in honky-tonks at night. He told *Original Cool,* "Joe Leonard got me on a few big shows here and there, but I was pretty much on my own. I did my own booking and just went from town-to-town and club to club and played every knock down drag-out hole-in-the-wall joint from the Mississippi River to the West Coast. … Of course, I did play in a few real nice clubs, but they were few."

Top Attraction in Alaska

Eventually Starr caught a break in 1960 that kept his family fed. "Well, I peaked out in Alaska," he recalled in *Original Cool.* "I was hired to go there on a club date [at the Hi Hat Club]. I signed a six-month contract and stayed five years! I was the bandleader, in charge of entertainment, making real good money. Then I flew back to Nashville and recorded every once in a while for Joe Leonard again."

Leonard leased Starr's music to Kapp and Holiday Inn before putting him back on Lin in 1963. But once out of the music mainstream, Starr's recording career suffered. Worse, being a name performer in Alaska provided Starr with an excuse to succumb to the twin demons of drugs and alcohol. He told *Original Cool,* "Playing music six, seven nights a week, you've got to have something to keep you going. People don't care whether you're sick or not, they want you to get up there and entertain. … I got into that real bad and had to get out of it."

Starr left Alaska in 1965, and tried to make another go of it in Los Angeles, where he played as Frankie & The Blue Notes. By then, the British Invasion had made him a pop music anachronism. After a recording deal and movie offer fell through, he departed for the Pacific Northwest, where he worked in a sawmill and played music on the weekends for the better part of 18 years.

Took Erratic Path

In 1972 the singer legally changed his name to Frank Starr because "I got tired of being called one thing and signing my name as something else." A short time later he formed the "Church of America" and began giving religious testimony to prisoners while cutting a live album for his own label. During that period he released the 1973 LP *Frank Starr Sings Patterson & Starr.* Recorded with co-writer Harry Patterson, its simple acoustic approach showed what a fine country and blues singer Starr could be under the right circumstances.

Rollin' Rock's Ron Weiser released an EP of some of Starr's unreleased Lin masters to the delight of rockabilly aficionados in 1975, but if the singer took any notice of the growing rockabilly revival, he didn't act upon it. Making increasingly unusual decisions, he announced he was a candidate for the state senate in Idaho in 1974, and ran as a protest candidate in the U.S. Presidential race in 1978. In 1996 he again declared himself a candidate for the land's highest office. During this time Starr also released a cassette of poorly crafted salacious songs titled *Good Stuff (Rated XXX),* and a protest album called *Uncle $am $ucks.*

Although Starr's early records—compiled on Bear Family's 1995 release *Dig Them Squeaky Shoes*—were loved by rockabilly enthusiasts the world over, the artist himself never reaped the benefits of the genre's revival. Erratic and in constant poor health, he seldom performed outside of Arkansas, and when European promoters came calling, he would ask for exorbitant fees. During the late 1990s he leased some sides to old friends and fellow cult rockers Bobby Wayne and Don Weise. By then Starr wanted to make a comeback, but his penchant for making unrealistic demands had caught up with him and there were no takers.

A Final Moment in the Sun

Married again and with his health on the rebound, Starr caught a break when Steve Haggard's Wild Oats label in Nashville came calling. Haggard's wife, artist Gail Lloyd of the rockabilly/swing combo Gail & the Tricksters, had admired Starr's early sides and wanted to work with him. It took some doing, but Haggard got Starr up to Nashville, put a solid roots band behind him, and recorded eleven songs, one a duet with Lloyd. Four of those tunes were released on the 2003 compilation album *Starr Struck,* which also featured performances by Lloyd and another group, the Haywoods. For a few precious moments during each song he demonstrated the bluesy spark that made his early records so good.

A few months before his death, Starr wrote a letter to the editor of a local Arkansas newspaper. With justifiable pride, he told of being called to Nashville to record an album. His final words provided his epitaph. "My message to the public is this: Don't ever give up on your dreams and your ambitions. Especially you young people. Stay in school. Get a good education and believe in yourself."

"I never went looking for Nashville," Starr continued. "Nashville came looking for me. Why? Because of 50 years of hard work and dedication I had given to the music industry. I am now 70 years of age and it looks like a whole world of opportunities have opened up for me. Respectfully, Frank Starr." Frank "Andy" Starr died from complications of a staph infection on September 12, 2003.

Selected discography

Singles

"Dig Them Squeaky Shoes," Lin, 1955.
"Rockin' Rollin' Stone," MGM, 1956.
"She's a Goin' Jessie," MGM, 1956.
"Give Me a Woman," MGM, 1956.
"One More Time," MGM, 1957.
"Do it Right Now," Kapp, 1957.
"Knees Shakin'," Holiday Inn, 1961.
"Pledge of Love," Lin, 1963.

Albums

(With the Wilson-McKinley Band) *You Can't Disguise Religion,* Starr, 1972.
In Concert at the Idaho State Penitentiary, Starr, 1973.
Frank Starr Sings Patterson & Starr, Starr, 1973.
Frank Starr Live at Wanda's Club, Starr, 1973.
Good Stuff (Rated XXX), Starr, 1990.

Uncle $am $ucks, Starr, 1992.
Dig Them Squeaky Shoes, Bear Family, 1995.
Don Weise: Hillbilly Cat—Special Guest Andy Starr, Spitfire, 1998.
Starr Struck: Frank "Andy" Starr, The Haywoods, Gail & the Tricksters, Wild Oats, 2003.
The Rockin' Return of Frank "Andy" Starr, Wild Oats, 2004.

Sources

Books

Morrison, Craig, *Go Cat Go: Rockabilly Music and Its Makers,* University of Illinois Press, 1996.

Periodicals

Goldmine, September 8, 1989.
Kicks #7, 1992.
Original Cool #44, December/January 2001.

Online

"Andy Starr," RCS Artist Discography, http://www.rcs.law. emory.edu/rcs/artists/s/star5500.htm (January 8, 2004).
"Frank 'Andy' Starr," Rockabilly Hall of Fame, http://www. rockabillyhall.com/AndyStarr.html (February 4, 2004).

Additional information was obtained through phone interviews and e-mails with the artist's brother Bob Gulledge, sister-in-law Mildred Gulledge, and Starr's daughter Linda Hone.

—Ken Burke

Stereolab

Pop group

Stereolab singer Laetitia Sadier told *Pulse!*: "We're a pop band in the sense that being pop is about knowing how to steal from the past and bring your own personality and ideas into it." Stereolab established itself as a cult favorite, partly because the band "stole" from an eclectic combination of largely ignored musical forms. But while other acts that share their passion for "Space-Age Bachelor Pad Music," easy listening, and other previously debased styles—mostly from the 1950s and '60s—Stereolab have refused to indulge in camp. Instead, they have taken the adventurous thread of such recordings and followed it into new sonic territory. Meanwhile, Sadier's lyrics have explored political and social issues with a surrealist's sense of poetry. "The whole effect is one of a shiny silver bubble," ventured Kathy Mancall in *Addicted to Noise*, "an erotically charged Jetsonian '60s vision of the future."

The band began in 1988, when Sadier met British guitarist-songwriter Tim Gane in Paris. Gane, then a member of the moody pop band McCarthy, used some translated lyrics of Sadier's on his band's final album, and the two were both musically and romantically involved shortly thereafter. By 1991 they formed Stereolab, which took its name from a record company of the "hi-fi" era that specialized in recordings designed to exploit the sonic capabilities of stereo equipment. Gane and Sadier also created their own label, Duophonic. Fascinated by the inventive, atmospheric recordings of such composers as Juan Esquivel and Martin Denny, who fused "exotic," symphonic, and avant-garde textures as well as such pop innovators as Brian Wilson of the Beach Boys, Stereolab began searching for new sounds.

The group's approach leaned heavily on out-of-date keyboards, especially old organs. Gane and company took the already spooky tone of such vintage gear and further modified it with other musical effects. "That roughed-up organ, put through an amp and distorted—I don't know why, but I'm always attracted to that kind of sound," Gane told the *Los Angeles Times*. "I don't like things too clean. I like a bit of spillage." Sadier noted to the newspaper's Lorraine Ali that the ensemble "didn't look for that particular sound, we kind of stumbled on it. We happened to find this Farfisa organ, a great big plastic thing from the '70s, in a thrift shop," she added. The sound of this organ—generally considered outdated since its long-vanished heyday—appealed strongly to the Stereolab sensibility.

With a shifting crew of personnel that has included singer/guitarist Mary Hansen, bassist Duncan Brown, drummer Andy Ramsay, keyboardist/singer Katharine Gifford, multi-instrumentalist Sean O'Hagan, and a score of guest performers, Stereolab began constructing their idiosyncratic sound. "Basically, Tim writes the music on a 4-track (tape machine) and gets a very thin, sort of skeleton of a song," Sadier noted of their approach in *Grip*. "And I write some lyrics on top of that, and then we have the bones of the song. And then we either take time to practice it and then take to the studio, or we go straight to the studio and bring flesh to it there. Basically, when we record we've not really worn the songs in, it's really the birth of them."

After a couple of indie releases began to generate a cult following, Stereolab were signed to Elektra Records. Their major label debut, *Transient Random-Noise Bursts with Announcements,* stunned critics and suggested that the group's ambitions were expanding. Sadier recalled in *Pulse!* that the album "was a nightmare to record—even talking about it brings a pain to my stomach." Yet by the time of 1994's follow-up, *Mars Audiac Quintet,* she added, Stereolab was "much more in control. You always need to f*** up somewhere to then be able to do something that's right."

At the time of the *Mars* release, Gane outlined some of his musical preferences to Lorraine Ali of the *Los Angeles Times*. "I like music made for utilitarian reasons, like elevator music," he asserted. "You can take it out of its original purpose, then it's just strange and very avant-garde. It's like an odd little art world, but the people who made that music didn't think it was strange at the time." In *Addicted to Noise,* he argued that "People are ready to look for something else [besides] mainstream rock music, and trying to find something for themselves, taking a chance and finding things that aren't forced down your throat." Ali of the *Los Angeles Times* characterized the group's work as "easy-listening music for a generation raised on [alternative

Members include **Duncan Brown** (group member, 1993-96), bass; **Joe Dilworth** (group member, 1991-92), drums; **Tim Gane** (born on July 12, 1964), guitar, keyboards; **Katharine Gifford** (group member, 1993-95), keyboards, vocals; **Mary Hansen** (joined group, 1992; died on December 9, 2002), guitar, keyboards, vocals; **Richard Harrison** (joined group, 1996), bass; **Martin Kean** (group member, 1991-93), bass; **Morgan Lhote** (joined group, c. 1995), organ; **Sean O'Hagan** (group member, 1993), keyboards, guitar; **Andy Ramsay** (joined group, c. 1992), drums, percussion, vocals; **Laetitia Sadier** (born on May 6, 1968), vocals, keyboards.

Group formed in London, England, c. 1991; released debut recordings on own label, Duophonic; released debut album *Switched On Stereolab,* on Too Pure label, 1992; signed to Elektra Records and released *Transient Random-Noise Bursts with Announcements,* 1993; provided music for exhibit by sculptor Charles Long, 1995; participated in Lollapalooza traveling music festival, 1995; released *Emperor Tomato Ketchup,* 1996; released *Dots and Loops,* 1997; released *Sound Dust,* 2001; released *Margarine Eclipse,* 2004.

Addresses: *Record company*—Elektra Records, 75 Rockefeller Plaza, New York, NY 10019. *Website*— Stereolab Official Website: http://www.stereolab.co.uk.

noise-rockers] Sonic Youth." This proved accurate; Stereolab toured on the second stage of the traveling alternative music festival Lollapalooza. Yet such widespread exposure didn't prevent them from providing music for an art exhibit by a little-known sculptor, Charles Long.

Rather than exploit the kitsch value of "hi-fi" eccentrics like Esquivel, Denny, Les Baxter, and others—as a burgeoning circle of indie "lounge" bands had done— Stereolab took their influences seriously. "There's supposedly a trashy quality to it," Sadier told *Pulse!,* "but to us it actually means a lot. We don't feel it's kitsch. Some of these records are actually really good, with good music and ideas. Things that take you somewhere. These records were looking into the future with enthusiasm and great hope, and we like to look at the future that way."

Meanwhile, over sonic collages inspired by such eclectic sources, Sadier wrote lyrics—in French and English—of social confusion and loss. She was nonetheless bemused that critics persisted in labeling her a Marxist. However, her questioning stance did suggest a politically subversive agenda. "I'm not coming up with answers," she claimed in *Strobe,* "but surely there are answers to our problems. After having asked all the right questions, you'll want to take action. It's up to us, there's no big written solution, there's no God, and no ideologies either. There's only ourselves that we can rely on."

Stereolab expanded its following considerably with its subsequent releases, especially the much-praised *Emperor Tomato Ketchup.* Newly inspired by European progressive rock and the avant-jazz of Sun Ra and Don Cherry, the group once again explored new sonic territory. "The new songs are similar to what we always do with repetition and minimalism," Gane told *Newsday.* "But this time I wanted them to be bouncy, more rubbery. I wanted to have more of a swing." *Musician* deemed *Emperor* "extraordinary," while England's *Melody Maker* called it "bloody essential." *Entertainment Weekly* proclaimed that "They may be influenced by obscure German groups, they may sing partially in French, but Stereolab's kitsch pop is enjoyable even without a foreign language degree."

Following the release of *Emperor Tomato Ketchup,* bassist Duncan Brown departed, and was replaced by Richard Harrison. He made his first full-length recording with the group, *Dots and Loops,* in 1997. The group's lineup was enhanced by guests Jan St. Werner, a member of the German techno band Mouse on Mars, and producer and musician John McEntire from the band Tortoise. In addition to the Moog and Farfisa keyboards usually associated with Stereolab, the group also introduced an EMS Vocoder into their instrumental lineup. "People usually use it for vocals or keyboards," Gane told *Guitar Player,* "But an EMS Vocoder is great with drums or drum machines and guitar or organ. What comes out is a strange amalgamation. It's like the film *The Fly,* when the guy goes through the transformation. When it comes out it's a perfect blend of fly and human." Gane and Sadier put the group on hiatus afterwards in order to spend time with their first child. In 1999, they enlisted producers John McIntire and Jim O'Rourke for *Cobra and Phases Group Play Voltage in the Milky Night.*

Stereolab activities in the first years of the 21st century included the release of *Sound-Dust* in 2001 and a collection of live BBC Radio performances, *ABC Music: The Radio 1 Sessions* in 2002. Following the release of the latter album, singer-guitarist Mary Hansen died in London, England, after being hit by a truck while riding her bike. She was 36. Stereolab soldiered on in her absence, however, and released the critically acclaimed *Margarine Eclipse* in early 2004. *Entertainment Weekly* critic Elisabeth Vincentelli proclaimed the album the group's best release since *Emperor Tomato Ketchup:* "Returning to its roots, the band strikes a graceful balance between rockers that charge forward with exhilarating abandon and pop tunes that float about with delightful melodic inventiveness. It's like greeting old friends who'd been held hostage by free-jazz playing aliens for seven years."

Selected discography

Switched On Stereolab, Too Pure, 1992.
Peng!, Too Pure, 1992.
The Groop Played Space Age Bachelor Pad Music, Too Pure, 1993.
Transient Random-Noise Bursts with Announcements, Elektra, 1993.
Mars Audiac Quintet, Elektra, 1994.
Refried Ectoplasm, Duophonic, 1995.
Emperor Tomato Ketchup, Elektra, 1996.
Dots and Loops, Drag City, 1997.
Cobra and Phases Group Play Voltage in the Milky Night, Duophonic, 1999.
Sound-Dust, Elektra, 2001.
ABC Music: The BBC Radio 1 Sessions, Koch, 2002.
Margerine Eclipse, Elektra, 2004.

Sources

Periodicals

Addicted to Noise, June 1996.
College Music Journal (CMJ), April 1996.
Entertainment Weekly, January 23, 2004.
Grip, June 1996.
Los Angeles Times, August 6, 1994; April 24, 1996; April 27, 1996.
Melody Maker, March 16, 1996.
Musician, June 1996.
Newsday, May 20, 1996.
Option, July 1993.
Pitchfork, June 1996.
Progressive, July 1, 1996.
Pulse!, September 1994.
Spin, August 1996.
Strobe, September 1994.
Guitar Player, December 1997.

Online

"Stereolab," *All Music Guide,* http://www.allmusic.com/ (February 8, 2004).
"Stereolab," VH1, http://www.vh1.com/artists/az/stereolab/bio.jhtml (February 8, 2004).

—Simon Glickman and Bruce Walker

Lew Tabackin

Saxophonist, flutist

Lew Tabackin was first exposed to jazz as a child, when his mother took him to movies at Philadelphia's Earl Theater. In addition to films, each day's feature also included a live stage show. "The stage shows usually involved a band, and I can still remember seeing bands like Cab Calloway and Lionel Hampton," Tabackin recalled to Martin Richards in *Jazz Journal International.*

Tabackin's interest in the musical form was piqued, and when he entered middle school he joined the school band hoping to play the clarinet. When the clarinet wasn't available, he was switched to the flute. "Not too many people wanted a flute," he explained to Richards. "It wasn't exactly a macho thing, and where I grew up in south Philadelphia guys didn't play the flute. Nobody even knew what it was! Anyway, I was stuck with this instrument, but it was something to do so I started playing."

Tabackin learned to play the tenor saxophone at 15 when Frankie Avalon, a fellow Philadelphian, needed one for his band. Too young to enter the clubs they played, Tabackin scored fake identification to get in. After high school, he attended the Philadelphia Conservatory of Music, where he returned to the flute—the school didn't teach saxophone. He also began to study with composer Vincent Persichetti during this time.

After graduating from the conservatory in 1962, Tabackin was drafted into the army—and even while serving in South Carolina and New Jersey he found time to jam with fellow musicians. Upon his discharge in 1964, Tabackin headed straight for New York. "That's when my real musical life began," he told Richards. "I went to New York with $400 and found a place to stay and I figured that the only way I would be able to do anything was to force myself to go places and sit in." Soon he began playing with Elvin Jones, the Thad Jones–Mel Lewis Big Band and others, often substituting for saxophonist Joe Farrell when Farrell couldn't make a gig.

In 1965 or 1966 Tabackin joined Cab Calloway's band and, from there, began playing with trumpet players Maynard Ferguson and Clark Terry. In 1967 composer and pianist Toshiko Akiyoshi invited him to join her for a concert at New York's Town Hall. Contrary to popular legend, Tabackin declined the gig to tour with the Alan Mills Band. Afterward he and Akiyoshi reunited and began collaborating; he also joined saxophonist Doc Severinsen's *Tonight Show* band. In 1969 Tabackin and Akiyoshi married; the following year they went to Los Angeles.

The move came at an opportune time, since the social and political factors of the time, Tabackin told Fred Jung of the All About Jazz website, made work for white jazz musicians hard to find. "New York was very strange because there was almost like a black revolution happening. Martin Luther King was assassinated ... [as was] Malcolm X and it was very difficult for white jazz musicians. It was really tough and I respected it and I understood it and I didn't have any bitterness, but I remember Duke Pearson was trying to get me a contract with Blue Note and they weren't interested in white musicians. It was rough."

Tabackin stayed with Severinsen's band for only a short while before jumping to the *Dick Cavett Show.* In 1970-71 he and Akiyoshi toured her home country of Japan. In 1973 Tabackin, Akiyoshi, and other Los Angeles musicians began to rehearse Akiyoshi's compositions, with Tabackin on both flute and saxophone. The ensemble rented the Wilshire Ebell Theater for their first concert later that year, where they were joined by drummer Shelly Manne. The group then recorded *Kogun* as the Toshiko Akiyoshi-Lew Tabackin Big Band. The album was released by BMG in Japan, where its fusion of eastern and western sounds became a major hit, selling 30,000 copies. Their album *Long Yellow Road* was released domestically the same year. The Big Band drew its first major attention in the United States when it was invited to play at the 1975 Monterey Jazz Festival.

The Big Band remained active throughout the 1970s and 1980s, and Tabackin also pursued solo and small group projects with both Manne and Billy Higgins. His first solo album, *Tabackin,* was released on RCA in 1974 and featured Akiyoshi and pianist Roland Hanna. *Dual Nature,* released on the smaller Inner City label the following year, emphasized Tabackin's split musical personality. His mystically tinged, eastern-influenced flute playing spans one side of the album, while his hard bop tenor sax fills the other. While the early albums are difficult to track down, later releases from Tabackin's longstanding relationship with the Concord Jazz label are more readily available. This fruitful partnership began with 1989's *Desert Lady,* which features pianist Hank Jones, bassist Dave Holland, and drummer Victor Lewis.

Tabackin and Akiyoshi returned to New York in the early 1980s, seeking creative reinvigoration and additional performing opportunities. Tabackin told the All About Jazz website that his time in Los Angeles had been crucial to his musical development, however. "[W]hen I was in New York, I was involved in everyone else's projects. I played in so many bands at the same time, but I never focused on my own thing. In Los Angeles, I felt that I had to make an attempt to create my own little world, which I did.... There were some wonderful things that happened and it forced me to find out who I was because I had to create my own identity, so the ten years we spent in L.A. were quite important. But I felt like I had to get back to a certain energy that I missed in New York."

Tabackin primarily pursued independent projects in the late 1980s and through the 1990s, although the Big Band became more active around its thirtieth anniversary in 2003. In addition to major retrospectives at the Detroit Symphony's Orchestra Hall, Chicago's Jazz Showcase, Lincoln Center, and Carnegie Hall, the ensemble released two CDs on BMG: *Tanuki's Night Out* and *Tales of a Courtesan.* Tabackin has also focused on his international jazz trio, featuring Russian bassist Boris Kozlov and British drummer Mark Taylor. Even after four decades, Tabackin makes it clear his sound is still evolving—and that his sense of humor is intact. "I am trying to find ways to be more expressive and reach a larger audience without doing anything stupid," he told Jung. "I am trying to develop little projects and trying to keep my music as pure as possible."

Selected discography

Solo

Tabackin, RCA, 1974.
Dual Nature, Inner City, 1976.
Tenor Gladness, Inner City, 1976.
Trackin', RCA 1976
(With Toshiko Akiyoshi Orchestra) *Road Time,* RCA, 1976.

Rites of Pan, Inner City, 1977.
Black and Tan Fantasy, Ascent, 1979.
Desert Lady, Concord Jazz, 1989.
I'll Be Seeing You, Concord Jazz, 1992.
What a Little Moonlight Can Do, Concord Jazz, 1994.
Tenority, Concord Jazz, 1996.
In a Sentimental Mood, Camerata, 1998.
My Old Flame, Atlas, 1999.
Pyramid, Koch, 1999.

With Toshiko Akiyoshi-Lew Tabackin Big Band

Kogun, RCA, 1974.
Long Yellow Road, BMG, 1974.
Insights, BMG, 1976.
March of the Tadpoles, BMG, 1977.
Toshiko Akiyoshi-Lew Tabackin Big Band Live, RCA, 1977.
Tales of a Courtesan, BMG, 2003.
Tanuki's Night Out, BMG, 2003.

Sources

Periodicals

Down Beat, June 3, 1976.
Jazz Journal International, January 1989; February 1989.

Online

"A Fireside Chat with Lew Tabackin," All About Jazz, http://www.allaboutjazz.com (February 1, 2004).
"Lew Tabackin," *All Music Guide,* http://www.allmusic.com (February 1, 2004).
"Lew Tabackin," *Grove Dictionary of Music,* http://www.grovemusic.com (February 1, 2004).
Lew Tabackin Official Website, http://www.lewtabackin.com (January 30, 2004).

—*Kristin Palm*

Sister Rosetta Tharpe

Gospel singer

© Terry Cryer/Corbis. Reproduced by permission.

Sister Rosetta Tharpe was an American gospel music pioneer with a long list of firsts in the genre. Most notably she was the first gospel artist to achieve mainstream popularity. She was a singer and guitarist whose powerful and unique musicianship and charismatic stage presence have continued to inspire contemporary musicians, both religious and secular.

Jason Ankeny wrote in *All Music Guide,* "Sister Rosetta Tharpe is widely acclaimed among the greatest Sanctified gospel singers of her generation." Ankeny added that as a "flamboyant performer whose music often flirted with the blues and swing, she was also one of the most controversial talents of her day, shocking purists with her leap into the secular market—by playing nightclubs and theatres, she not only pushed spiritual music into the mainstream, but in the process also helped pioneer the rise of pop-gospel."

Born Rosetta Nubin in either 1915 or 1921—sources differ on her birth year and she perpetually dodged the question—Tharpe was the daughter of a traveling missionary for the Church of God in Christ, who was known as "Mother Bell." Katie Bell Nubin sang and played mandolin, and her daughter often accompanied her. Tharpe was a guitar prodigy who began playing publicly at the age of six, and was known as "Little Sister Nubin." The family relocated to Chicago in 1920.

Born to Praise the Lord

Tharpe performed at various Holiness gatherings and toured extensively between 1923 and 1934 with her mother, as part of the Rev. F.W. McGee's itinerant revival group. Tharpe was profoundly influenced by another musician in this group: Arizona Dranes, a blind pianist who was well known for her rousing performances. Tharpe also counted her mother as a formidable musical influence.

She moved to Harlem in the mid-1930s, where she affiliated with another church and married its pastor, Thomas J. Thorpe, a leader in the Holiness Church. Her husband reportedly could not accept Tharpe's desire to perform, and the marriage did not last. When the marriage ended she kept his name, but changed its spelling to "Tharpe."

Tony Heilbut, in his book *The Gospel Sound: Good News and Bad Times,* wrote that Tharpe "could pick blues guitar like a Memphis Minnie." He added that "her song style was filled with blues inversions, and a resonating vibrato. She bent her notes like a horn player, and syncopated in swing band manner. Above all, she had showmanship. ... And, starting in 1938, she triumphed as no gospel singer has done since."

Began Successful Recording Career

Tharpe signed with the Decca label in 1938. Her first records—including "Rock Me," which she recorded

Born Rosetta Nubin on March 20, 1915 (some sources say 1921), in Cotton Plant, AR; died on October 9, 1973, in Philadelphia, PA; married Thomas J. Thorpe (divorced); married Forrest Allen (divorced); married Russell Morrison, 1951.

Toured extensively with mother, 1923-34; signed recording contract with Decca, 1938; recorded V-Discs, c. 1940; "Up Above My Head" became hit, 1941; recorded blues numbers, 1950s; part of major all-gospel concert, 1960; performed at Newport Folk Festival, 1967.

The 1940s were considered a "golden era" for gospel. Tharpe's popularity was such that during World War II she and the Golden Gate Quartet were the only black gospel groups to record V-Discs, recordings sent to American soldiers overseas. She continued to record for Decca and formed a collaborative relationship with Samuel "Sammy" Price, who was the label's staff pianist and arranger. They would work together until 1951. She also married Forrest Allen, a gospel booking agent, at some point during this decade.

Tharpe continued to pursue her eclectic career, touring with the Dixie Hummingbirds, a popular gospel group, and recording with Sammy Price. Their record "Strange Things Happening Every Day" appeared in *Billboard* magazine's Top Ten list for "race records." Ankeny described this as "a rare feat for a gospel act and one which she repeated several more times during the course of her career," including a 1946 recording of "Up Above My Head" with Madame Marie Knight, another gospel singer who had sung with Mahalia Jackson and was also Tharpe's backup vocalist.

"We traveled all through the deep South together, for 25 years, playing to white and black audiences, strictly segregated," said Knight, in an interview with *Paste*. "I remember many times working with the sheriff at the front door of the church, with the whites on one side and the blacks on the other. The [police] came because they said they didn't want a riot. I don't know where they got the idea from—I've never heard of a riot at a gospel concert—but they wanted to make sure there was peace and order."

Tharpe was married a third time, to Russell Morrison, the former manager of The Ink Spots, in an elaborate ceremony in Washington D.C. in 1951. Guests paid to attend, and the event, which featured a gospel concert after the vows, was also recorded and issued on vinyl. Gayle Wald in *American Quarterly* pronounced the event a failure "as both a wedding and a concert. Indeed, it offended precisely to the degree that it was both and neither at the same time." This was purportedly Tharpe's most successful marriage. But it was the end of her working relationship with Knight, who felt snubbed when not asked to perform at the wedding, although she was a member of the wedding party.

with Lucius "Lucky" Millinder's big band, and "This Train"—were instant hits. She frequently rearranged traditional spirituals such as "Didn't It Rain" and "Down by the Riverside." Tharpe found popularity among mainstream audiences and performed on bills with artists such as Cab Calloway, Bill "Bojangles" Robinson, and Benny Goodman. She performed in such legendary New York City venues as the Cotton Club in Harlem and at New York City's Carnegie Hall. "She led an almost schizophrenic existence, remaining in the good graces of her core audience by recording material like 'Precious Lord,' 'Beams of Heaven' and 'End of My Journey' while also appealing to her growing white audience by performing rearranged, uptempo spirituals," wrote Ankeny. "There's something about the gospel blues that's so deep the world can't stand it," Tharpe told Heilbut, as reported in *The Gospel Sound*.

Despite her training in religious music, which clearly favored singing for the Lord rather than for the world, Tharpe also embraced bits and pieces of secular society. She "sang in clubs and theatres, broadcast the dangers of venereal disease, invented pop gospel, became a household name and ... everybody's sister," according to Heilbut. She performed during a unique musical era. When the electric guitar came to prominence, she took up the instrument, although she also played piano. "She figured out ways to work a guitar to bring an audience—even a huge, stadium size audience—to its feet," said Gayle Wald in *Sing Out!*. "She was extraordinarily brave in the manner of Bessie Smith or Billie Holiday—women who also had to confront social disapprobation for their social/musical choices." Tharpe also dressed more like an entertainer than an evangelizing missionary. She typically dyed her hair or wore vivid wigs, and wore feathered boas and finery with her gowns that "smack of rent parties and honky-tonks," observed Heilbut.

Tharpe embarked on extensive touring during the next several years. It took her to churches throughout the United States and then to Europe in the 1950s. She was the first gospel performer to tour Europe, where she remained for nearly a year. As Lynell George observed in the *Los Angeles Times*, "As an African-American, she was crossing color lines. As a woman, she was going places and performing in a fashion that had previously been unheard of—not to mention making mockery of the term 'ladylike.' Tharpe … was a sanctified gospel singer who ladled up big servings of the blues and sang and raised many an eyebrow doing so."

Embraced the Blues

In the early 1950s Tharpe decided to record several tracks of straight blues numbers. This outraged her gospel fans and, according to Ankeny, "her credibility and popularity were seriously damaged. Not only did her record sales drop off and her live engagements become fewer and farther between, but many purists took Tharpe's foray into the mainstream as a personal affront; the situation did not improve, and she spent over a year touring clubs in Europe, waiting for the controversy to die down." At the same time, Tharpe was leaving a deep impression on young musicians, her style cutting across color lines and musical genres. These included Chuck Berry, Little Richard, Jerry Lee Lewis, Johnny Cash, Sleepy LaBeef, and B.B. King.

The situation had improved by 1960, and Tharpe appeared in a prominent all-gospel concert at the legendary Apollo Theatre on a bill with the Caravans and James Cleveland. "By now her voice had lowered an octave, and she chanted more than she sang," wrote Heilbut. "It made no difference." She continued to tour, and performed at the prestigious Newport Folk Festival in 1967.

Despite this seeming reversal of professional fortunes, the last years of Tharpe's life were personally difficult. Her mother died in 1969 while Tharpe was touring Europe. In 1970, Tharpe suffered a stroke but continued to tour. Complications from the stroke resulted in the amputation of a leg, but she continued to tour through early 1973. Mahalia Jackson, the gospel legend and a personal friend, died in 1972. Tharpe then had a stroke just prior to a planned recording session, and died on October 9, 1973, in Philadelphia, Pennsylvania.

Beginning in the late 1990s, it seemed there was a resurgent interest in Tharpe and her music. She was often cited by contemporary blues musicians, particularly Maria Muldaur, as a formidable influence. Record labels seized upon this interest, spurring a spate of reissues and tribute recordings such as *Shout, Sister, Shout,* produced in part by Muldaur and released in 2002. A clip from one of her performances also appeared in *Amélie,* an internationally popular French film. Her achievements were remarkable. As pointed out in *Notable Black American Women,* Tharpe was "the first nationally known gospel singer; first gospel singer to record with a major company … first to go

public with gospel by performing on the secular stage; and first to perform gospel in a theatre."

Selected discography

Solo

The Lonesome Road: Gospel Songs and Other Favorites Sung by Rosetta Tharpe Accompanying Herself on the Guitar (five 78 RPM discs), Decca, c. 1941.
Gospel Hymns (four 78 RPM discs), Decca, 1947.
(With Marie Knight) *Beams of Heaven,* Decca, 1948.
Wedding ceremony of Sister Rosetta Tharpe and Russell Morrison, Decca, 1951.
Spirituals in Rhythm, Spinorama, 1956; reissued, Collectors Choice, 2003.
Gospels in Rhythm, Coronet, 1960.
Live in 1960, Southland, 1960; reissued, 1991; reissued, 1994.
Sister on Tour (live), Verve, 1961.
Sister Rosetta Tharpe, MGM, 1963.
Sister Rosetta Tharpe Live in Paris, 1964, Esoldun-INA/Wotre Music, 1988.
Live at the Hot Club de France, Milan America/BMG Music, 1966; reissued, 1991; reissued, 1996.
The Best of Sister Rosetta Tharpe, Savoy/Arista, 1979.
Sincerely, Sister Rosetta Tharpe, Rosetta, 1988; reissued, 1992.
Gospel Train, Lection/PolyGram, 1989.
Gospel Train, Vol. II, Lection/PolyGram, 1989.
Gospel and Negro Spirituals, Tuxedo Music, 1990.
Complete Recorded Works, Vol. 1 (1938-1941), Document, 1995.
Complete Recorded Works, Vol. 2 (1942-1944), Document, 1995.
Precious Memories, Savgos, 1997.
Complete Recorded Works, Vol. 3, Document, 1998.
Precious Memories, Savoy, 1998.
Up Above My Head, Indigo, 1999.
Gospel 1938-1943, Fremeaux & Associés, 2002.
Integrale Sister Rosetta Tharpe, Vol. 1: 1938-1943 (live), Fremeaux & Associés, 2002.
Integrale Sister Rosetta Tharpe, Vol. 2: 1943-1967 (live), Fremeaux & Associés, 2002.
The Original Soul Sister, Proper, 2002.
Singing in My Soul, Proper, 2002.
This Train, Proper, 2002.
Rock Me, Proper, 2002.
The Gospel of the Blues, MCA/Decca, 2003.
I Saw the Light, Direct Source, 2003.

With Lucky Millinder and His Orchestra

Lucky Days—1941-1945, MCA, 1941; reissued 1980.
Lucky Millinder and His Orchestra—1943-1947, Classics, 1998.
Lucky Millinder and His Orchestra, Jazz Archives, 1999.

With various artists

You Gotta Move, Decca, 1950.
Brighten the Corner Where You Are: Black and White Urban Hymnody, New World, 1978.

Shout, Sister, Shout! A Tribute to Sister Rosetta Tharpe, M.C. Records, 2003.

Sources

Books

Heilbut, Tony, *The Gospel Sound: Good News and Bad Times,* Simon and Schuster, 1971.

Jackson, Jerma A., *Singing in My Soul: Black Gospel Music in a Secular Age,* University of North Carolina Press, 2004.

Notable Black American Women, Book 1, Gale, 1992.

Periodicals

American Quarterly, September 2003.
Los Angeles Times, October 19, 2003.
Paste, October-November 2003.
Sing Out!, Winter 2004.

Online

"Sister Rosetta Tharpe," *All Music Guide,* http://www. allmusic.com (January 17, 2004).

—*Linda Dailey Paulson*

13th Floor Elevators

Psychedelic rock group

Often considered the first psychedelic rock group as well as the first underground band to achieve commercial success, the 13th Floor Elevators were a Texas-based outfit that combined folk/rock, R&B, and hard-driving rock 'n' roll with mystical lyrics that espoused the virtues of drugs. Although many of their songs are based around the concept that ingesting LSD and other substances can take the user to a higher plane of consciousness, the Elevators' biggest—and only—hit was "You're Gonna Miss Me," a song that has nothing to do with drugs. A forceful, pulsating rocker about the end of a relationship, it features the intense tenor vocals and blood-curdling screams of Roky Erickson and the percussive electric jug-playing of Tommy Hall. The tune reached number 56 on the national *Billboard* charts in 1966.

Although the Elevators have influenced punk and alternative rock bands for almost 40 years, as a group they lasted just over three. During this time, they released three studio albums—*Psychedelic Sounds of the 13th Floor Elevators, Easter Everywhere,* and *Bull of the Woods*—as well as a "live" album that actually was a collection of studio outtakes with tacked-on audience participation. The band's first two albums are considered classics of the garage and psychedelic rock genres; the third is considered a worthy addition to their canon. Their lead vocalist, Roky Erickson, an eccentric musical genius in the vein of Brian Wilson of the Beach Boys and Syd Barrett of Pink Floyd, is also a diagnosed schizophrenic known for legendary drug-taking exploits. He is regarded as an outstanding singer and gifted songwriter whose post-Elevators solo work includes moments of brilliance as well as disturbing, horror- and occult-tinged subject matter and imagery.

Elevators Up

The 13th Floor Elevators were formed by Tommy Hall in late 1965. A student of philosophy, psychology, and chemical engineering at the University of Texas at Austin, Hall had begun to experiment with drugs such as peyote and mescaline that were local to Texas and that were legal at the time. After moving to illegal substances such as LSD, he began to believe that drugs could enhance his personal and spiritual growth. He began to write song lyrics, and decided to make a popular local skiffle band, the Lingsmen, the mouthpiece for his theories. The Lingsmen were made up of guitarist Stacy Sutherland, bassist/electric violinist Benny Thurman, drummer John Ike Walton, and vocalist Max Rainey. When Rainey left the group, Hall invited Erickson, a 17-year-old wunderkind in the R&B band the Spades, to join as lead singer and rhythm guitarist.

Shortly before the formation of the Elevators, the Spades had released Erickson's song "You're Gonna Miss Me" on Zero Records, a local label. The Lingsmen decided to change their approach to reflect the tougher sounds of bands like the Rolling Stones and the Kinks as well as the mind-expanding experiences that they were having with acid, pot, and other drugs. Thurman dropped the electric violin to concentrate on bass, and Hall began to blow into a jug to which he had duct-taped a microphone, thus creating the electric jug, a new sound in pop music. The Lingsmen changed their name to the 13th Floor Elevators, named for the thirteenth letter of the alphabet, "M," which stood for marijuana, and for the missing floor in American high-rise buildings.

The Elevators developed a reputation for ferocious live shows, and they became hugely popular in Texas. Their rerecorded version of Erickson's punk anthem—released nationally by International Artists Records, a Houston-based label run by Lelan Rogers, the brother of pop singer Kenny Rogers—brought them popularity around the country. However, the Elevators were less than popular with the Texas Rangers and other local authorities, who were unhappy with the group's personal drug use and public support of getting high. In 1966 the band was arrested for possession of marijuana but was released on a technicality. Shortly thereafter they relocated to San Francisco without Thurman, who decided to stay in Texas; he was replaced by Ronnie Leatherman.

Elevators Down

In San Francisco, the Elevators became influential figures on the nascent psychedelic scene; they helped

Members include **Roger Kynard "Roky" Erickson** (born on July 15, 1947, in Dallas, TX; son of an architect/engineer and Evelyn Erickson, an opera singer; married Dana Gaines; children: Spring, Jegar, Cydne), vocals, rhythm guitar; **Dan Galindo** (born in TX; joined group, 1967), bass; **Tommy Hall** (born on September 21, 1943; married Clementine Tausch; divorced), electric jug; **Ronnie Leatherman** (born in TX; joined group, 1966), bass; **Stacy Sutherland** (born in Kerrville, TX; died on August 24, 1978, in Houston, TX), lead guitar; **Danny Thomas** (born in SC; joined group, 1966), drums; **Benny Thurman** (born in Austin, TX), bass; **John Ike Walton** (born in Kerrville, TX), drums.

Group formed in Austin, TX, 1965; released single "You're Gonna Miss Me," a rerecording of a song that lead singer/guitarist Roky Erickson had written for his previous group, the Spades, 1966; group released first album, *Psychedelic Sounds of the 13th Floor Elevators,* later that year; band moved to San Francisco and performed with several well known artists, including singer Janis Joplin; performed on television programs *American Bandstand* and *Where the Action Is* as well as at the Fillmore West and Avalon Ballroom; returned from California and released second LP, *Easter Everywhere,* 1967; "live" LP (actually studio outtakes enhanced by a recorded audience) and third studio album *Bull of the Woods* released, 1968; band broke up, 1969; resurgence of interest in band begun when *Nuggets* compilation of garage and early psychedelic rock is released, 1972; Erickson reformed band for a short period and began a solo career; Elevators lead guitarist Stacy Sutherland killed by his wife, 1978; reunion show featuring some surviving members took place in Houston, 1984; tribute album released, 1999; Erickson won lawsuit granting him master tapes and publishing rights for his work with the Elevators, 1999; "You're Gonna Miss Me" featured in film *High Fidelity,* 2000.

Addresses: *Record company*—Trance Syndicate Records USA, P.O. Box 49771, Austin, TX 78765, phone: (512) 454-3265. *Website*—Roky Erickson Official Website: http://www.rokyerickson.net.

create the "San Francisco sound," psychedelic music that would receive critical acclaim and commercial success. Allegedly the first group to go onstage under the influence of LSD, they played at the Fillmore West and the Avalon Ballroom with bands such as the Byrds, Grateful Dead, Jefferson Airplane, and Big Brother and the Holding Company. The lead singer of Big Brother, Janis Joplin, was asked to join Erickson as the Elevators' second vocalist. She declined, but always noted Erickson as a major influence.

In mid-1966, International Artists released *Psychedelic Sounds of the 13th Floor Elevators,* considered a groundbreaking debut. Writing on the Vinyl Junkie website, collector Karl Ikola stated, "[T]he depths of soul evident in the debut are still so richly filled with an hypnotic 'n' spine-tingling-blast-off life-odyssey paradox that I'd like to be buried with an original white-label promo copy right across my chest." However, due to the fact that International Artists decided not to publicize the band in order to retain their "mystique," the album failed to reach a mainstream audience.

Shortly after the release of *Psychedelic Sounds,* the band's rhythm section left; they were replaced by Elevator fans Dan Galindo on bass and Danny Thomas on drums. The group returned to Texas in late 1966 but went back to San Francisco several times over the next two years. In 1967 the Elevators released their second album, *Easter Everywhere.* Thought to be more focused and even more lysergically enhanced than their first release, *Easter Everywhere* usually is considered the group's best record. Cub Koda of *All Music Guide to Rock* suggested, "Anyone wanting a real psychedelic album from the '60s should head right to the counter and grab this one."

By this time, though, the band was starting to unravel. The crowning blow came on the occasion that Erickson decided to go home while high on acid. His mother, a former opera singer who had released a local 45-inch single, had him committed to the Austin State Hospital, where he underwent shock treatment. After this incident, Erickson's behavior became erratic and unpredictable; the rest of the band also showed signs that their drug use was catching up with them. Offered a chance to tour England with guitarist Jimi Hendrix, they refused so that they could stay at home, stoned. Hall and Erickson, wrecked on acid, were found waiting in line to buy tickets for one of their own shows in Austin.

Late in 1968, Erickson was busted for a single joint. In order to avoid being placed in the Texas state prison, he claimed to be a Martian. The authorities placed him in Rusk Hospital for the Criminally Insane in Rusk, Texas, where he was subjected to treatment with Thorazine and other psychotropic drugs for three years. In the meantime, International Artists released the pseudo-live album and *Bull of the Woods,* a record that features songs by lead guitarist Stacy Sutherland

and unreleased compositions from the band's first two albums; though praised for Sutherland's straight-ahead songwriting and musical prowess, the work generally is considered the least effective of the group's studio efforts. Like Erickson, Sutherland and lyricist/jug player Hall were busted for drugs, but each did jail time.

You're Gonna Miss Them

In 1969 the Elevators decided to disband. Hall, who wanted to write a treatise about his philosophies, moved to San Francisco with his wife Clementine, a lyricist and occasional vocalist for the group; the couple are now divorced. Most of the rest of the band remained in Texas, playing music semiprofessionally or not at all. After his release from Rusk in 1972, Erickson attempted to reform the Elevators with Sutherland, original drummer Walton, and second bassist Leatherman, but the band fell apart after a short time. A fan of horror and science fiction comics, films, and television programs as well as of arcane literature, Erickson began writing songs about demons, vampires, aliens, two-headed dogs, and other supernatural creatures. Doug Sahm of the Texas rock band the Sir Douglas Quintet took him into the studio as a solo artist, and Stu Cook, bassist of roots-rock group Creedence Clearwater Revival, also produced several tracks.

In 1972 rock historian/guitarist Lenny Kaye featured the Elevators' "You're Gonna Miss Me" on his garage/psych compilation *Nuggets: Original Artyfacts from the First Psychedelic Era, 1965–1968,* a release that helped the Elevators become legends in the burgeoning punk movement. The New York band Television performed the Elevators' song "Fire Engine" in concert, and the group was cited by poet/songwriter Patti Smith and art rockers Pere Ubu. Copies of the band's albums began to fetch high prices among collectors. In 1978 Stacy Sutherland, a former heroin addict, was shot and killed by his estranged wife in a domestic dispute; his tombstone reads "The Lead Guitarist of the 13th Floor Elevators."

By the early 1990s, Erickson—who, like the other Elevators, never had received royalties for his work with the band—was living at a subsistence level. He started to work with a variety of backing bands, such as Bleib Alien, the Explosives, and the Resurrectionists, and to record solo albums on a semiregular basis; he also produced two books of poetry, the second of which was published by writer/punk musician Henry Rollins. In 1984 an Elevators' reunion concert featuring Erickson, Leatherman, and Walton was held in Houston. Five years later Erickson was arrested for mail fraud; apparently, he collected mail for an apartment complex and neglected to give it to the addressees. The judge presiding over the case failed to believe that he had a mental condition and sent him to Missouri for "testing." A year later the album *Where the Pyramid Meets the Sky: A Tribute to Roky Erickson* was issued by Sire

Records; it contained songs by such groups as R.E.M., ZZ Top, the Butthole Surfers, and the Jesus and Mary Chain, all of whom cited Erickson and the Elevators as influences. An expanded version of *Nuggets* was released in 1998 by Rhino Records, a move that brought the Elevators to a new audience. In 1999 a case against International Artists was decided in Erickson's favor; he received master tapes and publishing rights to the songs he wrote for the Elevators. The following year "You're Gonna Miss Me" was featured in the film *High Fidelity* and appeared on its soundtrack.

The Circle Remains Unbroken

Reviewers regard the Elevators as architects of acid rock as well as a group whose exploits led to their demise. Writing in *All Music Guide to Rock,* Mark Deming noted that they "were trailblazers in the psychedelic rock scene, and in time they'd pay a heavy price for exploring the outer edges of musical and psychedelic possibility ..." Rock musician Steven Van Zant on the website Little Steven's Underground Garage called the Elevators "true rock visionaries. They were exceptional in a variety of respects, first appearing out of the wilds of Texas, featuring wildly unusual instrumentation, and a true genius/madman in the form of guitarist/vocalist Roky Erickson." Writing on Erickson's Website, Lenny Kaye noted "[I]f I had anything to do with keeping the flame alive, then that is the payback that happens when one artist touches another and they give each other a ride on the 'Fire Engine' of life. I'm glad this work is remembered because it was unique and visionary, even in a U-and-V time." In an essay on the Texas Ghetto website, Gerry Storm commented, "[T]he Elevators showed that it could be done, that small-time Texas kids could become leaders of the pop culture." Interviewed by Mike McDowell for *Blitz Magazine,* Erickson concluded, "I always refer to the Elevators' albums for inspiration. I pick little things out of the arrangements for my new songs... I'm not really trying for an Elevators sound, as I'm more into horror now. But the way I write songs hasn't changed since then."

Selected discography

Singles

"(I've Got) Levitation" b/w "Before You Accuse Me," International Artists, 1966.
"Reverberation (Doubt)" b/w "Fire Engine," International Artists, 1966.
"You're Gonna Miss Me" b/w "Tried to Hide," Contact, 1966; Hanna-Barbera, 1966; International Artists, 1966.
"She Lives (in a Time of Her Own)" b/w "It's All Over Now, Baby Blue," International Artists, 1967.
"Slip Inside This House" b/w "Splash I," International Artists, 1967.
"Livin' On" b/w "Scarlet and Gold," International Artists, 1968.

Albums

Psychedelic Sounds of the 13th Floor Elevators, International Artists, 1966.
Easter Everywhere, International Artists, 1967.
13th Floor Elevators Live!, International Artists, 1968.
Bull of the Woods, International Artists, 1968.

Sources

Books

Bogandov, Vladimir, Chris Woodstra, and Stephen Thomas Erlewine, editors, *All Music Guide to Rock: The Definitive Guide to Pop, Rock, and Soul,* All Media Guide/Backbeat, 2002.
Joynson, Vernon, *Fuzz, Acid, and Flowers: A Comprehensive Guide to American Garage, Psychedelic, and Hippie Rock (1964–1975),* Borderline, 1995.
Larkin, Colin, editor, *Encyclopedia of Popular Music,* 3rd edition, MUZE, 1998.
Unterberger, Richie, *Unknown Legends of Rock 'n' Roll: Psychedelic Unknowns, Mad Geniuses, Punk Pioneers, Lo-Fi Mavericks, and More,* Backbeat, 1998.

Periodicals

Blitz Magazine, March/April 1982.

Online

"13th Floor Elevators," Little Steven's Underground Garage, http://www.littlestevensundergroundgarage.com/psychedelic/13thfloorelevators.html (February 2, 2004).
"Austin Music Scene '65–'69," Texas Ghetto, http://www.texasghetto.com/Music6569.htm (March 31, 2004).
"Lenny Kaye on the 13th Floor Elevators," Roky Erickson Official Website, http://www.rokyerickson.net (February 16, 2004).
"Reverends of Karmic Youth: A 13th Floor Elevators Primer" (two parts), Flagpole Magazine Online, http://www.flagpole.com/Issues/09.23.98/ort.html (March 31, 2004).
"Roky Erickson FAQ v. 2.0," Perfect Sounds Forever: Online Music Magazine, http://www.furious.com/perfect/roky.html (March 14, 2004).
"The Origins of Psychedelic Music in Austin, Texas, Part 1," Good Rockin' Tonight: The Premier Internet Site for Collectors of Records, http://www.goodrockintonight.com/articles/article_view.chtml?artid=2514 (February 2, 2004).

—*Gerard J. Senick*

Doris Troy

Singer, songwriter

No other "one-hit wonder" can boast a record of survival as impressive as Doris Troy's. Best known for the 1963 hit single "Just One Look," the soul chanteuse kept an enviable career going long after the majority of her contemporaries had packed it in. A songwriter, in-demand backup vocalist, and seasoned club performer, she was paid the ultimate compliment when her sister wrote a long-running musical stage play based on her life called *Mama, I Want to Sing.* More than 40 years after its debut her one American hit remained popular in commercials and on oldies stations worldwide.

Born Doris Higginsen on January 6, 1937, in New York City, she sang in several choirs while growing up, especially in the Mount Calvary Church, where her Barbados-born father was the minister. Although no secular music was allowed in their strictly run home, their proximity to the Apollo Theater made it difficult for young Doris to stay away from jazz and R&B. At 16 she fibbed about her age and got a job as an Apollo usherette, where she soaked up influences from some of the greatest female stars of all time: Pearl Bailey, Etta James, Dinah Washington, and especially Sarah Vaughan, who occasionally hired her to do a little sewing.

Higginsen's mother made her quit the usherette job, but apparently couldn't stop her from forming a jazz vocal trio called the Halos with a couple of friends. The group didn't last long, but the youngster was not discouraged. Using her grandmother's name, Payne, she began writing and pitching songs to various artists.

Through sheer youthful nerve, she got a song through to R&B/pop hitmaker Dee Clark—best known for such hits as "Hey Little Girl" and "Nobody But You"—and scored a hundred-dollar advance for "How About That." Clark's 1960 Abner/Vee Jay recording of the song, complete with his trademark happy flute, was a respectable hit, climbing to 33 on the pop charts and ten on the R&B charts. Soul stars Chuck Jackson and Jackie Wilson also recorded some of her material, although none of those compositions charted.

"Just One Look"

Higginsen learned that the best way for a singer to stay connected to the recording industry was to work as a backup vocalist. Teaming with friends Dionne and Dee Dee Warwick, she supplied gospel-fed harmonies for recordings by Solomon Burke, the Drifters, Chuck Jackson, and Ben E. King. This not only supplied a steady paycheck, it gave her opportunities for solo recordings. Billed as Doris Payne, she recorded her first single, "I Want to Be Loved," for the Everest label, and, as part of a duo known as Jay & Dee, released "Heart" on Arliss Records. Both releases stiffed, but in the process, a legend was born.

According to the book *One-Hit Wonders,* no less a personage than Soul Brother Number One—James Brown himself—saw Higginsen perform in a nightclub and walked her into Atlantic Records. Years later she told David Nathan a different story for his book *Soulful Divas.* After working up a studio demo of a song she cowrote with Gregory Carroll called "Just One Look, " she took it to the head of Sue Records. "He just sat on the tape," she told Nathan, "so I took it over to Jerry Wexler at Atlantic Records, and they flipped out! Next thing I know, they put it out in the form we recorded it, as a demo!" For the record's release she officially changed her stage name to Doris Troy—although she still wrote under the name Payne.

A true classic of early 1960s pop, "Just One Look" was youthful enough for teens and seductive enough for adult listeners with a contralto gospel edge that caught the R&B crowd. Touring as an opening act and backup singer for Chuck Jackson—then cresting on a string of hits—helped turn the song into a bona fide hit, hitting number ten on the pop charts and number three on the R&B charts. Stardom seemed to be within her grasp.

Recorded for the Beatles' Apple Label

Despite this success, Troy's next single "Whatcha Gonna Do About It?" flopped. Worse, her debut album, a first-class blend of northern soul and classy uptown R&B, fizzled. She fared better with Atlantic's *Apollo Saturday Night,* a live 1964 album featuring established stars like the Coasters, the Falcons, Ben E. King, Otis Redding, and Rufus Thomas. To the delight

For the Record . . .

Born Doris Higginsen on January 6, 1937, in New York, NY; died on February 16, 2004, in Las Vegas, NV.

Began singing as a child in her father's church; joined a vocal jazz trio called the Halos, late 1950s; wrote "How About That" for Dee Clark, 1960; sang backup for Chuck Jackson, Solomon Burke, and James Brown, early 1960s; recorded as part of Jay & Dee, wrote and recorded the top-ten pop hit "Just One Look" for Atlantic Records, 1963; recorded for the Apple label, 1970; recorded for Polydor, 1972–74; starred in a musical inspired by her life, *Mama, I Want to Sing*, 1984; cofounded the MAMA Foundation for the Arts, 1998; appeared in the stage musical *Gospel Is … !*, 1999.

Awards: Pioneer Award, Rhythm & Blues Foundation, 1996.

Addresses: *Record company*—Atlantic Records, 1290 Avenue of the Americas, New York, NY 10104, website: http://www.atlanticrecords.com. *Office*—MAMA Foundation for the Arts, 149 W. 126th St,, Harlem, New York, 10027, phone: (212) 280-1045, fax: (212) 280-1045, website: http://www.mamafoundation.org. *Website*—Doris Troy Official Website: http://www.doristroy.com.

Finding enthusiastic audiences for her work, Troy eventually moved to England, touring Europe and Japan from her new base; her singles for Cameo, Capitol, and Calla, unfortunately, failed to make an impression in the United States. Further discouraged by disappointingly small royalty payments for her hits, Troy focused more on singing backup than writing during this time. A session with keyboard wizard Billy Preston led to a contract with the Beatles record label Apple. Despite its reputation as a failed, irresponsibly run experiment, Troy told Richie Unterberger in his book *Unknown Legends of Rock 'n' Roll* that it was a fun, creative place for collaboration.

"We really got into taking care of business and writing good tunes," she informed Unterberger. "Some of the stuff we did in the studio, I'd be messing around on the piano and somebody would walk over and say, what is that? I'd say, this what I got so far. And they'd so [sic], okay, try this, try this, and that's how come on the [songwriting credits] you see Ringo [Starr] on some of it, Stephen Stills on some of it, and George [Harrison]. Nobody stopped to say, well, you can't do this or you're signed to this company or you're signed to that company. We were all just doing it."

The album, simply titled *Doris Troy,* featured some of that era's biggest stars: Eric Clapton, Delaney & Bonnie, Peter Frampton, Leon Russell, and the Beatles' Harrison and Starr. The fusion of soul and rock should have been a star-making relaunch of her career, but during the Beatle's messy public breakup, their record label withered for want of attention.

Mama, I Want to Sing

Troy never stopped working and never gave up hope. She continued singing backup on sessions for the likes of Long John Baldry, Jimmy Cliff, the Spencer Davis Group, Humble Pie, Tom Jones, and Gary Wright. The most famous examples of her work as a background singer are on Carly Simon's 1972 smash "You're So Vain," where Troy supplies both harmony and the famed gospel counterpoint vocal, as well as Pink Floyd's classic 1973 LP *Dark Side of the Moon,* one of the biggest-selling concept albums of all time.

Polydor Records gave Troy and her new group the Gospel Truth a chance to apply their talents to a 1972 album called *Rainbow Testament.* A deeply spiritual project, the live set featured Troy at her mature best, singing soulful renditions of such popular contemporary hits as "Games People Play," "Put Your Hand in the Hand," "Rose Garden," and Troy's intense performance of "Steal Away." It didn't sell. She tried again two years later with *Stretching Out,* a strong reggae-influenced disc that highlighted her mellower side. Because it was poorly distributed and barely promoted, though, these high-water marks in her solo career

of her hometown crowd, Troy held her own with these legendary figures, delivering a jazzy version of "Misty" before rousing the Harlem faithful with the churchy "Say Yeah." If Atlantic took any notice of her burgeoning star power, it wasn't apparent in their actions. A little over a year after "Just One Look" slipped off the charts, the label dropped her from their roster.

Meanwhile, Troy received a strong boost overseas. A British Invasion group called the Hollies cut a hit version of "Just One Look" in 1964 that soared to number two on the British charts, and the Small Faces scored their first English hit with "Whatcha Gonna Do About It?" in 1965. Many Brits of that era were simply mad for American R&B, and they sent Troy's original of "Whatcha Gonna Do About It?" into their top 40 lists twice: number 37 in 1964 and number 38 in 1965. Heartened, the singer flew to London to appear on that country's premier pop music telecast *Ready, Steady, Go!*

faded into obscurity. With bills to pay, she settled in Las Vegas and took a job singing backup for Lola Falana's stage show, and did session work when she could.

In 1981 her sister Vy Higginsen, a popular New York deejay, cowrote an inspirational tribute to Doris's life and career called *Mama, I Want to Sing*. Filled with true-life events and uplifting musical numbers, the stage show—which sometimes included star turns by Chaka Kahn and Deniece Williams—proved a long-running off Broadway success, and was novelized for a 1992 Scholastic book. "I absolutely couldn't believe what I was seeing," Troy is quoted on the MAMA Foundation website. "Vy was a baby when our father died, yet she had come so close to completely capturing the essence of what he was about.... I cried when I first saw the first show. In fact, after joining the cast for the first three weeks I cried especially during the funeral scene." Playing the role of her own mother in 1984, Troy stole the show nightly and toured with the production on and off for over a decade.

The success helped Troy and her sister in form the MAMA Foundation for the Arts, a community-focused organization that helps train and employ people for work in music and theater. Their second full-scale production, *Gospel Is … !*, gave Troy a chance to show off her still-formidable chops. Despite needing an off-stage oxygen tank between numbers, she imbued her performance with sanctified soul and flair. Health problems continued to plague her, but, she told the *New York Amsterdam News* her future lay in helping her foundation's students. "That's why I'm going to be one of the teachers in the school of music," she told journalist Arlene McKanic. "With the experience I have from 1963 till today, I can show them how to do the song-writing, the stage presence, so there's a place for me." Emphysema claimed her life on February 16, 2004.

Selected discography

Just One Look, Atlantic, 1963.
(With others) *Apollo Saturday Night,* Atco, 1964.
Doris Troy, Capitol, 1970.
Rainbow Testament, Polydor, 1972.
Stretching Out, Polydor, 1997.
Just One Look: The Best of Doris Troy, Soul Classics, 1994.

Sources

Books

Brown, Tony, Jon Kutner, and Neil Warwick, *Complete Book of the British Carts: Singles and Albums,* Omnibus, 1999.
Jancik, Wayne, *Billboard Book of One-Hit Wonders,* revised and expanded, Billboard Books, 1998.
Nathan, David, *Soulful Divas,* Billboard Books, 1998.
Unterberger, Richie, *Unknown Legends of Rock 'n' Roll,* Backbeat, 1998.

Periodicals

Los Angeles Times, July 27, 1996; November 6, 1996.
New York Amsterdam News, October 14, 1999; October 30, 2003.
People, March 11, 2002.
USA Today, June 11, 1996.

Online

"Doris Troy," *All Music Guide,* http://www.allmusic.com (February 7, 2004).
"Doris Troy," MAMA Foundation for the Arts, http://www.mamafoundation.org (January 28, 2004).
Doris Troy Official Website, http://www.doristroy.com (January 8, 2004).
"R&B star Doris Troy Dead at 67," CNN, http://www.cnn.com/2004/showbiz/music/02/19/obit.doris.troy.reut/index.html (February 23, 2004).

—*Ken Burke*

Mitsuko Uchida

Pianist

Mitsuko Uchida's playing tempts the listener to imagine that the piano may be an extension of her personality. The idea sounds absurd, since we know that pianists, and performing artists in general, "merely" connect the listener with musical works. In Uchida's case, however, mere interpretation is not only artistry of the highest rank but also a mysterious, even supernatural, transformation that rewards the listener with unforgettable spiritual experiences. For example, when Uchida plays Mozart, even the experienced (and perhaps a little jaded) Mozart aficionado hears the familiar music of this great composer as a breathtaking revelation. Only a powerful and original artistic personality can effect this magical transformation of a familiar work into a resplendent vision. Perhaps it is better to say—since spatial terms poorly describe the essence of music—that the piano is thoroughly dominated by Uchida's personality.

As a performer, Uchida has been described as reticent, discreet, even reserved. If so, this is the reticence of an artist who knows that the lightest touch, as evidenced, for example, in her magisterial reading of Claude Debussy's *Etudes*, can reveal entire worlds of untold splendor, that the softest voice can reach the core of a person's being. The obvious paradox notwithstanding, Uchida demonstrates that listening to music is not a physical act. Indeed, as Alex Ross remarked in the *New Yorker,* anyone with the appropriate training can play the right notes. "It is another thing," Ross continued, "to play the thoughts within the notes, the light around them, the darkness behind them, the silence at the end of the phrase. That is what inspires awe." Thus,

the smallest gesture, the almost imperceptible turn of phrase, or the slightest hesitation reveal unfathomable feelings that no intellectual faculties can either measure or translate into words. Indeed, Uchida never lacks the courage to face the mysterious, even disconcerting, infinity of thought, feeling, energy, and inspiration in a great work of musical art.

Arrival in Vienna

Born near Tokyo, into a not particularly musical family, Mitsuko Uchida nevertheless received piano lessons as a young child. In 1961, when she was twelve, her father became Japan's ambassador to Austria, and the family moved to Vienna, the city of Mozart and Beethoven. The piano lessons continued, but this time at the venerable Hochschule für Musik (Vienna Academy of Music) with Richard Hauser. Her Viennese teacher must have recognized her immense talent immediately, for she gave her first concert at the Vienna Musikverein (concert hall) when she was only fourteen. In 1965 her father was transferred back to Japan, but she stayed in Vienna to continue her musical studies. Recognition came in 1969 when she won first prize at the Beethoven Competition.

The following year brought her a second prize at the Chopin Competition in Warsaw. According to some critics, this may have reflected the jury's perception that Uchida was a pianist destined to conquer the world. In 1973, deciding that she was a mature and independent artist, and no longer willing to conform to the extreme and exclusive traditionalism of Vienna's musical establishment, Uchida took control of her career. She moved to London, leaving Vienna and piano lessons behind.

After Uchida walked away from the 1975 Leeds Competition with a second prize, she turned her focus from the pursuit of a traditional concert career, including the struggle for recognition, to a dialogue with a great musical genius—Mozart. She spent years studying his music, intentionally ignoring received wisdom, pianistic tradition, and the established ways of playing Mozart "correctly." She went to the source, playing the music and studying the cultural context of Mozart's creative life. Finally, in 1982, she performed the composer's complete piano sonatas in series of recitals in London and Tokyo to immense critical and popular acclaim. Immediately approached by the Philips label, Uchida eventually recorded the sonatas, as well as his piano concertos, establishing what many claim is the unsurpassed standard for Mozart's piano works.

Golden Touch

While, for Uchida, Mozart remained a reference point and a constant source of inspiration (evidenced by the fact she is always involved in once Mozart project or another), critics and audiences quickly realized that her artistic vision transcended particular traditions: she was inspired by genius. Thus, for example, when she ventured outside the Viennese tradition, which many deemed her natural domain, she produced, in 1990, a magnificent disc of Debussy's Etudes, which were hailed as one of the greatest recordings of Debussy's music.

During the 1990s, Uchida offered extraordinarily original and suggestive readings, in recitals and recordings of Schubert's piano sonatas. Unlike Mozart and Beethoven, whose piano music in many ways defines their repertoire, Schubert is known primarily for his songs and piano miniatures, in which he displays his exquisite charm, dramatic intensity, and supreme melodic inventiveness. Once again approaching Schubert's music directly, without any preconceptions, Uchida successfully tapped into the spiritual vastness and metaphysical power of this great composer's piano sonatas. "Uchida," wrote Alex Ross, "is a great Schubertian because she takes the music at face value, discarding stereotypes of the composer as a twee [overly dainty] melodist or a doleful martyr."

In an effort to demonstrate that modern music—even in its desire to establish a sonic universe in which tonality (the consistent and predicable presence of clearly defined keys) gives way to an atonal musical language devoid of keys—never completely repudiates its sources, Uchida began to juxtapose Schubert and Schoenberg in her recitals. While critics questioned her truly unorthodox, even unsettling, programming, audiences, without analyzing her decision, appreciated her ability to illuminate the inner worlds of two profoundly different representatives of the Viennese tradition.

The Future: Mozart

Uchida's busy schedule and varied performances also include chamber music, and it is hardly surprising that one such engagement was the performance of Mozart's violin sonatas with violinist Mark Steinberg. The duo performed the complete cyle at London's Wigmore Hall, followed by smaller performances throughout Europe. During the 2002-2003 season she participated in a Japanese chamber music project along with Yo-Yo Ma, Steinberg, and Maria Picinini.

In 2003, after becoming artist in residence with the Cleveland Orchestra, Uchida undertook yet another long-term project: she decided to perform all of Mozart's piano concertos the way Mozart performed them—conducting the orchestra while she played the piano. She featured Mozart and other Viennese composers at Carnegie Hall in April 2004, as part of a chamber music series entitled "Mitsuko Uchida: Vienna Revisited." A laureate of numerous recording awards, Uchida is featured in the Great Pianists of the Twentieth Century CD series.

Selected discography

(Beethoven) *Piano Concertos / Klavierkonzerte Nos. 3 & 4,* Philips, 1996.
Mozart Piano Sonatas, Vol. 17, Philips Complete Mozart Edition series, Philips, 1996.
(Schubert) *Impromptus Op. 90 & Op. 142,* Philips, 1997.
(Schubert) *Piano Sonata D. 960,* Philips, 1998.
(Schubert) *Piano Sonatas D. 840 and D. 894,* Philips, 1998.
(Schubert) *Piano Sonatas D. 958 and D. 959,* Philips, 1998.
(Beethoven) *Piano Concerto No. 5,* Philips, 2000.
(Schubert) *Piano Sonatas D. 845 and D. 575,* Philips, 2000.
(Mozart) *The Great Piano Concertos, Vol 1,* Philips, 2001.
(Mozart) *The Great Piano Concertos, Vol. 2,* Philips, 2001.
(Schoenberg) *Piano Concerto,* Philips, 2001.
(Schubert) *Piano Sonata D. 568,* Philips, 2002.
(Schubert) *Piano Sonatas D. 537 and D. 664,* Philips, 2002.
(Mozart) *Early Piano Concertos,* Philips, 2003.
(Mozart) *Great Piano Concertos, Vol. 3,* Philips, 2003.

Sources

Books

Sadie, Stanley, editor, *The New Grove Dictionary of Music and Musicians,* Macmillan, 2001.

Periodicals

American Record Guide, March-April, 1996; September-October, 1997; March-April 1999; May-June, 2003.
Gramophone, February 2000.
Guardian (London), October 20, 2000; March 28, 2001.
New Yorker, March 17, 2003.
La Scena Musicale, July 10, 1999.
Time, March 25, 1999.

—*Zoran Minderovic*

Luther Vandross

Rhythm and blues singer Luther Vandross is best known for his soulful renditions of emotionally charged love ballads. Vandross' wide singing range runs from lush tenor to robust baritone and represents only one of his various talents. He has won numerous Grammy awards, while maintaining complete artistic control of his work. His musical compositions and arrangements have been recorded by many of the greatest American pop singers. Vandross, in addition to his fame as a solo artist, gained notoriety as one of the most talented backup singers in modern music. He released an astonishing 13 platinum albums in succession, beginning with his first major release.

Vandross was born in New York on Manhattan's Lower East Side on April 20, 1951. The youngest of four siblings, he was the son of an upholsterer who died from diabetes when Vandross was just eight. As a result, Vandross developed a close relationship with his mother, Mary Ida Vandross. The Vandross children were musically inclined, a trait that was encouraged by their parents. His mother recognized Vandross' particular musical bent and saw to his musical education when he was still very young, beginning his piano lessons at age three.

One of Vandross' older sisters sang with the Crests as a teenager, and although she left home while Vandross was still a child, he cultivated a particular love and respect for the female singing styles. He was drawn in particular to the late 1960s moods of Diana Ross, Dionne Warwick, and Aretha Franklin. Vandross saw that the unrestrained emotion of female singers was a magnificent faculty rarely found in the work of male pop vocalists. When Vandross was 13 he moved with his mother to the South Bronx in New York where he attended Taft High School. His interest in music became overpowering by his senior year, and although he enrolled at Western Michigan University in Kalamazoo, Michigan, he abandoned his formal education after by the end of his second semester, opting instead to embark on a musical career.

Luck and Talent

From that point Vandross achieved prominence through a delicate combination of talent and luck. One of his compositions, "Everybody Rejoice," was incorporated into the score of the Broadway musical *The Wiz* in 1972. Two years later he attended some taping sessions for rock star David Bowie in the company of a friend who worked as part of the Bowie entourage. As Vandross observed the taping sessions he expressed personal observations about Bowie's musical arrangements. Vandross used his own voice to illustrate his ideas, and his comments were taken seriously by Bowie, who encouraged Vandross to join the company as a backup artist on Bowie's album *Young Americans*.

Singer, songwriter

AP/Wide World Photos. Reproduced by permission.

Born on April 20, 1951, in New York, NY; son of an upholsterer and Mary Ida Vandross; youngest of four siblings. *Education:* Attended Western Michigan University, Kalamazoo, MI.

Wrote "Everybody Rejoice" for *The Wiz,* 1972; backup singer on David Bowie's *Young Americans;* toured with David Bowie, 1974; Atlantic Records, backup vocalist for Bette Midler, Carly Simon, Barbra Streisand, Roberta Flack, and others, 1974-81; singer/songwriter of commercial jingles, started group, Bionic Boogie and sang with Change, 1974; signed group, Luther, with Cotillion records, 1975; signed with Sony's Epic Records, released 13 consecutive platinum selling albums, 1981-1997; performed "In the Spotlight" from Royal Albert Hall for Public Broadcasting System, 1994; moved to Virgin Records in 1998; released *I Know* on Virgin, 1998; released *Smooth Love* on AMW label, 2000; moved to J-Records, released *Luther Vandross,* 2001; released J-Records albums *Dance With My Father* and *Live 2003 at Radio City Music Hall,* 2003.

Awards: Grammy Awards, Best Male Vocalist, 1979; Best Male R&B Vocal Performance for "Here and Now," 1990; Best R&B Song for "Power of Love," 1991; Best Male R&B Vocal Performance for "Power of Love," 1991; Best Male R&B Vocal Performance for *Your Secret Love,* 1996; Song of the Year for "Dance With My Father," 2003; Best R&B Album for *Dance With My Father,* 2003; Best Male R&B Vocal Performance for "Dance With My Father," 2003; Best R&B Performance by a Duo or Group with Vocals (with Beyoncé Knowles) for "The Closer I Get to You," 2003.

Addresses: Record company—J-Records, 745 Fifth Ave., New York, NY 10151, website: http://www.jrecords.com. *Website*—Luther Vandross Official Website: http://www.luthervandross.com.

Eventually Vandross was invited to tour with Bowie, as a warm up for Bowie's act. Vandross accepted the offer, but soon complained that the experience was exhausting, and expressed apprehension. The stress of performance caused him to be nervous and overwrought. He felt anxious at the thought of facing an audience of strangers. Bowie, convinced of Vandross' potential, influenced Vandross to persevere, emphasizing to Vandross that the experiences of live performance would be critical to his future success as an entertainer.

In time Bowie referred Vandross to Bette Midler who arranged to hire Vandross as a backup singer. Vandross embarked on a career as a backup singer for many popular artists including Carly Simon, Barbra Streisand, and the Average White Band. He also made a lucrative living singing jingles for television commercials. During this time Vandross sang with the disco band Change and created a group called Bionic Boogie, a studio production of sound mixes, all performed by Vandross—a virtual one-man band.

Began Solo Career

Vandross formed his own R&B group, Luther, in 1975. With the influence of Arif Mardin the group Luther signed to record with Cotillion Records. Luther was a short-lived enterprise, their records falling well short of expectations. Vandross, meanwhile, aspired to a recording contract that would allow him complete creative control over his recordings. Vandross signed with Epic Records in 1981 and his popularity, both as a singer and a songwriter, flourished steadily from that point forward.

Over the years Vandross wrote songs for other artists such as Aretha Franklin, Diana Ross, and Dionne Warwick, while his own singing career blossomed steadily. By 1991 his double album, *The Best of Luther Vandross, The Best of Love,* became a double platinum seller, and Vandross' success was assured. In 1991-92 Vandross embarked on a tour of the United States that culled a total attendance of 650,000 spectators nationwide and earned $15 million in box office receipts. In 1994 he performed a television special for the Public Broadcasting System called *In the Spotlight,* at Royal Albert Hall in London. He released a Christmas album in 1995, featuring seven new co-written songs, along with a variety of classic carols. In 1996 Vandross performed at the Essence Music Festival. He received the honor of singing the national anthem at the 1997 NFL Super Bowl, and that same year went on a five-city tour beginning in Las Vegas and culminating in Washington D.C.

Ended Epic Partnership

Vandross parted ways with Epic in 1998, after a 16-year partnership during which Vandross released 12 hit albums and sent 22 of singles into the top ten of the R&B charts. The separation from Epic's parent company, Sony, attributed to a dispute over artistic freedom, led to a new contract for Vandross with Virgin Records. His debut with Virgin, 1998's *I Know,* featured a bevy of stars including Stevie Wonder, Cassandra Wilson, and Bob James. The album received generally excellent reviews. Despite achieving super-stardom as a solo artist, Vandross continued to sing as a back up from time to time for a number of notable singers.

Vandross received four Grammy awards from 1990-98, including two for "Power of Love." All together he received three Grammy nominations in 1994, four nominations in 1995; three nominations in 1996, and three in 1997. Vandross made an acting debut in 1993 in the Robert Townsend film *The Meteor Man* and co-hosted the Soul Train Music Awards.

I Know turned out to be Vandross's last, as well as first, album for Virgin. After cutting 2000's *Smooth Love* with the AMW label, he moved to J-Records, where he found a more permanent home. He debuted on that label with a self-titled album in 2001. The new label proved to be a good match for Vandross, and he hit the road for a highly successful concert tour following the release of *Luther Vandross.* The album went platinum, and Vandross sold out Radio City Music Hall for eight nights.

Taking advantage of his new-found artistic freedom at his new label, Vandross released the very personal *Dance With My Father,* in whose title cut he wishes for one last chance to spend time with his father. Said Vandross of this album on the J-Records website, "I wrote the songs as we went along so it's definitely fresh and reflects where I'm at musically, lyrically and creatively."

Vandross suffered a debilitating stroke in early 2003, and spent the next several months slowly recovering away from the public eye. *Dance With My Father* was nominated for five Grammy Awards in 2003, and though Vandross was still too ill to attend the ceremony in early 2004, he was there in spirit as he took home four Grammys, including the award for Song of the Year. The Grammy ceremony also included a tribute to Vandross perfomed by Alicia Keys and Celine Dion. In a taped appearance, Vandross made his first public statement since his stroke to the Grammy audience and home viewers. "I wish I could be with you there tonight. I want to thank everyone for your love and support. And remember, when I say goodbye it's never for long, because I believe in the power of love."

Selected discography

Albums

Never Too Much, Epic, 1981.
Forever, For Always, For Love, Epic, 1982.
Busy Body, Epic, 1983.
The Night I Fell in Love, Columbia, 1985.
Any Love, Epic, 1988.

Power of Love, Epic/Legacy, 1991.
Never Let Me Go, Epic, 1993.
Songs, Epic, 1994.
This is Christmas, Sony, 1995.
Your Secret Love, Sony, 1996.
I Know, Virgin, 1998.
Smooth Love, AMW, 2000.
Luther Vandross, J-Records, 2001.
Home for Christmas, Sony Special, 2002.
Stop to Love, Sony Special, 2002.
Dance With My Father, J-Records, 2003.
Live 2003 at Radio City Music Hall, J-Records, 2003.

EPs and Singles

Give Me the Reason, Epic/Legacy, 1986.
Power of Love, Sony, 1991.
Don't Want to Be a Fool, Sony, 1991.
Never Too Much, Sony, 1991.
The Rush, Sony, 1991.
May Christmas Bring You Happiness, Atlantic, 1991.
Best Things in Life Are Free, A&M, 1992.
Sometimes It's Only Love, Sony, 1992.
Heaven Knows, Sony, 1993.
Never Let Me Go, Sony, 1993.
Always & Forever/Power of Love, Sony, 1994.
Always & Forever/Here & Now, Sony, 1994.
Endless Love, Sony, 1994.
Love the One You're With, Sony, 1995.
Going in Circles, Sony, 1995.
Your Secret Love, Sony, 1996.
I Can Make It Better, Sony, 1996.
Are You Using Me, EMI, 1998.
Heart of a Hero, Sony, 1999.
Take You Out, J-Records, 2001.
Can Heaven Wait?, J-Records, 2001.

Compilations

The Best of Luther Vandross, The Best of Love, Epic, 1989.
Best Remixes, Alex, 1991.
To Love, AMW, 1995.
Never Too Much/Forever, For Always, For Love/Busy Body, Sony, 1995.
Luther Vandross 1981-1995 Greatest Hits, Epic, 1996.
One Night With You: The Best of Love II, Epic, 1997.
Love Is on the Way, One Way, 1998.
Night I Fell in Love/Give Me the Reason/Power of Love, Sony, 1998.
Always & Forever: The Classics, LV/Epic, 1998.
Greatest Hits, Epic, 1999.
Super Hits, Sony, 2000.
The Ultimate Luther Vandross, Epic, 2001.
The Very Best of Luther Vandross, Sony, 2002.
The Very Best of Love, Madacy, 2002.
The Essential Luther Vandross, Epic/Legacy, 2003.

Sources

Books

Clarke, Donald, editor, *The Penguin Encyclopedia of Popular Music,* Viking, 1989.

Stambler, Irwin, editor, *Encyclopedia of Pop, Rock & Soul,* St. Martin's, 1989.

Periodicals

Arizona Republic, December 19, 1997.
Baltimore Afro-American, November 30, 1996.
Detroit News, September 1, 1998.
Gannett News Service, November 27, 1994.
Independent, March 7, 1997, p. 10(2).
Rocky Mountain News, September 5, 1997, p. 18D.
St. Louis Post-Dispatch, September 4, 1997, p. 5.
Sacramento Observer, January 22, 1997.
Tulsa World, August 7, 1998.

Online

"Luther Vandross," Virgin Records, http://www.virginrecords.com/artists/VR.cgi?ARTIST_NAME=Luther_Vandross (October 5, 1998).

"Luther Vandross Biography," Sony Music, http://www.sonymusic.com/artists/LutherVandross/biography.html (September 23, 1998).

Luther Vandross Official Website, http://www.luthervandross.com/ (January 24, 2004).

"Luther Vandross: Still Hungry for Hits," dotmusic, http://www.dotmusic.co.uk/MWtalentluther.html (September 10, 1998).

Recording Academy Grammy Awards, http://www.grammy.com/ (January 24, 2004).

—*Gloria Cooksey and Michael Belfiore*

Speedy West

Pedal steel guitar player, producer

Legendary pedal steel guitar player Speedy West was "one of the greatest virtuosos that country music has ever produced," according to *All Music Guide.* Leo Fender and Don Bigsby made innovations in the still-new instrument specifically for West, including the placement of all four pedals in a row. Best known for his recordings with Jimmy Bryant, he was also in demand as a session player. Throughout his career, West played with well-known artists such as Spade Cooley, Tennessee Ernie Ford, Hank Penny, and many others.

Wesley Webb West was born on January 25, 1924, in Springfield, Missouri, to Finley G. and Sue Arthur West. The elder West worked as a linotype operator for a gospel publishing company, and played guitar and sang gospel music as hobbies. With a supportive musical environment of family and neighbors surrounding him, West began to play guitar at the age of nine. West eventually asked his father for a National steel guitar, an expensive purchase for the family, and his father sacrificed his own guitar to purchase the instrument for his son.

Headed West

After his marriage in 1941, West lived in St. Louis, Missouri, for a year and took a factory job while continuing to play music. A year later his family moved to a farm owned by West's father in Strafford, Missouri. Because of World War II, farming was a vital occupation, and West was exempt from the draft. He contin-

ued to farm after the war, but was much more interested in playing music. A Grand Ole Opry traveling show featuring Eddy Arnold and Minnie Pearl arrived in Springfield, Missouri, in 1946, and West attended. He drew inspiration from Little Roy Wiggins, Arnold's steel guitar player, and began thinking more about a career in music, especially after he heard that musicians in Southern California could earn as much as $25 a night. He purchased a seven-string, doubleneck steel guitar, in order to try and emulate Wiggins's playing. Other important influences on his musical development were players such as Leon McAuliffe, Bashful Brother Oswald Kirby, Joaquin Murphy, Billy Robinson, and others. While West was playing at a radio station-sponsored jam session, the master of ceremonies introduced him as "Speedy West," a name that proved fitting and which he would adopt later in his career.

West and his family moved to Los Angeles in 1946, where he worked both day and night jobs. "First thing I did was get a job in a dry-cleaning plant," said West in a 1991 *Tulsa World* interview. "I worked dry-cleaning by day, beer joints by night. Counting driving time, it was an 18-hour day for two years." As he continued to play, West sought to develop his own style. He also bought a whole new set-up in 1947, purchasing a customized, three-neck pedal steel guitar with four foot pedals from instrument maker Paul Bigsby, and an amplifier from Leo Fender. The instrument was only the second Bigsby had made. As explained on the Rockabilly Hall of Fame website, "The four pedals were side by side, a design that would later influence all pedal guitars." Created in 1939, the instrument was still relatively new, and West was in fact the first country artist to play pedal steel guitar regularly.

With the new instrument and his own unique style, "West bridged the western swing and rockabilly eras with eye-popping steel guitar," proclaimed *All Music Guide.* "Adept at boogie, blues, and Hawaiian ballads, West played with an infectious joy and daring improvisation that, at its most adventurous, could be downright experimental. It's doubtful whether anyone could collect all of Speedy's solos under one roof, but it was his sessions of the 1950s and early '60s—especially those with Jimmy Bryant—that found his genius at its most freewheeling and dazzling."

Became a Full-time Musician

While working one night in 1947, West first met guitar player Jimmy Bryant. They were working at nearby clubs, and after each heard the other play, they became interested in working together, although this would not come to pass for several more years. Spade Cooley, the country big band leader, was keeping West busy. West regularly played dances with the band and performed on Cooley's television variety show. Cooley had a reputation for being difficult, particularly when drinking. He first fired, then tried to rehire West, calling

Born Wesley Webb West on January 25, 1924, in Springfield, MO; died on November 15, 2003, in Broken Bow, OK; son of Finley G. (a linotype operator and guitar player) and Sue (Arthur) West; married Opal Mae, 1941 (divorced, 1964); married Mary, 1966; children: two.

Began playing guitar, 1933; moved to Los Angeles, 1946; purchased custom equipment, 1947; met Jimmy Bryant, 1947; hired as session musician by Capitol Records, 1949; under contract to Capitol, began session work with Bryant, 1951; recorded *Two Guitars Country Style,* 1954; last work with Bryant, 1956; played estimated 6,000+ sessions for Capitol, 1950-55; Grand Ole Opry debut, 1951; moved to Tulsa, OK, 1960; last session for Capitol, 1962; moved to Broken Arrow, OK, 1971; ceased playing after stroke, 1981.

Awards: Inducted into Steel Guitar Hall of Fame, 1980.

him constantly for a year. "We worked shows together after that, but I never would return to work for him," West told Rich Kienzle in *Southwest Shuffle: Pioneers of Honky-Tonk, Western Swing, and Country Jazz.* West never recorded with Cooley because of a union recording ban that lasted through 1948.

West's talents had come to the attention of Cliffie Stone, who worked for Capitol Records, and West was hired by the label as a session musician in 1949. According to the Rockabilly Hall of Fame website, "One of the first lessons he learned was to play 'commercial,' and produce the sound expected by the producer. Speedy learned very quickly that he would not be able to develop his potential for session work if he continued to focus on his own style and try to dazzle everyone with his own talent."

However, West was able to stretch creatively in Hank Penny's western swing outfit. Penny appreciated West's work in The Penny Serenaders. "Speedy was brave," Penny told Kienzle. "He had distinctive ideas of his own. He was very good at tone and dynamics, young and full of vinegar. He would come in like a storm and did one hell of a job." Later that year, Stone hired West away from Penny. Stone and his band had a daily radio program called the *Dinner Bell Roundup,* plus a regular weekly dance program and later a television program. According to the Rockabilly Hall of Fame website, Stone "allowed and encouraged

Speedy, as well as other band members, to be creative and expand their talents as much as possible. Many performers launched their careers with the help of Cliffie Stone's *Hometown Jamboree,* such as Tennessee Ernie Ford, Merle Travis, Eddie Kirk, and many others." Stone was also very supportive of West. "Cliffie is the guy that probably opened more doors for me than anyone for recording and TV," he told Kienzle. "He wanted every person on that stage to be a star in their own right and have their own following. I owe him an awful lot." West would record his first solo instrumental, "Steel Strike," during a 1950 recording session for Stone.

Paired With Bryant

West also recorded in sessions for popular artists such as Tennessee Ernie Ford and Kay Starr. Capitol offered West a contract in 1951, and Bryant soon joined him. West and Bryant not only contributed to Ford's recordings, they appeared on a lengthy list of artists' recordings—everyone from Gene Autry to Sheb Wooley. Most notable of these was "Sixteen Tons," which was a crossover hit for Ford. According to *Country Music: The Rough Guide,* "During the '50s, West and Bryant were a practically unbeatable guitar team who played together not just on their own mind-blowing recordings, but on countless gun-for-hire sessions." The list included country and popular vocalists such as Doris Day, Betty Hutton, Wanda Jackson, Frank Sinatra, Johnny Horton, Spike Jones, Frankie Laine, Ferlin Huskey, and Roy Rogers and Dale Evans. David Gates in *Newsweek* called them "the [Dizzy] Gillespie and [Charlie] Parker of country."

Nick Tosches wrote in *Country: The Twisted Roots of Rock 'n' Roll,* "Pedal steel guitars were harder to master than conventional guitars. Men sat at this strange shining tool, their fingers gleaming with metal—doctoral, they seemed, and mystical, too." Tosches added, "In two 1952 recordings, Hank Thompson's 'Waiting in the Lobby of Your Heart' (Capitol) and Slim Whitman's 'Song of the Old Water Wheel' (Imperial), Speedy West used a bizarre, high-volume wah-wah effect that got the attention of the industry. Soon the pedal steel work heard in records coming from Nashville was louder, more emphatic than it had been." West was doing this without some of the modern equipment musicians now take for granted, such as electronic effects. Amplification was still relatively new as well. Kienzle observed, "Speedy generated all their adventurous sounds with nothing more than nimble hands and fingers, picks, and fertile and creative minds."

According to *Country Music: The Rough Guide,* "The sounds introduced by West … were like nothing country music had ever heard before—or has ever heard since. While an amplified steel guitar had been used to add color and depth to country music since the '30s, West's pedal-steel work was from another galaxy entirely—his solos a wild, unchained, and sometimes zany torrent of sonic loops, leaps, curves, hums and gallops." Roy Harte, a drummer who had played with Stone's outfit, remarked on the style of the Bryant-West pairing. "You know what it was? ...These guys had six ears. Most of us have only two," he said in *Southwest Shuffle.* "They could hear what was coming as well as what they were playing and what was past."

Their first duo recording was 1954's *Two Guitars Country Style.* It was the only album to be recorded under both their names. They released an estimated 50-plus instrumental recordings between 1951 and 1956. These included originals such as "Stratosphere Boogie" and "Caffeine Patrol." West alone would play on an estimated six thousand-plus recordings between 1950 and 1955, for 177 different artists. "I broke the all-time record for anyone playing any instrument," he told *Tulsa World.* He kept his own session log, noting details of each job in his own handwriting. West continued to perform on *Hometown Jamboree,* but also made many appearances on different network television variety programs including those hosted by Red Foley, Bob Crosby, Dinah Shore, and Lawrence Welk. He made his Grand Ole Opry debut in 1951.

West and Bryant made their final recording session for Capitol in October of 1956. Although the team was no longer intact, West continued to play for Capitol under a new contract and did so until 1960. Stone's *Hometown Jamboree* program was cancelled in 1959. West and the other musicians formed Billy and the Kids, which was a regular band on the Nevada club circuit. West was often called in to produce. One spring day in the 1960s, West was asked to produce an unknown female singer who showed up with her husband in tow. Early in the session, the young woman impressed West. He suggested hiring a better group of musicians and a better studio for the single, and brought in Roy Lanham, Harold Hensley, Roy Harte and Billy Liebert. He also suggested that, like Patti Page, she overdub her own harmonies. The recording was "Honky Tonk Girl"; the vocalist was Loretta Lynn.

When country music session work in Los Angeles tapered off, West began exploring other career options. Pedal steel had fallen out of favor in country recordings during this period. He moved to Tulsa, Oklahoma, in 1960, to manage a warehouse for Fender Musical Instruments, while continuing to play part-time. He recorded for Capitol until 1962, and worked with Leo Fender as a steel guitar design consultant. In 1971 he moved to Broken Bow, Oklahoma, with his second wife, Mary. West still continued to play and record, and was inducted into the Steel Guitar Hall of Fame in

1980. Following a stroke in 1981, West was no longer able to play, although he continued to attend events devoted to steel guitar playing. His health deteriorated, and West died on November 15, 2003, in Broken Bow, Oklahoma.

Selected discography

Solo

West of Hawaii, Capitol, 1958.
Steel Guitar, Capitol, 1960.
Guitar Spectacular, Longhorn, 1962.
Steel Guitar from Outer Space, See for Miles, 1989.

With Jimmy Bryant

Two Guitars Country Style, Capitol, 1954.
For the Last Time, Step One, 1990.
Stratosphere Boogie: The Flaming Guitars of Speedy West & Jimmy Bryant (compilation), Razor & Tie, 1995.
Flamin' Guitars (box set), Bear Family, 1997.
Swingin' on the Strings: The Speedy West & Jimmy Bryant Collection, Vol. 2, Razor & Tie, 1999.
There's Gonna Be a Party (compilation), Jasmine, 2000.

Sources

Books

Doggett, Peter, *Are You Ready for the Country,* Penguin, 2000.
Kienzle, Rich, *Southwest Shuffle: Pioneers of Honky-Tonk, Western Swing, and Country Jazz,* Routledge, 2003.
Tosches, Nick, *Country: The Twisted Roots of Rock 'n' Roll,* 2nd edition, Da Capo, 1998.
Wolff, Kurt, *Country Music: The Rough Guide,* Rough Guides, 2000.

Periodicals

Los Angeles Times, November 18, 2003.
Newsweek, November 13, 1995.
Tulsa World, November 16, 2003.

Online

"Speedy West," *All Music Guide,* http://www.allmusic.com/ (January 13, 2004).
"Speedy West," Rockabilly Hall of Fame, http://www.rockabillyhall.com/SpeedyWest.html (January 13, 2004).

—*Linda Dailey Paulson*

Wilco

Alternative country group

Wilco was initially an offshoot of Uncle Tupelo, a progressive country band that broke apart in 1994; one of the group's cofounders, Jeff Tweedy, formed a new band that held on to its country roots while adopting a more pop/rock sound. As the band progressed, however, it became clear "country" was far too limited a term to encapsulate Tweedy's musical vision. In 2002, the band's experimental album *Yankee Hotel Foxtrot,* although dropped by its previous record label, was a swirling, chanting, experimental work that landed atop the *Village Voice*'s annual Pazz & Jop Critics' Poll.

Wilco's roots were in a combination of country and punk music, and a band called Uncle Tupelo. In 1988, two longtime friends with a passion for traditional country and punk music, who were both natives of Belleville, Illinois, a decaying blue-collar suburb east of St. Louis, Missouri, Jay Farrar and Jeff Tweedy formed Uncle Tupelo. Prior to Uncle Tupelo, the two had formed a punk band, the Primitives, which broke up when Farrar's brother enlisted in the United States Army. Both men shared responsibility for writing music and lyrics, creating a persuasive blend of country punk, an intense style of punk-informed rural music, and were joined by drummer Mike Heidorn (later replaced by Ken Coomer).

The group toured on the Midwestern club circuit for a couple of years before releasing their debut album, *No Depression* in 1990, followed by *Still Feel Gone* in 1991, both for the independent Rockville label. These releases brought the group an instant cult following of both country and rock fans, as well as critical accolades from music magazines such as *Rolling Stone*. Tweedy, who played bass for the group, and Farrar, who served as lead guitarist and vocalist, each provided the group with a distinct sensibility. While Tweedy held the sweeter instincts and a critical interest in music, Farrar added soul to Uncle Tupelo's songs with his grand, indignant voice and pained tone. The group returned in 1992 with a more subdued, acoustic album of traditional folk tunes entitled *March 16-20, 1992,* produced by R.E.M. guitarist Peter Buck, which also earned favorable critical attention. After signing with a major label, Warner Brothers' Sire/Reprise, Uncle Tupelo released *Anodyne* in 1993, considered the group's best album. Here, the group placed country in the background and opted for a more progressive sound.

Despite the band's newfound commercial appeal, major label contract, and growing popularity, Farrar abruptly left Uncle Tupelo in 1994 and formed a new American folk/country group called Son Volt. Neither of the men would elaborate on the exact circumstances of the split, but Tweedy did suggest that "I think it was a personal decision for Jay, but he wasn't very communicative about anything to us, which was fairly normal for Jay," as quoted by Alan Sculley in the *St. Louis Post-Dispatch*. "I mean, a lot of things that were used as explanations were fairly contradictory so I wouldn't really be able to comment on it." Even though Tweedy and Farrar had worked together for years, Tweedy further commented that their relationship centered around music, rather than a personal friendship.

From the moment Farrar announced his departure, the remaining members knew that they loved making music together and did not want to stop. Thus, Tweedy took the leading role as guitarist and vocalist and renamed the group Wilco. The former members of Uncle Tupelo, which also included drummer Coomer, fiddler and mandolin and banjo player Max Johnston, and bassist John Stirratt, were later joined by a second guitarist, Jay Bennett (formerly of the group Titanic Love Affair). After closing the door on Uncle Tupelo, the newly-formed Wilco felt truly liberated. "Certain things, I think, would kind of be tossed out before they ever became a song, just on the idea that it wouldn't really fit in on an Uncle Tupelo record or really didn't work next to Jays songs—things like that," Tweedy told Sculley.

Originally, Wilco earned a reputation as a no frills rock band, and Tweedy became known as a simple, per-

sonal, and uncomplicated storyteller. But the band hinted at its future musical exploration even early in its career. With a new sense of creative freedom, Wilco seemed determined to include all styles of music into their new band. In 1995, they joined the H.O.R.D.E. (Horizons of Rock Developing Everywhere) tour, playing some old Uncle Tupelo songs, as well as some new songs that later appeared on their debut release.

After relocating to Chicago from St. Louis, Wilco released their first album, *A.M.,* in 1995 on the Sire/Reprise label. For the debut, the group, joined by guest guitarist Brian Henneman of the group the Bottle Rockets, maintained its country roots, but also added more pop and rock influences. Consisting of 13 tracks, 12 of which were written by Tweedy, *A.M.* opens with four solid rock songs, including "Box Full of Letters," which deals with separation (perhaps in regards to Farrar's leaving), and "Casino Queen," a rock song full of unbridled energy. Throughout the rest of the album, the music deepens in scope, moving back and forth between heavier rock songs and mid-tempo ballads, such as the love songs "Pick Up the Change," "That's Not the Issue," "Should've Been in Love," and "Too Far Apart." Bassist and rhythm guitarist Stirratt wrote and sang one song for the album entitled "It's Just That Simple," a tearful, traditional country tune. Later that year, multi-instrumentalist Johnson left Wilco, and fiddler and guitarist Bob Egan joined the band.

The following year, Wilco released their second album, a 19-track double CD entitled *Being There*. Publications such as *Rolling Stone* and the *Los Angeles Times* raved about the group's latest collection, using catch phrases like "album of the year" and "ambitious versatility," and their music received airplay on alternative rock radio stations across the United States. Like their debut, *Being There* included music from several genres, from neo-punk to rockabilly on top of their firm progressive country foundation. For example, the song "Monday" recalled the swinging rock of the Rolling Stones' hit "Brown Sugar," "Outta Mind (Outta Sight)" took inspiration from West Coast 1960s pop, and "Kingpin" boasted the sounds of swaggering country.

The band went back into the studio in 1997 to begin work on their third album. In the meantime, they took time off to work on a project with British folk singer and musician Billy Bragg in Dublin. In 1998, Bragg and Wilco released the critically acclaimed *Mermaid Avenue,* a collection of Woodie Guthrie lyrics for which the musicians wrote their own original music. The concept for the album came about in 1995 when Guthrie's daughter, Nora Guthrie, gave Bragg reams of her father's handwritten song lyrics and asked him to write music for them. Although Guthrie had composed some of the music for the lyrics, he did not have the chance to write the notes down before he died in 1967 following a long battle with a rare nervous disorder called Huntington's chorea. The resulting album, with music co-written by Wilco and Bragg, combined the folk blueprint of Bragg with the soul and genre-bending tendencies of Wilco. (Wilco and Bragg would revisit this formula on *Mermaid Avenue Vol. II,* in 2000, including even-more-obscure Guthrie originals such as "Stetson Kennedy" and "Black Wind Blowing.")

Subsequently, Wilco returned to Chicago to complete recording songs for *Summer Teeth,* released in 1999. A strong 1960s pop element came though in tracks like "I'm Always in Love," "ELT," and "Summer Teeth." However, Tweedy contrasted Wilco's bright pop songs with dark, often disturbing lyrics, although the overall feel of the album was upbeat. "There's a darkness to the lyrical half of the the record and there's an overwhelming brightness to the music," Tweedy informed Curtis Ross in the *Tampa Tribune.* "The effort was to make the record more hopeful as it progressed." Like the group's prior work, *Summer Teeth* received critical praise and further solidified Tweedy's reputation as one of America's most stellar songwriters. Also that year, Wilco toured Europe and the United States, opening for the group R.E.M. in larger arenas and headlining their own show at smaller venues.

Wilco seemed to be on a path to success. "I've always wanted a band where everybody felt invested and welcomed contributions, have it be fulfilling and as much of a democracy as it can be," Tweedy told the *Denver Post.* "With this current band, I've gotten closer to it than it's ever been. It's satisfying. But I admit it—I've learned to this point by f***ing it up!"

But Tweedy's enthusiasm didn't carry over to everybody else in the band. Although Wilco was in the studio recording what many consider its masterpiece, *Yankee Hotel Foxtrot,* multi-instrumentalist and key sound architect Bennett was starting to distance himself from the rest of the band. Then, a music-industry soap opera commenced after the band finished the album and submitted it to its longtime label, Reprise Records, which once had a reputation for releasing adventurous music. Reprise executives rejected the album as not commercial enough; the band pleaded its case in the media and wound up selling it to Nonesuch (which, oddly, was owned by Warner Bros., which also owns Reprise). The album's soaring, repetitive tracks sound absolutely nothing like the straightforward country-rock of *A.M.* or Uncle Tupelo, and songs such as "I Am Trying to Break Your Heart" and "Heavy Metal Drummer" resembled nothing else in rock 'n' roll at the time. Critics loved it.

Although Bennett appears on *Foxtrot,* he quit the band shortly thereafter and went on to work on several solo projects, including three albums scheduled for release in 2004. His departure of the band is achingly chronicled on *I Am Trying to Break Your Heart,* a bittersweet, Sam Jones-directed documentary film about the *Foxtrot* sessions. ("Jay wore out his welcome in a lot of ways," Tony Margherita, the band's manager,

says in the film.) More departures followed Bennett; veteran Wilco keyboardist Leroy Bach (who himself had replaced Bennett) and steel guitarist Bob Egan announced their departure from the group in early 2004. In early 2004, Wilco was in the studio recording a follow-up to *Foxtrot, A Ghost is Born,* to be released in the summer of 2004.

Despite Wilco's success after breaking away from Uncle Tupelo, Tweedy insisted that he still remains an ordinary guy. "I'm not some big rock star, but I do run into fans every now and then who think I'm this super-special person ... and it's weird, because you can't be who they think you are." Nevertheless, he admitted to acting "freaked out" when he met one of his musical heroes in 1996, when Wilco shared a bill with Johnny Cash at a show in New York City. "I don't know if someone coached him on my name or something, but he actually walked into the room and said, 'Where's Jeff?' and my heart stopped," Tweedy recalled to Thor Christensen of the *Dallas Morning News.* "After you've made a few records, you think you could meet [famous] people and not act goofy. But when I'm around a guy like Johnny Cash, there's no way I can act or talk normally."

Selected discography

A.M., Sire/Reprise, 1995.
Being There, Reprise, 1996.
(With Billy Bragg) *Mermaid Avenue,* Elektra, 1998.
Summer Teeth, Reprise, 1999.
(With Billy Bragg) *Mermaid Avenue Vol. II,* Reprise, 2000.
Yankee Hotel Foxtrot, Nonesuch, 2002.
A Ghost is Born, Nonesuch, 2004.

Sources

Books

Kingsbury, Paul, editor, *Encyclopedia of Country Music,* Oxford University Press, 1998.
MusicHound Rock: The Essential Album Guide, Visible Ink, 1999.
Robbins, Ira A., editor, *Trouser Press Guide to '90s Rock,* Fireside/Simon & Schuster, 1997.

Periodicals

Capital Times (Madison, WI), February 5, 1997, p. 1D.
Dallas Morning News, November 3, 1996, p. 1C; November 8, 1996, p. 33A; June 21, 1998, p. 1C.
Denver Post, September 8, 2002.
Independent, April 2, 1999, p. 11.
Independent on Sunday, March 30, 1997.
New Statesman, March 26, 1999.
Newsday, June 13, 1995, p. B02; February 17, 1997, p. B07.
The Record (Bergen County, NJ), June 14, 1995, p. F09.
Rolling Stone, June 24, 1999.

St. Louis Post-Dispatch, March 23, 1995, p. 04G; April 21, 1995, p. 06E; November 2, 1995, p. 11; January 1, 1997, p. 14; August 19, 1999, p. 26; October 11, 2002.

Spin, May 1999, p. 55.

Tampa Tribune, August 27, 1999, p. 18.

Toronto Sun, April 14, 1999, p. 63.

Wisconsin State Journal, April 8, 1999, p. 16.

Online

"Wilco," *All Music Guide,* http://www.allmusic.com (February 9, 2004).

Wilco Official Website, http://www.wilcoworld.net (February 9, 2004).

—*Laura Hightower and Steve Knopper*

Rob Zombie

Singer, songwriter

One of the most recognizable figures in the world of hard rock, Rob Zombie follows in the ghoulish footsteps of musicians that have mashed theatrical rock into a macabre mix of audiovisual stimuli. Zombie has sold millions of records, won an MTV video music award, and even ventured into horror films and comic books. Since 1985 the multitalented monster-loving frontman has translated the loud, gross, and gory into visual spectacles with unique soundtracks.

Rob Zombie was born Robert Cummings on January 12, 1965, in Haverhill, Massachusetts. Although he may have not initially envisioned himself a musician, he knew, even as a youngster, that he was determined to avoid the mundane. As the dread-headed singer explained to *Stuff Magazine,* "I always knew since I was a kid that all I ever wanted to do was make movies, draw comics, work in a wax museum, or wear a big animal suit at Disney... I just knew I wanted to do something like that. I never had any aspirations to do something that wasn't fun." Influenced by late 1960s kitsch horror programs like *The Munsters* and *The Addams Family* as well as theatrical shock rockers of the 1970s such as Alice Cooper and Kiss, Cummings always intended to find a way to parlay his unique interests into a career.

Immediately after graduating from high school, Cummings moved to New York's seedy lower east side. He took a series of jobs to pay the rent, including layout for a soft-core pornographic magazine, *Celebrity Sleuth,* and work as a production assistant for the then-popular children's television show *Pee Wee's Playhouse.* Cummings met Sean Yseult in 1985, and the two became romantically involved. The two formed White Zombie, with Cummings, now known as Rob Zombie, on vocals, and Yseult, who had no previous musical experience, on bass; completing the original line-up were musicians Tom Guay on guitar and Ivan de Prume on drums.

Named after a 1932 Bela Lugosi horror film, White Zombie meshed metal with monster affection and stomped through New York's rock scene, attracting much attention from both clubgoers and the local press. Zombie, who was inspired by both horror and theatrics, knew from the outset the importance of visuals to rock acts. As Zombie explained to *City Link Magazine* years later, "You can't have a great rock band with no visuals. Just like you can't have a great rock band with only visuals. If you look back through the history of rock music whether it's Elvis or The Beatles or Led Zeppelin or Jimi Hendrix or Kiss. Musically they were great but visually they were great too. They had it covered on every level."

Marketing themselves, however, was another problem. When White Zombie formed in the early eighties, few groups—with the exception of well-known acts such as the Misfits and the Cramps—were doing highly visual

Born Robert Cummings on January 12, 1965, in Haverhill, MA.

Formed rock band White Zombie in New York; released several albums, EPs, and singles independently, 1985-89; band signed to Geffen Records, 1990; released debut album *La Sexorcisto: Devil Music Vol. 1*, 1992; parted with all members of White Zombie except drummer John Tempesta, 1995; worked with famous cartoon series creator Mike Judge on the movie *Beavis and Butt-Head Do America*, 1986; released first solo effort *Hellbilly Deluxe: 13 Tales of Cadaverous Cavorting Inside the Spookshow International*, 1998; wrote and directed film *House of 1000 Corpses*, 2000 (released, 2003); released *Sinister Urge*, 2001; published horror comic book series, *Spook Show International*, 2003; released greatest hits album, *Past Present and Future*, 2003.

Awards: MTV Video Award, Best Hard Rock Video, for "More Human than Human," 1995.

Addresses: *Record company*—Geffen/Universal Music, 2220 Colorado Ave., Santa Monica, CA 90404. *Publicist*—Deborah Radel Public Relations, 1123 N. Flores St., Ste. 12, Los Angeles CA 90069.

performances. Regardless, White Zombie put out two singles and several works on their own label, Silent Explosion, prior to being discovered by independent Caroline Records who put out their next few releases.

After releasing the independent LP *Make Them Die Slowly*, the group embarked on a European tour, which they followed with the 1989 EP *God of Thunder*. The release got the attention of executives at Geffen Records, and the group signed a recording contract in 1990. White Zombie's major label debut, *La Sexorcisto: Devil Music Vol. 1*, was released in 1992. The band's B-movie slasher magic fused with metal riffs made their first single "Thunder Kiss '65" a staple on MTV and propelled the album into the top 40. To support the album, White Zombie embarked on an ambitious tour, playing more than 350 shows. The album eventually went platinum, and "Thunder Kiss '65" was nominated for a Grammy for Best Hard Rock Performance.

The band's 1995 triple-platinum follow-up, *Astro Creep: 2000, Songs of Love, Destruction and Other Synthetic Delusions of the Electric Head* debuted on the top ten album charts and stayed there for over two months before retreating to the *Billboard* Top 200, where it sat for over 89 weeks. A single from the album, "More Human than Human" was nominated for a Grammy, and won an MTV Video Music Award. *Supersexy Swinging Sounds*, which featured *Astro-Creep* remixes, arrived in 1996 and went platinum as well.

Zombie, who had creative control of the band's ventures, directing their videos and designing both artwork and stage shows, began to branch out on his own. While still on tour for *Astro Creep,* he worked with cartoonist Mike Judge on the 1996 movie *Beavis and Butt-Head Do America,* a film version of the popular television series of the same name that prominently featured the band. Zombie performed "The Great American Nightmare" on the *Private Parts* soundtrack with shock-rock deejay Howard Stern and sang "The Hands of Death" with horror-rock legend Alice Cooper on *Songs in the Key of X: Music from and Inspired by "The X-Files."* The latter was nominated for a Grammy and competed against (unsuccessfully) against yet another Zombie track, "I'm Your Boogieman" from the platinum soundtrack to *The Crow: City of Angels.*

Resentment began to build among White Zombie members, and the tension and burnout from being together for over 10 years eventually split the group. Zombie and drummer John Tempesta left to form their own act, with Zombie now in total control. Although the sound changed slightly, he kept his loud, horror-rock theatrical edge, much to the delight of his fans. "When White Zombie broke up it was at the height of the band's success, not on its way down," explained Zombie to the *Jersey Alive.* "That in itself is kind of a crazy thing to do, because you work your whole life to get somewhere and then it falls apart right at that moment. So going solo was tough to do but it worked out great. I have no complaints."

In 1998 Zombie released his first solo album, *Hellbilly Deluxe: 13 Tales of Cadaverous Cavorting Inside the Spookshow International,* which immediately went into the *Billboard* top five and eventually sold over three million copies. With his theatrical rants and extravagant stage show, Rob Zombie was just as successful solo as he'd been with his band. To promote *Hellbilly,* Zombie joined the multiact metal tour Ozzfest in 1999.

In April of 2000 Zombie began to write and direct *House of 1000 Corpses,* featuring cult movie stars Karen Black, Sid Haig, and Michael J. Pollard. The studio, however, claimed the violent, sadistic film would require an NC-17 rating, which they refused to accept. Zombie was skeptical. "I was really upfront with them," he told the *Guardian.* "They had the script ... They saw the dailies.... [I]t's not like they didn't know what I was doing." Universal stood their ground and refused to release the film.

Undeterred, Zombie went back to the studio in 2001 to record his new album *Sinister Urge* (named for a 1961 Ed Wood crime flick). Boasting an impressive list of guest performers including Ozzy Osbourne, Mötley Crüe drummer Tommy Lee, and Slayer guitarist Kerry King among others the album debuted at number 11 on the *Billboard* chart, confirming Zombie's consistent popularity. He took his show on the road, embarking on the Merry Mayhem tour with the legendary Ozzy Osbourne.

In 2003 Lions Gate Entertainment agreed to release *Night of 1000 Corpses,* fulfilling Zombie's dream and scoring major points with his fans, although it was panned by the critics. (Zombie began to work on the sequel in 2004.) In 2003 Zombie also released a greatest hits collection and launched his own comic book line, *Rob Zombie's Spook Show International.*

Although some have accused him of building on his exaggerated image, Zombie argues that he's simply being true to himself. "I try never to portray myself as something that isn't me. Onstage it's kind of a hyped up version of myself because I'm trying to reach the guy on the lawn but I am trying to keep it real because it's hard to live some lie." Zombie continues to remain a formidable spook in the haunted house of heavy metal.

Selected discography

With White Zombie

Soul Crusher, Caroline, 1987.
Make Them Die Slowly, Caroline, 1988.
God of Thunder (EP), Caroline, 1989.
La Sexorcisto: Devil Music Vol. 1, Geffen, 1992.
Astro Creep 2000: Songs of Love, Destruction and Other Synthetic Delusions of the Electric Head, Geffen, 1995.
Super Sexy Swingin' Sounds (remix), Geffen, 1996.

Solo

Hellbilly Deluxe: 13 Tales of Cadaverous Cavorting Inside the Spookshow International, Geffen, 1998.
American Made Music to Strip By, Interscope, 1999.

Sinister Urge, Universal, 2001.
Past, Present, and Future (compilation), Geffen, 2003.

Sources

Periodicals

Blender, January/February 2002.
Chicago Sun Times, December 8, 2001.
Circus Magazine, March 26, 2002.
Citi-Link, November 21, 2001.
College Times, April 9-15, 2003.
Daily Variety, March 20, 2002; May 8, 2003; December 9, 2003.
Entertainment Weekly, March 14, 2003; April 4, 2003.
Guardian (London), September 19, 2003.
Guitar World, January 2002.
Hit Parader, January 2002.
Hollywood Reporter, May 8, 2003; October 10, 2003.
Los Angeles Times, March 21, 2002.
Meltdown, October/December 2001.
Metal Edge, February 2002.
Request, October/December 2001.
Rolling Stone, December 12, 2001; November 27, 2003.
Record, December 21, 2001.
Transworld Stance, May 2002.

Online

"Movies Put the R back in Horror," *Los Angeles Times,* http://www.latimes.com/ (July 14, 2003).
"Rob Zombie to Write Comic about Bigfoot, Sinister Metal Band," MTV, http://www.mtv.com/news/articles/1481061/ 20031211/zombie_rob. jhtml?headlines=true (December 12, 2003).
"Rob Zombie's New Creep Show," *RollingStone.com,* http://www.rollingstone.com/news/newsarticle.asp?nid=19077 (December 12, 2003).
"Rob Zombie's 'Spookshow' 1 & 2 Sells Out, Series Goes Monthly," Comic Book Resources, http://www.comicbook resources.com/news/printthis.cgi?id=3069 (December 19, 2003).
"Six Debuts Rocket to Top of the Charts," *New York Daily News,* http://www.nydailynews.com/entertainment/story.12 2621p-110192c.html (October 2, 2003).
"Un-Dead Head," *New York Post,* http://newyorkpost.com/ entertainment/56683.htm (April 19, 2003).

Additional information was obtained from materials provided by Deborah Radel Public Relations and Geffen Records, 2004.

—Nicole Elyse

Cumulative Subject Index

Volume numbers appear in **bold**

Vaughan, Stevie Ray **1**
Waits, Tom **27**
  Earlier sketch in CM **12**
  Earlier sketch in CM **1**
Walker, Joe Louis **28**
Walker, T-Bone **5**
Wallace, Sippie **6**
Washington, Dinah **5**
Waters, Ethel **11**
Waters, Muddy **24**
  Earlier sketch in CM **4**
Watson, Johnny "Guitar" **41**
Wells, Junior **17**
Weston, Randy **15**
Whitfield, Mark **18**
Whitley, Chris **16**
Whittaker, Hudson **20**
Williams, Joe **11**
Williamson, Sonny Boy **9**
Wilson, Gerald **19**
Winter, Johnny **5**
Witherspoon, Jimmy **19**
ZZ Top **2**

Cajun/Zydeco

Ball, Marcia **15**
Beausoleil **37**
Brown, Clarence "Gatemouth" **11**
Buckwheat Zydeco **34**
  Earlier sketch in CM **6**
Chavis, Boozoo **38**
Chenier, C. J. **15**
Chenier, Clifton **6**
Doucet, Michael **8**
Hackberry Ramblers **43**
Landreth, Sonny **16**
Queen Ida **9**
Richard, Zachary **9**
Rockin' Dopsie **10**
Savoy, Ann **47**
Simien, Terrance **12**
Sonnier, Jo-El **10**
Sturr, Jimmy **33**

Cello

Casals, Pablo **9**
Chang, Han-Na **33**
Darling, David **34**
DuPré, Jacqueline **26**
Feigelson, Yosif **35**
Harrell, Lynn **3**
Holland, Dave **27**
Lavelle, Caroline **35**
Ma, Yo Yo **24**
  Earlier sketch in CM **2**
Mørk, Truls **38**
Rasputina **26**
Rostropovich, Mstislav **17**
Savall, Jordi **44**
Silva, Alan **45**
Starker, Janos **32**

Children's Music

Bartels, Joanie **13**
Cappelli, Frank **14**
Chapin, Tom **11**
Chenille Sisters, The **16**
Haack, Bruce **37**
Harley, Bill **7**
Lehrer, Tom **7**
Nagler, Eric **8**
Penner, Fred **10**
Raffi **8**
Riders in the Sky **33**
Rogers, Fred **46**
Rosenshontz **9**

Sharon, Lois & Bram **6**
Wiggles, The **42**

Christian Music

Anointed **21**
Arends, Carolyn **45**
Ashton, Susan **17**
Audio Adrenaline **22**
Avalon **26**
Becker, Margaret **31**
Boltz, Ray **33**
Boone, Debby **46**
Card, Michael **40**
Carman **36**
Champion, Eric **21**
Chapman, Steven Curtis **47**
  Earlier sketch in CM **15**
Chevelle **44**
Crosse, Clay **38**
dc Talk **18**
Delirious? **33**
Driscoll, Phil **45**
Duncan, Bryan **19**
Elms, The **44**
Eskelin, Ian **19**
4Him **23**
Grant, Amy **7**
Green, Keith **38**
Hammond, Fred **36**
Innocence Mission, The **46**
Jars of Clay **20**
Joy Electric **26**
Keaggy, Phil **26**
King's X **7**
Knapp, Jennifer **43**
Lewis, Crystal **38**
McGuire, Barry **45**
Moore, Geoff **43**
Morgan, Cindy **36**
Mullen, Nicole C. **44**
Mullins, Rich **35**
MxPx **33**
Newsboys, The **24**
Nordeman, Nichole **47**
Norman, Larry **42**
O.C. Supertones, The **40**
Orrico, Stacie **47**
Out of the Grey **37**
Paris, Twila **39**
  Earlier sketch in CM **16**
Patti, Sandi **7**
Petra **3**
PFR **38**
Phillips, Craig & Dean **45**
Plus One **43**
P.O.D. **33**
Point of Grace **21**
Resurrection Band **36**
Rice, Chris **25**
Roe, Michael **41**
  Also see Seventy Sevens, The
Seventy Sevens, The **46**
Sixpence None the Richer **26**
Smith, Michael W. **11**
St. James, Rebecca **26**
Stonehill, Randy **44**
Stryper **2**
Taylor, Steve **26**
Third Day **34**
Tumes, Michelle **37**
Velasquez, Jaci **32**
Watermark **43**
Waters, Ethel **11**
Winans, BeBe and CeCe **32**

Clarinet

Adams, John **8**
Bechet, Sidney **17**

Bilk, Acker **47**
Braxton, Anthony **12**
Brötzmann, Peter **26**
Byron, Don **22**
Carter, John **34**
DeFranco, Buddy **31**
D'Rivera, Paquito **46**
Fountain, Pete **7**
Goodman, Benny **4**
Herman, Woody **12**
Koffman, Moe **34**
Russell, Pee Wee **25**
Scott, Tony **32**
Segundo, Compay **45**
Shaw, Artie **8**
Stoltzman, Richard **24**
Sturr, Jimmy **33**
Vandermark, Ken **28**

Classical

Abbado, Claudio **32**
Ahn Trio **45**
Ameling, Elly **24**
Anderson, June **27**
Anderson, Marian **8**
Argerich, Martha **27**
Arrau, Claudio **1**
Ashkenazy, Vladimir **32**
Assad, Badi **36**
Austral, Florence **26**
Baker, Janet **14**
Barber, Samuel **34**
Barenboim, Daniel **30**
Barrueco, Manuel **39**
Beecham, Thomas **27**
Beltrán, Tito **28**
Berio, Luciano **32**
Bernstein, Leonard **2**
Birtwistle, Harrison **38**
Bond **43**
Bonfiglio, Robert **36**
Bonney, Barbara **33**
Boulez, Pierre **26**
Boyd, Liona **7**
Bream, Julian **9**
Britten, Benjamin **15**
Brodsky Quartet **41**
Bronfman, Yefim **6**
Canadian Brass, The **4**
Carter, Elliott **30**
Carter, Ron **14**
Casals, Pablo **9**
Chailly, Riccardo **35**
Chang, Han-Na **33**
Chang, Sarah **7**
Chanticleer **33**
Chung, Kyung Wha **34**
Church, Charlotte **28**
Clayderman, Richard **1**
Cliburn, Van **13**
Conlon, James **44**
Copland, Aaron **2**
Corigliano, John **34**
Davis, Anthony **17**
Davis, Chip **4**
Davis, Colin **27**
DuPré, Jacqueline **26**
Dvorak, Antonin **25**
Emerson String Quartet **33**
Ensemble Modern **39**
Eroica Trio **47**
Feigelson, Yosif **35**
Fiedler, Arthur **6**
Fleming, Renee **24**
Galimir, Felix **36**
Galway, James **3**
Gardiner, John Eliot **26**
Gingold, Josef **6**

Grusin, Dave **7**
Guaraldi, Vince **3**
Gubaidulina, Sofia **39**
Hall, Jim **35**
Hamlisch, Marvin **1**
Hammer, Jan **21**
Hancock, Herbie **25**
  Earlier sketch in CM **8**
Handy, W. C. **7**
Hanna, Roland, Sir **45**
Hardiman, Ronan **35**
Hargrove, Roy **15**
Harris, Barry **32**
Harris, Eddie **15**
Hartke, Stephen **5**
Hassell, Jon **43**
Hemphill, Julius **34**
Henderson, Fletcher **16**
Herrmann, Bernard **14**
Hill, Andrew **41**
Horvitz, Wayne **42**
Hovhaness, Alan **34**
Hunter, Alberta **7**
Hyman, Dick **39**
Ibrahim, Abdullah **24**
Isham, Mark **14**
Ives, Charles **29**
Jacquet, Illinois **17**
Jamal, Ahmad **32**
Janis, Tim **46**
Jarre, Jean-Michel **2**
Jarrett, Keith **36**
  Earlier sketch in CM **1**
Jenkins, Leroy **39**
Johnson, Buddy **44**
Johnson, J.J. **33**
Johnson, James P. **16**
Johnston, Phillip **36**
Jones, Hank **15**
Jones, Howard **26**
Jones, Quincy **20**
  Earlier sketch in CM **2**
Joplin, Scott **10**
Jordan, Stanley **1**
Kancheli, Giya **40**
Kander, John **33**
Kang, Eyvind **28**
Kater, Peter **35**
Kenny G **14**
Kenton, Stan **21**
Kern, Jerome **13**
Kitaro **36**
  Earlier sketch in CM **1**
Kottke, Leo **13**
Kropinski, Uwe **31**
Lacy, Steve **23**
Lasar, Mars **39**
Lateef, Yusef **16**
Lee, Peggy **8**
Legg, Adrian **17**
Lewis, John **29**
Lewis, Ramsey **14**
  Also see Urban Knights
Lincoln, Abbey **42**
  Earlier sketch in CM **9**
Little, Booker **36**
Lloyd, Charles **22**
Lloyd Webber, Andrew **6**
Loesser, Frank **19**
Lopez, Israel "Cachao" **34**
  Earlier sketch in CM **14**
Luening, Otto **37**
Mancini, Henry **20**
  Earlier sketch in CM **1**
Mandel, Johnny **28**
Marsalis, Branford **10**
Marsalis, Ellis **13**

Marsalis, Wynton **20**
  Earlier sketch in CM **6**
Martino, Pat **17**
Mascagni, Pietro **25**
Masekela, Hugh **7**
Matz, Peter **43**
McBride, Christian **17**
McLean, Jackie **41**
McPartland, Marian **15**
Mendes, Sergio **40**
Menken, Alan **10**
Menotti, Gian Carlo **37**
Metheny, Pat **26**
  Earlier sketch in CM **2**
Miles, Ron **22**
Mingus, Charles **9**
Minott, Sugar **31**
Moby **27**
  Earlier sketch in CM **17**
Monk, Meredith **1**
Monk, Thelonious **6**
Montenegro, Hugo **18**
Montsalvatge, Xavier **39**
Moore, Undine Smith **40**
Morricone, Ennio **15**
Morton, Jelly Roll **7**
Mulligan, Gerry **16**
Nancarrow, Conlon **32**
Nascimento, Milton **6**
N'Dour, Youssou **41**
  Earlier sketch in CM **6**
  Also see Orchestra Baobab
Newman, Randy **4**
Niblock, Phill **43**
Nyman, Michael **15**
O'Hearn, Patrick **40**
  Also see Missing Persons
Oldfield, Mike **18**
Orff, Carl **21**
O'Rourke, Jim **31**
Osby, Greg **21**
Ott, David **2**
Palmieri, Eddie **15**
Parker, Charlie **5**
Parks, Van Dyke **17**
Pärt, Arvo **40**
Partch, Harry **29**
Penderecki, Krzysztof **30**
Perez, Danilo **25**
Peterson, Oscar **11**
Piazzolla, Astor **18**
Ponty, Jean-Luc **8**
Porter, Cole **10**
Post, Mike **21**
Previn, André **15**
Puente, Tito **14**
Pullen, Don **16**
Reich, Steve **8**
Reinhardt, Django **7**
Riley, Terry **32**
Ritenour, Lee **7**
Rivers, Sam **29**
Roach, Max **12**
Roach, Steve **41**
Rollins, Sonny **7**
Rosnes, Renée **44**
Rota, Nino **13**
Rouse, Christopher **41**
Royal, Billy Joe **46**
Saariaho, Kaija **43**
Sakamoto, Ryuichi **19**
Salonen, Esa-Pekka **16**
Samuelsson, Marie **47**
Sánchez, David **40**
Sanders, Pharoah **28**
  Earlier sketch in CM **16**
  Also see Music Revelation Ensemble

Satie, Erik **25**
Satriani, Joe **4**
Sawhney, Nitin **46**
Scelsi, Giacinto **47**
Schickele, Peter **5**
Schifrin, Lalo **29**
Schuman, William **10**
Schütze, Paul **32**
Schwarz, Gerard **45**
Sebesky, Don **33**
Shankar, Ravi **38**
  Earlier sketch in CM **9**
Shapey, Ralph **42**
Shaw, Artie **8**
Shearing, George **28**
Shorter, Wayne **45**
  Earlier sketch in CM **5**
  Also see Weather Report
Shostakovich, Dmitry **42**
Silver, Horace **19**
Smith, Tommy **28**
Solal, Martial **4**
Sondheim, Stephen **8**
Sousa, John Philip **10**
Stern, Leni **29**
Stockhausen, Karlheinz **36**
Story, Liz **45**
  Earlier sketch in CM **2**
Strauss, Richard **25**
Stravinsky, Igor **21**
Strayhorn, Billy **13**
Strouse, Charles **43**
Styne, Jule **21**
Summers, Andy **3**
  Also see Police, The
Sun Ra **27**
  Earlier sketch in CM **5**
Sylvian, David **27**
Takemitsu, Toru **6**
Talbot, John Michael **6**
Tan Dun **33**
Tatum, Art **17**
Tavener, John **45**
Taylor, Billy **13**
Taylor, Cecil **9**
Tesh, John **20**
Thielemans, Toots **13**
Threadgill, Henry **9**
Tilson Thomas, Michael **24**
Tobin, Amon **32**
Towner, Ralph **22**
Tristano, Lennie **30**
Turnage, Mark-Anthony **31**
Tyner, McCoy **7**
Ung, Chinary **46**
Vangelis **21**
Van Hove, Fred **30**
Vollenweider, Andreas **30**
von Trapp, Elisabeth **29**
Wakeman, Rick **27**
  Also see Strawbs
  Also see Yes
Waldron, Mal **43**
Walker, George **34**
Wallace, Bennie **31**
Walton, William **44**
Was, Don **21**
  Also see Was (Not Was)
Washington, Grover, Jr. **5**
  Also see Urban Knights
Weber, Eberhard **41**
Weill, Kurt **12**
Wells, Bill **34**
Weston, Randy **15**
Whelan, Bill **20**
Whiteman, Paul **17**
Wildhorn, Frank **31**

Kronos Quartet, The **38**
  Earlier sketch in CM **5**
Lanz, David **42**
Lasar, Mars **39**
Legg, Adrian **17**
Liebert, Ottmar **33**
Line, Lorie **34**
Merzbow **31**
Mogwai **27**
Nightnoise **45**
O'Hearn, Patrick **40**
  Also see Missing Persons
Riley, Terry **32**
Roach, Steve **41**
Roth, Gabrielle **26**
Schroer, Oliver **29**
Sete, Bola **26**
Sissel **42**
Story, Liz **45**
  Earlier sketch in CM **2**
Summers, Andy **3**
  Also see Police, The
Tangerine Dream **12**
Tesh, John **20**
Tingstad & Rumbel **44**
Vollenweider, Andreas **30**
Winston, George **43**
  Earlier sketch in CM **9**
Winter, Paul **10**
Yanni **11**

Cornet
Adderley, Nat **29**
Armstrong, Louis **4**
Beiderbecke, Bix **16**
Braff, Ruby **43**
Cherry, Don **10**
  Also see Codona
Davison, Wild Bill **34**
Handy, W. C. **7**
Oliver, King **15**
Vaché, Warren, Jr. **22**

Country
Acuff, Roy **2**
Adams, Ryan **38**
  Also see Whiskeytown
Adkins, Trace **31**
Akins, Rhett **22**
Alabama **21**
  Earlier sketch in CM **1**
Allan, Gary **41**
Allison, Joe **42**
Anderson, Bill **32**
Anderson, John **5**
Andrews, Jessica **34**
Arnold, Eddy **10**
Asleep at the Wheel **29**
  Earlier sketch in CM **5**
Atkins, Chet **26**
  Earlier sketch in CM **5**
Auldridge, Mike **4**
Autry, Gene **25**
  Earlier sketch in CM **12**
Barnett, Mandy **26**
Bellamy Brothers, The **13**
Berg, Matraca **16**
Berry, John **17**
Black, Clint **5**
BlackHawk **21**
Blue Mountain **38**
Blue Rodeo **18**
Blue Sky Boys **46**
Boggs, Dock **25**
Bogguss, Suzy **11**
Bonamy, James **21**
Bond, Johnny **28**

Boone, Pat **13**
Boxcar Willie **41**
Boy Howdy **21**
Brandt, Paul **22**
Brannon, Kippi **20**
BR5-49 **35**
Brooks, Garth **25**
  Earlier sketch in CM **8**
Brooks & Dunn **25**
  Earlier sketch in CM **12**
Brown, Junior **15**
Brown, Marty **14**
Brown, Tony **14**
Buckner, Richard **31**
Buffett, Jimmy **42**
  Earlier sketch in CM **4**
Byrd, Tracy **39**
Byrds, The **8**
Cale, J. J. **16**
Calexico **33**
Campbell, Glen **2**
Campi, Ray **44**
Carter, Carlene **8**
Carter, Deana **25**
Carter Family, The **3**
Cary, Caitlin **46**
  Also see Whiskeytown
Cash, Johnny **46**
  Earlier sketch in CM **17**
  Earlier sketch in CM **1**
Cash, June Carter **6**
Cash, Rosanne **2**
Cash Brothers **47**
Chambers, Kasey **36**
Chapin Carpenter, Mary **25**
  Earlier sketch in CM **6**
Chapman, Beth Nielsen **42**
Chapman, Gary **33**
Chesney, Kenny **20**
Chesnutt, Mark **13**
Clark, Guy **17**
Clark, Roy **1**
Clark, Terri **44**
  Earlier sketch in CM **19**
Clements, Vassar **18**
Cline, Patsy **5**
Coe, David Allan **4**
Collie, Mark **15**
Commander Cody and His Lost Planet Airmen **30**
Confederate Railroad **23**
Cooder, Ry **2**
  Also see Captain Beefheart and His Magic Band
Coolidge, Rita **40**
Cowboy Junkies **38**
  Earlier sketch in CM **4**
Crawford, Randy **25**
Crowe, J. D. **5**
Crowell, Rodney **8**
Cyrus, Billy Ray **11**
Dalton, Lacy J. **43**
Daniels, Charlie **6**
Davies, Gail **38**
Davis, Linda **21**
Davis, Skeeter **15**
Dean, Billy **19**
DeMent, Iris **13**
Denver, John **22**
  Earlier sketch in CM **1**
Derailers, The **37**
Desert Rose Band, The **4**
Diamond Rio **35**
  Earlier sketch in CM **11**
Dickens, Hazel **35**
Dickens, Little Jimmy **7**

Diffie, Joe **27**
  Earlier sketch in CM **10**
Dillards, The **45**
Dixie Chicks **26**
Downing, Big Al **45**
Dusty, Slim **39**
Dylan, Bob **21**
  Earlier sketch in CM **3**
Earle, Steve **43**
  Earlier sketch in CM **16**
Estes, John **25**
Evans, Sara **27**
Farrar, Jay **46**
  Also see Son Volt
  Also see Uncle Tupelo
Feathers, Charlie **40**
Flatlanders, The **43**
Flatt, Lester **3**
Flores, Rosie **16**
Flying Burrito Brothers **44**
Ford, Tennessee Ernie **3**
Foster, Radney **16**
Fricke, Janie **33**
Friedman, Kinky **35**
Frizzell, Lefty **10**
Frost, Edith **40**
Gayle, Crystal **1**
Gentry, Bobbie **46**
Germano, Lisa **18**
Giant Sand **30**
Gill, Vince **34**
  Earlier sketch in CM **7**
Gilley, Mickey **7**
Gilman, Billy **34**
Gilmore, Jimmie Dale **11**
Gordy, Emory, Jr. **17**
Greenwood, Lee **12**
Griffith, Nanci **3**
Griggs, Andy **40**
Haggard, Merle **39**
  Earlier sketch in CM **2**
Hall, Tom T. **26**
Hancock, Wayne **45**
Handsome Family, The **30**
Harris, Emmylou **36**
  Earlier sketch in CM **4**
Hartford, John **37**
  Earlier sketch in CM **1**
Hay, George D. **3**
Hazlewood, Lee **45**
Herndon, Ty **20**
Hiatt, John **35**
  Earlier sketch in CM **8**
Highway 101 **4**
Hill, Faith **18**
Hinojosa, Tish **44**
  Earlier sketch in CM **13**
Hot Club of Cowtown **46**
Howard, Harlan **15**
Howard, Rebecca Lynn **41**
Hubbard, Ray Wylie **38**
Jackson, Alan **25**
  Earlier sketch in CM **7**
Jackson, Wanda **42**
Jason & the Scorchers **45**
Jennings, Waylon **4**
Jones, George **36**
  Earlier sketch in CM **4**
Jordanaires, The **44**
Judds, The **2**
Keith, Toby **40**
  Earlier sketch in CM **17**
Kentucky Headhunters, The **5**
Kershaw, Sammy **15**
Ketchum, Hal **14**
King, Pee Wee **30**
Kinleys, The **32**

Fiddle

Carthy, Eliza **31**
Ivers, Eileen **30**
Krauss, Alison **41**
  Earlier sketch in CM **10**
MacIsaac, Ashley **21**
MacMaster, Natalie **37**

Film Scores

Anka, Paul **2**
Arlen, Harold **27**
Bacharach, Burt **20**
  Earlier sketch in CM **1**
Badalamenti, Angelo **17**
Barry, John **29**
Baxter, Les **47**
Bergman, Alan and Marilyn **30**
Berlin, Irving **8**
Bernstein, Elmer **36**
Bernstein, Leonard **2**
Blanchard, Terence **13**
Britten, Benjamin **15**
Byrne, David **8**
  Also see Talking Heads
Cahn, Sammy **11**
Cliff, Jimmy **8**
Copeland, Stewart **14**
  Also see Police, The
Copland, Aaron **2**
Crouch, Andraé **6**
Dibango, Manu **14**
Dolby, Thomas **10**
Donovan **9**
Eddy, Duane **9**
Elfman, Danny **9**
Ellington, Duke **2**
Ferguson, Maynard **7**
Froom, Mitchell **15**
Gabriel, Peter **16**
  Earlier sketch in CM **2**
  Also see Genesis
Galás, Diamanda **16**
Gershwin, George and Ira **11**
Goldsmith, Jerry **40**
Gould, Glenn **9**
Grusin, Dave **7**
Guaraldi, Vince **3**
Hamlisch, Marvin **1**
Hancock, Herbie **25**
  Earlier sketch in CM **8**
Harrison, George **2**
  Also see Beatles, The
Hayes, Isaac **10**
Hedges, Michael **3**
Herrmann, Bernard **14**
Horner, James **38**
Isham, Mark **14**
Jones, Quincy **20**
  Earlier sketch in CM **2**
Kander, John **33**
Knopfler, Mark **25**
  Earlier sketch in CM **3**
  Also see Dire Straits
Lahiri, Bappi **42**
Lennon, John **9**
  Also see Beatles, The
Lerner and Loewe **13**
Loesser, Frank **19**
Mancini, Henry **20**
  Earlier sketch in CM **1**
Marsalis, Branford **10**
Matz, Peter **43**
Mayfield, Curtis **8**
McCartney, Paul **32**
  Earlier sketch in CM **4**
  Also see Beatles, The
Menken, Alan **10**
Mercer, Johnny **13**

Metheny, Pat **26**
  Earlier sketch in CM **2**
Montenegro, Hugo **18**
Morricone, Ennio **15**
Nascimento, Milton **6**
Newman, Randy **27**
  Earlier sketch in CM **4**
Nilsson **10**
Nyman, Michael **15**
Parks, Van Dyke **17**
Peterson, Oscar **11**
Porter, Cole **10**
Previn, André **15**
Reznor, Trent **13**
  Also see Nine Inch Nails
Richie, Lionel **2**
Robertson, Robbie **2**
Rollins, Sonny **7**
Rota, Nino **13**
Sager, Carole Bayer **5**
Sakamoto, Ryuichi **18**
Sawhney, Nitin **46**
Schickele, Peter **5**
Schütze, Paul **32**
Shankar, Ravi **38**
  Earlier sketch in CM **9**
Silvestri, Alan **37**
Strouse, Charles **43**
Taj Mahal **6**
Tan Dun **33**
Waits, Tom **27**
  Earlier sketch in CM **12**
  Earlier sketch in CM **1**
Weill, Kurt **12**
Williams, John **28**
  Earlier sketch in CM **9**
Williams, Paul **26**
  Earlier sketch in CM **5**
Willner, Hal **10**
Young, Neil **15**
Zimmer, Hans **34**

Flugelhorn

Bowie, Lester **29**
Mangione, Chuck **23**
Sandoval, Arturo **15**

Flute

Abou-Khalil, Rabih **38**
Galway, James **3**
Hofmann, Holly **41**
Jethro Tull **8**
Koffman, Moe **34**
Lateef, Yusef **16**
Laws, Hubert **38**
Mangione, Chuck **23**
Mann, Herbie **16**
Mirabal, Robert **45**
Moody, James **34**
Najee **21**
Nakai, R. Carlos **24**
Rampal, Jean-Pierre **6**
Tabackin, Lew **47**
Torres, Nestor **36**
Ulmer, James Blood **42**
  Earlier sketch in CM **13**
  Also see Music Revelation Ensemble
Valentin, Dave **33**
Wilson, Ransom **5**
Zamfir, Gheorghe **41**

Folk/Traditional

Abou-Khalil, Rabih **38**
Adam, Margie **39**
Alberstein, Chava **37**
Altan **44**
  Earlier sketch in CM **18**

America **16**
Anonymous 4 **23**
Arjona, Ricardo **43**
Arnaz, Desi **8**
Axton, Hoyt **28**
Baca, Susana **32**
Baez, Joan **1**
Battlefield Band, The **31**
Beamer, Keola **43**
Belafonte, Harry **8**
Belle and Sebastian **28**
Black, Mary **15**
Black 47 **37**
Blades, Ruben **2**
Bloom, Luka **14**
Bloomfield, Michael **40**
Blue Rodeo **18**
Boggs, Dock **25**
Brady, Paul **8**
Bragg, Billy **7**
Brave Combo **31**
Bromberg, David **18**
Brown, Carlinhos **32**
Buckley, Tim **14**
Buffalo Springfield **24**
Bulgarian State Female Vocal
  Choir, The **10**
Burns Sisters **41**
Byrds, The **8**
Campbell, Sarah Elizabeth **23**
Caravan **24**
Carter Family, The **3**
Carthy, Eliza **31**
Carthy, Martin **34**
  Also see Steeleye Span
Cassidy, Eva **35**
Ceili Rain **34**
Chandra, Sheila **16**
Chapin, Harry **6**
Chapman, Tracy **20**
  Earlier sketch in CM **4**
Chenille Sisters, The **16**
Cherish the Ladies **38**
Cherry, Don **10**
Chesnutt, Vic **28**
Chieftains, The **36**
  Earlier sketch in CM **7**
Childs, Toni **2**
Clancy Brothers and Tommy Makem, The **39**
Clannad **23**
Clegg, Johnny **8**
Cockburn, Bruce **8**
Cohen, Leonard **3**
Cohn, Marc **43**
Collins, Judy **4**
Collister, Christine **42**
Colvin, Shawn **38**
  Earlier sketch in CM **11**
Cotten, Elizabeth **16**
Crosby, David **3**
  Also see Byrds, The
  Also see Crosby, Stills, and Nash
Cruz, Celia **22**
  Earlier sketch in CM **10**
Curtis, Catie **31**
Dalaras, George **40**
de Lucia, Paco **1**
DeMent, Iris **13**
DiFranco, Ani **43**
  Earlier sketch in CM **17**
Donegan, Lonnie **42**
Donovan **9**
Drake, Nick **17**
Driftwood, Jimmy **25**
Dr. John **7**
Dylan, Bob **21**
  Earlier sketch in CM **3**

Parker, Maceo **46**
  Earlier sketch in CM **7**
Prince **40**
  Earlier sketch in CM **14**
  Earlier sketch in CM **1**
Red Hot Chili Peppers **29**
  Earlier sketch in CM **7**
Sly and the Family Stone **24**
Stone, Sly **8**
  Also see Sly and the Family Stone
Toussaint, Allen **11**
Tower of Power **40**
Worrell, Bernie **11**
Wu-Tang Clan **19**

Fusion
Anderson, Ray **7**
Avery, Teodross **23**
Beck, Jeff **4**
  Also see Yardbirds, The
Clarke, Stanley **3**
Codona **44**
Coleman, Ornette **5**
Corea, Chick **6**
Davis, Miles **1**
Dulfer, Candy **35**
Fishbone **7**
Hancock, Herbie **25**
  Earlier sketch in CM **8**
Harris, Eddie **15**
Johnson, Eric **19**
Lewis, Ramsey **14**
  Also see Urban Knights
Mahavishnu Orchestra **19**
McLaughlin, John **12**
Metheny, Pat **26**
  Earlier sketch in CM **2**
O'Connor, Mark **1**
Ponty, Jean-Luc **8**
Reid, Vernon **2**
  Also see Living Colour
Ritenour, Lee **7**
Shorter, Wayne **45**
  Earlier sketch in CM **5**
  Also see Weather Report
Soft Machine **36**
Summers, Andy **3**
  Also see Police, The
Washington, Grover, Jr. **5**
  Also see Urban Knights

Gospel
Anderson, Marian **8**
Armstrong, Vanessa Bell **24**
Baylor, Helen **20**
Boone, Pat **13**
Brown, James **2**
Caesar, Shirley **40**
  Earlier sketch in CM **17**
Carter Family, The **3**
Charles, Ray **24**
  Earlier sketch in CM **1**
Cleveland, James **1**
Cooke, Sam **1**
  Also see Soul Stirrers, The
Cox Family **44**
Crouch, Andraé **9**
Dixie Hummingbirds, The **41**
Dorsey, Thomas A. **11**
Eartha **44**
Five Blind Boys of Alabama **12**
Florida Boys, The **42**
Ford, Tennessee Ernie **3**
4Him **23**
Franklin, Aretha **17**
  Earlier sketch in CM **2**
Franklin, Kirk **22**

Gaither Vocal Band **38**
Golden Gate Quartet **25**
Greater Vision **26**
Green, Al **9**
Hawkins, Tramaine **17**
Houston, Cissy **26**
  Earlier sketch in CM **6**
Imperials, The **43**
Jackson, Mahalia **8**
Johnson, Blind Willie **26**
Jordanaires, The **44**
Kee, John P. **15**
Knight, Gladys **1**
Little Richard **1**
Louvin Brothers, The **12**
Mary Mary **39**
McClurkin, Donnie **35**
Mighty Clouds of Joy, The **17**
Oakland Interfaith Gospel Choir **26**
Oak Ridge Boys, The **7**
Paris, Twila **39**
  Earlier sketch in CM **16**
Persuasions, The **47**
Pickett, Wilson **10**
Presley, Elvis **1**
Redding, Otis **5**
Reese, Della **13**
Robbins, Marty **9**
Soul Stirrers, The **11**
Sounds of Blackness **13**
Staples, Mavis **13**
Staples, Pops **11**
Staton, Candi **45**
Swan Silvertones, The **39**
Sweet Honey In The Rock **26**
  Earlier sketch in CM **1**
Take 6 **39**
  Earlier sketch in CM **6**
Tharpe, Sister **47**
Waters, Ethel **11**
Watson, Doc **2**
Williams, Deniece **1**
Williams, Marion **15**
Winans, BeBe and CeCe **32**
Winans, The **12**
Womack, Bobby **5**

Guitar
Abercrombie, John **25**
Ackerman, Will **3**
Adamson, Barry **28**
Adé, King Sunny **18**
Adkins, Trace **31**
Allen, Daevid **28**
  Also see Gong
  Also see Soft Machine
Allison, Luther **21**
Alvin, Dave **17**
  Also see Blasters, The
  Also see X
Anastasio, Trey **47**
  Also see Phish
Armik **41**
Assad, Badi **36**
Atkins, Chet **26**
  Earlier sketch in CM **5**
Autry, Gene **25**
  Earlier sketch in CM **12**
Axton, Hoyt **28**
Badly Drawn Boy **33**
Bailey, Derek **40**
Barnes, Roosevelt "Booba" **23**
Barrett, Syd **37**
  Also see Pink Floyd
Barrueco, Manuel **39**
Beamer, Keola **43**
Beck, Jeff **4**
  Also see Yardbirds, The

Beck **41**
  Earlier sketch in CM **18**
Belew, Adrian **5**
Benoit, Tab **31**
Benson, George **9**
Berry, Chuck **33**
  Earlier sketch in CM **1**
Berry, John **17**
Bishop, Elvin **41**
Bishop, Jeb **28**
Blake, Norman **47**
Blegvad, Peter **28**
Block, Rory **18**
Bloom, Luka **14**
Bloomfield, Michael **40**
Bond, Johnny **28**
Boyd, Liona **7**
Bream, Julian **9**
Bromberg, David **18**
Brooks, Garth **25**
  Earlier sketch in CM **8**
Brooks, Meredith **30**
Broom, Bobby **38**
Brötzmann, Caspar **27**
Brown, Junior **15**
Brown, Norman **29**
Buckethead **34**
Buckingham, Lindsey **8**
  Also see Fleetwood Mac
Buckner, Richard **31**
Buffett, Jimmy **42**
  Earlier sketch in CM **4**
Burnside, R. L. **34**
  Earlier sketch in CM **1**
Burrell, Kenny **11**
Campbell, Glen **2**
Carlton, Larry **38**
Carter, Deana **25**
Cat Power **30**
Chadbourne, Eugene **30**
Chapin-Carpenter, Mary **25**
  Earlier sketch in CM **6**
Chaquico, Craig **23**
Chesney, Kenny **20**
Chesnutt, Mark **13**
Chesnutt, Vic **28**
Christian, Charlie **11**
Clapton, Eric **11**
  Earlier sketch in CM **1**
  Also see Cream
  Also see Yardbirds, The
Clark, Roy **1**
Clark, Terri **44**
  Earlier sketch in CM **19**
Cochran, Eddie **43**
Cockburn, Bruce **8**
Collie, Mark **15**
Collins, Albert **19**
  Earlier sketch in CM **4**
Collins, John **39**
Colvin, Shawn **38**
  Earlier sketch in CM **11**
Cooder, Ry **2**
  Also see Captain Beefheart and His
  Magic Band
Cook, Jesse **33**
Cornelius **44**
Cotten, Elizabeth **16**
Cray, Robert **46**
  Earlier sketch in CM **8**
Cropper, Steve **12**
Curtis, Catie **31**
Dahl, Jeff **28**
Dale, Dick **13**
Daniels, Charlie **6**
Dave, Edmunds **28**
Davis, Reverend Gary **18**

Robbins, Marty **9**
Robertson, Robbie **2**
Robillard, Duke **2**
Rodgers, Nile **8**
  Also see Chic
Rose, Tim **41**
Royal, Billy Joe **46**
Rush, Otis **12**
Sahm, Doug **30**
  Also see Texas Tornados, The
Salem, Kevin **32**
Sambora, Richie **24**
  Also see Bon Jovi
Santana, Carlos **43**
  Earlier sketch in CM **19**
  Earlier sketch in CM **1**
Satriani, Joe **4**
Scofield, John **7**
Scruggs, Randy **28**
Secola, Keith **45**
Segovia, Andres **6**
Segundo, Compay **45**
Sete, Bola **26**
Setzer, Brian **32**
Sexsmith, Ron **27**
Sharrock, Sonny **15**
Shelton, Blake **45**
Shepherd, Kenny Wayne **22**
Shines, Johnny **14**
Simon, Paul **16**
  Earlier sketch in CM **1**
  Also see Simon and Garfunkel
Skaggs, Ricky **43**
  Earlier sketch in CM **5**
Smith, Elliott **28**
Smog **28**
Springsteen, Bruce **25**
  Earlier sketch in CM **6**
Starr, Andy **47**
Stern, Leni **29**
Stern, Mike **29**
Stills, Stephen **5**
  Also see Buffalo Springfield
  Also see Crosby, Stills, and Nash
Stuart, Marty **9**
Summers, Andy **3**
  Also see Police, The
Tampa Red **25**
Tedeschi, Susan **45**
Terrell **32**
Thielemans, Toots **13**
Thompson, Richard **7**
Thorogood, George **34**
Tippin, Aaron **12**
Toure, Ali Farka **18**
Towner, Ralph **22**
Townshend, Pete **1**
  Also see Who, The
Traoré, Boubacar **38**
Travis, Merle **14**
Trynin, Jen **21**
Tubb, Ernest **4**
Ulmer, James Blood **42**
  Earlier sketch in CM **13**
  Also see Music Revelation Ensemble
Vai, Steve **5**
Van Ronk, Dave **12**
Van Zandt, Steven **29**
Vaughan, Jimmie **24**
  Also see Fabulous Thunderbirds, The
Vaughan, Stevie Ray **1**
Wachtel, Waddy **26**
Wagoner, Porter **13**
Waits, Tom **27**
  Earlier sketch in CM **12**
  Earlier sketch in CM **1**
Walker, Jerry Jeff **13**

Walker, Joe Louis **28**
Walker, T-Bone **5**
Walsh, Joe **5**
  Also see Eagles, The
Wariner, Steve **18**
Waters, Muddy **24**
  Earlier sketch in CM **4**
Watson, Doc **2**
Watson, Johnny "Guitar" **41**
Weller, Paul **14**
White, Lari **15**
Whitfield, Mark **18**
Whitley, Chris **16**
Whittaker, Hudson **20**
Wilson, Brian **24**
  Also see Beach Boys, The
Winston, George **43**
  Earlier sketch in CM **9**
Winter, Johnny **5**
Wiseman, Mac **19**
Wray, Link **17**
Yamashita, Kazuhito **4**
Yoakam, Dwight **21**
  Earlier sketch in CM **1**
York, Andrew **15**
Young, Neil **15**
  Earlier sketch in CM **2**
Zappa, Frank **17**

Harmonica
Adler, Larry **35**
Barnes, Roosevelt "Booba" **23**
Bonfiglio, Robert **36**
Cotton, James **35**
Dylan, Bob **21**
  Earlier sketch in CM **3**
Foster, Willie **36**
Guthrie, Woody **2**
Horton, Walter **19**
Lewis, Huey **9**
Little Walter **14**
McClinton, Delbert **14**
Musselwhite, Charlie **13**
Reed, Jimmy **15**
Riley, Billy Lee **43**
Thielemans, Toots **13**
Thompson, Hank **43**
Waters, Muddy **24**
  Earlier sketch in CM **4**
Wells, Junior **17**
Williamson, Sonny Boy **9**
Wonder, Stevie **17**
  Earlier sketch in CM **2**
Young, Neil **15**

Heavy Metal
AC/DC **4**
Aerosmith **37**
  Earlier sketch in CM **22**
  Earlier sketch in CM **1**
Alice in Chains **10**
Anthrax **41**
  Earlier sketch in CM **11**
Black Sabbath **9**
Blue Oyster Cult **16**
Cinderella **16**
Circle Jerks **17**
Coal Chamber **35**
Cradle of Filth **37**
Danzig **7**
Deep Purple **11**
Def Leppard **40**
  Earlier sketch in CM **3**
Disturbed **42**
Dokken **16**
Faith No More **7**
Fear Factory **27**

Fishbone **7**
Flying Luttenbachers, The **28**
Ford, Lita **9**
  Also see Runaways, The
Great White **44**
Guns n' Roses **2**
Iron Maiden **10**
Judas Priest **10**
Kilgore **24**
King's X **7**
Kiss **25**
  Earlier sketch in CM **5**
Led Zeppelin **1**
L7 **12**
Machine Head **32**
Megadeth **9**
Melvins **46**
  Earlier sketch in CM **21**
Metallica **33**
  Earlier sketch in CM **7**
Monster Magnet **39**
Mötley Crüe **35**
  Earlier sketch in CM **1**
Motörhead **10**
Mudvayne **42**
Neurosis **28**
Nugent, Ted **2**
  Also see Amboy Dukes, The
Osbourne, Ozzy **39**
  Earlier sketch in CM **3**
  Also see Black Sabbath
Pantera **13**
Petra **3**
Queensryche **8**
Reid, Vernon **2**
  Also see Living Colour
Reznor, Trent **13**
  Also see Nine Inch Nails
Rollins, Henry **35**
  Earlier sketch in CM **11**
Roth, David Lee **1**
  Also see Van Halen
Runaways, The **44**
Saliva **38**
Sepultura **12**
Sevendust **37**
Skinny Puppy **17**
Slayer **10**
Soulfly **33**
Soundgarden **6**
Spinal Tap **8**
Staind **31**
Stryper **2**
Suicidal Tendencies **15**
System of a Down **36**
Tool **21**
Type O Negative **27**
Warrant **17**
Wendy O. Williams and The Plasmatics **26**
Whitesnake **5**
White Zombie **17**

Humor
Borge, Victor **19**
Coasters, The **5**
Dr. Demento **23**
Friedman, Kinky **35**
Jones, Spike **5**
Lehrer, Tom **7**
Moxy Früvous **45**
Nixon, Mojo **32**
Pearl, Minnie **3**
Russell, Mark **6**
Sandler, Adam **19**
Schickele, Peter **5**
Shaffer, Paul **13**
Spinal Tap **8**
Stevens, Ray **7**

Incognito **16**
Isham, Mark **14**
Jackson, Milt **15**
Jacquet, Illinois **17**
Jamal, Ahmad **32**
James, Boney **21**
James, Harry **11**
Jarreau, Al **1**
Jarrett, Keith **36**
  Earlier sketch in CM **1**
Jenkins, Leroy **39**
Jensen, Ingrid **22**
Jobim, Antonio Carlos **19**
Johnson, Buddy **44**
Johnson, J.J. **33**
Johnson, James P. **16**
Johnson, Lonnie **17**
Johnston, Phillip **36**
Jones, Elvin **9**
Jones, Etta **37**
Jones, Hank **15**
Jones, Philly Joe **16**
Jones, Quincy **20**
  Earlier sketch in CM **2**
Jones, Thad **19**
Jordan, Marc **30**
Jordan, Stanley **1**
Kang, Eyvind **28**
Kennedy, Nigel **47**
  Earlier sketch in CM **8**
Kenny G **14**
Kent, Stacey **28**
Kenton, Stan **21**
Kirk, Rahsaan Roland **6**
Kitt, Eartha **9**
Klugh, Earl **10**
Koffman, Moe **34**
Konitz, Lee **30**
Kowald, Peter **32**
Krall, Diana **27**
Kronos Quartet, The **38**
  Earlier sketch in CM **5**
Kropinski, Uwe **31**
Krupa, Gene **13**
Laine, Cleo **10**
Lambert, Hendricks and Ross **28**
Lateef, Yusef **16**
Laws, Hubert **38**
Lee, Peggy **8**
Lewis, John **29**
Lewis, Ramsey **14**
  Also see Urban Knights
Lincoln, Abbey **42**
  Earlier sketch in CM **9**
Liquid Soul **42**
Little, Booker **36**
Lloyd, Charles **22**
London, Julie **32**
Lopez, Israel "Cachao" **34**
  Earlier sketch in CM **14**
Los Hombres Calientes **29**
Lovano, Joe **13**
Mahavishnu Orchestra **19**
Mahogany, Kevin **26**
Malone, Russell **27**
Mancini, Henry **20**
  Earlier sketch in CM **1**
Mangione, Chuck **23**
Manhattan Transfer, The **42**
  Earlier sketch in CM **8**
Mann, Herbie **16**
Marsalis, Branford **10**
Marsalis, Ellis **13**
Marsalis, Wynton **20**
  Earlier sketch in CM **6**
Martino, Pat **17**
Masekela, Hugh **7**

Matsui, Keiko **35**
McBride, Christian **17**
McCorkle, Susannah **27**
McFerrin, Bobby **3**
McKinney's Cotton Pickers **16**
McLaughlin, John **12**
McLean, Jackie **41**
McNeely, Big Jay **37**
McPartland, Marian **15**
McRae, Carmen **9**
McShann, Jay **41**
Medeski, Martin & Wood **32**
Metheny, Pat **26**
  Earlier sketch in CM **2**
Mingus, Charles **9**
Monheit, Jane **33**
Monk, Thelonious **6**
Montgomery, Wes **3**
Moody, James **34**
Moran, Jason **44**
Moreira, Airto **44**
Morgan, Frank **9**
Morton, Jelly Roll **7**
Muhammad, Idris **40**
Mulligan, Gerry **16**
Murray, Dave **28**
  Also see Music Revelation Ensemble
  Also see World Saxophone Quartet
Music Revelation Ensemble **43**
Najee **21**
Nascimento, Milton **6**
Navarro, Fats **25**
NOJO **47**
Northwoods Improvisers **31**
Norvo, Red **12**
O'Day, Anita **21**
O'Farrill, Chico **31**
Oliver, King **15**
Oregon **30**
O'Rourke, Jim **31**
Oxley, Tony **32**
Palmer, Jeff **20**
Palmieri, Eddie **15**
Parker, Charlie **5**
Parker, Evan **28**
  Also see Brotherhood of Breath
Parker, Leon **27**
Parker, Maceo **46**
  Earlier sketch in CM **7**
Parker, William **31**
Pass, Joe **15**
Paul, Les **2**
Payton, Nicholas **27**
Pepper, Art **18**
Perez, Danilo **25**
Peterson, Oscar **11**
Ponty, Jean-Luc **8**
Portuondo, Omara **42**
Powell, Bud **15**
Previn, André **15**
Professor Longhair **6**
Puente, Tito **14**
Pullen, Don **16**
Purim, Flora **45**
Ralph Sharon Quartet **26**
Rampal, Jean-Pierre **6**
Rebirth Brass Band **35**
Redman, Dewey **32**
Redman, Joshua **25**
  Earlier sketch in CM **12**
Reeves, Dianne **16**
Reid, Vernon **2**
  Also see Living Colour
Reinhardt, Django **7**
Ribot, Marc **30**
Rich, Buddy **13**
Rippingtons **38**

Rivers, Sam **29**
Roach, Max **12**
Roberts, Marcus **6**
Robillard, Duke **2**
Rodney, Red **14**
Rollins, Sonny **7**
Roney, Wallace **33**
Rosnes, Renée **44**
Rova Saxophone Quartet **42**
Rumba Club **36**
Rushing, Jimmy **37**
Russell, Pee Wee **25**
Saluzzi, Dino **23**
Sanborn, David **28**
  Earlier sketch in CM **1**
Sánchez, David **40**
Sanders, Pharoah **28**
  Earlier sketch in CM **16**
  Also see Music Revelation Ensemble
Sandoval, Arturo **15**
Santamaria, Mongo **28**
Santana, Carlos **43**
  Earlier sketch in CM **19**
  Earlier sketch in CM **1**
Schuur, Diane **6**
Schweizer, Irène **46**
Scofield, John **7**
Scott, Jimmy **14**
Scott, Tony **32**
Scott-Heron, Gil **13**
Sebesky, Don **33**
Severinsen, Doc **1**
Sharrock, Sonny **15**
Shaw, Artie **8**
Shaw, Woody **27**
Shearing, George **28**
Shepp, Archie **43**
Shorter, Wayne **45**
  Earlier sketch in CM **5**
  Also see Weather Report
Silva, Alan **45**
Silver, Horace **19**
Simone, Nina **11**
Sims, Zoot **37**
Sloane, Carol **36**
Smith, Jimmy **30**
Smith, Jocelyn B. **30**
Smith, Tommy **28**
Soft Machine **36**
Solal, Martial **4**
Sommer, Günter "Baby" **31**
Soulive **44**
Spyro Gyra **34**
Stanko, Tomasz **47**
Stern, Leni **29**
Stern, Mike **29**
Strayhorn, Billy **13**
String Trio of New York **40**
Summers, Andy **3**
  Also see Police, The
Sun Ra **27**
  Earlier sketch in CM **5**
Tabackin, Lew **47**
Take 6 **39**
  Earlier sketch in CM **6**
Tate, Buddy **33**
Tatum, Art **17**
Taylor, Billy **13**
Taylor, Cecil **9**
Teagarden, Jack **10**
Terry, Clark **24**
Thielemans, Toots **13**
Thornton, Teri **28**
Threadgill, Henry **9**
Tin Hat Trio **41**
Torme, Mel **4**
Torres, Nestor **36**

Church, Charlotte **28**
Copeland, Stewart **14**
  Also see Police, The
Cotrubas, Ileana **1**
Davis, Anthony **17**
Domingo, Placido **20**
  Earlier sketch in CM **1**
Eaglen, Jane **36**
Evans, Anne **46**
Fleming, Renee **24**
Freni, Mirella **14**
Gershwin, George and Ira **11**
Gheorghiu, Angela **38**
Graham, Susan **40**
Graves, Denyce **16**
Groban, Josh **47**
Hampson, Thomas **12**
Hendricks, Barbara **10**
Heppner, Ben **23**
Herrmann, Bernard **14**
Horne, Marilyn **9**
Jo, Sumi **37**
Licitra, Salvatore **46**
Malfitano, Catherine **45**
McNair, Sylvia **15**
Menotti, Gian Carlo **37**
Nilsson, Birgit **31**
Norman, Jessye **7**
Pavarotti, Luciano **20**
  Earlier sketch in CM **1**
Price, Leontyne **6**
Quasthoff, Thomas **26**
Safina, Alessandro **42**
Scholl, Andreas **38**
Sills, Beverly **5**
Solti, Georg **13**
Sutherland, Joan **13**
Tan Dun **33**
Te Kanawa, Kiri **2**
Terfel, Bryn **31**
Toscanini, Arturo **14**
Upshaw, Dawn **9**
Voigt, Deborah **42**
von Karajan, Herbert **1**
von Otter, Anne Sofie **30**
Watson, Russell **37**
Weill, Kurt **12**
Zimmerman, Udo **5**

Percussion
Aronoff, Kenny **21**
Baker, Ginger **16**
  Also see Cream
  Also see Hawkwind
Barretto, Ray **37**
Blackman, Cindy **15**
Blakey, Art **11**
Brown, Carlinhos **32**
Burton, Gary **10**
Collins, Phil **20**
  Earlier sketch in CM **2**
  Also see Genesis
Connors, Norman **30**
Copeland, Stewart **14**
  Also see Police, The
DeJohnette, Jack **7**
Gerhard-García, Alexandra **41**
Glennie, Evelyn **33**
Gurtu, Trilok **29**
Hampton, Lionel **6**
Hart, Mickey **39**
  Also see Grateful Dead, The
Henley, Don **3**
Hussain, Zakir **32**
Jones, Elvin **9**
Jones, Philly Joe **16**
Jones, Spike **5**
Krupa, Gene **13**

Mo', Keb' **21**
Moreira, Airto **44**
N'Dour, Youssou **41**
  Earlier sketch in CM **6**
  Also see Orchestra Baobab
Otis, Johnny **16**
Oxley, Tony **32**
Palmieri, Eddie **15**
Parker, Leon **27**
Puente, Tito **14**
Quaye, Finley **30**
Qureshi, Ustad Alla Rakha **29**
Rich, Buddy **13**
Roach, Max **12**
Santamaria, Mongo **28**
Scharin, Doug **32**
Schütze, Paul **32**
Sheila E. **3**
Singh, Talvin **44**
Sommer, Günter "Baby" **31**
Starr, Ringo **24**
  Earlier sketch in CM **10**
  Also see Beatles, The
Turner, Roger **32**
Walden, Narada Michael **14**
Webb, Chick **14**

Piano
Abrams, Muhal Richard **37**
Adamson, Barry **28**
Adès, Thomas **30**
Akiyoshi, Toshiko **38**
Allen, Geri **10**
Allison, Mose **17**
Amos, Tori **42**
  Earlier sketch in CM **12**
Apple, Fiona **28**
Argerich, Martha **27**
Arrau, Claudio **1**
Ashkenazy, Vladimir **32**
Axton, Hoyt **28**
Bacharach, Burt **20**
  Earlier sketch in CM **1**
Ball, Marcia **15**
Barber, Patricia **40**
Barenboim, Daniel **30**
Barron, Kenny **37**
Basie, Count **2**
Baxter, Les **47**
Ben Folds Five **20**
Benoit, David **40**
  Also see Rippingtons
Berlin, Irving **8**
Bey, Andy **45**
Blake, Eubie **19**
Blake, Ran **38**
Bley, Carla **8**
  Also see Golden Palominos
Bley, Paul **14**
Borge, Victor **19**
Brendel, Alfred **23**
Brickman, Jim **22**
Britten, Benjamin **15**
Bronfman, Yefim **6**
Brooks, Hadda **43**
Brubeck, Dave **8**
Buckwheat Zydeco **34**
  Earlier sketch in CM **6**
Burns, Ralph **37**
Bush, Kate **4**
Caine, Uri **31**
Carpenter, Richard **24**
  Also see Carpenters
Charles, Ray **24**
  Earlier sketch in CM **1**
Chestnut, Cyrus **47**
Clayderman, Richard **1**
Cleveland, James **1**

Cliburn, Van **13**
Cohen, Avishai **42**
Cole, Freddy **35**
Cole, Nat King **3**
Collins, Judy **4**
Collins, Phil **20**
  Earlier sketch in CM **2**
  Also see Genesis
Connick, Harry, Jr. **36**
  Earlier sketch in CM **4**
Crispell, Marilyn **47**
Crouch, Andraé **9**
Davies, Dennis Russell **24**
DeJohnette, Jack **7**
Denny, Martin **44**
Domino, Fats **2**
Dr. John **7**
Dupree, Champion Jack **12**
Ellington, Duke **2**
Esquivel, Juan **17**
Evans, Bill **17**
Evans, Gil **17**
Feinstein, Michael **6**
Feldman, Morton **42**
Ferrell, Rachelle **17**
Five for Fighting **36**
Flack, Roberta **5**
Flanagan, Tommy **16**
Flynn, Frank Emilio **37**
Frey, Glenn **3**
Gaillard, Slim **31**
Galás, Diamanda **16**
Garner, Erroll **25**
Gayle, Charles **35**
Glass, Philip **47**
  Earlier sketch in CM **1**
Gould, Glenn **9**
Green, Benny **17**
Grimaud, Hélène **35**
Grusin, Dave **7**
Guaraldi, Vince **3**
Hamelin, Marc-André **33**
Hamlisch, Marvin **1**
Hammill, Peter **30**
Hancock, Herbie **25**
  Earlier sketch in CM **8**
Hanna, Roland, Sir **45**
Harris, Barry **32**
Harris, Teddy **22**
Helfgott, David **19**
Henderson, Fletcher **16**
Hill, Andrew **41**
Hinderas, Natalie **12**
Hines, Earl "Fatha" **12**
Horn, Shirley **7**
Hornsby, Bruce **25**
  Earlier sketch in CM **3**
Horowitz, Vladimir **1**
Horvitz, Wayne **42**
Hough, Stephen **40**
Hyman, Dick **39**
Ibrahim, Abdullah **24**
Jackson, Joe **22**
  Earlier sketch in CM **4**
Jamal, Ahmad **32**
James, Skip **24**
Jarrett, Keith **36**
  Earlier sketch in CM **1**
Joel, Billy **12**
  Earlier sketch in CM **2**
John, Elton **20**
  Earlier sketch in CM **3**
Johnson, Buddy **44**
Johnson, James P. **16**
Jones, Hank **15**
Jones, Howard **26**
Joplin, Scott **10**

Dalton, Nic **31**
Dave, Edmunds **28**
Davies, Gail **38**
Dimitri from Paris **43**
Dixon, Willie **10**
Dolby, Thomas **10**
Dr. Dre **15**
  Also see N.W.A.
Dupri, Jermaine **25**
Dust Brothers **32**
Edmonds, Kenneth "Babyface" **12**
Eicher, Manfred **38**
Elliott, Missy **30**
Enigma **32**
  Earlier sketch in CM **14**
Eno, Brian **8**
  Also see Roxy Music
Ertegun, Ahmet **10**
Ertegun, Nesuhi **24**
Foster, David **13**
Fripp, Robert **9**
Froom, Mitchell **15**
Gabler, Milton **25**
Gabriel, Ana **44**
Gabriel, Juan **31**
Garnier, Laurent **29**
Gordy, Emory, Jr. **17**
Granz, Norman **37**
Gray, F. Gary **19**
Grusin, Dave **7**
Hardcastle, Paul **20**
Horn, Trevor **33**
Iglauer, Bruce **37**
Iovine, Jimmy **46**
Jackson, Millie **14**
Jerkins, Rodney **38**
Jimmy Jam and Terry Lewis **11**
Jones, Booker T. **8**
  Also see Booker T. & the M.G.'s
Jones, Donell **43**
Jones, Quincy **20**
  Earlier sketch in CM **2**
Jordan, Montell **26**
Kelly, R. **44**
  Earlier sketch in CM **19**
Kool Herc **45**
Krasnow, Bob **15**
Lange, Mutt **47**
Lanois, Daniel **8**
Lasar, Mars **39**
Laswell, Bill **14**
Leiber and Stoller **14**
Lillywhite, Steve **13**
Lynne, Jeff **5**
Mandel, Johnny **28**
Marley, Rita **10**
Martin, George **6**
Master P **22**
Mayfield, Curtis **8**
McKnight, Brian **22**
McLaren, Malcolm **23**
Meek, Joe **46**
Miller, Marcus **38**
Miller, Mitch **11**
Most, Mickie **29**
Neptunes, The **45**
Oakenfold, Paul **32**
Orbit, William **30**
O'Rourke, Jim **31**
Osby, Greg **21**
Pablo, Augustus **37**
Parks, Van Dyke **17**
Parsons, Alan **12**
Paul, Prince **29**
Post, Mike **21**

Prince **40**
  Earlier sketch in CM **14**
  Earlier sketch in CM **1**
Queen Latifah **24**
  Earlier sketch in CM **6**
Reid, Antonio **44**
Riley, Teddy **14**
Robertson, Robbie **2**
Rodgers, Nile **8**
Rosnes, Renée **44**
Rubin, Rick **9**
Rundgren, Todd **11**
Salem, Kevin **32**
Sawhney, Nitin **46**
Scruggs, Randy **28**
Sermon, Erick **44**
  Also see EPMD
Sherwood, Adrian **31**
Shocklee, Hank **15**
Simmons, Russell **47**
  Earlier sketch in CM **7**
Singh, Talvin **44**
Size, Roni **31**
Skaggs, Ricky **43**
  Earlier sketch in CM **5**
Spector, Phil **4**
Sure!, Al B. **13**
Sweat, Keith **13**
Tall Paul **36**
Timbaland **42**
Too $hort **16**
Toussaint, Allen **11**
Tricky **18**
Vandross, Luther **47**
  Earlier sketch in CM **24**
  Earlier sketch in CM **2**
Van Dyk, Paul **35**
Van Helden, Armand **32**
Van Zandt, Steven **29**
Vasquez, Junior **16**
Vig, Butch **17**
Wachtel, Waddy **26**
Walden, Narada Michael **14**
Was, Don **21**
  Also see Was (Not Was)
Watt, Mike **22**
Wexler, Jerry **15**
Whelan, Bill **20**
Wildhorn, Frank **31**
Willner, Hal **10**
Wilson, Brian **24**
  Also see Beach Boys, The
Winbush, Angela **15**
Wolf, Peter **31**
Woods-Wright, Tomica **22**

Promoters
Clark, Dick **25**
  Earlier sketch in CM **2**
Cohen, Lyor **29**
Geldof, Bob **9**
Graham, Bill **10**
Hay, George D. **3**
Meek, Joe **46**
Simmons, Russell **47**
  Earlier sketch in CM **7**

Ragtime
Johnson, James P. **16**
Joplin, Scott **10**

Rap
Arrested Development **14**
Austin, Dallas **16**
AZ **44**
Bambaataa, Afrika **42**
  Earlier sketch in CM **13**

Basehead **11**
Beastie Boys **25**
  Earlier sketch in CM **8**
Big Punisher **43**
Big Tymers, The **42**
Biz Markie **10**
Blackalicious **39**
Black Eyed Peas **45**
Black Sheep **15**
Bone Thugs-N-Harmony **18**
Bow Wow **45**
Busta Rhymes **18**
Campbell, Luther **10**
Cam'ron **39**
Cappadonna **43**
Cherry, Neneh **4**
Combs, Sean "Puffy" **25**
  Earlier sketch in CM **16**
Common **23**
Coolio **19**
Cypress Hill **11**
Da Brat **30**
Das EFX **14**
De La Soul **37**
  Earlier sketch in CM **7**
Del the Funky Homosapien **30**
Digable Planets **15**
Digital Underground **9**
DJ Jazzy Jeff and the Fresh Prince **5**
DMX **25**
Dr. Dre **15**
  Also see N.W.A.
Dupri, Jermaine **25**
Eazy-E **13**
  Also see N.W.A.
E-40 **46**
Elliott, Missy **30**
Eminem **28**
EPMD **10**
Eric B. and Rakim **9**
ESG **45**
Evans, Faith **25**
Eve **34**
Fabolous **47**
Fat Boys, The **47**
Fat Joe **42**
Franti, Michael **16**
Fugees, The **17**
Gang Starr **13**
Geto Boys, The **11**
Ghostface Killah **33**
Goodie Mob **24**
Grandmaster Flash **14**
Gravediggaz **23**
Hammer, M.C. **5**
Heavy D **10**
House of Pain **14**
Ice Cube **10**
  Also see N.W.A.
Ice-T **7**
Insane Clown Posse **22**
Jackson, Millie **14**
Ja Rule **36**
Jay-Z **47**
  Earlier sketch in CM **28**
Jeru the Damaja **33**
Jurassic 5 **42**
Juvenile **36**
Kane, Big Daddy **7**
Kid 'n Play **5**
Kid Rock **27**
Knight, Suge **15**
Kool Herc **45**
Kool Moe Dee **9**
Kris Kross **11**
KRS-One **8**
Kurupt **35**

Collins, Phil **2**
  Also see Genesis
Colvin, Shawn **38**
  Earlier sketch in CM **11**
Cooder, Ry **2**
  Also see Captain Beefheart and His
  Magic Band
Cooke, Sam **1**
  Also see Soul Stirrers, The
Cooper, Alice **8**
Cope, Julian **16**
Costello, Elvis **40**
  Earlier sketch in CM **12**
  Earlier sketch in CM **2**
Cotten, Elizabeth **16**
Coverdale, David **34**
  See Deep Purple
  Also see Whitesnake
Crenshaw, Marshall **5**
Croce, Jim **3**
Cropper, Steve **12**
Crosby, David **3**
  Also see Byrds, The
  Also see Crosby, Stills, and Nash
Crosse, Clay **38**
Crow, Sheryl **40**
  Earlier sketch in CM **18**
Crowe, J. D. **5**
Crowell, Rodney **8**
Curtis, Catie **31**
Dahl, Jeff **28**
Dalton, Nic **31**
Daniels, Charlie **6**
Davies, Gail **38**
Davies, Ray **5**
  Also see Kinks, the
Davis, Alana **36**
DeBarge, El **14**
de Burgh, Chris **22**
DeMent, Iris **13**
Denver, John **22**
  Earlier sketch in CM **1**
DeShannon, Jackie **40**
Des'ree **24**
  Earlier sketch in CM **15**
Diamond, Neil **1**
Dickerson, Deke **44**
Diddley, Bo **3**
Dido **46**
Diffie, Joe **27**
  Earlier sketch in CM **10**
DiFranco, Ani **43**
  Earlier sketch in CM **17**
Dion **4**
Dixon, Willie **10**
DMX **25**
Doc Pomus **14**
Doiron, Julie **41**
Domino, Fats **2**
Donelly, Tanya **39**
  Also see Belly
  Also see Breeders
  Also see Throwing Muses
Donovan **9**
Dorsey, Thomas A. **11**
Doucet, Michael **8**
Drake, Nick **17**
Dube, Lucky **17**
Dulli, Greg **17**
  Also see Afghan Whigs, The
Dury, Ian **30**
Dylan, Bob **21**
  Earlier sketch in CM **3**
Earle, Steve **43**
  Earlier sketch in CM **16**
Edmonds, Kenneth "Babyface" **12**
Elfman, Danny **9**

Ellington, Duke **2**
Elliott, Ramblin' Jack **32**
Emmanuel, Tommy **21**
English, Michael **23**
Enigma **32**
  Earlier sketch in CM **14**
Enya **32**
  Earlier sketch in CM **6**
Erickson, Roky **16**
Ertegun, Ahmet **10**
Escovedo, Alejandro **37**
  Earlier sketch in CM **18**
Estefan, Gloria **15**
  Earlier sketch in CM **2**
Etheridge, Melissa **16**
  Earlier sketch in CM **4**
Evans, Sara **27**
Everlast **27**
Fabian, Lara **34**
Faithfull, Marianne **14**
Farrar, Jay **46**
  Also see Son Volt
  Also see Uncle Tupelo
Ferry, Bryan **1**
Finn, Neil **34**
  Also see Crowded House
Five for Fighting **36**
Flack, Roberta **5**
Flatt, Lester **3**
Fogelberg, Dan **4**
Fogerty, John **2**
  Also see Creedence Clearwater Revival
Fordham, Julia **15**
Foster, David **13**
Frampton, Peter **3**
  Also see Humble Pie
Franti, Michael **16**
Frey, Glenn **3**
  Also see Eagles, The
Fripp, Robert **9**
Frizzell, Lefty **10**
Frost, Edith **40**
Gabriel, Ana **44**
Gabriel, Juan **31**
Gabriel, Peter **16**
  Earlier sketch in CM **2**
  Also see Genesis
Gaines, Jeffrey **34**
Gainsbourg, Serge **41**
Garcia, Jerry **4**
  Also see Grateful Dead, The
Gaye, Marvin **4**
Geldof, Bob **9**
Gershwin, George and Ira **11**
Gibson, Bob **23**
Gibson, Deborah **24**
  Earlier sketch in CM **1**
  Also see Gibson, Debbie
Gift, Roland **3**
Gill, Vince **34**
  Earlier sketch in CM **7**
Gilley, Mickey **7**
Goffin-King **24**
Gold, Julie **22**
Goodman, Benny **4**
Gordy, Berry, Jr. **6**
Gorka, John **18**
Grant, Amy **7**
Gray, David **30**
Gray, Macy **32**
Green, Al **9**
Green, Keith **38**
Greenwood, Lee **12**
Griffin, Patty **24**
Griffith, Nanci **3**
Guthrie, Arlo **6**
Guthrie, Gwen **26**

Guthrie, Woodie **2**
Guy, Buddy **4**
Haack, Bruce **37**
Hagen, Nina **25**
Haggard, Merle **39**
  Earlier sketch in CM **2**
Hall, Tom T. **26**
  Earlier sketch in CM **4**
Hamlisch, Marvin **1**
Hammer, M.C. **5**
Hammill, Peter **30**
Hancock, Herbie **25**
  Earlier sketch in CM **8**
Hancock, Wayne **45**
Hanna, Kathleen **45**
Hardin, Tim **18**
Harding, John Wesley **6**
Hardy, Françoise **43**
Harley, Bill **7**
Harper, Ben **17**
Harper, Roy **30**
Harris, Emmylou **36**
  Earlier sketch in CM **4**
Harris, Jesse **47**
Harrison, George **2**
  Also see Beatles, The
Harry, Deborah **4**
  Also see Blondie
Hart, Beth **29**
Hartford, John **37**
  Earlier sketch in CM **1**
Harvey, PJ **43**
  Earlier sketch in CM **11**
Hatfield, Juliana **37**
  Earlier sketch in CM **12**
  Also see Lemonheads, The
Hawkins, Dale **45**
Hawkins, Screamin' Jay **29**
  Earlier sketch in CM **8**
Hayes, Isaac **10**
Hazlewood, Lee **45**
Healey, Jeff **4**
Hedges, Michael **3**
Hendrix, Jimi **2**
Henley, Don **3**
  Also see Eagles, The
Henry, Joe **37**
  Earlier sketch in CM **18**
Hiatt, John **35**
  Earlier sketch in CM **8**
Hill, Lauryn **25**
  Also see Fugees, The
Hinojosa, Tish **44**
  Earlier sketch in CM **13**
Hitchcock, Robyn **9**
Holly, Buddy **1**
Hornsby, Bruce **25**
  Earlier sketch in CM **3**
Houston, Penelope **28**
Howard, Harlan **15**
Howard, Rebecca Lynn **41**
Hubbard, Ray Wylie **38**
Ian, Janis **24**
  Earlier sketch in CM **5**
Ice Cube **10**
  Also see N.W.A.
Ice-T **7**
Idol, Billy **3**
Imbruglia, Natalie **27**
Isaak, Chris **33**
  Earlier sketch in CM **6**
Jackson, Alan **25**
  Earlier sketch in CM **7**
Jackson, Janet **36**
  Earlier sketch in CM **16**
  Earlier sketch in CM **3**

Cumulative Musicians Index

Volume numbers appear in **bold**

Andrews, Maxene
　See Andrews Sisters, The
Andrews, Patty
　See Andrews Sisters, The
Andrews, Revert
　See Dirty Dozen Brass Band
Andrews Sisters, The **9**
Andriano, Dan
　See Alkaline Trio
Andrus, Sherman
　See Imperials, The
Andy
　See Ex, The
Andy, Horace
　See Massive Attack
Angel, Ashley Parker
　See O-Town
Angel, Jerry
　See Blasters, The
Anger, Darol
　See Turtle Island String Quartet
Angus, Colin
　See Shamen, The
Animals, The **22**
Anka, Paul **2**
Anointed **21**
Anonymous, Rodney
　See Dead Milkmen
Anonymous 4 **23**
Anselmo, Philip
　See Pantera
Ant, Adam
　See Adam Ant
Anthony, Larry
　See Dru Hill
Anthony, Marc **33**
　Earlier sketch in CM **19**
Anthony, Michael
　See Massive Attack
Anthony, Michael
　See Van Halen
Anthrax **41**
　Earlier sketch in CM **11**
Antin, Jesse
　See Chanticleer
Anton, Alan
　See Cowboy Junkies, The
Antoni, Mark De Gli
　See Soul Coughing
Antunes, Michael
　See Beaver Brown Band, The
Anu, Christine **34**
Anway, Susan
　See Magnetic Fields, The
A1 **41**
Aphex Twin **14**
Apl.de.Ap
　See Black Eyed Peas
Aponte, Charlie
　See El Gran Combo
Appice, Vinnie
　See Black Sabbath
Apple, Fiona **28**
Apples in Stereo **30**
Appleton, Natalie
　See All Saints
Appleton, Nicole
　See All Saints
April, Johnny
　See Staind
April Wine **43**
Aqua **34**
Aqua Velvets **23**
Aquabats, The **22**
Arab Strap **33**
Araya, Tom
　See Slayer

Arbulu, Shia
　See La Ley
Archer, Al
　See Dexy's Midnight Runners
Archer, Gem
　See Oasis
Archers of Loaf **21**
Arden, Jann **21**
Ardito, Douglas
　See Puddle of Mudd
Ardolino, Tom
　See NRBQ
Arellano, Rod
　See Aquabats, The
Arena, Tina **21**
Arends, Carolyn **45**
Arentzen, Jamie
　See American Hi-Fi
Argent, Rod
　See Zombies, The
Argerich, Martha **27**
Arias, Raymond
　See Ceili Rain
Arjona, Ricardo **43**
Arkenstone, David **40**
　Earlier sketch in CM **20**
Arlen, Harold **27**
Arm, Mark
　See Mudhoney
Armaou, Lindsay
　See B*Witched
Armatrading, Joan **4**
Armerding, Jake
　See Northern Lights
Armerding, Taylor
　See Northern Lights
Armik **41**
Armstrong, Billie Joe
　See Green Day
Armstrong, Louis **4**
Armstrong, Paul
　See Country Joe and the Fish
Armstrong, Robbie
　See Royal Trux
Armstrong, Rollo
　See Faithless
Armstrong, Tim
　See Rancid
Armstrong, Vanessa Bell **24**
Arnaz, Desi **8**
Arni, Stefan
　See Gus Gus
Arnold, Brad
　See 3 Doors Down
Arnold, Eddy **10**
Arnold, James
　See Four Lads, The
Arnold, Kristine
　See Sweethearts of the Rodeo
Aronoff, Kenny **21**
Arrau, Claudio **1**
Arrested Development **14**
Arson, Nicholaus
　See Hives, The
Art of Noise **22**
Art Ensemble of Chicago, The **23**
Arthur, Brian
　See Goldfinger
Arthur, Davey
　See Fureys, The
Arthurs, Paul "Bonehead"
　See Oasis
Artifacts **23**
Ash **34**
Ash, Daniel
　See Bauhaus
　Also see Love and Rockets

Ashanti **45**
Ashcroft, Richard
　See Verve, The
Ashford, Jack
　See Funk Brothers
Ashford, Rosalind
　See Martha and the Vandellas
Ashkenazy, Vladimir **32**
Ashley, Bob
　See Guess Who
Ashton, John
　See Psychedelic Furs
Ashton, Nick
　See Northwoods Improvisers
Ashton, Susan **17**
Asian Dub Foundation **30**
Asleep at the Wheel **29**
　Earlier sketch in CM **5**
Assad, Badi **36**
Astbury, Ian
　See Cult, The
Asthana, Shivika
　See Papas Fritas
Astley, Rick **5**
Aston, Jay "J"
　See Gene Loves Jezebel
Aston, Michael
　See Gene Loves Jezebel
Astro
　See UB40
Asuo, Kwesi
　See Arrested Development
Aswad **34**
At The Drive-In **32**
Atari Teenage Riot **27**
A*Teens **36**
Aterciopelados **38**
Atkins, Chet **26**
　Earlier sketch in CM **5**
Atkins, Erica
　See Mary Mary
Atkins, Martin
　See Killing Joke
　Also see Pigface
Atkins, Tina
　See Mary Mary
Atkins, Victor "Red"
　See Los Hombres Calientes
Atkinson, Lyle
　See Brave Combo
Atkinson, Paul
　See Zombies, The
Atkinson, Sweet Pea
　See Was (Not Was)
Atomic Fireballs, The **27**
ATR
　See Boredoms, The
Attisso, Barthelemy
　See Orchestra Baobab
Audio Adrenaline **22**
Auf Der Maur, Melissa
　See Smashing Pumpkins
　Also see Hole
Auge, Jymn
　See His Name Is Alive
Augustyniak, Jerry
　See 10,000 Maniacs
Auldridge, Mike **4**
　Also see Country Gentlemen, The
　Also see Seldom Scene, The
Austin, Cuba
　See McKinney's Cotton Pickers
Austin, Dallas **16**
Austin, Kenneth
　See Rebirth Brass Band
Austin, Patti **47**
Austin, Sherrié **34**

Barber, Keith
  See Soul Stirrers, The
Barber, Patricia **40**
Barber, Samuel **34**
Barbero, Lori
  See Babes in Toyland
Barbieri, Gato **22**
Barbirolli, Lady Evelyn
  See Rothwell, Evelyn
Barbot, Bill
  See Jawbox
Bardens, Peter
  See Camel
Bardo Pond **28**
Barenaked Ladies **39**
  Earlier sketch in CM **18**
Barenboim, Daniel **30**
Bargeld, Blixa
  See Einstürzende Neubauten
Bargeron, Dave
  See Blood, Sweat and Tears
Barham, Meriel
  See Lush
Barile, Jo
  See Ventures, The
Barker, Andrew
  See 808 State
Barker, Paul
  See Ministry
Barker, Travis Landon
  See Aquabats, The
  Also see Blink 182
Barksdale, Charles
  See Dells, The
Barlow, Andy
  See Lamb
Barlow, Barriemore
  See Jethro Tull
Barlow, Bruce
  See Commander Cody and His Lost
    Planet Airmen
Barlow, Lou **20**
  Also see Dinosaur Jr.
  Also see Folk Implosion, The
  Also see Sebadoh
Barlow, Tommy
  See Aztec Camera
Barnes, Danny
  See Bad Livers, The
Barnes, Don
  See .38 Special
Barnes, Jeffrey
  See Brave Combo
Barnes, Jeremy
  See Neutral Milk Hotel
Barnes, Jimmy
  See Cold Chisel
Barnes, Micah
  See Nylons, The
Barnes, Neil
  See Leftfield
Barnes, Prentiss
  See Moonglows, The
Barnes, Roosevelt "Booba" **23**
Barnett, Mandy **26**
Barnwell, Duncan
  See Simple Minds
Barnwell, Ysaye Maria
  See Sweet Honey in the Rock
Barocas, Zach
  See Jawbox
Barr, Al
  See Dropkick Murphys
Barr, Jess
  See Slobberbone
Barr, Ralph
  See Nitty Gritty Dirt Band, The

Barradas, Miggy
  See Divine Comedy, The
Barre, Martin
  See Jethro Tull
Barrere, Paul
  See Little Feat
Barret, Charlie
  See Fixx, The
Barrett, Dicky
  See Mighty Mighty Bosstones
Barrett, Mike
  See Lettermen, The
Barrett, Robert "T-Mo"
  See Goodie Mob
Barrett, Syd **37**
  Also see Pink Floyd
Barrett, Tina
  See S Club 7
Barretto, Ray **37**
Barron, Christopher
  See Spin Doctors
Barron, Kenny **37**
Barrow, Geoff
  See Portishead
Barrueco, Manuel **39**
Barry, John **29**
Barry, Mark
  See BBMak
Barson, Mike
  See Madness
Bartek, Steve
  See Oingo Boingo
Bartels, Joanie **13**
Barthol, Bruce
  See Country Joe and the Fish
Bartholomew, Simon
  See Brand New Heavies, The
Bartoli, Cecilia **12**
Barton, Lou Ann
  See Fabulous Thunderbirds, The
Barton, Rick
  See Dropkick Murphys
Bartos, Karl
  See Kraftwerk
Barzelay, Eef
  See Clem Snide
Basehead **11**
Basement Jaxx **29**
Basher, Mick
  See X
Basia **5**
Basie, Count **2**
Bass, Colin
  See Camel
Bass, Lance
  See 'N Sync
Bass, Ralph **24**
Bastida, Ceci (Cecilia)
  See Tijuana No!
Batchelor, Kevin
  See Big Mountain
  Also see Steel Pulse
Batel, Beate
  See Einstürzende Neubauten
Bateman, Bill
  See Blasters, The
Bates, Stuart "Pinkie"
  See Divine Comedy, The
Batiste, Lionel
  See Dirty Dozen Brass Band
Batoh, Masaki
  See Ghost
  Also see Pearls Before Swine
Battin, Skip
  See Byrds, The
Battle, Kathleen **6**

Battle, Phyllis
  See Fifth Dimension
Battlefield Band, The **31**
Batty, Cody
  See Fugs, The
Baucom, Terry
  See IIIrd Tyme Out
Bauer, Johannes **32**
Bauer, Judah
  See Jon Spencer Blues Explosion
Bauermeister, Chris
  See Jawbreaker
Bauhaus **27**
Baum, Kevin
  See Chanticleer
Baumann, Peter
  See Tangerine Dream
Bautista, Roland
  See Earth, Wind and Fire
Baxter, Adrian
  See Cherry Poppin' Daddies
Baxter, Jeff
  See Doobie Brothers, The
Baxter, Les **47**
Baxter, Steve
  See Daniel Amos
Bayer Sager, Carole
  See Sager, Carole Bayer
Bayliss, Michael
  See Saints, The
Baylor, Helen **20**
Baylor, Marcus
  See Yellowjackets
Baynton-Power, David
  See James
Bazilian, Eric
  See Hooters
Bazz, John
  See Blasters, The
BBMak **38**
Beach Boys, The **1**
Beale, Michael
  See Earth, Wind and Fire
Beamer, Keola **43**
Beard, Annette
  See Martha and the Vandellas
Beard, Frank
  See ZZ Top
Beasley, Les
  See Florida Boys, The
Beasley, Paul
  See Mighty Clouds of Joy, The
Beastie Boys **25**
  Earlier sketch in CM **8**
Beat Farmers **23**
Beat Happening **28**
Beatles, The **2**
Beau Brummels **39**
Beauford, Carter
  See Dave Matthews Band
Beausoleil **37**
Beautiful South **19**
Beauvoir, Jean
  See Wendy O. Williams and The Plasmatics
Beaver Brown Band, The **3**
Bechdel, John
  See Fear Factory
Bechet, Sidney **17**
Beck **41**
  Earlier sketch in CM **18**
Beck, Jeff **4**
  Also see Yardbirds, The
Beck, William
  See Ohio Players
Beckenstein, Jay
  See Spyro Gyra

Best, Brent
　See Slobberbone
Best, Nathaniel
　See O'Jays, The
Best, Pete
　See Beatles, The
Beta Band, The **27**
Betha, Mason
　See Mase
Bethea, Ken
　See Old 97's
Bettencourt, Nuno
　See Extreme
Better Than Ezra **19**
Bettie Serveert **17**
Bettini, Tom
　See Jackyl
Betts, Dicky
　See Allman Brothers, The
Bevan, Alonza
　See Kula Shaker
Bevan, Bev
　See Black Sabbath
　Also see Electric Light Orchestra
Bever, Pete
　See Workhorse Movement, The
Bevis Frond **23**
Bey, Andy **45**
Bezozi, Alan
　See Dog's Eye View
B-52's, The **4**
Bhag-dad-a, Omar
　See Lane, Fred
Biafra, Jello **18**
　Also see Dead Kennedys
Bibey, Alan
　See IIIrd Tyme Out
Bidini, Dave
　See Rheostatics
Big Audio Dynamite **18**
Big Bad Voodoo Daddy **38**
Big Head Todd and the Monsters **20**
Big Mike
　See Geto Boys, The
Big Money Odis
　See Digital Underground
Big Mountain **23**
Big Paul
　See Killing Joke
Big Punisher **43**
Big Star **36**
Big V
　See Nappy Roots
Big Youth **43**
Biger, Guenole
　See Les Négresses Vertes
Bigham, John
　See Fishbone
Big Tymers, The **42**
Bilk, Acker **47**
Bill Wyman & the Rhythm Kings **26**
Billingham, Mickey
　See Dexy's Midnight Runners
Bingham, John
　See Fishbone
Bin Hassan, Umar
　See Last Poets
Binks, Les
　See Judas Priest
Biondo, George
　See Steppenwolf
Birch, Rob
　See Stereo MC's
Birchfield, Benny
　See Osborne Brothers, The
Bird
　See Parker, Charlie

Bird, Andrew **46**
Birdsong, Cindy
　See Supremes, The
Birdstuff
　See Man or Astroman?
Birgisson, Jón Pór
　See Sigur Rós
Birmingham, Mark
　See Saints, The
Birtwistle, Harrison **38**
Biscuits, Chuck
　See Circle Jerks
　Also see Danzig
　Also see D.O.A.
　Also see Social Distortion
Bishop, Elvin **41**
Bishop, Jeb **28**
　Also see Flying Luttenbachers, The
Bishop, Michael
　See Gwar
Bishop, Steven
　See Powderfinger
Bitney, Dan
　See Tortoise
Bitts, Mike
　See Innocence Mission, The
Bixler, Cedric
　See At The Drive-In
Biz Markie **10**
BizzyBone
　See Bone Thugs-N-Harmony
Bjelland, Kat
　See Babes in Toyland
Bjerregard, Marty
　See Saints, The
Bjork, Brant
　See Fu Manchu
Björk **39**
　Earlier sketch in CM **16**
　Also see Sugarcubes, The
Black, Bobby
　See Commander Cody and His Lost
　　Planet Airmen
Black, Clint **5**
Black, Frank **14**
　Also see Pixies, The
Black, Jet
　See Stranglers, The
Black, Jimmy Carl "India Ink"
　See Captain Beefheart and His Magic Band
Black, Lori
　See Melvins
Black, Lorne
　See Great White
Black, Mary **15**
Black, Tommy
　See Paloalto
Black, Vic
　See C + C Music Factory
Black Eyed Peas **45**
Black Flag **22**
Black 47 **37**
Black Francis
　See Black, Frank
Black Sabbath **9**
Black Sheep **15**
Black Uhuru **41**
　Earlier sketch in CM **12**
Blackalicious **39**
Blackburn, Paul
　See Gomez
Black Crowes, The **35**
　Earlier sketch in CM **7**
BlackHawk **21**
Blackman, Cindy **15**
Blackman, Nicole
　See Golden Palominos

Blackman, Tee-Wee
　See Memphis Jug Band
Blackmore, Ritchie
　See Deep Purple
　Also see Rainbow
Blackstreet **23**
Blackwell, Chris **26**
Blackwood, Sarah
　See Dubstar
Blackwood, Terry
　See Imperials, The
Bladd, Stephen Jo
　See J. Geils Band
Blades, Ruben **2**
Blair, Ron
　See Tom Petty and the Heartbreakers
Blake, Eubie **19**
Blake, Katharine
　See Mediaeval Baebes
Blake, Norman **47**
Blake, Norman
　See Teenage Fanclub
Blake, Ran **38**
Blake, Tim
　See Gong
Blakely, Paul
　See Captain Beefheart and His Magic Band
Blakey, Art **11**
Blakey, Colin
　See Waterboys, The
Blanchard, Terence **13**
Bland, Bobby "Blue" **12**
Blasters, The **41**
Blatt, Melanie
　See All Saints
Blegen, Jutith **23**
Blegvad, Peter **28**
Blessid Union of Souls **20**
Bley, Carla **8**
　Also see Golden Palominos
Bley, Paul **14**
Blige, Mary J. **35**
　Earlier sketch in CM **15**
Blind Melon **21**
Blink 182 **27**
Bliss, Lang
　See Ceili Rain
Bloch, Alan
　See Concrete Blonde
Bloch, Kurt
　See Fastbacks, The
Block, Ken
　See Sister Hazel
Block, Norman
　See Rasputina
Block, Rory **18**
Blocker, Joe
　See Love
Blonde Redhead **28**
Blondie **27**
　Earlier sketch in CM **14**
Blondy, Alpha **40**
Blood, Dave
　See Dead Milkmen
Blood, Johnny
　See Magnetic Fields, The
Blood, Sweat and Tears **7**
Bloodhound Gang, The **31**
Bloom, Eric
　See Blue Oyster Cult
Bloom, Luka **14**
Bloomfield, Michael **40**
Blount, Herman "Sonny"
　See Sun Ra
Blue, Buddy
　See Beat Farmers

Bracken, Ben
See Northwoods Improvisers
Brad **21**
Brad Daddy X
See Kottonmouth Kings
Bradbury, John
See Specials, The
Bradbury, Randy
See Pennywise
Bradfield, James Dean
See Manic Street Preachers
Bradley, Michael
See Undertones, The
Bradley, Robert
See Robert Bradley's Blackwater Surprise
Bradshaw, Kym
See Saints, The
Bradshaw, Tim
See Dog's Eye View
Bradstreet, Rick
See Bluegrass Patriots
Brady, Paul **8**
Braff, Ruby **43**
Bragg, Billy **7**
Bragg, Todd
See Caedmon's Call
Braggs, Larry
See Tower of Power
Brahem, Anouar **46**
Brain, Matt
See Grapes of Wrath, The
Braithwaite, Stuart
See Mogwai
Bramah, Martin
See Fall, The
Bramlett, Bekka
See Fleetwood Mac
Bramley, Clyde
See Hoodoo Gurus
Branca, Glenn **29**
Branch, Michelle **47**
Brand New Heavies, The **14**
Brandt, Paul **22**
Brandy **19**
Branigan, Laura **2**
Brannon, Kippi **20**
Brant, Henry **39**
Brantley, Junior
See Roomful of Blues
Brave Combo **31**
Braxton, Anthony **12**
Braxton, Toni **44**
Earlier sketch in CM **17**
Bread **40**
Breadman, Scott
See Rippingtons
B-Real
See Cypress Hill
Bream, Julian **9**
Breaux, Jimmy
See Beausoleil
Brecker, Michael **29**
Breeders **19**
Bregante, Merel
See Nitty Gritty Dirt Band, The
Brendel, Alfred **23**
Brennan, Ciaran
See Clannad
Brennan, Maire
See Clannad
Brennan, Paul
See Odds
Brennan, Pol
See Clannad
Brennan, Steve
See Dexy's Midnight Runners

Brenner, Simon
See Talk Talk
Breuker, Willem
See Willem Breuker Kollektief
Brevette, Lloyd
See Skatalites, The
Brewer, Don
See Grand Funk Railroad
BR5-49 **35**
Brickell, Edie **3**
Brickman, Jim **22**
Bridgeman, Noel
See Waterboys, The
Bridgewater, Dee Dee **18**
Briggs, David
See Pearls Before Swine
Briggs, James Randall
See Aquabats, The
Briggs, Vic
See Animals, The
Bright, Garfield
See Shai
Bright, Ronnie
See Coasters, The
Bright, William
See Dixie Hummingbirds, The
Bright Eyes **42**
Brightman, Sarah **45**
Earlier sketch in CM **20**
Briley, Alex
See Village People, The
Brindley, Paul
See Sundays, The
Brinsley Schwarz **40**
Britt, Michael
See Lonestar
Britten, Benjamin **15**
Brittingham, Eric
See Cinderella
Brix
See Fall, The
Broadly, Whit
See Paladins, The
Brock, Dave
See Hawkwind
Brock, Isaac
See Modest Mouse
Brock, Jesse
See Lynn Morris Band
Brockenborough, Dennis
See Mighty Mighty Bosstones
Brockie, Dave
See Gwar
Brodsky Quartet **41**
Broemel, Carl
See My Morning Jacket
Brokop, Lisa **22**
Brom, Marti **46**
Bromberg, David **18**
Bronfman, Yefim **6**
Brook, Rachel
See Flying Saucer Attack
Brooke, Jonatha
See Story, The
Brooker, Gary
See Bill Wyman & the Rhythm Kings
Brooker, Nicholas "Natty"
See Spacemen 3
Brookes, Jon
See Charlatans, The
Brookes, Steve
See Jam, The
Brookins, Steve
See .38 Special
Brooks, Arthur
See Impressions, The

Brooks, Baba
See Skatalites, The
Brooks, DJ
See Citizen King
Brooks, Garth **25**
Earlier sketch in CM **8**
Brooks, Hadda **43**
Brooks, Leon Eric "Kix" III
See Brooks & Dunn
Brooks, Meredith **30**
Brooks, Richard
See Impressions, The
Brooks, Stuart
See Pretty Things, The
Brooks & Dunn **25**
Earlier sketch in CM **12**
Broom, Bobby **38**
Broonzy, Big Bill **13**
Brotherdale, Steve
See Joy Division
Also see Smithereens, The
Brötzmann, Caspar **27**
Brötzmann, Peter **26**
Broudie, Ian
See Lightning Seeds
Broussard, Jules
See Lavay Smith and Her Red Hot
Skillet Lickers
Broussard, Russ
See Continental Drifters
Brown, Alison **44**
Brown, Amanda
See Go-Betweens, The
Brown, Bobby **4**
Brown, Brooks
See Cherry Poppin' Daddies
Brown, Bundy K.
See Tortoise
Brown, Carlinhos **32**
Brown, Clarence "Gatemouth" **11**
Brown, Clifford **24**
Brown, Dan
See Royal Trux
Brown, Dan K.
See Fixx, The
Brown, Danny Joe
See Molly Hatchet
Brown, Dennis **29**
Brown, Donny
See Verve Pipe, The
Brown, Duncan
See Stereolab
Brown, Earle **41**
Brown, Eddie "Bongo"
See Funk Brothers
Brown, Foxy **25**
Brown, George
See Kool & the Gang
Brown, Greg
See Cake
Brown, Harold
See War
Brown, Heidi
See Treadmill Trackstar
Brown, Ian
See Stone Roses, The
Brown, James **16**
Earlier sketch in CM **2**
Brown, Jimmy
See UB40
Brown, Junior **15**
Brown, Lawrence **23**
Brown, Marty **14**
Brown, Melanie
See Spice Girls
Brown, Mick
See Dokken

Brown, Morris
  See Pearls Before Swine
Brown, Norman **29**
Brown, Norman
  See Mills Brothers, The
Brown, Paula
  See Giant Sand
Brown, Rahem
  See Artifacts
Brown, Ray **21**
Brown, Robin
  See Cousteau
Brown, Rob
  See Autechre
Brown, Ruth **13**
Brown, Selwyn "Bumbo"
  See Steel Pulse
Brown, Steven
  See Tuxedomoon
Brown, Tim
  See Boo Radleys, The
Brown, Tony **14**
Browne, Ian
  See Matthew Good Band
Browne, Jackson **3**
  Also see Nitty Gritty Dirt Band, The
Brownstein, Carrie
  See Sleater-Kinney
Brownstone **21**
Brubeck, Dave **8**
Bruce, Aaron
  See Four Lads, The
Bruce, Don
  See Jordanaires, The
Bruce, Dustan
  See Chumbawamba
Bruce, Jack
  See Cream
  Also see Golden Palominos
  Also see Soft Machine
Bruce, Joseph Frank
  See Insane Clown Posse
Bruford, Bill
  See King Crimson
  Also see Yes
Bruno, Gioia
  See Exposé
Bruschini, Angelo
  See Blue Aeroplanes, The
Bruster, Thomas
  See Soul Stirrers, The
Bryan, David
  See Bon Jovi
Bryan, Karl
  See Skatalites, The
Bryan, Mark
  See Hootie and the Blowfish
Bryant, Elbridge
  See Temptations, The
Bryant, Jeff
  See Ricochet
Bryant, Jimmy
  See Dixie Hummingbirds, The
Bryant, Junior
  See Ricochet
Brydon, Mark
  See Moloko
Bryson, Bill
  See Desert Rose Band, The
Bryson, David
  See Counting Crows
Bryson, Peabo **11**
Bryson, Wally
  See Raspberries
Brzezicki, Mark
  See Ultravox
B2K **42**

Buchanan, Wallis
  See Jamiroquai
Buchholz, Francis
  See Scorpions, The
Buchignani, Paul
  See Afghan Whigs
Buck, Mike
  See Fabulous Thunderbirds, The
Buck, Peter
  See R.E.M.
Buck, Robert
  See 10,000 Maniacs
Buckethead **34**
Buckingham, Lindsey **8**
  Also see Fleetwood Mac
Buckland, John
  See Coldplay
Buckler, Rick
  See Jam, The
Buckley, Betty **16**
  Earlier sketch in CM **1**
Buckley, Jeff **22**
Buckley, Tim **14**
Buckner, David
  See Papa Roach
Buckner, Richard **31**
Buckwheat Zydeco **34**
  Earlier sketch in CM **6**
Budgie
  See Siouxsie and the Banshees
Buell, Garett
  See Caedmon's Call
Buerstatte, Phil
  See White Zombie
Buffalo Springfield **24**
Buffalo Tom **18**
Buffett, Jimmy **42**
  Earlier sketch in CM **4**
Built to Spill **27**
Buitrago, Héctor
  See Aterciopelados
Bulgarian State Radio and Television Female
    Vocal Choir
  See Bulgarian State Female Vocal Choir, The
Bulgarian State Female Vocal Choir, The **10**
Bulgin, Lascelle
  See Israel Vibration
Bulloch, Martin
  See Mogwai
Bullock, Craig "DJ Homicide"
  See Sugar Ray
Bumbry, Grace **13**
Bumpus, Cornelius
  See Doobie Brothers, The
Bunch, Jon
  See Sense Field
Bundrick, John "Rabbit"
  See Free
Bunford, Huw "Bunf"
  See Super Furry Animals
Bunker, Clive
  See Jethro Tull
Bunkley, John
  See Atomic Fireballs, The
Bunnell, Dewey
  See America
Bunnett, Jane **37**
Bunskoeke, Herman
  See Bettie Serveert
Bunton, Emma
  See Spice Girls
Burch, Curtis
  See New Grass Revival, The
Burch, Rich
  See Jimmy Eat World
Burchill, Charlie
  See Simple Minds

Burden, Ian
  See Human League, The
Burdon, Eric **14**
  Also see Animals, The
  Also see War
Burger, Rob
  See Tin Hat Trio
Burgess, Paul
  See Camel
  Also see 10cc
Burgess, Sonny **42**
Burgess, Tim
  See Charlatans, The
Burgman, Richard
  See Saints, The
Burke, Clem
  See Blondie
  Also see Romantics, The
Burke, Solomon **36**
Burkum, Tyler
  See Audio Adrenaline
Burleson, Jason
  See Blue Highway
Burnel, J.J.
  See Stranglers, The
Burnett, Carol **6**
Burnett, T Bone **13**
Burnette, Billy
  See Fleetwood Mac
Burnham, Charles
  See String Trio of New York
Burnham, Hugo
  See Gang of Four
Burning Spear **15**
Burns, Annie
  See Burns Sisters
Burns, Barry
  See Mogwai
Burns, Bob
  See Lynyrd Skynyrd
Burns, Christian
  See BBMak
Burns, Jeannie
  See Burns Sisters
Burns, Joey
  See Calexico
  Also see Giant Sand
Burns, Karl
  See Fall, The
Burns, Keith
  See Trick Pony
Burns, Marie
  See Burns Sisters
Burns, Ralph **37**
Burns, Sheila
  See Burns Sisters
Burns, Terry
  See Burns Sisters
Burns, Vinnie
  See Ultravox
Burns Sisters **41**
Burnside, R. L. **34**
Burr, Clive
  See Iron Maiden
Burrell, Boz
  See Bad Company
Burrell, Kenny **11**
Burrell, Raymond "Boz"
  See King Crimson
Burroughs, William S. **26**
Burrows, Jeff
  See Tea Party
Burse, Charlie
  See Memphis Jug Band
Burse, Robert
  See Memphis Jug Band

Burtch, Aaron
  See Grandaddy
Burtnik, Glen
  See Styx
Burton, Cliff
  See Metallica
Burton, Gary **10**
Burton, Tim
  See Mighty Mighty Bosstones
  Also see Promise Ring, The
Busby, Jheryl **9**
Buschman, Carol
  See Chordettes, The
Bush **38**
  Earlier sketch in CM **18**
Bush, Dave
  See Elastica
  Also see Fall, The
Bush, John
  See Anthrax
Bush, Kate **4**
Bush, Roger
  See Flying Burrito Brothers
Bush, Sam
  See New Grass Revival, The
Bushwick, Bill
  See Geto Boys, The
Busseri, Frank
  See Four Lads, The
Busta Rhymes **18**
Butala, Tony
  See Lettermen, The
Butcher, Bilinda
  See My Bloody Valentine
Butler, Bernard
  See Suede
Butler, Jerry
  See Impressions, The
Butler, Joe
  See Lovin' Spoonful
Butler, Richard
  See Love Spit Love
  Also see Psychedelic Furs
Butler, Terry "Geezer"
  See Black Sabbath
Butler, Tim
  See Love Spit Love
  Also see Psychedelic Furs
Butterfield, Paul **23**
Butterfly
  See Digable Planets
Butthole Surfers **16**
Buttrey, Kenneth
  See Pearls Before Swine
Buxton, Felix
  See Basement Jaxx
Buynak, John
  See Rusted Root
Buzzcocks, The **9**
B*Witched **33**
Byers, Roddy
  See Specials, The
Byrd, Tracy **39**
Byrds, The **8**
Byrne, Chris
  See Black 47
Byrne, David **8**
  Also see Talking Heads
Byrne, Dermot
  See Altan
Byrne, Nicky
  See Westlife
Byrom, Larry
  See Steppenwolf
Byron, David
  See Uriah Heep
Byron, Don **22**

Byron, Lord T.
  See Lords of Acid
C + C Music Factory **16**
Caballe, Monserrat **23**
Cabaret Voltaire **18**
Cable, John
  See Nitty Gritty Dirt Band, The
Cable, Stuart
  See Stereophonics
Cachao
  See Lopez, Israel "Cachao"
Cadogan, Kevin
  See Third Eye Blind
Caedmon's Call **39**
Caesar, Shirley **40**
  Earlier sketch in CM **17**
Café Tacuba **45**
Cafferty, John
  See Beaver Brown Band, The
Caffey, Charlotte
  See Go-Go's, The
Cage, John **8**
Caggiano, Rob
  See Anthrax
Cahn, Sammy **11**
Cain, Jeffrey
  See Remy Zero
Cain, Jonathan
  See Journey
Caine, Uri **31**
Caivano, Phil
  See Monster Magnet
Cake **27**
Calandra, Joe
  See Monster Magnet
Calderon, Mark
  See Color Me Badd
Caldwell, Tommy
  See Marshall Tucker Band
Caldwell, Toy
  See Marshall Tucker Band
Cale, J. J. **16**
Cale, John **9**
  Also see Velvet Underground, The
Calexico **33**
Calhoun, Will
  See Living Colour
California, Randy
  See Spirit
Calire, Mario
  See Wallflowers, The
Callahan, Ken
  See Jayhawks, The
Callahan, Ray
  See Wendy O. Williams and The Plasmatics
Callas, Maria **11**
Calleros, Juan
  See Maná
Callis, Jo
  See Human League, The
Calloway, Cab **6**
Calvert, Bernie
  See Hollies, The
Calvert, Bob
  See Hawkwind
Calvert, Robert **30**
Camaro, Vivian
  See Lanternjack, The
Camel **21**
Camel, Abdul Ben
  See Lane, Fred
Cameron, Clayton
  See Ralph Sharon Quartet
Cameron, Dave "Tito"
  See Brave Combo
Cameron, Duncan
  See Sawyer Brown

Cameron, G. C.
  See Spinners, The
Cameron, Matt
  See Pearl Jam
  Also see Soundgarden
Cameron, Timothy
  See Silk
Camp, Greg
  See Smash Mouth
Campbell, Ali
  See UB40
Campbell, Eddie
  See Texas
Campbell, Glen **2**
Campbell, Isobel
  See Belle and Sebastian
Campbell, Kerry
  See War
Campbell, Luther **10**
Campbell, Martyn
  See Lightning Seeds
Campbell, Mike
  See Tom Petty and the Heartbreakers
Campbell, Phil
  See Motörhead
Campbell, Robin
  See UB40
Campbell, Sarah Elizabeth **23**
Campbell, Scott
  See Paladins, The
Campbell, Sterling
  See Duran Duran
Campbell, Tevin **13**
Campbell, Vivian
  See Def Leppard
Campeau, Don
  See Lettermen, The
Campi, Ray **44**
Cam'ron **39**
Can **28**
Canadian Brass, The **4**
Canavase, Matthias
  See Les Négresses Vertes
Candlebox **32**
Canler, Coz
  See Romantics, The
Cann, Warren
  See Ultravox
Canned Heat **44**
Cantrell, Blu **45**
Cantrell, Jerry
  See Alice in Chains
Canty, Brendan
  See Fugazi
Capaldi, Jim
  See Traffic
Capleton **40**
Cappadonna **43**
  Also see Wu-Tang Clan
Cappelli, Frank **14**
Cappos, Andy
  See Built to Spill
Capps, Bobby
  See .38 Special
Captain Beefheart and His Magic Band **26**
  Earlier sketch in CM **10**
Caravan **24**
Carbonara, Paul
  See Blondie
Card, Michael **40**
Cardew, Cornelius
  See AMM
Cardigans **19**
Cardwell, Joi **22**
Carey, Danny
  See Tool

Cavalera, Igor
  See Sepultura
Cavalera, Max
  See Sepultura
  Also see Soulfly
Cavanaugh, Frank
  See Filter
Cave, Nick 43
  Earlier sketch in CM 10
Cavoukian, Raffi
  See Raffi
Cazares, Dino
  See Fear Factory
Cease, Jeff
  See Black Crowes, The
Ceili Rain 34
Cervenka, Exene
  See X
Cesare, DJ
  See Stereo MC's
Cetera, Peter
  See Chicago
Chad, Dominic
  See Mansun
Chadbourne, Eugene 30
Chailly, Riccardo 35
Chainsaw Kittens, The 33
Chali 2na
  See Jurassic 5
Chamberlain, Jerry
  See Daniel Amos
Chamberlin, Jimmy
  See Smashing Pumpkins
Chambers, Guy
  See Waterboys, The
Chambers, Jimmy
  See Mercury Rev
Chambers, Kasey 36
Chambers, Martin
  See Pretenders, The
Chambers, Paul 18
Chambers, Terry
  See XTC
Champion, Eric 21
Champion, Will
  See Coldplay
Chan, Spencer
  See Aqua Velvets
Chance, David "Davinch"
  See Ruff Endz
Chance, Slim
  See Cramps, The
Chancellor, Justin
  See Tool
Chandler, Chas
  See Animals, The
Chandler, Gene 46
Chandler, Knox
  See Golden Palominos
Chandler, Tim
  See Daniel Amos
Chandra, Sheila 16
Chandrasonic
  See Asian Dub Foundation
Chaney, Jimmy
  See Jimmie's Chicken Shack
Chang, Han-Na 33
Chang, Sarah 7
Channing, Carol 6
Chanticleer 33
Chao, Manu 41
Chapin, Harry 6
Chapin, Tom 11
Chapin Carpenter, Mary 25
  Earlier sketch in CM 6
Chaplin, Nick
  See Slowdive

Chapman, Beth Nielsen 42
Chapman, Dave
  See Blue Aeroplanes, The
Chapman, Gary 33
Chapman, Steven Curtis 47
  Earlier sketch in CM 15
Chapman, Tony
  See Rolling Stones, The
Chapman, Tracy 20
  Earlier sketch in CM 4
Chaquico, Craig 23
  Also see Jefferson Starship
Charig, Marc
  See Brotherhood of Breath
  Also see Soft Machine
Charlatans, The 13
Charles, Gerry C. "Baby Gerry"
  See Full Force
Charles, Ray 24
  Earlier sketch in CM 1
Charles, Yolanda
  See Aztec Camera
Charm Farm 20
Charman, Shaun
  See Wedding Present, The
Charmichael, Chris
  See Ceili Rain
Chasez, Joshua Scott "JC"
  See 'N Sync
Chastain, Paul
  See Velvet Crush
Chater, Eos
  See Bond
Chater, Kerry
  See Gary Puckett and the Union Gap
Chatwood, Stuart
  See Tea Party
Chauncey, Danny
  See .38 Special
Chavis, Boozoo 38
Chayanne 44
Chea, Alvin "Vinnie"
  See Take 6
Cheap Trick 12
Cheatam, Aldolphus "Doc"
  See McKinney's Cotton Pickers
Checker, Chubby 7
Che Colovita, Lemon
  See Jimmie's Chicken Shack
Cheeks, Julius
  See Soul Stirrers, The
Chemical Brothers 20
Cheney, Chris
  See Living End, The
Cheng, Chi
  See Deftones
Chenier, C. J. 15
Chenier, Clifton 6
Chenille Sisters, The 16
Cher 35
  Earlier sketch in CM 1
  Also see Sonny and Cher
Cherise, Cyd
  See Lane, Fred
Cherish the Ladies 38
Cherone, Gary
  See Extreme
  Also see Van Halen
Cherry, Don 10
  Also see Codona
Cherry, Neneh 4
Cherry Poppin' Daddies 24
Chesney, Kenny 20
Chesnutt, Mark 13
Chesnutt, Vic 28
Chess, Leonard 24

Chesterman, Ron
  See Strawbs
Chesters, Eds D.
  See Bluetones, The
Chestnut, Cyrus 47
Cheung, Jacky 33
Chevalier, Dave
  See O.C. Supertones, The
Chevalier, Maurice 6
Chevelle 44
Chevron, Phillip
  See Pogues, The
Chew, Chris
  See North Mississippi Allstars
Chic 39
Chicago 3
Chicks on Speed 47
Chief Xcel
  See Blackalicious
Chieftains, The 36
  Earlier sketch in CM 7
Chiffons, The 43
Child, Desmond 30
Childish, Billy 28
Childress, Ross
  See Collective Soul
Childress Saxton, Shirley
  See Sweet Honey in the Rock
Childs, Euros
  See Gorky's Zygotic Mynci
Childs, Megan
  See Gorky's Zygotic Mynci
Childs, Toni 2
Chilton, Alex 10
  Also see Big Star
  Also see Box Tops, The
Chimes, Terry
  See Clash, The
Chin
  See Quickspace
Chin, Tony
  See Big Mountain
Chipperfield, Sheila
  See Elastica
Chisholm, Melanie
  See Spice Girls
Chopmaster J
  See Digital Underground
Chordettes, The 34
Choy, Nalani
  See Na Leo
Chris
  See Apples in Stereo
Chrisman, Andy
  See 4Him
Chrisman, Paul "Woody Paul"
  See Riders in the Sky
Christ, John
  See Danzig
Christian, Charlie 11
Christian Death 28
Christina, Fran
  See Fabulous Thunderbirds, The
  Also see Roomful of Blues
Christo, Guy-Manuel de Homem
  See Daft Punk
Chuck D
  See Public Enemy
Chud, Dr.
  See Misfits, The
Chud
  See Mudvayne
Chumbawamba 21
Chung, Kyung Wha 34
Chung, Mark
  See Einstürzende Neubauten
Church, Charlotte 28

Cole, David
 See C + C Music Factory
Cole, Freddy **35**
Cole, Holly **18**
Cole, Lloyd **9**
Cole, Nat King **3**
Cole, Natalie **21**
 Earlier sketch in CM **1**
Cole, Nate
 See Plus One
Cole, Paula **20**
Cole, Ralph
 See Nylons, The
Cole, Rich
 See Romantics, The
Coleman, Helen
 See Sweet Honey in the Rock
Coleman, Jaz
 See Killing Joke
Coleman, Kevin
 See Smash Mouth
Coleman, Michael
 See Seldom Scene, The
Coleman, Ornette **5**
Coles, Dennis
 See Ghostface Killah
Coletta, Kim
 See Jawbox
Colin, Charlie
 See Train
Collective Soul **16**
Collen, Phil
 See Def Leppard
Colletti, Dominic
 See Bevis Frond
Colley, Dana
 See Morphine
Collie, Mark **15**
Colligan, Michael
 See Flying Luttenbachers, The
Collingwood, Chris
 See Fountains of Wayne
Collins, Albert **19**
 Earlier sketch in CM **4**
Collins, Allen
 See Lynyrd Skynyrd
Collins, Bootsy **8**
 Also see Golden Palominos
Collins, Chris
 See Dream Theater
Collins, Edwyn **47**
Collins, John **39**
Collins, John
 See Powderfinger
Collins, Judy **4**
Collins, Mark
 See Charlatans, The
Collins, Max
 See Eve 6
Collins, Mel
 See Camel
 Also see King Crimson
Collins, Phil **20**
 Earlier sketch in CM **2**
 Also see Genesis
Collins, Rob
 See Charlatans, The
Collins, Sandra **41**
Collins, William
 See Collins, Bootsy
Collister, Christine **42**
Colomby, Bobby
 See Blood, Sweat and Tears
Colon, Willie **37**
Color Me Badd **23**
Colt, Johnny
 See Black Crowes, The

Colthart, Chris
 See Papas Fritas
Coltrane, John **4**
Colvin, Shawn **38**
 Earlier sketch in CM **11**
Colwell, David
 See Bad Company
Coma, Franche
 See Misfits, The
Combs, Gabe
 See Plus One
Combs, Sean "Puffy" **25**
 Earlier sketch in CM **16**
Comess, Aaron
 See Spin Doctors
Commander Cody
 See Commander Cody and His Lost
  Planet Airmen
Commander Cody and His Lost
 Planet Airmen **30**
Commodores, The **23**
Common **23**
Como, Perry **14**
Comparelli, Phil
 See 54-40
Compulsion **23**
Concrete Blonde **32**
Condo, Ray
 See Ray Condo and His Ricochets
Confederate Railroad **23**
Congo Norvell **22**
Conlon, James **44**
Conneff, Kevin
 See Chieftains, The
Connell, Andy
 See Swing Out Sister
Connelly, Chris
 See KMFDM
 Also see Pigface
Conner, Gary Lee
 See Screaming Trees
Conner, Van
 See Screaming Trees
Conner, William "Pete"
 See Swan Silvertones, The
Connick, Harry, Jr. **36**
 Earlier sketch in CM **4**
Conniff, Ray **37**
Connolly, Brian
 See Sweet
Connolly, Buddy
 See Ceili Rain
Connolly, Deirdre
 See Cherish the Ladies
Connolly, John
 See Sevendust
Connolly, Pat
 See Surfaris, The
Connor, Chris **30**
Connors, Clare
 See Spiritualized
Connors, Marc
 See Nylons, The
Connors, Norman **30**
Conrad, David
 See Black 47
Considine, Craig
 See Rumba Club
Conte, Bruce
 See Tower of Power
Conti, Neil
 See Prefab Sprout
Continental Drifters **39**
Convertino, John
 See Calexico
 Also see Giant Sand

Conway, Billy
 See Morphine
Conway, Dave
 See My Bloody Valentine
Conway, Gerry
 See Pentangle
Cooder, Ry **2**
 Also see Captain Beefheart and His Magic
 Band
Coogan, Mary
 See Cherish the Ladies
Cook, David Kyle
 See Matchbox 20
Cook, Frank
 See Canned Heat
Cook, Greg
 See Ricochet
Cook, Jeffrey Alan
 See Alabama
Cook, Jesse **33**
Cook, Mark
 See Daniel Amos
Cook, Murray
 See Wiggles, The
Cook, Paul
 See Sex Pistols, The
Cook, Steve
 See Soft Machine
Cook, Stuart
 See Creedence Clearwater Revival
Cook, Teddy
 See Great White
Cook, Wayne
 See Steppenwolf
Cooke, Mick
 See Belle and Sebastian
Cooke, Sam **1**
 Also see Soul Stirrers, The
Cool, Tre
 See Green Day
Cooley, Dave
 See Citizen King
Cooley, Mike
 See Drive-By Truckers
Cooley, Steve
 See Dillards, The
Coolidge, Rita **40**
Coolio **19**
Coombes, Gary
 See Supergrass
Coombes, Rod
 See Strawbs
Coomer, Ken
 See Uncle Tupelo
 Also see Wilco
Coomes, Sam
 See Quasi
Cooney, Rory **6**
Cooper, Alice **8**
Cooper, Jason
 See Cure, The
Cooper, Martin
 See Orchestral Manoeuvres in the Dark
Cooper, Michael
 See Third World
Cooper, Paul
 See Nylons, The
Cooper, Ralph
 See Air Supply
Coore, Stephen
 See Third World
Cope, Julian **16**
Copeland, Andrew
 See Sister Hazel
Copeland, Stewart **14**
 Also see Police, The
Copland, Aaron **2**

Cross, Tim
  See Sponge
Crosse, Clay 38
Crouch, Andraé 9
Crover, Dale
  See Melvins
Crow, Sheryl 40
  Earlier sketch in CM 18
Crowded House 12
Crowe, J. D. 5
Crowell, Rodney 8
Crowley, Martin
  See Bevis Frond
Cruikshank, Gregory
  See Tuxedomoon
Crump, Bruce
  See Molly Hatchet
Cruz, Anthony
  See AZ
Cruz, Celia 22
  Earlier sketch in CM 10
Crystal Method, The 35
Cua, Rick
  See Ceili Rain
Cuccurullo, Warren
  See Duran Duran
  Also see Missing Persons
Cuddy, Jim
  See Blue Rodeo
Cuevas, Alberto "Beto"
  See La Ley
Cuffee, Ed
  See McKinney's Cotton Pickers
Cugat, Xavier 23
Culbertson, Brian 40
Cullinan, Tom
  See Quickspace
Culp, Dennis
  See Five Iron Frenzy
Culp, Jennifer
  See Kronos Quartet, The
Cult, The 16
Culture Club 37
Culver, Joe
  See Bardo Pond
Cumming, Graham
  See Bevis Frond
Cummings, Burton
  See Guess Who
Cummings, Danny
  See Dire Straits
Cummings, David
  See Del Amitri
Cummings, John
  See Mogwai
Cummings, Mike "Spider One"
  See Powerman 5000
Cumplido, J. C.
  See La Ley
Cunniff, Jill
  See Luscious Jackson
Cunningham, Abe
  See Deftones
Cunningham, Bill
  See Box Tops, The
Cunningham, Blair
  See Echo and the Bunnymen
Cunningham, Johnny
  See Nightnoise
  Also see Silly Wizard
Cunningham, Phil
  See Silly Wizard
Cunningham, Ruth
  See Anonymous 4
Cuomo, Rivers
  See Weezer

Cure, The 20
  Earlier sketch in CM 3
Curiel, Marcos
  See P.O.D.
Curl, Langston
  See McKinney's Cotton Pickers
Curless, Ann
  See Exposé
Curley, John
  See Afghan Whigs
Curnin, Cy
  See Fixx, The
Curran, Ciaran
  See Altan
Curran, Doug
  See Lettermen, The
Currie, Alannah
  See Thompson Twins
Currie, Billy
  See Ultravox
Currie, Cherie
  See Runaways, The
Currie, Justin
  See Del Amitri
Currie, Kevin
  See Supertramp
Currie, Steve
  See T. Rex
Curry, Tim 3
Curtis, Barry
  See Kingsmen, The
Curtis, Catie 31
Curtis, Chris
  See Searchers, The
Curtis, Ian
  See Joy Division
Curtis, King 17
Curulewski, John
  See Styx
Curve 13
Custance, Mickey
  See Big Audio Dynamite
Cut Chemist
  See Jurassic 5
Cuthbert, Scott
  See Everclear
Cutler, Chris
  See Pere Ubu
Cypress Hill 11
Cyran, T.C.
  See Hot Club of Cowtown
Cyrus, Billy Ray 11
Czukay, Holger
  See Can
D Generation 26
Da Brat 30
D'abaldo, Chris
  See Saliva
Dachert, Peter
  See Tuxedomoon
Dacus, Donnie
  See Chicago
Dacus, Johnny
  See Osborne Brothers, The
Daddy G
  See Massive Attack
Daddy Mack
  See Kris Kross
Daellenbach, Charles
  See Canadian Brass, The
Daft Punk 33
Dahl, Jeff 28
Dahlgren, Erik
  See Wannadies, The
Dahlheimer, Patrick
  See Live

Daisley, Bob
  See Black Sabbath
  Also see Rainbow
Dalaras, George 40
Dale, Dick 13
Daley, Paul
  See Leftfield
Daley, Richard
  See Third World
Dall, Bobby
  See Poison
Dallin, Sarah
  See Bananarama
Dalton, John
  See Kinks, The
Dalton, Lacy J. 43
Dalton, Nic 31
  Also see Lemonheads, The
Daltrey, Roger 3
  Also see Who, The
Damiani, Victor
  See Cake
Dammers, Jerry
  See Specials, The
Damned, The 34
Damon and Naomi 25
Damone, Vic 33
D'Amour, Paul
  See Tool
Danbom, Scott
  See Slobberbone
Dando, Evan
  See Lemonheads, The
Dandy Warhols 22
Danell, Dennis
  See Social Distortion
D'Angelo 20
D'Angelo, Greg
  See Anthrax
Dangerous, Chris
  See Hives, The
Daniel, Britt
  See Spoon
Daniel, Casey
  See Seven Mary Three
Daniel Amos 44
Danielian, Barry
  See Tower of Power
Daniels, Charlie 6
Daniels, Jack
  See Highway 101
Daniels, Jerry
  See Ink Spots
Danko, Rick
  See Band, The
Danny Boy
  See House of Pain
Danze, William "Billy"
  See M.O.P.
Danzig 7
Danzig, Glenn
  See Danzig
  Also see Misfits, The
Dap, Bill The Kid
  See Lane, Fred
Dara, Olu 46
Darbone, Luderin
  See Hackberry Ramblers
D'Arby, Terence Trent 3
Darin, Bobby 4
Dark Star 29
D'Arko, Joe
  See Godsmack
Darling, David 34
Darling, Eric
  See Weavers, The

Del Tredici, David **35**
de Lucia, Paco **1**
Del Vikings, The **35**
DeMarcus, Jay
  See Rascal Flatts
DeMent, Iris **13**
Demeski, Stanley
  See Luna
De Meyer, Jean-Luc
  See Front 242
Deming, Michael
  See Pernice Brothers
DeMone, Gitane
  See Christian Death
Demos, Greg
  See Guided By Voices
Dempsey, Michael
  See Cure, The
Demsey, Travis
  See Living End, The
Denison, Duane
  See Jesus Lizard
Deniz, Claire
  See Strawbs
Dennis, Garth
  See Black Uhuru
Dennis, Rudolph "Garth"
  See Wailing Souls
Denny, Martin **44**
Denny, Sandy
  See Fairport Convention
  Also see Strawbs
Denov, Ernie
  See Liquid Soul
Densmore, John
  See Doors, The
Dent, Cedric
  See Take 6
Dente, Christine
  See Out of the Grey
Dente, Scott
  See Out of the Grey
Denton, Sandy
  See Salt-N-Pepa
d'Enton, Steve
  See Quickspace
Denver, John **22**
  Earlier sketch in CM **1**
De Oliveria, Laudir
  See Chicago
Depeche Mode **35**
  Earlier sketch in CM **5**
Depew, Don
  See Cobra Verde
de Prume, Ivan
  See White Zombie
Derailers, The **37**
Derakh, Amir
  See Orgy
Derhak, Rob
  See moe.
Derosier, Michael
  See Heart
Desaulniers, Stephen
  See Scud Mountain Boys
Desbrow, Audie
  See Great White
Deschamps, Kim
  See Blue Rodeo
Desert Rose Band, The **4**
DeShannon, Jackie **40**
Desjardins, Claude
  See Nylons, The
Desmond, Paul **23**
Des'ree **24**
  Earlier sketch in CM **15**
Destiny's Child **33**

Destri, Jimmy
  See Blondie
Detar, Brett
  See Juliana Theory, The
Dettman, John
  See Swell
Dettmar, Del
  See Hawkwind
Deupree, Jerome
  See Morphine
Deurloo, Hermine
  See Willem Breuker Kollektief
Deutrom, Mark
  See Melvins
Deutsch, Stu
  See Wendy O. Williams and The Plasmatics
DeVille, C. C.
  See Poison
Devito, Nick
  See Four Seasons, The
Devito, Tommy
  See Four Seasons, The
Devlin, Adam P.
  See Bluetones, The
Devo **13**
Devoto, Howard
  See Buzzcocks, The
Dewees, James
  See Get Up Kids
DeWitt, Lew C.
  See Statler Brothers, The
Dexter X
  See Man or Astroman?
Dexy's Midnight Runners **46**
DeYoung, Dennis
  See Styx
de Young, Joyce
  See Andrews Sisters, The
Diagram, Andy
  See James
Diallo, Medoune
  See Orchestra Baobab
Diamond, "Dimebag" Darrell
  See Pantera
Diamond, Mike "Mike D"
  See Beastie Boys, The
Diamond, Neil **1**
Diamond Rio **35**
  Earlier sketch in CM **11**
Di'anno, Paul
  See Iron Maiden
Diaz, Tim
  See Robert Bradley's Blackwater Surprise
Dibango, Manu **14**
Dick, Bob
  See Front Range
Dick, Coby
  See Papa Roach
Dick, Magic
  See J. Geils Band
Dickaty, Raymond
  See Spiritualized
Dickens, Hazel **35**
Dickens, Little Jimmy **7**
Dickerson, B.B.
  See War
Dickerson, Deke **44**
Dickerson, Lance
  See Commander Cody and His Lost
    Planet Airmen
Dickinson, Cody
  See North Mississippi Allstars
Dickinson, Luther
  See North Mississippi Allstars
Dickinson, Paul Bruce
  See Iron Maiden

Dickinson, Rob
  See Catherine Wheel
Diddley, Bo **3**
Didier, Daniel
  See Promise Ring, The
Dido **46**
Dieckmeyer, Marty
  See Daniel Amos
Dieng, Ndiouga
  See Orchestra Baobab
Dierksen, Uwe
  See Ensemble Modern
Diermaier, Werner
  See Faust
Dietrich, Marlene **25**
Dif, René
  See Aqua
Diffie, Joe **27**
  Earlier sketch in CM **10**
Difford, Chris
  See Squeeze
di Fiore, Vince
  See Cake
DiFranco, Ani **43**
  Earlier sketch in CM **17**
Digable Planets **15**
Diggle, Steve
  See Buzzcocks, The
Diggs, Robert "RZA" (Prince Rakeem)
  See Gravediggaz
  Also see Wu-Tang Clan
Digital Underground **9**
Digweed, John **44**
Dillard, Doug
  See Dillards, The
Dillard, Rodney
  See Dillards, The
Dillards, The **45**
Dilling, Steve
  See IIIrd Tyme Out
Dillon, James
  See Caustic Resin
  Also see Built to Spill
Dillon, Jerome
  See Nine Inch Nails
Dilworth, Joe
  See Stereolab
DiMambro, "Angry" John
  See Down By Law
DiMant, Leor
  See House of Pain
Di Meola, Al **12**
Dimitri from Paris **43**
DiMucci, Dion
  See Dion
Dinger, Klaus
  See Neu!
DiNizo, Pat
  See Smithereens, The
Dinning, Dean
  See Toad the Wet Sprocket
Dinosaur Jr. **10**
Dio, Ronnie James
  See Black Sabbath
  Also see Rainbow
Dion **4**
Dion, Celine **25**
  Earlier sketch in CM **12**
Diop, Massamba
  See Afro Celt Sound System
Dire Straits **22**
Dirks, Michael
  See Gwar
Dirnt, Mike
  See Green Day
Dirty Dozen Brass Band **23**
Dirty Three **31**

Driscoll, Gary
  See Rainbow
Driscoll, Phil **45**
Drive-By Truckers **45**
D'Rivera, Paquito **46**
Drivin' N' Cryin' **31**
Droge, Pete **24**
Dropkick Murphys **26**
Drozd, Stephen
  See Flaming Lips
Dru Hill **25**
Drucker, Eugene
  See Emerson String Quartet
Drumbago
  See Skatalites, The
Drumdini, Harry
  See Cramps, The
Drummond, Don
  See Skatalites, The
Drummond, Tom
  See Better Than Ezra
Dryden, Spencer
  See Jefferson Airplane
Dryden, Tim
  See Grandaddy
Dryer, Debroah
  See Skunk Anansie
Dubbe, Berend
  See Bettie Serveert
Dube, Lucky **17**
Dubeau, Angèle **47**
Dubstar **22**
Duce, Adam
  See Machine Head
Dudley, Anne
  See Art of Noise
Duenas, Fain
  See Radio Tarifa
Dufay, Rick
  See Aerosmith
Duffey, John
  See Country Gentlemen, The
  Also see Seldom Scene, The
Duffy, Billy
  See Cult, The
Duffy, Keith
  See Boyzone
Duffy, Martin
  See Primal Scream
Dufresne, Mark
  See Confederate Railroad
Duggan, Noel
  See Clannad
Duggan, Paidraig
  See Clannad
Duhon, Edwin
  See Hackberry Ramblers
Duke, John
  See Pearls Before Swine
Dukowski, Chuck
  See Black Flag
Dulfer, Candy **35**
Dulli, Greg
  See Afghan Whigs
Dumont, Tom
  See No Doubt
Dunbar, Aynsley
  See Jefferson Starship
  Also see Journey
  Also see Whitesnake
Dunbar, Sly
  See Sly and Robbie
  Also see Black Uhuru
Duncan, Bryan **19**
Duncan, Gary
  See Quicksilver Messenger Service

Duncan, Malcolm "Molly"
  See Average White Band
Duncan, Steve
  See Desert Rose Band, The
Duncan, Stuart
  See Nashville Bluegrass Band
Dunckel, Jean-Benoit
  See Air
Dunham, Nathanel "Brad"
  See Five Iron Frenzy
Dunlap, Slim
  See Replacements, The
Dunlop, Andy
  See Travis
Dunn, Donald "Duck"
  See Booker T. & the M.G.'s
Dunn, Holly **7**
Dunn, Larry
  See Earth, Wind and Fire
Dunn, Ronnie Gene
  See Brooks & Dunn
Dunne, Brian
  See Average White Band
Dunning, A.J.
  See Verve Pipe, The
Dunning, Brian
  See Nightnoise
DuPré, Jacqueline **26**
Dupree, Champion Jack **12**
Dupree, Jesse James
  See Jackyl
Dupri, Jermaine **25**
Duque, Alejandro
  See Aterciopelados
Dural, Stanley Jr.
  See Buckwheat Zydeco
Duran Duran **45**
  Earlier sketch in CM **4**
Durante, Mark
  See KMFDM
Duritz, Adam
  See Counting Crows
Durrill, Johnny
  See Ventures, The
Durst, Fred
  See Limp Bizkit
Durutti Column, The **30**
Dury, Ian **30**
Dust Brothers **32**
Dusty, Slim **39**
Dutt, Hank
  See Kronos Quartet, The
Dutton, Garrett
  See G. Love
Dutton, Lawrence
  See Emerson String Quartet
Dvorak, Antonin **25**
Dyble, Judy
  See Fairport Convention
Dylan, Bob **21**
  Earlier sketch in CM **3**
Dylan, Jakob
  See Wallflowers, The
Dyrason, Orri Páll
  See Sigur Rós
E., Sheila
  See Sheila E.
Eacrett, Chris
  See Our Lady Peace
Eaglen, Jane **36**
Eagles, The **46**
  Earlier sketch in CM **3**
Eaglestone, Robin
  See Cradle of Filth
Earl, Roger
  See Foghat

Earl, Ronnie **5**
  Also see Roomful of Blues
Earle, Steve **43**
  Earlier sketch in CM **16**
Early, Ian
  See Cherry Poppin' Daddies
Earth, Wind and Fire **12**
Eartha **44**
Easton, Elliot
  See Cars, The
Easton, Lynn
  See Kingsmen, The
Easton, Sheena **2**
Eazy-E **13**
  Also see N.W.A.
Ebright, Randy
  See Molotov
Echeverri, Andrea
  See Aterciopelados
Echeverria, Rob
  See Helmet
Echo and the Bunnymen **32**
Echobelly **21**
Echols, John
  See Love
Ecker, Haylie
  See Bond
Eckstine, Billy **1**
Ed, John
  See Monster Magnet
Eddy, Chris
  See Ceili Rain
Eddy, Duane **9**
Eden, Sean
  See Luna
Eder, Linda **30**
Edge, Graeme
  See Moody Blues, The
Edge, The
  See U2
Edison, Harry "Sweets" **29**
Edmonds, Kenneth "Babyface" **12**
Edmonds, Lu
  See Damned, The
Edmonton, Jerry
  See Steppenwolf
Edmunds, Dave **28**
Edson, Richard
  See Sonic Youth
Edward, Scott
  See Bluetones, The
Edwards, Bernard
  See Chic
Edwards, Dennis
  See Temptations, The
Edwards, Edgar
  See Spinners, The
Edwards, Gordon
  See Kinks, The
  Also see Pretty Things, The
Edwards, Johnny
  See Foreigner
Edwards, John
  See Spinners, The
Edwards, John
  See Status Quo
Edwards, Leroy "Lion"
  See Mystic Revealers
Edwards, Mark
  See Aztec Camera
Edwards, Michael James
  See Jesus Jones
Edwards, Mike
  See Electric Light Orchestra
Edwards, Nokie
  See Ventures, The

Fogerty, Thomas
See Creedence Clearwater Revival
Foghat **45**
Folds, Ben
See Ben Folds Five
Foley
See Arrested Development
Folk Implosion, The **28**
Fonseca, Celso **47**
Fontana, Carl **47**
Foo Fighters **20**
Foote, Dick
See Lane, Fred
Forbes, Derek
See Simple Minds
Forbes, Graham
See Incredible String Band
Ford, Frankie
See Pretty Things, The
Ford, John
See Strawbs
Ford, Lita **9**
Also see Runaways, The
Ford, Marc
See Black Crowes, The
Ford, Maya
See Donnas, The
Ford, Mike
See Moxy Früvous
Ford, Penny
See Soul II Soul
Ford, Robert "Peg"
See Golden Gate Quartet
Ford, T-Model **41**
Ford, Tennessee Ernie **3**
Forde, Brinsley "Dan"
See Aswad
Fordham, Julia **15**
Foreigner **21**
Foreman, Chris
See Madness
Forrester, Alan
See Mojave 3
Forsi, Ken
See Surfaris, The
Forster, Robert
See Go-Betweens, The
Forte, Juan
See Oakland Interfaith Gospel Choir
Fortune, Jimmy
See Statler Brothers, The
Fortus, Richard
See Love Spit Love
Fossen, Steve
See Heart
Foss-Rose, Rayna
See Coal Chamber
Foster, David **13**
Foster, Malcolm
See Pretenders, The
Foster, Murray
See Moxy Früvous
Foster, Paul
See Soul Stirrers, The
Foster, Radney **16**
Foster, Willie **36**
Fountain, Clarence
See Five Blind Boys of Alabama
Fountain, Pete **7**
Fountains of Wayne **26**
4Him **23**
Four Lads, The **41**
Four Seasons, The **24**
Four Tops, The **11**
Fowler, Bruce "Fossil Fowler"
See Captain Beefheart and His Magic Band

Fowler, Buren
See Drivin' N' Cryin'
Fowlkes, Jeff
See Robert Bradley's Blackwater Surprise
Fox, Jackie
See Runaways, The
Fox, Ken
See Jason & the Scorchers
Fox, Lucas
See Motörhead
Fox, Oz
See Stryper
Fox, Samantha **3**
Foxton, Bruce
See Jam, The
Foxwell Baker, Iain Richard
See Jesus Jones
Foxx, John
See Ultravox
Foxx, Leigh
See Blondie
Fraiture, Nikolai
See Strokes, The
Frame, Roddy
See Aztec Camera
Frampton, Peter **3**
Also see Humble Pie
Francis, Barrington
See Saints, The
Francis, Black
See Black, Frank
Francis, Connie **10**
Francis, David "Panama" **37**
Francis, Michael
See Asleep at the Wheel
Franco **39**
Francolini, Dave
See Dark Star
Franey, Ian
See 54-40
Franke, Chris
See Tangerine Dream
Frankenstein, Jeff
See Newsboys, The
Frankie Goes to Hollywood **31**
Frankie Lymon and The Teenagers **24**
Franklin, Adam
See Swervedriver
Franklin, Aretha **17**
Earlier sketch in CM **2**
Franklin, Elmo
See Mighty Clouds of Joy, The
Franklin, Farrah
See Destiny's Child
Franklin, Kirk **22**
Franklin, Larry
See Asleep at the Wheel
Franklin, Melvin
See Temptations, The
Franti, Michael **16**
Also see Spearhead
Frantz, Chris
See Gorillaz
Also see Talking Heads
Fraser, Andy
See Free
Fraser, Elizabeth
See Cocteau Twins, The
Frater, Shaun
See Fairport Convention
Frazier, Keith "Bass Drum Shorty"
See Rebirth Brass Band
Frazier, Philip
See Rebirth Brass Band
Frazier, Stan
See Sugar Ray

Frederic, Dreux "Li'l Fizz"
See B2K
Frederiksen, Lars
See Rancid
Fredriksson, Marie
See Roxette
Free **44**
Freed, Alan **36**
Freed, Audley
See Black Crowes, The
Freel, David
See Swell
Freeman, Aaron
See Ween
Freeman, Matt
See Rancid
Freeman, Russ
See Rippingtons
Freese, Josh
See Suicidal Tendencies
Also see 3 Doors Down
Frehley, Ace
See Kiss
Freiberg, David
See Jefferson Starship
Also see Quicksilver Messenger Service
Fremerman, Elana
See Hot Club of Cowtown
French, Frank
See Cake
French, John "Drumbo"
See Captain Beefheart and His Magic Band
French, Mark
See Blue Rodeo
Frenett, John
See Laika
Frenette, Matthew
See Loverboy
Freni, Mirella **14**
Fresh, Mannie
See Big Tymers, The
Freshwater, John
See Alien Sex Fiend
Frey, Glenn **3**
Also see Eagles, The
Fricke, Janie **33**
Fricker, Sylvia
See Ian and Sylvia
Fridmann, Dave
See Mercury Rev
Friedman, Kinky **35**
Friedman, Marty
See Megadeth
Friel, Tony
See Fall, The
Friend, Eric
See Spoon
Friesen, David **41**
Fripp, Robert **9**
Also see King Crimson
Frischmann, Justine Elinor
See Elastica
Also see Suede
Frisell, Bill **15**
Frith, Fred **19**
Also see Golden Palominos
Fritzsche, Chris
See Chanticleer
Frizzell, Lefty **10**
Frobusch, Nichole
See Mediaeval Baebes
Froese, Edgar
See Tangerine Dream
Froggatt, Thomas
See VAST
Frogs, The **31**
Fröhlich, Frank **32**

Gay, Marc
　　See Shai
Gayden, Mac
　　See Pearls Before Swine
Gaye, Angus "Drummie Zeb"
　　See Aswad
Gaye, Marvin **4**
Gayle, Charles **35**
Gayle, Crystal **1**
Gaynor, Adam
　　See Matchbox 20
Gaynor, Gloria **36**
Gaynor, Mel
　　See Simple Minds
Gayol, Rafael "Danny"
　　See BoDeans
Geary, Paul
　　See Extreme
Geddes, Chris
　　See Belle and Sebastian
Gedge, David
　　See Wedding Present, The
Gee, Rosko
　　See Can
　　Also see Traffic
Geffen, David **8**
Geils, J.
　　See J. Geils Band
Gelb, Howe
　　See Giant Sand
Geldof, Bob **9**
Gendel, Keith
　　See Papas Fritas
Gene Loves Jezebel **27**
Genensky, Marsha
　　See Anonymous 4
Genesis **4**
Genn, Dave
　　See Matthew Good Band
Gentling, Matt
　　See Archers of Loaf
Gentry, Bobbie **46**
Gentry, Teddy Wayne
　　See Alabama
Gentry, Troy
　　See Montgomery Gentry
George, Boy
　　See Culture Club
George, Brian "B-Fine"
　　See Full Force
George, Jr., Lucien "Bow-Legged Lou"
　　See Full Force
George, Lowell
　　See Little Feat
George, Paul Anthony
　　See Full Force
George, Rocky
　　See Suicidal Tendencies
George, Stephen
　　See Swervedriver
Georges, Bernard
　　See Throwing Muses
Georgiev, Ivan
　　See Tuxedomoon
Geraldine Fibbers **21**
Gerber, Scott
　　See Giant Sand
Gerhard-García, Alexandra **41**
Germano, Lisa **18**
Gerrard, Lisa
　　See Dead Can Dance
Gerrard, Vic
　　See Derailers, The
Gershwin, George and Ira **11**
Gessle, Per
　　See Roxette
Get Up Kids **41**

Geto Boys, The **11**
Getz, Stan **12**
Gheorghiu, Angela **38**
Ghomeshi, Jian
　　See Moxy Früvous
Ghost **24**
Ghostface Killah **33**
　　Also see Wu-Tang Clan
Giammalvo, Chris
　　See Madder Rose
Gianni, Angelo
　　See Treadmill Trackstar
Giant Sand **30**
Gibb, Barry
　　See Bee Gees, The
Gibb, Maurice
　　See Bee Gees, The
Gibb, Robin
　　See Bee Gees, The
Gibbins, Mike
　　See Badfinger
Gibbons, Beth
　　See Portishead
Gibbons, Billy
　　See ZZ Top
Gibbons, Ian
　　See Kinks, The
Gibbons, John
　　See Bardo Pond
Gibbons, Michael
　　See Bardo Pond
Gibbs, Rich
　　See Oingo Boingo
Gibbs, Terry **35**
Giblin, John
　　See Simple Minds
Gibson, Bob **23**
Gibson, Debbie
　　See Gibson, Deborah
Gibson, Deborah **24**
　　Earlier sketch in CM 1
Gibson, Wilf
　　See Electric Light Orchestra
Gifford, Alex
　　See Propellerheads
　　Also see Electric Light Orchestra
Gifford, Katharine
　　See Stereolab
Gifford, Peter
　　See Midnight Oil
Gift, Roland **3**
　　Also see Fine Young Cannibals
Gift of Gab
　　See Blackalicious
Gil, Gilberto **26**
Gilbert, Bruce
　　See Wire
Gilbert, Gillian
　　See New Order
Gilbert, John
　　See Rebirth Brass Band
Gilbert, Nick
　　See Felt
Gilbert, Nicole Nicci
　　See Brownstone
Gilbert, Ronnie
　　See Weavers, The
Gilbert, Simon
　　See Suede
Gilberto, Astrud **44**
Gilberto, João **33**
Gilchrist, Chad
　　See His Name Is Alive
Giles, Michael
　　See King Crimson
Gilkinson, Jeff
　　See Dillards, The

Gilkyson, Tony
　　See X
Gill, Andy
　　See Gang of Four
Gill, George
　　See Wire
Gill, Janis
　　See Sweethearts of the Rodeo
Gill, Johnny **20**
Gill, Ped
　　See Frankie Goes To Hollywood
Gill, Pete
　　See Motörhead
Gill, Vince **34**
　　Earlier sketch in CM **7**
Gillan, Ian
　　See Deep Purple
　　Also see Black Sabbath
Gillard, Doug
　　See Cobra Verde
Gillespie, Bobby
　　See Jesus and Mary Chain, The
　　Also see Primal Scream
Gillespie, Dizzy **6**
Gillette, Mic
　　See Tower of Power
Gilley, Mickey **7**
Gillies, Ben
　　See Silverchair
Gillingham, Charles
　　See Counting Crows
Gillis, Steve
　　See Filter
Gilman, Billy **34**
Gilmore, Jimmie Dale **11**
　　Also see Flatlanders, The
Gilmore, Mike
　　See Northwoods Improvisers
Gilmore, Skillet
　　See Whiskeytown
Gilmour, David
　　See Pink Floyd
Gilvear, Marcus
　　See Gene Loves Jezebel
Gin Blossoms **18**
Gingold, Josef **6**
Ginn, Greg
　　See Black Flag
Ginsberg, Allen **26**
Ginuwine **34**
Gioia
　　See Exposé
Gipp, Cameron "Big Gipp"
　　See Goodie Mob
Gipson, Barney
　　See Dixie Hummingbirds, The
Gipsy Kings, The **8**
Giraldo, Andres
　　See Aterciopelados
Giraudy, Miquette
　　See Gong
Girls Against Boys **31**
Gittleman, Joe
　　See Mighty Mighty Bosstones
Glabicki, Michael
　　See Rusted Root
Glamorre, Matthew
　　See Minty
Glascock, John
　　See Jethro Tull
Glaser, Gabby
　　See Luscious Jackson
Glass, Daniel
　　See Royal Crown Revue
Glass, David
　　See Christian Death

Gray, David **30**
Gray, Del
  See Little Texas
Gray, Doug
  See Marshall Tucker Band
Gray, Eddie
  See Tommy James and the Shondells
Gray, Ella
  See Kronos Quartet
Gray, Ellen
  See Two Dollar Pistols
Gray, F. Gary **19**
Gray, James
  See Blue Rodeo
Gray, Luther
  See Tsunami
Gray, Macy **32**
Gray, Paul
  See Slipknot
Gray, Tom
  See Country Gentlemen, The
  Also see Seldom Scene, The
Gray, Walter
  See Kronos Quartet
Gray, Wardell
  See McKinney's Cotton Pickers
Great Big Sea **45**
Great White **44**
Greater Vision **26**
Grebenshikov, Boris **3**
Grech, Rick
  See Traffic
Greco, Paul
  See Chumbawamba
Greco, Ron
  See Flamin' Groovies
Green, Al **9**
Green, Benny **17**
Green, Carlito "Cee-lo"
  See Goodie Mob
Green, Charles
  See War
Green, David
  See Air Supply
Green, Douglas "Ranger Doug"
  See Riders in the Sky
Green, Gardner Ray
  See Rebirth Brass Band
Green, Grant **14**
Green, James
  See Dru Hill
Green, Jeremiah
  See Modest Mouse
Green, Keith **38**
Green, Peter
  See Fleetwood Mac
Green, Susaye
  See Supremes, The
Green, Urbie **36**
Green, Willie
  See Neville Brothers, The
Green Day **40**
  Earlier sketch in CM **16**
Greenall, Rupert
  See Fixx, The
Greene, Karl Anthony
  See Herman's Hermits
Greenfield, Dave
  See Stranglers, The
Greenhalgh, Tom
  See Mekons, The
Greensmith, Domenic
  See Reef
Greenspoon, Jimmy
  See Three Dog Night
Greentree, Richard
  See Beta Band, The

Greenway, Brian
  See April Wine
Greenwood, Al
  See Foreigner
Greenwood, Colin
  See Radiohead
Greenwood, Gail
  See Belly
Greenwood, Jonny
  See Radiohead
Greenwood, Lee **12**
Greer, Jim
  See Guided By Voices
Gregg, Dave
  See D.O.A.
Gregg, Paul
  See Restless Heart
Gregory, Bryan
  See Cramps, The
Gregory, Dave
  See XTC
Gregory, Gerald
  See Spaniels, The
Gregory, Keith
  See Wedding Present, The
Gregory, Troy
  See Prong
Greller, Al
  See Yo La Tengo
Grey, Charles Wallace
  See Aquabats, The
Grice, Gary "The Genius"
  See Wu-Tang Clan
Griffin, A.C. "Eddie"
  See Golden Gate Quartet
Griffin, Bob
  See BoDeans, The
Griffin, Dale "Buffin"
  See Mott the Hoople
Griffin, Gus
  See Paladins, The
Griffin, James
  See Bread
Griffin, Kevin
  See Better Than Ezra
  Also see NRBQ
Griffin, Mark
  See MC 900 Ft. Jesus
Griffin, Patty **24**
Griffin, Rodney
  See Greater Vision
Griffith, John Thomas
  See Cowboy Mouth
Griffith, Johnny
  See Funk Brothers
Griffith, Nanci **3**
Griffiths, Donald "Benjamin"
  See Aswad
Griffiths, Marcia **45**
Griffiths, Martin
  See Hawkwind
Grigg, Chris
  See Treadmill Trackstar
Griggs, Andy **40**
Grillo, Carmen
  See Tower of Power
Grimaud, Hélène **35**
Grisman, David **17**
Groban, Josh **47**
Grohl, Dave
  See Foo Fighters
  Also see Nirvana
Grondin, Jack
  See .38 Special
Groove Armada **39**
Grossman, Rick
  See Hoodoo Gurus

Grotberg, Karen
  See Jayhawks, The
Grothman, Steve
  See Whiskeytown
Groucutt, Kelly
  See Electric Light Orchestra
Grove, George
  See Kingston Trio, The
Grover, Charlie
  See Sponge
Growcott, Andy
  See Dexy's Midnight Runners
Gruber, Craig
  See Rainbow
Grundler, James
  See Paloalto
Grundy, Hugh
  See Zombies, The
Grusin, Dave **7**
Guaraldi, Vince **3**
Guard, Dave
  See Kingston Trio, The
Gubaidulina, Sofia **39**
Gudmundsdottir, Björk
  See Björk
  Also see Sugarcubes, The
Güereña, Luis
  See Tijuana No!
Guerin, John
  See Byrds, The
Guess Who **23**
Guest, Christopher
  See Spinal Tap
Guetig, K.C.
  See My Morning Jacket
Guided By Voices **18**
Gun, John
  See X-Ray Spex
Gunn, Nicholas **39**
Gunn, Trey
  See King Crimson
Gunning, John Francis
  See Country Joe and the Fish
Guns n' Roses **2**
Gunther, Cornell
  See Coasters, The
Gunther, Ric
  See Bevis Frond
Gurewitz, Brett
  See Bad Religion
Gurtu, Trilok **29**
  Also see Oregon
Guru
  See Gang Starr
Gus Gus **26**
Guss, Randy
  See Toad the Wet Sprocket
Gustafson, John
  See Roxy Music
Gustafson, Steve
  See 10,000 Maniacs
Guster **29**
Gut, Grudrun
  See Einstürzende Neubauten
Guthrie, Arlo **6**
Guthrie, Gwen **26**
Guthrie, Robin
  See Cocteau Twins, The
Guthrie, Woody **2**
Guttermouth **39**
Guug
  See Mudvayne
Guy, Billy
  See Coasters, The
Guy, Buddy **4**
Guy, Geordie
  See Killing Joke

Harper, Tony
  See Slobberbone
Harrell, Andre **16**
Harrell, Lynn **3**
Harrell, Todd
  See 3 Doors Down
Harrell, Tom **28**
Harrington, Ayodele
  See Sweet Honey in the Rock
Harrington, Carrie
  See Sounds of Blackness
Harrington, David
  See Kronos Quartet, The
Harris, Addie "Micki"
  See Shirelles, The
Harris, Barry **32**
Harris, Bill
  See Clovers, The
Harris, Corey **41**
Harris, Damon Otis
  See Temptations, The
Harris, Eddie **15**
Harris, Emmylou **36**
  Earlier sketch in CM **4**
Harris, Eric
  See Olivia Tremor Control
Harris, Evelyn Maria
  See Sweet Honey in the Rock
Harris, Gerard
  See Kool & the Gang
Harris, James
  See Echobelly
Harris, Jason "Moose"
  See New Model Army
Harris, Jason
  See Damned, The
Harris, Jeff
  See Big Bad Voodoo Daddy
Harris, Jesse **47**
Harris, Jet
  See Shadows, The
Harris, Jody
  See Golden Palominos
Harris, Joey
  See Beat Farmers
Harris, Kevin
  See Dirty Dozen Brass Band
Harris, Lee
  See Talk Talk
Harris, Mark
  See 4Him
Harris, Mary
  See Spearhead
Harris, Nigel
  See Jam, The
Harris, R. H.
  See Soul Stirrers, The
Harris, Shawntae
  See Da Brat
Harris, Steve
  See Iron Maiden
Harris, Teddy **22**
Harrison, George **2**
  Also see Beatles, The
Harrison, Jerry
  See Talking Heads
Harrison, John
  See Hawkwind
Harrison, Nigel
  See Blondie
Harrison, Richard
  See Stereolab
Harry, Deborah **4**
  Also see Blondie
Harry, Neil
  See Giant Sand

Harsh, Eddie
  See Black Crowes, The
Hart, Alvin Youngblood **27**
Hart, Beth **29**
Hart, Chuck
  See Surfin' Pluto
Hart, Douglas
  See Jesus and Mary Chain, The
Hart, Emerson
  See Tonic
Hart, Grant
  See Hüsker Dü
Hart, Hattie
  See Memphis Jug Band
Hart, Lorenz
  See Rodgers, Richard
Hart, Mark
  See Crowded House
Hart, Mickey **39**
  Also see Grateful Dead, The
Hart, Robert
  See Bad Company
Hart, Tim
  See Steeleye Span
Hart, William Cullen
  See Olivia Tremor Control
Hartford, John **37**
  Earlier sketch in CM **1**
Hartgrove, Mike
  See IIIrd Tyme Out
Hartke, Stephen **5**
Hartley, Matthieu
  See Cure, The
Hartman, Bob
  See Petra
Hartman, Dave
  See Southern Culture on the Skids
Hartman, John
  See Doobie Brothers, The
Hartnoll, Paul
  See Orbital
Hartnoll, Phil
  See Orbital
Hartridge, Jimmy
  See Swervedriver
Harvey, Bernard "Touter"
  See Inner Circle
Harvey, PJ **43**
  Earlier sketch in CM **11**
Harvey, Philip "Daddae"
  See Soul II Soul
Harvey, Polly Jean
  See Harvey, PJ
Harvie, Iain
  See Del Amitri
Harwell, Steve
  See Smash Mouth
Harwood, Justin
  See Luna
Haseltine, Dan
  See Jars of Clay
Hashian
  See Boston
Haskell, Gordon
  See King Crimson
Haskins, Kevin
  See Bauhaus
  Also see Love and Rockets
Haslinger, Paul
  See Tangerine Dream
Haslip, Jimmy
  See Yellowjackets
Hassan, Norman
  See UB40
Hasselhoff, Evil "Jared"
  See Bloodhound Gang, The
Hassell, Jon **43**

Hassilev, Alex
  See Limeliters, The
Hassman, Nikki
  See Avalon
Hastings, Jimmy
  See Caravan
Hastings, Pye
  See Caravan
Hatch, Kerry
  See Oingo Boingo
Hatfield, Juliana **37**
  Earlier sketch in CM **12**
  Also see Lemonheads, The
Hathaway, Donny **42**
Hathaway, Jane
  See Lane, Fred
Hathaway, Richard
  See Nitty Gritty Dirt Band, The
Hatherley, Charlotte
  See Ash
Hatori, Miho
  See Cibo Matto
  Also see Gorillaz
Haug, Ian
  See Powderfinger
Hauser, Tim
  See Manhattan Transfer, The
Havens, Richie **11**
Haveron, Andrew
  See Brodsky Quartet
Hawes, Dave
  See Catherine Wheel
Hawken, John
  See Strawbs
Hawkes, Greg
  See Cars, The
Hawkins, Coleman **11**
Hawkins, Dale **45**
Hawkins, Derrek
  See Stabbing Westward
Hawkins, Erskine **19**
Hawkins, Hoyt
  See Jordanaires, The
Hawkins, Lamont "U-God"
  See Wu-Tang Clan
Hawkins, Nick
  See Big Audio Dynamite
Hawkins, Richard (Dick)
  See Gene Loves Jezebel
Hawkins, Roger
  See Traffic
Hawkins, Ronnie **36**
Hawkins, Screamin' Jay **29**
  Earlier sketch in CM **8**
Hawkins, Sophie B. **21**
Hawkins, Taylor
  See Foo Fighters
Hawkins, Tramaine **17**
Hawkins, Xian
  See Silver Apples
Hawkwind **41**
Hawtin, Richie **45**
Hay, Colin
  See Men at Work
Hay, George D. **3**
Hay, Ivor
  See Saints, The
Hay, Roy
  See Culture Club
Hayden, Victor "The Mascara Snake"
  See Captain Beefheart and His Magic Band
Haydn, Lili **46**
Haydock, Eric
  See Hollies, The
Haye, George "Buddy"
  See Wailing Souls

Hidalgo, David
  See Los Lobos
Hield, Nehemiah
  See Baha Men
Hield, Omerit
  See Baha Men
Higgins, Billy **35**
Higgins, Terence
  See Dirty Dozen Brass Band
Highway 101 **4**
Hijbert, Fritz
  See Kraftwerk
Hilah
  See Boredoms, The
Hill, Andrew **41**
Hill, Brendan
  See Blues Traveler
Hill, Brian "Beezer"
  See Frogs, The
Hill, Dave
  See Cobra Verde
Hill, Dusty
  See ZZ Top
Hill, Faith **18**
Hill, Ian
  See Judas Priest
Hill, John
  See Apples in Stereo
Hill, Kim
  See Black Eyed Peas
Hill, Lauryn **25**
  Also see Fugees, The
Hill, Michael
  See Slobberbone
Hill, Scott
  See Fu Manchu
Hill, Stuart
  See Shudder to Think
Hillage, Steve
  See Orb, The
  Also see Gong
Hillier, Steve
  See Dubstar
Hillman, Bones
  See Midnight Oil
Hillman, Chris
  See Byrds, The
  Also see Desert Rose Band, The
  Also see Flying Burrito Brothers
Hilton, Eric
  See Thievery Corporation
Hinderas, Natalie **12**
Hinds, David
  See Steel Pulse
Hines, Earl "Fatha" **12**
Hines, Gary
  See Sounds of Blackness
Hinojos, Paul
  See At The Drive-In
Hinojosa, Tish **44**
  Earlier sketch in CM **13**
Hinton, Milt **33**
Hirsh, Chicken
  See Country Joe and the Fish
Hirst, Rob
  See Midnight Oil
Hirt, Al **5**
His Name Is Alive **43**
Hitchcock, Robyn **9**
Hitchcock, Russell
  See Air Supply
Hite, Bob
  See Canned Heat
Hitt, Bryan
  See REO Speedwagon
Hives, The **44**

Hlubek, Dave
  See Molly Hatchet
Hobson, Motor
  See Lane, Fred
Hodge, Alex
  See Platters, The
Hodges, Johnny **24**
Hodges, Warner
  See Jason & the Scorchers
Hodgson, Roger **26**
  Also see Supertramp
Hodo, David
  See Village People, The
Hoed, Pat
  See Down By Law
Hoenig, Michael
  See Tangerine Dream
Hoerig, Keith
  See Five Iron Frenzy
Hoerner, Dan
  See Sunny Day Real Estate
Hofeldt, Brian
  See Derailers, The
Hoffman, Ellen
  See Oakland Interfaith Gospel Choir
Hoffman, Erika
  See His Name Is Alive
Hoffman, Guy
  See BoDeans, The
  Also see Violent Femmes
Hoffman, Kristian
  See Congo Norvell
Hoffman, Sam
  See Captain Beefheart and His Magic Band
Hoffs, Susanna
  See Bangles, The
Hofmann, Holly **41**
Hogan, Mike
  See Cranberries, The
Hogan, Noel
  See Cranberries, The
Hoke, Jim
  See NRBQ
Holder, Gene
  See dB's, The
  Also see Yo La Tengo
Holdsworth, Alan
  See Soft Machine
Hole **14**
Holiday, Billie **6**
Holland, Annie
  See Elastica
Holland, Brian
  See Holland-Dozier-Holland
Holland, Bryan "Dexter"
  See Offspring
Holland, Dave **27**
Holland, Dave
  See Judas Priest
Holland, Eddie
  See Holland-Dozier-Holland
Holland, Gary
  See Great White
Holland, Julian "Jools"
  See Squeeze
Holland, Steve
  See Molly Hatchet
Holland-Dozier-Holland **5**
Hollies, The **39**
Hollinger, Kyle
  See Crazy Town
Hollingsworth, Kyle
  See String Cheese Incident, The
Hollis, Mark
  See Talk Talk
Hollister, Dave
  See Blackstreet

Holloway, Brenda **45**
Holly, Buddy **1**
Holm, Georg
  See Sigur Rós
Holmes, David **31**
Holmes, Malcolm
  See Orchestral Manoeuvres in the Dark
Holmes, Sherman
  See Holmes Brothers, The
Holmes, Tim
  See Death in Vegas
Holmes, Wendell
  See Holmes Brothers, The
Holmes Brothers, The **35**
Holmstrom, Peter
  See Dandy Warhols
Holsapple, Peter
  See Continental Drifters
  Also see dB's, The
Holsapple, Randy
  See Caedmon's Call
Holt, Cully
  See Jordanaires, The
Holt, David Lee
  See Mavericks, The
Holy Goat
  See Lanternjack, The
Homme, Joshua
  See Queens of the Stone Age
  Also see Screaming Trees
Honda, Yuka
  See Cibo Matto
Honeyman, Susie
  See Mekons, The
Honeyman-Scott, James
  See Pretenders, The
Honolulu
  See Minty
Hood, David
  See Traffic
Hood, Patterson
  See Drive-By Truckers
Hoodoo Gurus **33**
Hook, Peter
  See Joy Division
  Also see New Order
Hooker, John Lee **26**
  Earlier sketch in CM **1**
Hooks, Rosie Lee
  See Sweet Honey in the Rock
Hoon, Shannon
  See Blind Melon
Hooper, Chris
  See Grapes of Wrath, The
Hooper, Dave
  See Rippingtons
Hooper, Nellee
  See Massive Attack
  Also see Soul II Soul
Hooper, Tom
  See Grapes of Wrath, The
Hooper, Tony
  See Ceili Rain
  Also see Strawbs
Hooters **20**
Hootie and the Blowfish **18**
Hoover, Jamie
  See Spongetones, The
Hope, Dave
  See Kansas
Hope, Gavin
  See Nylons, The
Hopkins, Doug
  See Gin Blossoms
Hopkins, Lightnin' **13**
Hopkins, Nicky
  See Quicksilver Messenger Service

Ieuan, Dafydd "Daf"
　See Catatonia
　Also see Super Furry Animals
If, Owen
　See Stereo MC's
Iglauer, Bruce **37**
Iglesias, Enrique **27**
Iglesias, Julio **20**
　Earlier sketch in CM **2**
Iha, James
　See Smashing Pumpkins
Illsley, John
　See Dire Straits
Image, Joey
　See Misfits, The
Imbruglia, Natalie **27**
Immergluck, David
　See Monks of Doom
Immerwahr, Steve
　See Ida
Imperial Teen **26**
Imperials, The **43**
Impressions, The **36**
Incognito **16**
Incredible String Band **23**
Incubus **23**
India.Arie **41**
Indigenous **31**
Indigo Girls **20**
　Earlier sketch in CM **3**
Inez, Mike
　See Alice in Chains
Infante, Frank
　See Blondie
Ingber, Elliot "Winged Eel Fingerling"
　See Captain Beefheart and His Magic Band
Inge, Edward
　See McKinney's Cotton Pickers
Ingebrigtsen, Christian
　See A1
Ingram, Bobby
　See Molly Hatchet
Ingram, Jack
　See Incredible String Band
Ingram, James **11**
Ink Spots **23**
Inner Circle **15**
Innes, Andrew
　See Primal Scream
Innes, Neil
　See Bonzo Dog Doo-Dah Band
Innis, Dave
　See Restless Heart
Innocence Mission, The **46**
Insane Clown Posse **22**
Interior, Lux
　See Cramps, The
Intveldt, James
　See Blasters, The
INXS **21**
　Earlier sketch in CM **2**
Iommi, Tony
　See Black Sabbath
Iovine, Jimmy **46**
Irish Tenors, The **36**
Irmler, Hans-Joachim
　See Faust
Iron Maiden **10**
Irons, Jack
　See Pearl Jam
　Also see Red Hot Chili Peppers
Isaak, Chris **33**
　Earlier sketch in CM **6**
Isabelle, Jeff
　See Guns n' Roses
Isacsson, Jonas
　See Roxette

Isbell, Jason
　See Drive-By Truckers
Isbin, Sharon **33**
Isham, Mark **14**
Isles, Bill
　See O'Jays, The
Isley, Ernie
　See Isley Brothers, The
Isley, Marvin
　See Isley Brothers, The
Isley, O'Kelly, Jr.
　See Isley Brothers, The
Isley, Ronald
　See Isley Brothers, The
Isley, Rudolph
　See Isley Brothers, The
Isley Brothers, The **47**
　Earlier sketch in CM **8**
Israel Vibration **21**
Ithier, Rafael
　See El Gran Combo
Ivers, Eileen **30**
　Also see Cherish the Ladies
Ives, Burl **12**
Ives, Charles **29**
Ivey, Michael
　See Basehead
Ivins, Michael
　See Flaming Lips
J.
　See White Zombie
J, David
　See Bauhaus
　Also see Love and Rockets
J. Geils Band **25**
Ja Rule **36**
Jabs, Matthias
　See Scorpions, The
Jackson, Alan **25**
　Earlier sketch in CM **7**
Jackson, Al
　See Booker T. & the M.G.'s
Jackson, Chuck
　See Del Vikings, The
Jackson, Clive
　See Ray Condo and His Ricochets
Jackson, Eddie
　See Queensryche
Jackson, Freddie **3**
Jackson, Jackie
　See Jacksons, The
Jackson, Janet **36**
　Earlier sketch in CM **16**
　Earlier sketch in CM **3**
Jackson, Jermaine
　See Jacksons, The
Jackson, Joe **22**
　Earlier sketch in CM **4**
Jackson, Karen
　See Supremes, The
Jackson, Mahalia **8**
Jackson, Marlon
　See Jacksons, The
Jackson, Martin
　See Swing Out Sister
Jackson, Michael **44**
　Earlier sketch in CM **17**
　Earlier sketch in CM **1**
　Also see Jacksons, The
Jackson, Millie **14**
Jackson, Milt **15**
Jackson, Pervis
　See Spinners, The
Jackson, Quentin
　See McKinney's Cotton Pickers
Jackson, Randy
　See Jacksons, The

Jackson, Ronald Shannon
　See Music Revelation Ensemble
Jackson, Stevie
　See Belle and Sebastian
Jackson, Tito
　See Jacksons, The
Jackson, Tony
　See Searchers, The
Jackson, Wanda **42**
Jackson, Willie
　See Spaniels, The
Jackson 5, The
　See Jacksons, The
Jacksons, The **7**
Jackyl **24**
Jacobs, Alan
　See Fugs, The
Jacobs, Christian Richard
　See Aquabats, The
Jacobs, Jeff
　See Foreigner
Jacobs, Nick
　See Blue Aeroplanes, The
Jacobs, Parker
　See Aquabats, The
Jacobs, Walter
　See Little Walter
Jacox, Martin
　See Soul Stirrers, The
Jacquet, Illinois **17**
Jade 4U
　See Lords of Acid
Jaffee, Rami
　See Wallflowers, The
Jagged Edge **36**
Jagger, Mick **7**
　Also see Rolling Stones, The
Jaheim **42**
Jairo T.
　See Sepultura
Jalal
　See Last Poets
Jam, Jimmy
　See Jimmy Jam and Terry Lewis
Jam, The **27**
Jam Master Jay
　See Run DMC
Jamal, Ahmad **32**
Jamerson, James
　See Funk Brothers
James **12**
James, Alex
　See Blur
James, Andrew "Bear"
　See Midnight Oil
James, Boney **21**
James, Brian
　See Damned, The
James, Cheryl
　See Salt-N-Pepa
James, David
　See Alien Sex Fiend
　Also see Spearhead
James, Denise
　See His Name Is Alive
James, Doug
　See Roomful of Blues
James, Elmore **8**
James, Etta **6**
James, Gregg
　See D.O.A.
James, Harry **11**
James, Jesse
　See Jackyl
James, Jim
　See My Morning Jacket

Johnson, Mike
  See Dinosaur Jr.
Johnson, Patricia
  See Sweet Honey in the Rock
Johnson, Ralph
  See Earth, Wind and Fire
Johnson, Robert 6
Johnson, Robert
  See KC and the Sunshine Band
Johnson, Scott
  See Gin Blossoms
Johnson, Shirley Childres
  See Sweet Honey in the Rock
Johnson, Tamara "Taj"
  See SWV
Johnson, Vince
  See Mediaeval Baebes
Johnson, Willie
  See Golden Gate Quartet
Johnston, Bruce
  See Beach Boys, The
Johnston, Doug
  See Loverboy
Johnston, Freedy 20
Johnston, Howie
  See Ventures, The
Johnston, Max
  See Uncle Tupelo
  Also see Wilco
Johnston, Mike
  See Northwoods Improvisers
Johnston, Phillip 36
Johnston, Sonnie
  See Five Iron Frenzy
Johnston, Tom
  See Doobie Brothers, The
JoJo
  See Jodeci
  Also see K-Ci & JoJo
Jolly, Bill
  See Butthole Surfers
Jolly, Herman
  See Sunset Valley
Jolson, Al 10
Jon B. 41
Jon Spencer Blues Explosion 18
Jones, Adam
  See Tool
Jones, Anthony
  See Humble Pie
Jones, Benny
  See Dirty Dozen Brass Band
Jones, Booker T. 8
  Also see Booker T. & the M.G.'s
Jones, Brian
  See Rolling Stones, The
Jones, Busta
  See Gang of Four
Jones, Calvin "Fuzz"
  See Music Revelation Ensemble
Jones, Claude
  See McKinney's Cotton Pickers
Jones, Craig
  See Slipknot
Jones, Daniel
  See Savage Garden
Jones, Darryl
  See Rolling Stones, The
Jones, Davy
  See Monkees, The
Jones, Denise
  See Point of Grace
Jones, Donell 43
Jones, Elvin 9
Jones, Etta 37
Jones, Geoffrey
  See Sounds of Blackness

Jones, George 36
  Earlier sketch in CM 4
Jones, Gordon
  See Silly Wizard
Jones, Grace 9
Jones, Hank 15
Jones, Howard 26
Jones, Jab
  See Memphis Jug Band
Jones, Jamie
  See All-4-One
Jones, Jim
  See Pere Ubu
Jones, John Paul
  See Led Zeppelin
Jones, Kelly
  See Stereophonics
Jones, Kendall
  See Fishbone
Jones, Kenny
  See Faces, The
  Also see Who, The
Jones, Kimberly
  See Lil' Kim
Jones, Marshall
  See Ohio Players
Jones, Maxine
  See En Vogue
Jones, Michael
  See Kronos Quartet
Jones, Mick
  See Clash, The
Jones, Mick
  See Foreigner
Jones, Mick
  See Tommy James and the Shondells
Jones, Mic
  See Big Audio Dynamite
  Also see Clash, The
Jones, Orville
  See Ink Spots
Jones, Paul
  See Catatonia
  Also see Elastica
Jones, Philly Joe 16
Jones, Quincy 20
  Earlier sketch in CM 2
Jones, Randy
  See Village People, The
Jones, Richard
  See Stereophonics
Jones, Rickie Lee 4
Jones, Robert "Kuumba"
  See Ohio Players
Jones, Robin
  See Beta Band, The
Jones, Rod
  See Idlewild
Jones, Ronald
  See Flaming Lips
Jones, Russell "Ol' Dirty Bastard"
  See Ol' Dirty Bastard
  Also see Wu-Tang Clan
Jones, Sandra "Puma"
  See Black Uhuru
Jones, Simon
  See Verve, The
Jones, Spike 5
Jones, Stacy
  See American Hi-Fi
  Also see Letters to Cleo
  Also see Veruca Salt
Jones, Steve
  See Sex Pistols, The
Jones, Teren
  See Del the Funky Homosapien
  Also see Gorillaz

Jones, Terry
  See Point of Grace
Jones, Thad 19
Jones, Tom 11
Jones, Uriel
  See Funk Brothers
Jones, Vincent
  See Grapes of Wrath, The
Jones, Will "Dub"
  See Coasters, The
Jonsson, Magnus
  See Gus Gus
Joplin, Janis 3
Joplin, Scott 10
Jordan, Cyril
  See Flamin' Groovies
Jordan, Dante "Chi"
  See Ruff Endz
Jordan, Ken
  See Crystal Method, The
Jordan, Lonnie
  See War
Jordan, Louis 11
Jordan, Marc 30
Jordan, Montell 26
Jordan, Stanley 1
Jordanaires, The 44
Jordison, Joey
  See Slipknot
Jorgensen, Mikal
  See Wilco
Jorgenson, John
  See Desert Rose Band, The
Jos
  See Ex, The
Josefowicz, Leila 35
Joseph, Charles
  See Dirty Dozen Brass Band
Joseph, Kirk
  See Dirty Dozen Brass Band
Joseph-I, Israel
  See Bad Brains
Josephmary
  See Compulsion
Jourgensen, Al
  See Ministry
Journey 21
Joy Division 19
Joy Electric 26
Joyce, Don
  See Negativland
Joyce, Mike
  See Buzzcocks, The
  Also see Smiths, The
Juanes 43
Juanita
  See Les Négresses Vertes
Judas Priest 47
  Earlier sketch in CM 10
Judd, Naomi
  See Judds, The
Judd, Wynonna
  See Judds, The
  Also see Wynonna
Judds, The 2
Judy, Eric
  See Modest Mouse
Jugg, Roman
  See Damned, The
Juhlin, Dag
  See Poi Dog Pondering
Jukebox
  See Geto Boys, The
Juliana Theory, The 43
Juliano, Thomas
  See Seven Mary Three

Kentucky Headhunters, The **5**
Kerman, Elliott
  See Rockapella
Kern, Jerome **13**
Kerr, Don
  See Rheostatics
Kerr, Jim
  See Simple Minds
Kerr, Scott
  See Five Iron Frenzy
Kerr, Stuart
  See Texas
Kershaw, Sammy **15**
Kessel, Barney **47**
Kessel, Kenny
  See Loud Family, The
Ketchum, Hal **14**
Key, Cevin
  See Skinny Puppy
Keys, Alicia **46**
Keyser, Alex
  See Echobelly
Khaled **33**
Khalsa, Giti
  See Seven Mary Three
Khan, Ali Akbar **34**
Khan, Chaka **19**
  Earlier sketch in CM **9**
Khan, Nusrat Fateh Ali **13**
Khan, Praga
  See Lords of Acid
Kibble, Joey
  See Take 6
Kibble, Mark
  See Take 6
Kibby, Walter
  See Fishbone
Kick, Johnny
  See Madder Rose
Kid 'n Play **5**
Kid Rock **27**
Kidjo, Angelique **39**
  Earlier sketch in CM **17**
Kidney, Robert
  See Golden Palominos
Kid606 **36**
Kiedis, Anthony
  See Red Hot Chili Peppers
Kiftmeyer
  See Green Day
Kihlstedt, Carla
  See Tin Hat Trio
Kilbey, Steve
  See Church, The
Kilbourn, Duncan
  See Psychedelic Furs
Kilgallon, Eddie
  See Ricochet
Kilgore **24**
Kilkenny, Giorgio
  See Dexy's Midnight Runners
Killian, Tim
  See Kronos Quartet
Killing Joke **30**
Kimball, Jennifer
  See Story, The
Kimball, Jim
  See Jesus Lizard
Kimble, Paul
  See Grant Lee Buffalo
Kimbrough, Junior **41**
Kinard, Tulani Jordan
  See Sweet Honey in the Rock
Kincaid, Jan
  See Brand New Heavies, The
Kinchen, Ricky
  See Mint Condition

Kinchla, Chan
  See Blues Traveler
Kinde, Geoff
  See Atomic Fireballs, The
King, Albert **2**
King, Andy
  See Hooters
King, B.B. **24**
  Earlier sketch in CM **1**
King, Ben E. **7**
  Also see Drifters, The
King, Bob
  See Soul Stirrers, The
King, Carole **6**
  Also see Goffin-King
King, Chris Thomas **43**
King, Earl **44**
King, Ed
  See Lynyrd Skynyrd
King, Freddy **17**
King, John
  See Dust Brothers
King, Jon
  See Gang of Four
King, Kerry
  See Slayer
King, Pee Wee **30**
King, Philip
  See Lush
King, Simon
  See Hawkwind
King, Stove
  See Mansun
King, William Jr.
  See Commodores, The
King Ad-Rock
  See Horovitz, Adam
King Crimson **17**
King Missile **22**
Kingins, Duke
  See Atomic Fireballs, The
King's X **7**
Kingsmen, The **34**
Kingsmill, Mark
  See Hoodoo Gurus
Kingston Trio, The **9**
Kininger, Sam
  See Soulive
Kinks, The **15**
Kinley, Heather
  See Kinleys, The
Kinley, Jennifer
  See Kinleys, The
Kinleys, The **32**
Kinney, Kevn
  See Drivin' N' Cryin'
Kinney, Sean
  See Alice in Chains
Kippenberger, Karl
  See Shihad
Kirchen, Bill
  See Commander Cody and His Lost
    Planet Airmen
Kircher, Pete
  See Status Quo
Kirk, Rahsaan Roland **6**
Kirk, Richard H.
  See Cabaret Voltaire
Kirkby, Emma **35**
Kirke, Simon
  See Bad Company
  Also see Free
Kirkendall, Terry
  See Derailers, The
Kirkland, Mike
  See Prong

Kirkland, Scott
  See Crystal Method, The
Kirkpatrick, Chris
  See 'N Sync
Kirkpatrick, Sean
  See Swell
Kirkwood, Cris
  See Meat Puppets, The
Kirkwood, Curt
  See Meat Puppets, The
Kirtley, Peter
  See Pentangle
Kirwan, Danny
  See Fleetwood Mac
Kirwan, Larry
  See Black 47
Kiss **25**
  Earlier sketch in CM **5**
Kisser, Andreas
  See Sepultura
Kissin, Evgeny **6**
Kitaro **36**
  Earlier sketch in CM **1**
Kitchener, Lord **29**
Kitsos, Nick
  See BoDeans
Kitt, Eartha **9**
Kjartansson, Siggi
  See Gus Gus
Kleiman, Jon
  See Monster Magnet
Klein, Danny
  See J. Geils Band
Klein, Jon
  See Siouxsie and the Banshees
Klein, Mark
  See Cobra Verde
Kleinow, "Sneaky" Pete
  See Flying Burrito Brothers
Klett, Peter
  See Candlebox
Klezmatics, The **18**
Klugh, Earl **10**
Kmatsu, Bravo
  See Pizzicato Five
KMFDM **18**
Knack, The **35**
Knapp, Jennifer **43**
Knechtel, Larry
  See Bread
Knight, Gladys **1**
Knight, Jon
  See New Kids on the Block
Knight, Jordan
  See New Kids on the Block
Knight, Larry
  See Spirit
Knight, Peter
  See Steeleye Span
Knight, Phil
  See Shihad
Knight, Steve
  See Mountain
Knight, Suge **15**
Knight, Susan
  See Ensemble Modern
Knighton, Willie "Khujo"
  See Goodie Mob
Knopfler, David
  See Dire Straits
Knopfler, Mark **25**
  Earlier sketch in CM **3**
  Also see Dire Straits
Know, Dr.
  See Bad Brains
Knowledge
  See Digable Planets

Lambert, Ben
  See Carter USM
Lambert, Dave
  See Lambert, Hendricks and Ross
  Also see Strawbs
Lambert, Hendricks and Ross **28**
Lamble, Martin
  See Fairport Convention
Lamm, Robert
  See Chicago
Lamond, Mary Jane **33**
Lampkin, Troy
  See Oakland Interfaith Gospel Choir
Lancaster, Alan
  See Status Quo
Lancaster, Brian
  See Surfin' Pluto
Landers, Paul
  See Rammstein
Landreth, Sonny **16**
Lane, Brian
  See Slobberbone
Lane, David
  See You Am I
Lane, Fred **28**
Lane, Jani
  See Warrant
Lane, Jay
  See Primus
Lane, Ronnie **46**
  Also see Faces, The
Lane, Shawn
  See Blue Highway
Lanegan, Mark
  See Screaming Trees
Lang, Damian
  See His Name Is Alive
Lang, Jonny **27**
lang, kd **25**
  Earlier sketch in CM **4**
Langan, Gary
  See Art of Noise
Langdon, Antony
  See Spacehog
Langdon, Royston
  See Spacehog
Lange, Mutt **47**
Langford, Jon
  See Mekons, The
Langford, Willie
  See Golden Gate Quartet
Langley, Gerard
  See Blue Aeroplanes, The
Langley, John
  See Blue Aeroplanes, The
  Also see Mekons, The
Langlois, Paul
  See Tragically Hip, The
Langosch, Paul
  See Ralph Sharon Quartet
Langston, Leslie
  See Throwing Muses
Langton, Huw Lloyd
  See Hawkwind
Lanier, Allen
  See Blue Oyster Cult
Lanker, Dustin
  See Cherry Poppin' Daddies
Lanois, Daniel **8**
Lanternjack, The **31**
Lantz, Mike
  See Front Range
Lanz, David **42**
LaPread, Ronald
  See Commodores, The
Lardie, Michael
  See Great White

LaRizza, Archie
  See Saints, The
Larkey, Charles
  See Fugs, The
Larkin, Patty **9**
Larkin, Tom
  See Shihad
Larkins, Tom
  See Giant Sand
Larsen, Marit
  See M2M
Larson, Chad Albert
  See Aquabats, The
Larson, Nathan
  See Shudder to Think
LaRue, Florence
  See Fifth Dimension
LaSalle, Denise **43**
Lasar, Mars **39**
Lash, Tony
  See Sunset Valley
Lassiter, Richard
  See Ida
Last Poets **21**
Laswell, Bill **14**
  Also see Golden Palominos
Lataille, Rich
  See Roomful of Blues
Lateef, Yusef **16**
Latham, Billy Ray
  See Dillards, The
Latimer, Andrew
  See Camel
Lauderdale, Jim **29**
Laughner, Peter
  See Pere Ubu
Laughren, Matt
  See Cold
Lauper, Cyndi **11**
Laurence, Lynda
  See Supremes, The
Lava, Larry
  See Lanternjack, The
Lavay Smith and Her Red Hot
  Skillet Lickers **32**
Lavelle, Caroline **35**
Lavery, Dan
  See Tonic
Lavin, Christine **6**
Lavis, Gilson
  See Squeeze
Lavitz, T.
  See Dixie Dregs
Lawler, Feargal
  See Cranberries, The
Lawnge
  See Black Sheep
Lawrence, John
  See Gorky's Zygotic Mynci
Lawrence, Tracy **11**
Lawry, John
  See Petra
Laws, Hubert **38**
Laws, Roland
  See Earth, Wind and Fire
Lawson, Doyle
  See Country Gentlemen, The
Lawson, Jerry
  See Persuasions, The
Lawson, Ricky
  See Yellowjackets
Layzie Bone
  See Bone Thugs-N-Harmony
Le Mystère des Voix Bulgares
  See Bulgarian State Female Vocal Choir, The
Leadbelly **6**

Leader, Ted
  See Chainsaw Kittens, The
Leadon, Bernie
  See Eagles, The
  Also see Flying Burrito Brothers
  Also see Nitty Gritty Dirt Band, The
Lear, Graham
  See REO Speedwagon
Leary, Paul
  See Butthole Surfers
Leary, Vinnie
  See Fugs, The
Leatherman, Ronnie
  See 13th Floor Elevators
Leavell, Chuck
  See Allman Brothers, The
LeBlanc, Fred
  See Cowboy Mouth
Le Bon, Simon
  See Duran Duran
Leckenby, Derek "Lek"
  See Herman's Hermits
Led Zeppelin **1**
Ledbetter, Huddie
  See Leadbelly
LeDoux, Chris **12**
Lee, Alex
  See Blue Aeroplanes, The
Lee, Arthur
  See Love
Lee, Barbara
  See Chiffons, The
Lee, Ben **26**
Lee, Beverly
  See Shirelles, The
Lee, Brenda **5**
Lee, Buddy
  See Less Than Jake
Lee, Buddy
  See McKinney's Cotton Pickers
Lee, CoCo **36**
Lee, Garret
  See Compulsion
Lee, Geddy
  See Rush
Lee, Hunter
  See Ceili Rain
Lee, Jon
  See S Club 7
Lee, Mark
  See Third Day
Lee, Peggy **8**
Lee, Pete
  See Gwar
Lee, Rita **37**
Lee, Sara
  See Gang of Four
Lee, Stan
  See Incredible String Band
Lee, Tommy
  See Mötley Crüe
Lee, Tony
  See Treadmill Trackstar
Leeb, Bill
  See Delerium
  Also see Front Line Assembly
Leen, Bill
  See Gin Blossoms
Leese, Howard
  See Heart
Leeway, Joe
  See Thompson Twins
Leftfield **29**
Legg, Adrian **17**
Legowitz, Herr
  See Gus Gus

Little Feat **4**
Little Richard **1**
Little Texas **14**
Little Walter **14**
Littleton, Daniel
  See Ida
Littleton, Michael "Miggy"
  See Ida
Littrell, Brian
  See Backstreet Boys
Live **14**
Livgren, Kerry
  See Kansas
Living Colour **7**
Living End, The **42**
Livingston, Edwin
  See Los Hombres Calientes
L.L. Cool J **46**
  Earlier sketch in CM **5**
Llanas, Sam
  See BoDeans
Lloyd, Charles **22**
Lloyd, Geoff
  See Matthew Good Band
Lloyd, Mick
  See Felt
Lloyd, Richard
  See Television
Lloyd Webber, Andrew **6**
Lo Fidelity All Stars **27**
Locke, John
  See Spirit
Lockhart, Keith **36**
Locking, Brian
  See Shadows, The
Lockley, Jayne
  See Wedding Present, The
Lockwood, Robert, Jr. **10**
Lodge, John
  See Moody Blues, The
Loeb, Lisa **23**
  Earlier sketch in CM **19**
Loeffler, Joe
  See Chevelle
Loeffler, Pete
  See Chevelle
Loeffler, Sam
  See Chevelle
Loesser, Frank **19**
Loewe, Frederick
  See Lerner and Loewe
Loewenstein, Jason
  See Sebadoh
Lofgren, Nils **25**
Logan, Jack **27**
Logan, Melissa
  See Chicks on Speed
Loggins, Kenny **20**
  Earlier sketch in CM **3**
Logic, Laura
  See X-Ray Spex
Lohner, Danny
  See Nine Inch Nails
Lombardo, Dave
  See Slayer
Lonberg-Holm, Fred
  See Flying Luttenbachers, The
London, Frank
  See Klezmatics, The
London, Julie **32**
Lonestar **27**
Loney, Roy
  See Flamin' Groovies
Long, Donna
  See Cherish the Ladies
Longley, Ty
  See Great White

Lopes, Lisa "Left Eye"
  See TLC
Lopez, Angel
  See Son by Four
Lopez, Israel "Cachao" **34**
  Earlier sketch in CM **14**
Lopez, Jennifer **27**
Lord, Jon
  See Deep Purple
Lords of Acid **20**
Lorenz, Flake
  See Rammstein
Loria, Steve
  See Spirit
Lorimer, Roddy
  See Spiritualized
  Also see Waterboys, The
Lorson, Mary
  See Madder Rose
Los Hombres Calientes **29**
Los Lobos **36**
  Earlier sketch in CM **2**
Los Reyes
  See Gipsy Kings, The
Lou Dog
  See Kottonmouth Kings
Loud Family, The **31**
Loughlin, Jim
  See moe.
Loughnane, Lee
  See Chicago
Louison, Steve
  See Massive Attack
Louris, Gary
  See Jayhawks, The
Louvin, Charlie
  See Louvin Brothers, The
Louvin, Ira
  See Louvin Brothers, The
Louvin Brothers, The **12**
Lovano, Joe **13**
Love **34**
Love, Courtney
  See Hole
Love, Darlene **46**
Love, Gerry
  See Teenage Fanclub
Love, Laura **20**
Love, Mike
  See Beach Boys, The
Love, Rollie
  See Beat Farmers
Love and Rockets **15**
Love Spit Love **21**
Loveless, Patty **21**
  Earlier sketch in CM **5**
Loverboy **46**
Lovering, David
  See Cracker
  Also see Pixies, The
Lovett, Lyle **28**
  Earlier sketch in CM **5**
Lovin' Spoonful **37**
Low **37**
Lowe, Chris
  See Pet Shop Boys
Lowe, Nick **25**
  Earlier sketch in CM **6**
  Also see Brinsley Schwarz
Lowe, Victoria
  See Tuxedomoon
Lowell, Charlie
  See Jars of Clay
Lowenstein, Evan
  See Evan and Jaron
Lowenstein, Jaron
  See Evan and Jaron

Lowery, Clint
  See Sevendust
Lowery, David
  See Cracker
Lowry, Mark
  See Gaither Vocal Band
Lozano, Conrad
  See Los Lobos
L7 **12**
Luc
  See Ex, The
Luca, Nick
  See Giant Sand
Lucas, Gary
  See Captain Beefheart and His Magic Band
Lucas, Jr., Harold
  See Clovers, The
Lucas, Kirk
  See Northwoods Improvisers
Lucas, Trevor
  See Fairport Convention
Luccketta, Troy
  See Tesla
Lucero, Nick
  See Queens of the Stone Age
Lucia, Paco de
  See de Lucia, Paco
Lucia, Peter
  See Tommy James and the Shondells
Luciano **41**
Luciano, Felipe
  See Last Poets
Luck, Greg
  See IIIrd Tyme Out
Luckett, LaToya
  See Destiny's Child
Ludacris **38**
Luening, Otto **37**
Lugo, Frank
  See ? and the Mysterians
Luke
  See Campbell, Luther
Lukin, Matt
  See Melvins
  Also see Mudhoney
Lulu **32**
Lumholdt, Sara
  See A*Teens
Luna **18**
Lund, Sara
  See Unwound
Lunsford, Bret
  See Beat Happening
Lupo, Pat
  See Beaver Brown Band, The
LuPone, Patti **8**
Lupton, Karen
  See Mediaeval Baebes
Lupu, Radu **36**
Luscious Jackson **27**
  Earlier sketch in CM **19**
Lush **13**
Luster, Ahrue
  See Machine Head
Luttell, Terry
  See REO Speedwagon
Lydon, John **9**
  Also see Golden Palominos
  Also see Sex Pistols, The
Lyfe, DJ
  See Incubus
Lymon, Frankie
  See Frankie Lymon and The Teenagers
Lynam, Ron
  See Front Range
Lynch, David
  See Platters, The

Manson, Shirley
  See Garbage
Mansun **30**
Manuel, Richard
  See Band, The
Many, Trey
  See His Name Is Alive
Manzanera, Phil
  See Roxy Music
Manzarek, Ray
  See Doors, The
Mapfumo, Thomas **39**
Marazzi, Paul
  See A1
Marc **7**
  See Jurassic 5
March, Kevin
  See Shudder to Think
Marcy Playground **31**
Marhevka, Glenn
  See Big Bad Voodoo Daddy
Marie, Buffy Sainte
  See Sainte-Marie, Buffy
Marienthal, Eric
  See Rippingtons
Marilyn Manson **44**
  Earlier sketch in CM **18**
Marine, Mitch
  See Brave Combo
Marini, Lou, Jr.
  See Blood, Sweat and Tears
Marinos, Jimmy
  See Romantics, The
Marker, Steve
  See Garbage
Marks, Toby
  See De Gaia, Banco
Marley, Bob **3**
Marley, Damian **39**
Marley, Rita **10**
Marley, Ziggy **47**
  Earlier sketch in CM **3**
Marquez, Carlos
  See Aterciopelados
Marr, Johnny
  See Smiths, The
  Also see The The
Marriner, Neville **7**
Marriott, Steve
  See Humble Pie
Mars, Chris
  See Replacements, The
Mars, Derron
  See Less Than Jake
Mars, Mick
  See Mötley Crüe
Marsalis, Branford **10**
Marsalis, Ellis **13**
Marsalis, Jason
  See Los Hombres Calientes
Marsalis, Wynton **20**
  Earlier sketch in CM **6**
Marsh, Ian Craig
  See Human League, The
Marsh, Randy
  See Northwoods Improvisers
Marshal, Cornel
  See Third World
Marshall, Amanda **27**
Marshall, Arik
  See Red Hot Chili Peppers
Marshall, Brian
  See Creed
Marshall, Chan
  See Cat Power
Marshall, David Alan
  See Chanticleer

Marshall, Jeff
  See Clem Snide
Marshall, Jenell
  See Dirty Dozen Brass Band
Marshall, Jeremy
  See Cold
Marshall, John
  See Soft Machine
Marshall, Steve
  See Gene Loves Jezebel
Marshall Tucker Band **43**
Martensen, Vic
  See Captain Beefheart and His Magic Band
Martha and the Vandellas **25**
Martin, Barbara
  See Supremes, The
Martin, Bardi
  See Candlebox
Martin, Barrett
  See Screaming Trees
Martin, Billy
  See Good Charlotte
Martin, Carl
  See Shai
Martin, Christopher
  See Kid 'n Play
Martin, Chris
  See Coldplay
Martin, Dean **1**
Martin, Dewey
  See Buffalo Springfield
Martin, George **6**
Martin, Greg
  See Kentucky Headhunters, The
Martin, Jeff
  See Tea Party
Martin, Jimmy **5**
  Also see Osborne Brothers, The
Martin, Jim
  See Faith No More
Martin, Johnney
  See Mighty Clouds of Joy, The
Martin, Jordan
  See Great White
Martin, Kevin
  See Candlebox
Martin, Luci
  See Chic
Martin, Mary **27**
Martin, Phonso
  See Steel Pulse
Martin, Ricky **26**
Martin, Ronnie
  See Joy Electric
Martin, Sarah
  See Belle and Sebastian
Martin, Sennie
  See Kool & the Gang
Martin, Tony
  See Black Sabbath
Martinez, Angie **43**
Martinez, Anthony
  See Black Flag
Martinez, Christina
  See Boss Hog
Martinez, Cliff
  See Captain Beefheart and His Magic Band
Martinez, Robert
  See ? and the Mysterians
Martinez, S. A.
  See 311
Martini, Jerry
  See Sly & the Family Stone
Martino, Pat **17**
Martsch, Doug
  See Built to Spill
Martyn, John **43**

Marvin, Hank B.
  See Shadows, The
Marx, Richard **21**
  Earlier sketch in CM **3**
Mary Mary **39**
Mascagni, Pietro **25**
Mascis, J
  See Dinosaur Jr.
Masdea, Jim
  See Boston
Mase **27**
Masekela, Hugh **7**
Maseo
  See De La Soul
Masi, Nick
  See Four Seasons, The
Mason, Bob
  See Fugs, The
Mason, Dave
  See Fleetwood Mac
  Also see Traffic
Mason, Nick
  See Pink Floyd
Mason, Stephen
  See Beta Band, The
Mason, Steve
  See Jars of Clay
Mason, Terry
  See Joy Division
Masse, Laurel
  See Manhattan Transfer, The
Massey, Bobby
  See O'Jays, The
Massey, Graham
  See 808 State
Massi, Nick
  See Four Seasons, The
Massive Attack **17**
Masta Ace **40**
Mastelotto, Pat
  See King Crimson
Master D
  See Asian Dub Foundation
Master P **22**
Masur, Kurt **11**
Matchbox 20 **27**
Material
  See Laswell, Bill
Matheson, David
  See Moxy Früvous
Mathias, Nathaniel "Jerry"
  See Toots and the Maytals
Mathis, Johnny **2**
Mathus, Jim
  See Squirrel Nut Zippers
Matlock, Glen
  See Sex Pistols, The
Maïtra, Shyamal
  See Gong
Matsui, Keiko **35**
Mattacks, Dave
  See Fairport Convention
Mattea, Kathy **37**
  Earlier sketch in CM **5**
Matterson, J. B.
  See Dixie Hummingbirds, The
Matthew Good Band **34**
Matthews, Cerys
  See Catatonia
Matthews, Chris
  See Shudder to Think
Matthews, Dave
  See Dave Matthews Band
Matthews, Donna Lorraine
  See Elastica
Matthews, Eric **22**

McDowell, Hugh
 See Electric Light Orchestra
McDowell, Mississippi Fred 16
McDowell, Smilin' Jay
 See BR5-49
McDuffie, Chris
 See Apples in Stereo
McElhaney, Kevin
 See Chainsaw Kittens, The
McElhone, John
 See Texas
McElroy, Sollie
 See Flamingos, The
McEntire, John
 See Tortoise
McEntire, Reba 38
 Earlier sketch in CM 11
McErlaine, Ally
 See Texas
McEuen, John
 See Nitty Gritty Dirt Band, The
McFadden, Bryan
 See Westlife
McFarlane, Elaine
 See Mamas and the Papas
McFee, John
 See Doobie Brothers, The
McFerrin, Bobby 3
McFessel, Sean
 See Cake
MC5, The 9
McGarrigle, Kate and Anna 35
McGearly, James
 See Christian Death
McGee, Brian
 See Simple Minds
McGee, Jerry
 See Ventures, The
McGeoch, John
 See Siouxsie and the Banshees
McGill, Lucius
 See Dells, The
McGill, Michael
 See Dells, The
McGinley, Raymond
 See Teenage Fanclub
McGinniss, Will
 See Audio Adrenaline
McGrath, Mark
 See Sugar Ray
McGraw, Tim 42
 Earlier sketch in CM 17
McGuigan, Paul
 See Oasis
McGuinn, Jim
 See McGuinn, Roger
McGuinn, Roger 35
 Also see Byrds, The
McGuinness
 See Lords of Acid
McGuire, Andy
 See Spoon
McGuire, Barry 45
McGuire, Christine
 See McGuire Sisters, The
McGuire, Dorothy
 See McGuire Sisters, The
McGuire, Mike
 See Shenandoah
McGuire, Phyllis
 See McGuire Sisters, The
McGuire Sisters, The 27
McIntosh, Robbie
 See Average White Band
McIntosh, Robbie
 See Pretenders, The

McIntyre, Jim
 See Apples in Stereo
McIntyre, Joey 34
 Also see New Kids on the Block
McIntyre, Owen "Onnie"
 See Average White Band
McJohn, Goldy
 See Steppenwolf
McKagan, Duff
 See Guns n' Roses
McKahey, Liam
 See Cousteau
McKay, Al
 See Earth, Wind and Fire
McKay, John
 See Siouxsie and the Banshees
McKean, Michael
 See Spinal Tap
McKee, Julius
 See Dirty Dozen Brass Band
McKee, Maria 11
McKeehan, Toby
 See dc Talk
McKenna, Greg
 See Letters to Cleo
McKennitt, Loreena 24
McKenzie, Christina "Licorice"
 See Incredible String Band
McKenzie, Derrick
 See Jamiroquai
McKenzie, Scott
 See Mamas and the Papas
McKernan, Ron "Pigpen"
 See Grateful Dead, The
McKinney, Andy
 See Molly Hatchet
McKinney, William
 See McKinney's Cotton Pickers
McKinney's Cotton Pickers 16
McKnight, Brian 22
McKnight III, Claude V.
 See Take 6
McLachlan, Sarah 34
 Earlier sketch in CM 12
McLagan, Ian
 See Faces, The
McLaren, Malcolm 23
McLaughlin, David
 See Lynn Morris Band
McLaughlin, John 12
 Also see Mahavishnu Orchestra
McLean, A. J.
 See Backstreet Boys
McLean, Dave 24
McLean, Don 7
McLean, Jackie 41
McLean, John
 See Beta Band, The
McLemore, Lamonte
 See Fifth Dimension
McLennan, Grant 21
 Also see Go-Betweens, The
McLeod, Rory
 See Roomful of Blues
McLoughlin, Jon
 See Del Amitri
McMackin, Bryon
 See Pennywise
McMeel, Mickey
 See Three Dog Night
McMurray, Rick
 See Ash
McMurtry, James 10
McNabb, Sean
 See Great White
McNabb, Travis
 See Better Than Ezra

McNair, Sylvia 15
McNally, James
 See Afro Celt Sound System
McNally, Joe
 See Voodoo Glow Skulls
McNally, John
 See Searchers, The
McNally, Ste
 See BBMak
McNeely, Big Jay 37
McNeill, Brian
 See Battlefield Band, The
McNeilly, Mac
 See Jesus Lizard
McNew, James
 See Yo La Tengo
McPartland, Marian 15
McPhatter, Clyde 25
 Also see Drifters, The
McPherson, Graham "Suggs"
 See Madness
McPherson, Scott
 See Sense Field
McPherson, Todd
 See Kingsmen, The
McQuater, Matthew
 See Clovers, The
McQuillar, Shawn
 See Kool & the Gang
McRae, Carmen 9
McReynolds, Jesse
 See McReynolds, Jim and Jesse
McReynolds, Jim and Jesse 12
McReynolds, Jim
 See McReynolds, Jim and Jesse
McRobbie, Stephen
 See Pastels, The
McShane, Ronnie
 See Chieftains, The
McShann, Jay 41
McShee, Jacqui
 See Pentangle
McSpadden, Gary
 See Imperials, The
McTaggert, Ed
 See Daniel Amos
McTell, Blind Willie 17
McVie, Christine
 See Fleetwood Mac
McVie, John
 See Fleetwood Mac
McWhinney, James
 See Big Mountain
McWhinney, Joaquin
 See Big Mountain
Mdletshe, Geophrey
 See Ladysmith Black Mambazo
Mead, Chuck
 See BR5-49
Meade, Tyson
 See Chainsaw Kittens, The
Meagher, Ron
 See Beau Brummels
Meat Loaf 12
Meat Puppets, The 13
Medeski, John
 See Medeski, Martin & Wood
Medeski, Martin & Wood 32
Mediaeval Baebes 47
Medley, Bill 3
Medlock, James
 See Soul Stirrers, The
Meehan, Tony
 See Shadows, The
Meek, Joe 46
Megadeth 9
Mehldau, Brad 27

Mehta, Zubin 11
Meifert, Arnulf
  See Faust
Meine, Klaus
  See Scorpions, The
Meisner, Randy
  See Eagles, The
Mekons, The 15
Melanie 12
Melax, Einar
  See Sugarcubes, The
Melchiondo, Mickey
  See Ween
Mellencamp, John 20
  Earlier sketch in CM 2
Mellino, Iza
  See Les Négresses Vertes
Mellino, Stéfane
  See Les Négresses Vertes
Melton, Barry
  See Country Joe and the Fish
Melvin, Eric
  See NOFX
Melvins 46
  Earlier sketch in CM 21
Melvoin, Jonathan
  See Smashing Pumpkins
Memphis Jug Band 25
Memphis Minnie 25
Men at Work 34
Menck, Ric
  See Velvet Crush
Mendel, Nate
  See Foo Fighters
  Also see Sunny Day Real Estate
Mendes, Sergio 40
Mengede, Peter
  See Helmet
Menken, Alan 10
Menotti, Gian Carlo 37
Menuhin, Yehudi 11
Menza, Nick
  See Megadeth
Mercado, Scott
  See Candlebox
Mercer, Jerry
  See April Wine
Mercer, Johnny 13
Merchant, Jimmy
  See Frankie Lymon and The Teenagers
Merchant, Natalie 25
  Also see 10,000 Maniacs
Mercier, Peadar
  See Chieftains, The
Mercurio, Robert
  See Galactic
Mercury, Freddie
  See Queen
Mercury Rev 28
Merman, Ethel 27
Merrick, Bryn
  See Damned, The
Merrill, Robbie
  See Godsmack
Merritt, Brad
  See 54-40
Merritt, Stephin
  See Magnetic Fields, The
Mertens, Paul
  See Poi Dog Pondering
Merzbow 31
Mesaros, Michael
  See Smithereens, The
Messecar, Dek
  See Caravan
Messina, Jim
  See Buffalo Springfield

Messina, Jo Dee 26
Messina, Joe
  See Funk Brothers
Metallica 33
  Earlier sketch in CM 7
Meters, The 14
Methembu, Russel
  See Ladysmith Black Mambazo
Metheny, Pat 26
  Earlier sketch in CM 2
Method Man 31
  Also see Wu-Tang Clan
Mettler, Darren
  See O.C. Supertones, The
Metzger, Mark
  See Chainsaw Kittens, The
Mew, Sharon
  See Elastica
Meyer, Edgar 40
Meyer, Eric
  See Charm Farm
Meyers, Augie
  See Texas Tornados, The
Mhaonaigh, Mairead Ni
  See Altan
Mhire, Jeremy
  See Plus One
Michael, George 9
Michaels, Bret
  See Poison
Michel, Luke
  See Emmet Swimming
Michel, Prakazrel "Pras"
  See Fugees, The
Michiles, Malcolm
  See Citizen King
Middlebrook, Ralph "Pee Wee"
  See Ohio Players
Middleton, Darren
  See Powderfinger
Middleton, Malcolm
  See Arab Strap
Middleton, Mark
  See Blackstreet
Midler, Bette 8
Midnight Oil 11
Midori 7
Mighty Mighty Bosstones 20
Mighty Clouds of Joy, The 17
Miguel, Luis 34
Mihm, Danny
  See Flamin' Groovies
Mike D
  See Diamond, Michael
Mike & the Mechanics 17
Mikens, Dennis
  See Smithereens, The
Mikens, Robert
  See Kool & the Gang
Milchem, Glenn
  See Blue Rodeo
Miles, Chris
  See Northern Lights
Miles, David
  See ESG
Miles, Richard
  See Soul Stirrers, The
Miles, Ron 22
Millar, Deborah
  See Massive Attack
Miller, Buddy 31
Miller, Charles
  See War
Miller, Dan
  See O-Town
Miller, David
  See Asleep at the Wheel

Miller, Glenn 6
Miller, Jacob "Killer"
  See Inner Circle
Miller, Jerry
  See Moby Grape
Miller, Keith
  See Elms, The
Miller, Kevin
  See Fuel
Miller, Marcus 38
Miller, Mark
  See Sawyer Brown
Miller, Mitch 11
Miller, Rhett
  See Old 97's
Miller, Rice
  See Williamson, Sonny Boy
Miller, Rick
  See Southern Culture on the Skids
Miller, Robert
  See Supertramp
Miller, Roger 4
Miller, Ryan
  See Guster
Miller, Scott
  See Loud Family, The
Miller, Steve 2
Milli Vanilli 4
Milliken, Catherine
  See Ensemble Modern
Mills, Bryan
  See Divine Comedy, The
Mills, Crispian
  See Kula Shaker
Mills, Donald
  See Mills Brothers, The
Mills, Fred
  See Canadian Brass, The
Mills, Harry
  See Mills Brothers, The
Mills, Herbert
  See Mills Brothers, The
Mills, John, Jr.
  See Mills Brothers, The
Mills, John, Sr.
  See Mills Brothers, The
Mills, Mike
  See R.E.M.
Mills, Sidney
  See Steel Pulse
Mills, Stephanie 21
Mills Brothers, The 14
Milo, Nick
  See Tower of Power
Milsap, Ronnie 2
Milton, Doctor
  See Alien Sex Fiend
Mingus, Charles 9
Ministry 10
Minnelli, Liza 19
Minns, Danielle
  See Minty
Minogue, Kylie 32
Minott, Sugar 31
Mint Condition 29
Minton, Phil 29
Minty 32
Minutemen, The 31
Mirabal, Robert 45
Miranda, Freddi
  See El Gran Combo
Misfits, The 32
Miskulin, Joey "The Cowpolka King"
  See Riders in the Sky
Miss Kier Kirby
  See Lady Miss Kier
Missing Persons 39

Mister Rogers
  See Rogers, Fred
Mistry, Jagdish
  See Ensemble Modern
Mitchell, Alex
  See Curve
Mitchell, Billy
  See Clovers, The
Mitchell, Bruce
  See Durutti Column, The
Mitchell, Burt
  See Ceili Rain
Mitchell, Elizabeth
  See Ida
Mitchell, John
  See Asleep at the Wheel
Mitchell, Joni **42**
  Earlier sketch in CM **17**
  Earlier sketch in CM **2**
Mitchell, Katrina
  See Pastels, The
Mitchell, Keith
  See Mazzy Star
Mitchell, Mike
  See Kingsmen, The
Mitchell, Mitch
  See Guided By Voices
Mitchell, Roscoe
  See Art Ensemble of Chicago, The
Mittoo, Jackie
  See Skatalites, The
Mize, Ben
  See Counting Crows
Mizell, Jay "Jam Master Jay"
  See Run DMC
Mo', Keb' **21**
Moberley, Gary
  See Sweet
Moby **27**
  Earlier sketch in CM **17**
Moby Grape **12**
Modeliste, Joseph "Zigaboo"
  See Meters, The
Modest Mouse **30**
moe. **34**
Moerlen, Pierre
  See Gong
Moffat, Aidan
  See Arab Strap
Moffatt, Gary
  See .38 Special
Moffatt, Katy **46**
  Earlier sketch in CM **18**
Moginie, Jim
  See Midnight Oil
Mogwai **27**
Mohan, John
  See Felt
Mohr, Todd
  See Big Head Todd and the Monsters
Mojave 3 **26**
Molino, Vincent
  See Radio Tarifa
Molko, Brian
  See Placebo
Molla, Chris
  See Monks of Doom
Molland, Joey
  See Badfinger
Molloy, Matt
  See Chieftains, The
Molly Hatchet **37**
Moloko **37**
Moloney, Paddy
  See Chieftains, The
Molotov **47**
Momus **47**

Monahan, Pat
  See Train
Monahan, Thom
  See Pernice Brothers
Monarch, Michael
  See Steppenwolf
Monch, Pharoahe **29**
Money, Bob
  See Jordanaires, The
Money, Eddie **16**
Money B
  See Digital Underground
Monheit, Jane **33**
Monica **26**
Monifah **24**
Monk, Meredith **1**
Monk, Thelonious **6**
Monkees, The **7**
Monks of Doom **28**
Monro, Diane
  See String Trio of New York
Monroe, Bill **1**
Monster, Drunkness
  See Len
Monster Magnet **39**
Montana, Country Dick
  See Beat Farmers
Montana, Patsy **38**
Montana, Tony
  See Great White
Montand, Yves **12**
Monte, Marisa **38**
Montenegro, Hugo **18**
Montes, George
  See Son by Four
Montes, Javier
  See Son by Four
Montgomery, Eddie
  See Montgomery Gentry
Montgomery, John Michael **14**
Montgomery, Ken "Dimwit"
  See D.O.A.
Montgomery, Little Brother **26**
Montgomery, Wes **3**
Montgomery Gentry **34**
Monti, Steve
  See Curve
Montoya, Craig
  See Everclear
Montrose, Ronnie **22**
Montroy, Roy
  See Resurrection Band
Montsalvatge, Xavier **39**
Moody, James **34**
Moody, Spencer
  See Murder City Devils
Moody Blues, The **18**
Moog, Robert A. **46**
Moon, Doug
  See Captain Beefheart and His Magic Band
Moon, Keith
  See Who, The
Mooney, Malcolm
  See Can
Mooney, Michael
  See Spiritualized
Mooney, Tim
  See American Music Club
Moonglows, The **33**
Moor, Davey Ray
  See Cousteau
Moore, Alan
  See Judas Priest
Moore, Angelo
  See Fishbone
Moore, Archie
  See Velocity Girl

Moore, Chante **21**
Moore, Geoff **43**
Moore, Glen
  See Oregon
Moore, Johnny "Dizzy"
  See Skatalites, The
Moore, Johnny
  See Drifters, The
Moore, Josh
  See Caedmon's Call
Moore, Kevin
  See Dream Theater
Moore, LeRoi
  See Dave Matthews Band
Moore, Mandy **35**
Moore, Melba **7**
Moore, Russell
  See IIIrd Tyme Out
Moore, Sam
  See Sam and Dave
Moore, Sean
  See Manic Street Preachers
Moore, Stanton
  See Galactic
Moore, Thurston
  See Sonic Youth
Moore, Undine Smith **40**
Moorer, Allison **40**
Moorse, Kiki
  See Chicks on Speed
M.O.P. **34**
Morales, Angela
  See Na Leo
Morales, Armond
  See Imperials, The
Morales, Mark
  See Fat Boys, The
Morales, Richie
  See Spyro Gyra
Morales, Rudy
  See Rumba Club
Moran, Jason **44**
Morand, Grace
  See Chenille Sisters, The
Moraz, Patrick
  See Moody Blues, The
  Also see Yes
Morcheeba **25**
Moreira, Airto **44**
  Also see Weather Report
Morello, Tom
  See Rage Against the Machine
Moreno, Chino
  See Deftones
Moreno-Primeau, Soni
  See Ulali
Moretti, Fabrizio
  See Strokes, The
Moreve, Rushton
  See Steppenwolf
Morgan, Brad
  See Drive-By Truckers
Morgan, Cindy **36**
Morgan, Frank **9**
Morgan, Jane **30**
Morgan, John Russell
  See Steppenwolf
Morgan, Lorrie **41**
  Earlier sketch in CM **10**
Morgenstein, Rod
  See Dixie Dregs
Morginsky, Matt
  See O.C. Supertones, The
Morisey, Dick
  See Soft Machine
Morissette, Alanis **39**
  Earlier sketch in CM **19**

O'Hara, Helen
See Dexy's Midnight Runners
O'Hara, Mary 47
O'Hare, Brendan
See Mogwai
Also see Teenage Fanclub
O'Hearn, Patrick 40
Also see Missing Persons
Ohio Players 16
Oingo Boingo 39
O'Jays, The 13
Oje, Baba
See Arrested Development
O'Keefe, Laurence
See Dark Star
Ol' Dirty Bastard 42
Also see Wu-Tang Clan
Olafsson, Bragi
See Sugarcubes, The
Olafunke, Carlene
See Black Uhuru
Olander, Jimmy
See Diamond Rio
Olatunji, Babatunde 45
Olaverra, Margot
See Go-Go's, The
Old 97's 33
Olde-Wolbers, Christian
See Fear Factory
Oldfield, Mike 18
Oldham, Jack
See Surfaris, The
Oldham, Sean
See Cherry Poppin' Daddies
Oldham, Will 32
Olds, Brent
See Poi Dog Pondering
O'Lionaird, Iarla
See Afro Celt Sound System
Oliver, Joe
See Oliver, King
Oliver, Karin
See His Name Is Alive
Oliver, King 15
Oliveri, Nick
See Queens of the Stone Age
Oliveros, Pauline 47
Olivia Tremor Control 28
Olley, Chris
See Six by Seven
Ollis, Terry
See Hawkwind
Ollu, Franck
See Ensemble Modern
Olsdal, Stefan
See Placebo
Olson, Carla 45
Olson, Jeff
See Village People, The
Olson, Mark
See Jayhawks, The
Olsson, Nigel
See Spencer Davis Group
Oltman, Matt
See Chanticleer
O'Malley, Tony
See 10cc
O'Meara, Jo
See S Club 7
Ommer, Nobert
See Ensemble Modern
Onassis, Blackie
See Urge Overkill
Ondras, Charlie
See Boss Hog
O'Neill, Damian
See Undertones, The

O'Neill, Jerry
See Voodoo Glow Skulls
O'Neill, John
See Undertones, The
Ono, Yoko 47
Earlier sketch in CM 11
Opokuwaa, Akua
See Sweet Honey in the Rock
Orange, Walter "Clyde"
See Commodores, The
Orange County Supertones
See O.C. Supertones, The
Orb, The 18
Orbison, Roy 2
Orbit, William 30
Orbital 20
Orchestra Baobab 42
Orchestral Manoeuvres in the Dark 21
O'Reagan, Tim
See Jayhawks, The
Oregon 30
Orff, Carl 21
Organ, Chad
See Flying Luttenbachers, The
Orgy 27
Orioles, The 35
O'Riordan, Cait
See Pogues, The
O'Riordan, Dolores
See Cranberries, The
Orlando, Tony 15
örn, Einar
See Sugarcubes, The
örnolfsdottir, Margret
See Sugarcubes, The
O'Rourke, Jim 31
Orr, Benjamin
See Cars, The
Orr, Casey
See Gwar
Orrall, Frank
See Poi Dog Pondering
Orrico, Stacie 47
Ortega, Leonor "Jeff"
See Five Iron Frenzy
Ortega, Micah
See Five Iron Frenzy
Ortiz, Bill
See Lavay Smith and Her Red Hot
Skillet Lickers
Ortiz, Domingo "Sunny"
See Widespread Panic
Ortmann, Mark
See Bottle Rockets
Ortoli
See Les Négresses Vertes
Orton, Beth 26
Orton, Mark
See Tin Hat Trio
Orzabal, Roland
See Tears for Fears
Osborn, Jinny
See Chordettes, The
Osborn, Kassidy
See SHeDAISY
Osborn, Kelsi
See SHeDAISY
Osborn, Kristyn
See SHeDAISY
Osborne, Bob
See Osborne Brothers, The
Osborne, Buzz
See Melvins
Osborne, David
See 54-40
Osborne, Joan 19

Osborne, Neil
See 54-40
Osborne, Sonny
See Osborne Brothers, The
Osborne Brothers, The 8
Osbourne, Ozzy 39
Earlier sketch in CM 3
Also see Black Sabbath
Osby, Greg 21
Oskar, Lee
See War
Oskay, Billy
See Nightnoise
Oslin, K. T. 3
Osman, Mat
See Suede
Osmond, Donny 3
Ostin, Mo 17
Oswald, Hunter
See Down By Law
Otis, Johnny 16
O'Toole, Mark
See Frankie Goes To Hollywood
O-Town 44
Ott, David 2
Ottewell, Ben
See Gomez
Otto, John
See Limp Bizkit
Our Lady Peace 22
Out of the Grey 37
OutKast 33
Outler, Jimmy
See Soul Stirrers, The
Ovenden, Emily
See Mediaeval Baebes
Overstreet, Paul 33
Overton, Nancy
See Chordettes, The
Owen, Randy Yueull
See Alabama
Owen, Scott
See Living End, The
Owens, Buck 2
Owens, Campbell
See Aztec Camera
Owens, Fred
See Dixie Hummingbirds, The
Owens, Henry
See Golden Gate Quartet
Owens, Jack 30
Owens, Paul
See Dixie Hummingbirds, The
Also see Swan Silvertones, The
Owens, Ricky
See Temptations, The
Owens, Tim
See Jay-Z
Oxley, Tony 32
Oyewole, Abiodun
See Last Poets
P. Diddy
See Combs, Sean "Puffy"
Pablo, Augustus 37
Pace, Amedeo
See Blonde Redhead
Pace, Simone
See Blonde Redhead
Page, Greg
See Wiggles, The
Page, Jimmy 4
Also see Led Zeppelin
Also see Yardbirds, The
Page, Patti 11
Page, Steven
See Barenaked Ladies

Peek, Dan
  See America
Peel, John **43**
Peeler, Ben
  See Mavericks, The
Peeples, Philip
  See Old 97's
Peet, Joe
  See Cousteau
Pegg, Dave
  See Fairport Convention
  Also see Jethro Tull
Pegrum, Nigel
  See Steeleye Span
Peligro, Darren H.
  See Dead Kennedys
Pelletier, Mike
  See Kilgore
Peña, Adela
  See Eroica Trio
Pence, Jeff
  See Blessid Union of Souls
Pender, Mike
  See Searchers, The
Penderecki, Krzysztof **30**
Pendergast, George
  See Dishwalla
Pendergrass, Teddy **3**
Pendleton, Brian
  See Pretty Things, The
Pengilly, Kirk
  See INXS
Penick, Trevor
  See O-Town
Peniston, CeCe **15**
Penn, Michael **4**
Penner, Fred **10**
Pennywise **27**
Penrod, Guy
  See Gaither Vocal Band
Pentangle **18**
Pentland, Patrick
  See Sloan
People Under The Stairs **39**
Pepper, Art **18**
Perahia, Murray **35**
  Earlier sketch in CM **10**
Pere Ubu **17**
Peretz, Jesse
  See Lemonheads, The
Perez, Arturo
  See Redbone
Perez, Danilo **25**
Perez, Eddie
  See El Gran Combo
Perez, Louie
  See Los Lobos
Peris, Don
  See Innocence Mission, The
Peris, Karen
  See Innocence Mission, The
Perkins, Al
  See Flying Burrito Brothers
Perkins, Carl **9**
Perkins, John
  See XTC
Perkins, Percell
  See Five Blind Boys of Alabama
Perkins, Steve
  See Jane's Addiction
  Also see Porno for Pyros
Perko, Lynn
  See Imperial Teen
Perlemuter, Vlado **41**
Perlman, Itzhak **37**
  Earlier sketch in CM **2**

Perlman, Marc
  See Jayhawks, The
Pernice, Bob
  See Pernice Brothers
Pernice, Joe
  See Pernice Brothers
  Also see Scud Mountain Boys
Pernice Brothers **33**
Peron, Jean-Hervé
  See Faust
Perry, Brendan
  See Dead Can Dance
Perry, Doane
  See Jethro Tull
Perry, Jason
  See Plus One
Perry, Joe
  See Aerosmith
Perry, John G.
  See Caravan
Perry, Linda **38**
Perry, Phil **24**
Perry, Steve
  See Cherry Poppin' Daddies
Perry, Steve
  See Journey
Perry, Virgshawn
  See Artifacts
Person, Eric
  See World Saxophone Quartet
Persson, Nina
  See Cardigans
Persuasions, The **47**
Pet Shop Boys **5**
Peter, Paul & Mary **4**
Peters, Bernadette **27**
  Earlier sketch in CM **7**
Peters, Dan
  See Mudhoney
Peters, Gretchen **45**
Peters, Joey
  See Grant Lee Buffalo
Peters, Mike
  See Alarm
Petersen, Chris
  See Front Line Assembly
Peterson, Debbi
  See Bangles, The
Peterson, Dick
  See Kingsmen, The
Peterson, Garry
  See Guess Who
Peterson, John
  See Beau Brummels
Peterson, Michael **31**
Peterson, Oscar **11**
Peterson, Steve
  See Kingsmen, The
Peterson, Sylvia
  See Chiffons, The
Peterson, Vicki
  See Bangles, The
  Also see Continental Drifters
Petersson, Tom
  See Cheap Trick
Petito, Scott
  See Fugs, The
Petkovic, John
  See Cobra Verde
Petra **3**
Petratos, Dave
  See Romantics, The
Petri, Tony
  See Wendy O. Williams and The Plasmatics
Petrucci, John
  See Dream Theater

Petty, Tom **9**
  Also see Tom Petty and the Heartbreakers
Peverett, Dave
  See Foghat
Pfaff, Kristen
  See Hole
Pfahler, Adam
  See Jawbreaker
Pfeiffer, Darrin
  See Goldfinger
Pfeiffer, Rob
  See Sense Field
Pfisterer, Alban
  See Love
PFR **38**
Phair, Liz **14**
Phantom, Slim Jim
  See Stray Cats, The
Pharcyde, The **17**
Phelps, David
  See Gaither Vocal Band
Phelps, Doug
  See Kentucky Headhunters, The
Phelps, Kelly Joe **36**
Phelps, Ricky Lee
  See Kentucky Headhunters, The
Phife
  See Tribe Called Quest, A
Phil, Gary
  See Boston
Philbin, Greg
  See REO Speedwagon
Philips, Anthony
  See Genesis
Phillips, Chris
  See Squirrel Nut Zippers
Phillips, Chynna
  See Wilson Phillips
Phillips, Craig & Dean **45**
Phillips, Esther **46**
Phillips, Glenn
  See Toad the Wet Sprocket
Phillips, Grant Lee
  See Grant Lee Buffalo
Phillips, Harvey **3**
Phillips, John
  See Mamas and the Papas
Phillips, Mackenzie
  See Mamas and the Papas
Phillips, Mark
  See Down By Law
Phillips, Michelle
  See Mamas and the Papas
Phillips, Paul
  See Puddle of Mudd
Phillips, Randy
  See Phillips, Craig & Dean
Phillips, Sam **12**
Phillips, Sam **5**
Phillips, Scott
  See Creed
Phillips, Shawn **41**
Phillips, Shelley
  See Point of Grace
Phillips, Simon
  See Judas Priest
Phipps, Sam
  See Oingo Boingo
Phish **25**
  Earlier sketch in CM **13**
Phungula, Inos
  See Ladysmith Black Mambazo
Piaf, Edith **8**
Piazza, Sammy
  See Quicksilver Messenger Service
Piazzolla, Astor **18**

Presley, Elvis **1**
Prestia, Francis "Rocco"
  See Tower of Power
Preston, Aaron
  See Chainsaw Kittens, The
Preston, Joe
  See Melvins
Preston, Leroy
  See Asleep at the Wheel
Preston, Mark
  See Lettermen, The
Prestwich, Steven
  See Cold Chisel
Pretenders, The **8**
Pretty Things, The **26**
Previn, André **15**
Prévost, Eddie
  See AMM
Price, Alan
  See Animals, The
Price, Kelly **34**
Price, Leontyne **6**
Price, Lloyd **25**
Price, Louis
  See Temptations, The
Price, Mark
  See Archers of Loaf
Price, Martin
  See 808 State
Price, Ray **11**
Price, Rick
  See Electric Light Orchestra
Price, Rod
  See Foghat
Pride, Charley **4**
Priest, Gretchen
  See Ceili Rain
Priest, Maxi **20**
Priest, Steve
  See Sweet
Prima, Louis **18**
Primal Scream **14**
Primettes, The
  See Supremes, The
Primrose, Neil
  See Travis
Primus **11**
Prince **40**
  Earlier sketch in CM **14**
  Earlier sketch in CM **1**
Prince, Prairie
  See Journey
Prince, Vivian
  See Pretty Things, The
Prince Be
  See P.M. Dawn
Princess Superstar **39**
Prine, John **7**
Prior, Maddy
  See Steeleye Span
Priske, Rich
  See Matthew Good Band
Pritchard, Chris
  See Silly Wizard
Proclaimers, The **13**
Proctor, Mark
  See Seventy Sevens, The
Prodigy **22**
Professor Longhair **6**
Promise Ring, The **28**
Prong **23**
Propatier, Joe
  See Silver Apples
Propellerheads **26**
Propes, Duane
  See Little Texas
Prophet, Chuck **32**

Prosper, Marvin
  See Baha Men
Prout, Brian
  See Diamond Rio
Pryce, Guto
  See Super Furry Animals
Pryor, Matthew
  See Get Up Kids
Psychedelic Furs **23**
Ptacek, Rainer
  See Giant Sand
Pte
  See Indigenous
Public Enemy **4**
Puccini, Giacomo **25**
Puckett, Gary
  See Gary Puckett and the Union Gap
Puddle of Mudd **45**
Puente, Tito **14**
Puff Daddy
  See Combs, Sean "Puffy"
Pullen, Don **16**
Pulp **18**
Pulsford, Nigel
  See Bush
Pura Fé
  See Ulali
Purcell, John
  See World Saxophone Quartet
Purim, Flora **45**
Pusey, Clifford "Moonie"
  See Steel Pulse
Pyle, Andy
  See Kinks, The
Pyle, Artemis
  See Lynyrd Skynyrd
Pyle, Chris
  See Royal Trux
Pyle, Pip
  See Gong
Pyres, Gian
  See Cradle of Filth
Pyro, Howie
  See D Generation
Q-Ball, D.J.
  See Bloodhound Gang, The
Q-Tip
  See Tribe Called Quest, A
Quaid, Johnny
  See My Morning Jacket
Quaife, Peter
  See Kinks, The
Quasi **24**
Quasthoff, Thomas **26**
Quatro, Suzi **47**
Quaye, Finley **30**
Queen **6**
Queen Ida **9**
Queen Latifah **24**
  Earlier sketch in CM **6**
Queens, Hollis
  See Boss Hog
Queens of the Stone Age **31**
Queensryche **8**
Queralt, Steve
  See Ride
Querfurth, Carl
  See Roomful of Blues
? and the Mysterians **44**
Quick, Clarence
  See Del Vikings, The
Quicksilver Messenger Service **23**
Quickspace **30**
Quiles, Pedro
  See Son by Four
Quinn, Mickey
  See Supergrass

Qureshi, Ustad Alla Rakha **29**
R. Prophet
  See Nappy Roots
Raaymakers, Boy
  See Willem Breuker Kollektief
Rabbitt, Eddie **24**
  Earlier sketch in CM **5**
Rabin, Trevor
  See Yes
Race, Tony
  See Felt
Radalj, Rod
  See Hoodoo Gurus
Radio Tarifa **40**
Radiohead **24**
Radley, Kate
  See Spiritualized
Rae, Terry
  See Flamin' Groovies
Raekwon
  See Wu-Tang Clan
Rafferty, Mary
  See Cherish the Ladies
Raffi **8**
Rage Against the Machine **37**
  Earlier sketch in CM **18**
Raheem
  See Geto Boys, The
Rainbow **40**
Raines, Jeff
  See Galactic
Rainey, Ma **22**
Rainey, Sid
  See Compulsion
Rainford, Simone
  See All Saints
Rainwater, Keech
  See Lonestar
Rainwater, Lonnie
  See Hackberry Ramblers
Raitt, Bonnie **23**
  Earlier sketch in CM **3**
Rakim **46**
  Also see Eric B. and Rakim
Raleigh, Don
  See Squirrel Nut Zippers
Ralph Sharon Quartet **26**
Ralphs, Mick
  See Bad Company
  Also see Mott the Hoople
Ramirez, Twiggy
  See Marilyn Manson
Rammstein **25**
Ramone, C. J.
  See Ramones, The
Ramone, Dee Dee
  See Ramones, The
Ramone, Joey
  See Ramones, The
Ramone, Johnny
  See Ramones, The
Ramone, Marky
  See Ramones, The
Ramone, Ritchie
  See Ramones, The
Ramone, Tommy
  See Ramones, The
Ramones, The **41**
  Earlier sketch in CM **9**
Rampage, Randy
  See D.O.A.
Rampal, Jean-Pierre **6**
Ramsay, Andy
  See Stereolab
Ranaldo, Lee
  See Sonic Youth
Rancid **29**

Reynolds, Robert
  See Mavericks, The
Reynolds, Sheldon
  See Earth, Wind and Fire
Reznor, Trent 13
  Also see Nine Inch Nails
Rheostatics 37
Rhoad, Herbert
  See Persuasions, The
Rhodes, Louise
  See Lamb
Rhodes, Nick
  See Duran Duran
Rhodes, Philip
  See Gin Blossoms
Rhodes, Todd
  See McKinney's Cotton Pickers
Rhone, Sylvia 13
Rhys, Gruff
  See Super Furry Animals
Ribot, Marc 30
Rice, Chris 25
Rice, Jeff
  See Whiskeytown
Rice, Syl
  See Flatlanders, The
Rich, Buddy 13
Rich, Charlie 3
Rich, Jeff
  See Status Quo
Rich, John
  See Lonestar
Richard, Cliff 14
Richard, Zachary 9
Richards, Aled
  See Catatonia
Richards, Edward
  See Shamen, The
Richards, J.R.
  See Dishwalla
Richards, Keith 11
  Also see Rolling Stones, The
Richards, Lee
  See Godsmack
Richardson, Geoffrey
  See Caravan
Richardson, Kevin
  See Backstreet Boys
Richey, Kim 20
Richie, Lionel 2
  Also see Commodores, The
Richling, Greg
  See Wallflowers, The
Richman, Jonathan 12
Richrath, Gary
  See REO Speedwagon
Richter, Johnny
  See Kottonmouth Kings
Rick, Dave
  See King Missile
Ricochet 23
Riddle, Paul
  See Marshall Tucker Band
Ride 40
Riders in the Sky 33
Ridley, Greg
  See Humble Pie
Riebling, Scott
  See Letters to Cleo
Rieckermann, Ralph
  See Scorpions, The
Riedel, Oliver
  See Rammstein
Rieflin, William
  See Ministry
  Also see Pigface

Rieger, Andrew
  See Elf Power
Rieu, André 26
Rigby, Will
  See dB's, The
Riles, Kelly
  See Velocity Girl
Riley, Billy Lee 43
Riley, Herman
  See Lavay Smith and Her Red Hot
  Skillet Lickers
Riley, Kristian
  See Citizen King
Riley, Teddy "Street" 14
  See Blackstreet
Riley, Terry 32
Riley, Timothy Christian
  See Tony! Toni! Toné!
Rillera, Butch
  See Redbone
Rimes, LeAnn 46
  Earlier sketch in CM 19
Ringenberg, Jason
  See Jason & the Scorchers
Rippingtons 38
Rippon, Steve
  See Lush
Ritchie, Brian
  See Violent Femmes
Ritchie, Jean 4
Ritchie, John Simon
  See Sid Vicious
Ritchie, Robert
  See Kid Rock
Ritenour, Lee 7
Ritter, Tex 37
Ritts-Kirby, Freya
  See Ensemble Modern
Rivas, Jerry
  See El Gran Combo
Rivera, Freddie
  See El Gran Combo
Rivers, Sam 29
Rivers, Sam
  See Limp Bizkit
Rivers, Sam
  See Music Revelation Ensemble
Rizzo, Joe
  See D Generation
Rizzo, Peter
  See Gene Loves Jezebel
Roach, Max 12
Roach, Steve 41
Roback, David
  See Mazzy Star
Robbins, Charles David
  See BlackHawk
Robbins, J
  See Jawbox
Robbins, Marty 9
Roberson, LaTavia
  See Destiny's Child
Robert Bradley's Blackwater Surprise 35
Roberts, Brad
  See Crash Test Dummies
Roberts, Brad
  See Gwar
Roberts, Dan
  See Crash Test Dummies
Roberts, Jason
  See Asleep at the Wheel
Roberts, Ken
  See Charm Farm
Roberts, Marcus 6
Roberts, Mark
  See Catatonia

Roberts, Matt
  See 3 Doors Down
Roberts, Nathan
  See Flaming Lips
Roberts, Paul
  See Stranglers, The
Roberts, Rick
  See Flying Burrito Brothers
Robertson, Allison
  See Donnas, The
Robertson, Brian
  See Motörhead
  Also see Thin Lizzy
Robertson, Ed
  See Barenaked Ladies
Robertson, Robbie 2
  Also see Band, The
Robertson, Rowan
  See VAST
Robeson, Paul 8
Robi, Paul
  See Platters, The
Robie, Milton
  See Memphis Jug Band
Robillard, Duke 2
  Also see Roomful of Blues
Robinson, Arnold
  See Nylons, The
Robinson, Chris
  See Black Crowes, The
Robinson, Cynthia
  See Sly & the Family Stone
Robinson, Darren
  See Fat Boys, The
Robinson, David
  See Cars, The
Robinson, Dawn
  See En Vogue
Robinson, Louise
  See Sweet Honey in the Rock
Robinson, Prince
  See McKinney's Cotton Pickers
Robinson, R. B.
  See Soul Stirrers, The
Robinson, Rich
  See Black Crowes, The
Robinson, Romye "Booty Brown"
  See Pharcyde, The
Robinson, Smokey 1
Robinson, Tony "Gad"
  See Aswad
Roche, Maggie
  See Roches, The
Roche, Suzzy
  See Roches, The
Roche, Terre
  See Roches, The
Roches, The 18
Rochester, Cornell
  See Music Revelation Ensemble
Rock, D.
  See Len
Rock, Richie
  See Boyzone
Rockapella 34
Rockenfield, Scott
  See Queensryche
Rocker, Lee
  See Stray Cats, The
Rockett, Rikki
  See Poison
Rockin' Dopsie 10
Rodford, Jim
  See Kinks, The
Rodgers, Jimmie 3
Rodgers, Nile 8
  Also see Chic

Rudolph, Paul
  See Hawkwind
Rue, Caroline
  See Hole
Ruff Endz 41
Ruffin, David 6
  Also see Temptations, The
Ruffin, Tamir
  See Dru Hill
Ruffins, Kermit
  See Rebirth Brass Band
Ruffy, Dave
  See Aztec Camera
  Also see Waterboys, The
Ruiz, Francis
  See Great White
Ruley, Yuri
  See MxPx
Rumba Club 36
Rumbel, Nancy
  See Tingstad & Rumbel
Rumsey, Vern
  See Unwound
Run
  See Run DMC
Run DMC 25
  Earlier sketch in CM 4
Runaways, The 44
Rundgren, Todd 11
RuPaul 20
Rusby, Kate 29
Rush 8
Rush, Otis 12
Rushakoff, Harry
  See Concrete Blonde
Rushing, Jimmy 37
Rushlow, Tim
  See Little Texas
Russel
  See Gorillaz
Russell, Alecia
  See Sounds of Blackness
Russell, Alistair
  See Battlefield Band, The
Russell, Graham
  See Air Supply
Russell, Hal
  See Flying Luttenbachers, The
Russell, Jack
  See Great White
Russell, John
  See Steppenwolf
Russell, Joseph
  See Persuasions, The
Russell, Leon 35
Russell, Mark 6
Russell, Martin
  See Afro Celt Sound System
Russell, Mike
  See Shudder to Think
Russell, Pee Wee 25
Russell, Tom 26
Russo, Jeff
  See Tonic
Russo, Marc
  See Yellowjackets
Rust Epique
  See Crazy Town
Rusted Root 26
Rutherford, Mike
  See Genesis
  Also see Mike & the Mechanics
Rutherford, Paul
  See Frankie Goes To Hollywood
Rutmanis, Kevin
  See Cows, The

Rutsey, John
  See Rush
Ryan, Cathie
  See Cherish the Ladies
Ryan, David
  See Lemonheads, The
Ryan, Mark
  See Country Joe and the Fish
  Also see Quicksilver Messenger Service
Ryan, Mick
  See Dave Clark Five, The
Ryan, Pat "Taco"
  See Asleep at the Wheel
Rybska, Agnieszka
  See Rasputina
Ryder, Mitch 23
  Earlier sketch in CM 11
Ryland, Jack
  See Three Dog Night
Rzab, Greg
  See Black Crowes, The
Rzeznik, Johnny
  See Goo Goo Dolls, The
S Club 7 37
Saariaho, Kaija 43
Sabo, Dave
  See Bon Jovi
Sade 37
  Earlier sketch in CM 2
Sadier, Laetitia
  See Stereolab
Saffery, Anthony
  See Cornershop
Saffron
  See Republica
Safina, Alessandro 42
Sage, Danny
  See D Generation
Sager, Carole Bayer 5
Sahir, Kadim al- 44
Sahm, Doug 30
  Also see Texas Tornados, The
Saint Etienne 28
Saint Vicious
  See Kottonmouth Kings
Sainte-Marie, Buffy 11
Saints, The 40
Saint-Saëns, Camille 25
Sakamoto, Ryuichi 19
Salazar, Arion
  See Third Eye Blind
Salem, Kevin 32
Salerno-Sonnenberg, Nadja 3
Saliers, Emily
  See Indigo Girls
Salisbury, Peter
  See Verve, The
Saliva 38
Sally, Zak
  See Low
Salmon, Michael
  See Prefab Sprout
Saloman, Nick
  See Bevis Frond
Salonen, Esa-Pekka 16
Salt-N-Pepa 6
Saltzman, Jeff
  See Sunset Valley
Saluzzi, Dino 23
Salv
  See Carter USM
Sam and Dave 8
Sambora, Richie 24
  Also see Bon Jovi
Sampson, Doug
  See Iron Maiden

Sams, Dean
  See Lonestar
Samuels, Dave
  See Spyro Gyra
Samuelson, Gar
  See Megadeth
Samuelsson, Marie 47
Samwell-Smith, Paul
  See Yardbirds, The
Sanborn, David 28
  Earlier sketch in CM 1
Sanchez 38
Sánchez, David 40
Sanchez, Michel
  See Deep Forest
Sanchez, Paul
  See Cowboy Mouth
Sanctuary, Gary
  See Aztec Camera
Sanders, Ed
  See Fugs, The
Sanders, Pharoah 28
  Earlier sketch in CM 16
  Also see Music Revelation Ensemble
Sanders, Ric
  See Fairport Convention
Sanders, Steve
  See Oak Ridge Boys, The
Sandison, Michael
  See Boards of Canada
Sandler, Adam 19
Sandman, Mark
  See Morphine
Sandmel, Ben
  See Hackberry Ramblers
Sandoval, Arturo 15
Sandoval, Hope
  See Mazzy Star
Sandoval, Sonny
  See P.O.D.
Sands, Aaron
  See Jars of Clay
Sanford, Gary
  See Aztec Camera
Sangare, Oumou 22
Sanger, David
  See Asleep at the Wheel
Sant' Ambrogio, Sara
  See Eroica Trio
Santamaria, Mongo 28
Santana, Carlos 43
  Earlier sketch in CM 19
  Earlier sketch in CM 1
Santiago, Herman
  See Frankie Lymon and The Teenagers
Santiago, Joey
  See Pixies, The
Santos, Domingo
  See El Gran Combo
Sanz, Alejandro 35
Sapphire, Cylindra
  See Mediaeval Baebes
Saraceno, Blues
  See Poison
Sargent, Gray
  See Ralph Sharon Quartet
Sasaki, Mamiko
  See Pizzicato Five
  Also see Pulp
Sasha 39
Satchell, Clarence "Satch"
  See Ohio Players
Satie, Erik 25
Satriani, Joe 4
Saunders, Peter
  See Dexy's Midnight Runners

Secrest, Wayne
  See Confederate Railroad
Sed, Billy
  See Giant Sand
Sedaka, Neil **4**
Seeger, Peggy **25**
Seeger, Pete **38**
  Earlier sketch in CM **4**
  Also see Weavers, The
Seger, Bob **15**
Seger, David
  See Giant Sand
Segovia, Andres **6**
Segundo, Compay **45**
Seidel, Martie
  See Dixie Chicks
Selberg, Shannon
  See Cows, The
Seldom Scene, The **4**
Selena **16**
Seligman, Matthew
  See Thompson Twins
Sellars, Rodney
  See Sense Field
Sellers, Jim
  See Stabbing Westward
Selway, Phil
  See Radiohead
Semisonic **32**
Sen Dog
  See Cypress Hill
Senior, Milton
  See McKinney's Cotton Pickers
Senior, Russell
  See Pulp
Sense Field **39**
Sensi
  See Soul II Soul
Sensible, Captain
  See Damned, The
Sepultura **12**
Seraphine, Daniel
  See Chicago
Sergeant, Will
  See Echo and the Bunnymen
Sermon, Erick **44**
  Also see EPMD
Serneholt, Marie
  See A*Teens
Serrato, Eddie
  See ? and the Mysterians
Setari, Craig
  See Sick of It All
Sete, Bola **26**
Setzer, Brian **32**
  Also see Stray Cats, The
Setzer, Philip
  See Emerson String Quartet
Seven Mary Three **39**
Sevendust **37**
Seventy Sevens, The **46**
Severin, Steven
  See Siouxsie and the Banshees
Severinsen, Doc **1**
Sex Pistols, The **5**
Sexsmith, Ron **27**
Sexton, Chad
  See 311
Sexton, Martin **41**
Seymour, Neil
  See Crowded House
Shabalala, Ben
  See Ladysmith Black Mambazo
Shabalala, Headman
  See Ladysmith Black Mambazo
Shabalala, Jockey
  See Ladysmith Black Mambazo

Shabalala, Joseph
  See Ladysmith Black Mambazo
Shabo, Eric
  See Atomic Fireballs, The
Shade, Will
  See Memphis Jug Band
Shadow, DJ **19**
Shadows, The **22**
Shaffer, James
  See Korn
Shaffer, Paul **13**
Shaggs, The **46**
Shaggy **37**
  Earlier sketch in CM **19**
Shaggy 2 Dope
  See Insane Clown Posse
Shaham, Gil **35**
Shai **23**
Shakespeare, Robbie
  See Sly and Robbie
  Also see Black Uhuru
Shakira **33**
Shakur, Tupac
  See 2Pac
Shallenberger, James
  See Kronos Quartet
Shamen, The **23**
Shane, Bob
  See Kingston Trio, The
Shangri-Las, The **35**
Shanice **14**
Shankar, Anoushka **46**
Shankar, Ravi **38**
  Earlier sketch in CM **9**
Shannon, Del **10**
Shannon, Sarah
  See Velocity Girl
Shannon, Sean
  See Molly Hatchet
Shannon, Sharon
  See Waterboys, The
Shanté **10**
Shapey, Ralph **42**
Shapiro, Jim
  See Veruca Salt
Shapiro, Lee
  See Four Seasons, The
Shapiro, Steve
  See Imperials, The
Shapps, Andre
  See Big Audio Dynamite
Sharkey, Feargal
  See Undertones, The
Sharon, Lois & Bram **6**
Sharon, Ralph
  See Ralph Sharon Quartet
Sharp, Alexander
  See Orioles, The
Sharp, Dave
  See Alarm
Sharp, Laura
  See Sweet Honey in the Rock
Sharpe, Matt
  See Weezer
Sharpe, Trevor
  See Mediaeval Baebes
Sharpe, Trevor
  See Minty
Sharrock, Chris
  See Lightning Seeds
Sharrock, Sonny **15**
Shaw, Adrian
  See Bevis Frond
Shaw, Artie **8**
Shaw, Ethan
  See Derailers, The

Shaw, Martin
  See Jamiroquai
Shaw, Robert **32**
Shaw, Tommy
  See Styx
Shaw, Woody **27**
Shea, Tom
  See Scud Mountain Boys
Sheaff, Lawrence
  See AMM
Shearer, Harry
  See Spinal Tap
Shearing, George **28**
Shears, Steve
  See Ultravox
SHeDAISY **36**
Shedden, Iain
  See Saints, The
Sheehan, Bobby
  See Blues Traveler
Sheehan, Fran
  See Boston
Sheep on Drugs **27**
Sheik, Duncan **32**
Sheila E. **3**
Sheldon, George
  See Blue Mountain
Sheldon, Scott
  See Guttermouth
Shellac **46**
Shellenberger, Allen
  See Lit
Shelley, Peter
  See Buzzcocks, The
Shelley, Steve
  See Sonic Youth
Shelton, Blake **45**
Shelton, Seb
  See Dexy's Midnight Runners
Shenandoah **17**
Shenandoah, Joanne **33**
Shepard, Kevin
  See Tonic
Shepard, Vonda **35**
Shepherd, Brad
  See Hoodoo Gurus
Shepherd, Hunter "Ben"
  See Soundgarden
Shepherd, John
  See Northwoods Improvisers
Shepherd, Kenny Wayne **22**
Shepp, Archie **43**
Sheppard, Rodney
  See Sugar Ray
Sherba, John
  See Kronos Quartet, The
Sherinian, Derek
  See Dream Theater
Sherman, Jack
  See Red Hot Chili Peppers
Sherwood, Adrian **31**
Shezbie, Derrick
  See Rebirth Brass Band
Shields, Kevin
  See My Bloody Valentine
Shifty Shellshock
  See Crazy Town
Shihad **34**
Shilton, Paul
  See Quickspace
Shimada, Noriko
  See Ensemble Modern
Shines, Johnny **14**
Shinoda, Mike
  See Linkin Park
Shipp, Matthew **31**
Shirelles, The **11**

Sleet, Nicole
See Mediaeval Baebes
Slesinger, Bruce "Ted"
See Dead Kennedys
Slichter, Jake
See Semisonic
Slick, Grace **33**
Also see Jefferson Airplane
Slick Rick **27**
Slijngaard, Ray
See 2 Unlimited
Slipknot **30**
Sloan **28**
Sloan, Allen
See Dixie Dregs
Sloan, Eliot
See Blessid Union of Souls
Sloane, Carol **36**
Sloas, Jimmie Lee
See Imperials, The
Slobberbone **38**
Slocum, Matt
See Sixpence None the Richer
Slovak, Hillel
See Red Hot Chili Peppers
Slowdive **40**
Sly, Randy "Ginger"
See Atomic Fireballs, The
Sly and Robbie **13**
Sly & the Family Stone **24**
Small, Heather
See M People
Small, Phil
See Cold Chisel
Smalley, Dave
See Down By Law
Smalley, Dave
See Raspberries
Smalls, Derek
See Spinal Tap
Smart, Terence
See Butthole Surfers
Smart II, N.D.
See Mountain
Smash, Chas
See Madness
Smash Mouth **27**
Smashing Pumpkins **36**
Earlier sketch in CM **13**
Smear, Pat
See Foo Fighters
Smelly
See NOFX
Smith, Aaron
See Seventy Sevens, The
Smith, Adrian
See Iron Maiden
Smith, Allen
See Lavay Smith and Her Red Hot
Skillet Lickers
Smith, Bessie **3**
Smith, Brad
See Blind Melon
Smith, Chad
See Red Hot Chili Peppers
Smith, Charles
See Kool & the Gang
Smith, Chas
See Cobra Verde
Smith, Clifford
See Method Man
Smith, Curt
See Tears for Fears
Smith, Debbie
See Curve
Also see Echobelly
Smith, Elliott **28**

Smith, Fran
See Hooters
Smith, Fred
See Blondie
Smith, Fred
See MC5, The
Smith, Fred
See Television
Smith, Garth
See Buzzcocks, The
Smith, Greg
See Rainbow
Smith, James "Smitty"
See Three Dog Night
Smith, Jerome
See KC and the Sunshine Band
Smith, Jimmy **30**
Smith, Jocelyn B. **30**
Smith, Joe
See McKinney's Cotton Pickers
Smith, Keely **29**
Smith, Kevin
See dc Talk
Smith, Lavay
See Lavay Smith and Her Red Hot
Skillet Lickers
Smith, "Legs" Larry
See Bonzo Dog Doo-Dah Band
Smith, Mark E.
See Fall, The
Smith, Martin
See Delirious?
Smith, Michael W. **11**
Smith, Mike
See Dave Clark Five, The
Smith, Mike
See Paul Revere & The Raiders
Smith, Parrish
See EPMD
Smith, Patti **17**
Earlier sketch in CM **1**
Smith, Paul
See Imperials, The
Smith, Rick
See Underworld
Smith, Robert
See Cure, The
Smith, Robert
See Spinners, The
Smith, Roger
See Tower of Power
Also see Siouxsie and the Banshees
Smith, Scott
See Loverboy
Smith, Shannon
See Imperials, The
Smith, Shawn
See Brad
Smith, Simon
See Wedding Present, The
Smith, Smitty
See Three Dog Night
Smith, Spike
See Damned, The
Smith, Steve
See Journey
Smith, Stewart
See Delirious?
Smith, Tommy **28**
Smith, Tweed
See War
Smith, Tyler
See Guttermouth
Smith, Wendy
See Prefab Sprout
Smith, Whit
See Hot Club of Cowtown

Smith, Will **26**
Also see DJ Jazzy Jeff and the Fresh Prince
Smith, Zachary
See Loud Family, The
Smithereens, The **14**
Smiths, The **3**
Smog **28**
Smyth, Gilli
See Gong
Smyth, Joe
See Sawyer Brown
Smythe, Danny
See Box Tops, The
Sneed, Floyd Chester
See Three Dog Night
Snoop Dogg **44**
Earlier sketch in CM **17**
Snoop Doggy Dogg
See Snoop Doog
Snouffer, Alex "Alex St. Clair"
See Captain Beefheart and His Magic Band
Snow **23**
Snow, Don
See Squeeze
Snow, Hank **29**
Snow, Phoebe **4**
Snyder, Richard "Midnight Hatsize Snyder"
See Captain Beefheart and His Magic Band
Soan, Ashley
See Del Amitri
Sobule, Jill **20**
Social Distortion **27**
Earlier sketch in CM **19**
Sodergren, Kurt
See Big Bad Voodoo Daddy
Soft Cell **43**
Soft Machine **36**
Sokolof, Alan
See Four Lads, The
Solal, Martial **4**
Solas **34**
Solem, Phil
See Rembrandts, The
Sollenberger, Isobel
See Bardo Pond
Soloff, Lew
See Blood, Sweat and Tears
Solowka, Peter
See Wedding Present, The
Solti, Georg **13**
Sommer, Günter "Baby" **31**
Son by Four **35**
Son Volt **21**
Sondheim, Stephen **8**
Sonefeld, Jim
See Hootie and the Blowfish
Sonic Youth **26**
Earlier sketch in CM **9**
Sonique **45**
Sonnenberg, Nadja Salerno
See Salerno-Sonnenberg, Nadja
Sonni, Jack
See Dire Straits
Sonnier, Jo-El **10**
Sonnier, Lennis
See Hackberry Ramblers
Sonny and Cher **24**
Sons of the Desert **44**
Soraya **46**
Sorum, Matt
See Cult, The
Sosa, Mercedes **3**
Sosna, Rudolf
See Faust
Soucie, Michael
See Surfin' Pluto
Soul Asylum **10**

Steele, Michael "Micki"
  See Bangles, The
  Also see Runaways, The
Steele, Peter
  See Type O Negative
Steeleye Span 19
Steely Dan 29
  Earlier sketch in CM 5
Steen, Scott
  See Royal Crown Revue
Stefani, Gwen
  See No Doubt
Stefansson, Baldur
  See Gus Gus
Steier, Rick
  See Warrant
Stein, Andy
  See Commander Cody and His Lost
    Planet Airmen
Stein, Chris
  See Blondie
Stein, Hal
  See Lavay Smith and Her Red Hot
    Skillet Lickers
Stein, Laura
  See Pernice Brothers
Steinberg, Lewis
  See Booker T. & the M.G.'s
Steinberg, Sebastian
  See Soul Coughing
Steinhardt, Robby
  See Kansas
Stephens, Jody
  See Big Star
Stephenson, Van Wesley
  See BlackHawk
Steppenwolf 20
Sterban, Richard
  See Oak Ridge Boys, The
Stereo MC's 34
Stereolab 47
  Earlier sketch in CM 18
Stereophonics 29
Sterling, Jay
  See Love
Sterling, Lester
  See Skatalites, The
Stern, Isaac 7
Stern, Leni 29
Stern, Mike 29
Steve
  See Carter USM
Steve
  See Fun Lovin' Criminals
Stevens, April
  See Nino Tempo & April Stevens
Stevens, Cat 3
Stevens, Rachel
  See S Club 7
Stevens, Ray 7
Stevens, Rick
  See Tower of Power
Stevens, Roger
  See Blind Melon
Stevens, Tony
  See Foghat
Stevens, Vol
  See Memphis Jug Band
Stevenson, Bill
  See Black Flag
Stevenson, Don
  See Moby Grape
Stevenson, James
  See Gene Loves Jezebel
Steward, Pat
  See Odds

Stewart, Andy M.
  See Silly Wizard
Stewart, Bill
  See Lavay Smith and Her Red Hot
    Skillet Lickers
Stewart, Dave
  See Eurythmics
Stewart, Derrell
  See Florida Boys, The
Stewart, Derrick "Fatlip"
  See Pharcyde, The
Stewart, Eric
  See 10cc
Stewart, Freddie
  See Sly & the Family Stone
Stewart, Ian
  See Rolling Stones, The
Stewart, Jamie
  See Cult, The
Stewart, John
  See Kingston Trio, The
Stewart, Larry
  See Restless Heart
Stewart, Reggie
  See Rebirth Brass Band
Stewart, Rex
  See McKinney's Cotton Pickers
Stewart, Robert
  See Lavay Smith and Her Red Hot
    Skillet Lickers
Stewart, Rod 20
  Earlier sketch in CM 2
  Also see Faces, The
Stewart, Ron
  See Lynn Morris Band
Stewart, Sylvester
  See Sly & the Family Stone
Stewart, Tommy
  See Godsmack
Stewart, Tyler
  See Barenaked Ladies
Stewart, Vaetta
  See Sly & the Family Stone
Stewart, William
  See Third World
Stewart, Winston "Metal"
  See Mystic Revealers
St. Hubbins, David
  See Spinal Tap
St. Hubbins, David
  See Spinal Tap
Stiff, Jimmy
  See Jackyl
Stills, Stephen 5
  Also see Buffalo Springfield
  Also see Crosby, Stills, and Nash
Sting 41
  Earlier sketch in CM 19
  Earlier sketch in CM 2
  Also see Police, The
Stinson, Bob
  See Replacements, The
Stinson, Tommy
  See Replacements, The
Stipe, Michael
  See Golden Palominos
  Also see R.E.M.
Stirratt, John
  See Uncle Tupelo
  Also see Wilco
Stirratt, Laurie
  See Blue Mountain
St. James, Rebecca 26
St. John, Mark
  See Kiss
St. Marie, Buffy
  See Sainte-Marie, Buffy

St. Nicholas, Nick
  See Steppenwolf
Stockberger, John
  See Sense Field
Stockhausen, Karlheinz 36
Stockman, Shawn
  See Boyz II Men
Stockwood, Kim 26
Stoeckel, Steve
  See Spongetones, The
Stoker, Gordan
  See Jordanaires, The
Stoll
  See Clannad
  Also see Big Mountain
Stoller, Mike
  See Leiber and Stoller
Stoltz, Brian
  See Neville Brothers, The
Stoltzman, Richard 24
Stonadge, Gary
  See Big Audio Dynamite
Stone, Angie 37
Stone, Curtis
  See Highway 101
Stone, David
  See Rainbow
Stone, Doug 10
Stone, Kim
  See Rippingtons
  Also see Spyro Gyra
Stone, Sly 8
Stone Temple Pilots 36
  Earlier sketch in CM 14
Stonehill, Randy 44
Stone Roses, The 16
Stookey, Paul
  See Peter, Paul & Mary
Story, Liz 45
  Earlier sketch in CM 2
Story, The 13
Stotts, Richie
  See Wendy O. Williams and The Plasmatics
Strachan, Andy
  See Living End, The
Stradlin, Izzy
  See Guns n' Roses
Strain, Sammy
  See O'Jays, The
Strait, George 38
  Earlier sketch in CM 5
Stranglers, The 31
Stratton, Dennis
  See Iron Maiden
Strauss, Richard 25
Stravinsky, Igor 21
Straw, Syd 18
  Also see Golden Palominos
Strawbs 37
Stray Cats, The 11
Strayhorn, Billy 13
Street, Richard
  See Temptations, The
Streisand, Barbra 35
  Earlier sketch in CM 2
Strickland, Keith
  See B-52's, The
String Trio of New York 40
String Cheese Incident, The 34
Stringer, Gary
  See Reef
Strokes, The 37
Strouse, Charles 43
Strummer, Joe
  See Clash, The
Stryi, Wolfgang
  See Ensemble Modern

Taylor, Dan
　See Silver Apples
Taylor, Dave
　See Pere Ubu
Taylor, Dick
　See Rolling Stones, The
Taylor, Earl
　See Country Gentlemen, The
Taylor, Gene
　See Blasters, The
Taylor, Isaiah
　See Baha Men
Taylor, James "J.T."
　See Kool & the Gang
Taylor, James **25**
　Earlier sketch in CM **2**
Taylor, Johnnie
　See Soul Stirrers, The
Taylor, John
　See Duran Duran
Taylor, Kate **30**
Taylor, Koko **43**
　Earlier sketch in CM **10**
Taylor, Larry
　See Canned Heat
Taylor, Leroy
　See Soul Stirrers, The
Taylor, Madelaine
　See Silly Wizard
Taylor, Melvin
　See Ventures, The
Taylor, Mick
　See Rolling Stones, The
　Also see Pretty Things, The
Taylor, Paul
　See Rippingtons
Taylor, Philip "Philthy Animal"
　See Motörhead
Taylor, Roger Meadows
　See Queen
Taylor, Roger
　See Duran Duran
Taylor, Steve **26**
Taylor, Steve
　See Fugs, The
Taylor, Steve
　See Ray Condo and His Ricochets
Taylor, Teresa
　See Butthole Surfers
Taylor, Terry
　See Daniel Amos
Taylor, Wayne
　See Blue Highway
Taylor, Zola
　See Platters, The
Tea Party **38**
Teagarden, Jack **10**
Tears for Fears **6**
Technotronic **5**
Tedeschi, Susan **45**
Teel, Jerry
　See Boss Hog
Teenage Fanclub **13**
Te Kanawa, Kiri **2**
Television **17**
Teller, Al **15**
Temirkanov, Yuri **26**
Tempesta, John
　See White Zombie
Tempesta, Mike "M33"
　See Powerman 5000
Temple, Johnny
　See Girls Against Boys
Temple, Michelle
　See Pere Ubu
Tempo, Nino
　See Nino Tempo & April Stevens

Temptations, The **3**
10cc **43**
Tench, Benmont
　See Tom Petty and the Heartbreakers
Tench, Bobby
　See Humble Pie
Tennant, Neil
　See Pet Shop Boys
Tennison, Chalee **36**
10,000 Maniacs **3**
Tepper, Jeff "Morris"
　See Captain Beefheart and His Magic Band
Terfel, Bryn **31**
Terminator X
　See Public Enemy
Terrell **32**
Terrell, Jean
　See Supremes, The
Terrie
　See Ex, The
Terry, Boyd
　See Aquabats, The
Terry, Clark **24**
Terry, Steven
　See Whiskeytown
Terusa, Tony
　See O.C. Supertones, The
Tesh, John **20**
Tesla **15**
Texas **27**
Texas Tornados, The **8**
Thacher, Jeff
　See Rockapella
Thacker, Rocky
　See Shenandoah
Thain, Gary
　See Uriah Heep
Thalia **38**
Tharp, Al
　See Beausoleil
Tharpe, Sister **47**
Thatcher, Jon
　See Delirious?
Thayil, Kim
　See Soundgarden
The The **15**
Theaker, Drachen
　See Love
Theremin, Leon **19**
Thes One
　See People Under The Stairs
They Might Be Giants **7**
Thibaudet, Jean-Yves **24**
Thielemans, Toots **13**
Thievery Corporation **31**
Thighpaulsandra
　See Spiritualized
Thile, Chris
　See Nickel Creek
Thi-Lihn Le
　See Golden Palominos
Thin Lizzy **13**
Third Day **34**
Third Eye Blind **25**
IIIrd Tyme Out **40**
Third World **13**
Thirsk, Jason
　See Pennywise
.38 Special **40**
Thistlethwaite, Anthony
　See Waterboys, The
Thomas, Alex
　See Earth, Wind and Fire
Thomas, Banner
　See Molly Hatchet
Thomas, Bob
　See Silly Wizard

Thomas, Chris
　See Elms, The
Thomas, Danny
　See 13th Floor Elevators
Thomas, David Clayton
　See Clayton-Thomas, David
Thomas, David
　See Pere Ubu
Thomas, David
　See Take 6
Thomas, Dennis "D.T."
　See Kool & the Gang
Thomas, George "Fathead"
　See McKinney's Cotton Pickers
Thomas, Irma **16**
Thomas, Jacqueline
　See Brodsky Quartet
Thomas, John
　See Captain Beefheart and His Magic Band
Thomas, Michael
　See Brodsky Quartet
Thomas, Mickey
　See Jefferson Starship
Thomas, Olice
　See Five Blind Boys of Alabama
Thomas, Owen
　See Elms, The
Thomas, Paul
　See Good Charlotte
Thomas, Ray
　See Moody Blues, The
Thomas, Richard
　See Jesus and Mary Chain, The
Thomas, Rob
　See Matchbox 20
Thomas, Rob
　See String Trio of New York
Thomas, Rozonda "Chilli"
　See TLC
Thompson, Beachey
　See Dixie Hummingbirds, The
Thompson, Chester
　See Tower of Power
Thompson, Chester
　See Weather Report
Thompson, Danny
　See Pentangle
Thompson, Dennis
　See MC5, The
Thompson, Dougie
　See Supertramp
Thompson, Hank **43**
Thompson, Lee
　See Madness
Thompson, Les
　See Nitty Gritty Dirt Band, The
Thompson, Mayo
　See Pere Ubu
Thompson, Mick
　See Slipknot
Thompson, Paul
　See Concrete Blonde
　Also see Roxy Music
Thompson, Porl
　See Cure, The
Thompson, Richard **7**
　Also see Fairport Convention
　Also see Golden Palominos
Thompson, Rudi
　See X-Ray Spex
Thompson, Tony
　See Chic
Thompson Twins **43**
Thomson, Kristin
　See Tsunami
Thoranisson, Biggi
　See Gus Gus

Tritsch, Christian
  See Gong
Tritt, Travis **7**
Trojanowski, Mark
  See Sister Hazel
Trosper, Justin
  See Unwound
Trotter, Kera
  See C + C Music Factory
Troy, Doris **47**
Trucks, Butch
  See Allman Brothers, The
Trugoy the Dove
  See De La Soul
Trujillo, Robert
  See Suicidal Tendencies
Truman, Dan
  See Diamond Rio
Trynin, Jen **21**
Trytten, Lorre Lynn
  See Willem Breuker Kollektief
Tse, Nicholas **44**
Tsunami **21**
Tubb, Ernest **4**
Tubbs, Hubert
  See Tower of Power
Tubridy, Michael
  See Chieftains, The
Tuck & Patti **44**
Tucker, Corin
  See Sleater-Kinney
Tucker, Ira
  See Dixie Hummingbirds, The
Tucker, Jim
  See Turtles, The
Tucker, Mick
  See Sweet
Tucker, Moe
  See Velvet Underground, The
Tucker, Sophie **12**
Tucker, Tanya **3**
Tucker, William
  See Ministry
  Also see Pigface
Tufnel, Nigel
  See Spinal Tap
Tull, Bruce
  See Scud Mountain Boys
Tumes, Michelle **37**
Turbin, Neil
  See Anthrax
Turgon, Bruce
  See Foreigner
Turnage, Mark-Anthony **31**
Turnbull, Alex
  See 23 Skidoo
Turnbull, Johnny
  See 23 Skidoo
Turner, Big Joe **13**
Turner, Dale
  See Oingo Boingo
Turner, Elgin "Masta Killa"
  See Wu-Tang Clan
Turner, Erik
  See Warrant
Turner, Ike and Tina **24**
Turner, Ike
  See Turner, Ike and Tina
Turner, Joe Lynn
  See Deep Purple
  Also see Rainbow
Turner, Mark **40**
Turner, Mick
  See Dirty Three
Turner, Mike
  See Our Lady Peace

Turner, Nik
  See Hawkwind
Turner, Roger **32**
Turner, Sam "Segundo"
  See Rumba Club
Turner, Sonny
  See Platters, The
Turner, Steve
  See Mudhoney
Turner, Tina **29**
  Earlier sketch in CM **1**
  Also see Turner, Ike and Tina
Turpin, Will
  See Collective Soul
Turre, Steve **22**
Turrentine, Stanley **42**
Turtle Island String Quartet **9**
Turtles, The **29**
Tutton, Bill
  See Geraldine Fibbers
Tutuska, George
  See Goo Goo Dolls, The
Tuxedomoon **21**
Twain, Shania **42**
  Earlier sketch in CM **17**
Tweedy, Jeff
  See Uncle Tupelo
  Also see Wilco
23, Richard
  See Front 242
23 Skidoo **31**
Twist, Nigel
  See Alarm
Twitty, Conway **6**
Two Dollar Pistols **41**
2 Unlimited **18**
2D
  See Gorillaz
2Pac **17**
  Also see Digital Underground
Two-Tone Tommy
  See My Morning Jacket
Tyagi, Paul
  See Del Amitri
Tyler, Kraig
  See Crazy Town
Tyler, Steve
  See Aerosmith
Tynan, Ronan
  See Irish Tenors, The
Tyner, McCoy **7**
Tyner, Rob
  See MC5, The
Type O Negative **27**
Tyrese **34**
Tyson, Ian
  See Ian and Sylvia
Tyson, Ron
  See Temptations, The
UB40 **4**
Uchida, Mitsuko **47**
Ulali **38**
Ulmer, James Blood **42**
  Earlier sketch in CM **13**
  Also see Music Revelation Ensemble
Ulrich, Lars
  See Metallica
Ultravox **38**
Ulvaeus, Björn
  See Abba
Um Romao, Dom
  See Weather Report
Uncle Kracker **42**
Uncle Tupelo **37**
Undertones, The **39**
Underwood, Jacob
  See O-Town

Underwood, Scott
  See Train
Underworld **26**
Ungerman, Bill
  See Royal Crown Revue
Unitt, Victor
  See Pretty Things, The
Unruh, N. U.
  See Einstürzende Neubauten
Unwound **41**
Uosikkinen, David
  See Hooters
Upchurch, Greg
  See Puddle of Mudd
Upshaw, Dawn **9**
Urban, Keith **44**
Ure, Midge
  See Ultravox
Urge Overkill **17**
Uriah Heep **19**
Urlik, Ed
  See Down By Law
U-Roy **37**
Usher **23**
US3 **18**
Utley, Adrian
  See Portishead
Utsler, Joseph
  See Insane Clown Posse
U2 **34**
  Earlier sketch in CM **12**
  Earlier sketch in CM **2**
Vaché Jr., Warren **22**
Vachon, Chris
  See Roomful of Blues
Vai, Steve **5**
  Also see Whitesnake
Valdes, Bebo **42**
Valdès, Chucho **25**
Vale, Jerry **30**
Vale, Mike
  See Tommy James and the Shondells
Valens, Ritchie **23**
Valensi, Nick
  See Strokes, The
Valenti, Dino
  See Quicksilver Messenger Service
Valentin, Dave **33**
Valentine, Gary
  See Blondie
Valentine, Hilton
  See Animals, The
Valentine, Kathy
  See Go-Go's, The
Valentine, Rae
  See War
Valentino, Sal
  See Beau Brummels
Valenzuela, Jesse
  See Gin Blossoms
Valley, Jim
  See Paul Revere & The Raiders
Valli, Anthony
  See Crazy Town
Valli, Frankie **10**
  Also see Four Seasons, The
Vallier, Monte
  See Swell
Vallin, Sergio
  See Maná
Valory, Ross
  See Journey
Van Asch, Rachel
  See Mediaeval Baebes
Van Halen **25**
  Earlier sketch in CM **8**

Waldron, Mal **43**
Waldroup, Jason
  See Greater Vision
Wales, Ashley
  See Spring Heel Jack
Walford, Britt
  See Breeders
Walker, Clay **20**
Walker, Colin
  See Electric Light Orchestra
Walker, Don
  See Cold Chisel
Walker, Ebo
  See New Grass Revival, The
Walker, George **34**
Walker, Greg
  See Fifth Dimension
Walker, James
  See Dixie Hummingbirds, The
Walker, Jeff
  See Imperials, The
Walker, Jerry Jeff **13**
Walker, Joe Louis **28**
Walker, Junior **30**
Walker, Mark
  See Oregon
Walker, Matt
  See Filter
  Also see Smashing Pumpkins
Walker, Ray
  See Jordanaires, The
Walker, T-Bone **5**
Wall, Jeremy
  See Spyro Gyra
Wallace, Bennie **31**
Wallace, Bill
  See Guess Who
Wallace, Ian
  See King Crimson
Wallace, Richard
  See Mighty Clouds of Joy, The
Wallace, Sippie **6**
Waller, Charlie
  See Country Gentlemen, The
Waller, Dave
  See Jam, The
Waller, Fats **7**
Wallflowers, The **20**
Wallinger, Karl **11**
  Also see Waterboys, The
Wallis, Gary
  See 10cc
Wallis, Larry
  See Motörhead
Walls, Chris
  See Dave Clark Five, The
Walls, Denise "Nee-C"
  See Anointed
Walls, Greg
  See Anthrax
Walser, Don **35**
Walsh, Joe **5**
  Also see Eagles, The
Walsh, Marty
  See Supertramp
Walsh, Steve
  See Kansas
Walsh, Tim
  See Brave Combo
Walter, Tommy
  See eels
Walter, Weasel
  See Flying Luttenbachers, The
Walters, Josh
  See Juliana Theory, The
Walters, Nathan
  See Plus One

Walters, Pat
  See Spongetones, The
Walters, Richard
  See Slick Rick
Walters, Robert "Patch"
  See Mystic Revealers
Walton, John Ike
  See 13th Floor Elevators
Walton, Mark
  See Boyzone
Walton, Mark
  See Continental Drifters
Walton, Mark
  See Giant Sand
Walton, William **44**
Wanbdi
  See Indigenous
Wandscher, Phil
  See Whiskeytown
Wannadies, The **29**
War **14**
Ward, Algy
  See Damned, The
Ward, Alistair
  See Saints, The
Ward, Andy
  See Bevis Frond
  Also see Camel
Ward, Billy
  See Knack, The
Ward, Bill
  See Black Sabbath
Ward, Jim
  See At The Drive-In
Ward, Michael
  See Wallflowers, The
Ward, Scooter
  See Cold
Ware, Billy
  See Beausoleil
Ware, Martyn
  See Human League, The
Wareham, Dean
  See Galaxie 500
  Also see Luna
Warfield, William **33**
Wariner, Steve **18**
Warmling, Hans
  See Stranglers, The
Warner, Les
  See Cult, The
Warnes, Jennifer **3**
Warnick, Kim
  See Fastbacks, The
Warrant **17**
Warren, Brad
  See Warren Brothers, The
Warren, Brett
  See Warren Brothers, The
Warren, Diane **21**
Warren, Ernest
  See Spaniels, The
Warren, George W.
  See Five Blind Boys of Alabama
Warren, Mervyn
  See Take 6
Warren G **33**
Warren Brothers, The **34**
Warwick, Clint
  See Moody Blues, The
Warwick, Dionne **2**
Was, David
  See Was (Not Was)
Was, Don **21**
  Also see Was (Not Was)
Was (Not Was) **6**

Wash, Martha
  See C + C Music Factory
Washington, Chester
  See Earth, Wind and Fire
Washington, Dinah **5**
Washington, Grover, Jr. **5**
  Also see Urban Knights
Washington, Jayotis
  See Persuasions, The
Wasserman, Greg "Noodles"
  See Offspring
Watanabe, Sadao **39**
Waterboys, The **27**
Watermark **43**
Waters, Crystal **15**
Waters, Ethel **11**
Waters, Muddy **24**
  Earlier sketch in CM **4**
Waters, Roger
  See Pink Floyd
Watkins, Christopher
  See Cabaret Voltaire
Watkins, Sara
  See Nickel Creek
Watkins, Sean
  See Nickel Creek
Watkins, Tionne "T-Boz"
  See TLC
Watley, Jody **26**
  Earlier sketch in CM **9**
Watson, Doc **2**
Watson, Guy
  See Surfaris, The
Watson, Ivory
  See Ink Spots
Watson, Johnny "Guitar" **41**
Watson, Rob
  See Daniel Amos
Watson, Russell **37**
Watt, Ben
  See Everything But The Girl
Watt, Mike **22**
  Also see fIREHOSE
  Also see Minutemen, The
Watters, Sam
  See Color Me Badd
Watts, Bari
  See Bevis Frond
Watts, Charlie
  See Rolling Stones, The
Watts, Eugene
  See Canadian Brass, The
Watts, Lou
  See Chumbawamba
Watts, Pete "Overend"
  See Mott the Hoople
Watts, Raymond
  See KMFDM
Watts, Todd
  See Emmet Swimming
Weather Report **19**
Weaver, Blue
  See Strawbs
Weaver, Louie
  See Petra
Weaver, Mark A.
  See Two Dollar Pistols
Weavers, The **8**
Webb, Chick **14**
Webb, Dean
  See Dillards, The
Webb, Derek
  See Caedmon's Call
Webb, Jimmy **12**
Webb, Nick
  See Acoustic Alchemy

Whitley, Keith **7**
Whitman, Slim **19**
Whittaker, Hudson **20**
Whittaker, Roger **41**
Whitten, Chris
  See Dire Straits
Whittington, Melvan
  See Love
Whitwam, Barry
  See Herman's Hermits
Whity, Damien "Whit"
  See Spiderbait
Who, The **3**
Wichnewski, Stephen
  See Yo La Tengo
Wickham, Steve
  See Waterboys, The
Widenhouse, Je
  See Squirrel Nut Zippers
Widespread Panic **39**
Wiedlin, Jane
  See Go-Go's, The
Wieneke, Paul
  See Loud Family, The
Wiesner, Dietmar
  See Ensemble Modern
Wiget, Ueli
  See Ensemble Modern
Wiggin, Betty
  See Shaggs, The
Wiggin, Dorothy
  See Shaggs, The
Wiggin, Helen
  See Shaggs, The
Wiggins, Dwayne
  See Tony! Toni! Toné!
Wiggins, Raphael
  See Tony! Toni! Toné!
Wiggles, The **42**
Wiggs, Josephine
  See Breeders
Wiggs, Pete
  See Saint Etienne
Wikso, Ron
  See Foreigner
Wiksten, Pär
  See Wannadies, The
Wilborn, Dave
  See McKinney's Cotton Pickers
Wilborn, Marshall
  See Lynn Morris Band
Wilbur, James "Jim"
  See Superchunk
Wilburn, Doyle
  See Wilburn Brothers, The
Wilburn, Ishmael
  See Weather Report
Wilburn, Teddy
  See Wilburn Brothers, The
Wilburn Brothers, The **45**
Wilco **47**
  Earlier sketch in CM **27**
Wilcox, David **38**
Wilcox, Imani
  See Pharcyde, The
Wild, Chuck
  See Missing Persons
Wilde, Danny
  See Rembrandts, The
Wilde, Phil
  See 2 Unlimited
Wilder, Alan
  See Depeche Mode
Wilder, Philip
  See Chanticleer
Wildhorn, Frank **31**

Wildwood, Michael
  See D Generation
Wiley, Derek "Dirt"
  See Rebirth Brass Band
Wiley, Howard
  See Lavay Smith and Her Red Hot
    Skillet Lickers
Wilhelm, Mike
  See Flamin' Groovies
Wilk, Brad
  See Rage Against the Machine
Wilkeson, Leon
  See Lynyrd Skynyrd
Wilkie, Chris
  See Dubstar
Wilkie, Franklin
  See Marshall Tucker Band
Wilkinson, Amanda
  See Wilkinsons, The
Wilkinson, Geoff
  See US3
Wilkinson, Keith
  See Squeeze
Wilkinson, Kevin
  See Waterboys, The
Wilkinson, Peter
  See Saints, The
Wilkinson, Steve
  See Wilkinsons, The
Wilkinson, Tyler
  See Wilkinsons, The
Wilkinsons, The **30**
Will, David
  See Imperials, The
Willem Breuker Kollektief **28**
Will.I.Am
  See Black Eyed Peas
Williams, Adam "Adam 12"
  See Powerman 5000
Williams, Andy **2**
Williams, Andy
  See Doves
Williams, Boris
  See Cure, The
Williams, Brian "Baby"
  See Big Tymers, The
Williams, Claude "Fiddler" **42**
Williams, Cliff
  See AC/DC
Williams, Dana
  See Diamond Rio
Williams, Dar **21**
Williams, Deniece **1**
Williams, Don **4**
Williams, Eric
  See Blackstreet
Williams, Fred
  See C + C Music Factory
Williams, Hank, III **38**
Williams, Hank, Jr. **1**
Williams, Hank, Sr. **4**
Williams, James "Diamond"
  See Ohio Players
Williams, Jessica **39**
Williams, Jez
  See Doves
Williams, Joe **11**
Williams, John **28**
  Earlier sketch in CM **9**
Williams, John
  See Solas
Williams, Kiely
  See 3LW
Williams, Lamar
  See Allman Brothers, The
Williams, Lenny
  See Tower of Power

Williams, Lucinda **24**
  Earlier sketch in CM **10**
Williams, Marion **15**
Williams, Mars
  See Liquid Soul
Williams, Michelle
  See Destiny's Child
Williams, Milan
  See Commodores, The
Williams, Otis
  See Temptations, The
Williams, Paul **26**
  Earlier sketch in CM **5**
Williams, Paul
  See Temptations, The
Williams, Pete
  See Dexy's Midnight Runners
Williams, Pharrell
  See Neptunes, The
Williams, Phillard
  See Earth, Wind and Fire
Williams, Ralph
  See Orioles, The
Williams, Rich
  See Kansas
Williams, Robbie **25**
Williams, Robert
  See Captain Beefheart and His Magic Band
Williams, Rozz
  See Christian Death
Williams, Sam, III
  See Down By Law
Williams, "Slim" and "Baby" **31**
Williams, Stokley
  See Mint Condition
Williams, Terry
  See Dire Straits
Williams, Tony **6**
Williams, Tony
  See Platters, The
Williams, Vanessa **10**
Williams, Victoria **17**
Williams, Walter
  See O'Jays, The
Williams, Wendy O.
  See Wendy O. Williams and The Plasmatics
Williams, Wilbert
  See Mighty Clouds of Joy, The
Williams, William Elliot
  See Artifacts
Williams, Willie
  See Fifth Dimension
Williams, Yasmeen
  See Sweet Honey in the Rock
Williamson, Gloria
  See Martha and the Vandellas
Williamson, Malcolm **45**
Williamson, Robin **39**
  Also see Incredible String Band
Williamson, Sonny Boy **9**
Willie D.
  See Geto Boys, The
Willie the New Guy
  See Bloodhound Gang, The
Willis, Clarence "Chet"
  See Ohio Players
Willis, Cody
  See Murder City Devils
Willis, Eddie
  See Funk Brothers
Willis, Kelly **12**
Willis, Larry
  See Blood, Sweat and Tears
Willis, Pete
  See Def Leppard
Willis, Rick
  See Foreigner

Wretzky, D'Arcy
 See Smashing Pumpkins
Wright, Adrian
 See Human League, The
Wright, Aggi
 See Pastels, The
Wright, Chely **35**
Wright, David "Blockhead"
 See English Beat, The
Wright, David
 See Flamin' Groovies
Wright, Finbar
 See Irish Tenors, The
Wright, Heath
 See Ricochet
Wright, Hugh
 See Boy Howdy
Wright, Jimmy
 See Sounds of Blackness
Wright, Kevin
 See Rockapella
Wright, Natascha
 See La Bouche
Wright, Norma Jean
 See Chic
Wright, Norman
 See Country Gentlemen, The
 Also see Del Vikings, The
Wright, Rick
 See Pink Floyd
Wright, Simon
 See AC/DC
Wright, Tim
 See Pere Ubu
Wupass, Reverend
 See Rube Waddell
Wurster, Jon
 See Superchunk
Wurzel
 See Motörhead
Wusthoff, Gunter
 See Faust
Wu-Tang Clan **19**
Wuv
 See P.O.D.
Wyatt, Keith
 See Blasters, The
Wyatt, Robert **24**
 Also see Soft Machine
Wyman, Bill
 See Bill Wyman & the Rhythm Kings
 Also see Rolling Stones, The
Wyndorf, Dave
 See Monster Magnet
Wynette, Tammy **24**
 Earlier sketch in CM **2**
Wynn, Steve **31**
Wynn, Steve
 See Dexy's Midnight Runners
Wynne, Philippe
 See Spinners, The
Wynonna **11**
 Also see Judds, The
Wysocki, Jon
 See Staind
X **11**
Xefos, Chris
 See King Missile
Xenakis, Iannis **34**
X-Ray Spex **31**
XTC **26**
 Earlier sketch in CM **10**
Xzibit **31**
Ya Kid K
 See Technotronic
Yale, Brian
 See Matchbox 20

Yamamoto, Hiro
 See Soundgarden
Yamamoto, Seichi
 See Boredoms, The
Yamano, Atsuko
 See Shonen Knife
Yamano, Naoko
 See Shonen Knife
Yamashita, Kazuhito **4**
Yamataka, Eye
 See Boredoms, The
Yamauchi, Tetsu
 See Faces, The
 Also see Free
Yamazaki, Iwao
 See Ghost
Yang, Naomi
 See Damon and Naomi
 Also see Galaxie 500
Yankovic, "Weird Al" **7**
Yanni **11**
Yanovsky, Zal
 See Lovin' Spoonful
Yarbrough, Glenn
 See Limeliters, The
Yardbirds, The **10**
Yarrow, Peter
 See Peter, Paul & Mary
Yates, Bill
 See Country Gentlemen, The
Yates, Stephen
 See Mediaeval Baebes
Yauch, Adam
 See Beastie Boys, The
Yearsley, Thomas
 See Paladins, The
Yearwood, Trisha **25**
 Earlier sketch in CM **10**
Yella
 See N.W.A.
Yellowjackets **36**
Yellowman **42**
Yes **8**
Yester, Jerry
 See Lovin' Spoonful
Yeston, Maury **22**
Yo La Tengo **24**
Yo Yo **9**
Yoakam, Dwight **21**
 Earlier sketch in CM **1**
Yoot, Tukka
 See US3
York, Andrew **15**
York, John
 See Byrds, The
York, Paul
 See Dillards, The
York, Pete
 See Spencer Davis Group
Yorke, Thom E.
 See Radiohead
Yorn, Pete **45**
Yoshida, Tatsuya
 See Flying Luttenbachers, The
Yoshikawa, Toyohito
 See Boredoms, The
Yoshimi
 See Boredoms, The
You Am I **35**
Young, Adrian
 See No Doubt
Young, Angus
 See AC/DC
Young, Brian
 See Fountains of Wayne
Young, Cliff
 See Caedmon's Call

Young, Curtis
 See Jordanaires, The
Young, Danielle
 See Caedmon's Call
Young, Faron **7**
Young, Fred
 See Kentucky Headhunters, The
Young, Gary
 See Pavement
Young, Grant
 See Soul Asylum
Young, James
 See Styx
Young, Jeff
 See Megadeth
Young, La Monte **16**
Young, Lester **14**
Young, Malcolm
 See AC/DC
Young, Neil **15**
 Earlier sketch in CM **2**
 Also see Buffalo Springfield
Young, Paul
 See Mike & the Mechanics
Young, Richard
 See Kentucky Headhunters, The
Young, Robert "Throbert"
 See Primal Scream
Young M.C. **4**
Youth
 See Killing Joke
Youth, Todd
 See D Generation
Youtz, Raif
 See Built to Spill
Yow, David
 See Jesus Lizard
Yseult, Sean
 See White Zombie
Yslas, Ray
 See Rippingtons
Yule, Doug
 See Velvet Underground, The
Z, Rachel **40**
Zaakir/Soup
 See Jurassic 5
Zamfir, Gheorghe **41**
Zander, Robin
 See Cheap Trick
Zankey, Glen
 See Bluegrass Patriots
Zap Mama **14**
Zappa, Frank **17**
 Earlier sketch in CM **1**
Zawinul, Josef
 See Weather Report
Zé, Tom **43**
Zender, Stuart
 See Jamiroquai
Zevon, Warren **9**
Zhane **22**
Zilinskas, Annette
 See Bangles, The
Zim Zum
 See Marilyn Manson
Zimmer, Hans **34**
Zimmerman, Udo **5**
Ziskrout, Jay
 See Bad Religion
Zombie, Rob **47**
Zombie, Rob
 See White Zombie
Zombies, The **23**
Zoom, Billy
 See X